# HIDDEN ®

# Colorado

"Besides the obvious, author Richard Harris looks also to spots beyond the tourist track."

—*New Orleans Times-Picayune*

"*Hidden Colorado* is part of the excellent and reliable Hidden series. I never fail to take a *Hidden* book on my travels."

—*Rocky Mountain News*

# HIDDEN®

# Colorado

### Including Denver, Boulder, Aspen, Vail, Rocky Mountain National Park & Mesa Verde National Park

## Richard Harris

**FIFTH EDITION**

Ulysses Press®

BERKELEY, CALIFORNIA

Published by:
ULYSSES PRESS
P.O. Box 3440
Berkeley, CA 94703
www.ulyssespress.com

ISSN 1521-8384
ISBN 1-56975-428-4

Printed in Canada by Transcontinental Printing

10 9 8 7 6

MANAGING EDITOR: Claire Chun
COPY EDITORS: Katherine Wright, Lily Chou
EDITORIAL ASSOCIATES: Leona Benten, Laura Brancella, Jay Chung,
    Lisa Kester, James Meetze
TYPESETTER: Steven Schwartz
CARTOGRAPHY: Pease Press
HIDDEN BOOKS DESIGN: Sarah Levin
COVER DESIGN: Leslie Henriques
INDEXER: Sayre Van Young
FRONT COVER PHOTOGRAPHY: SuperStock (Yankee Boy Basin,
    Uncompahgre National Forest)
ILLUSTRATOR: Doug McCarthy

Distributed in the United States by PublishersGroup West
and in Canada by Raincoast Books

# Write to us!

If in your travels you discover a spot that captures the spirit of Colorado, or if you live in the region and have a favorite place to share, or if you just feel like expressing your views, write to us and we'll pass your note along to the author.

We can't guarantee that the author will add your personal find to the next edition, but if the writer does use the suggestion, we'll acknowledge you in the credits and send you a free copy of the new edition.

ULYSSES PRESS
P.O. Box 3440
Berkeley, CA 94703
E-mail: readermail@ulyssespress.com

# What's Hidden?

At different points throughout this book, you'll find special listings marked with a hidden symbol:

◄ *HIDDEN*

This means that you have come upon a place off the beaten tourist track, a spot that will carry you a step closer to the local people and natural environment of Colorado.

The goal of this guide is to lead you beyond the realm of everyday tourist facilities. While we include traditional sightseeing listings and popular attractions, we also offer alternative sights and adventure activities. Instead of filling this guide with reviews of standard hotels and chain restaurants, we concentrate on one-of-a-kind places and locally owned establishments.

Our authors seek out locales that are popular with residents but usually overlooked by visitors. Some are more hidden than others (and are marked accordingly), but all the listings in this book are intended to help you discover the true nature of Colorado and put you on the path of adventure.

# Contents

# Maps

## OUTDOOR ADVENTURE SYMBOLS

The following symbols accompany national, state and regional park listings, as well as beach descriptions throughout the text.

| | | | | |
|---|---|---|---|---|
| ▲ | Camping | | | Snorkeling or Scuba Diving |
| | Hiking | | | Waterskiing |
| | Biking | | | Windsurfing |
| | Horseback Riding | | | Canoeing or Kayaking |
| | Downhill Skiing | | | Boating |
| | Cross-country Skiing | | | Boat Ramps |
| | Swimming | | | Fishing |

# ONE

# Colorado

That first view of Colorado's 14,000-foot mountain summits stirs a traveler's soul with the kind of elation and awe that the "Pikes Peak or Bust" pioneers with their covered wagons must have felt. You're driving across the midwestern plains on a fast, straight interstate highway when suddenly Pikes Peak stands in massive solitude. Or you're crossing the piñon-studded redrock canyonlands of the Navajo country when the San Juans rise up in the hazy distance in jagged majesty like misplaced Swiss Alps. Or you look out the window of the plane taking you to Aspen, see that from horizon to horizon among the granite crags and evergreen slopes there is not a single road in sight and realize in that moment that there are still places in these mountains where no human has ever set foot. The Colorado Rockies are big in the way that an ocean is big. From any one place, the eye can see only a small part of them, and the unseen part tantalizes the imagination. They reach up high into a world apart from the one in which most of us live. Their alpine lakes and forest trails hold out the promise of cool respite from the humid summer heat of the flatlands, and in winter their high-speed slopes gleam with packed powder and their cross-country ski trails lead through crystal fantasies.

It's easy to think of Colorado as one huge public park. Thirty-six percent of the state is public land, much of it ideal for recreation. On any highway, many cars are clearly bound for the great outdoors, mounted with roof racks carrying skis, kayaks or mountain bikes, depending on the season. Horseback riders are a common sight along back roads and busy thoroughfares alike. Along a thousand creeks and lakeshores, fishing enthusiasts cast for rainbow trout. It is not unusual to spot deer, elk and pronghorn antelopes grazing within sight of the highway. Tourism brings more money into Colorado's economy than mining, and almost as much as cattle.

Yet tourism is just one of Colorado's multiple facets. The state boasts a diversified economy that runs the gamut from computer companies to llama and buffalo ranches. Colorado is the most prosperous state in the Mountain West as well as the most populous. Between 1990 and 2002, the population grew to 4,507,000 people—an increase of 29 percent. The vast majority of Coloradoans live in the cities of the Front Range Corridor, a narrow band of development that clings to Route 25 from Fort Collins in the north to Pueblo in the south. Denver, the state capital and commercial hub, has a population density of 3616 per square mile. Yet not far away lie several of the dozen Colorado counties that have fewer than two human residents per square mile.

*Hidden Colorado* is designed to help you explore every part of the state. It covers popular, "must-see" places, offering advice on how best to enjoy them. It also tells you about many off-the-beaten-path spots, the kind you would find by talking with folks at the local café or with someone who has lived in the area all his or her life. It describes the region's history, its natural areas and its residents, both human and animal. It suggests places to eat, to lodge, to play, to camp. Taking into account varying interests, budgets and tastes, it provides the information you need whether your vacation style involves backpacking, mountain biking, playing golf, museum browsing, shopping or all of the above.

This book covers Colorado in eight sections. Each region of the state is so different from the others that whether your taste in travel destinations runs to the sophistication of the big city, the glamorous seclusion of a chic year-round resort, the rugged majesty of 14,000-foot-high mountain peaks, the whisper of history through ghost-town streets, the solitude of redrock desert canyons or the pure relaxation of picturesque creeks and alpine lakes, you're bound to find a part of Colorado that fits your vacation dreams perfectly.

The traveling part of the book begins in Chapter Two with the sightseeing highlights of metropolitan Denver, the natural starting point for most Colorado explorations. Chapter Three expands the focus to the Front Range, the region along the eastern perimeter of the mountains that includes the booming university towns of Boulder and Fort Collins as well as the casinos of Central City and Black Hawk and the family-style resort town of Estes Park, gateway to Rocky Mountain National Park—all within an hour's drive of Denver.

Chapter Four takes you over the Continental Divide to North Central Colorado's world-renowned ski resorts, including Aspen, Vail, Steamboat Springs, Winter Park and Breckenridge in the heart of the Colorado Rockies, where they are easily reached via Route 70. Chapter Five continues the journey into Northwestern Colorado, beginning with a descent from the high country down Glenwood Canyon to the town whose claim to fame is the state's largest hot spring and follows the Colorado River westward through dramatic canyon and mesa country, best known for dinosaur bones.

The last third of this book covers the southern and far eastern part of the state, beginning in Chapter Six with the Colorado Springs and Pikes Peak Region, the state's oldest tourist area and still one of the most popular, where vacation fun can include such diverse options as mountain climbing, whitewater rafting, gold panning and blackjack. Chapter Seven broadens the look at South Central Colorado to take in such destinations as the spectacular Great Sand Dunes, the ghost-town-turned-ski-resort of Crested Butte and the remote mountain hideaways of Lake City and Creede. Chapter Eight presents the mystery and majesty of Southwestern Colorado, from the cliff dwellings at Mesa Verde National Park and an array of

Colorado

lesser-known ancient ruins to the vast wilderness areas of the San Juans surrounding such unique mountain towns as Silverton, Ouray and Telluride. Chapter Nine examines the Eastern Plains, revealing an array of little-known roadside attractions as well as a few natural areas so far off the beaten path that even most native Coloradoans have never heard of them.

What you choose to see and do is up to you. The old cliché that "there is something for everyone" pretty well rings true in Colorado. In this book, you'll find free campgrounds with hiking trails and fantastic views as well as several plush playgrounds for the wealthy and well-known. You can take a chairlift to a high alpine ridge and then coast down on a mountain bike. Or check into a bed and breakfast that has delightful little galleries and boutiques within walking distance. Whether you're a first-time visitor setting out on your dream vacation or a long-time resident searching for that proverbial undiscovered spot, *Hidden Colorado* will help you experience for yourself a wealth of exciting places and adventures.

▼▼▼▼▼▼▼▼▼▼▼▼▼▼▼

## The Story of Colorado

### GEOLOGY

The rock that forms the Colorado Rockies is mainly granite, which is an igneous rock. That means it is a combination of several different minerals—quartz, feldspar and granite, along with traces and veins of metals such as gold, silver, lead and zinc—blended deep within the earth countless millennia ago under conditions of great heat. Long after the other major mountain chains in the United States had already been formed, the massive layer of granite that would become the Rocky Mountains lay beneath the sandy floor of a great sea.

Very slowly, inexorably, two tectonic plates that make up most of the North American continent—the Canadian Shield and the Pacific Plate—drifted toward each other, floating on molten rock far under the earth's surface. In a slow collision, the plates crushed against each other and started to crumple, pushing the granite layer upward. Dinosaurs, which were abundant in the area at that time, would have experienced this phenomenon as occasional earthquakes.

Sixty million years ago, around the time dinosaurs became extinct, the granite mass cracked through the red sandstone surface that had been beaches and marshy wetlands. In many places along the edges of the uplift, the fractured sandstone was thrust skyward to create the spires and hogback formations that characterize the Front Range of the Colorado Rockies today. The collision of tectonic plates and the uplifting of the granite rock continues even now, though the process is imperceptible.

The mountains as we see them today were shaped by glaciers. A series of Ice Ages, the last of which ended 10,000 years ago—a mere eyeblink in geological time—covered the high country in accumulations of snow and ice that flowed down the mountainsides slowly in solid frozen rivers that gouged deep valleys called moraines, creating steep mountain faces and marking the courses for the turbulent rivers that would slice canyons hundreds of feet deep.

The lofty mountains attract storm clouds like a magnet, making for rainfall and snowfall many times greater than in the deserts and arid prairies at the foot of the mountains. Runoff from the melting snowpack in spring and the thunderstorms of summer gives birth to several of the West's great rivers—the Colorado, Río Grande, Arkansas and South Platte. It is the rivers that give significance to the Continental Divide, the dotted line on maps that meanders through the wilderness connecting Colorado's highest mountain passes.

> The movement of tectonic plates and granite rock is so slow that the Rockies have only gained a few inches in height during the time humans have walked the earth.

All precipitation that falls east of the Continental Divide flows eventually to the Gulf of Mexico or the Atlantic Ocean, while west of the Divide it flows to the Pacific. Elsewhere in the western states, the backbone of the continent may be marked by nothing more spectacular than a point-of-interest sign at a roadside rest area. But in Colorado the Continental Divide is a formidable barrier bisecting the entire state. Crossing it means either driving through a tunnel beneath the mountains or climbing a switchback road up a wall of granite to the summit of a pass more than two miles above sea level.

**AMERICAN INDIANS**  Anywhere you go in Colorado, particularly in the southwestern part of the state, you'll find reminders of the American Indian people who used to roam the region's mountains, mesas and prairies. In the glass cases of Denver's big art, history, and natural history museums as well as in small-town historical museums across the state, you'll see 19th-century Indian artifacts. Then, too, you will find souvenir stores everywhere selling turquoise-and-silver Indian-made jewelry (state law prohibits displaying the ubiquitous "authentic Indian design" or "replica" Indian jewelry alongside the genuine item), as well as pottery, beadwork, and other arts and crafts. It's enough to make one wonder why visitors so rarely see a living American Indian in Colorado.

**HISTORY**

Indian petroglyphs (designs chipped into rock) and pictographs (paintings on rock) are found in several lowland areas of the state, particularly the southeast and northwest corners. Some of the images are thought to be as much as 4500 years old. Little is known of the early people who created them beyond the fact that they hunted large mammals using spears and throwing sticks with flaked flint points. Artistic differences suggest that the plains people on the east side of the Continental Divide and the desert people on the west side had little or no contact with one another. Anthropologists are particularly puzzled by rock art found in the canyons of Colorado's southeastern plains, which bear an inexplicable resemblance to the system of writing used in ancient Ireland.

Civilization came to southwestern Colorado around A.D. 800, when the Anasazi (a Navajo name meaning "ancient enemies"), presumably descendants of early nomads, began growing corn and building permanent houses. They built monumental cliff dwellings and pueblos such as the ones visitors see today at Mesa Verde National Park, the Anasazi Heritage Center near Dolores, and the Ute Mountain Tribal Park. They accomplished impressive feats of astronomy and architecture, and they established trade networks that reached all the way to the Toltec cities of central Mexico. Mysteriously, around A.D. 1250, the Anasazi suddenly abandoned the region, moving south into New Mexico, where their descendants now live at Acoma Pueblo near Grants. Why they left the communities where their people had lived for more than 400 years remains one of the most puzzling questions in American archaeology.

For centuries, the Colorado high country was the domain of the Ute people, who touched the mountains lightly and with reverence. Living as nomads, they huddled around fires in bison-leather tents through thousands of long, brutal winters in the canyonlands of southwestern Colorado, waiting to follow the spring snowmelt into hidden canyons and ancient forests of the high country along the Continental Divide. The Indian population of the Colorado region was never large. The Utes laid claim to virtually all the mountain country of Colorado—yet numbered only about as many as there are year-round residents of Aspen today. With such a vast territory to roam, the mountain tribes rarely came into conflict with one another. In fact, they rarely encountered each other at all except on purpose, in intertribal powwows held at traditional times and places for purposes of trade, social contests, spiritual ceremonies and political diplomacy. At the same time the nomadic Cheyenne and Arapaho tribes followed the bison herds across the plains of northeastern Colorado, as they had since the dawn of memory.

Warfare among the Indian tribes took place mainly along the eastern edge of the mountains, where Plains tribes such as the Arapaho and Cheyenne would send hunting parties into the rich high-country valleys of the mountain people. Before the arrival of non-Indians, intertribal battles bore little resemblance to the bloodbaths that would come later. War parties were generally small and had no firearms, steel or horses. The limited supply of arrows a warrior could carry did not last long in battle, and it was better to save them for hunting if possible, since each handmade arrow represented many hours of work.

At least two non-Indian influences—horses and guns—began to change the Indian way of life long before the first white man set foot in the Rockies at the beginning of the 19th century. Horses first came into Indian hands in northern New Mexico in 1680, when Pueblo people revolted against their Spanish oppressors, looting and burning every settler's home. Navajo and Apache groups agreed to help the Pueblos drive the Spaniards out; in exchange, they could keep all the livestock they could round up from the Spanish ranches and farms—including thousands of horses. Many more horses driven off from the ranches were never captured, but instead went wild to spawn the herds of mustangs that inhabit remote areas of western Colorado even today. As neighbors of the Navajo, the Ute people got their first horses around 1700, and within the next sixty years, virtually every tribe in the Rocky Mountain West had bought, captured or stolen enough horses to breed its own herd.

> Horses let the Indians travel much farther and faster, bringing more frequent contact—whether friendly or hostile—between tribes.

Guns spread more slowly among the Indians. In the British and French settlements along America's east coast, armies of both colonial powers gave rifles to tribes that helped fight the Seven Years War (1756–1763), also known as the French and Indian War. Guns meant power to conquer other tribes to the west who did not have them. Fur traders on what was then the American frontier found that the self-defense needs of Indian tribes made guns extremely valuable as items of exchange, even as they empowered Indian hunters to hunt more efficiently and bring larger quantities of valuable furs to trade for more guns. As Indians got guns by trading with non-Indians from the east, they often turned the guns against rival tribes to the west in order to expand their hunting territory. In this way, firearms often made their way westward ahead of the first non-Indian explorers.

In 1851, as more and more non-Indian homesteaders came into the region, the Cheyenne and Arapaho people signed the Fort Laramie Treaty, granting them spacious reservation lands along the Front Range, including the land where Denver now sits. Ten years later, as the first settlers began homesteading in that area, the government canceled the treaty and relocated the Indians to an arid reservation near Las Animas in southeastern Colorado. Starvation set in, and parties of Indian men left the reservation to scour the countryside for food, alarming the non-Indian settlers, many of whom could not communicate with the Indians and feared them. In a solitary instance, a farm family south of Denver was killed by a small party of Indians.

Colorado was settled at the height of the U.S. government's military campaigns against the Indians, and with few exceptions, the Indians were either relocated or exterminated within a few years after Colorado became a state. Colonel John Chivington of the Colorado National Guard took punitive action against the Cheyenne and Arapaho people in November 1864, leading a cavalry company in a dawn raid on a reservation village and killing 123 people, mostly women and children. News of the raid, which is now remembered as the Sand Creek Massacre, was received with mixed emotions. Chivington was awarded a Medal of Honor by the Territorial Governor and hailed as a hero by some settlers, but he was simultaneously court-martialed by the U.S. Army and drummed out of military service. The Cheyenne and Arapaho people were relocated to reservations in Nebraska and South Dakota, but renegade Cheyenne "dog" soldiers terrorized the Colorado plains for five years before their leader, Tall Bull, was killed in a battle with the cavalry.

> Twenty-three-year-old army scout Buffalo Bill Cody was inaccurately given credit for killing Tall Bull in a bestselling dime novel that established Cody's spurious reputation as an Indian fighter.

Meanwhile, Kit Carson, a legitimately legendary Indian fighter who commanded the garrison at Fort Garland in southern Colorado's San Luis Valley, led actions in the southeastern plains against small, elusive parties of Comanche, Kiowa and Prairie Apache warriors who had been driven from their homelands in West Texas. There was no major, decisive battle. Little by little, the renegades were confined to reservation lands in Oklahoma—or killed.

In 1868, the U.S. government made a treaty with the Ute people granting them a magnificent 6000-square-mile reservation that contained all of the San Juan Mountains, including the sites of present-day Durango, Silverton, Ouray, Telluride and Montrose. Their leader, Chief Ouray, settled down on a farm that is now the site of Ute Indian Museum and Chipeta Park near Montrose and became one of the most eloquent spokesmen and negotiators for the Indian cause.

But five years later, in 1873, soon after gold was discovered in the San Juans, the government rescinded the treaty, and the Utes were forced to move—some to a reservation south of Vernal, Utah, others to the narrow bands of piñon-covered hills and mesas that lie between the desert and Sleeping Ute Mountain on the southern fringe of their former homeland. The Southern Ute and Ute Mountain reservations are now the only Indian lands in Colorado, and the instrument of retribution for past injustices seems to be at hand, for the Ute people now operate the only gambling casino in southern Colorado, the Ute Mountain Casino in Towaoc. When Colorado legalized casino gambling in Cripple Creek, Central City and Black Hawk in 1993, under federal law casinos automatically became legal on the Ute reservations.

**EXPLORERS AND MOUNTAIN MEN**    A vast area of North America, from the Mississippi River to the Pacific Northwest coast, including all of Colorado, was claimed sight unseen as Spanish territory in 1769, even though no Spanish settlement was ever established beyond the port city of New Orleans. France acquired the Louisiana Territory from Spain by treaty in 1800, but except for small trading expeditions up the river, the French found it impossible to occupy—or even explore and map—the territory, and in 1803 they sold it to the United States for $12 million dollars. Two years later, the first French trapper/traders reached the Rocky Mountains; they had been in the wilderness so long that they did not know the region had been sold to America, nor did it matter much, since virtually all of the estimated 150 French frontiersmen who went west found homes among the Indians and never returned to civilization.

No American expedition reached Colorado until 1806, when the U.S. government sent an expedition under the leadership of Captain Zebulon Pike to trace the Arkansas River to its source. After seeing—and failing in attempts to climb—the peak that would later bear his name, Pike was arrested as a spy by the Mexican army and imprisoned in Santa Fe. He was released only after making an unauthorized agreement that henceforth the Arkansas River would be recognized as the border between U.S. and Mexican territory—an agreement that would hold in the Rocky Mountain region for the next 43 years.

As the Bent brothers and other entrepreneurs established trading posts along the Arkansas and South Platte rivers of eastern Colorado, hundreds of freelance adventurers set off to probe deeper into the mountains in search of pelts. These "mountain men," as they were called, explored virtually every valley in the Colorado Rockies during the next thirty years, bringing back more than half a million beaver pelts each year. In order to kill animals in such phenomenal numbers, the mountain men not only set their own traps but also traded gunpowder and bullets to the Indians for more furs. By the 1840s, beavers had become nearly extinct in the territory. The last of the old-time fur trappers either became guides for army expeditions and pioneer wagon trains or established their own trading posts, where they continued to sell ammunition to the Indians—a practice that would soon become controversial and then illegal.

**PIONEERS AND PROSPECTORS**    Colorado missed out on the great pioneer migrations of the 1840s and 1850s because its high mountain passes posed an impossible obstacle to wagon trains. Colorado was settled later than any of its neighboring states because mountain winters made it a hard place to survive in. But almost overnight, rumors of gold turned the eastern slope of the Colorado Rockies into the region's main population center. A trickle of prospectors started arriving in the territory in 1849, a year after the discovery of gold at Sutter's Mill in California proved that gold existed in United States territory.

The gold find that touched off the 1858 "Pikes Peak or Bust" gold rush turned out to be a bust—a discovery of about $200 worth of gold flakes in Cherry Creek, where no more gold has been seen since. Large numbers of gold hunters made their way to Colorado's Front Range chasing exaggerated reports of the find, and many newcomers starved that winter.

But the following May saw the first of a seemingly endless string of fabulous finds in the canyon country along the route of present-day Route 70. Idaho Springs, Central City, Georgetown—boom towns appeared ever deeper in the forbidding mountains. By 1861, two years after the first find, claims had been staked along every foot of Clear Creek's banks, and the goldfields of Colorado were producing 150,000 ounces of gold a year (worth about $60 million today).

The gold rush only lasted for a few years. By the end of the Civil War in 1865, Colorado's gold production was already declining. By 1868, it had dwindled to almost nothing, leaving the miners to scramble after lesser minerals like silver, lead and even coal. In all, the "Pikes Peak or Bust" gold rush produced about one-sixteenth the amount of gold that came from California during the same years.

People had flocked to gold and silver boom towns such as Central City and Leadville, as well as the Front Range towns of Denver and Colorado City (now part of Colorado Springs) in such numbers that Colorado—a region previously inhabited only by Indians and fur traders—was declared a territory in 1862, just three years after the gold rush began, and a state 14 years later on the centennial of the Declaration of Independence, giving rise to the nickname, "the Centennial State."

The years following the Civil War saw the construction of four major railroads. The Santa Fe Railway followed the old Santa Fe Trail through Lamar, La Junta and Trinidad on its way to New Mexico Territory. The Colorado Central connected Golden, Colorado, with the transcontinental Union Pacific Railroad at Cheyenne, Wyoming, and soon the Kansas Pacific linked Denver with the Union Pacific. Shorter railroad lines soon linked the main rail arteries to Denver and Colorado City (now part of Colorado Springs), and within a few more years a network of narrow-gauge railroads connected mining towns throughout the mountains. Finally, in the early 1870s, the Denver & Rio Grande began extending service between Denver and the communities of southern Colorado.

At the same time that bison were being exterminated to feed railroad work crews, leaving boundless empty grazing land, the new transportation network made cattle and sheep ranching feasible in the Rockies. Starting in the mid-1870s, vast cattle ranches that measured in the millions of acres were established on the northeastern plains under absentee ownership. These ranches thrived, employing thousands of cowboys and earning their owners bigger profits, in many cases, than the gold mines of Colorado had ever yielded. On some ranches, cattle came to number in the millions—on paper, at least. The unfenced rangeland was so big that actually counting the cattle—let alone rounding them up and branding them—was impossible.

In the 1870s, gold continued to lure prospectors into the mountains, from Leadville to the San Juan Mountains of southwestern Colorado, but once there, most would-be gold hunters found that the real fortunes were being made in silver and more mundane metals such as zinc and lead. Stories were common of newcomers buying fraudulent "salted" gold mines—where small amounts of gold were fired into an exposed wall with a shotgun to falsify assays—only to dig a little farther and find rich silver lodes.

**THE DECLINE OF THE OLD WEST**   The end of the great ranches came in the brutal winter of 1887–88, when a single blizzard heaped snow higher than cattle's heads and was followed by weeks of record cold temperatures. When the spring thaw came, few cattle could be found alive. Many ranch owners went bankrupt, leaving the former ranches unsupervised. Newcomers rushed in to seize pieces of the abandoned ranches. Many started their own ranches on a more modest scale. Legal title to lands that had been part of bankrupt ranches was vague at best, so violent clashes erupted between cowboys, sheepmen and farmers (known as grangers). The lawlessness was made worse by the fact that some cowboys from the early ranches turned to crime after losing their jobs, forming outlaw bands that lived by armed robbery. Rampant lawlessness continued into the early years of the 20th century. Eventually, when landholders had occupied their ranches and farms long enough to file for legal title under the law of adverse possession, the violence faded.

The mining districts of northern Colorado continued to flourish until 1893, when the U.S. Congress ended silver subsidies, bringing about a collapse in the silver market. Towns that depended mainly on silver mining, such as Aspen and Leadville, were all but abandoned within a few years. Many miners moved to the new-

### THE COLOR OF MONEY

Gold hunters poked into every canyon and creek of the Rocky Mountain labyrinth. Wherever a trace of "color" was found, a gold camp would appear, and if the discovery proved significant enough to become a mine, the camp would instantly become a town complete with shops, saloons, hotels, newspapers and lots of lawyers.

found goldfields of Cripple Creek, site of the West's last major gold boom.

Bob Womack, a cowboy living in a lonely line shack on the west side of Pikes Peak, found the first nuggets of gold in a stream called Cripple Creek on the back side of Pikes Peak in 1879, but it took eleven years for him to convince anyone that his find was genuine. By the time he finally found a backer and proved his gold find, he had become known as "Crazy Bob," and his credibility was so low that he was only able to sell his interest for $500; within the next year, it produced more than $200,000 in gold ore. Womack is memorialized today by the Cripple Creek casino named after him. Between 1890 and 1896, Cripple Creek grew to become—briefly—Colorado's second-largest city.

Still, gold mining was rarely a profitable business. Of nearly 100,000 people who flocked to the Cripple Creek goldfields, 28 became millionaires from their gold claims. Only one was a professional prospector and none were miners; most were shopkeepers, construction workers, lawyers, pharmacists and real estate agents. All made their millions by selling their claims to mining corporations, which rarely recovered as much gold as they paid for the claims.

The main reason mining companies were interested in Colorado gold at all was that it was easy to sell stock in gold mines. The United States was on the Gold Standard in those days, meaning that the nation's economy could only expand as fast as gold was produced. Even a money-losing mine was good for the national economy, inspiring eastern politicians to pour money into gold production. In Cripple Creek, of the 5000 exploratory holes that were dug, 700 became working mines. Yet more than 12,000 mining corporations were selling stock on the (now-defunct) Colorado Springs stock exchange.

Violence became commonplace in the Cripple Creek District as labor union organizers battled against enforcers hired by the

## GOLD IN THEM THAR HILLS?

A lot of old-time Coloradoans believe the legendary gold veins of the Cripple Creek District were a mere offshoot of an immense mother lode hidden deep beneath the Pikes Peak massif. Amateur and professional geologists have been debating this theory's likelihood for decades, since tunneling beneath the mountain to find out would be so enormously costly that nobody is likely to actually do it. Even scoffers agree that there is probably more gold under the hills of Cripple Creek today than the $412,974,848 worth of ore (that's about 1,200,000 ounces of gold, worth something like $5 billion today) mined there between 1890 and 1950.

mine owners. Dynamite was the weapon of choice, and the outcome of the conflict was inconclusive. The gold-mining industry prospered until 1933, when it, too, came to an abrupt end as a change in federal law ruined the market for the precious metal.

**MODERN TIMES**   The introduction of the railroads made it easy for vacationers to visit Colorado and the Rocky Mountains. Tourism came to the Pikes Peak and Glenwood Springs areas around 1885 and to Estes Park around 1900. In those days, however, the West was much more remote than the African veldt or the Australian outback is today—the exclusive province of adventurers, tycoons and wealthy dilettantes. It was not until the 1920s, when many Americans bought automobiles and the first main highways were paved, that tourists began heading for Colorado in large numbers. Tourism has become central to the economy of Colorado and has increased steadily for more than a century now.

But as enticing to tourists as the wild, pristine Colorado mountains were already proving to be, other forces were less ecologically benign. As early as the 1880s, large seams of high-quality coal had been discovered in Colorado, allowing Coloradoans to cheaply heat the high-ceilinged houses that came into vogue at that time and enabling the Rockefeller family to establish Colorado Fuel and Iron, which would become one of the nation's leading steel producers, in Pueblo. Coal mining grew to become a huge industry in Colorado—more profitable than gold, and more destructive to the environment.

In 1933, the United States went off the Gold Standard but still regulated gold prices at levels too low for profitable mining. Nearly all gold mines in Colorado shut down. Gold prices were deregulated in 1976 and instantly jumped from $35 an ounce to around $400 an ounce. But because of the huge equipment investments required, few mines have been reopened. Instead, gold companies use high-tech cyanide leeching methods to extract more gold from old mine and refinery slag heaps. Today, fortune-seekers are more likely to play the Colorado Lottery (the odds are better) and mining companies are content to leave most of Colorado's remaining gold in the ground—for now.

Energy booms have swept across 20th-century Colorado with the frenetic but fleeting quality of earlier gold rushes. In the 1950s, atomic bombs and the glowing promise of nuclear power made a previously unheard-of mineral called uranium one of the most valuable commodities known to humanity. Scattered deposits of the stuff were found in the Colorado backcountry from Grand Junction west to Utah and south to the New Mexico state line, luring a new generation of prospectors driven by fantasies of striking it rich. Though there was still plenty radioactive ore waiting to be found, rising costs, lower prices and reduced government subsidies brought the collapse of Colorado's uranium industry around 1960.

Tourism got a major boost with the development of Aspen, Vail and a host of other ski resorts that have created a second tourist season in the winter, bringing millions of additional visitors to the state. These winter-season resorts, in turn, began to experiment with other kinds of facilities designed to stimulate the local economy during the roughly seven months of the year when the ski slopes were closed. Conference centers, golf courses and alpine slides popped up in every ski town. Finally, in the early 1980s, a single stunt—an impromptu race up a jeep road and over a mountain pass from Crested Butte to Aspen on battered old bicycles—spawned the mountain bike industry, which has since transformed summer sports in many areas of the Rockies, providing an ideal way to experience the mountain magnificence around many ski resort towns in the summertime.

With the late 1960s and early 1970s, population growth and development came to Colorado's Front Range in a big way, making it one of the fastest-growing areas in the United States. Many surrounding communities doubled in size in a year, then doubled again the next year. With this rampant development came skyrocketing prices for land in the nearby mountains, and soon formerly remote areas were being filled with paved roads, vacation homes and condominiums.

By the time the 1970s energy crisis came along, energy-aware prospectors had attracted the notice of major oil companies with a rock called oil shale, so permeated with petroleum that it could actually be set on fire. Huge-scale operations were undertaken in the canyons north of Parachute to prove that oil could be mined in the form of shale as cheaply as drilling for it. But soon the international chess game of petroleum made both oil wells and shale operations in the American West unprofitable, and Parachute, Colorado's last mining boom town, changed overnight into a modern-day ghost town just off the interstate.

Saving the natural landscape from real estate development and other forms of economic exploitation has become a primary concern in Colorado in recent years with some of the nation's strictest environmental laws, including the only statewide ban on clearcutting in the national forests. The tension between developers and conservationists remains a polarizing reality in Colorado.

**FLORA**     Altitude makes all the difference when it comes to Colorado plant life. At lower elevations—low in this region meaning a mile or less above sea level—the environment consists of arid prairies with vegetation so sparse that it takes as much as 60 acres to graze a single cow. The reason is that the Rocky Mountains cast a "rain shadow"; as weather patterns move from west to east, clouds dump most of their rain or snow on the high, cool mountains, leaving little moisture to fall on the prairies. The closer the land is to the base of the mountains, the drier it is, with natural vegetation that consists mainly of thin veneers of grass punctuated by prickly pear cactus. In some areas, especially northeastern Colorado, farmers have transformed this seeming wasteland into fields of wheat, sugar beets and other crops made possible by irrigation wells that tap into huge underground aquifers fed by the moisture that falls in the mountains and then seeps into the earth.

The foothills along the Front Range are even drier than the prairies, since they are not only in the mountains' rain shadow but also steep enough so that whatever rain does fall quickly spills away like water off a duck's back. The foothills are just high enough, however, so that cooler temperatures let snow melt more slowly, seeping into the top layer of earth to sustain scrub, or small trees that may reach a mature height of only five or six feet. The most common scrub tree in the foothills is Gambel oak (commonly called "scrub" oak), a diminutive cousin of the stately oak trees found in lowland forests of the eastern United States. Other scrub trees include juniper and, in the southern foothills, piñon.

> The aspen is a delicate tree that cannot tolerate high or low altitude extremes. Attempts to use aspens for landscaping in lower places like Denver and Colorado Springs almost always end in failure.

Mountain forests, too, change with elevation, forming three distinct bands. On the lower slopes of the mountains, ponderosa pine stand 50 feet tall and more. Douglas fir and blue spruce dominate the higher reaches of the mountains. Between the two bands of evergreen forest, shimmering stands of aspen trees fill the mountainsides and paint them bright yellow in early October. The aspen, perhaps the most intriguing and distinctive tree in the Colorado Rockies, is what forestry experts call an opportunistic species: stands grow wherever clearings appear in the evergreen woods—usually because of forest fires or pine beetle infestations. Gradually, over a span of centuries, the taller evergreens will crowd out old aspen stands as new stands appear elsewhere.

The upper boundary of the deep green forests of spirelike Douglas fir is known as timberline, the elevation above which temperatures drop below freezing at night year-round and trees can't grow. Timberline is around 10,500 to 11,000 feet in the southern Colorado Rockies and lower the farther north you go. Above timberline lies the alpine tundra, a delicate world of short grasses and other green plants rooted in permafrost where tiny flowers appear for brief moments each summer. At the highest elevations, around 14,000-foot mountain summits, summer freezing prevents even the small plants of the tundra from growing. Up there, clinging to the granite cliffs and boulders, grows lichen, a symbiotic combination of two plants that survive in partnership: a type of moss forms a leathery, sheltering shell that protects an algae, which in turn provides nutrients by photosynthesis to feed the moss. This ingenious arrangement is perhaps the ultimate tribute to life's amazing capacity for adapting to even the harshest environments.

**FAUNA**

The abundance of wildlife is one of Colorado's greatest attractions. You are most likely to get a good look at large animals in the national parks, where long-standing prohibitions against hunting have helped them lose their fear of humans. The wildlife populations are about the same in national forests, but sightings are much less common because animals generally keep their distance from roads, trails, and any human scent.

The eastern foothills, high plains and mountain parks (not the kind with rangers, but flat grasslands surrounded by mountain ranges) are a favorite habitat of jackrabbits, coyotes and pronghorn antelope, as well as prairie birds such as hawks, grouse and pheasants. Coyotes are abundant in Colorado; they are commonly seen not only in open grasslands but also on the outskirts of urban areas, including the suburbs of Denver. Intelligent and curious, coyotes can often be spotted observing humans from a distance. They are not dangerous to humans, though they may sometimes attack small pets.

Pronghorn antelope, once hunted nearly to extinction and until recently listed as a threatened species under the federal Endangered Species Act, have multiplied to the point that they are now a common sight on the high plains of eastern Colorado and in grassland areas in the northwestern part of the state. Although these tan, black and white deerlike creatures with short legs and large heads are commonly called antelope, they are not related to the true antelope of Africa and Asia. In fact, they are not related to any other living species.

American bison, more often called buffalo although they are unrelated to Asian buffalo, once roamed throughout Colorado's eastern prairies and mountain parks. Today they are only found in captive herds, mostly on buffalo ranches, a growing industry along the Front Range.

## THE HIGHER THE PRESSURE, THE BIGGER THE LITTER

Coyote populations are on the increase just about everywhere in the West. Scientists have discovered that as the number of coyotes in an area declines, the number of coyote pups born in a litter increases to compensate; so although states have paid hundreds of thousands of dollars annually for nearly a century to eliminate these wild canines because ranchers believe they may pose a threat to livestock, there are now more coyotes than ever.

There are also rattlesnakes in the foothills and high plains. The good news is that they rarely venture into the mountains. Snakes and other reptiles are cold-blooded and cannot function in low temperatures, so they are hardly ever found at elevations above about 7000 feet. When hiking at lower elevations, walk loudly and never put your hand or foot where you can't see it.

Deer, mountain lions and bobcats inhabit the western plateaus and, in lesser numbers, the eastern foothills. While deer may be spotted anywhere in the mountains, they prefer to graze in areas where scrub oak grows. Mountain lions hunt deer and prefer areas with high rocks, where they can spot both dangers and prey a long ways away. Since mountain lions are nocturnal and reclusive, it's a stroke of luck to glimpse one darting across the road in your headlights at night. They have not been known to attack humans in the Colorado Rockies, though several recent incidents in Southern California have proved that they can be dangerous. Wild horses also graze the remote plateaus and mesas of western Colorado.

In mountain forests and meadows, common small mammals include squirrels, chipmunks, raccoons and porcupines. Large animals include elk and black bears. Since elk prefer high mountain meadows in the warm months, they are usually seen in the summer only by serious hikers who venture deep into the wilderness. Sightings are more common in winter, when they descend to lower elevations where grass is easier to reach under the snow. In some areas, usually marked by signs and sometimes observation areas, herds of elk can often be spotted from the road in winter. Moose are rarely found in Colorado.

As for black bears, they are elusive but more common than most hikers realize. In times of drought, when food becomes scarce, it's not unusual for a bear to raid trash cans along the fringes of civilization. Black bears rarely attack people, but they are unpredictable and can be dangerous because of their size. Most injuries involving bears happen because campers store their food inside tents with them at night. When camping in the forest, it's a better idea to leave all food inside a closed vehicle or suspended from a tree limb. Grizzly bears are believed to be extinct, or at least very rare, in Colorado, though several unconfirmed sightings have been reported in the San Juan Mountains. Unconfirmed sightings have provided evidence to support rumors that timber wolves were also reintroduced surreptitiously to the San Juans by radical environmentalists in the 1980s.

Beavers once inhabited virtually every stream in Colorado. Trapped by the millions for their pelts in the early 19th century, these largest of North American rodents once stood on the brink of extinction. In more recent times, they have too often been considered pests because their habit of damming streams to create ponds surrounding their dome-shaped sticks-and-mud lodges floods the most desirable areas of mountain valleys. Landowners persisted for many years in poisoning the beavers or dynamiting their dams and putting up low electric fences to keep them away. Now a protected species in Colorado, beavers seem to be making a slow comeback. It's not unusual to discover beaver ponds on backcountry streams, and if you watch a pond near sunset, you may get a look at the animals themselves.

The smaller animals most commonly seen above timberline are golden marmots, large, chubby rodents nicknamed "whistlepigs" because they communicate with shrill whistles.

Above timberline, Rocky Mountain bighorn sheep are common and easy to spot in alpine meadows. Herds of ewes are protected by a single ram, while other males lead a solitary existence elsewhere until mating season, when the high crags echo with the crash of horns as young rams challenge their elders for dominance over the female herd. In areas with vehicle traffic, such as Pikes Peak, Mount Evans and Rocky Mountain National Park's Trail Ridge, the sheep vanished in the 1950s because the rams were so distracted by the noise of cars that they became impotent. New herds were brought from the Collegiate Range in central Colorado, which had become overpopulated with sheep, and they have made a successful comeback, particularly on Pikes Peak. Mountain goats—shaggy, snow-white and solitary, may also be seen in some high mountain areas, especially Rocky Mountain and Glacier National Parks. Small rodents called picas colonize high-altitude rockpiles, where swarms of hundreds of them are sometimes seen.

**Where to Go**

Most visitors from out of state, whether they arrive by car, plane or train, begin their Colorado explorations in **Denver**, the region's largest city and main transportation center. The largest city in Colorado—and, indeed, within 600 miles in any direction—Denver has the biggest museums, the best shopping malls and the most restaurants in the state. Here you'll find such popular attractions as the Denver Art Museum and Elitch Gardens, as well as such lesser known sights as the old-time stagecoach station at Four Mile Historic Park and the Denver Museum of Miniatures, Toys and Dolls.

Chapter Three includes the cities of the **Front Range** and the nearby mountains. Just beyond the Denver metropolitan area you will find towering mountain peaks, old mining towns and plenty of scenery and history. Denver and most other Front Range municipal and county governments have cooperated to set aside vast expanses of mountain parklands, protecting their skylines from both mining exploitation and subdivision development and offering both popular and little-known wilderness getaways within a half-hour's drive of the city. Rocky Mountain National Park, adjoining the town of Estes Park, is the biggest tourist destination in the area. Visitors can also take their pick among dozens of other historic, scenic and entertainment attractions ranging from the old-time gold mines of Idaho Springs to the recently resurrected gambling casinos of Central City and Black Hawk. The region's main features also include the state's largest and liveliest university towns, Boulder and Fort Collins.

Chapter Four takes you through the Eisenhower Tunnel under the Continental Divide and directly into the heart of the mountains, home of such world-class ski resorts as Vail, Breckenridge, Aspen and Steamboat Springs. The scene of the great mid-19th-century gold and silver strikes, **North Central Colorado** is a region steeped in history and change, where within a span of a few generations entire cities of brick buildings and Victorian homes have appeared in the wilderness only to be abandoned as the mineral wealth played out. Travelers who choose to explore beyond the booming resorts of today can explore the historic mining town where such famous Colorado historical figures as Leadville Johnny Brown and Horace Tabor struck it rich. Other adventure options include watching for bighorn sheep on Guanella Pass, mountain biking on the old railroad bed over Boreas Pass, and hiking in the Eagle's Nest Wilderness. More vacationers come to this region of Colorado in winter than in summer. Millions of ski enthusiasts each year pay top dollar for lodging and lift tickets to experience the thrill of plunging thousands of feet down mountain slopes, while others put on cross-country skis to discover budget-priced exhilaration and the natural beauty of winter in the high country. Summer brings off-season bargains at northern Colorado's luxury mega-resorts, as most ski areas keep chairlifts running, offering an amazingly easy way to climb mountains.

One of Colorado's fastest-growing tourist areas, Glenwood Springs, invites you to hike or bike on the newly created Glenwood Canyon Trail, then relax in one of the region's largest hot-springs pools. From here Chapter Five works its way down the Colorado River through **Northwestern Colorado** to Grand Junction, the largest city on the western slope of the Colorado Rockies. Along the way, short side trips from the interstate highway lead to some of the least-visited mountain scenery in the state, including the high, cool "islands" in the sky of Grand Mesa and the Flattops. A longer detour takes travelers into the rugged, unpopulated northwestern corner of the state to explore the backcountry of Dinosaur National Monument and Brown's Park.

The **Pikes Peak Region** just west of and including Colorado Springs, explored in Chapter Six, is an old-timer where tourism is concerned. Several sightseeing attractions have been in continuous operation since the end of the 19th century, when Aspen and Durango were forgotten, nearly abandoned mining towns and Vail had not yet been imagined. Tourists have been climbing the peak for more than 120 years. The Royal Gorge has been attracting visitors for nearly as long. In recent times, the face of tourism in the region has been transformed by river rafting on the Arkansas River, the most popular whitewater run in the world, and by the resurrection of the once-abandoned gold-mining city of Cripple Creek as a casino gambling mecca. Hidden spots abound in this part of the state, from hot springs and hidden canyons to wild drives on mountain roads that were once narrow-gauge railroad beds.

Pikes Peak is named after the first American explorer to set foot in Colorado.

Chapter Seven covers **South Central Colorado** from Pueblo, Trinidad and the San Luis Valley to Alamosa, Creede and the area around Gunnison and Crested Butte. Although tourism in this part of the state happens on a much smaller scale than in northern Colorado, the Pikes Peak Region or the Durango area, the recreational options this area has to offer are impressive, from such awesome sights as the Great Sand Dunes and the Black Canyon of the Gunnison to scenic steam train trips on the narrow-gauge Cumbres and Toltec Railroad and boating on Colorado's largest lake in Curecanti National Recreation Area. The area around the skiing-and-mountain-biking town of Crested Butte boasts some of the West's most interesting ghost towns.

**Southwestern Colorado**, a region with a distinctly different character from any other part of Colorado, is the subject of Chapter Eight. The hub of the region is Durango, departure point of the Durango & Silverton Narrow-Gauge Railway, and starting point for driving tours on the San Juan Skyway, one of America's most scenic highway trips. The San Juan Mountains contain several of Colorado's largest and most spectacular wilderness areas, and though they are becoming increasingly well known, the picturesque towns of Silverton, Ouray and Telluride are certainly among Colorado's most "hidden" communities in the geographic sense. Durango is also a good base from which to explore the ancient cliff dwelling ruins at Mesa Verde National Park as well as less-visited sites such as Hovenweep and the Lowry Ruins.

Chapter Nine covers the three major highway routes across the **Eastern Plains**—Route 76, which follows the old Overland Trail along the South Platte River; Route 70, which traces the earliest railroad route straight across the plains; and Route 50, which follows the old Santa Fe Trail along the Arkansas River. This seemingly featureless farm and ranch country covers more than a third of the state, and hardly anybody would consider it as a potential vacation destination. In fact, just about the only way most people see the eastern plains is through a windshield. But the traveler who finds wide open roads thrilling, who takes time to seek out secret glimpses of the past and to appreciate the subtle natural beauty of this magnificent emptiness, will find that the prairie holds a few roadside surprises such as the Living Tree sculptures of Sterling, the County Carousel in Burlington, and the unexplained Celtic-style rock art found at Picture Canyon in the Comanche National Grassland.

Though it may sound romantic, springtime in the Colorado Rockies is less than appealing in reality. Cold winds, occasional avalanches, brown vegetation and plenty of mud are a few of the reasons that most Coloradoans in the tourist business shut down their shops and motels in April and take their own vacations in more southerly climes. Just about any other time of year, however, the climate is ideal for one kind of outdoor recreation or another, giving rise to Colorado's distinctive summer-and-winter double tourist season.

## When to Go

### SEASONS

The traditional summer tourist season, which runs from Memorial Day to Labor Day, is characterized by cool nights, mild days, colorful wildflowers and sudden, brief afternoon rainstorms. In all mountain areas, it's a good idea to start outdoor activities early and carry ponchos or waterproof tarps on all-day hikes, since rain is almost inevitable in the afternoon. In a common, peculiar phenomenon, wind currents called "waves" can carry precipitation for long distances from clouds hidden behind the mountains, causing "sun showers." Old-timers say that if it rains while the sun is shining, it will rain again tomorrow. This adage almost always holds true—but then, if it doesn't rain in the sunshine, it's still likely to rain tomorrow. The good news is, summer rains rarely last more than one hour, and skies generally clear well before sunset.

Along the Front Range, clouds typically build in the early afternoon and then burst into thunder, lightning, and sometimes hail. In mountain areas west of the Continental Divide, storms tend to be smaller, more scattered, and much more frequent. In the San Juan Mountains of southwestern Colorado, it's not unusual to encounter five or six brief rainstorms in a single day. Above timberline, temperatures fall below freezing at night through the whole summer and typically reach only 40° to 50°F at midday. High mountain roads such as the Pikes Peak Highway, Independence Pass and Rocky Mountain National Park's Trail Ridge Road may be closed by blizzards even in August, sometimes stranding motorists for an hour or two before snowplows clear the road.

Early fall—around the end of September—is one of the most delightful times to visit Colorado, as the turning of the aspens paints the mountainsides in yellow with splashes of orange and red, brilliant against a deep green background of evergreen forests. The weather is generally dry and cool at this time of year, making it a great time to take a long wilderness hike or mountain-bike excursion. The first light snowfall can be expected in the high country around the first week of October and along the Front Range around the third week; the first heavy snow typically comes around Halloween. November is hunting season, a good time to keep out of the mountains unless you're armed and dangerous.

The official ski season in Colorado runs from Thanksgiving through March 15. This is the period for which all ski areas expect a reliable snow base. All ski events and package tours are scheduled within this time period, and if you're planning ahead for a major ski vacation, you'll want to schedule it between these dates, too. In reality, snowfall amounts, as well as winter temperatures in the mountains, can vary a lot from year to year, so the actual dates of operation at various ski areas are somewhat unpredictable. These days, the huge artificial snowmaking capacity of most ski areas almost always assures a Thanksgiving opening day. While snowmaking usually ceases after mid-March when advance-reservation business slows down, skiing continues until spring temperatures rise enough to erode the snow base. In some years, at some ski areas, late-season skiing may continue well into April, and even later in parts of the northern Rockies. Uncrowded ski trails, discount lift tickets and lots of sunshine make this late season a favorite time for many local ski enthusiasts.

> In early fall, mountain highways tend to be crowded with carloads of leaf-gawkers on weekends but not on weekdays, while hiking and biking traffic on forest trails is much lighter than during the summer.

## CALENDAR OF EVENTS

**JANUARY**   **Denver**  The National Western Stock Show and Rodeo, the world's largest rodeo, features top-name country-and-western music concerts and a parade through the streets of Denver.

**North Central Colorado**  Ullrfest in Breckenridge honors the Norse god of snow with a fireworks, torchlight skiing and cross-country ski competitions. Aspen's five-day Winterskol features a parade, torchlight skiing, fireworks and skydiving. In Steamboat Springs, the Cowboy Downhill pits professional rodeo cowboys against each other in a unique triathlon of skiing, roping and horse racing.

**Southwestern Colorado**  The events of Snowdown are divided between Durango and nearby Purgatory Ski Area; besides ski competitions, they include a chili cook-off and odd events such as a waiter/waitress obstacle race.

**FEBRUARY**   **Front Range**  The city of Loveland observes St. Valentine's Day with the Sweetheart Sculpture Show, exhibiting works by local and nationally known sculptors with an emphasis on romance.

**North Central Colorado**  Fishermen compete for prize money at the North Park Ice Fishing Contest. The week-long Steamboat

Springs Winter Carnival includes ski races, contests and street celebrations.

**South Central Colorado**  Walsenburg's municipal golf course is the scene of a **Groundhog Brunch** on Groundhog Day.

**Southwestern Colorado**  Telluride hosts **Ski Forever Week,** a celebration and competition for mature skiers, during the first week of February. Later in the month Pagosa Springs celebrates **Winterfest,** a weekend of contests and street events.

**Denver**  Denver's **St. Patrick's Day Parade,** the second-largest in the nation, features more than 5000 horses as well as floats and marching bands.

**MARCH**

**North Central Colorado**  Leadville's **Crystal Carnival,** the oldest winter celebration in the West, features ski joring, an activity in which a skier is pulled by a horse and rider along snow-covered Main Street and goes off jumps in the road. Legendary skiers compete in 65 events at Vail's **American Ski Classic.** A week later, snowboarders compete in **Unvailed** at Vail's Golden Peak Terrain Park.

**South Central Colorado**  The **Monte Vista Crane Festival** celebrates the migration of sandhill and whooping cranes with art shows, naturalist speakers and bus tours of the Rio Grande Wildlife Refuge.

**Southwestern Colorado**  Telluride hosts **Extreme Ski Week** early in the month, then marks the last days of the ski season with **Surf the Rockies.**

**Pikes Peak Region**  Thousands attend the spectacular **Easter Sunrise Pageant** at Garden of the Gods in Colorado Springs.

**APRIL**

**South Central Colorado**  Crested Butte marks the end of the ski season with **Flauschink,** featuring a parade and a coronation ball.

**Eastern Plains**  Birdwatchers flock to Wray to witness the **greater prairie chicken courtship dances** that take place on private land (info: 970-332-5063) in the area.

**Denver**  **Cinco de Mayo,** Mexico's national patriotic celebration, is observed in Denver with fiestas downtown and along Santa Fe Drive.

**MAY**

**Front Range**  A big **Cinco de Mayo** celebration is also held in Greeley. Boulder hosts the **Kinetic Conveyance Sculpture Race.** Later in the month, the **Bolder Boulder 10K Marathon** is the state's largest footrace, with more than 35,000 runners.

**Northwestern Colorado**  Craig celebrates **Grand Olde West Days** with bluegrass and country music contests and a "wild game and roadkill" cookoff.

**Pikes Peak Region**  **Territory Days** celebrates the era when Colorado Springs' Old Colorado City Historic District was the territorial capital. **Music and Blossom Festival and Royal Gorge Rodeo**

packs Cañon City's Main Street with band performances, parades and a carnival; the rodeo is one of the oldest in Colorado. Buena Vista sponsors **Arkansas River Peak Season Days**—the best time of year for whitewater rafting.

**South Central Colorado**   Art shows, bluegrass music and samples of cuisine from local restaurants highlight **A Taste of Creede**, which coincides with a **Mountain Man Rendezvous** outside of town.

**Southwestern Colorado**   Durango's **Iron Horse Bicycle Classic**, a grueling three-day series of bike races on roads and trails, draws more than 2000 competitors from around the world. The **Telluride Mountain Film Festival** focuses on mountain and outdoor adventure movies.

**Eastern Plains**   Rocky Ford celebrates **Cinco de Mayo** with food, street dancing and a mariachi Mass.

**JUNE**

**Denver**   Denver's **Capitol Hill People's Fair** showcases the work of more than 550 artists and crafters, along with live music on six stages.

**Front Range**   Evergreen kicks off the summer rodeo season in Colorado with **Rodeo Weekend**. Fort Collins hosts the **Colorado Brewers' Festival**. **The Greeley Independence Stampede** fills the two weeks leading up to July 4th with family fun, including foot races, fireworks, parades, street breakfasts and the world's largest Fourth of July rodeo. Weavers and wool producers from around the world meet in Estes Park for the annual **Wool Market**, with contests, exhibits and a livestock show of sheep, llamas and angora rabbits.

**North Central Colorado**   The three-day **Aspen Food and Wine Classic** features wine tastings, lectures and seminars, along with cooking demonstrations and a dessert extravaganza. Late June marks the start of the **Aspen Music Festival**, the premier music festival in the United States, with opera, jazz, classical and chamber music performances daily for nine weeks. The summer rodeo season kicks off with Steamboat Springs' PRCA **ProRodeo Series** and Walden's **Never Summer Rodeo**.

**Northwestern Colorado**   Glenwood Springs' **Strawberry Days**, Colorado's oldest town celebration, lasts three days and includes a rodeo, talent show, live entertainment and a parade followed by a street feast of strawberries and cream.

**Pikes Peak Region**   The high point of Colorado Springs' **Springspree** weekend is a bed race through downtown. Salida's **FIBArk Boat Race** is the oldest, longest and most famous kayak race anywhere; the four-day event also includes raft, foot and bike races, live entertainment and a parade.

**South Central Colorado**   **Fiesta del Rio** in Pueblo features bluegrass performances on the banks of the Arkansas River. In Trinidad, the **Santa Fe Trail Festival** features historical re-creations, live entertainment and a quilt show. Monte Vista's **Sunshine Festival** features an arts and crafts fair, food booths and live entertainment.

**Southwestern Colorado**   The **Telluride Bluegrass Festival**, the granddaddy of Telluride festivals, fills the town with big-name musicians and enormous crowds of festival-goers. Later in the month comes the **Telluride Wine Festival**, with formal tastings and connoisseurs' seminars and the **Telluride Theatre Festival**, featuring new plays, theater arts workshops and seminars. The **Music in Ouray Chamber Concert Series** presents nine days of chamber music. Silverton's **Jubilee Folk Music Festival** focuses on bluegrass and folk music.

**Eastern Plains**   Fort Morgan sponsors the **Tin Man Triathlon**, a swimming, biking and running competition. Sterling hosts **Hay Days**, extolling the crop's virtues with exhibits, booths and baling demonstrations. Kit Carson, a small town an hour's drive southeast of Limon, hosts a **Mountain Man Rendezvous** with black-powder shooting contests, tomahawk throws and buckskin-clad storytellers.

**Denver**   The **Cherry Creek Arts Festival** showcases nearly 200 Colorado artists and crafters as well as entertainment and cooking demonstrations. Later in the month, the **Denver Black Arts Festival** presents work by African-American artists and crafters.

**JULY**

**Front Range**   The small mountain town of Empire hosts its annual **Frog Rodeo** (no kidding). The **Greeley Independence Stampede** culminates on July 4th with myriad festivities. The renowned **Central City Opera Festival** begins, with three operas in English presented in rotation through August. Boulder fairly bursts with live cultural performances—the overlapping **Colorado Dance Festival, Colorado Music Festival** and **Colorado Shakespeare Festival**.

**North Central Colorado**   The hills are alive with the sound of music as the National Repertory Orchestry presents **The Breckenridge Music Festival**. Winter Park stages its **American Music Festival**, Aspen opens its six-week **Dance/Aspen Festival** and Vail presents the **Bravo Colorado Music Festival**. The **Carbondale Mountain Fair** features artists and crafters along with live entertainment and kids activities. Steamboat Springs hosts **Rainbow Weekend**, when more than 50 hot-air balloons fill the sky while musicians and arts-and-crafts exhibits liven up the downtown.

**Northwestern Colorado**   In Grand Junction, **Dinosaur Days** presents a dinosaur parade and paleontology lectures, and the public is invited to help dig for fossils.

**Pikes Peak Region**   In Colorado Springs, the **Pikes Peak or Bust Rodeo** kicks off with a street breakfast and parade. Woodland Park presents the **Ute Trail Stampede Rodeo & Parade**. Llama races as well as burro races highlight Fairplay's **Burro Days**.

**South Central Colorado**    **Aerial Weekend** in Crested Butte focuses on hot-air ballooning, hang gliding and skydiving events.

**Southwestern Colorado**    Silverton's **Kendall Mountain Run** is one of the top mountain running events in the state.

**Eastern Plains**    Fort Morgan sponsors a three-day **Festival in the Park**.

**AUGUST**    **Front Range**    Musicians come from all over the United States and Europe to participate in the three-day **Central City Jazz Festival**. Fort Collins' big local festival, **New West Fest**, features food, music, arts and crafts, and contests. Bluegrass, folk and country musicians break out their guitars and banjos for Estes Park's **Rocky Mountain Folks Festival**.

**North Central Colorado**    Hundreds of fine American wines, as well as cuisine from Colorado's top chefs, are available for sampling at Winter Park's **Rocky Mountain Wine and Food Festival**. Grand Lake is the site of one of the region's most improbable sporting events, the **Daven Haven Downs Turtle Race**. Celebrities flock to Vail for the **Ford Cup Golf Invitational**. Leadville celebrates **Boom Days** with a parade, carnival, street fair, 22-mile burro pack race and mining contests.

**Northwestern Colorado**    Glenwood Springs observes **Doc Hollidays** with a re-enactment of the OK Corral gunfight and a party at the local bar Holliday ran. Palisade, near Grand Junction, celebrates the top local crop in the **Palisade Peach Festival** with a barbecue, band concert, parade and tour of fruit stands and wineries.

**Pikes Peak Region**    Manitou Springs hosts a big bluegrass event, the **Mountain Music Festival**. The **Pikes Peak Or Bust Rodeo** is in Colorado Springs. Buena Vista's **Gold Rush Days & Burro Jamboree** offers burro pack races, outhouse and bed races, gold panning, street dancing and the area's largest rock and gem show.

**South Central Colorado**    Pueblo is the site of the **Colorado State Fair**. A street celebration, **Noche de Fiesta**, takes place the night before the opening of the fair. In Crested Butte, a five-day **Mountain Man Rendezvous** features period costumes, rough-and-tumble contests and music.

**Southwestern Colorado**    Telluride events include the **Telluride Chamber Music Festival**, the **Telluride Jazz Celebration** and the **Telluride Mushroom Festival**. Ouray holds its **Artists Alpine Holiday**, a nine-day juried show of local and national artwork.

**Eastern Plains**    Colorado's oldest local fair, the **Arkansas Valley Fair**, held in Rocky Ford, features a Chicano fiesta and a watermelon feast.

**Denver**   The **Festival of Mountain and Plain** marks the end of
summer with food and entertainment.

**SEPTEMBER**

**Front Range**   Golden celebrates **Goldenfest** in mid-September.
Estes Park hosts a **Scottish-Irish Highland Festival** complete with
bagpipes, dancing and traditional Celtic contests.

**North Central Colorado**   **Oktoberfest** livens up the Vail Valley
with food, entertainment and children's activities. Steamboat
Springs hosts the **Steamboat Vintage Auto Race and Concours
d'Elegance** on Labor Day weekend.

**Northwestern Colorado**   Glenwood Springs' **Fall Arts Festival**
has separate competitions for amateur and professional artists.
Meeker hosts the **National Border Collie Finals,** America's top
sheepdog competition. Palisade, in the heart of western Colorado's fruit-growing country, hosts the **Colorado Mountain
Winefest.** In Delta, the **Council Tree Pow Wow & Cultural
Festival** is the state's largest American Indian event.

**Pikes Peak Region**   The **Colorado Springs Hot-Air Balloon Classic,** featuring more than 100 balloons, is the largest such event
in Colorado. Manitou Springs hosts the **Colorado Wine Festival.**

**South Central Colorado**   Crested Butte celebrates **Vinotok,** an
Eastern European fall festival, with storytelling, polka dancing
and a feast of traditional Slavic foods.

**Southwestern Colorado**   Twenty-one southwestern Colorado
communities join together to stage the spectacular **Colorfest,** with
more than 70 special events plus hikes, jeep trips and auto tours
to see the fall colors. The **Airmen's Rendezvous** is the world's
largest and most spectacular hang gliding event. Also here is the
**Telluride Film Festival.**

**Eastern Plains**   Burlington holds an **Outback Hoedown** with
food and western entertainment on Labor Day weekend. Limon
holds its annual **James Dean Daze & Classic Car Show.** La Junta's
**Early Settler's Day Celebration** features arts and crafts booths
and street dancing. Sterling hosts an arts and crafts fair for **Sugar
Beet Days.**

**Denver**   The three-day **Colorado Performing Arts Festival** in
Denver presents free music, dance and theater events. Later in
the month, the city hosts the **Denver International Film Festival**
and the **Great American Beer Festival.**

**OCTOBER**

**Northwestern Colorado**   A farmers market, parade, live entertainment and an outdoor meat-and-potatoes feast are highlights
of Carbondale's annual community festival, **Potato Day.** Cedaredge, a small fruit-growing town north of Montrose and Delta,
celebrates the harvest with **Applefest.**

**Southwestern Colorado**   Ouray hosts a lively **Oktoberfest.** The
**Western Arts, Film and Cowboy Poetry Gathering** takes place in
Durango. Not to be outdone, Silverton celebrates the **Bordello
Costume Ball.**

**Eastern Plains**  Haxtun, a small town east of Sterling, holds its annual **Corn Festival**, featuring a parade, crafts show, races and an ice cream social.

**NOVEMBER**  **Denver**  Beginning around Thanksgiving and lasting through the National Western Stock Show in January, downtown Denver's city and county buildings are festooned with the World's Largest Christmas Lighting Display for **Winterfest**.

**Front Range**  A standout among the Christmas lighting ceremonies on Thanksgiving weekend is Estes Park's **Catch the Glow**, which includes a parade.

**North Central Colorado**  Georgetown has a **Christmas Tree Lighting** on Thanksgiving weekend.

**Pikes Peak Region**  **Victorian Christmas at Miramont Castle** opens in Manitou Springs to run through Christmas.

**South Central Colorado**  Creede celebrates self-indulgence with its annual **Chocolate Festival**. Pueblo has a nighttime **Christmas Parade of Lights**, as well as a traditional Mexican-style **Las Posadas** procession.

**Southwestern Colorado**  Montrose is the scene of the **Black Canyon Balloon Classic**, a four-day hot-air ballooning event.

**DECEMBER**  **Denver**  Winterfest continues in December with the **Larimer Square Christmas Walk**, re-creating the ambience of a traditional Victorian Christmas, and the downtown **Parade of Lights**, an illuminated nighttime parade with floats and marching bands.

**North Central Colorado**  Georgetown's **Christmas Market** features food, horse-drawn carriage rides and a Santa Lucia processional. Leadville sponsors an all-day **Victorian Christmas Home Tour** complete with an elegant brunch and a candlelight dinner. Snowmass hosts the **Surge Boardfest**, one of the biggest snowboarding events anywhere.

**Southwestern Colorado**  In Silverton, local children and visitors are invited to take part in a traditional **Yule Log Festival**.

**Eastern Plains**  Burlington observes the holiday season with **Old Town Country Christmas**. Near La Junta, Bent's Old Fort re-enacts **Christmas 1846**.

▼▼▼▼▼▼▼▼▼▼▼
## Before You Go

**VISITORS CENTERS**

For free visitor information packages including maps and current details on special events, accommodations and camping, contact the **Colorado Tourism Board**. ~ 1625 Broadway, Suite 1700, Denver, CO 80202; 303-892-3485 or 800-265-6723; www.colorado.com. The state operates **Welcome Centers** that provide tourist information at major points of entry including Burlington, Lamar, Dinosaur, Trinidad, Fruita and Cortez. State and local tourist information centers are usually not open on weekends.

There is such an abundance of Colorado visitors' information on the world wide web that you could spend your entire vacation browsing through it and never leave home. A good starting point is the state's collection of links found at www.colorado.gov/rec reation.htm. You'll find the **Colorado Travel and Tourism** official website, which lets you order the **Colorado Vacation Guide** on-line and receive it by snail mail, at www.colorado.com. The **Department of Transportation** website, www.dot.state.co.us, provides maps, travel advisories and road conditions. There are links to more than 90 local **chambers of commerce** at www.state.co.us/business_dir/chambers.html, as well as links to more than 70 "unofficial" **community websites** at www.state.co.us/communities_dir/communities.html.

The old adage that you should take along twice as much money and half as much stuff as you think you'll need is sound advice as far as it goes. Bear in mind, though, that even in the more remote reaches of Colorado you might come across a store selling something more substantial than beef jerky and country-and-western cassettes . . . well . . . every once in a while.

Westerners are casual in their dress and expect the same of visitors. Once you leave the Denver metropolitan area, restaurants with dress codes are few and far between, though major resort towns such as Vail and Aspen cater to such upmarket vacationers that you might want to wear sport clothes a little more chic than a plaid flannel shirt and old Levis. Then again, you might not. They'll never know if you might be an eccentric billionaire.

> Vail and Aspen in particular seem to fancy themselves the Paris and Rome of winter sports-wear; otherwise, hardly anybody comes to the Rocky Mountains to show off their clothes.

When packing clothes, plan to dress in layers. Colorado's temperatures can turn hot or cold in a flash. During the course of a single summer vacation day in the mountains, you can expect to start wearing a heavy jacket, a sweater or flannel shirt and a pair of jeans, peeling down to a T-shirt and shorts as the day warms up, then putting the extra layers back on as the late afternoon shadows set in.

Other essentials to pack or buy along the way include a good sunscreen and high-quality sunglasses. Cool temperatures often lull newcomers into forgetting that thin high-altitude air filters out far less of the sun's ultraviolet rays; above timberline, exposed skin will get sunburned faster than it would on a Florida beach. If you are planning to camp in the mountains during the summer months, you'll be glad you brought mosquito repellent. Umbrellas are considered an oddity. You'll hardly ever see one, and you'll get funny looks from the locals if you carry one. The approved means of keeping chilly afternoon rain from running down the back of your neck is a cowboy hat.

For outdoor activities, tough-soled hiking boots are more comfortable than running shoes on rocky terrain. Even RV travelers and those who prefer to spend most nights in motels may want to take along a backpacking tent and sleeping bag for irresistible urges to stay out under Colorado's star-spangled skies. A canteen, first-aid kit, flashlight and other routine camping gear are also likely to come in handy. Both cross-country and downhill ski rentals are available everywhere you look during the winter, though serious skiers may find that the quality and condition of rental skis leaves something to be desired. In the summer, mountain bikes can be rented in just about any small town in the Colorado Rockies, but bike rentals are much harder to come by in other areas, so cycling enthusiasts who plan to explore the eastern plains or the northwest quadrant of the state should bring their own bikes. Other outdoor recreation equipment—a kayak, fishing tackle, golf clubs or a gold pan—generally cannot be rented, so you'll want to bring the right gear for your special sporting passion.

A camera is essential for capturing your travel experience; of equal importance is a good pair of binoculars, which let you explore distant landscapes from scenic overlooks and bring wildlife up close. And don't, for heaven's sake, forget your copy of *Hidden Colorado*.

**LODGING**  Lodgings in Colorado run the gamut from tiny one-room cabins to luxury hotels that blend traditional alpine lodge ambience with contemporary elegance. Bed and breakfasts can be found in almost all Colorado mountain towns you're likely to visit—not only chic destinations like Aspen and Telluride but also such off-the-beaten-path places as Sterling and Creede. They come in all types, sizes and price ranges. Typical of the genre are lovingly restored

## HOME ON THE RANCH

A vacation option can be found at guest ranches throughout the mountain areas of the state. Horseback riding is the common theme of all these ranches. Some offer luxury lodging, spa facilities and a full range of activities that may include fishing, boating, swimming and even tennis. Others operate as working ranches, provide lodging in comfortably rustic cabins and offer the opportunity to participate in roundups and other ranching activities. Rates at most guest ranches are comparatively expensive but include all meals and use of recreational facilities. Most guest ranches have minimum stay requirements ranging from three days to a week.

Victorian-era mansions comfortably furnished with period decor, usually with fewer than a dozen rooms. Some bed and breakfasts, however, are guest cottages or rooms in nice suburban homes, while others are larger establishments, approaching hotel size, of the type sometimes referred to as country inns.

In many parts of Colorado, you'll find lavishly restored historic hotels that date back to the gold boom days of the late 19th century. Many of these places combine affordable rates with plenty of antique decor and authentic personality.

The abundance of motels in towns along all major highway routes presents a range of choices, from name-brand motor inns to traditional mom-and-pop establishments that have endured for the more than half a century since motels were invented. While rather ordinary motels in the vicinity of major tourist destinations can be pricey, lodging in small towns away from major resorts and interstate routes can offer friendliness, quiet and comfort at ridiculously affordable rates.

At the other end of the price spectrum, peak season rates at leading ski resorts can be phenomenally high. Ways to skirt this problem include staying in more affordable lodging as much as an hour away and commuting in to the ski slopes during the day, or planning your ski vacation at the beginning or end of the season when rates are somewhat lower. Even though summer is a lively time in many ski towns, there is such a surplus of accommodations that room rates during the summer months are often a small fraction of winter rates.

Whatever your preference and budget, you can probably find something to suit your taste with the help of this book. Remember, rooms can be scarce and prices may rise during peak season, which is summer throughout most of the region and winter in ski resorts. Travelers planning to visit a place in peak season should either make advance reservations or arrive early in the day, before the "No Vacancy" signs start lighting up.

Accommodations in this book are organized by region and classified according to price. Rates referred to are summer high-season rates; in ski resorts where rooms cost significantly more in winter than in summer, ranges are given for both seasons. If you're looking for off-season bargains, it's good to inquire. *Budget* lodgings generally run less than $60 per night for two people and are satisfactory and clean but modest. *Moderate* hotels range from $60 to $110; what they have to offer in the way of luxury will depend on where they are located, but they generally offer larger rooms and more attractive surroundings. At *deluxe*-priced accommodations, you can expect to spend between $110 and $180 for a homey bed and breakfast or a double in a hotel or resort. In hotels of this price you'll generally find spacious rooms, a fashionable lobby, a restaurant and often a bar or nightclub. *Ultra-deluxe* facilities, priced above $180, are the finest in the region, offering all the amenities of a deluxe hotel plus plenty of extras.

Room rates vary as much with locale as with quality. Some of the trendier destinations have no rooms at all in the budget price range. In other communities—those where rates are set with truck drivers in mind and those in out-of-the-way small towns—every motel falls into the budget category, even though accommodations may range from $19.95 at run-down, spartan places to $45 or so at the classiest motor inn in town. The price categories listed in this book are relative, designed to show you where to get the most out of your travel budget, however large or small it may be.

**DINING**    Fine dining in most Colorado towns tends to focus on the region's traditional cuisine—beef and trout. You can also count on finding Mexican restaurants in just about every town you come to. More unusual cuisine is to be found in the major resort areas, such as Aspen and Vail, for restaurant business is fierce. There you'll find menus featuring everything from duck *à l'orange* to grilled elk. In Denver and some other areas of Colorado, buffalo meat is emerging as a specialty thanks to a growing number of ranches that have turned to raising this tasty, lean, low-cholesterol alternative to beef. If your idea of an ideal vacation includes savoring epicurean delights, then by all means seize opportunities whenever they arise. When traveling in the Colorado Rockies, you can go for days between gourmet meals.

Within a particular chapter, restaurants are categorized by region, with each restaurant entry describing the establishment according to price. Dinner entrées at *budget* restaurants usually cost $8 or less. The ambience is informal, service usually speedy and the crowd often a local one. *Moderate*-priced restaurants range between $8 and $16 at dinner; surroundings are casual but pleasant, the menu offers more variety and the pace is usually slower. *Deluxe* establishments tab their entrées from $16 to $24; cuisines may be simple or sophisticated, depending on the location, but the decor is plusher and the service more personalized. *Ultra-deluxe* dining rooms, where entrées begin at $24, are often the gourmet places; here cooking has become a fine art and the service should be impeccable.

Some restaurants change hands often and are occasionally closed in low seasons. Efforts have been made in this book to include places with established reputations for good eating. Breakfast and lunch menus vary less in price from restaurant to restaurant than evening dinners.

**DRIVING**    Some first-time visitors to Colorado wonder why so many mountain roads do not have guard rails to separate motorists from thousand-foot drop-offs. The fact is, highway safety studies have found that far fewer accidents occur where there are no guard rails. Statistically, edgy, winding mountain roads are much safer than straight, fast interstate highways. Unpaved roads are another story. While many are wide and well-graded, weather conditions or the wear and tear of heavy seasonal use can create unexpected road hazards. Some National Forest Service and Bureau of Land Management roads are designated for four-wheel-drive or high-clearance vehicles only. If you see a sign indicating four-wheel drive only, believe it. These roads can be very dangerous in a standard passenger car without the high ground clearance and extra traction afforded by four-wheel drive—and there may be no safe place to turn around if you get stuck.

If your car does not seem to run well at high elevations, the solution is probably to have the carburetor adjusted at the next service station. The air at Rocky Mountain altitudes is "thin"—that is, it contains considerably less oxygen in a given volume than air at lower altitudes. The carburetor or fuel injection unit should be set leaner to achieve an efficient fuel-to-air mixture. Another common problem when climbing mountain passes is vapor lock, a condition in which low atmospheric pressure combined with high engine temperatures causes gasoline to evaporate in the fuel lines, making bubbles that prevent the fuel pump from functioning. The result is that your car's engine coughs and soon stops dead. The solution is to pull over to the side of the road and wait until the fuel system cools down. A damp rag held against the fuel line will speed up the process and get you back on the road more quickly.

The most serious hazard of mountain driving is brake failure. Drivers of motor homes and heavily loaded trucks must be constantly alert to this risk, which is why mountain passes have "Trucks Use Lower Gear" signs—and runaway truck ramps. It can happen in a passenger car, too, if the driver "rides" the brakes while going down a steep mountain road. With heat buildup from friction, brakes quickly "fade" and lose their stopping power. To avoid this, descend steep grades in a lower gear and keep your foot away from the brake pedal. When you do brake, as for a

## WHEN IT SNOWS

In the winter months, mountain passes frequently become snowpacked, and under these conditions tire chains are required by law in Colorado, even on main highways. The chain law goes into effect regularly on Route 70 west of Denver. State patrolmen will make you turn back if your car is not equipped with chains, so make sure you have them. In winter it is also wise to travel with a shovel and blankets in your car.

switchback curve, bring the car's speed way down quickly and let it start picking up momentum as you begin the turn, minimizing the time your foot is on the brake pedal. If the brakes start feeling questionable or you smell a strange odor, pull over and feel the temperature inside one of the wheels. Hot brakes? Let them cool down before proceeding.

**TRAVELING WITH CHILDREN**  Any place that has wild animals, cowboys, rocks to climb and limitless room to run is bound to be a hit with youngsters. Plenty of family adventures are available in Colorado, from manmade attractions to experiences in the wilderness. A few guidelines will help make travel with children a pleasure.

Book reservations in advance, making sure that the places you stay accept children. Many bed and breakfasts do not. If you need a crib or extra cot, arrange for it ahead of time. A travel agent can be of help here, as well as with most other travel plans.

If you are traveling by air, try to reserve bulkhead seats where there is plenty of room. Take along extras you may need such as diapers, changes of clothing, snacks and toys or small games. When traveling by car, be sure to take along the extras, too. Make sure you have plenty of water and juices to drink; dehydration can be a subtle but serious problem. Most towns have all-night convenience stores that carry diapers, baby food, snacks and other essentials; national parks and some state parks also have such stores, though they usually close early.

A first-aid kit is a must for any trip. Along with adhesive bandages, antiseptic cream and something to stop itching, include any medicines your pediatrician might recommend to treat allergies, colds, diarrhea or any chronic problems your child may have. Mountain sunshine is intense, so take extra care. Children's skin is usually more tender than adult skin, and severe sunburn can happen before you realize. A hat is a good idea, along with a reliable sunblock.

Many national parks and monuments offer special activities designed just for children. Visitor center film presentations and rangers' campfire slide shows can help inform children about the

**PREPARE FOR SAFETY**

Some side roads will take you far from civilization, so be sure to have a full radiator and tank of gas. Carry spare fuel, water and food. Should you become stuck, local people are usually helpful about offering assistance to stranded vehicles, but in case no one else is around, for extended backcountry driving a CB radio or a car phone would not be a bad idea.

natural history of an area and head off some questions. Still, kids tend to find a lot more things to wonder about than adults have answers for. To be as prepared as possible, seize every opportunity to learn more—particularly about wildlife, a constant curiosity for young minds.

Colorado is big dog country, and you'll probably notice more **TRAVELING** travelers accompanied by their pets than in other regions. Pets are **WITH PETS** permitted on leashes in virtually all campgrounds. Most bed and breakfasts and guest ranches will not accept them, and more run-of-the-mill motels, particularly in Colorado tourist areas, seem to be adopting No Pets policies each year. Otherwise, the main limitation of traveling with a canine companion is that national parks and monuments prohibit pets on trails or in the backcountry. You are supposed to walk your dog on the roadside, then leave him in the car while you hike in the woods. Make sure the poor creature has adequate ventilation and water. Fortunately, dogs are free to run everywhere in national forests, and leashes are only required in designated camping and picnic areas.

Wildlife can pose special hazards for pets in the backcountry. At lower elevations in the plains and foothills, campers should not leave a cat or small dog outside at night because coyotes sometimes attack small pets. In remote forest areas, it's especially important to keep an eye on your dog at all times. Bears are upset by dogs barking at them and may attack even very large dogs. Porcupines, common in pine forests, are tempting to chase and slow enough to be easy to catch; if your dog *does* catch one, a mouthful of quills means painfully pulling them out one by one with a pair of pliers or making an emergency visit to a veterinary clinic in the nearest town.

In the greater Denver and Colorado Springs areas, the incidence **WOMEN** of crimes against women is substantially the same as in other mid- **TRAVELING** dle American cities of comparable size. Sexual assaults are rare but **ALONE** not unheard of in less populated parts of the state, including ski towns, gambling towns, wilderness areas and national parks.

Hitchhiking—or picking up hitchhikers—can be hazardous to one's personal safety on all Colorado highways and back roads. Personal security is one reason, though not among the most compelling ones, to avoid hiking or camping alone in remote areas. Unless your goal is absolute solitude—with its risks as well as its rewards—as a single traveler you can feel safer by sticking to larger established campgrounds and well-used trails. If you are hassled or threatened in some way, never be reluctant to scream for assistance.

It's a good idea to carry change for a phone call. Many Colorado organizations provide 24-hour help in case of emergency.

Metro Denver has the **Rape Assistance & Awareness Program** (303-329-9922) and there's the **Comitis Crisis Center** (303-343-9890) in Aurora. Other help lines include the **Rape Crisis Team of Boulder County** (303-442-7300); **Fort Collins Helpline** (970-586-5050); the **Colorado Springs Rape Crisis Center** (719-444-7540), the **Pueblo Rape Crisis Center** (719-544-1133); the **Rape Crisis Center of Grand Junction** (303-243-0290) and the **Durango Rape Intervention Team** (970-247-5400). When in doubt, dial 911 anywhere in the state.

**GAY & LESBIAN TRAVELERS**

Colorado achieved national notoriety in 1994 when it became the first state to pass an anti-gay rights law forbidding municipalities from enacting ordinances to protect gay and lesbian individuals from discrimination. The state supreme court ruled the new law unconstitutional, but not before public outrage resulted in a devastating tourist boycott.

Every story has two sides. Orchestrated by conservative religious groups, the anti-gay rights referendum was a backlash to the fact that several towns, including Boulder and Aspen, had just been among the first to pass progressive ordinances

On the web, you'll find an extensive listing of gay and lesbian resources in Colorado at www.gayrocky mountains.com.

*protecting* gay and lesbian civil rights. These gay-rights ordinances, and others passed in other cities and towns since the referendum, remain in full force today, protecting against discrimination in employment and housing—including travelers' lodging.

In general, gay and lesbian travelers will find open, multilayered alternative communities in major cities, including Denver, Boulder and Colorado Springs, and friendly attitudes in most resort towns. Bigotry is not dead in this part of the Wild West, though, and if you find yourself surrounded by people wearing cowboy hats, "don't tell" is still the safest policy.

Leading gay and lesbian periodicals in Colorado are the bi-weekly **Out Front** (723 Sherman Street, Denver, CO 80203; 303-778-7900 or 808-827-1915; www.outfrontcolorado.com) and the monthly **H Ink Magazine** (Quest Publications/H Ink Magazine, PO Box 18325, Denver, CO 80218; 303-752-4300; www.denvergay.com).

One of the state's most unusual gay groups, the **Colorado Gay Ice Hockey Association** is the home of the Colorado Climax hockey team. ~ 3939 Wyandot Street, 303-919-9860; www.climaxhockey.org.

**SENIOR TRAVELERS**

Colorado is a hospitable place for older vacationers, many of whom migrate from hotter climates to enjoy the cool summers. National parks and monuments invite persons age 62 and older to save considerable money with a **Golden Age Passport**, which allows free admission. Apply for one in person at any national park unit that charges an entrance fee. The passports are also good for a 50 percent discount on fees at most national forest campgrounds. Many private sightseeing attractions also offer significant discounts for seniors.

Colorado residents age 62 and up can buy an **Aspen Leaf Pass**, which eliminates the $4 day-use fee in state parks and permits free camping on weekdays. The annual pass costs $10; free to those over 72.

The **American Association of Retired Persons (AARP)** offers membership to anyone over 50 years old. AARP's benefits include travel discounts with a number of firms. ~ 1301 Pennsylvania Street #200, Denver, CO 80203; 303-830-2277, 800-424-3410; www.aarp.org.

**Elderhostel** offers educational courses that are all-inclusive packages at colleges and universities. In Colorado, Elderhostel courses are available in numerous locations including Rocky Mountain National Park, Cortez and Lake City. Among the dozens of subjects available are photography, archaeology, geology, railroads, birding, bicycling, skiing and hot springs. ~ 11 Avenue de Lafayette, Boston, MA 02111; 978-323-4141, 877-426-8056; www.elderhostel.org.

Be extra careful about health matters. High altitude is the biggest risk factor. Since many driving routes through the Colorado Rockies involve crossing mountain passes at 10,000 to 12,000 feet above sea level, it's advisable to ask your physician first. People with heart problems are commonly advised to avoid all physical exertion above 10,000 feet, and those with respiratory conditions such as emphysema may not be able to visit high altitudes at all. In the changeable climate of the Rockies, seniors are more at risk of suffering hypothermia. Many tourist destinations in the region are a long way from any hospital or other health care facility.

In addition to the medications you ordinarily use, it's a good idea to bring along the prescriptions for obtaining more. Consider carrying a copy of your medical record with you, including your history and current medical status as well as your doctor's name, phone number and address. Make sure that your insurance covers you while you are away from home.

**DISABLED TRAVELERS**

Colorado strives to make public areas fully accessible to persons with disabilities. Parking spaces and restroom facilities for the physically challenged are provided according to both state law and national park regulations. National parks and monuments also post signs that tell which trails are wheelchair-accessible. Some recreation areas have Braille nature trails with marked points of interest appealing to the senses of touch and smell.

Golden Access Passports, good for free entry to all national parks and monuments as well as discounts at most federal public campgrounds, are available at no charge to persons who are blind or who have another permanent disability. Apply in person at any national park or monument that charges an entrance fee.

The Columbine Pass, an annual state parks pass, costs $12.50 a year and is available to Colorado residents who are totally and permanently disabled. The pass is only available through parks department regional offices, not at the individual parks. ~ Colorado State Parks Department, Division Headquarters, 1313 Sherman, Room 618, Denver, CO 80203; 303-866-3437; www.parks.state.co.us.

Providing helpful information for disabled travelers are Accessible Travel & Hospitality, publishers of *Open World Magazine*, at 347 5th Avenue, Suite 610, New York, NY 10016, 212-447-7284, fax 212-725-8253, www.sath.org; and the Travel Disabilities Information Service at 1200 West Tabor Road, Philadelphia, PA 19141, 215-456-9900, www.mossresourcenet.org/travel.

Access-Able Travel Service provides worldwide information online. ~ P.O. Box 1796, Wheat Ridge, CO 80034; 303-232-2979; www.access-able.com.

**FOREIGN TRAVELERS**

**Passports and Visas**    Most foreign visitors, other than Canadian citizens, need a passport and tourist visa to enter the United States. Contact your nearest U.S. Embassy or Consulate well in advance to obtain a visa and to check on any other entry requirements.

**Customs Requirements**    Foreign travelers are allowed to carry in the following: 200 cigarettes (1 carton), 50 cigars, or 2 kilograms (4.4 pounds) of smoking tobacco; one liter of alcohol for personal use only (you must be 21 years of age to bring in alcohol); and US$100 worth of duty-free gifts that can include an additional quantity of 100 cigars. You may bring in any amount of currency, but must fill out a form if you bring in over US$10,000. Carry any prescription drugs in clearly marked containers. (You may have to produce a written prescription or doctor's statement for the custom's officer.) Meat or meat products, seeds, plants, fruits and narcotics are not allowed to be brought into the United States. Contact the United States Customs Service for further information. ~ 1301 Constitution Avenue NW, Washington, DC 20229; 202-927-6724; www.customs.treas.gov.

**Driving**    If you plan to rent a car, obtain an international driver's license before arriving in the United States. Some car rental agencies require both a foreign license and an international driver's license. Virtually all require a lessee to be at least 25 years of age and to present a major credit card. Seat belts are mandatory for the driver and all passengers. Children under the age of

# Secrets of Wildlife Watching

Most of us are probably city dwellers who rarely encounter wildlife more exotic than park pigeons in our everyday lives. One of the things that makes a trip on Colorado's back roads and trails so special is the chance it provides to see abundant—and often large—wild animals in a variety of habitat.

The state has no less than nine distinct life zones, each shaped by altitude and water availability, and each with its own set of animal inhabitants. A drive of just a few hours can take you through most of these zones—from riparian wetlands with white-tailed deer and beaver, up into the subalpine forest domain of elk and black bears, then higher yet to alpine tundra where mountain goats and bighorn sheep roam free, then down into the semidesert shrublands of the western slope where coyotes and pronghorn antelope are common sights.

*Hidden Colorado* contains dozens of tips for particularly good places to watch wildlife. Spotting large mammals is easiest in state parks and national parks and monuments, because game species possess an uncanny sense of where they are safe from human hunters. Fall hunting is permitted in the national forests, including in designated wilderness areas, so forest inhabitants such as deer and bears usually avoid encounters with humans.

The National Forest Service has set up viewing stations in some areas where there is an exceptional likelihood of seeing elk, pronghorn antelope, bighorn sheep, and even moose. State and federal governments have also set aside wetland reserves for migrating birds, and many of these provide havens for deer and other animals. In backcountry areas, the best places to look for wildlife are in open meadows with streams or lakes. Campgrounds, too, attract deer, raccoons and other animals who forage for food there. Avoid feeding deer, who have lost their natural fear of humans. Human food quickly impairs their ability to digest the leaves and bark that are their natural food, leaving many deer to starve to death during the off-season in tourist areas.

The best time for wildlife viewing is the first hour after sunrise and the last hour before sunset. Armed with binoculars or a telephoto camera lens, sit quietly, motionlessly and, above all, patiently. Animals notice sudden movements the most, and often pay no attention to motionless objects. A car can provide an effective blind, concealing sounds, scents or small movements that could alarm wildlife.

six or under 60 pounds should be in the back seat in approved child-safety restraints.

**Currency**   United States money is based on the dollar. Bills generally come in denominations of $1, $5, $10, $20, $50 and $100. Every dollar is divided into 100 cents. Coins are the penny (1 cent), nickel (5 cents), dime (10 cents) and quarter (25 cents). Half-dollar and dollar coins exist but are rarely used. You may not use foreign currency to purchase goods and services in the United States. Consider buying travelers checks in dollar amounts. You may also use credit cards affiliated with an American company such as Interbank, Barclay Card, Visa and American Express.

> In many areas, campers may find it convenient to keep a single location for as much as a week and explore surrounding areas on day trips.

**Electricity and Electronics**   Electric outlets use currents of 110 volts, 60 cycles. For appliances made for other electrical systems, you need a transformer or other adapter. Travelers who use laptop computers for telecommunication should be aware that modem configurations for U.S. telephone systems may be different than their European counterparts. Similarly, the U.S. format for videotapes is different than in Europe; National Park Service visitor centers and other stores that sell souvenir videos often have them available in European format on request.

**Weights and Measures**   The United States uses the English system of weights and measures. American units and their metric equivalents are: 1 inch = 2.5 centimeters; 1 foot (12 inches) = 0.3 meter; 1 yard (3 feet) = 0.9 meter; 1 mile (5280 feet) = 1.6 kilometers; 1 ounce = 28 grams; 1 pound (16 ounces) = 0.45 kilogram; 1 quart (liquid) = 0.9 liter.

## Outdoor Adventures

### CAMPING

RV or tent camping is a great way to tour Colorado during the summer months. Besides saving substantial sums of money, campers enjoy the freedom to watch sunsets from beautiful places, spend nights under spectacularly starry skies and wake up to find themselves in lovely surroundings that few hotels can match.

Most towns have commercial RV parks of some sort, and long-term mobile home parks often rent spaces to RVers by the night. But unless you absolutely need cable television, none of these places can compete with the wide array of public campgrounds available in national and state parks, monuments and forests. Federal campground sites are typically less developed: you won't find electric, water or sewer hookups in national forest, national monument or national recreation area campgrounds. As for national parks, the campground at Mesa Verde has some sites with full hookups, but Rocky Mountain National Park, with five large campgrounds totaling almost 600 sites, has no hookups. In Colorado, only a few state park campgrounds at major recreation lakes near cities have hookups; most do not. The largest public campgrounds, such as those in national parks, offer tent camping loops separate from RV loops, as well as hike-in backcountry camping by permit.

Colorado state park campgrounds operate on a reservation system; they are usually full on weekends but nearly empty on weekdays. Reservations are available from three days to six months in advance. ~ 303-470-1144, 800-678-2267; www.reserve america.com.

While most federal campgrounds do not take reservations, Rocky Mountain National Park does through a fairly cumbersome system. You can make reservations by phone (800-365-2267) up to five months in advance—but only on the fifth, 15th or 25th day of each month. On those days, the reservation line is extremely busy, and you should expect to wait on hold interminably. It's easier to make reservations through the National Park Service website (reservations.nps.gov). Whether you make them by phone or by internet, a credit card is required.

For Mesa Verde, Black Canyon and Great Sand Dunes national parks, as well as all national monument and national forest campgrounds, the rule is still first-come, first-served, even though they fill up practically every night in peak season. For campers, this means traveling in the morning and reaching your intended campground by early afternoon. In a few resort areas where housing is very expensive, particularly Aspen, don't expect to find a campsite no matter how early in the day you arrive; students working seasonal jobs and other long-term visitors monopolize the public campgrounds all summer, trading locations every two weeks to avoid maximum-stay limitations.

For a listing of state parks with camping facilities and reservation information, contact **Colorado State Parks**. ~ 1313 Sherman Street, Room 618, Denver, CO 80203; 303-866-3437; www.col oradoparks.org. Information on camping in the national forests is available from ten national forest headquarters around the state. Camping information for national parks and monuments is available from **National Park Service Intermountain Regional Headquarters**. ~ 12795 Alameda Parkway, Denver, CO 80225; 303-969-2500. A list of private campgrounds is available from **Colorado Adventure Guide**. ~ 303-422-4539; www.coloradovacation.com.

**PERMITS**

Colorado has well over two million acres in federally designated wilderness areas, most of which have been created quite recently. When the United States Congress passed the original Wilderness Act in 1964, only five areas in the state—La Garita, Mount Zirkel, Maroon Bells–Snowmass, Rawah and West Elk—were granted federal wilderness protection. They totaled less than 300,000 acres. Since then, wilderness protection has been expanded by the Colorado Wilderness Act of 1980, which set aside an additional 1.4 million acres, and the Wilderness Act of 1993, which extended wilderness protection to another 600,000 acres in the state. Today, Colorado boasts 33 designated wilderness areas, several of which are so new that they do not yet appear on most maps. Another 500,000 acres in 15 wilderness study areas enjoy temporary protection pending evaluation as future wilderness areas.

The Arkansas River is the most-used whitewater recreation river in the United States.

To be considered for federal wilderness protection, an area must consist of at least five contiguous square miles of public land without a road of any kind. Once it has been declared a wilderness area, its use is limited to uses that existed as of that date. Since most wilderness areas in the Rockies were created quite recently it is generally the highest peaks, where roads are few and far between, that qualify for wilderness status. Besides protecting ancient forests from timber cutting by newly developed methods like skylining or helicopter airlifting, the main significance of federal wilderness designation is that it prohibits all mechanized transportation—no jeeps, motorcycles or all-terrain vehicles and, after years of heated controversy, no mountain bikes. Wilderness areas usually have well-developed trail networks for hiking, cross-country skiing, and pack trips using horses or llamas.

You no longer need a permit to hike or camp in national forest or BLM wilderness areas, but plan to stop at a ranger station anyway for trail maps and advice on current conditions and fire regulations. Tent camping is allowed without restriction in wilderness areas and most other backcountry areas of national forests, except where signs are posted prohibiting it. Throughout the national forest in dry season and in certain wilderness areas at all times, regulations may prohibit campfires and sometimes ban cigarette smoking, with stiff enforcement penalties.

For backcountry hiking in most national parks and monuments, you must first obtain a permit from the ranger at the front desk in the visitor center. The permit procedure is simple and free. It helps park administrators measure the impact on sensitive ecosystems and distribute use evenly among major trails to prevent overuse.

**BOATING**

Many large manmade lakes in Colorado are administered as state parks, while others are National Recreation Areas supervised by the U.S. Army Corps of Engineers. Federal boating safety regulations may vary slightly from state regulations. Indian reservations have separate rules for boating on tribal lakes. More significant than any differences between federal, state and tribal regulations are the local rules in force for any particular lake, which are posted near boat ramps. Ask for applicable boating regulations at a local marina or fishing supply store or use the addresses and phone numbers listed in "Parks" or other sections of each chapter in this book to contact the headquarters for lakes where you plan to use a boat.

Boats, from small motorized skiffs to big, fast bass boats and sometimes even houseboats, can be rented by the half-day, 24-hour day or longer at marinas on many of the larger lakes. At most marinas, you can get a boat on short notice if you come on a weekday, since much of their business comes from local week-end recreation.

River rafting is a very popular sport in many parts of Colorado, notably the Arkansas River between Salida and Cañon City; the Roaring Fork River between Aspen and Glenwood Springs; and, for week-long backcountry float trips, the Yampa River in Dinosaur National Monument. Independent rafters are welcome, but because of the bulky equipment and specialized knowledge of river hazards involved, most adventurous souls stick with group tours offered by many rafting companies throughout the region.

Rafters, as well as people using canoes, kayaks, sailboards or inner tubes, are required by state and federal regulations to wear life jackets.

**FISHING**

Colorado boasts 7000 miles of streams and more than 2100 lakes. The more accessible a shoreline is, the more anglers you're likely to find there, especially during the summer months. You can beat the crowds by hiking a few miles into the backcountry or, to some extent, by planning your fishing days during the week.

Fish hatcheries in Colorado keep busy stocking streams with trout, particularly rainbows, the most popular game fish throughout the West. More than 22 million rainbow trout are stocked annually. Many cold-water mountain lakes also offer fishing for cutthroat trout and kokanee salmon. Catch-and-release flyfishing is the rule in some popular areas, allowing more anglers a chance at bigger fish. Be sure to inquire locally about eating the fish you catch, since some seemingly remote streams and rivers have contamination problems from old mines and mills.

The larger reservoirs, especially those at lower elevations, offer an assortment of sport fish, including carp, crappie, channel catfish, largemouth bass, smallmouth bass, white bass, bluegill, bull-head, perch, walleye and northern pike.

For copies of state fishing regulations, inquire at a local fishing supply or marina, or contact the **Colorado Division of Wildlife**. ~ 6060 Broadway, Denver, CO 80216; 303-297-1192; www.wildlife.state.co.us. State fishing licenses are required for fishing in national parks, national forests and national recreation areas, but not on Indian reservations, where daily permits are sold by the tribal governments.

# Denver

Passengers arriving by plane at Denver International Airport first glimpse Denver as a hazy sprawl that blurs the boundary between the flat prairie that stretches eastward and the jagged granite peaks of the central Rockies rising like castle walls and parapets just west of the city's edge. To motorists arriving from the east, north or south, the city is usually hidden by its murky atmosphere until the last possible moment, when the freeway plunges headlong into the dirty urban air, and suddenly the mountains fade away, replaced by the plate-glass canyons and steel pinnacles of the downtown skyline.

In recent years, Denver has topped all other American cities in air quality improvement. The problem is the city's location; the same mountains that offer Denverites so much natural beauty so close at hand also create air inversions that trap the smog, preventing it from blowing away. Despite the pollution, heavy traffic, suburban sprawl and other big-city drawbacks, Denver is actually a fun and easy place to visit. Colorado's largest museums, skyscrapers and amusement parks are located here, and the range of shopping and nightlife possibilities is unrivaled in the entire Rocky Mountain region. To reduce Denver to a set of sightseeing highlights worth searching for on a quick visit is to overlook the essential nature of the place, for its vast expanse and complexity make the city as unique and awe-inspiring as any mountain range or wilderness area in this book.

Just as modern travelers bound for almost any place in the Colorado Rockies are likely to come through Denver first, the city served as the main gateway through which miners, traders and homesteaders made their way into the mountains and where they often returned—sometimes wealthy. The Victorian-era mansions of the fortunate few who struck it rich still stand in the stately, shaded residential neighborhoods around the city center. During its early growth years, Denver developed strictly segregated ethnic neighborhoods. This cowboy-style discrimination even led to a landmark school desegregation case in which the U.S. Supreme Court outlawed Denver's practice of drawing district lines to create not only all-white and all-black schools but also separate Chicano, Asian, German, Italian and

Jewish schools. Today, old prejudices have faded, and Denverites take considerable pride in the city's multiethnic heritage; yet visitors who explore the residential areas of the city will soon discover the traditional ethnic enclaves that remain a key part of the city's character.

Denver got its start 1858, when prospector William Green Russell made the first gold discovery in Colorado along a tributary of Cherry Creek. Although the amount of gold dust panned from the creekbed proved insignificant and early prospectors soon moved higher into the mountains, they were quickly replaced by hordes of settlers chasing exaggerated rumors of wealth for the taking. Developers who had chartered the towns of Denver and Auraria (now Aurora) on paper several years before, sight unseen, rushed in to take charge as founding fathers of the tent communities that had sprung up on opposite banks of Cherry Creek.

Although its promoters billed it as "The Queen City of the Plains," Denver was slow to emerge as a town of any special importance. In the early years, it had no apparent advantages over other Front Range communities such as Colorado City, Boulder and Greeley. Central City, not Denver, was generally expected to emerge as the main cultural, political and financial center of the territory. To make matters worse, Denver burned to the ground in an 1863 fire. The following year, a flood sent a "wall of water" down Cherry Creek, devastating the town. Denver's aspirations as a commercial center were dashed when the builders of the first transcontinental railroad decided to bypass Denver and go through Cheyenne, Wyoming, instead. Observers of the developing West dismissed Denver as "a city without reason for being." Newspaper editor Horace Greeley went so far as to assert that there were " . . . more brawls, more fights, more pistol-shots with criminal intent in this log city of one hundred and fifty dwellings, not three-fourths completed nor two-thirds inhabited, nor one-third fit to be, than in any community of equal numbers on earth."

Little by little, however, mainly by developing a network of short-line railroads to serve the mining towns and building smelters and foundries that manufactured the heavy equipment needed for large-scale gold and silver mining in the mountains, Denver emerged as the economic hub of the region. Growth has followed the same pattern of Western-style sprawl as Los Angeles, as independent municipalities including Aurora, Lakewood, Westminster, Brighton, Englewood, Commerce City and Wheat Ridge—many larger in themselves than almost any other city in the state—have grown together to produce a five-county megalopolis. Today, with a population of almost two million, the Denver metro area is home to 54 percent of all Coloradoans.

## Downtown Denver

Set at a 45-degree angle to the conventional north–south streets and east–west avenues of the rest of the metropolis, downtown Denver dazzles visitors with a diversity of venerable Victoriana, '80s mirrored skyscrapers and stately government buildings. Best of all, it is tailor-made for walking. A few hours in the heart of the city provide an opportunity to admire Colorado's gold-plated state capitol, wander through the largest art museum in the Rocky Mountain region, stand in the room where "Unsinkable" Molly Brown held lavish society balls and stroll the steel-and-glass canyon of pedestrians-only 16th Street.

**SIGHTS**

A good landmark from which to begin exploring downtown Denver is the **Colorado State Capitol**, conventional in design but unique for its gleaming dome gilded with 200 ounces of 24-carat gold from the mines of Colorado, worth $4000 when it was completed in 1908, and nearly $120,000 today. Denver is known as the Mile-High City, and a plaque on the west steps of the capitol marks the elevation as exactly 5280 feet above sea level. Free tours start on the half hour weekdays, and every 45 minutes during the school year. Tours up into the dome, 180 feet above the ground floor, have been discontinued until further notice for security reasons. ~ Sherman Avenue between 14th and East Colfax avenues; 303-866-2604.

Stone lions flank the front door of the **Molly Brown House**, three blocks east of the capitol building. The mansion belonged to Leadville Johnny Brown, who struck it rich in the goldfields, and his wife, Molly, who achieved local fame as a survivor of the *Titanic* disaster. Their story became a hit Broadway musical and movie, *The Unsinkable Molly Brown*. Now restored to its turn-of-the-20th-century glory, the house radiates conspicuous consumption from its gold-leafed parlor ceilings to its lavish third-floor ballroom. Closed Mondays off-season. Admission. ~ 1340 Pennsylvania Street; 303-832-4092; mollybrown.org.

West of the capitol building stand a group of municipal buildings collectively known as the **Denver Civic Center**, erected around a Greek amphitheater commonly frequented by picnickers and street preachers. Southeast of the Civic Center, the **Colorado History Museum** presents changing exhibits on the state's heritage assembled from the museum's large collection of documents and antiques. Permanent displays include Plains Indian artifacts, Mesa Verde pottery and an exhibit about Cheyenne Indian "dog soldiers." The museum's centerpiece is a huge scale model of Denver as it looked in 1860 before the original wooden buildings were destroyed by fire. There are also models of cavalry forts and gold mines, along with real covered wagons and a wall from a pioneer sod house. Admission. ~ 1300 Broadway; 303-866-3682; www.coloradohistory.org.

The six-story free-form building gleaming with glass tiles at the south end of the Civic Center is the **Denver Art Museum**. It takes all day to see everything in this huge museum. Wings are devoted to pre-Columbian and Spanish Colonial art, Asian art, 19th-century art of the American West and decorative arts, among others. The museum's pride is an American Indian collection, said by many

*Text continued on page 50.*

# Denver Area

to Boulder

287

128

120th Ave

BRIGHTON

Barr Lake
State Park

Barr Lake

85

Henderson

WESTMINSTER

THORNTON

25

76

6

Denver
International
Airport

Peña Blvd

36

95

287

6

ARVADA

121

76

85

270

COMMERCE
CITY

6

85

WHEAT RIDGE

70

391

Blvd

Blvd

Blvd

40

W Colfax Ave

33

2

Blvd

City
Park

E Colfax Ave

287 40

70

6

6th
Ave

DENVER

LAKEWOOD

AURORA

W Alameda Ave

E
St

York St

Colorado

Alameda Ave

E Mississippi Ave

30

26

Wadsworth

Sheridan

Federal

Evans Ave

Four-Mile
Historic Park

Chambers Rd

Rd

Rd

225

ENGLEWOOD

Hampden Ave

Buckley

Tower

Quincy Ave

285

121

S Broadway

Blvd

88

Cherry Creek
Reservoir

Cherry Creek
State Park

Leetsdale Dr

85

University

177

88

Cherry Creek

470

75

25

470

LITTLETON

470

470

Chatfield
State
Park

121

Chatfield
Lake

Titan Rd

Santa Fe Dr

83

E Parker Rd

Kassler

Rampart Rd

South Platte River

Roxborough Park

Roxborough
State Park

85

Sedalia

N

Pike

National

Park

67

105

Castle Rock

86

Franktown

83

Castlewood
Canyon
State Park

25

0          10 miles

0          10 kilometers

*One-day Getaway*

## Denver with Kids

For most Colorado travelers, a visit to Denver is hard to avoid. Luckily the city has a wealth of riches when it comes to art and history museums, cultural events, shopping, fine dining—and other things that make many kids yawn. If your family finds itself in Denver on a summer day, here's a plan for having fun as you explore the city.

- Start with a visit to the **Denver Zoo** (page 64) before the day gets hot. If you're staying in the suburbs, where accommodations tend to be more family-friendly, take a surface street—Colfax Avenue or Colorado Boulevard—to reach City Park (the freeways get clogged during morning rush hour). Allow one and a half to two hours.

- City Park is also the place for family-oriented museums. Depending on your youngsters' interests, you can see dinosaurs and gold nuggets at the **Denver Museum of Nature and Science** (page 64) or amazing dollhouses at the **Denver Museum of Miniatures, Dolls and Toys** (page 64). Allow one and a half hours.

- From the west entrance of City Park, a left turn puts you on York Street, which heads directly to **Cherry Creek Shopping Center** (page 70). More than 50 restaurants in the mall and its immediate vicinity serve lunch. After your meal, stop in at the Cherry Creek location of the **Tattered Cover Book Store** (page 71) and browse through one of the largest selections of children's books in the United States.

- Now that the educational part of the day is out of the way, it's time to play. You could head for **Six Flags Elitch Gardens Amusement Park** (page 53) or its older, more affordable rival, **Lakeside Amusement Park** (page 66), but if it's a hot summer afternoon I recommend **Water World**. With more than 40 water slides, wave pools and tube rides, it's one of the best water parks in the country. Take Route 25 north to 84th Avenue (Exit 219), turn west (left) to Pecos Street, then north (right) to 88th Avenue. Admission. ~ 8800 Pecos, Thornton; 303-427-7873. Allow most of the afternoon.

- Head out to **Casa Bonita** (page 70) in Lakewood for dinner. The buffet and nonstop entertainment make this huge restaurant a lively, family-friendly dining experience. If you're coming from Water World, take Route 25 south back to Colfax Avenue (Exit 209), then take Colfax west to Casa Bonita.

- If your kids are still raring to go, check out Colorado's largest video arcade, **Red & Jerry's**, where they have soccer, stock car, monster truck and roller coaster simulators along with brand-new and vintage interactive games. From Casa Bonita, take Colfax Avenue east to Federal Boulevard, then turn right, go south to Oxford Street, and turn left. ~ 1840 West Oxford Street, Englewood; 303-783-0655.

to be the finest in the world. A major renovation in 1997 added a floor of European paintings and textiles as well as a café. A much more ambitious project, the Hamilton Building, will double the museum's exhibit space when it opens in 2006. Meanwhile, the new building's bold (some say bizarre) architecture by Daniel Libeskind, who was also chosen to design the reborn World Trade Center site, is a continuing source of controversy. Admission. ~ 100 West 14th Avenue Parkway, 720-865-5000; www.denver artmuseum.org.

The art museum's design faces tough competition thanks to the recent expansion of the **Denver Public Library**. Contrasting round and square elements, the architects used various colors of masonry to create a complex skyline of turrets, towers and pyramids that seems to mirror the kaleidoscopic character of Denver's downtown architecture. The largest library between Chicago and Los Angeles, it boasts 47 miles of bookshelves, including the seemingly boundless resources of the Gates Western History Reading Room. Rows of computers provide free public internet access. (The library does not allow people to check their e-mail, though.) ~ 10 West 14th Avenue Parkway; 720-865-1111; www.denver.lib.co.us.

Located behind the art museum, the **Byers-Evans House** is the property of the Colorado Historical Society. Built in 1883 by William Byers, founder of the *Rocky Mountain News*, it was lived in until 1981 by the Evans family of Denver philanthropists, including Anne Evans, founder of the Denver Art Museum. The house has been restored to its pre–World War I opulence and contains the Denver History Museum as well as family heirlooms. Closed Monday. Admission. ~ 1310 Bannock Street; 303-620-4933.

A block west of the Civic Center, the **United States Mint** is where the government makes more than 30 million coins a day. Just in case the nation ever needs to start making gold coins again, the mint also serves as the United States' second-largest gold repository (after Fort Knox). Closed for several years for security reasons, the mint has resumed public tours on the strictest conditions imaginable. You must be a U.S. citizen and be sponsored by your senator or congressman. Such sponsorship is routine, but you must apply at least three weeks in advance to allow time for the security check. The long list of items you can't bring along on the tour includes purses, backpacks, cameras, tobacco products and knitting needles. For complete details on tour restrictions, visit their website. ~ 320 West Colfax Avenue; 303-405-4764; www.usmint.gov.

HIDDEN ►    Any present or former kid who has ever dreamed of becoming a firefighter can fuel that fantasy at the **Denver Firefighters Museum**, in Denver's old fire station (c. 1906). Closed Sunday.

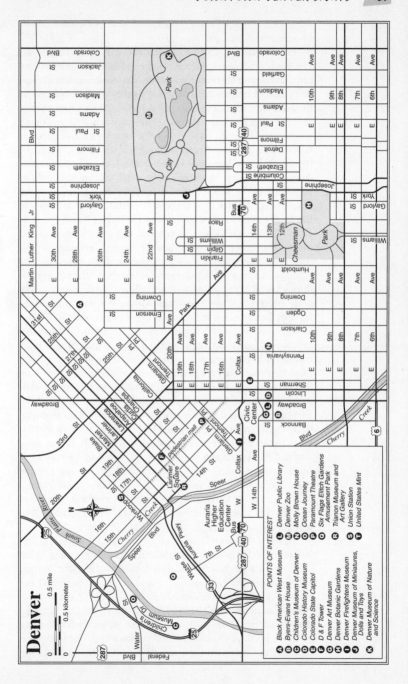

# Denver

0.5 mile
0.5 kilometer

*POINTS OF INTEREST*

- **A** Black American West Museum
- **B** Byers-Evans House
- **C** Children's Museum of Denver
- **D** Colorado History Museum
- **E** Colorado State Capitol
- **F** D & F Tower
- **G** Denver Art Museum
- **H** Denver Botanic Gardens
- **I** Denver Firefighters Museum
- **J** Denver Museum of Miniatures, Dolls and Toys
- **K** Denver Museum of Nature and Science
- **L** Denver Public Library
- **M** Denver Zoo
- **N** Molly Brown House
- **O** Ocean Journey
- **P** Paramount Theatre
- **Q** Six Flags Elitch Gardens Amusement Park
- **R** Trianon Museum and Art Gallery
- **S** Union Station
- **T** United States Mint

Admission. ~ 1326 Tremont Place; 303-892-1436; www.denver firefightersmuseum.org.

Head west on Colfax Avenue across Cherry Creek to the **Auraria Higher Education Center**, a large college campus shared by the University of Colorado at Denver, Metropolitan State College and Denver Community College and used by 30,000 students. At the northwest edge of the campus is a shady block of beautifully restored older residences that were preserved when the rest of the neighborhood was demolished to make room for the college buildings. Known as **Ninth Street Historic Park**, the block contains 14 homes, each in a different architectural style from Denver's early days, with signs on the front lawns to tell visitors about them. Highlights of the park include a small 1911 duplex owned by the center, which was once the home of Israeli leader Golda Meir and has been restored as a museum, and the former Tivoli Brewery, with its flamboyant 1860s architecture and seven-story mansard tower. The brewery now houses the **Starz FilmCenter**. ~ 900 Aurora Parkway; 303-820-3456; www.starzfilmcenter.com.

Skyscrapers turn the downtown streets into echoing canyons through which streams of humanity flow. The pedestrians-only **16th Street Mall**, the most people-friendly route through the heart of the city, starts at Broadway two blocks north of the Civic Center and runs northwest for the entire one-mile length of downtown. Cafés and shops line the mall, and free frequent shuttle buses run from one end to the other. Points of interest along the way include the **Paramount Theatre**, the city's only surviving motion-picture palace, now used for plays, rock concerts, children's shows and film festivals, as well as several blocks of department stores and refurbished commercial buildings that date back to the late 1800s. ~ 1631 Glenarm Place; 303-623-0106; www.historicparamounttheatre.com. The **D & F Tower**, now dwarfed by skyscrapers nearby, was the tallest building west of the Mississippi when it was completed in 1910 as part of the Daniels & Fisher department store (which later merged with the May Company to create Denver's leading department store, May D & F). The renovated tower is part of the Tabor Center office and condominium complex. ~ 1601 Arapahoe Street.

At the northwest end of the 16th Street Mall is Writer Square, a modern development that integrates retail, office and living space. It is the gateway to the **Lower Downtown Historic District**, usually referred to as "LoDo." The area of historic buildings from the late 1800s starts at **Larimer Square**, Denver's oldest commercial block. Restored in 1964, it was one of the first officially designated historic districts in the United States. Today, Larimer Square is filled with restaurants and unique shops. The LoDo Historic District continues for about six blocks to grand old **Union**

**Station**, still used by Amtrak and ski-train passengers. In the basement of the station, one of the world's largest model-train collections is open to the public on the last Friday evening of every month. ~ 1701 Wynkoop Street.

The **Trianon Museum and Art Gallery** contains French paintings and furniture from the 17th and 18th centuries in a 1910 Colorado Springs gold rush–era mansion modeled after the palace of Marie Antoinette and later moved to its present location. The museum also has Asian art of the same period. Closed Sunday. Admission. ~ 335 14th Street; 303-623-0739.

Elsewhere in the downtown area, the **Black American West Museum** traces the roles African American pioneers, cowboys, miners, soldiers and politicians played in settling the West. The museum is housed in the former office and residence of Dr. Justina Ford, a black woman physician who practiced in Denver for 50 years. Admission. ~ 3091 California Street; 303-292-2566; www.blackamericanwest.org.

"Not to see Elitch's is not to see Denver" was the familiar slogan of the old Elitch Gardens, a Denver landmark that dated back to the 1890s and had not only amusement park rides but also lavish fresh-flower displays, a big-band ballroom and a theater where generations of Broadway stars performed. In 1993, however, Elitch's closed down and began the two-year task of disassembling its rides, including a 70-year-old carousel and parts of its original roller coaster (to be incorporated in a new, higher, faster roller coaster), and relocating to the present **Six Flags Elitch Gardens Amusement Park**, located at the confluence of Cherry Creek and the South Platte River just west of downtown Denver. There are six entertainment stages, four game arcades, six restaurants, a plethora of curio stands and 27 major rides including three roller coasters—one a wooden replica of the classic coaster at the old Elitch Gardens—as well as a 220-foot free-fall tower, a bungee jump, the world's highest free-fall swing, a halfpipe snowboard simulator and a "flying coaster" on which you ride prone, as well as a water park called Island Kingdom. Bereft of most of its historical charm, the new Elitch Gardens is as state-of-the-art as an amusement park can be—and costs three times as much as its longtime rival, Lakeside Amusement Park (see "Suburban Denver"). Admission. ~ 2000 Elitch Circle (Route 25 at Speer Boulevard); 303-595-4386; www.sixflags.com/parks/elitchgardens.

The most unusual feature at the Children's Museum of Denver is Kidslope, an artificial ski slope with a separate admission charge, where children can take ski lessons from a pro year-round.

Located just across the river from Elitch's, off Route 25 at the 7th Street exit, is the **Children's Museum of Denver**. Exhibits include CompuLAB, where visitors can create programs and access the internet; Wild Oats Community Market, an interactive kid-size supermarket, and Planet Zoo, featuring animals such as hedgehogs, chameleons and turtles. The museum also offers children's inline-skating lessons spring through fall and ski and snowboard lessons year-round. Closed Monday except during the summer. Admission. ~ 2121 Children's Museum Drive; 303-433-7444; www.cmdenver.org.

Also across the river from Elitch's is **Ocean Journey**, a unique, state-of-the-art aquarium that re-creates settings above the water's surface as well as below, incorporating thousands of live plants, birds and mammals including a pair of Sumatran tigers. Circulating one million gallons of fresh and salt water, the aquarium simulates the courses of two great rivers on opposite sides of the world—the Colorado River and Indonesia's Kampar River—as they make their way from headwaters to the sea. Opened in 1999 as a nonprofit institution, the aquarium was immensely popular; yet due to its $93 million construction cost, it went bankrupt within a year. Finding that it's not easy to attract a buyer for a million-gallon fishtank complete with fish, the bankruptcy trustee finally auctioned the facility—ironically, to the corporation that owns the world's largest chain of seafood restaurants—for about 5 percent of its construction cost. It's now back in operation. Admission. ~ 700 Water Street; 305-561-4444; www.oceanjourney.com.

The **Forney Transportation Museum**, just off Route 70 Exit 275, displays electric streetcars that once carried passengers through Denver's streets, as well as antique cars such as Theodore Roosevelt's Renault and Arab prince Aly Khan's Rolls-Royce. There are railroad coaches and cabooses, the world's largest steam locomotive and a vintage McCormick reaper. Admission. ~ 4303 Brighton Boulevard; 303-297-1113; www.forneymuseum.com, e-mail forney@frii.net.

**LODGING**    Although rates for lodging in downtown Denver tend to be very expensive, those traveling on minimal funds can find budget-priced beds at the **Denver International Youth Hostel**, a 160-bed hostel offering separate dormitory-style accommodations for men and women. Guests must furnish their own sheets or rent them, but both the prices and the location—just four blocks from the capitol—are hard to beat. Reservations are generally not necessary. ~ 630 East 16th Avenue; 303-832-9996; e-mail denver@youth hostels.com. BUDGET.

Toward the other end of the lodging spectrum, the **Brown Palace Hotel** has enjoyed a reputation as Denver's finest hotel ever since it was built in 1892, when cattle barons and railroad tycoons made this their home away from home. In those days, the seven-story red stone structure with its distinctive triangular shape dominated the downtown skyline. Renovated for its 100th birthday in 1992, the 241-room hotel still stands proud among the steel-and-glass faces of neighboring skyscrapers. A lofty, eight-story-high stained glass atrium makes the hotel far more impressive inside than out. Guest rooms are individually decorated in a variety of styles spanning the lifetime of the hotel: gracious Victorian, lively art deco and bright contemporary. ~ 321 17th Street; 303-297-3111, 800-321-2599; www.brownpalace. com, e-mail brownpalace@brownpalace.com. ULTRA-DELUXE.

Connected to the Brown Palace by a second-floor walkway, the **Comfort Inn Downtown Denver** offers somewhat lower rates for centrally located downtown lodgings. The 229 rooms are modern, with bright, contemporary furnishings, and hotel services include 24-hour room service and valet parking. The prices include a continental-plus breakfast. ~ 401 17th Street; 303-296-0400, 800-221-2222, fax 303-312-5941; www.comfortinn.com, e-mail cisales@brownpalace.com. DELUXE.

Located a short stroll from the Denver Art Museum in the same stately old residential neighborhood as the Molly Brown House, the turreted three-story red sandstone **Capitol Hill Mansion Bed & Breakfast Inn** dates back to 1891. It was among the last grand mansions built before the silver crash toppled Denver's mining prosperity. Some of the eight guest rooms and suites feature fireplaces, balconies, whirlpool tubs or queen-size canopy beds, and all have refrigerators and high-speed wireless internet access. Rooms are individually decorated and range from the all-white Paintbrush Room, with air-conditioning as well as a ceiling fan, to the Snowlover Balcony Room, with its floor-to-ceiling wraparound mural of an aspen forest. ~ 1207 Pennsylvania; 303-

**AUTHOR FAVORITE**

The architect of the Brown Palace also designed the smaller, 81-room **Oxford Hotel**, located in the LoDo historic district. It prospered for decades as the grand hotel closest to Union Station. In the 1930s a top-to-bottom renovation transformed it into an art-deco masterpiece. The hotel deteriorated with the decline of train travel and finally was closed down for restoration in 1979. Today, the sterling-silver chandeliers have been stripped of layers of paint and faithful copies of the original carpets grace the hotel's corridors after a $12 million effort restored the glory of this elegant small hotel. The 80 guest rooms have dark wood antique furnishings and soft-hued floral patterns; some have canopied beds and fireplaces. ~ 1600 17th Street; 303-628-5400, 800-228-5838, fax 303-628-5413; www.the oxfordhotel.com, e-mail reservations@theoxfordhotel.com. ULTRA-DELUXE.

839-5221 or 800-839-9329, fax: 303-839-9046; www.capitolhill mansion.com, e-mail Info@capitolhillmansion.com. DELUXE TO ULTRA-DELUXE.

**Hotel Teatro** has seen as many changes as an actor in a French farce. Originally the local tramway building, the place morphed into the governor's mansion, then university headquarters and finally a theater workshop space. Now a stunning boutique hotel just across from the Denver Performing Arts Complex, the 1911 building features original detail work and preserved costumes from its stint as a rehearsal space. The 111 rooms have 12-foot ceilings, art-deco decor and custom-built furniture draped with rich, textured fabrics. It ain't cheap, but it's worth every penny. ~ 1100 14th Street; 303-228-1100, 888-727-1200, fax 303-228-1101; www.hotelteatro.com, e-mail general manager@hotelteatro.com. ULTRA-DELUXE.

Most modern hotels in the downtown area are brand-name highrises geared toward business travelers. Room rates are high and reservations essential during the workweek, but on Friday, Saturday and Sunday nights the cost typically drops by 50 percent or more, so you can realize significant savings if you make your Denver sightseeing visit on a weekend. For instance, the rates at the **Executive Tower Hotel**, a 337-room skyscraper across the street from the Denver Convention Center, run in the ultra-deluxe range on weeknights but come down all the way to the moderate range on weekends for spacious, bright rooms with mountain or cityscape views. Guest facilities at this sleek, contemporary hotel include an indoor swimming pool and an outdoor running track, exercise equipment and tennis, squash and racquetball courts. ~ 1405 Curtis Street; 303-571-0300, 800-525-6651, fax 303-825-4301; www.exectowerhotel.com, e-mail inquiries@exectowerhotel. com. MODERATE TO ULTRA-DELUXE.

Located near 16th Street Mall, the **Holiday Inn Denver Downtown** shows the results of a major renovation of the venerable

---

### A ROYAL RESPITE

One of Denver's best bed and breakfasts is **Castle Marne**, an 1889 Richardsonian Romanesque stone mansion five minutes from downtown. This nine-room inn is thought to be the finest remaining example of Victorian architect William Lang's work. Rooms are furnished with family antiques and decorated with vintage and local artwork; some rooms have balconies with jacuzzis. Rates include a complete gourmet breakfast and afternoon tea. ~ 1572 Race Street; 303-331-0621, 800-926-2763, fax 303-331-0623; www.castlemarne.com, e-mail info@castlemarne.com. DELUXE TO ULTRA-DELUXE.

Hotel Denver Downtown, which was the largest hotel in the city for many years. The 21-story highrise has spacious, modern rooms decorated in soft hues, many with views overlooking the capitol dome. Amenities include a fitness center and rooftop swimming pool, as well as such business conveniences as in-room data ports and secretarial service on call 24 hours a day. ~ 1450 Glenarm Place; 303-573-1450, 800-423-5128, fax 303-572-1113; www. hoteldenver.net, e-mail information@hoteldenver.net. DELUXE.

Located four blocks from downtown in Denver's Clement Historic District, the **Queen Anne B&B Inn** consists of two Victorian-era houses with porches, turrets, sundeck, hot tub, gardens and patio. One of the 14 rooms has a fireplace and all are distinctively decorated with flowery motifs and four-poster brass beds to create a romantic ambience. ~ 2147 Tremont Place; 303-296-6666, 800-432-4667, fax 303-296-2151; www.queenannebnb.com, e-mail travel@queenannebnb.com. MODERATE TO ULTRA-DELUXE.

The brownstone **Holiday Chalet** was originally built in 1896 as the Bohm mansion, residence of one of Denver's first jewelers. Its ten rooms are furnished with heirloom antiques and have individual kitchens and baths. A renovation added new wood floors and decorative touches. Rates include a self-serve breakfast. ~ 1820 East Colfax Avenue; 303-321-9975, 800-626-4497, fax 303-377-6556; e-mail holidaychalet@aol.com. MODERATE TO DELUXE.

The high-rise **Red Lion Hotel Downtown West** is about two miles from downtown near the new Invesco Stadium, home of the Denver Broncos football team. Six Flags Elitch Gardens is located across the street. There is an outdoor pool and a restaurant; a complimentary shuttle runs to and from downtown. Following a complete remodeling in 1996, the 171 rooms look brand-new in warm hues. ~ 1975 Bryant Street; 303-433-8331, 800-388-5381, fax 303-455-7061; www.redliondenverdowntown.com, e-mail info@redliondenverdowntown.com. MODERATE.

**Strings** serves imaginative contemporary cuisine à la carte and offers patio dining. Sample dishes include baby spinach and mint salad with berries, *penne bagutta* (homemade pasta with chicken and mushrooms in a spicy sauce), an heirloom tomato and caviar tower and salmon ceviche. The clientele presents a striking cross section of Denverites—on any evening you're likely to see diners wearing everything from T-shirts to tuxedos. ~ 1700 Humboldt Street; 303-831-7310. DELUXE.

**DINING**

**Pete's Kitchen** has been serving fast and delicious American diner food since 1942. Housed in a historic landmark building, Pete's attracts all-night crowds on Friday and Saturday nights, when the doors remain open all night long. ~ 1962 East Colfax Avenue; 303-321-3139. BUDGET.

HIDDEN ▶    The **Bump & Grind Café** is a retro neighborhood eatery that combines '50s kitsch with modern styling. At the weekend Petticoat Brunch, your eggs roulade, roasted vegetable pie or cowgirl tofu scramble is served by men in drag. ~ 439 East 17th Avenue; 303-861-4841. BUDGET TO MODERATE.

Occupying two separate converted houses in the trendily resurrected "Golden Triangle" neighborhood, **Cuba Cuba** is Denver's only Cuban restaurant. The tastefully tropical ambience is as cool as the minty *mojitos* that the bartender concocts. You'll find the menu full of subtle flavor with just a hint of the tropics. Try the plantain chips with *habanero mojo* and avocado salad, mahi-mahi painted with Bacardi or the *piccadillo con arroz y Madura*, a ground-beef dish with tomatoes, raisins and potatoes served with plantain cakes. This enormously popular restaurant does not take reservations, so come prepared for a long wait. Dinner only. Closed Sunday. ~ 1173 Delaware Street; 303-605-2822. MODERATE.

Many Denver gourmands contend that the **Imperial Chinese Seafood Restaurant** is the best Chinese restaurant in the Rocky Mountain region. It certainly has the most elaborate decor, from the papier-mâché lions that guard the front entrance to the high-style Hong Kong glitz of the dining area. Seafood is the specialty. Try the Dungeness crab in Szechuan spices and scallops stir-fried with vegetables. ~ 431 South Broadway; 303-698-2800. DELUXE.

Recently opened on the premises that formerly housed the late, lamented Denver Buffalo Company, a gourmet Mexican restaurant named **Cielo** (Spanish for "sky" or "heaven") showcases such fare as *huachinango* (red snapper) in a spicy seafood sauce and tamales filled with turkey chorizo. The restaurant is painted in a skylike motif of blended blues and bathed in romantic golden light. ~ 1109 Lincoln Street; 303-597-2435. DELUXE.

When the longtime favorite Denver Buffalo Company closed its doors, the low-fat red-meat niche was promptly filled by **Ted's**

### AUTHOR FAVORITE

I'm usually a little ambivalent about French restaurants. Sure, the French have elevated cuisine to a fine art, but most restaurants that serve it tend to be expensive and snooty. Not so **Le Central**, where the ambience is modest, the service is polite, the price is right and the Provence-style food is out of this world. The menu, which changes often to take advantage of seasonally available ingredients, always features meat and seafood selections, entrée salads and vegetarian specials. The wine list is extensive but not expensive, and a separate menu offers a variety of clams and mussels, served with all the french fries you can eat. ~ 112 East 8th Avenue; 303-863-8094. MODERATE.

**Montana Grille**. "Ted" is media mogul Ted Turner, whose ranches raise about 70 percent of the estimated quarter-million living bison on earth. Decorated in dark polished wood and displaying Old West artworks, the restaurant serves everything from sandwiches and burgers (try the big buffalo burger with bleu cheese, bacon and mushrooms), to barbecued bison ribs and the bison Delmonico. ~1404 Larimer Street; 303-893-0654. MODERATE TO DELUXE.

The **Fourth Story**, upstairs in the LoDo District's legendary Tattered Cover Bookstore, offers gourmet cheeses and the city's longest by-the-glass wine list in a librarylike atmosphere that provides an ideal hideaway from the noise and bustle of downtown Denver. ~ 2955 East First Avenue; 303-322-1824. MODERATE.

In part of the historic building that was once Denver's grand Paramount Theatre, rescued from demolition with all artwork and original gilding still intact, **Paramount Café** is a lively bar and grill specializing in buffalo burgers and sandwiches. Dining is either inside or on the patio. The café shares the premises with a five-table pool room. ~ 519 16th Street; 303-893-2000. BUDGET.

You'll find Cajun cuisine reputed to be the best in town at **Bayou Bob's**. Plastic tablecloths highlight the decor, but no frills are necessary. Fried catfish and spicy gumbo have made this place a favorite of the downtown weekday lunch bunch; it's also open for dinner. Closed Sunday. ~1635 Glenarm Place; 303-573-6828. BUDGET.

Located in the elegant grace of Hotel Teatro, the award-winning **Restaurant Kevin Taylor** will wow you with its Parisian decor and atmosphere (think chandeliers and striped-silk brocade furnishings). The menu follows suit with French-influenced offerings such as lavender honey–roasted ranch venison with Peruvian potatoes, anjou pears and a peppery cider reduction. And if you can't find what you want from their 5000-bottle wine cellar, maybe it just doesn't exist. Dinner only. Closed Sunday. ~ 1100 14th Street; 303-820-2600; www.hotelteatro.com, e-mail general manager@hotelteatro.com. ULTRA-DELUXE.

At **Jou Jou**, Hotel Teatro's other award-winning eatery, the feel is slightly more casual; the bistro setting is accented with 18-foot ceilings and windows everywhere you turn. The food's just as good: try the arugula and tomato fettuccine with sweet corn and garlic basil sauce. For breakfast they have homemade granola with steamed milk. Breakfast, lunch and dinner. ~ 1100 14th Street; 303-228-0770; www.hotelteatro.com, e-mail generalmanager@hotel teatro.com. MODERATE TO DELUXE.

The quaint, Old World–style **Little Russian Cafe** on Larimer Square features authentic Russian food. Favorites are caviar, chicken Kiev and Siberian *pelmeni* (beef dumplings). Also available are European wines and beers and plenty of vodkas. There's patio dining in summer. ~ 1424 Larimer Street; 303-595-8600. MODERATE.

The strangest decor in a downtown restaurant-and-bar is at the **Croc's Mexican Grill**, where a 20-foot-long artificial crocodile dangles from the ceiling and leers at diners. The scene is lively after five, as happy-hour sloshes its way toward the dinner hour. The menu features Mexican food along with sandwiches and seafood. Shrimp is a specialty—in fajitas or enchiladas, smothered in a Mazatlan-style sauce, or fried and served by the bucket. ~ 1630 Market Street; 303-436-1144. BUDGET.

The **Wynkoop Brewing Company** is Colorado's oldest brewpub (a genre that has become ubiquitous in the Denver–Boulder area). Located in an old warehouse in the LoDo district, the establishment brews its own beer—more beer, they claim, than any other brewpub in the country—and serves it in a traditional tavern atmosphere along with English and Scottish food selections such as shepherd's pie, as well as more American entrées such as elk medallions and portobello sandwiches. ~ 1634 18th Street; 303-297-2700; www.wynkoop.com, e-mail info@wynkoop.com. MODERATE.

The big buzz in the Denver restaurant scene, **Adega** opened in 2002 to instant national acclaim: *Gourmet* magazine and *The New York Times* featured it, *Food & Wine* magazine gave it a Best New Chef award and *Esquire* ranked it among the Best New Restaurants in the United States. The name means "wine cellar" in Portuguese, and that's a big part of what this place is about, with its huge, glassed-in wine storage area and its list of 800 wines, including nearly 50 available by the glass. The cuisine is whimsically French in style, featuring such "wine-friendly" fare as veal cheek marsala and fricassee of rabbit with farfallini, smaller tasting plates of delicacies like quail eggs Benedict, gnocci with duck confit and bacon-wrapped, almond-stuffed dates, as well as a lavish six-course chef's tasting plate. Reservations are a must. ~ 1700 Wynkoop Street; 303-534-2222. ULTRA-DELUXE.

Vegetarians are well-advised to steer clear of **The Buckhorn Exchange**, but other visitors discover a unique brand of Old West elegance here. Denver's oldest restaurant, it was started in 1893 by a former frontier scout, who began decorating the restaurant with hunting trophies (still common practice in some parts of Colorado). The collection grew over the years until today the Buckhorn displays more than 500 stuffed animals and birds. The menu, too, may remind you of a museum of natural history, with its emphasis on exotic meats such as rattlesnake marinated in chile and lime, Rocky Mountain oysters with horseradish, and pheasant breast sautéed in a cinnamon-marmalade sauce. ~ 1000 Osage Street; 303-534-9505; www.buckhorn.com. ULTRA-DELUXE.

**SHOPPING**     As the largest city in the Rocky Mountain states, Denver caters to many people who live in small ranch, mining and oil communities and come to "the big city," often traveling hundreds of miles, for special-occasion shopping sprees. Nowhere is this phenomenon more vividly apparent than along the **16th Street Mall**, a major downtown street that has been closed to traffic for its entire one-mile length. There are buskers, fashion boutiques, Parisian-style sidewalk cafés, numerous sporting goods shops and outdoorsy clothiers along this commercialized shopping strip. With the preponderance of franchise name stores and restaurants, the mall is a center of entertainment and shopping activity in downtown Denver. Anchoring one end of the mall is the **Denver Pavilions**, where you'll find a multiplex movie theater, stores like Nike Town, Banana Republic and Talbot's, and upscale eateries such as Wolfgang Puck Café and Maggiano's Little Italy. Near the northwest end of 16th Street Mall is **Tabor Center**, a two-block-long, three-story atrium containing 65 specialty stores. ~ 16th and Lawrence streets; 303-572-6868. Also here is **Bridge Market**, where vendors sell such wares as T-shirts, imports, paintings and electronic novelties from pushcarts.

> The free 16th Street shuttle, which runs from Civic Center to Union Station in LoDo, makes shopping along the 16th Street Mall a breeze.

Larimer Street, at the northwest end of 16th Street Mall just past Tabor Center, was Denver's original main street. It had deteriorated into the city's skid row by the 1960s, when a massive urban-renewal effort transformed it into a showpiece historic district of red-brick Victorian restorations. Two shopping blocks, **Writer Square** and **Larimer Square**, offer an ever-changing kaleidoscope of specialty stores ideal for gift shopping. Among the fine art galleries in Writer Square are **Gallery One** (303-629-5005), with works by leading contemporary artists such as Native American painter R. C. Gorman and Spanish Impressionist Royo, and **Third Canyon Gallery** (303-893-3936). ~ 1512 Larimer Street. In Larimer Square, check out cozy **Cry Baby Ranch** (1422 Larimer Square; 303-623-3979), where whimsical frontier-themed goods such as Happy Trails lunchboxes, cowboy kitchen plates and Buckaroo hats stock the shelves. **John Atencio** (1440 Larimer Street; 303-534-4277) has the award-winning custom-designed jewelry of goldsmith John Atencio. ~ 14th and Larimer streets.

In the same neighborhood, check out the antique furniture and welcoming fireplace at the **Tattered Cover Book Store**, Colorado's largest independent bookseller, to see just how comfortable a superstore can be. ~ 1628 16th Street; 303-436-1070; www.tatteredcover.com.

Just south of downtown, **Gart Bros. Sports Castle**, the world's largest sporting goods store, has equipment for every known sport except perhaps skydiving and curling. It has its own tennis court, golf driving cage and ski mountain, as well as a rooftop basketball court and test area for rollerblades and bikes. Shoppers can ride around the huge store on golf carts. ~ 1000 Broadway; 303-861-1122.

**NIGHTLIFE**    The **Denver Performing Arts Complex**, commonly known as "The Plex," covers four city blocks and has 9000 seats in ten theaters and performance spaces. Within the arts complex, theater productions are presented at the **Helen Bonfils Theatre Complex**, which is associated with the National Theatre Conservatory. (Helen Bonfils, heiress to the Denver Post publishing empire, was one of Denver's leading philanthropists and theatrical producers.) Musical performances are offered at the Denver Center for the Performing Arts by the **Colorado Symphony Orchestra** (303-292-5566; www.coloradosymphony. org), **Opera Colorado** (303-778-1500; www.operacolorado.org) and the **Colorado Ballet** (303-837-8888; www.coloradoballet.org). For a complete rundown on current performances at the complex, call 303-893-4000. ~ 14th and Champa streets; 303-893-4100.

> The Denver Performing Arts Complex is second only to Lincoln Center in audience capacity.

As for nightclubs, Denver has plenty of them. **Comedy Works** features nationally known standup comics Wednesday through Sunday and has an open-mike night on Tuesday. Closed Monday. Cover. ~ 1226 15th Street; 303-595-3637. **Impulse Theater**, downstairs from the Wynkoop Brewing Company brewpub, presents improvisational comedy Thursday, Friday and Saturday nights. Cover. ~ 1634 18th Street; 303-297-2111; www.impulsetheater.com.

**Brendan's Market Street Pub**, in the LoDo district, features live blues Monday through Saturday and live funk on Sunday. ~ 1624 Market Street; 303-595-0609.

The "67" in **Blue 67** is for the number of different kinds of martinis at this mellow, ultra-trendy LoDo saloon, whose exclusive admission policy means you may want to dress up for happy hour. ~ 1475 Lawrence; 303-260-7505

A prime location on 16th Street Mall helps make **Rock Bottom and Walnut Brewery** one of downtown's liveliest young professional happy-hour hangouts, presents live jazz later in the evening on Friday and Saturday nights during the summer. ~ 1001 16th Street; 303-534-7616.

**Rock Island** is a popular club for alternative dance music from hip-hop to slammin'. Cover. ~ 1614 15th Street; 303-572-7625; www.rockislandclub.com.

**El Chapultepec** features live jazz nightly. Cover. ~ 1962 Market Street; 303-295-9126. **Mercury Café** also offers jazz Tuesday through Sunday, an open stage for drumming and storytelling on Wednesday, poetry readings and performance art on Friday, and a tango and swing club. Cover. ~ 2199 California Street; 303-294-9281; www.mercurycafe.com.

Probably *the* most anachronistic trend to appear on the Denver nightlife scene in decades is the "gentlemen's cabaret" concept. The largest, conveniently located just a block from the Convention Center, is the **Diamond Cabaret**. With "over 150 of the world's most gorgeous entertainers," this place may not win any prizes for political correctness, but it's a far cry from the sleazy strip joints found farther east along Colfax Avenue. It has more in common with the Playboy Clubs of decades past. The club features an elegantly appointed dining area that specializes in steaks. After dinner, you can enjoy a cigar from the club's private humidor, which features more than 50 makes and styles. (There are no comparable clubs for gentlewomen around the Convention Center.) ~ 1222 Glenarm Place; 303-571-4242.

With its vintage sign, the **Skylark Lounge** is retro cool simply because the comfortable watering hole actually *has* been around for more than 60 years. The jukebox features an eclectic mix of swing, alternative rock, legendary crooners, rockabilly and country that appeals to the young hipsters and hoary regulars who frequent this joint. The Skylark recently relocated to a larger space a couple of blocks down Broadway—and somehow managed to bring its distinctive ambience along. ~ 140 South Broadway; 303-722-7844.

The **Red Room** is a real find that brings downtown style to the Capital Hill neighborhood for folks who don't want to brave the Lodo scene. This Colfax gem is trendy, but the ruby walls and friendly staff are inviting to all in search of a comfortable bar and a tasty late night menu that includes spicy vegetarian green chile, deliciously garlicky mussels and chips with smoky salsa. ~ 320 East Colfax Avenue; 303-830-7050.

**GAY SCENE**   **60 South**, long said to be the best of Denver's two dozen gay and lesbian clubs, features live comics and performing artists on Tuesday and Saturday, with deejayed dance music other evenings; Wednesday's ladies' night features "drag king" shows. ~ 60 South Broadway; 303-777-0193. A hot new contender to upstage 60 South is **Serengeti**, with its mix of gays and straights, mostly glitzy; if it's Thursday, don't miss Drag Queen Bingo with the house improv group. ~ 1037 Broadway; 303-534-0222. A young, mixed crowd enjoys electrifying music and active mingling at **JR.'s**, a long-established Denver boys' bar recently moved to a spacious new location. The two-story video bar is a wildly popular after-work watering hole, but also attracts a weekend following. ~ 1669 Clarkson Street; 303-831-0459. The **Wave Nightclub** doesn't get going until after midnight but then becomes the city's hottest gay men's dance club. ~ 2101 Champa Street; 303-299-9283. For a down and dirty time, head to the **Wrangler**. ~ 1700 Logan Street; 303-877-1075; www.denverwrangler.com.

▼▼▼▼▼▼▼▼▼▼▼▼▼▼
**Suburban Denver**

Hemmed in by mountains on its west side, the city of Denver has historically grown south and east, spreading from the banks of the South Platte River and Cherry Creek. For decades, the city's politicians annexed every new development that was built, so the city limits today enclose more than 300 square miles. Eventually, however, the city filled all the land in Denver County and could not expand farther. So when a population explosion hit the Denver area in the 1960s, when the completion of a pipeline tunnel through the Continental Divide greatly expanded the water supply, most newcomers settled in sprawling independent suburbs in neighboring Arapahoe, Jefferson and Adams counties. For the most part, visitors are likely to find Denver's 'burbs short on points of interest, with hotels geared for business travelers and restaurants designed for a local family trade. The older residential neighborhoods of Denver have more to offer in terms of parks, museums and historic sites.

**SIGHTS**

Foremost among Denver's sightseeing highlights located away from the downtown is **City Park**, in a pretty, shady old residential neighborhood about three and a half miles east of downtown, off Colorado Boulevard between 17th and 23rd avenues. The park is the setting for the **Denver Museum of Nature and Science** (see page 65) and the **Denver Zoo**. The zoo has more than 1700 animals from around the world, some caged and others in open habitats. Admission. ~ 2300 Steele Street (main entrance on 23rd Avenue); 303-376-4800, fax 303-376-4801; www.denverzoo.org.

Just across the street from the west boundary of City Park, the **Denver Museum of Miniatures, Dolls and Toys** exhibits some of the largest and most lavish dollhouses ever created, including reproductions in miniature of an adobe Indian pueblo, a mansion complete with working electric lights, and an exact replica of the Kingsgate Mansion in Maine. Visitors will also find collections of American Indian kachinas and teddy bears. Closed Monday. Admission. ~ 1880 Gaylord Street; 303-322-1053.

About a mile southwest of City Park is **Cheesman Park**, home of the **Denver Botanic Gardens**, with its array of indoor and outdoor environments including a Japanese garden, a habitat for nesting birds, a "Plants of the Bible" scripture garden and a re-creation of a tropical rainforest. Of special interest is the alpine rock garden, which contains more than 3500 species of high-mountain plants from around the world. Admission. ~ 1005 York Street; 720-865-3500; www.botanicgardens.org.

Farther toward the east side of town, little **Cranmer Park** is interesting for its large terrazzo model of the Continental Divide. The park also makes a peaceful spot for an urban picnic. ~ East 3rd Avenue at Bellaire Street.

The **Mizel Museum of Judaica** is dedicated to using the arts to present the continuum of the Jewish experience within a multicultural context. There is a permanent collection, as well as educational programs. Exhibits such as "Rites of Passage" and "Ceremonies and Festivals" explore the traditions and customs of several ethnic groups that settled in Colorado; other exhibits like "Jewish Traders of the Silk Road" reveal little-known aspects of Jewish history worldwide. The museum is closed during construction of a new building due to open in 2005. ~ Jewish Community Center, 350 South Delia Street; 303-399-2660; www.mizelmuseum.org.

The oldest building in Denver is the former stagecoach station at **Four-Mile Historic Park.** The station, which was in the middle of nowhere when it was built in 1860, is now surrounded by the affluent southeast Denver neighborhood of Glendale. Volunteers in period costume show visitors around the main travelers' inn as well as the barn and other outbuildings, some of which have been reconstructed with 19th-century tools and construction methods. Farm animals wander through the 14-acre park. On weekends, visitors can ride in a stage coach drawn by draft horses. Closed Monday and Tuesday. Admission. ~ 715 South Forest Street; 303-399-1859.

In the early 20th century, thousands of people migrated northward from Mexico and New Mexico to work in the Colorado sugar beet fields. Many stayed to make their homes in Denver's *barrio* southwest of downtown, and the Latino population soon grew to become the city's largest ethnic minority. Located in the heart of the traditional Spanish-speaking district, the **Museo de las Americas** presents changing exhibits on Latino art, history and

◀ *HIDDEN*

**AUTHOR FAVORITE**

*sights*

As a child growing up in the Colorado Rockies, I'd eagerly look forward to family trips to Denver because it meant a visit to the Denver Museum of Natural History. The elaborate dioramas of landscapes ranging from Arctic ice to African veldt captured my young imagination like nothing else. I suspect it was my first step toward a career in travel writing. Since renamed the **Denver Museum of Nature and Science**, the place is as magical as ever. Besides nature dioramas, displays range from skeletons of dinosaurs and a great blue whale to a life-size Navajo hogan and Eskimo igloo. The museum's gold collection features the largest gold nugget ever found in Colorado, weighing eight and a half pounds. Admission. ~ 2001 Colorado Boulevard; 303-322-7009, 800-925-2250; www.dmnh.org.

cultural heritage in Colorado, the Southwest and Latin America. Closed Sunday and Monday. ~ 861 Santa Fe Drive; 303-571-4401; www.museo.org.

With 3 coasters (including a classic Cyclone), 25 other major rides and 15 kiddie rides, **Lakeside Amusement Park** vies with Six Flags Elitch Gardens for the distinction of being Colorado's largest. The quaint art-deco park hasn't changed much for half a century, and the cost of admission and unlimited rides is about one-third of the price at the newer Elitch's. The miniature train ride around Lake Rhoda has created sentimental memories for generations of native Denverites. Open daily Memorial Day through Labor Day and weekends only in May. Admission. ~ 4601 Sheridan Boulevard; 303-477-1621; www.lakesideamuse mentpark.com.

More than 85 percent of Denver metropolitan area residents live outside the Denver city limits in 13 adjoining suburbs—Aurora to the east; Englewood, Greenwood Village and Littleton to the south; Lakewood, Wheat Ridge and Arvada to the west; and Commerce City, Northglenn, Thornton, Federal Heights, Westminster and Broomfield to the north.

Aurora is Colorado's largest city in area and third-largest in population. Once known for its farms and military bases, it is now quintessential suburbia on a vast scale. Besides miles and miles of lookalike houses, Aurora has its own freeway—Route 225—and one of the largest shopping malls in the state, Aurora Mall. The **Aurora History Museum** focuses on the city's history from the 1800s to the present day. Aurora residents have donated many of the items on display, such as old army uniforms, military paraphernalia and agricultural implements, as well as 1950s memorabilia. Admission. ~ 15001 East Alameda Drive, Aurora; 303-739-6660.

Englewood, Greenwood Village and Littleton are part of an older suburban area, where most homes date back to the post–World War II era. The economy in these communities received a much-needed boost when General Dynamics Space Systems bought Martin Marietta, the largest employer in the area, creating thousands of new jobs. Englewood looks better than ever following an urban-renewal facelift, and Littleton has done a good job of historical preservation on its quaint small-town main street. The **Littleton Historical Museum** has developed two working farms into an open-air museum where 19th-century agricultural methods and lifestyles are preserved. Sheep, cows, horses, pigs and chickens can be seen on the grounds. Friendly, informative staff members clothed in pioneer-era garb do farm chores in between visitors' questions. The museum also has rotating history and art exhibits. Closed Monday. ~ 6028 South Gallup Street, Littleton; 303-795-3950; www.littletongov.org/museum.

Although Lakewood, Wheat Ridge and Arvada make up the most industrialized part of the greater Denver area, neighborhoods in this part of town are considered attractive because they are close to the mountains, making weekend escapes easy. The Denver Federal Center, located in Lakewood, is the largest employer in Jefferson County, and Lakewood is on the verge of surpassing Denver itself as Colorado's most populous city.

Sightseeing attractions are few in this part of town; the best bet is the art gallery at the **Arvada Center for the Arts and Humanities**, which features two exhibition halls of contemporary works by Colorado artists and crafters. The center also has an outdoor amphitheater and an auditorium that is used as a venue for a packed schedule of community and special-interest programs ranging from AIDS benefits and women's consciousness workshops to cowboy poetry readings. The center also hosts plays, musicals and concerts. ~ 6901 Wadsworth Boulevard, Arvada; 720-898-7200; www.arvadacenter.org.

Commerce City, Northglenn, Thornton, Westminster, Federal Heights, and Broomfield, on the north side, form Denver's most economically diverse area, where both smoke-stack and high-tech factories punctuate green farm and ranch lands along the fringes of the city's sprawl. **Rocky Mountain Arsenal**, a former U.S. Army chemical weapons complex, was recently designated as a national wildlife refuge. Today, Denverites take the kids to ride the shuttle buses that run through the arsenal grounds on Saturday mornings; reservations are required.

> The Rocky Mountain Arsenal contains a Superfund cleanup site said to be the most polluted square mile on earth.

During the winter, visitors come to view the bald eagles. Recently, however, whistleblowers' reports of past illegal nuclear dumping have raised serious questions about whether Rocky Flats is safe for either wildlife or human visitors. ~ 72nd and Quebeck streets, Commerce City; 303-289-0232. In Westminster, the **Arabian Horse Trust** has an art gallery and small museum dedicated to the breed many riders and breeders consider the world's most beautiful horses. Closed weekends. ~ 12000 Zuni Street, Westminster; 303-450-4710; www.arabianhorses.org.

**Loews Denver Hotel** is an Italian-style hotel ten minutes from downtown in the Glendale area. The lobby's large vaulted ceiling, chandelier, columns and murals evoke an atmosphere of ancient Rome. The 183 rooms have either a king-size or two queen-size beds. Weekend rates include a continental breakfast. ~ 4150 East Mississippi Avenue; 303-782-9300, fax 303-758-6542; www.loews hotels.com. ULTRA-DELUXE.

**LODGING**

Aurora has a full complement of chain motor inns, most offering room rates that are a fraction of the price for comparable lodging in downtown Denver. Characteristic and conveniently located, the **Hampton Inn Denver East/Aurora** has 132 modern, spacious mini-suites, and guests can rent refrigerators or microwaves. There is a large heated swimming pool. ~ 1500 South Abilene Street, Aurora; 303-369-8400, 800-426-7866, fax 303-369-0324; www.hamptoninn.com. MODERATE.

In the Englewood/Littleton area, major hotels cluster around the Denver Tech Center off Route 25 at the south edge of the city. Not surprisingly, all of these hotels are oriented toward business travelers and are state-of-the-art modern and ultrastylish in a corporate way. A standout is the **Inverness Hotel and Golf Club**. The 191 guest rooms are so bright and seemingly brand-new that you'll almost feel as though you shouldn't touch anything. The sporting facilities, second to none in the Denver area, include lighted tennis courts, indoor and outdoor swimming pools, saunas and whirlpool spas, a complete fitness club and an 18-hole golf course that hosts the prestigious annual Colorado Open golf tournament. ~ 200 Inverness Drive West, Englewood; 303-799-5800, 800-832-9053, fax 303-799-5874; www.invernesshotel.com. MODERATE TO ULTRA-DELUXE.

Lakewood can be a convenient place for vacationers to stay while exploring the Denver area. Rates run much lower than in the city center, and Route 70 can put you downtown within a matter of minutes or, with equal simplicity, take you into the heart of the Colorado Rockies. **The Four Points by Sheraton Denver West**, an attractive motor inn near the Denver Federal Center, has rooms that are large, modern and thoroughly conventional, as well as an exercise room, spa and outdoor swimming pool. A hotel shuttle offers free transportation within a five-mile radius. ~ 137 Union Boulevard, Lakewood; 303-969-9900, 800-222-8733, fax 303-989-9847; www.sheraton.com. MODERATE.

One of the few notable lodgings in the north part of metro Denver, the **Radisson North Denver Graystone Castle**, is located at Route 25 Exit 223, and you can't miss it. The exterior styling of this five-story motor inn re-creates a medieval castle, and the motif is carried through the common areas of the hotel—restaurant, pub, pool and spa area—until you may start to feel as if you're spending the night in a theme park. Fortunately, though, you can leave the Arthurian ambience outside the door of one of the 137 large, thoroughly modern (if rather bland) guest rooms. ~ 83 East 120th Avenue, Thornton; 303-451-1002 or 800-333-3333, fax 303-452-1962; www.radisson.com. MODERATE.

**DINING**    Looking for the best pizza in Denver? Locals, especially students at the nearby University of Denver, agree that the place to find it is the **Bonnie Brae Tavern**. Run by the same family since 1934, it wasn't always a pizza joint; while the menu fare has changed over the years, the traditional pub atmosphere has endured. No reservations; expect to wait for a table. Closed Monday. ~ 740 South University Boulevard; 303-777-2262. MODERATE.

With no Chinatown in Denver, you'd have to search far and wide to find a place as authentic as the **Sunny China Café**, located    ◄ HIDDEN
on a thoroughfare known more for its antiques than its restaurants. Don't let the drab interior fool you: the fare here is so good that the restaurant was selected to provide food for Chinese premier Zhu Rongji and his entourage during a recent visit to Denver. The menu separates Americanized dishes from traditional fare for folks who may not want to sample the deep-fried oysters, jellyfish or spicy garlic pig ears. ~ 1156 South Broadway; 303-722-9968. MODERATE TO DELUXE.

Situated in a neighborhood where Spanish is spoken more often than English, **El Noa Noa** is filled with local residents and    ◄ HIDDEN
gringos seeking real Mexican food. Exceptional items on the menu include *chile rellenos*, tacos with shredded meat and *sopapillas* with honey. Closed Sunday. ~ 722 Santa Fe Drive; 303-623-9968. BUDGET.

Vietnamese grocers, shops and small restaurants cluster west of downtown along Federal Boulevard. The longest-established eatery among them, the family **T-Wa Inn** offers a simple ambi-    ◄ HIDDEN
ence and outstanding, affordably priced Asian dishes with an emphasis on seafood. Try the seafood egg rolls and the succulent soft-shell crab. ~ 555 South Federal Boulevard; 303-922-2378. BUDGET TO MODERATE.

In the mood for something exotic? Try **India's**. A big tandoori oven forms the centerpiece in this casually elegant neighborhood restaurant. Tandoori cookery involves heating such an oven to more than 700°F and cooking the savory meat and fish entrées until precisely the right moment. Outstanding curry and vegetarian dishes are also available. No lunch on Sunday. ~ 3333 South Tamarack Drive; 303-755-4284. MODERATE.

**Mataam Fez** serves Moroccan food in a sumptuous Arabian Nights atmosphere with tented ceiling and decor from Morocco.

### MANGIA, MANGIA!

Long one of Denver's favorite Italian restaurants, **Carmine's on Penn** is in an older but far from elegant former residence hidden away on a side street near Washington Park. Though the decor may not be exceptional, the cuisine and presentation will knock your socks off. Besides a tantalizing range of pasta choices, meat, fowl and seafood specials change nightly; most dishes are prepared for two (but could easily feed six). Closed Monday. ~ 92 South Pennsylvania Street; 303-777-6443. DELUXE.

Diners are seated on the floor on pillows and leather puffs. The five-course prix-fixe meal includes a choice of entrées such as Cornish game hen in a sauce of honey and almonds or shrimp *pel-pel*, plus soup, salad, appetizer and fresh-fruit dessert. ~ 4609 East Colfax Avenue; 303-399-9283. DELUXE.

A restaurant considered by many to be the best in the greater Denver area is **The Swan** in the Inverness Hotel and Golf Club near the Denver Tech Center on the southern outskirts of the city. The restaurant's ambience is light and airy, minimal and chic. The serving staff is impeccably attentive. The bill of fare highlights continental house specialties such as châteaubriand and leg of lamb. There's a seafood buffet on Friday and Saturday evenings. ~ 200 Inverness Drive West, Englewood; 303-799-5800. ULTRA-DELUXE.

Certainly the most prominent restaurant in Lakewood, **Casa Bonita** serves a tasty, though predictable, range of Mexican dishes in an all-you-can-eat buffet. Its size alone makes this place remarkable; the 52,000-square-foot restaurant seats 1100 people. The real draw here, though, is its nonstop family-oriented (that is, mainly for kids) entertainment—Old West shootouts, wandering mariachis, puppet shows, magicians, prizes and fire-juggling cliff divers who leap from the top of a 30-foot artificial waterfall. ~ 6715 West Colfax Avenue, Lakewood; 303-232-5115; www.casa bonitadenver.com. BUDGET.

**SHOPPING**    The reigning queen of metropolitan Denver shopping malls is the **Cherry Creek Shopping Center**, located at University Avenue southeast of downtown. This one-million-square-foot indoor mall features such upscale chain department stores as Saks Fifth Avenue, Neiman Marcus and Lord & Taylor, along with more than 200 specialty shops and restaurants. ~ 3000 East 1st Avenue; 303-388-3900. The adjoining **Cherry Creek North** area along 3rd Avenue features one of the city's highest concentrations of fine-art galleries. PISMO specializes in contemporary glass work. ~ 235 Fillmore Street; 303-333-2879. **Show of Hands Gallery** showcases hand-dyed silks, stained glass, handmade furniture, jewelry, wearable art, garden sculpture and other creations, many

**AUTHOR FAVORITE**

Victoriana is perennially in vogue in Colorado, and since the state was sparsely populated until the late 20th century, most antiques are imported from elsewhere. To the extent that there are any authentic Colorado antiques to be found, the place to look for them is a six-block stretch along South Broadway where virtually every store sells vintage furniture and collectibles. See page 71 for selected antique shops.

by Colorado artisans. ~ 210 Clayton Street; 303-399-0201; www.
showofhandsdenver.com. **West Southwest** features arts, crafts
and accessories from (southwest) Seattle to Santa Fe. ~ 257 Fillmore Street; 303-321-4139. But the *sine qua non* for browsing
in the Cherry Creek area is the **Tattered Cover Book Store**, the
second location of one of the largest independent bookstores in
the United States (the other is in downtown Denver). The shelves
of the immense four-story store display an astonishing 400,000
volumes. ~ 2955 East 1st Avenue; 303-322-7727; www.tattered
cover.com.

Another must-see store in the Cherry Creek North area, the
**Artisan Center** presents an amazing array of arts-and-crafts gift
items—sushi plates, candles, painted and bejewelled glasses, unique
cards, funky jewelry, pottery—by more than 2500 contemporary
craftspeople, most of whom live and work in Colorado. Prices
range from supercheap to if-you-have-to-ask . . . . ~ 2757 East
3rd Avenue; 303-333-1201.

The six-block stretch of South Broadway known as the Antique District, about a mile south of the State Capitol, has one of
the largest concentrations of antique dealers anywhere. Though
quality varies, persistence will reveal some rare treasures. At the
heart of the district is the **Antique Guild & Antique Market**,
where nearly 400 dealers display their wares. ~ 1298 South
Broadway; 303-744-0281. These days, many of the dealers here
specialize in things like American Indian artifacts and cowboy
keepsakes. But besides the big antique markets, the area has many
wonderful shops such as **Packrat Antiques**, a museum-like showcase for scientific, nautical and medical instruments as well as
rarities like working manual typewriters. ~ 1594 South Broadway; 303-778-1211. Sometimes the shopkeepers are as unusual
as their wares: Stop by **Blinky's Antiques and Collectibles** to hear
reminiscences of owner Russell Scott, AKA Blinky the Clown, who
starred in a popular local kids' TV show for 38 years. ~ 1590
South Broadway; 303-778-7583.

**NIGHTLIFE**

On a Saturday night you may find more cowboys and ranch girls
in Denver area bars than ever rode the range. You'll find country-
and-western music nightly at the **Grizzly Rose Saloon & Dance
Hall**. There's a Family Night on Sunday, and free dance lessons
on Sunday and Wednesday. Cover. ~ 5450 North Valley Highway;
303-295-1330; www.grizzlyrose.com.

Perhaps the most spectacular western dance club in the area,
though, is the **Stampede Steak House & Dance Emporium**, a
larger-than-life place with a huge racetrack-shaped dancefloor, an
amazingly long antique saloon bar, double-sided video screens,
state-of-the-art disco lighting, and a second-floor balcony dining
area overlooking the action. Thursday is West Coast swing night.

Closed Sunday and Monday. Cover. ~ 2430 South Havana Street at Parker Road, Aurora; 303-696-7686.

The eclectic **Jimmy's Grille** offers live reggae and jazz. Closed Sunday and Monday. Cover. ~ 320 South Birch Street, Glendale; 303-322-5334. You'll find contemporary jazz at **Bourbon Street**, a sleek young professional hangout at the Denver Tech Center. ~ 10158 Parker Road; 303-805-7683.

For a family-oriented evening on the town, try the **Country Dinner Playhouse**, the state's only year-round professional dinner theater. The entertainment fare consists of recent and classic Broadway musicals. The reasonable ticket charge includes a dinner buffet. The playhouse is dark on Monday nights. Admission. ~ 6875 South Clinton Avenue, Englewood; 303-799-1410.

**PARKS**

**BARR LAKE STATE PARK** 🚶 🚴 🚤 🛥 🛶 This artificial lake was once part of Denver's sewer drainage system. Abandoned after a flooding South Platte River washed it out in 1965, the lake became lush, exceptionally fertile wetlands. Thirty-three years later, it provides habitat for about 300 bird species and is the favorite birdwatching spot in the Denver area. A nine-mile hiking and biking trail encircles the lake, and boating is permitted (10-horsepower or less). Fishing is good for trout, walleye, wiper and catfish. There's a nature center. Day-use fee, $6 per vehicle. ~ Take Route 76 for 23 miles northeast of downtown Denver, past the reservoir, to Bromley Lane (Brighton, Exit 22). Head east and follow Piccadilly Road South to the park entrance; 303-659-6005.

**CHATFIELD STATE PARK** 🚶 🚴 🏇 🛖 🚤 🛶 🎣 🚣 🛥 🛶 The Denver area's most popular recreational lake is shared by sailboats, windsurfers, waterskiers, fishermen, scuba divers and swimmers. It gets very crowded on sunny summer weekends. It also offers 24 miles of horseback and hiking trails through the surrounding foothills; portions of many trails are wheelchair-accessible. It is the starting point for the Denver Greenways Trail, a paved biking and jogging trail that follows the South Platte River for more than 20 miles to downtown Denver. Great blue herons are abundant in the area, as are birders. Fishing is fair to good for perch, crappie, bass, walleye, trout, bluegill and catfish. Facilities include a picnic area, restrooms, nature trails, an arboretum, horse rentals, limited groceries, a boat ramp and a marina that rents boats from May through mid-September and sells bait and tackle. Day-use fee, $6 per vehicle. ~ Located 25 miles southwest of downtown Denver in suburban Littleton. Take Wadsworth Boulevard or Route 470 to Route 121, which goes south through the park; 303-791-7275.

▲ There are 153 RV/tent sites (52 with electric hookups); $12 to $16 per night. Reservations: 303-470-1144, 800-678-2267.

# Colorado's Financial Heartbeat

From the mirrored skyscrapers that form a canyon around down-town Denver's 17th Street financial district to the sprawling corporate complexes that fill the Denver Tech Center on the city's southern edge, it's plain to see that the Mile High City is Colorado's economic hub. Almost 90 percent of the wealth from all in-state sources—mining, ranching, tourism, manufacturing and all the rest—eventually finds its way into Denver banks and boardrooms. What is less visible is the underlying economic shift that is presently transforming the state.

The get-rich-quick optimism of the gold-rush days is long gone. Ornate mountain-town mansions built by silver barons a century ago survive, if at all, as local museums or bed and breakfasts. Mineral extraction has continued to play an important if volatile role in Colorado's economy. Growing environmental and safety concerns have combined with changes in market demand to end uranium prospecting, shut down molybdenum mining and slam the doors on the state's only steel mill. Oil shale, once touted as the key to national energy independence, turned out to be a bust, leaving a new crop of ghost towns in the 1980s. Even coal mining, the most resilient of the state's extractive industries, is on the decline.

Colorado's other traditional key industry, agriculture, has also seen hard times recently. Beginning with the early 1980s, a national recession hit Colorado's economy especially hard, and those who suffered worst were independent farmers and ranchers, who went bankrupt in record numbers. Even large agribusiness corporations, including the sugar-beet conglomerate Holly Sugar, have collapsed.

Closures of Cold War–era weapons facilities have reduced the flow of federal money into the state, and even growth in summer and winter tourist economies has leveled out. Statistics show that while more tourists visit Colorado each year, they are spending less on the average as more travelers eschew traditional resort areas in favor of less-known, "hidden" destinations where they get more adventure for less money.

Despite such bearish trends, Colorado's natural appeal as a place to live and work has attracted high-tech companies and other clean industries as fast as the old industries have faded. With this economic diversi-fication, Colorado's urban population and standard of living are growing with the momentum of a new gold rush, and the state still reigns as the wealthiest in the Rockies.

**ROXBOROUGH STATE PARK** 🚶 🏕 This natural area is dominated by a series of hogback ridges thrust through the earth's crust by the same seismic upheavals that created Red Rocks west of Denver and the Garden of the Gods at Colorado Springs. Twelve miles of hiking trails wind through the canyons between the rock ridges; the Fountain Valley Trail is wheelchair-accessible. Cross-country skiers flock here after snowstorms. Facilities include a visitors center, restrooms and hiking, biking and cross-country ski trails. No pets are allowed in the park. Day-use fee, $6 per vehicle. ~ Located seven miles south of Chatfield State Park on North Roxborough Drive; 303-973-3959.

**CHERRY CREEK STATE PARK** 🚶 🐎 ⚓ 🏖 🛶 🚤 ⛵ The nearest large lake to Denver, now surrounded by suburbs on three sides, gets unbelievably crowded on weekends as tens of thousands of locals descend on Cherry Creek Reservoir for windsurfing, waterskiing, sailing, fishing, swimming and sunbathing at the small, sandy beach. Fishing is good for walleye, trout, perch, crappie, largemouth bass, catfish, pike and bluegill. Facilities include picnic areas, restrooms, hiking and horseback trails, a marina, boat rentals, and a swimming beach. Day-use fee, $6. ~ On Parker Road, one mile south of Route 225; 303-699-3860.

▲ There are 102 RV/tent sites (51 with electric hookups); $12 to $16 per night. Reservations: 303-470-1144, 800-678-2267.

**CASTLEWOOD CANYON STATE PARK** 🚶 About 20 miles upstream from Cherry Creek Reservoir is the site of an early reservoir that was destroyed by a flood in 1933. Today, the canyon where the lakebed used to be is thickly wooded with pine, fir, aspen and scrub oak protected by sheer sandstone cliffs. Relatively few visitors come to this idyllic area. Hidden as it is in the midst of dry, featureless prairie, you don't see the creek and woodlands until you reach the canyon rim. Birdwatching and hiking are the main attractions. The east side of the park has one mile of wheelchair-accessible trails. Facilities include a picnic area, restrooms, a visitors center and nature trails. Day-use fee, $6 per vehicle. ~ Located 27 miles southeast of downtown Denver off Route 83 (from Franktown, the main entrance is five miles south on Route 86); 303-688-5242.

▼▼▼▼▼▼▼▼▼▼▼▼▼

# Outdoor Adventures

### FISHING

The waters of Cherry Creek and Chatfield reservoirs are home to largemouth bass, trout, pike, channel catfish, bluegill, carp, bullhead, perch and crappie. **Cherry Creek Marina** has fishing boats for rent. ~ 303-779-6144; www.cherrycreekmarina.com. You can also rent fishing boats, along with bait and tackle, at **Chatfield Boat and Jet Ski Rentals.** ~ 303-791-5555.

Sailboats, power boats, paddleboats, pontoons and kayaks can be rented at **Cherry Creek Marina** for use on Cherry Creek Reservoir south of Denver from April through late October. ~ 303-779-6144; www.cherrycreekmarina.com. **Chatfield Boat and Jet Ski Rentals** on Chatfield Reservoir rents sailboats, pontoons, canoes, paddleboats and jet skis. ~ 303-791-5555.

**WATER SPORTS**

For ballooning aficionados, **Life Cycle Balloon Adventures** offers daily champagne flights along the Front Range out of various Denver locations. ~ 410 19th Street, Golden; 303-216-1990; www.lifecycleballoons.com.

**BALLOON RIDES**

Although there are no ski slopes in the immediate Denver area, some of the world's finest ski areas are within a couple of hours' drive (see Chapter Four for complete information). Downhill and cross-country ski rentals, as well as snowboard rentals, are available in Denver at many locations, including **Sports Rent**. ~ 8761 Wadsworth Boulevard, Westminster; 303-467-0200. **Breeze Ski Rentals** has seven locations in the greater Denver area. ~ 405 Urban Street #205, Lakewood; central reservations: 303-980-1223.

**SKIING**

Denver has 40 golf courses. Most have club and cart rentals. The 18-hole **City Park Golf Course** has cart rentals and, like all Denver municipal courses, offers reduced rates for Colorado residents. ~ East 25th Avenue at York Street; 303-295-4420. The 18-hole **Overland Park Golf Course** is favored by senior players because of the relatively flat terrain. ~ South Santa Fe Drive at Jewell Street; 303-698-4975. **Harvard Gulch Golf Course** is a nine-hole, par-3 course. There are no cart rentals. ~ 60 East Iliff and South Clarkson streets; 303-698-4078. **Kennedy Golf Course** also offers nine holes. ~ 10500 East Hampden Avenue; 303-751-0311. Other 18-hole courses open to the public include two long-established clubs, the **Wellshire Country Club** (3333 South Colorado Boulevard; 303-692-5636) and the spikeless **Park Hill Golf Club** (Colorado Boulevard at 35th Avenue; 303-333-5411). Robert Trent Jones, Jr., designed the beautiful—and pricey—**Arrowhead Golf Club** among the dramatic red sandstone rock formations in Roxborough State Park; carts are required and included in the fee. ~ 10850 West Sundown Trail, Littleton; 303-973-9614.

**GOLF**

Overland Park Golf Course, one of the first golf courses in the region, was built in 1895.

Denver has nine hard-surfaced, lighted courts at **City Park** (23rd and York streets) and eight more in **Washington Park** (East Louisiana Avenue at South Humboldt Street). For a complete listing, call Denver Parks and Recreation. ~ 303-964-2522.

**TENNIS**

**SWIMMING**    Public pools in Denver are at **Glenarm Recreation Center** (2800 Glenarm Place; 303-295-4475), **Martin Luther King Recreation Center** (3880 Newport Street; 303-331-4034), **Washington Park Recreation Center** (701 South Franklin Street; 303-698-4962) and, in summer only, the outdoor pool at **Eisenhower Recreation Center** (4300 East Dartmouth Avenue; 303-692-5650).

The city's splashiest swimmin' hole is 64-acre **Water World**. It's the largest water park in America, with river rapids, wave pools and huge spiral water slides; senior citizens get in free. Admission. Free parking. ~ 88th Avenue and Pecos Street; 303-427-7873.

Near downtown, Six Flags Elitch Gardens opened its big new **Island Kingdom Water Park** in 2002. It's included in the general amusement park admission. ~ 2000 Elitch Circle; 303-595-4386; www.sixflags.com/parks/elitchgardens.

**RIDING**       At Cherry Creek State Park you can rent horses from **Paint Horse**
**STABLES**      **Stables**. ~ 4201 South Parker Road, Aurora; 303-690-8235. For children too young to ride horses, **Precious Ponies** offers pony rides. ~ 5990 West Bowles Avenue, Littleton; 303-279-3049.

**BIKING**       Denver has an extensive urban trail system and was recognized by the League of American Bicyclists as one of the country's most bike-friendly cities. Though shared with hikers, joggers and equestrians, the more than 100 miles of trails that reach out from the city as far as Chatfield and Cherry Creek state parks are smooth, fairly level and perfect for cycling. Detailed bike route and urban trail maps are available from the **Colorado State Parks Division of Parks and Outdoor Recreation**. ~ 1313 Sherman Street #618; 303-866-3437.

Under construction and scheduled to open in early 2003, the **Denver Bikestation** is a half-million-dollar municipal project that will provide parking, bike rentals, repair and maintenance facilities and showers and will link to public buses, shuttles and trains. ~ Denver Union Terminal; 303-949-6000; www.bikestation.org.

**Bike Rentals**    **Arvada Bicycle Company**, located in a Denver suburb northwest of downtown, rents mountain and suspension bikes. ~ 6595 Wadsworth Boulevard, Arvada; 303-420-3854.

**HIKING**       Two parks in this chapter offer real hiking trails; however, they are interconnecting trail segments and not single long trails. Serious hikers should look for nearby trails in Chapter Three. All distances for hiking trails are one way unless otherwise noted.

**Roxborough State Park** near Littleton, a southwestern suburb of Denver, has a network of trails through the canyons formed between tall sandstone ridges. Although the longest trails run for only a mile or so one way, they interconnect to create hikes of up to eight miles. **Castlewood Canyon State Park** has a number of interconnected trails totaling about four miles through a green canyon carved into the prairie near Franktown, a southeastern suburb.

## Transportation

### CAR

**Route 25** is Denver's main north–south thoroughfare, leading south to Colorado Springs and north to Fort Collins. **Route 70** splits the city horizontally, running east–west, quickly bringing motorists to the mountain forests and rock cliffs of the Front Range. **Route 76** enters Denver from the northeast.

### AIR

The state-of-the-art **Denver International Airport** (DIA), which opened in 1995, is located so far east of the city that many Denverites actually live closer to the Colorado Springs Airport than the Denver one. At $5 billion, it is the most expensive airport ever built, and one of the most controversial. If you have spare time, stroll around the terminal and notice the unusual art: gargoyles, simulated fossils, Masonic symbols, murals depicting mind-altering plants and a giant green figure in a gas mask destroying a city. What does it all mean? Nobody seems to be too sure, but the strangeness and the high price tag gave rise to a local urban legend that a secret underground city was built here along with the airport. ~ 8500 Peña Boulevard, Denver; 303-342-2000; www.flydenver.com.

> Denver International Airport ranks as the world's largest airport, covering an area of 53 square miles—twice the size of Manhattan.

Denver International Airport is served by Air Canada, Air Europa, Airtran, Alaska Airways, America West, American Airlines, British Airways, Continental Airlines, Delta Air Lines, Frontier Airlines, Great Lakes Aviation, Iberia, Japan Airlines, Jet Blue, Lacsa, Lufthansa, Mexicana, Northwest, Qantas Airways, Sabena Belgium, Spirit Airlines, TACA, United Airlines and US Airways, as well as the commuter carriers Mesa Airlines, Midwest Express and United Express.

Airport transportation from Denver International Airport is by taxi or shuttle. The **Super Shuttle** (303-370-1300; www.super shuttledenver.com) runs shuttle vans from the airport to downtown hotels and to southeast Denver hotels. They can also schedule home pickups. Visitors traveling to the mountains can call **Colorado Mountain Express** (800-525-6363; www.cmex.com) for van service to Vail and Aspen. Reservations are recommended for the scheduled departures from DIA. The **RTD** (303-299-6000; www.rtd-denver.com) regional bus system offers low-cost bus service to and from the airport. For current ground transportation options, contact the **Ground Transportation Information Center**. ~ 303-342-4059, 800-247-2336.

**TRAIN**    Amtrak's "Zephyr" stops at Union Station on its run between Chicago and San Francisco. The portion of the route that crosses the Rockies between Denver and Glenwood Springs is one of the most spectacular rides on the Amtrak system. ~ 1701 Wynkoop Street; Denver; 303-825-2583 or 303-534-2812, 800-872-7245; www.amtrak.com.

**BUS**    **Greyhound Bus Lines** serves Denver's large, modern downtown bus terminal, departing several times daily in all four compass directions on Routes 70 and 25. ~ 1055 19th Street; 303-293-6555, 800-231-2222; www.greyhound.com.

**CAR RENTALS**    Among the many car-rental agencies at or near the Denver and Colorado Springs airports are **Alamo Rent A Car** (800-462-5266), **Avis Rent A Car** (800-230-4898), **Budget Rent A Car** (800-527-0700), **Dollar Rent A Car** (800-800-4000), **Enterprise Rent A Car** (800-736-8227), **Hertz Rent A Car** (800-654-3131) and **National Car Rental** (800-227-7368). Motor homes, RVs and motorcycles are for rent at **Cruise America**. ~ 8950 North Federal Boulevard, Denver; 303-650-2865.

**PUBLIC TRANSIT**    RTD (Regional Transportation District) provides bus service throughout the Denver metropolitan area. ~ 303-299-6000; www.rtd-denver.com.

**TAXIS**    Major cab companies that serve the greater Denver area include **Metro Taxi** (303-333-3333), **Yellow Cab** (303-777-7777) and **Freedom Cab** (303-444-4444).

## THREE

# The Front Range

Trace the Continental Divide on a map of Colorado and you'll notice that it veers due east from Steamboat Springs all the way to Rocky Mountain National Park. From there, the Divide extends southward for nearly a hundred miles as a 12,000-foot-high wall of solid granite before meandering westward again. The wall of mountains poses an obstacle so formidable that in pioneer days wagon trains journeyed hundreds of miles to the north or south to avoid it. As recently as the 1960s, the builders of the interstate highway system concluded that the only way to extend a four-lane freeway west from Denver was to forget about trying to cross over the Continental Divide and instead tunnel *through* it.

This mountain range, extending from Rocky Mountain National Park south to Hoosier Pass near Breckenridge, together with the lower mountains that step their way down the eastern slope from the Continental Divide to the plains, is officially known as the Front Range. It is the easternmost major mountain range in the Rockies—the first to be explored by mountain men, gold prospectors and early-day tourists, and the most populous mountain area in Colorado today. Besides accessibility, the lower elevations of the Front Range enjoy the mildest winter weather in the central Rockies thanks to the "rain shadow" cast by the higher mountains along the Continental Divide.

The Front Range has come to mean something different to most Coloradoans. "Front Range Corridor" has become the common term for the string of cities at the foot of the Front Range mountains, from the southern edge of the Denver metro area northward to Fort Collins, including Boulder, Longmont, Loveland and Greeley, as well as a number of increasingly suburban mountain towns such as Golden, Evergreen and Estes Park.

Nowhere else in Colorado will visitors find such diversity as along the Front Range. Even a cursory auto tour of this region, which could be accomplished in a single day, might include the state's richest farmland, its largest universities, its highest mountain roads, its oldest gold and silver boom towns, as well as high-tech industries, high-priced housing developments, tourist traps galore and vast expanses of alpine wilderness studded with peaks that present challenges to novice hikers and veteran mountain climber alike. All the towns and sights included in this chapter lie within an hour's drive west of Route 25.

## Denver Mountain Parks Area

The western suburbs of the greater Denver area collide with mountain forests and rock cliffs no more than 20 miles from the state capitol downtown. Thanks to this proximity, Denver's municipal government has been able to acquire areas outside the city over the years to create the Denver Mountain Parks System. As a result, today Denver has more municipal park acreage than any other city in the country, and the acquisition has been coordinated with county and state park departments and the national forest service to form a huge greenbelt including virtually all of the mountains visible from Denver on a smog-free day. Exploring these areas just west of Denver makes for memorable day trips—and a complete change of pace from the bustle of the city.

**SIGHTS**

**Golden** is set at the foot of Lookout Mountain, the low peak crowned by broadcast towers serving the Denver area. There are spectacular views of the city from the paved road that winds seven miles up the mountain to **Buffalo Bill's Grave and Memorial Museum**. William F. "Buffalo Bill" Cody began his career on the prairies of Kansas and Nebraska as a Pony Express rider, army scout, Indian fighter and bison hunter for construction crews laying the first railroad tracks to the West. Stretching the truth a little, dime novelist Ned Buntline made Cody famous as the hero of numerous best-selling tales of the American frontier. Cody cashed in on his reputation by producing a Wild West spectacular that featured a cast of hundreds including Annie Oakley, Chief Sitting Bull and several live bison. The hugely successful show toured the eastern United States and Europe for 30 years but finally collapsed into bankruptcy. Cody died a 70-year-old pauper in 1917 while staying with relatives in Denver. Exhibits in the museum at the gravesite show both sides of Cody's life—frontiersman and show-business promoter—including the flashy saddle and fringed buckskin suit he wore in his Wild West show. Admission. ~ 987 ½ Lookout Mountain Road, Golden; 303-526-0747; www. buffalobill.org.

Golden is best known for its largest employer, the **Adolph Coors Company**. Visitors can take a free tour of the brewery and see the huge vats where the beer is made. There is a tasting room. Tours, which run from 10 a.m. to 4 p.m. daily, are first-come, first-served; getting on one in summer can mean a long wait. ~ 13th and Ford streets, Golden; 303-277-2337; www.coors.com.

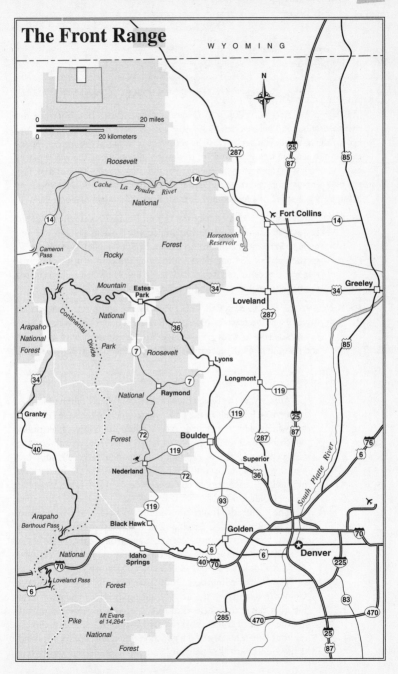

# The Front Range

WYOMING

N

0           20 miles

0          20 kilometers

*Roosevelt*

*Cache La Poudre River*

14

*National*

287

25

87

85

14

✈ Fort Collins

14

*Horsetooth Reservoir*

Cameron Pass

*Forest*

Rocky

34

Loveland

Greeley

34

*Mountain*

Estes Park

287

Arapaho National Forest

Continental Divide

*National*

Park

36

7

*Roosevelt*

Lyons

Longmont

85

119

34

7

National

Raymond

119

25

87

Granby

72

119

Boulder

76

6

40

119

Superior

Nederland

72

36

Arapaho

93

Berthoud Pass

119

Black Hawk

Golden

70

✈

National

Idaho Springs

6

Denver ★

225

Loveland Pass

70

40 70

6

*Forest*

83

470

*Pike*

▲ Mt Evans
el 14,264'

285

470

25

*National*

87

*Forest*

*South Platte River*

# Peaking Up the Front Range

This is the most scenic route from Denver to Estes Park. Though it's not the shortest (about 150 miles versus about 65 if you go there by way of Boulder and Lyons) this way lets you get as close as you want to some of the highest mountains in the state. In fact, you can drive to the top of one. Along the way it passes historic districts that preserve the memory of the gold and silver boom days. This can be a one-day trip, returning to Denver by the more direct Boulder route, or it can be the first leg of a longer trip through Rocky Mountain National Park.

**RED ROCKS PARK**     Head out of the city on Route 70 west (Route 25 intersects it just north of downtown, or you'll eventually join it if you drive toward the mountains on Colfax or 6th Avenue). Turn off the interstate at Exit 259 and drive south along the base of a long hogback ridge that leads to Red Rocks Park (page 84). Allow half an hour to see the natural amphitheater and the *Tyrannosaurus rex* tracks.

**MOUNT EVANS**     Leaving Red Rocks Park by the south gate puts you on Route 74 in the town of Morrison. Turn right and follow winding Bear Creek Canyon to **Evergreen** (page 85). Continue through the town and past the lake five more miles to **Bergen Park** (page 85), where the

Adjacent to the Coors brewery is a completely different kind of brewery—**Hakushika Sake** USA, where much of the sake (Japanese rice wine) sold in the United States is made and bottled. Hakushika, which has been making sake in Japan since 1662, established its U.S. plant in 1992. An exhibition of Japanese art, a gift shop and a tasting room are open to the public, and tours of the brewery are available by reservation a day in advance. ~ 4414 Table Mountain Drive, Golden; 303-279-7253.

The **Colorado Railroad Museum** provides an overview of 19th-century railroad development with maps, memorabilia and more than 50 locomotives, carriages and trolley cars. There is also a large model-train collection on display. ~ 17155 West 44th Avenue, Golden; 303-279-4591; www.crrm.org.

The **Rocky Mountain Quilt Museum**, the only museum in Colorado devoted to the art of quilting, presents changing exhibits that range from historical retrospectives to shows highlighting the work of contemporary craftspeople. A guide explains the quilts and their history, and a gift shop offers not only locally handmade quilts but also patterns and publications for do-it-your-paved Squaw Pass Road (Route 103) turns off to the left. The next part of the trip is not for drivers who are squeamish about mountain roads—another way of saying that the views are astonishing. At **Echo Lake** (page 86), 19 miles up the road, you can choose to turn left and keep climbing to the **Mount Evans** summit (page 86) or start your descent. Allow three hours for the drive if you plan to go to the mountaintop, two hours if you don't.

IDAHO SPRINGS AND CENTRAL CITY    After coming down from Mount Evans on Route 103, you'll find yourself in **Idaho Springs** (page 86). In spite of its location alongside the state's busiest interstate highway, Idaho Springs has a well-preserved historic district worth a one- to two-hour visit. Cross under the interstate and follow unpaved **Oh My God Road** (page 87) for nine exciting miles to Central City (page 93). Allow half an hour for the drive.

PEAK TO PEAK HIGHWAY    Continue through Central City to **Black Hawk** (page 96) and turn left (north) on Route 119, the **Peak to Peak Highway** (page 101). It merges with Route 72 in Nederland and continues north around the base of Long's Peak to **Estes Park** (page 106). The 65-mile drive to Estes Park takes about an hour and a half and offers dramatic vistas of the Continental Divide.

selfers. Closed Sunday and Monday. Admission. ~ 1111 Washington Avenue, Golden; 303-277-0377; www.rmqm.org.

Two other local-history museums offer a look at Golden in the 1860s, when it was the first capital of the Colorado Territory. One is the small **Golden Pioneer Museum**, with its collections of guns, antique furnishings and territorial documents. Admission. ~ 923 10th Street, Golden; 303-278-7151; www.goldenpioneer museum.com. Nearby the **Astor House Hotel Museum** was the first stone masonry hotel west of the Mississippi when it was built in 1867, and it is the oldest hotel in Colorado that is still standing, though it no longer rents rooms. Instead, it has been restored as a museum of 19th-century furniture and decorative art, with room after room of brass beds and baroque wallpaper and a sumptuous sitting room. Closed Sunday and Monday. Admission. ~ 822 12th Street, Golden; 303-278-3557.

Since 1871, Golden has been the site of one of the nation's leading colleges for geologists, the Colorado School of Mines. For the largest exhibit of minerals, fossils, gems and ores to be found anywhere in the state, visit the **Colorado School of Mines Geology**

**Museum**. The museum also exhibits mining drills and other equipment from the gold boom days. Of particular interest is the Thomas Allen Minelighting Collection, showing ingenious methods of underground lighting devised in the days before electricity. ~ 16th and Maple streets, Golden; 303-273-3823; www.mines. edu/academic/geology/museum. Also on the campus is the **U.S. Geological Survey National Earthquake Information Center**, where seismographs monitor earthquake activity throughout the world. Free tours, which must be arranged in advance, are available on weekdays. Visitors see the banks of machines that track the earth's rumblings, while a guide explains how the scientists at work there collect and organize all those squiggly lines into a coherent picture of geological activity and describes efforts to develop ways of predicting future quakes. ~ 1711 Illinois Street, Golden; 303-273-8500; neic.usgs.gov.

The visitors center of the **National Renewable Energy Laboratory** contains exhibits showing how technologies are being developed to transform the power of the sun and wind into electricity. Free tours of the laboratory facilities are offered daily. ~ 1617 Cole Boulevard, Golden; 303-275-3000; www.nrel.gov.

**Red Rocks Park** is located along the sandstone escarpment above the town of Morrison. To get there, take Route 285 west from Route 25 through Englewood, the major suburb on the south side of downtown Denver. Turn north on Route 8. The park is best known as the site of **Red Rocks Amphitheater**, one of the most important concert venues in the Rockies. Bruce Springsteen, U2 and the Beatles (on their first U.S. tour!) are among the performers who have stood on the stage. You can stand there, too, unless preparations are being made for a concert that night. The acoustics of the natural amphitheater surrounded by sandstone cliffs are so perfect that a person standing at the back of the 8000 seats can hear a ping-pong ball drop on the concrete stage—without a microphone. ~ Hogback Road; 303-640-7300; www.red rocksonline.com. Adjoining the 2700-acre park is **Dinosaur Ridge**, where visitors can see a working fossil dig and the actual footprints of a *Tyrannosaurus rex*. ~ 16821 West Alameda Parkway, Morrison; 303-640-7300.

Generations of kids (and their parents) have marveled at **Tiny Town**, a unique array of more than a hundred miniature houses, stores, churches, and other structures covering nearly 20 acres, best viewed from the little coal-fired steam train that carries sightseers around the grounds. Admission. ~ 6249 South Turkey Creek Road, Morrison; 303-697-6829.

To learn more about the plants, wildlife and fossils of the Red Rocks area, visit the **Morrison Natural History Museum** eight miles south of town. The museum is housed in the Cox Cabin, a

1945 replica of an old-time stagecoach stop. ~ South Turkey Creek Road, Morrison; 303-697-1873.

Ten miles up Bear Creek Canyon on serpentine Route 74 is **Evergreen,** a former ranching town next to an artificial lake at the foot of Mount Evans. The village is now the center of an exclusive bedroom community set among ponderosa pines and sandwiched between the Red Rocks Park backcountry on the east and the 4000-acre Mount Evans State Wildlife Area on the west.

The **Hiwan Homestead Museum** preserves a rustic log mansion in a narrow valley. The antique furnishings and decor of the interior span a 50-year period from 1889 to 1930. Exhibits tell about Evergreen's early settlers. The neighborhood of custom homes on five-acre lots surrounding the museum were once part of the ranch. Afternoon tours are available by advance reservation. ~ 4208 South Timberville Drive, Evergreen; 303-674-6262.

Five miles north of Evergreen on Route 74, the town of **Bergen Park** is the starting point of the road up Mount Evans. Bergen Park is only three miles from busy Route 70 (Exit 252). At Exit 253,

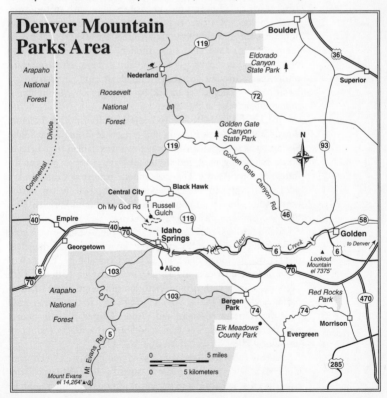

a mile east on the interstate, is **Genessee Park**, the oldest and largest park in the Denver Mountain Parks system, where a city-owned bison herd has roamed since 1914.

From Bergen Park, Route 103 climbs laterally across the steep north face of the mountain for 19 miles among aspen groves and tall fir forests to picture-perfect **Echo Lake**, just below timberline, where the paved **Mount Evans Road** (Route 5) turns off for its ascent to the 14,264-foot summit. Open only during the summer months, the 14-mile-long road over alpine tundra is the highest auto route in the Rocky Mountains, reaching 164 feet higher than the summit of Pikes Peak. Three miles up the road to the summit from Echo Lake is the trailhead for the **Mount Goliath Natural Area**, where an easy one-and-a-half-mile (one-way) nature trail leads through a rare forest of bristlecone pine, a small species of evergreen that grows only at timberline and is sculpted into strangely twisted forms by alpine winds. Some of the trees here are more than 1600 years old. Adventuresome visitors may wish to forgo the drive up the last steep, twisting mile to the summit, park at **Summit Lake** and climb the trail up the last 600 vertical feet of the mountain. Take your time, though. Strenuous exercise can bring on altitude sickness in the thin atmosphere, with symptoms of dizziness, fainting or nausea. Thunderstorms can also pose a hazard: more people are struck by lightning on Mount Evans than anyplace else in the state.

Mount Evans is only 169 feet shorter than Mount Elbert, the highest mountain in Colorado.

From Echo Lake, Route 103 continues for another 14 miles down Chicago Creek Canyon and returns to Route 70 at **Idaho Springs**. The springs for which the town was named feed a greenhouse swimming pool, individual tubs and a vapor pool at the **Indian Springs Resort**. The spa's unique feature is Club Mud, a pool where you can immerse your whole body in warm, earthy ooze. Admission. ~ 302 Soda Creek Road, Idaho Springs; 303-989-6666; www.indianspringsresort.com.

Idaho Springs, founded as the site of the first important gold strike in the Colorado Rockies, grew up as the hub of the silver district that included Black Hawk and Central City. The downtown **historic district** along Miner Street between 13th and 17th avenues is lined with ornate Victorian buildings, some of them dating back to the 1850s. For an introduction to the district, stop in at the **Heritage Museum and Visitors Center**, a 9000-square-foot facility that displays mining equipment, artifacts and memorabilia. ~ 2060 Miner Street; 303-567-4382.

Several sights recall the region's old mining days. The **Phoenix Gold Mine** offers tours of a family-owned gold mine that still operates on a small scale and utilizes traditional mining methods.

You'll be escorted 600 feet underground and shown a three-foot-long vein of gold ore. Feeling lucky? Gold panning is possible for a small fee. Admission. ~ Trail Creek Road, Idaho Springs; 303-567-0422; www.phoenixmine.com.

For a different slant on mining, visit the **Edgar Experimental Mine**, an 1870s shaft that the Colorado School of Mines in Golden has revived as an underground research and instruction facility where visitors can take a peek at the latest mining technology. It's used for classes during the school year and offers tours during summer vacation. Admission. ~ 365 8th Avenue, Idaho Springs; 303-567-2911.

Most of the gold ore mined in the Central City–Black Hawk area was transported through a tunnel more than four miles long for refining in Idaho Springs at the **Argo Mill and Museum**, the state's largest ore mill. Guides show visitors the furnaces where gold concentrate was turned into ingots and the vaults where it was stored, providing a vivid demonstration of the huge quantities of precious metal that poured out of the Colorado Rockies in the 19th century. Thoroughly commercialized today, the mill offers gold panning, curios and staged shootouts. Admission. ~ 2317 Riverside Drive, Idaho Springs; 303-567-2421; www.historicargotours.com.

An old-time assay office has been restored at the **Underhill Museum**. It now serves as the headquarters for the Idaho Springs Historical Society and displays photographs, documents and equipment used for analyzing ore. ~ 1416 Miner Street, Idaho Springs; 303-567-4709.

A mile west of town at Exit 238 from Route 70, the paved 12-mile Fall River Road leads to the ghost town of **Alice**, which dates back to the 1860s and was the site of the richest gold mine in the area. A 1915 schoolhouse and a scattering of old log cabins remain. Above the town site at the end of a half-mile walking trail, **St. Mary's Lake** shimmers at the foot of St. Mary's Glacier, one of the few true glaciers in Colorado, on the slope of Mount Kingston (12,136 feet).

◄ HIDDEN

From the Idaho Springs vicinity, the nine-mile **Oh My God Road** winds up through Virginia Canyon to Central City. It is unpaved but well maintained and can easily be driven in a passenger car. The part of the road above Central City is a gentle grade, while the part above Idaho Springs is steep. Uphill traffic has the right-of-way, and if you're at all squeamish about mountain driving, the trip is much less scary starting from the Idaho Springs end; if you start from Central City, you'll see where this spectacular drive got its name. Along the way are hundreds of old mines and the ghost town of **Russell Gulch**, which got its start in the 1860s and grew to a population of 2500, mostly immigrant min-

◄ HIDDEN

ers from the Italian and Austrian Alps. For motorists who are timid about mountain driving, an easier, paved road—Route 119—goes through Clear Creek Canyon to Central City from Exit 244 on Route 70, three miles east of Idaho Springs.

**LODGING**    While most visitors opt to stay in the Denver metro area while exploring the nearby mountains, Golden has several chain hotels and motor inns geared primarily toward business travelers that can make convenient havens beyond the reach of big-city traffic. For instance, the **Holiday Inn Denver West Village**, a modern 224-room hotel, is ideally located as a base for exploring areas west of Denver. The rooms are spacious and the furnishings are exactly what you'd expect from a first-class corporate motor inn—flawless and virtually identical. The indoor recreation center, including a swimming pool, whirlpool spa, exercise room, miniature golf, ping-pong and video games, makes it a good choice for families. ~ 14707 West Colfax Avenue, Golden; 303-279-7611, 800-729-2830, fax 303-278-1651; www.holiday-inn.com/denverwmills, e-mail dengwhi@aol.com. MODERATE.

Originally built in the early 1900s as a private mansion, the **Table Mountain Inn** was so extensively remodeled in 1992 that its original character is concealed by a no-expense-spared coat of Santa Fe style. Most of the 32 rooms have balconies or patios with views of the foothills, and some suites have jacuzzis. ~ 1310 Washington Avenue, Golden; 303-277-9898, 800-762-9898, fax 303-271-0298; www.tablemountaininn.com. DELUXE.

Inexpensive accommodations can be found in Golden at the **Mountain View Inn**, a low-slung highway motel that offers 34 clean, recently carpeted motel rooms, each with two double beds. Some rooms have refrigerators and bathtubs, and a few have efficiency kitchens. ~ 14825 West Colfax Avenue, Golden; 303-279-2526; www.mountain-view-inn.com. MODERATE.

**AUTHOR FAVORITE**

Hot water and history are both included in the room rate at **Indian Springs Resort**, a century-old Idaho Springs spa once known as the "Saratoga of the West." Franklin and Eleanor Roosevelt stayed here, as did Walt Whitman and Jesse James. The original rooms, dating back to 1905, have been refurbished to re-create a sense of yesteryear, complete with steam radiators and half-baths (no tub or shower—the hot springs are just a few steps away). Modern, slightly pricier rooms are also available. All guests can use the resort's big mineral-water swimming pool and get discounts on hot mineral baths and massages. There's a restaurant on the premises. ~ 302 Soda Creek Road, Idaho Springs; 303-989-6666; www.indianspringsresort.com. MODERATE.

Built from local sandstone in 1873, the **Cliff House Lodge** was originally the mansion of George Morrison, the founder of the town that bears his name. Today the mansion operates as a bed-and-breakfast establishment. Each of the six guest cottages is individually decorated with period antiques and has a fireplace and private indoor or outdoor hot tub. ~ 121 Stone Street, Morrison; 303-697-9732. DELUXE.

A real charmer of an Evergreen hideaway, the **Highland Haven Creekside Inn** has 16 rooms, suites and cottages, each one unique, and a broad range of rates. Standard rooms in the main log lodge have private baths and separate garden-level entrances. There are also two-bedroom suites with kitchens, sitting rooms and French windows or walkout balconies overlooking the gardens. Some suites and creekside cottages feature fireplaces, jacuzzis and CD players. The inn is located on the banks of Bear Creek within walking distance of Evergreen's main street. A full gourmet breakfast is served in the oldest cabin in Evergreen, now beautifully refurbished. ~ 4395 Independence Trail, Evergreen; 303-674-3577, 800-459-2406, fax 303-674-9088; www.highlandhaven.com, e-mail info@highlandhaven.com. MODERATE TO ULTRA-DELUXE.

Also located along the creek, and less than a mile from downtown Evergreen, **Bear Creek Cabins** offers accommodations in four rustic yet luxurious fourplex units surrounded by blue spruce trees. Each guest unit is a single large wood-paneled room with a fully equipped kitchen and dining area. Rates vary widely depending on the season and day of the week; there may be a minimum stay requirement at busy times. ~ 27400 Route 74, Evergreen; 303-674-3442; www.bearcreekcabinsco.com, e-mail proprietors@bearcreekcabinsco.com. DELUXE TO ULTRA-DELUXE.

**DINING**

In the Golden foothills, **Briarwood Inn** is considered one of the finest restaurants in the Denver area. It features Continental dining, candlelight, polished silver, fine china and lavish European-country decor. The menu offers prime rib, lobster, Dover sole and beef Wellington; all entrées include appetizers and dessert. ~ 16304 8th Street, Golden; 303-279-3121. ULTRA-DELUXE.

Another great dining option in Golden is the **Old Capital Grill**, a spin-off location of a perennially popular restaurant in Silverthorne. The food is all-American, featuring home-style ribs, chicken and fish. Guests get to grill some of the meat and fish entrées themselves on a stone slab. ~ 1122 Washington Street, Golden; 303-279-6390. MODERATE.

If you've never seen a buckskin-clad waitperson open a champagne bottle with a tomahawk, you'll have a chance to witness this spectacle at **The Fort**. Designed in Southwestern adobe style after Bent's Fort, the first trading post in Colorado, The Fort has a lovely setting near Red Rocks Park, an Indian tepee out front, a picturesque courtyard and round *horno*-style fireplaces. It serves more buffalo meat than any other restaurant, along with such other frontier delicacies as rattlesnake, roast buffalo marrow bone, and Rocky Mountain oysters (which, it should be mentioned, are not really oysters at all). Not a great place for vegetarians, though the appetizer menu does include peanut butter–stuffed jalapeños— yum! Dinner only. ~ 19192 Route 8, Morrison; 303-697-4771; www.thefort.com. DELUXE.

**Historic El Rancho Village**, a mountain lodge, has been a favorite special-occasion restaurant for generations of Front Range residents. Diners enjoy spectacular Continental Divide views from the main dining room, with its big picture windows, or from the Colorado Deck, an outdoor seating area that is plexiglassed in winter for year-round use. Primarily a steakhouse, El Rancho also serves prime rib and trout. El Rancho is also known for its lavish Sunday brunch. Although it has a Golden address, El Rancho is actually on a back-road route between Idaho Springs and Evergreen. ~ 29260 Route 40, Golden; 303-526-0661; www.historicelrancho.com. MODERATE TO DELUXE.

Save room for dessert at Historic El Rancho Village: all dinners come with an ice-cream sundae to top off the meal.

**Buffalo Restaurant and Bar** has a bar that dates back to 1860, a museum-like assemblage of memorabilia, a retail smoke house and trading post, and great views of Bridal Veil Falls from the back dining rooms. Formerly under the same management as the now-defunct but not forgotten Denver Buffalo Company, the Buffalo Restaurant continues to thrive with its eclectic menu, specializing in buffalo and also featuring salads, soups, pizza, Texas-style barbecue and Mexican food. ~ 1617 Miner Street, Idaho Springs; 303-567-2729; www.buffalorestaurant.com. MODERATE.

**SHOPPING**   If factory outlet shopping is your passion, you could spend your entire vacation maxing out your credit cards in Golden at **Colorado Mills**, one of the largest malls in Colorado, with hundreds of big-name retail stores including Ann Taylor Factory Store, Brooks Brothers Factory Store, Off 5th Saks Fifth Avenue Outlet, Eddie Bauer Outlet and Last Call from Neiman Marcus. ~ 14500 West Colfax Avenue, Golden; 303-384-3000.

Also in Golden, check out **Heritage Square**, a combination shopping center and theme park with an Old West motif. You can, if you wish, browse through mostly locally owned gift shops with an ersatz old-fashioned flavor while the kids get their thrills on the alpine slide and go-cart racetrack or try bungee jumping. The amusement park is open daily in summer and weekends in April, May, September and October. ~ Colfax Avenue, Golden; 303-279-2789.

Evergreen was an artsy-craftsy haven even before the town evolved into a high-priced bedroom community in the 1980s. Artisans who make their homes here tend to sell elsewhere these days, but an hour spent strolling Evergreen's main-street "historic district" will turn up the occasional locally made item among the pricey decorative imports that make up most of the inventory in the galleries and shops. Among the town's best galleries are **Evergreen Fine Art** (3042 Evergreen Parkway; 303-679-3610; www.evergreenfineart.com) and **The Evergreen Gallery** (downtown Evergreen at the light; 303-674-4871; www.theevergreen gallery.com). Also worth a look is the less upmarket **Evergreen Crafters & Village Casuals,** a gift and sportswear shop that has been in business in the same main-street location for more than 50 years. ~ 303-674-3153; www.evergreencrafters.com.

The **Little Bear Inn** in the center of Evergreen was the town's original saloon, a rowdy roadhouse that used to serve as a meeting place for bikers from all over the West. Though it retains a slightly disreputable look, the present-day clientele is more likely to be made up of lawyers and trust-fund kids than black-leather outlaws. There's live music nightly, featuring local and sometimes national rock and R&B bands. ~ 28075 Route 74, Evergreen; 303-674-9991.

**NIGHTLIFE**

**ARAPAHO NATIONAL FOREST** 🏃 🏊 ⚓ This 1,025,000-acre forest covers both sides of the Continental Divide and reaches from the southwestern outskirts of the Denver metropolitan area northwest almost to Steamboat Springs, a distance of 90 miles as the crow flies, spanning some of the Colorado Rockies' most rugged terrain. The forest's principal feature in the Denver Mountain Parks area is the Mount Evans Wilderness, a 74,000-acre roadless area that extends into Pike National Forest to the south and encompasses all of the mountain except for a pie-shaped corridor through which the Mount Evans Highway zigzags to the summit. Fishing is good for rainbow and other trout species, particularly in Chicago Creek and Echo Lake along the Mount Evans Highway and in Chicago Lake near the summit. The forest is under the same administration as Roosevelt National Forest. Facilities include picnic areas, restrooms, hiking trails and jeep trails. ~ The main road through this area of the forest is paved Route 103, the Mount Evans Highway. West Chicago Creek Campground is 6 miles southwest of Idaho Springs on this highway, and Echo Lake Campground is 14 miles from Idaho Springs on the same road; 303-567-2901.

**PARKS**

▲ There are two national forest campgrounds in this area. West Chicago Creek Campground has 11 RV/tent sites (no hookups), while Echo Lake Campground offers 18 RV/tent sites (no hookups). Both are open through mid-September and sometimes later, depending on the snowfall. Fees at both are $11 per night.

**RED ROCKS PARK** 🏃 Seventy-million-year-old splinters of sandstone broke through the earth's surface in the upheavals that created the Front Range to form 400-foot-tall rock formations shaped like the prows of sinking ships. Two of them wrap around a 8000-seat natural amphitheater that serves as one of the nation's most unusual rock and country concert venues. Although the amphitheater is the main sightseeing highlight, the surrounding 600-acre Denver Mountain Park offers paved roads to picnic spots and hiking trails through foothills covered with scrub oak and rock monoliths. As tempting as it may be to scale the rocks here, don't—rock climbing is prohibited. There are picnic areas, restrooms and a store. ~ The park is near the town of Morrison. From Route 70, take Exit 259 and follow Route 26 south to the well-marked park road. It can also be reached via Route 74; 303-640-2637.

**BEAR CREEK CANYON PARKS** 🏃 At different times throughout the 20th century, the Denver Mountain Parks system and Jefferson County Open Space Parks have acquired various tracts of land that now make up an almost unbroken strand along the banks of Bear Creek between Morrison and Evergreen. Among them are **Lair o' the Bear Park, O'Fallon Park, Little Park** and **Corwina Park**. Barely noticed side roads and stone bridges across the creek provide access to secluded canyons for hiking and picnicking. No use fees. ~ Route 74; 303-640-2637 and 303-697-4545.

**ELK MEADOWS COUNTY PARK AND DEDISSE PARK** 🏃 🚲 Elk Meadows, a Jefferson County Open Space Park, adjoins Bergen Peak State Wildlife Area on one side and Dedisse Park, part of the Denver Mountain Parks system, on the other to form one vast recreation area. An easy six-mile trail that loops through varied terrain—meadows, sunny mountain slopes and dark forest nooks—is a favorite of joggers and mountain bikers. There are plenty of benches at scenic overlooks, and longer trails climb into the wildlife area and wind south toward Dedisse Park, which has more well-worn hiking trails as well as picnic sites with stone fireplaces and shelters built in the 1930s by the WPA. There are picnic areas and restrooms at Dedisse Park. ~ Parking area and trailhead located along the west side of Route 74 about three miles north of Evergreen; 303-697-4545.

**MOUNT FALCON PARK** 🏃 🚲 This 1400-acre Jefferson County Open Space Park has ten miles of hiking and mountain-biking trails on the slopes of Mount Falcon, overlooking Denver and Red Rocks Park to the northeast and Mount Evans to the west.

The park was once part of the estate of John Brisbane Walker, publisher of *Cosmopolitan* magazine, who had a castlelike summer home here. In 1914, Walker began construction on a "Summer White House," which he planned to donate to the federal government as a vacation home for U.S. presidents. The vacation cabin was never completed, nor was it ever visited by any U.S. president, and Walker's own castle burned in 1918, leaving only stone walls. The ruins of both summer homes afford spectacular views. ~ Take Route 285 for 14 miles southwest of Denver to Indian Hills Road; turn north and go three and a half miles to the sign marking the park entrance; 303-697-4545.

## Central City Area

Central City, one of Colorado's preeminent historic mining towns, has a population of 335 today but was the largest city in the territory around the time of the U.S. Civil War: in the early 1860s Central City had 15,000 residents, well over Denver's 6000. It became the cultural center of the Colorado Rockies as well, with a theater district that included the grandest opera house in the West. When Colorado became a state in 1876, Central City was one of the top choices for the state capital and lost the honor by a close vote. Black Hawk, a tiny mining camp about a mile down canyon from Central City, was transformed into a real town in 1877, when a railroad spur made it that far but could not reach Central City. But the richest gold and silver ore ran out by 1880, and creeping unemployment brought about the city's agonizingly slow abandonment over a period of 50 years. The restoration of Central City's elegant hotel during the 1930s focused attention once more on the picturesque old town of Victorian brick buildings adorned with fluted columns and fanciful stonework that loom like wraiths out of a not-so-ancient past.

Although tourists have crowded the streets of Central City for decades, an economy based on seasonal curio shops and luncheon restaurants could not generate the kind of money needed to keep most of the old buildings from deteriorating. In 1990, Coloradoans voted to legalize $5-limit casino gambling in

### CENTRAL CITY'S SALOON LEGEND

The claim is often heard that the haunting "Face on the Barroom Floor" in the Teller House casino bar was the subject of H. Antoine D'Arcy's tragic 19th-century poem of the same name. But in fact it was the poem that inspired Colorado artist Herndon Davis, who restored the hotel's murals during the 1930s, to paint his wife's face on the floorboards.

Central City and Black Hawk as well as Cripple Creek, with the provision that casinos could be operated only in existing historic buildings. Given Central City's location, half an hour's drive from a city of a million people, it's no wonder that the casino idea has succeeded enormously in bringing money to the town and fixing up every building in sight. The controversial change also obscured much of Central City's unique historical character behind a veneer of glitz, clamor and greed, driving most old-timers to sell out and leave town.

During the first year of legalized gambling, virtually every commercial building in Central City and Black Hawk was converted into a casino. Today, the casinos are fewer (ten in Black Hawk, five in Central City). A Las Vegas–style sensibility has invaded the Black Hawk Historic District in the form of big-resort gaming establishments with architecture vaguely resembling the town's former buildings and names like the Riviera, Mardi Gras and Isle of Capri. With more historic structures that can't be torn down to make room for big casinos, Central City has become a ghost town once more, though tourist-oriented shops are starting to move back into the shells of abandoned casinos. The few surviving Central City gaming halls have a friendly, uncrowded, mom-and-pop feel that is worlds apart from Black Hawk just down the road. Some of the remaining locals believe that the economic situation will improve with the completion of a new four-lane highway into the towns, and plans have been announced for a new casino-hotel complex in downtown Central City.

**SIGHTS**

History still exists in Central City—if you look for it. The **Central City Opera House** has crystal chandeliers and elaborate wall murals. Although it was open for only about five years at the end of the mining boom, since its restoration in the 1930s it has been, and continues to be, Colorado's favorite place to see opera. Some of America's leading opera singers appear in the annual July and August performance season. There are no winter performances because the opera house lacks a heating system. Admission. ~ 124 Eureka Street, Central City; 303-582-6500, opera tickets: 303-292-6700, 800-851-8175; www.centralcityopera.org.

Next door to the opera, the **Teller House** was built in 1872 as a boardinghouse for miners, but when the sidewalk in front of the hotel was paved with silver ingots to welcome visiting President Ulysses S. Grant, it began to gain its reputation as the city's elegant hostelry. When silver baron and U.S. Senator Horace Tabor turned one floor of the hotel into a lavish suite for his mistress, Black Hawk divorcee Elizabeth "Baby Doe" (who would become his second wife and a legendary figure in Colorado history), he refurbished the hotel in a grand manner, redecorating

# Colorado's Casino Comeback

One of the most familiar images of Hollywood's version of the Old West is the smoke-filled saloon where cowboys and cardsharks face off around the poker table as women of ill repute make eyes at the winners. There is a lot of truth to the image. Gambling played an important role in 19th-century frontier life for many of Colorado's ranch and mine workers, who were so poorly paid that gaming tables offered the only chance, however illusory, to get together enough cash to buy land and start a better life. More often, of course, gambling merely perpetuated their poverty instead.

Most games of chance were declared illegal in Colorado early in the 20th century, partly due to the moralistic fervor that led to Prohibition, but also because of the social ills—notably, violent crime—associated with gambling.

Beginning in the mid-1970s, Colorado became one of the first states besides Nevada to relax its prohibitions against gambling. The state legislature passed the Colorado Lottery, and it unexpectedly generated more than $25 million in state revenues in its first 90 days of operation, winning renewed respectability for gambling. So it sounded reasonable when, in 1990, state legislators proposed legalizing limited-stakes casino gambling in three great old mining towns—Central City, Black Hawk and Cripple Creek—in hopes of generating funds for historic preservation in these towns. The first casinos opened in 1993, sparking a controversy that has raged ever since.

Slot machines, video poker screens and poker and blackjack tables suddenly packed every decrepit old building that was still standing and resulted in grand-scale refurbishment of the towns. The casinos also drove out the modest ma-and-pa cafés and small grocery stores that used to occupy the towns' storefronts and pushed old-time curio shops into bankruptcy. Crowd control needs and the threat of crime inspired Cripple Creek to quadruple the size of its police force. Traffic on the winding mountain routes to all three towns increased 20-fold. This, combined with drunk driving incidents, make them among the most dangerous roads in the state. In Central City, parking problems have helped reduce the number of casinos from 19 to five in the past few years.

Critics have amassed substantial proof that allowing the casinos was a mistake, but legislators don't want to face the political risk involved in repealing the casino gambling law. Casino revenues for all three towns hit a new low in 2003, followed by a record high in 2004. The future is . . . well . . . a gamble.

in opulent French Provincial style and lining the walls with 12-foot-tall diamond-dust mirrors imported from Italy and brought from the East Coast by wagon. When University of Denver students began restoration efforts in 1932, they found the mirrors still in place and part of the abandoned hotel in use as a chicken coop. Early in Central City's gambling revival, the Teller House was converted into the town's most lavish casino, but in 2000 it went out of business. The Opera Association conducts tours of both the opera house and the Teller House, including the famous "Face on the Barroom Floor" in the bar, Friday through Monday. Admission. ~ 120 Eureka Street, Central City; 303-582-3200.

The first Stetson hat ever manufactured was made in Central City.

Across from the Teller House, the **Thomas Historical House** was boarded up in 1917 and, like a huge time capsule, remained untouched until new owners reopened it 70 years later. Restored with original furnishings and period decor, the house operates as a museum. Since the original owners were local merchants, the exhibits emphasize 19th-century product packaging and advertisements. Friday through Monday. Admission. ~ 209 Eureka Street, Central City; 303-582-5283.

The **Gilpin County Historical Society Museum**, in the old high school building, displays artifacts and photographs from the mining era along with collections of Victorian clothing, dolls and toys. Admission. ~ 228 East High Street, Central City; 303-582-5283.

Less than a mile down the road from the eastern outskirts of Central City is the smaller town of **Black Hawk**, where the main sight to see is the **Lace House**, a restored 1863 Carpenter Gothic–style gabled home known locally as "the Gingerbread House." Its rooms are filled with household antiques from the mining-boom period. Admission. ~ 161 Main Street, Black Hawk; 303-582-5211.

Route 119/6, the Clear Creek Canyon Highway, parallels the newer interstate highway at a distance and goes downhill for 20 miles to the city of Golden. For a slower but more scenic and much less busy alternative, motorists may wish to try the Golden Gate Canyon Road (Route 46). It turns off from Route 119 at the Dory Hill campground, seven miles north of Black Hawk, and threads its way out of the mountains through a narrow canyon to the north side of Golden.

**LODGING**    The Central City area has a handful of small bed and breakfasts in restored Victorian-era houses. The best of the bunch, the Cajun-style **Chateau L'Acadienne** has three guest rooms—two with queen-size beds and one with a king-size. ~ 325 Spring Street, Central City; 303-582-5209, 800-834-5209. MODERATE. There are also three small, rather plain rooms in the **Shamrock Inn**. ~ 351 Gregory Street, Black Hawk; 303-582-5513. MODERATE.

The lodging situation changed in 1995 with the opening of what is now the **Fortune Valley Hotel and Resort**. This large modern hotel built up a hillside on the road into town is the closest thing to a Las Vegas–style resort hotel you'll find anywhere in Colorado. It's still the only casino hotel in town. The 118 guest rooms are decorated in soft earth tones, and some have good views overlooking the town. There's free parking—a rare find in Central City. ~ 321 Gregory Street, Central City; 303-582-0800, 800-924-6646, fax 303-582-5860. DELUXE.

A good bet among the several casino hotels in Black Hawk, **The Lodge Casino** is a standout with 50 luxury guest rooms and suites. The ground floor exemplifies what has come to pass for historic style preservation in this all-gambling town, with helter-skelter wood beams, exposed red brick and rustic touches contrasting with the clamor and flashing lights of more than 800 slot machines. ~ 240 Main Street, Black Hawk; 303-582-1771, fax 303-582-0239.

**DINING**

Although the last independent restaurants in the Central City/ Black Hawk area have closed down, dining does not seem to be a high priority at local casinos. Even at some of the largest resort hotels, the fare is limited to hot dogs or burgers and pizza by the slice. Still, gamblers have to eat sometime. Here are some places to find a satisfying meal in Black Hawk. For Chinese food, try the **Eureka Casino** ~ 211 Gregory, Black Hawk; 303-582-1040. MODERATE. You'll find Cajun food at the **Mardi Gras Casino**. ~ 280 Main Street, Black Hawk; 303-582-5600. MODERATE. There's Mexican food at the **Golden Gates Casino**. ~ 261 Main Street, Black Hawk; 303-582-1650. MODERATE. The nicest full-service restaurant in town, **Farradday's in the Isle of Capri**, specializes in steak and lobster. ~ 401 Main Street, Black Hawk; 303-998-7777. MODERATE. Among the half-dozen Las Vegas–style buffets in town, my pick is the **Riviera Casino's World Buffet**. ~ 444 Main Street, Black Hawk; 303-582-1000. MODERATE. When it comes to food in Central City, just about the only game in town is the small **Dostal Alley Brewpub and Casino**, which features pizza and beer, both made in-house. ~ 114 Main Street, Central City; 303-5821610. BUDGET.

**NIGHTLIFE**

Gambling casinos are the sole entertainment—indeed, the only industry of any kind—in Central City (five casinos) and Black Hawk (ten casinos). The betting limit is $5 at all casinos; only blackjack and poker tables are permitted, along with mechanical "one-armed bandits" and video gaming including poker, blackjack and keno machines.

Curiously, no Central City or Black Hawk casino presents Las Vegas–style shows—or live stage entertainment of any kind.

**PARKS**

**ARAPAHO AND ROOSEVELT NATIONAL FORESTS** 🚲 🏍
Central City is situated near the boundary between these two contiguous national forests. Extensive past mining and logging have scarred hillsides in the area but left an extensive network of roads suitable for four-wheel-drive vehicles and mountain bikes. Columbine Campground offers the only camping in the Central City area. You can fish for rainbow trout in Pine Creek and Missouri Creek. ~ Main roads through this part of the forest include the Peak to Peak Highway (Route 119) and Oh My God Road (County Road 279). Columbine Campground is two miles northwest of Central City on County Road 279; 303-567-2901.

▲ Columbine Campground has 47 RV/tent sites (no hookups); $11 per night. Closed from mid-October to late May.

**GOLDEN GATE CANYON STATE PARK** 🚶 🐎 🚣 This 14,000-acre expanse of mountain meadows and canyons is the largest of the many state, county and municipal mountain parks along the Front Range. It has 35 miles of hiking and horseback trails, many of which are open for cross-country skiing in winter. Fishing is good for rainbow trout. Panorama Point offers a spectacular view of the Continental Divide. The visitors center has interpretive exhibits on plant and animal life, history and geology. Parking spaces can be hard to find on summer weekends. There are picnic areas and restrooms. Day-use fee, $5. ~ From Golden, take Route 93 north for one and a half miles; then turn west on Golden Gate Canyon Road. This paved road runs for about 15 miles through the park and comes out on Route 119 between Central City and Nederland; 303-582-3707.

▲ There are 164 RV/tent sites (some with electric hookups); $12 to $16 per night; reservations, 303-470-1144 or 800-678-2267.

▼▼▼▼▼▼▼▼▼▼▼
**Boulder**

From Denver, the most direct route to Estes Park and Rocky Mountain National Park is through Boulder, a prosperous university town. Although Boulder, like Denver, was founded by gold prospectors immediately after the first gold was discovered along the Front Range in 1858, Boulder emerged as an educational center practically from the start. Colorado's first schoolhouse was built there in 1860. The University of Colorado started in Boulder in 1877 with a class of 64 freshmen, of which 7 would receive diplomas four years later. Adult education also began here in 1898 with the Chautauqua, a lecture and symposium series held each summer in the state's first conference center and whose goal it was to expose Westerners to the thoughts of the era's leading intellectuals and moralists. Today, in spite of explosive population growth that has all but merged the city into Denver's amorphous suburban sprawl, Boulder's unique character remains a blend of high technology, humanism and youthful exuberance.

The main campus of the University of Colorado sprawls across the south side of town, bounded by Foothills Parkway on the east and Broadway on the west. The easiest access is from 26th Street (Route 36, the main highway from Denver). At the heart of the campus, broad green quadrangles are shaded by century-old fir trees and flanked by massive stone buildings with Mediterranean-style red-tile roofs. One main visitors' attraction on the campus is the **University of Colorado Museum**, which displays a full range of collections from dinosaur fossils to plant specimens, including a treasure trove of southwestern artifacts. ~ Henderson Building, 15th Street and Broadway; 303-492-6892; www.colorado.edu/cumuseum.

The best show in Boulder is along **Pearl Street Mall**. In the 1970s, Boulder's main downtown street was the model for the kind of cute, café-lined, pedestrians-only historic district that has since sprung up in urban-renewal zones all over America. But the feel of Pearl Street remains unique thanks in large part to its street performers. Almost any day of the year finds folksingers playing for handouts beside the fountains and sculptures. On sunny summer weekends the mall is often completely lined with musicians, magicians, mimes and even acrobats performing in a dizzying impromptu circus. ~ Downtown between 11th and 15th streets.

The **Boulder Museum of History**, situated in the restored Harbeck Bergheim Mansion (circa 1899), features both permanent and changing exhibits from the society's 35,000-item local-heritage collection. Outstanding displays include a pre-electric kitchen, fully equipped in the Victorian manner, and an extensive array of antique clothing. Admission. ~ 1206 Euclid Avenue; 303-449-3464; www.boulderhistorymuseum.org.

**SIGHTS**

**AUTHOR FAVORITE**

Once upon a time I worked as a projectionist at the University of Colorado's **Fiske Planetarium**. Today, when I revisit it, I'm still struck by what an exceptional facility it is. The Zeiss star projector, one of the largest in the world, accurately simulates more than 3000 celestial bodies, and the special-effects projectors are state-of-the-art. Many people expect the planetarium to be a bit stodgy, the kind of place schoolchildren are dragged to on class field trips, but not so Fiske Planetarium, whose staggering star shows and rock-and-roll laser shows draw crowds of college students. Admission. ~ Regent Drive; 303-492-5001; www.colorado.edu/fiske.

Visitors are welcome to take a self-guided tour of the **National Center for Atmospheric Research**. The red sandstone building, set at the foot of the huge, slanted cliffs called the Flatirons on the southwest outskirts of the city, was designed by I. M. Pei, whom many consider to be America's finest living architect. Inside, exhibits cover everything from thunderstorms to global warming and offer a close-up look at the surface of the sun. Visitors can see two Cray supercomputers, whose speed of up to a billion calculations per second makes them the world's fastest computers at the time of this writing. ~ 1850 Table Mesa Drive; 303-497-1000; www.ncar.ucar.edu.

Two of Boulder's most unusual manufacturing firms strive to attract visitors. **Celestial Seasonings**, which produces herb teas, offers weekday factory tours revealing how its teas are invented, blended and packaged. The tour includes a luscious-smelling mint room and herb garden, an international collection of teapots and -cups, and original designs created for Celestial Seasonings tea boxes by top American illustrators. ~ 4600 Sleepytime Drive; 303-581-1202; www.celestialseasonings.com.

HIDDEN ►

**Leanin' Tree**, the leading publisher of Western greeting cards, has a free museum of Western art containing the originals of paintings reproduced on their cards as well as other cowboy paintings and sculptures. ~ 6055 Longbow Drive; 303-530-1442, 800-777-8716; www.leanintree.com.

For the best view of the Boulder area, take the paved, serpentine **Flagstaff Mountain Road** about three miles to a 7000-foot summit overlooking the city. Before entering wild Boulder Mountain Park with its dramatic cliffs and canyons, the road goes through **Chautauqua Park**. At the center of this large, grassy foothills park is a big, whitewashed wood community center that was built in 1898 and, like its namesake at Lake Chautauqua, New York, has been used for summer conferences, lectures and concerts ever since. ~ 900 Baseline Road; 303-442-3282.

Another scenic mountain drive from Boulder is Route 119, which winds for 16 miles up **Boulder Canyon**. Midway up the canyon, the creek plunges over **Boulder Falls**, a pretty spot anytime and most spectacular during the spring runoff. At the upper end of the canyon is the lakeside community of **Nederland**. The silver ore mined around Nederland was considered low-grade because it contained tungsten, which was hard to remove in the refining process. But with World War I the tungsten, a rare metal used to harden steel alloys, became much more valuable than silver had ever been, and Nederland experienced a belated—and short-lived—mining boom. In the 1970s, the town experienced a new flurry of activity as the site of Caribou Ranch, a famed recording studio used by such pop music legends as the Rolling

Stones and Elton John. In recent years, the block-long town has been engulfed by new custom-home development. At Nederland, motorists can join the **Peak to Peak Highway** and follow it 15 miles south to Central City or 42 miles north to Estes Park and the entrance to Rocky Mountain National Park. While this is not the most direct route from Boulder to the national park, much less the fastest, it is certainly the most scenic. ~ Route 72 North and Route 119 South.

**LODGING**

Built in 1908, the **Hotel Boulderado** has been painstakingly restored to the grandeur of earlier times, when such celebrities as Bat Masterson, Ethel Barrymore and Douglas Fairbanks, Jr., stayed here. Rich woodwork and overstuffed antique armchairs and sofas grace the lobby under a two-story-high stained glass canopy. The 160 rooms feature antique furnishings and flowery period decor as well as fresh flowers daily. ~ 2115 13th Street; 303-442-4344, 800-433-4344, fax 303-442-4378; www.boulderado.com, e-mail info@boulderado.com. ULTRA-DELUXE.

A few blocks east of the pedestrians-only part of downtown, the **Pearl Street Inn** offers eight antique-decorated rooms, all with private baths, fireplaces and private entrances, surrounding a peaceful central courtyard. Some rooms are in the historic main house dating back to 1898; others are in a contemporary annex built in 1985. Rates include a full breakfast. ~ 1820 Pearl Street; 303-444-5584, 888-810-1302, fax 303-444-6494; www.pearlstreet inn.com, e-mail kbeeman@msn.com. DELUXE.

Half of Boulder's population is under the age of 21.

Another Victorian-era home turned B&B in the downtown area, the **Briar Rose** has nine rooms—five in the main 1890-vintage house and four in a separate guest house. Some rooms have fireplaces, others have balconies or patios, and all have queen-size beds with feather comforters. A gourmet continental breakfast is served sitdown-style. ~ 2151 Arapahoe Avenue; 303-442-3007, fax 303-786-8440; www.briarrose bb.com, e-mail info@briarrosebb.com. DELUXE TO ULTRA-DELUXE.

While lodging rates in Boulder tend to run higher than in most communities in the state, affordable accommodations can be found at the **Foot of the Mountain Motel**, the oldest continuously operated motel in Boulder. The 18 rooms are in rustic cabins dating back to 1930. They have been nicely renovated and feature all the conveniences of a modern midrange motel. The location— at the mouth of Boulder Canyon and the start of the Boulder Creekpath—makes this motel special. ~ 200 Arapahoe Avenue; 303-442-5688, 866-773-5489, fax 303-442-5719; www.footof themountainmotel.com, e-mail info@footofthemountainmotel. com. MODERATE.

**DINING**     **Trios Grille & Wine Bar** serves gourmet Southwestern cuisine in a New Mexico–style setting with Santa Fe–style decor and picture windows overlooking Boulder and the mountains. The menu focuses on unique dishes like Atlantic salmon Napoleon and, for dessert, a caramelized lemon tart with raspberry syrup. The restaurant also features live jazz six nights a week. Dinner only. ~ 1155 Canyon Road; 303-442-8400. DELUXE.

The menu is heart-healthy and totally organic at **Q's**, the restaurant in what was the original dining room of the Hotel Boulderado, where Teddy Roosevelt once ate. Centrally located on Pearl Street Mall, it has been the site of a long succession of Boulder's favorite fine restaurants, and Q's has lasted longer than most. The fare, which changes seasonally, ranges from elaborate salads to gourmet cuisine, with a good selection of vegetarian dishes, complemented by an eclectic wine list. ~ Hotel Boulderado, 2115 13th Street; 303-442-4880; www.qsboulder.com. DELUXE.

The bright, cheerfully flowery **Sunflower Restaurant** is Boulder's premier natural foods eatery. The juices, produce, coffee and grains are all organic, as are the beer and wine; the poultry is free-range, and everything is cooked with with non-irradiated herbs and spices, Celtic sea salt, filtered water and aluminum-free cookware. There's a tantalizing selection of vegetarian, fish and meat dishes. Start with an ocean garden salad —baby greens and sea vegetables with lemon miso vinaigrette—and move on to an entrée such as the seitan and shiitake and portobello mushroom medallions in burgundy sauce or, for fowl fans, the sherry-marinated smoked duck breast. ~ 1701 Pearl Street; 303-440-0220. MODERATE TO DELUXE.

### ABOVE IT ALL

Boulder's ultimate fine-dining establishment is the **Flagstaff House Restaurant** on Mount Flagstaff 1000 feet above town. Floor-to-ceiling walls of glass give diners an unparalleled view, especially after dark, when dinner is served by candlelight and the city's lights along the Front Range have full impact. Dining is formal (no T-shirts or shorts, please), and the menu changes daily to make the most of fresh seasonal ingredients and locally grown organic produce. A typical dinner might include an appetizer of Kumomoto oysters, a main course of pan-seared venison loin and duck breast with shiitake mushrooms and cherry sauce and, for dessert, a pear and a baked almond tart with Chivas Regal ice cream. Dinner only. ~ 1138 Flagstaff Road; 303-442-4640; www.flagstaffhouse.com. ULTRA-DELUXE.

One of Colorado's most unusual restaurants, the **Boulder Dushanbe Teahouse** was a gift to the city of Boulder from the mayor of its sister city, Dushanbe, Tajikistan (just north of Afghanistan), where the entire building, with its ornately carved ceiling, traditional Persian plaster bas-reliefs and life-size fountain statues, was made by hand. It was then shipped in pieces and reassembled in Boulder. The menu features several Tajiki and traditional Persian dishes, such as tamarind fish kabobs, *kooftah*—meatballs stuffed with dried fruit, nuts and spices—and *plov*, a rice and beef dish. There is also fare from other parts of the world, including Thailand, Bolivia, Indonesia and Jamaica. ~ 1770 13th Street; 303-442-4993; www.boulderteahouse.com. MODERATE.

**SHOPPING**

Pearl Street Mall, Boulder's pedestrians-only downtown main street, is so full of life that shopping is almost incidental. Many of the small shops that line the street specialize in arts, crafts and unique gift items. **Von Eschen Gallery** showcases contemporary Western and wildlife art in various media including paintings, limited-edition prints, bronze sculptures and wood carvings. ~ 2920 Pearl Street; 303-443-9989. **Art Source International** is Colorado's largest dealer in historic photos and 19th-century prints and maps. ~ 1237 Pearl Street; 303-444-4080. Good selections of local arts and crafts can be found at the **Boulder Arts & Crafts Cooperative**. ~ 1421 Pearl Street; 303-443-3683. Also stop by **Handmade in Colorado** for crafts. ~ 1426 Pearl Street; 303-938-8394. For shoppers whose tastes run to the exotic, **Shankar Gallery** exhibits art with Eastern spiritual themes by prolific Indian artist S. S. Shankar. ~ 1840 Violet Street; 303-447-9606.

Antique dealers dominate the main street of tiny **Niwot**, midway between Boulder and Longmont on Route 119.

**NIGHTLIFE**

The University of Colorado sponsors a full range of events, most of them open to the public. Check the Boulder *Daily Camera*'s Friday edition or any of the many bulletin boards around town for current happenings.

University students dominate the Boulder bar scene. A popular, eclectic hangout is the **West End Tavern**, which features alternative music on Tuesday, jazz on Wednesday, comedy on Saturday and a deejay on other nights. Cover. ~ 926 Pearl Street; 303-444-3535. The **Walnut Brewery**, one of the town's many brewpubs, has live jazz and blues on Friday nights. ~ 1123 Walnut Street; 303-447-1345. **The Sink** serves up pizza, burgers, beer and, on weekends, live reggae or rock. ~ 1165 13th Street; 303-444-7465.

The **Fox Theatre and Café**, a 625-seat showcase concert club, features a variety of local and national acts, from jazz and folk to contemporary and alternative music nightly. Cover. ~ 1135 13th Street; 303-443-3399.

Look for live traditional Irish music, dart games and a pub atmosphere at **Conor O'Neill's**. ~ 1922 13th Street; 303-449-1922.

If you prefer a nonalcoholically hip club scene, the **Tonic Oxygen Bar** offers herbal cocktails, live enzyme drinks, herbal tea infusions and "smartinis" as well as oxygen sessions with aromatherapy. ~ 2011 10th Street, 303-544-0202.

When it comes to gay nightlife, Boulder has fewer options than you might expect. The town's only GLBT tavern, **The Yard** has a large dance floor, a separate smoking area, pool tables and video, with a deejay on Friday and Saturday and a great light show. ~ 2960 28th Street #C; 303-443-1987. Look for a mixed gay and straight crowd on the rooftop dance floor at **The Foundry**, with live music on Friday and Saturday nights. ~ 1109 Walnut Street, 303-447-1803.

**PARKS**

**BOULDER MOUNTAIN PARK** 🏃 Little by little, Boulder taxpayers' dollars have purchased the mountains that flank the west side of the city in order to protect this dramatic stretch of the Front Range from development. The park includes the huge slanted expanse of granite cliffs known as the Flatirons as well as Flagstaff Mountain, where a three-mile switchback road winds to the 1600-foot summit—a great spot for watching stars, the lights of Boulder or the breaking dawn. Several hiking trails start from Sunrise Circle Amphitheater. There are picnic areas and restrooms. Day-use fee, $5. ~ Follow Baseline Road west from Boulder; it becomes Flagstaff Mountain Road as it winds its way up to the trailhead and the summit; 303-441-3410.

**ROOSEVELT NATIONAL FOREST** 🏃 🚵 ⛺ The mountains west of Boulder are a checkerboard of national forest and state, county and municipal parks, many of them undeveloped. Numerous forest roads and jeep trails radiate into the park from the town of Nederland at the upper end of Boulder Canyon. Among the noteworthy is the Moffat Road, a four-wheel-drive and mountain-bike road that starts at Rollinsville south of Nederland and follows a former railroad route over Rollins Pass. The Indian Peaks Wilderness, a 70,000-acre area of alpine tundra with nearly 50 lakes, lies west of Nederland and adjoins the south boundary of Rocky Mountain National Park. It is the most popular wilderness area in Roosevelt National Forest; more hikers use its extensive trail network than all other trails in the national forest combined. Fishing is good for lake trout and kokanee salmon at Gross Reservoir, located southwest of Boulder, just beyond Boulder Mountain Park. ~ Forest access is provided by Routes 72 and 119 as well as the roads through Golden Gate State Park and

Boulder Mountain Park. Kelly Dahl Campground is three miles south of Nederland on Route 119; 303-444-6001.

▲ Kelly Dahl Campground has 48 lakeside RV/tent sites (no hookups), with a small campers store and coin laundromat; open mid-May through October; $13 per night.

**ELDORADO CANYON STATE PARK** 🚶‍♂️🚵‍♂️🐎⛵🎣 Rock climbers come from as far away as Europe to challenge the sheer, vertical 850-foot sandstone cliffs that enclose Eldorado Canyon. There are picnic areas along the creek at the canyon's bottom and ten miles of trails for hiking and mountain biking. Rainbow trout is the main catch here. Day-use fee, $6. ~ Located eight miles southwest of Boulder on Route 170, above the village of Eldorado Springs; 303-494-3943.

**Estes Park Area**

Estes Park is a world apart from the rest of the Front Range, though it's on a direct route to Rocky Mountain National Park and just 30 miles from Boulder, Longmont and Loveland. The sole point of interest along the way is the town of Lyons, at the intersection of Routes 7 and 36. The town has a spread-out historic district made up of 15 buildings dating back to the turn of the century, all constructed from locally quarried red sandstone.

**SIGHTS**

The starting point for sightseeing in Lyons is the **Lyons Redstone Museum**, where artifacts and photos from the town's early days are displayed in an old sandstone schoolhouse. The museum is the headquarters of the Lyons Historical Society, which offers a self-guided tour brochure of the Lyons Historic District. Closed October to June. ~ 340 High Street, Lyons; 303-823-5271.

**Estes Park** has thrived as a tourist town since Rocky Mountain National Park opened in 1915, and today it feels a little quaint with its old-fashioned curio shops full of ersatz Indian items, Asian-made Colorado ashtrays and souvenir rocks. Since there is no food or lodging within the national park, Estes Park is the place for noncampers who wish to spend more than a single day there. Visitors can ride the **Aerial Tramway** up 1200 feet from the middle of town to the top of Prospect Mountain for an overview of Estes Park, Lake Estes and the Big Thompson River. Admission. ~ 420 East Riverside Drive, Estes Park; 970-586-3675.

Perhaps the most interesting sight in Estes Park is the grand old **Stanley Hotel**. Even if you're not planning to stay there, stroll the lobby and grounds of this elegant, historic resort hotel. It was built in 1909, six years before the national park opened, by the man who invented the steam-powered automobile, the Stanley Steamer. The hotel is said to have inspired Stephen King's breakthrough novel, *The Shining*. ~ 333 Wonderview Avenue, Estes Park; 970-586-3371.

An original Stanley Steamer is on display in the recently expanded **Estes Park Area Historical Museum**, along with a 19th-century settler's log cabin, the original Rocky Mountain National Park headquarters building and exhibits on the town's history, including kitsch from the early years of tourism. Admission. ~ 200 4th Street, Estes Park; 970-586-6256.

The **MacGregor Ranch Museum** preserves the homestead of one of the Estes Park region's first settlers, Alexander MacGregor,

**sights**

**AUTHOR FAVORITE**

So many visitors climb Trail Ridge Road into the alpine heart of Rocky Mountain National Park that on many summer days the traffic is bumper-to-bumper. During peak season (no pun intended) I prefer the less-used **Old Fall River Road**, which was the main park road from 1915 (when Rocky Mountain National Park opened its gates to the public) to 1932 (when Trail Ridge Road was completed). The unpaved one-way (uphill) road branches off just inside the east entrance and follows Fall River for 12 miles through ancient forests of Douglas fir and blue spruce, nearing the river's source at Iceberg Lake, then scrambles up over Fall River Pass (11,796 feet) to join Trail Ridge Road at the Alpine Visitors Center.

who led the legal battle against a British earl who claimed all the area's land in the 1870s. Besides a complete documentary record of the land dispute, the museum has antique furnishings, ranch implements and a sizable collection of Western paintings—and it's still a working cattle ranch. Open June through August, Tuesday through Friday. ~ 180 MacGregor Lane, Estes Park; 970-586-3749; www.macgregorranch.org.

A best-selling mystery novel of the 1920s, *Seven Keys to Baldpate*, inspired another historic Estes Park hotel. Gordon and Charles Mace, who built it in 1917, named it the Baldpate Inn after the novel. Later, attorney Clarence Darrow started a tradition by declaring that each guest should contribute a key to the hotel. Over the years the collection grew to become the world's largest. The more than 20,000 keys in the **Baldpate Inn Key Room** include keys to Mozart's wine cellar, Jack Benny's dressing room and the Pentagon. ~ 4900 South Route 7, seven miles south of Estes Park; 970-586-6151.

Close by on the same highway, the **Enos Mills Cabin and Nature Study Area** was the 1885 homestead of the naturalist who persuaded Congress to create Rocky Mountain National Park. The old cabin, where Mills' writings and photographs are on display, sits within a 200-acre preserve laced with nature trails. ~ Route 7, Estes Park; 970-586-4706.

The 19 miles of Route 7 from Estes Park south to Raymond are part of the **Peak to Peak Highway**, which continues as Route 72 for another 37 miles through Nederland, at the upper end of Boulder Canyon, to Central City. The Route 7 portion skirts the Rocky Mountain National Park boundary, passing between two of the area's highest mountains, Mount Meeker (13,911 feet) and Longs Peak (14,256 feet). The latter marks the southeast corner of Rocky Mountain National Park.

While all the mountains that flank Colorado's busy Route 25 corridor are commonly referred to as the Front Range, the actual mountain range of that name runs through **Rocky Mountain National Park**. The most popular tourist spot in Colorado, the national park is where the Continental Divide reaches closest to the eastern Colorado plains. The park encompasses some of the highest, most rugged terrain in the Rockies. During the summer months, expect long lines of cars at the main park entrance on Route 36 just west of Estes Park. Every place that is accessible by car on the east side of the park is crowded at all times in tourist season and on weekends all year. Relatively few visitors wander far from the roadways, however, and with 76 mountain summits above 12,000 feet in elevation, the possibilities for exploring the wilderness on foot or horseback are practically endless. Admission. ~ Estes Park; 970-586-1206; www.nps.gov/romo.

As soon as you enter the park, you find yourself facing a fork in the road. A left turn takes you to **Moraine Park**, where the Big Thompson River meanders through a broad, grassy valley gouged by ancient glaciers and surrounded by mountain crags. The rustic **Moraine Park Museum** has exhibits that explain the natural history of Rocky Mountain National Park. The road climbs for ten miles, following Glacier Creek and passing numerous marked trailheads, to **Bear Lake**, a classic mountain lake surrounded by a paved nature trail and, most of the time, hundreds or even thousands of sightseers. It is typical of dozens of other fair-size natural lakes in the park, most of them accessible only by hiking or horseback trails. While motorists can drive their cars to Bear Lake and join others in a desperate search for parking spaces, an easier and more scenic option is to take one of the shuttle buses that run frequently from the Moraine Park Museum and stop at each trailhead on the way to the lake.

Take the right-hand fork inside the park entrance to drive up **Trail Ridge Road**, the highest continuous automobile road in North America. Completed in 1932, the 45-mile-long paved road traces an old Ute Indian migration route along a ridge high above timberline, paralleling the jagged, impassable rock-and-ice wall of the Continental Divide. Just beyond the highest point on the road (12,183 feet), the **Alpine Visitors Center** stands on the wind-swept brink of rocky cliffs where snowdrifts remain year-round. It has snacks, souvenirs and an observation deck. While most people turn around at the visitors center and return the way they came, the road continues over the Continental Divide to the town of Grand Lake at the park's west entrance (see "Winter Park–Grand Lake Area" in Chapter Four). Oddly enough, Milner Pass, where Trail Ridge Road crosses the Great Divide, is about 1200 feet *lower* than the Alpine Visitors Center.

**LODGING**    Right in town and as romantic as they come is the **Black Canyon Inn**. Accommodations are in a two-story 1929 lodge and separate one- to three-bedroom cabins, some with porches, kitchen facilities and fireplaces. The cabins require a four-night minimum stay; the lodge does not. Amenities include a heated pool, hot tub, fishing pond and barbecue area. ~ 800 MacGregor Avenue, Estes Park; 970-586-8113, 800-897-3730; www.blackcanyoninn.com, e-mail info@blackcanyoninn.com. DELUXE TO ULTRA-DELUXE.

The **Stanley Hotel** was built as a resort in 1909 by inventor F. O. Stanley (one of his Stanley Steamers, a steam-powered touring automobile, is on display in the lobby). Most of the 92 rooms in this hillside hotel have views of the Continental Divide or Lake Estes. A $4 million renovation in the 1990s has left the stately old

Rumor has it that the Stanley Hotel was the inspiration for Stephen King's famous novel *The Shining*.

hotel gleaming like new inside and out. Amenities include a swimming pool, hot tub and volleyball court. The hotel has hosted guests as diverse as the Emperor of Japan and Bob Dylan. ~ 333 Wonderview Avenue, Estes Park; 970-586-3371, 800-976-1337, fax 970-586-4694; www.stanleyhotel.com. ULTRA-DELUXE.

Built in 1917, the **Baldpate Inn** took its name from a best-selling mystery novel of the time called *Seven Keys to Baldpate*, which inspired its huge, world-famous key collection. Auto-graphed photos of celebrities who have been guests there are also on display. The 12 guest rooms and three individual cabins are rather small but nicely furnished with antiques and handmade quilts. Set at an elevation of 9000 feet, the inn commands a grand view of the valley below. ~ 4900 South Route 7, Estes Park; 970-586-6151; www.baldpateinn.com, e-mail baldpatein@aol.com. MODERATE TO DELUXE.

Colorado's largest log lodge is the **Aspen Lodge**. Set on 3000 acres of ranchland with a spectacular view of Longs Peak, the lodge offers a full range of sports activities for guests, including horseback riding, hayrides, barbecues, swimming, fishing, tennis, racquetball, hiking and sleigh rides (in season). Facilities also in-clude hot tubs and saunas. Some of the 59 guest rooms are in the main lodge, while others are in luxurious individual log cabins. There is a three-night minimum stay in summer. Rates include all three meals in summer, breakfast the rest of the year. ~ 6120 Route 7, Estes Park; 970-586-8133, 800-332-6867, fax 970-586-8133; www.aspenlodge.net. DELUXE TO ULTRA-DELUXE.

Built on land that formerly belonged to the Irish Earl of Dun-raven, **Tiny Town Cottages** has 20 cozy cottages set on the banks of the Big Thompson River, a great spot for trout fishing. The cottages feature queen- or king-size beds, kitchens and fireplaces. Rates include a continental breakfast. ~ 830 Moraine Road, Estes Park; 970-586-4249; www.tinytowncottages.com, e-mail info@tinytowncottages.com. MODERATE TO DELUXE.

Perhaps the most unabashedly romantic lodging in the Estes Park area is the **Antlers Pointe on the River**, a couples-only hide-away nestled in a grove of spruce and pine on the banks of the Fall River near the entrance to Rocky Mountain National Park. Each of the eight luxury one-bedroom cabins has a king-size bed, a jacuzzi, a cozy parlor with a fireplace and loveseat, and a deck at the water's edge. Southwestern-style furnishings emphasize logs, leather and polished oak. ~ 1515 Fish Hatchery Road, Estes Park; 970-586-8881, 800-638-8881, fax 970-586-2301; www. antlerspointe.com, e-mail info@antlerspointe.com. ULTRA-DELUXE.

The **Fawn Brook Inn**, four miles south of Estes Park, has a repu-tation for the finest dining in the vicinity. Open Friday, Saturday and Sunday only, this mountain lodge offers a changing selection

**DINING**

of wild-game dishes, veal, duck and seafood traditionally prepared with an Austrian flair. The contrast of the rugged setting and rustic old lodge with the elegant presentation and service makes the Fawn Brook Inn extra-special. Closed Monday through Thursday from October to mid-May. ~ Route 7, Allenspark; 303-747-2556. ULTRA-DELUXE.

Another longtime Estes Park favorite, the **Dunrovin Inn** serves Italian cuisine, showcasing traditional pasta dishes such as lasagna, cannelloni and ziti, and also offers a wide range of beef and seafood choices. The decor is striking, with dark wood, bright crimson accents and a carpet that may make you dizzy. Reservations are often necessary. ~ 2470 Route 66; 970-586-6409. The inn recently opened a second location with the same menu downtown at 101 West Elkhorn Avenue, Estes Park; 970-586-3818. MODERATE TO DELUXE.

For a more affordable feast, try **Nicky's,** an eclectic American-Greek-Italian restaurant specializing in prime-rib dinners in a clean, contemporary family-dining atmosphere. An open-air dining deck overlooks the river. The menu in the café-style Garden Room offers burgers, salads and pasta dishes. In the more elegant Cattlemen's Room, lit by crystal chandeliers that hang from a rustic wood-beam ceiling, the specialty is steak and lobster. ~ 1350 Fall River Road, Estes Park; 970-586-5376, 800-323-0031. MODERATE TO DELUXE.

Even more eclectic is the **Gazebo Restaurant,** next to Bond Park in downtown Estes Park. The international menu features specialties from Italy, Afghanistan, the Caribbean and Mexico among its 48 entrées. The environment is formal, with white-linen service for both lunch and dinner, and the decor is bursting with silk flowers and floral prints. ~ 225 Park Lane, Estes Park; 970-586-9564. DELUXE.

Giant breakfast burritos are the claim to fame at **Ed's Cantina & Grill,** which also serves burgers and Mexican favorites for lunch and dinner among baseball memorabilia and beer signs. ~ 362 East Elkhorn Avenue, Estes Park; 970-586-2919. BUDGET.

## WORK OF ART

The world's largest pewter casting studio is the **Michael Ricker Pewter Studio and Museum,** located at the base of Lake Estes Dam. With the help of 70 employees, artist Michael Ricker casts more than 25,000 sculptures a month. His work is on display in the White House, Walt Disney World and the Vatican, as well as in the museum adjacent to the studio. ~ 2050 Big Thompson Avenue, Estes Park; 970-586-2030.

Estes Park, where the tourism industry has thrived for more than a century, has every kind of gift and curio shop you can imagine. Venerable tourist traps selling authentic reproduction turquoise-and-silver Indian-design jewelry and "Colorful Colorado" ash-trays from Taiwan stand alongside sleek modern-art galleries and outdoor fashion boutiques. There are also clusters of arts and crafts retailers such as the **Old Church Shops**, which feature works by more than 75 Colorado craftspersons. ~ 157 West Elkhorn Avenue, Estes Park. There are also more sophisticated galleries such as the **Art Center of Estes Park**, which offers not only local and out-of-state artists' paintings and sculptures for sale but also art classes and painting trips. ~ 517 Big Thompson Avenue, Estes Park; 970-586-5882.

One of the oldest and most beloved stores in the Estes Park area—and still one of the best—is the **Eagle Plume Gallery** of Native American Arts ten miles south of town. Started in the 1930s by Charles Perkins (a native Coloradoan who was so proud to be one-fourth Blackfoot Indian that he changed his name to Charlie Eagle Plume to reflect his heritage), it was one of the first stores in America to deal exclusively in American Indian collectibles. The store continues to uphold Eagle Plume's reverence for Indian arts and traditions: it contains one of the world's finest private collections of Plains Indian artifacts and offers high-quality tourist-trade goods and collectibles for sale. Open daily in summer, weekends only in winter. ~ Route 7, Estes Park; 970-747-2861.

For a rowdy scene, check out **Lonigan's Saloon**, with live acoustic music on Tuesday and loud rock for dancing on Friday and Saturday evenings. ~ 110 West Elkhorn Avenue, Estes Park; 970-586-4346.

Area musicians perform contemporary, country or folk music every Wednesday and Thursday evening in summer at **Performance Park**. ~ West end of Elkhorn Avenue. The park is also the summer venue for the **Estes Park Music Festival**, which presents classical concerts by members of the Colorado Music Festival. ~ 304 East Elkhorn Avenue; 970-586-9203; www.estes arts.com/estesparkmusicfestival.htm. In the winter, the festival concerts move indoors to the **Stanley Concert Hall** adjoining the hotel. ~ 333 Wonderview Avenue, Estes Park; 970-586-3371.

**ROCKY MOUNTAIN NATIONAL PARK** 🧍🏇⛵ One of the premier areas in the U.S. National Park System, this 266,957-acre mountain recreation area reaches from meadows at 8000-foot elevation into the high mountains, containing 107 peaks over 12,000 feet. Major features include Bear Lake, a natural lake surrounded by a half-mile paved trail that connects to other, more ambitious hiking trails into the high country; Trail Ridge Road, one of Colorado's most scenic high-altitude routes; and Longs Peak, a legendary weekend climb that requires no special equipment in summer. Easy access from Denver and other Front Range cities makes this one of the most crowded summertime destinations in Colorado. Fishing is permitted for trout in backcountry lakes and streams. There are picnic areas, restrooms, visitors centers, campfire programs, a cafeteria, horse stables, shuttle buses and hiking trails (355 miles of them). Day-use fee $10, good for seven days. ~ The main east entrance is three miles west of Estes Park on Route 34/36. The west entrance is about two miles north of Grand Lake on Route 34; 970-586-1206.

▲ Camping is permitted in five public campgrounds totaling 577 sites (no hookups); $20 per night. In July and August, reservations are required for the two largest campgrounds, Glacier Basin and Moraine Park (800-365-2267; credit card required). A limited number of backcountry campsites are available by permit.

**ROOSEVELT NATIONAL FOREST** 🏃 ↙ This 788,000-acre forest spans the eastern slope of the Rockies from Central City to the Wyoming state line and wraps around three sides of Rocky Mountain National Park. Its most distinctive feature is a series of deep gorges, including Big Thompson Canyon below Estes Park. Two national forest wilderness areas—Indian Peaks Wilderness and Comanche Peak Wilderness—adjoin Rocky Mountain National Park. Fishing is good for native cutthroat, rainbow and brown trout species in Big Thompson Canyon. Facilities include picnic areas, hiking trails and jeep trails. ~ There is extensive forest access along Route 34 East (Big Thompson Canyon), Route 36 East, Route 7 South (Peak to Peak Highway) and Route 72. Trailheads for the Comanche Peaks Wilderness are off Devil's Gulch Road, which runs northeast from Estes Park. The Brainard Lake Road off Route 72 at Ward provides trailhead access to the Indian Peaks Wilderness. Olive Ridge Campground is 15 miles south of Estes Park on Route 7; 303-444-6001.

▲ The only national forest campground in the area, Olive Ridge Campground has 56 RV/tent sites (no hookups); $13 to $16 per night. Closed mid-September to mid-May. Reservations: 877-444-6777; www.reserveusa.com.

▼▼▼▼▼▼▼▼▼▼▼▼
**Fort Collins Area**    Along the northern part of the Front Range Corridor, agriculture is king. The major towns in the area—Loveland, Greeley and Fort Collins—were founded by farmers rather than gold prospectors. Fort Collins, for example, sprang up in 1873 when the army abandoned a small frontier outpost called Camp Collins and auctioned the land

to a utopian agricultural colony, which offered memberships to persons "of good moral character." Today, Fort Collins is the largest town in the area and the site of the state's "Aggie" school, Colorado State University. Traditionally, the major crop in this part of Colorado has been sugar beets. The juice of the beets was refined into white granulated sugar, and the pulp that remained was used to fatten cattle in vast feed lots. Declining demand for beet sugar has forced area farmers to diversify in recent years, and the region now produces everything from herbs and organic vegetables to experimental "beefalo," a cross between cattle and bison.

**SIGHTS**

The most direct route from Route 25 to Estes Park and Rocky Mountain National Park is through Loveland. The site of Colorado's first beet sugar mill in 1901, Loveland still has the look of a typical farm town, with its silos, cattle feedlots and railroad yards. But looks can be deceiving. Loveland has developed into the main artists' community on the Front Range. Visitors can watch bronze sculptures being poured at **Art Castings**. ~ 511 8th Street Southeast, Loveland; 970-667-1114; www.artcastings.com. See some of the locally made sculptures on exhibit in the city-owned **Benson Park Children's Sculpture Garden.** ~ 29th Street at Aspen Drive, Loveland; 970-663-2940.

Much of the **Loveland Museum and Gallery** is given over to showing the works of local artists. The museum also features a 2000-square-foot relief map of Big Thompson Canyon. You can see the lower portion of the canyon for yourself by taking Route 34 west toward Estes Park, a distance of 30 miles. If the name rings a bell, it is probably because the long, narrow canyon gained national notoriety in 1977 as the scene of one of Colorado's most terrible disasters, a huge flash flood in which scores of campers drowned. ~ 503 North Lincoln Avenue, Loveland; 970-962-2410; www.ci.loveland.co.us/museum/museum.htm.

Before heading into the mountains, travelers may wish to take a detour from Loveland 13 miles east to **Greeley** for a dose of history straight out of Colorado's richest farm country. The city was named for *New York Tribune* publisher Horace Greeley. Horace Greeley used his newspaper to recruit members for a utopian farming cooperative, the Union Colony, which, under the leadership of the *Tribune*'s agriculture editor, Nathan Meeker, founded the town in 1870 and developed the first large-scale irrigation system in Colorado to serve the community's farms. In an era when most Colorado communities seemed to exist primarily to provide booze, gambling and prostitution for area cowboys and miners, liquor and the other forms of entertainment that went with it were prohibited in Greeley, giving the town a reputation for clean living that it has yet to live down.

For a look at the early years of the Union Colony, visit the **1870 Meeker House Museum.** The original two-story adobe house built by the colony's leader became Greeley's first museum in 1929. Admission. ~ 1324 9th Avenue, Greeley; 970-350-9220. More

## WILDLIFE UP CLOSE

Because they have enjoyed protection from hunters for more than 75 years in Rocky Mountain National Park, wildlife both large and small is abundant and not too shy. You are more likely to see elk here than anywhere else in Colorado. Watch for them in high, distant meadows in the summer and in the lowlands of Moraine Park during the cold months. Bighorn sheep and mountain goats sometimes graze within sight of Trail Ridge Road; bald eagles and peregrine falcons ride updrafts where the wind meets the mountains; marmots whistle signals across the high tundra; and black bears roam deep in the forests. Chipmunks swarm around every scenic turnout, greedily stuffing their cheeks with tourist handouts, as camp-robber jays swoop down to grab their share. Be sure to bring binoculars and a loaded camera.

about the colony, including lots of documents and photographs, can be found nearby at the **Greeley Municipal Museum and Archives**. Admission. ~ 919 7th Street, Greeley; 970-350-9220.

While **Centennial Village** officially got its name because it was opened in 1976 on the 100th anniversary of Colorado statehood, it also recalls James A. Michener's fictionalized history of the region, *Centennial*. Michener, who taught at the University of Northern Colorado in Greeley from 1936 to 1941, used the town as the model for his fictitious town of Centennial. The village is actually a large, grassy park where historic buildings have been collected from throughout the northeastern plains and arranged in a chronology of 60 years of settlement. Included, among other structures, are an Indian teepee, a homesteader's house, a white-washed one-room schoolhouse, a Victorian residence, a firehouse and a blacksmith's shop. Admission. Open mid-April to mid-October. Closed Sunday and Monday. ~ 1475 A Street, Greeley; 970-350-9220.

Also in Greeley is **Houston Gardens**, where typical flora from four of the five life zones found in Colorado—all except alpine tundra—makes up a pleasant botanical garden. Admission. ~ 515 23rd Avenue, Greeley; 970-353-4837.

Twenty miles east of Greeley off Route 34, **Riverside Reservoir White Pelican Nesting Colony** draws birding enthusiasts from around the state during the nesting season. The reservoir is not open to recreational use, but a trail provides access to the shore. Bring binoculars, which will allow you to view the island in the middle of the lake, where about 500 pairs of white pelicans nest each spring.

◄ HIDDEN

Twelve miles north of Loveland via Route 25, **Fort Collins** is the site of **Colorado State University**, which includes the state's agricultural, forestry and veterinary schools. The town's original commercial district, which dates back to the 1870s, has been refurbished as the **Historic Old Town District**, a pretty town square lined with galleries, specialty shops and cafés, on Mountain Avenue between Remington Street and North College Avenue.

The **Fort Collins Museum** in Library Park displays artifacts from the city's early years as a fur trappers' outpost and a U.S. cavalry fort protecting pioneers on the Overland Trail. Outside the main museum in the peaceful, hidden-away little Heritage Compound, are two cabins—one of them the oldest in the state—and a one-room schoolhouse, all relocated from elsewhere in the county. Closed Monday. ~ 200 Matthews Street, Fort Collins; 970-221-6738.

Nearby, the 1879 Victorian **Avery House**, one of the city's grandest mansions, has been restored and furnished with antiques of the period. Franklin Avery, the original owner, laid out the exceptionally wide streets of Fort Collins and was the town banker.

Public tours are offered twice weekly, on Wednesday and Sunday afternoons. ~ 328 West Mountain Avenue, Fort Collins; 970-221-0533.

The **Fort Collins Municipal Railway**, the last of the old-time streetcars that provided public transportation in most Colorado cities from the 1930s through the 1950s, operates only on weekends and holidays from May through September. It travels a route between Historic Old Town and the **City Park** at Roosevelt Avenue and Oak Street. Admission. ~ 970-482-5821.

Free tours are offered at the **Anheuser-Busch Brewery**. More modern and high-tech than the Coors brewery in Golden but lacking Coors' ties to Colorado tradition, the Anheuser-Busch facility is worth a visit primarily because of its mascot Clydesdale team. The horses perform once a day (except Tuesday and Wednesday off-season), and all tours include a walk through their barn. The first Saturday of each month is Clydesdale Camera Day, when visitors can take photos of each other with the horses. ~ 2351 Busch Drive, Fort Collins; 970-490-4691.

East of town on the other side of the interstate is Fort Collins' most unusual sight, the **Swetsville Zoo**. The more than 70 "animals" in the park are actually life-size sculptures made from junkyard pieces of cars and farm machinery. ~ 4801 Harmony Road, Fort Collins; 970-484-9509.

Of the cities along the northern Colorado Front Range, Fort Collins is the only one not on a direct route to Rocky Mountain National Park. Instead, motorists who head west into the mountains from Fort Collins on Route 14 discover a less-traveled highway that runs north of the national park through the **Poudre River Canyon**, snaking along the Cache La Poudre River past campgrounds, picnic areas and fishing spots and through a long tunnel on its way up to the summit of **Cameron Pass** (10,276 feet). Turnouts on both sides of the pass afford dramatic views of the 2000-foot cliff faces of the **Nokhu Crags**, which mark the northwest corner of Rocky Mountain National Park. The area is mountain wilderness so rugged that even though the park boundary is less than five miles away from Cameron Pass, it is impossible to reach by road. The distance from Fort Collins to Cameron Pass is 68 miles.

**LODGING**    Located in the little antique-filled village of Windsor, the **Porter House Bed and Breakfast** was built in 1898 for a local doctor, who used it as both his home and his office. The steep-roofed, turreted Queen Anne Victorian-style house has four guest rooms with vintage furnishings and all the niceties a good B&B ought to have, from fresh flowers to goose-down comforters. Each room has a queen-size bed and a desk with a computer data port. One has its own fireplace, and another has a balcony. ~ 530

Main Street, Windsor; 970-686-5973, 888-686-5793, fax 970-686-7046. MODERATE TO DELUXE.

Another good B&B option in Loveland, the two-story neo-Victorian **Cattail Creek Inn Bed & Breakfast** stands with its back yard opening onto the seventh tee box of the Cattail Creek Golf Course. The inn is one block from Lake Loveland and within easy walking distance of the Benson Sculpture Park. Its eight guest rooms are individually decorated in motifs that range from mountain cabin rusticity to antique elegance. All rooms have private baths, and some have special features such as a fireplace, a private deck or a two-person whirlpool tub. ~ 2665 Abarr Drive, Loveland; 970-667-7600, 800-572-2466, fax 970-667-8968; www.cattailcreekinn.com. MODERATE TO DELUXE.

You won't find more unique lodging anywhere than at the **Heritage Inn,** located near Greeley in the small town of Evans. The 14 individually decorated rooms feature fantasy motifs that include a space capsule, a rainforest, an igloo and even a genuine '59 Cadillac. ~ 3301 West Service Road, Evans; 970-339-5900; www.fantasuiteco.com. DELUXE.

In Greeley, the **Sod Buster Inn Bed & Breakfast** was built in 1997 to harmonize with the existing Victorian homes of the Monroe Corridor historic district, which it does surprisingly well considering its unusual design. The three-story inn is octagonal in shape, with a wraparound verandah. Inside, a large open living room is lit by a skylight high overhead in the top of the rotunda, while a curved stairway winds up to the guest rooms. All ten rooms are individually decorated and have private baths with ether-jetted tubs or antique clawfoot tubs. ~ 1221 9th Avenue, Greeley; 970-392-1221, 888-300-1221, fax 970-392-1222; e-mail sodbuster@ctos.com. MODERATE TO DELUXE.

Lodgings in Fort Collins generally can't compare with those in Boulder for history or charm but are much less expensive. Try the **Mulberry Inn,** which has 120 motel-style rooms, all with queen-size beds and standard amenities. In addition, some rooms

### KING AND QUEEN OF HEARTS

Besides art, Loveland is known for its postmark. Every year before Valentine's Day, the local post office stamps "Loveland" on more than 100,000 greeting cards from all over the U.S. and remails them. (To do this, send your valentine by February 9, prestamped and preaddressed, in a larger envelope to Postmaster, Attn: Valentine, USPS, Loveland, CO 80538-9998.) Ted and Mabel Thompson, who started the valentine remailing program in 1946, are memorialized by a bas-relief sculpture in **Thompson Park.** ~ 4th Street, Loveland.

have jacuzzis, and suites have private sundecks. ~ 4333 East Mulberry Street, Fort Collins; 970-493-9000, 800-234-5548, fax 970-224-9636; www.mulberry-inn.com. BUDGET TO MODERATE.

The **Edwards House Bed & Breakfast** offers six attractively furnished guest rooms with shared baths in a three-story 1904 mansion. The inn doubles as a small conference center and features such high-tech conveniences as computer data ports in the rooms. ~ 402 West Mountain Avenue, Fort Collins; 970-493-9191, 800-281-9190, fax 970-484-0706; www.edwardshouse.com. MODERATE TO DELUXE.

Affordable and convenient to the CSU campus, the **Best Western University Inn** has 74 clean though plain motel rooms, cable TV and a heated pool. Guests have privileges at a nearby health club. Bland? Well, maybe so; welcome to Fort Collins. ~ 914 South College Avenue, Fort Collins; 970-484-1984, fax 970-484-1987. MODERATE.

**DINING**

The **Breakfast Club** isn't just a John Hughes teeny-bopper film. It's also an all-day (well, until 2 p.m.) breakfast diner in the heart of Loveland. Take your sweetheart, or your kids, for omelets, eggs and pancakes, with all the usual fixin's. (Don't leave without trying the Belgian waffles.) If it's something more substantial you want, there's a list of luscious burritos to linger over. Be forewarned, though, this is a *breakfast* place; look elsewhere for your soups and salads. The price is certainly right. ~ 1451 North Boise Avenue, Loveland; 970-461-1261. There's a second location in Fort Collins at 121 West Monroe Drive; 970-223-7193. BUDGET.

The **Silver Grill Cafe** has been a fixture in Fort Collins' Old Town Historic District since 1933. The café serves no-nonsense breakfasts from biscuits and gravy to steak and eggs. The lunch menu features daily grill specials and a choice of sandwiches. Refurbished in the recent gentrification of Old Town, the café still makes you feel as if you've stepped into an earlier era. ~ 218 Walnut Street, Fort Collins; 970-484-4656. BUDGET.

**AUTHOR FAVORITE**

At any time of year, the most romantic spot to take your valentine to dinner in Loveland is **The Parsonage**, a historic Victorian house built in 1900 for a local minister. The menu presents an impressive array of American and Continental dishes, and the ambience keeps its promise of candlelit intimacy. ~ 405 East 5th Street, Loveland; 970-962-9700. MODERATE.

Another local favorite is **Bisetti's Ristorante**, located a block south of Old Town. This cozy family-style Italian restaurant emphasizes Sicilian cuisine, with a menu that offers (on the one hand) heart-healthy selections and (on the other hand) homemade cheesecake so rich it's downright sinful. ~ 120 South College Avenue, Fort Collins; 970-493-0086. BUDGET TO MODERATE.

For fine dining in Fort Collins, it's **Braddy's Downtown Restaurant**. In an understated atmosphere of contemporary light wood furnishings, tropical plants and crisp white tablecloths, the restaurant features gamey haute cuisine like antelope steaks and bacon-wrapped red deer roulade, as well as more conventional selections such as filet mignon, maple-basted salmon and Muscovy duck breast. There's also a chef's tasting plate—three or five courses to be shared by a whole table—with dishes that are not available on the regular menu, wine optional. ~ 160 West Oak Street, Fort Collins; 970-498-0873. DELUXE TO ULTRA-DELUXE.

**SHOPPING**

In Fort Collins, the triangular **Old Town Square** has a handful of galleries. ~ Mountain and College avenues, Fort Collins. **Walnut Street Gallery** specializes in musician photographs and album cover art. ~ 217 Linden Street, Fort Collins; 970-221-2383; www.walnutst.com. Also stop by **Trimble Court Artisans**, an artists' cooperative featuring pottery, jewelry, wearable art and other local arts and crafts. ~ 118 Trimble Court, Fort Collins; 970-221-0051.

**NIGHTLIFE**

Fort Collins, the cultural hub of Colorado's northern farmlands, has its own symphony orchestra, which performs in a new arts complex called **Lincoln Center**. The center, which has an art gallery, an auditorium, and several other performance spaces, including an intimate little theater and an outdoor courtyard stage surrounded by gardens, also provides a venue for local theater and dance companies from several smaller communities in the area. Call for the current schedule and you'll usually find something going on here in the evening—unlike most other northern Colorado farm towns, which roll up the sidewalks when the sun goes down. Closed Saturdays in summer and Sundays year-round. ~ 417 West Magnolia Street, Fort Collins; 970-221-6735.

With its large college-student population, Fort Collins supports a beer-and-burgers sort of nightlife scene, though no place tries very hard to compete with the live music clubs of Boulder. Try **CooperSmith's Pub & Brewing and Billiards**—the name says it all. ~ 5 Old Town Square, Fort Collins; 970-498-0483.

**PARKS**

**BOYD LAKE STATE PARK** Just outside the Loveland city limits, this reservoir is used for swimming, waterskiing, sailing and windsurfing. Its soft sand beaches are perfect for sunbathing. Surrounded by prairie and numerous smaller lakes, Boyd Lake has a view of Rocky Mountain National Park on the distant western horizon. Facilities include picnic areas, restrooms and a marina with rentals. There's fishing for walleye, perch, crappie, catfish, bass, bluegill, pike, carp and bullhead. Day-use fee, $6 in summer, $5 the rest of the year. ~ Located one mile east of Loveland. From Eisenhower Boulevard, take Madison Avenue north and follow the signs; 970-669-1739.

▲ There are 148 RV/tent sites (no hookups); $16 per night.

## HORSETOOTH RESERVOIR AND HORSETOOTH MOUNTAIN PARK 🏃 🚣 ⚓ 🛶 🚤 ⛵ Long, narrow Horsetooth Reservoir hugs the foothills due west of Fort Collins. The lake has been a popular, often crowded water-sports area used for waterskiing, boating, windsurfing and swimming. A paved county road runs along the eastern shore, which in past years has often been lined with anglers trying for walleye, bass, bluegill and rainbow trout here. In 2000, the U.S. Bureau of Reclamation began a dam renovation project that has lowered the water level a full 33 feet— far out of reach of boat launch facilities—limiting recreation possibilities. It should be refilled by 2005. The lake is flanked on the west by the Lory State Park and Horsetooth Mountain Park. Facilities include picnic areas, restrooms, a marina and hiking trails. Day-use fee, $7. ~ From Bellvue, ten miles west of Fort Collins, County Road 23 heads south along the eastern shore of the lake; 970-679-4570.

▲ There are 115 RV sites (20 with water and electric hookups) and 100 tent sites around the lake. Camping costs $10 for tents, or $15 for RV sites with electrical hookups.

Newspaper editor Horace Greeley is often credited with coining the slogan "Go west, young man, go west." (Actually, the words were written by journalist John Babson Lane, but Greeley printed them.)

## LORY STATE PARK 🏃 🚵 🏇 An unpaved road and 30 miles of hiking trails wind among Lory State Park's arid foothills, grasslands and upthrust rock formations. Deer are abundant. A gravel trail, ideal for mountain biking, runs from the park boundary across the east face of nearby Horsetooth Mountain, named for its crowning rock formation, which some say resembles a horse's bicuspid. There are picnic areas and restrooms. Day-use fee, $5. ~ Shortly before reaching Horsetooth Reservoir, County Road 25G branches off westward to Lory State Park; 970-493-1623.

## ROOSEVELT NATIONAL FOREST 🏃 🛶 🚤 ⛵ The northern section of Roosevelt National Forest includes the Poudre River Canyon west of Fort Collins. While most of the canyon is accessible by paved highway, one of the most spectacular sections of the

canyon runs through the relatively small Cache La Poudre Wilderness and can only be reached on foot. A much larger wilderness area, the Rawah Wilderness, covers the eastern slope of the Medicine Bow Mountains on the west edge of the national forest. An abundance of lakes, especially in the Red Feather Lakes area, is a key feature of this part of Roosevelt National Forest. Two areas of the Cache La Poudre River in Poudre River Canyon are designated wild trout waters with native (not stocked) cutthroat, rainbow, brown and brook trout. Dowdy, Parvin and West lakes in the Red Feather Lakes area offer excellent kokanee salmon and cutthroat and rainbow trout fishing, as do Chambers and Barnes Meadow lakes at the headwaters of the Cache La Poudre River. There are picnic areas, restrooms, boat ramps, hiking trails and jeep trails. ~ The main recreational access is up the Poudre River Canyon on Route 14. Kelly Flats and Tom Bennett campgrounds are 26 miles west of Fort Collins on this highway. The Red Feather Lakes area is reached from the town of Livermore via paved Red Feather Lakes Road (County Road 74E); 970-498-2770.

▲ Among the nine small national forest campgrounds along the Cache La Poudre River are the 23-site Kelly Flats Campground ($14 per night) and 12-site Tom Bennett Campground ($9 per night). Both are closed from mid-October to mid-May. In the Red Feather Lakes area, Dowdy Lake Campground has 62 RV/tent sites ($12 per night); some sites here are open year-round. Reservations are accepted for Dowdy Lake: 877-444-6777; www.reserveusa.com.

## Outdoor Adventures

### FISHING

Most fishing along the Front Range is in warm-water reservoirs, where the catch includes walleye, largemouth bass, channel catfish, pike, bluegill, carp, bullhead, perch and crappie. **Boyd Lake Marina** offers boat rentals, bait and tackle for angling on Boyd Lake. ~ 970-669-1739.

### BALLOON RIDES

In Boulder, **Fair Winds** offers one-hour early morning balloon excursions with a champagne celebration afterwards. ~ Boulder; 303-939-9323; www.fairwindsinc.com. **Life Cycle Balloon Adventures** offers daily champagne flights over Boulder, as well as Winter Park, Castle Rock and South Park. ~ 410 19th Street, Golden; 303-216-1990; www.lifecycleballoons.com.

### SKIING

**Eldora Mountain Resort,** near the upper end of Boulder Canyon, may be modest in size as Colorado ski areas go, but with ten chairlifts and a vertical drop of 1400 feet, it is the largest ski area in the Front Range. The slopes are often packed with students from the

University of Colorado, a short drive away. There are three terrain parks for snowboarders. Open mid-November to mid-April. ~ Off Route 19, Nederland; 303-440-8700; www.eldora.com.

The region's best cross-country skiing trails are found within **Rocky Mountain National Park**.

**Ski Rentals**   Cross-country skis and guided tours within Rocky Mountain National Park are available at **Estes Park Mountain Shop**. ~ 358 East Elkhorn Avenue, Estes Park; 970-586-6548; www.estesparkmountainshop.com.

**ICE SKATING**

**Evergreen Lake**, just west of the town of Evergreen, is one of the most popular outdoor ice-skating spots in the state from mid-December until the ice gets too thin in the spring. Skate rentals are available at the lake. ~ 303-674-2677. Fort Collins has a fine indoor ice rink, open year-round, at the **Edora Pool Ice Center**. ~ 1801 Riverside Drive; 970-221-6683.

**GOLF**

Golden's new municipal golf course, the 18-hole **Fossil Trace Golf Club**, is a green oasis against the arid foothills. Red and white rock formations, some of them filled with fossils, stand throughout the course and surround the 12th hole like Stonehenge. ~ 3050 Illinois Street, Golden; 303-277-8750; www.fossiltrace.com.

In the mountains within an hour's drive west of Denver, Evergreen's 18-hole **Evergreen Golf Course** has narrow fairways and rock obstacles. It offers cart and club rentals. ~ 29614 Upper Bear Creek Road; 303-674-4128. There's also the **Hiwan Golf Club**, one of the region's finest golf courses. ~ 30671 Clubhouse Lane; 303-674-3366; prior arrangements necessary.

Located between Boulder and Longmont is the challenging 18-hole semiprivate **Lake Valley Golf Club**. ~ 4400 Lake Valley Drive, Longmont; 303-444-2114. You can also tee off at the beautiful **Flatirons Golf Course**, which dates back to the 1930s and has mature shade trees, with creeks, streams or ponds on 14 of the 18 holes. ~ 5706 Arapahoe Avenue; 303-442-7851. Loveland has two 18-hole public golf courses—the newer **Mariana Butte Golf Course** (701 Clubhouse Drive; 303-669-5800), which has been rated one of the top affordable golf courses in the country by *Golf Digest,* and **The Olde Course at Loveland** (2115 West 29th Street; 970-667-5256). Fort Collins has two nine-hole golf courses: **Mountain Vista Greens Golf Course** (2808 Northeast Frontage Road; 970-482-4847) and the **City Park Nine Golf Course** (411 South Bryan Avenue; 970-221-6650), both with pro shops that offer cart and club rentals. In Estes Park there's the **Estes Park Golf Club**, a traditional 18-hole mountain course that is cited by golf magazines as one of Colorado's best. ~ 1080 South Saint Vrain

Avenue; 970-586-8146. Also try the nine-hole par-3 **Lake Estes Executive Course.** ~ 690 Big Thompson Avenue; 970-586-8176. All these courses offer club rentals.

In Boulder, look for free lighted courts at **Chautauqua Park.** ~ 9th Street at Baseline Road. There are also courts lighted for night play at the **North Boulder Recreation Center;** fee for court reservations. ~ 3170 North Broadway; 303-441-3444. Estes Park has municipal courts at **Stanley Park.** ~ Community Drive. In Fort Collins, try **Warren Park.** ~ Lemay Street at Horsetooth Road.

**TENNIS**

In Fort Collins, hour-long guided rides around Lory State Park are available at **Double Diamond Stables** for riding on trails in the park. ~ Lory State Park; 970-224-4200. In the Estes Park area, the **Cowpoke Corner Corral** offers guided rides ranging from one to four hours on Grant Track Mountain, ~ 2166 Route 66, Estes Park; 970-586-5890. There's also **Elkhorn Stables.** ~ 650 West Elkhorn Avenue, Estes Park; 970-586-5525.

**RIDING STABLES**

**National Park Village Stables** leads small guided tours, limited to seven riders, including trips along Fall River and all-day rides to the top of Deer Mountain in Rocky Mountain National Park. ~ 4600 Fall River Road, Rocky Mountain National Park; 970-586-5269. Longmont, a farming and ranching town located midway between Boulder and Fort Collins, has more horse stables than any other town in the region. Although many specialize in boarding and training, more than a dozen offer horse rentals and western-style riding instruction, including **Apex Equestrian Center.** ~ 8939 Nelson Road, Longmont; 303-447-8290.

> You may never find solitude at the Rocky Mountain National Park, but you will find hundreds of miles of alpine trails through mountain scenery as spectacular as any you can imagine.

**Elk Meadows County Park** north of Evergreen has six miles of trails through varied terrain that are used by hundreds of mountain bikers daily (mostly local residents).

**BIKING**

The **Boulder Creekpath** forms the main artery of a 50-mile bicycle trail system throughout the Boulder area.

**Bike Rentals** In Boulder, **University Bicycles** rents mountain bikes, hybrids and three-speed town bikes. ~ 839 Pearl Street, Boulder; 303-444-4196.

In Estes Park, **Colorado Bicycling Adventures** has mountain bike rentals and also offers van-supported all-downhill tours in Rocky Mountain National Park. ~ 184 East Elkhorn Avenue, Estes Park; 970-586-4241, 800-607-6765; e-mail cbabike@frii.com. **Estes Park Marina** at Lake Estes rents mountain bikes, four-wheel surreys and tandems. ~ Estes Park; 970-586-2011.

**HIKING**     All distances listed for hiking trails are one way unless otherwise
noted.

**DENVER MOUNTAIN PARKS AREA**   Nearly ten miles of trails
meander among the eroded sandstone formations of Morrison's
**Red Rocks State Park.** In the Evergreen area, **Elk Meadows
County Park** has an easy six-mile loop trail through mountain
meadows and ponderosa-covered mountainsides shared by hikers, joggers and bikers. **Golden Gate Canyon State Park,** which
lies between Golden and Central City, offers 35 miles of hiking
trails through dramatic canyon country. **Arapaho National Forest**
in the vicinity of Idaho Springs and Georgetown has a truly vast
trail network. Among the best trails are the four-mile **Chicago
Lakes Trail** from Echo Lake on the Mount Evans Highway and
the 12-mile climb from the Echo Lake trailhead to the summit of
Mount Evans.

**BOULDER AREA**   The mountains on Boulder's western edge, including Boulder Mountain Park, offer some of the most accessible hiking trails in the Front Range. Major trailheads at Chautauqua Park and at Sunrise Amphitheater on Flagstaff Mountain
provide access to such backcountry routes as the **Enchanted Mesa
Trail** (3 miles) and longer trails leading to the Flatirons. There is
also good hiking just outside the city in **Sunshine Canyon,** at the
west end of Mapleton Street.

**ESTES PARK AREA**   Rangers estimate that only 15 percent of
visitors to Rocky Mountain National Park venture more than a
quarter-mile from their cars. Considering how many people visit
the park on a typical summer day, this still means that the main
trails see heavy use. Among the great trails in the national park
are the fairly easy **Bridal Veil Falls Trail** (3 miles), near the north
boundary of the park; the hike from the **Flattop Trail** starting at
Bear Lake on the **Fern Lake Trail** (3 miles); and the climb to the
summit of Longs Peak by either the more popular **East Longs
Peak Trail** (4 miles) or the longer, less crowded **North Longs
Peak Trail** (4.5 miles), which merges with the East Longs Peak
Trail about three miles below the summit.

**FORT COLLINS AREA**   In the Poudre River Canyon west of Fort
Collins, the **Greyrock Trail** (3 miles) makes a steep climb to a
spectacular viewpoint overlooking the canyon and the lofty mountain ranges to the west.

▼ ▼ ▼ ▼ ▼ ▼ ▼ ▼ ▼ ▼
**Transportation**

**CAR**

Every place described in this chapter is within about an
hour's drive from **Route 25,** which traces the edge of the
Rockies northward to Fort Collins and Cheyenne, Wyo-
ming, and southward to Colorado Springs, Pueblo and Trinidad.
Route 25 intersects east–west **Route 70** in Denver. Following
Route 70W will take you to Idaho Springs and Central City.

Boulder is reached via **Route 36**, which runs northwest from Denver. This highway continues into the mountains, ending in Estes Park.

**Denver International Airport** is the primary commercial airport serving the Front Range communities north and west of Denver.

Boulder has no commercial air service; the **Airporter** runs hourly shuttle vans between Boulder and the Denver airport. ~ 303-227-0000, 303-444-0808. RTD buses also go to the Denver airport from Boulder. ~ 303-299-6000. **Denver Mountain Express** operates shuttle vans to the Denver airport. ~ 877-933-4362, 800-950-3274. Continental Express flies to the **Fort Collins–Loveland Municipal Airport**. Area residents take one of these commercial flights to Denver and then make connections with interstate or international flights. The **Shamrock Airport Express** offers service to Denver International Airport from Fort Collins, Loveland and Longmont. ~ 970-482-0505, 970-772-5466.

**AIR**

**Greyhound Bus Lines** (800-231-2222; www.greyhound.com) serves Fort Collins. ~ Route 501 at Riverside Avenue; 970-221-1327.

**BUS**

Most air travelers visiting this region rent cars upon arrival at Denver International Airport. Among the many rental agencies at or near DIA are **Alamo Rent A Car** (800-462-5266), **Avis Rent A Car** (800-230-4898), **Budget Rent A Car** (800-527-0700), **Dollar Rent A Car** (800-800-4000), **Enterprise Rent A Car** (800-736-8227), **Hertz Rent A Car** (800-654-3131) and **National Car Rental** (800-227-7368).

**CAR RENTALS**

RTD (Regional Transportation District) provides bus service in the Denver, Evergreen, Boulder, Nederland and Longmont areas. ~ 303-299-6000. Public buses in Fort Collins are operated by **Transfort**. ~ 970-221-6620. Greeley also has public bus service, called simply **The Bus**. ~ 970-350-9751.

**PUBLIC TRANSIT**

In Boulder, **Boulder Yellow Cab** provides taxi service. ~ 303-442-2279. Cyclists can arrange shuttle service with **Boulder Bike Taxi**. ~ 1834 Grove Street; 303-545-5222.

**TAXIS**

**FOUR**

# North Central Colorado

From the last splash of gold October aspen leaves until the May thaw, a layer of snow up to 25 feet deep covers the mountain ridges along the Continental Divide. Half-burying the steep-slope forests of Douglas fir, gleaming unmarred and unreachable in the cold winter sunlight, it is this combination of phenomenal snowfall and mountain slopes of vast size that accounts for Colorado's unrivaled reputation as a winter resort destination.

Whether any of the state's ski areas can legitimately lay claim to being the world's best is a topic of endless debate, but one thing's for sure: the northern Colorado Rockies contain more major ski slopes than any other region of the United States—among them local favorites such as Arapaho, Loveland, Keystone, Cooper, and Copper Mountain, as well as the internationally renowned Winter Park, Breckenridge, Steamboat Springs and, above all, Aspen and Vail. All clustered within an area less than 80 miles in diameter, these sporty winter fantasylands boast a winter season so big and busy that the snowless summer months—peak tourist season in most of Colorado and the West—are considered the off-season here.

The huge scale of the hospitality industry that has grown up around Colorado's ski resorts means that visitors who come during the summer for high-country hiking, mountain biking, fishing or cultural events can enjoy a wide choice of luxury lodgings and exceptional restaurants at bargain prices with no waiting. The ski resort towns devote huge amounts of energy to promoting off-season events, from golf tournaments to theatrical performances and concert series, all with an eye toward filling some of the thousands of vacant hotel rooms and restaurant tables. They have devised ingenious ways of using ski lifts when the snow is gone (from alpine slides to mountaintop biking) and have developed other warm-weather thrill sports, such as hang-gliding and bungee jumping, that are well suited to mountainsides and sheer cliffs. Yet a hike across boundless alpine tundra sparkling with wildflowers in hues of scarlet, lavender, yellow and snow white surrounded by views that reach for a hundred miles is still perhaps the biggest thrill of all.

History, too, is all around. Long before the first ski lift was built, the northern Colorado Rockies were already booming, enjoying economic prosperity and attracting people from all over America with the promise of gold and silver there for the finding. From the first gold strikes in the Georgetown area in 1859 through the discovery in the 1870s of fabulous silver lodes that transformed grubby mining camps like Leadville and Aspen overnight into sizeable cities with opera houses and elegant Victorian mansions, the history of the area was a fantastic rags-to-riches tale. You can't go far without learning about the glamourous but doomed romance of prospector-turned-senator Horace Tabor and his lover, Baby Doe, or the dizzying climb of the Unsinkable Molly Brown from the miner's shack of her childhood to the pinnacle of Denver high society and international notoriety. The mining boom ended abruptly in 1893 because of a collapse in silver prices, and most towns in the northern Colorado Rockies were almost completely abandoned for more than 50 years. Although much of the gingerbread architecture and elegant decor has been preserved in mountain towns throughout the area, backroad excursions into more remote areas reveal the remains of camps where less fortunate miners and prospectors lived and died in far harsher conditions.

The destinations covered in this chapter lie along Route 70 or within an hour's drive on highways that exit from Route 70. They are presented from east to west in the order that motorists would exit Route 70 to reach them. The Continental Divide meanders through north central Colorado in a haphazard manner, so that although all the major ski resorts are west of the Divide, paradoxically, many of them actually lie to the east of nonskiing historic towns such as Georgetown and Leadville. In fact, if you visit all the major towns covered in this chapter in east-to-west sequence, you will cross the Continental Divide at least five times.

Leaving Route 70 at Empire (Exit 233), Route 40 will take you up a sweeping series of switchbacks to the top of 11,315-foot Berthoud Pass and then twist down the other side of the Continental Divide into

# Winter Park– Grand Lake Area

Winter Park, one of Colorado's most popular ski areas and one of the closest to Denver, just 67 miles away.

**SIGHTS**

If you're looking for a unique ski weekend and want to avoid the heavy ski-season traffic on Berthoud Pass, make reservations early for the **Rio Grande Ski Train**. Running from Denver's Union Station on ski-season weekends, the train carries passengers on a scenic two-hour trip through areas that are inaccessible by road in winter. The train also makes summer forays every Saturday from mid-June to mid-August. ~ 303-296-4754; www.skitrain.com. In the summer, the ski slopes at Winter Park offer chairlift rides and a 3000-foot **alpine slide** (Colorado's longest). ~ 970-726-5514.

With no old town to serve as a nucleus for the community, **Winter Park** has sprawled into a characterless agglomeration of condominiums and shopping centers where sporting goods stores are the specialty. Once virtually deserted outside of ski season,

Winter Park has recently gained renown as a mountain-bike mecca thanks to its 500-mile bike trail network, one of the largest in the state. Music festivals and Saturday-night rodeos also enliven the summer season.

The area's early days are recalled at the **Cozens Ranch House Museum,** located between Winter Park and Fraser. Started by a retired Central City sheriff in the late 1870s, the ranch also served as the stage stop and store for the Winter Park area for decades and had the only hotel in the valley. Today, the ranch buildings have been refurnished with simple frontier-style antiques of the period. Admission. ~ Route 40, Winter Park; 970-725-3939.

North of Winter Park, the highway becomes straight and level as it crosses **Middle Park,** one of the Colorado Rockies' three broad natural "parks"—high, grassy plains that form bowls in the surrounding mountains. North Park lies straight ahead, while South Park is described in Chapter Six. The idea of a huge mountain park sounds more idyllic than the reality. Middle Park, like North and South Parks, is windswept ranchland where the main industry is growing hay for sale as feed to other ranches all over the state. Haystacks, hay rolls, hay bales in heaps taller than a barn—the sheer quantity of hay visible from the highway is impressive. The park's ranch towns, Fraser, Granby and Kremmling, are not.

Granby, however, is an important crossroads in this rarely visited part of the state. If you continue on Route 40 as it veers westward in the direction of distant Steamboat Springs, you soon come to Hot Sulphur Springs, site of a spa of the same name that was popular in the 1920s, when trainloads of people arrived daily to take the waters. After decades of decrepitude, **Hot Sulphur Springs** has been completely renovated. It now has 16 outdoor pools and four private indoor pools fed by 104°F water. The spa also offers massages, facial and body wraps, and snacks. ~ Route 40, Hot Sulphur Springs; 970-725-3306, 800-510-6235; www.hotsulphursprings.com.

Located in a historic old schoolhouse, the **Grand County Museum** displays local history exhibits that range from prehistoric Indian artifacts to memorabilia from the early days of Hot Sulphur Springs, Fraser, Granby and Kremmling. The most noteworthy exhibit reveals the early history of recreational skiing in Colorado, reminding visitors that Hot Sulphur Springs was the site of the state's first ski area back in the 1920s, long before any skier made tracks down Aspen Mountain. ~ Route 40, Hot Sulphur Springs; 970-725-3939.

If you continue north from Granby on Route 125, you'll cross the Rabbit Ears Range back to the eastern slope of the Continental Divide over gentle, pine-clad 9621-foot Willow Creek Pass.

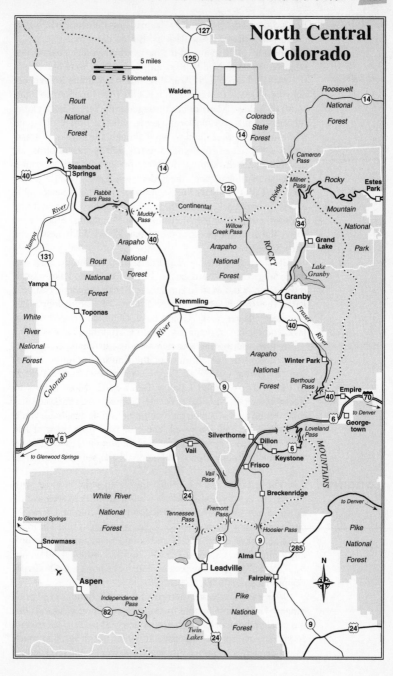

# North Central Colorado

0    5 miles

0    5 kilometers

HIDDEN ► Beyond the pass, the highway descends into **North Park**, bigger and broader than Middle Park, with even more hay.

The only place in any of the parks where you can experience what North Park, Middle Park and South Park were like before HIDDEN ► the arrival of ranching is **Arapaho National Wildlife Refuge**, occupying a broad area on both sides of the road for about 15 miles south of Walden. Many ponds throughout the refuge attract large numbers of migrating ducks and geese, which in turn attract quite a few hunters in the fall; in summer, though, the knee-high grasslands of the refuge are home to nearly 300 species of birds, including songbirds darting wherever you look as well as grouse and quail trotting through the underbrush. East across the plains rises the **Colorado State Forest**, most of it virtually inaccessible except on horseback, against the sheer, impassable ridge that forms the southern part of the Medicine Bow Mountains. To the west tower the dramatic peaks of the **Mount Zirkel Wilderness** in the Park Range.

Upon reaching the highway intersection at Granby, most travelers take Route 34 northeast to the town of **Grand Lake**, a small resort town at the western entrance to Rocky Mountain National Park. The town is set on the north shores of 12-mile-long, 400-foot-deep, glacier-carved **Grand Lake**, Colorado's largest natural lake, and the larger, manmade **Shadow Mountain Lake** nearby.

In town during the summer months, the chamber of commerce gives free guided tours of the **Kauffman House**, a two-story lodge that was the area's finest resort hotel from the 1890s to the 1920s. ~ Grand Lake; 970-627-3402. Most visitors to Rocky Mountain National Park enter from the Estes Park side and turn around after reaching the summit of Trail Ridge Road; you'll be surprised at how few people enter the park from the west side near Grand Lake, even at the peak of the summer season. For information on Rocky Mountain National Park, see Chapter Three.

**LODGING**   The **Viking Lodge** is a traditional European-style ski lodge with simply furnished wood-paneled rooms and suites as well as rustic, hostelish "nordic rooms." Facilities in the common areas include an inviting lobby fireplace, a sauna and a hot tub. The managers also have rental homes and condos available. ~ P.O. Box 89, Winter Park, CO 80482; 970-726-5356, 800-421-4013, fax 970-726-5773; www.skiwp.com/vikinglodge.html, e-mail skiwp@rkymtnhi.com. BUDGET TO DELUXE.

Winter Park offers a vast array of accommodations in all price ranges. The town is packed to capacity on winter weekends but has an abundance of lodging at other times. As at many ski resorts, room rates tend to be expensive in winter but drop by as much as 50 percent in summer. Among the several luxury ski lodges

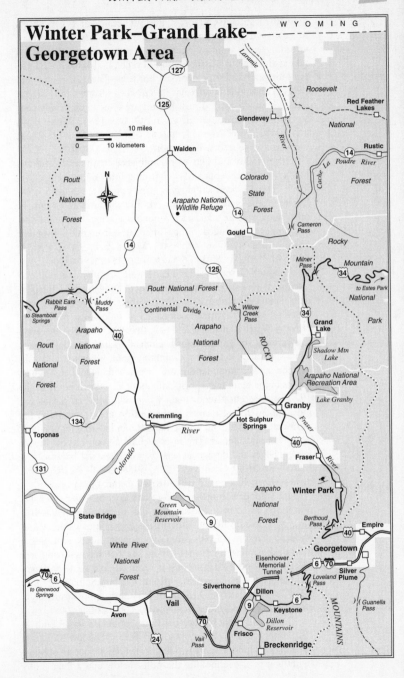

there, the **Iron Horse Resort** stands out because of its easy access to the main trail between the Winter Park and Mary Jane ski areas, affording from-your-doorstep skiing in winter and boundless biking and jogging possibilities in summer. It also has an indoor-outdoor pool and four open-air hot tubs. The 120 rooms and suites in this modern lodge have fireplaces, balconies and kitchenettes with microwave ovens. Rooms are done in cheerfully contemporary Southwestern decor. ~ P.O. Box 1286, Winter Park, CO 80482; 970-726-8851, 800-621-8190, fax 970-726-2321; www.ironhorse-resort.com. MODERATE TO ULTRA-DELUXE.

Affordability and Old World ambience combine at **Gasthaus Eichler**, an exact replica of a charming little alpine inn in Germany. The 15 continental-style guest rooms have down comforters on the beds, lace curtains on the windows and a host of other homey touches, and each room has a jacuzzi bath. Breakfast and dinner are included in the winter rates, from mid-November to mid-April. ~ 78786 Route 40, Winter Park; 970-726-5133, 800-543-3899, fax 970-726-5175. MODERATE TO DELUXE.

Although Granby itself is a cattle-shipping town with little to interest visitors aside from a sprinkling of budget-priced independent motels, a number of ranches in the area have evolved into first-class dude ranches. Located seven miles west of Granby, **Drowsy Water Ranch** specializes in horseback riding, with services running the gamut from beginners' lessons to all-day pack trips. The ranch also has a swimming pool, a hot tub and fishing ponds. Accommodations are in nine cabins and eight guest rooms in the main lodge, originally built as a ranch house in the 1920s and recently renovated. While this is by no means the most expensive guest ranch in the Granby area, rates are in the ultra-deluxe range, and a seven-day minimum-stay requirement applies in midsummer. The rates include all-you-can-eat breakfasts, lunches and dinners as well as your personal horse for the week. ~ Route 40, Granby; 970-725-3456, 800-845-2292; www.drowsywater.com, e-mail whoadwr@aol.com. ULTRA-DELUXE.

**Hot Sulphur Springs**—the spa, not the town—operates a 17-unit motel adjacent to the springs. The guest rooms themselves have lodgepole furnishings and the usual amenities (cable TV and phones). A restored 1840s cabin overlooking the spa rents in the ultra-deluxe range. It's the hot-springs spa that makes staying here special. Use of the 20 hot pools is included, and some packages include massages and wraps. ~ Route 40, Hot Sulphur Springs; 970-725-3306, fax 970-725-3206; www.hotsulphursprings.com, e-mail reservations@hotsulphursprings.com. MODERATE.

The **Grand Lake Lodge**, a historic mountain lodge built in 1925, offers fabulous views of Grand Lake and Shadow Mountain Lake from its hillside vantage point. Amenities include an outdoor swimming pool overlooking the valley below and a huge lobby fireplace to chase away the evening chill. Accommodations are in the main lodge and a string of rustic cabins, some with kitchenettes. The cabins have no TVs or phones. Closed mid-September through May. ~ 15500 Route 34, Grand Lake; 970-627-3967, fax 970-627-9495; www.grandlakelodge.com. MODERATE TO ULTRA-DELUXE.

Built from rough-hewn logs and local stone, **Shadowcliff Life Center** overlooks Grand Lake from an even more spectacular location at the top of a cliff. While there are three individual cabins with kitchenettes and fireplaces (bring your own sheets; six-night minimum stay), most accommodations are in the 19 lodge rooms containing four to eight bunk beds each and in youth hostel–style dorms. This is a popular spot for retreats. Closed October through May. ~ 405 Summerland Park Road, Grand Lake; phone/fax 970-627-9220; www.shadowcliff.org. BUDGET TO MODERATE.

**DINING**

Winter Park specializes in food with a German accent. For one of the finest dinners in town, make reservations at the **Gasthaus Eichler**. Situated on the ground floor of the small inn of the same name, the dining room has a distinctly Old World feeling and serves the most authentic *rindsrouladen, jägerschnitzel* and *kassler rippchen* in the Colorado ski country. ~ Route 40, Winter Park; 970-726-5133. MODERATE TO DELUXE.

The café-style **Carver Brothers Bakery** serves pastries, gourmet coffee, full breakfasts and, for lunch, homemade stews and soups, salads and submarine sandwiches, as well as vegetarian options. ~ Behind Cooper Creek Square, Winter Park; 970-726-8202. MODERATE.

The **Grand Lake Lodge Restaurant** lets you enjoy a fantastic view of Grand Lake and Shadow Mountain Lake along with your breakfast buffet, pasta luncheon special or elegant dinner. Nightly chef's specials include fish, lamb, wild-game entrées and steaks. ~ Route 34, Grand Lake; 970-627-3185. MODERATE.

In a restored 1909 historic lodge with a whitewater view of the Blue River, **The Rapids Restaurant** features gourmet interna-

**AUTHOR FAVORITE**

I know just where to head for comfort food. A long-established local favorite in Grand Lake, the **Mountain Inn** is in a cozy old knotty-pine log inn warmed by a big wood-burning stove. Choose from a char-broiled New York strip steak, a beef kebab, trout amandine or barbe-cued chicken. All dinners are served with soup, salad, biscuits and ice cream. Dinner only. ~ 612 Grand Avenue, Grand Lake; 970-627-3385. MODERATE.

tional cuisine such as fettuccine Alfredo and rice noodles with prawns in curry sauce. The only appetizer—which is also the house specialty—is a generous tray of boiled shrimp. Dessert specials change daily. Closed November and April. Dinner only. ~ 209 Rapids Lane, Grand Lake; 970-627-3707. MODERATE TO DELUXE.

The only town in North Park large enough to have a café or gas station is Walden, which is not on the direct route to any tourist destination and may be the least-visited town in the Colorado Rockies.

Fine dining is surprisingly affordable at **Caroline's Cuisine**. This casually elegant restaurant in the round alongside the headwaters of the Colorado River, north of Grand Lake, is worth the drive for its imaginative presentations of shellfish, duck and veal as well as roast beef, filet mignon and pasta dishes. ~ Soda Springs Ranch, 9921 Route 34, Grand Lake; 970-627-9404. DELUXE.

**SHOPPING**   This is not an area for recreational shopping, unless you're interested in sporting goods, available in abundance at Winter Park's shopping centers. Check out **Cascades of the Rockies**, a cheery gallery jam-packed with unique contemporary arts and crafts inside, with colorful lakeside flower gardens out back. ~ 1116 Grand Avenue; 970-627-8722.

In Grand Lake, the **Trail Ridge Art Company** exhibits art and fine crafts by about 50 Colorado artists. ~ Cooper Creek Square; 970-726-4959.

**NIGHTLIFE**   In ski season you'll find live music most evenings at a number of lively après-ski bars. In Winter Park these include **The Slope** (Route 40; 970-726-5727) and **The Derailer** (Winter Park Resort; 970-726-5514).

The most popular partying bar in the valley is the **Crooked Creek Saloon**, a rock-and-roll roadhouse in nearby Fraser where mountain bikers meet the local cowboys, get rowdy and remain so until 2 a.m. ~ 401 Zerex Street, Fraser; 970-726-9250.

The **Rocky Mountain Repertory Theatre** presents light, contemporary plays in Grand Lake nightly throughout the summer. ~ 1025 Grand Avenue, Grand Lake; 970-627-3421. Otherwise, when it comes to nightlife, Grand Lake is on the slow side. But you'll find a Western atmosphere and live country bands on weekends at the **Lariat Saloon**. ~ 1121 Grand Avenue, Grand Lake; 970-627-9965.

**PARKS**   **ARAPAHO NATIONAL FOREST** 🚶 🚵 🐎 ⛺ 🚗 The part of the forest around Winter Park includes the Vasquez Mountains, where a major system of horse pack trails connects several 12,000-foot peaks surrounding the scenic St. Louis Creek area. The forest just west of Winter Park has an extensive system of roads and trails that are good for mountain biking. Fishing is fair for trout in St. Louis Creek. Facilities include hiking trails, pack trails and jeep roads. ~ The main forest access in this area is on St. Louis Creek Road (County Road 73), off Route 40, one mile south of Winter Park; 970-887-4100.

▲ Idlewild Campground on Fraser River has 24 RV/tent sites (no hookups); open Memorial Day weekend to early September; $12 per night.

Georgetown began as a short-lived gold boom town in 1859. Although the gold ran out within two years and miners and prospectors began to drift away to richer digs, the first large silver strike in Colorado catapulted Georgetown and neighboring Silver Plume, two miles away, into prosperity that lasted for more than 30 years.

**Georgetown Area**

Until recently, the town's most famous visitor attraction was the Georgetown Loop Scenic Railroad, a narrow-gauge steam train that operated during the summer months. An impasse between train personnel and the Colorado Historical Society resulted in the railroad's equipment being relocated to the Royal Gorge (see Chapter Six) in October 2004, and the Georgetown route is not expected to reopen.

Today, the **Georgetown–Silver Plume Historic District** stands out because of the sheer number of Victorian buildings remaining there—thanks, it is said, to the town's well-organized volunteer fire brigade, which repeatedly saved Georgetown from the kind of fires that devastated many other early-day mining towns. The historic district has more than 200 19th-century residences and commercial buildings.

**SIGHTS**

Among the several elegant old structures that now serve as museums within the historic district, one of the most impressive is the **Hotel de Paris**. Much of the period decor and furnishings survives from the 1870s, when this posh hotel was ranked among the most luxurious lodgings in the West. Besides showing off some of the finest examples of Victorian decorative arts to be found anywhere in Colorado, the museum displays mementos of the hotel's founder, Louis Dupuy, a French philosopher and chef who came to Colorado hoping to strike gold. After he was crippled in a mine accident, the townspeople took up a collection to help him out, which financed his plan to convert a former bakery into a grand hotel. It is now a museum owned by the Society of Colonial Dames of America in Colorado. Exhibits include much of Dupuy's 3000-volume private library, in its day one of the largest collections of books in the Rocky Mountain West. Admission. ~ 6th and Taos streets, Georgetown; 303-569-2311; www.hoteldeparismuseum.org.

Nearby, the Gothic Revival **Hamill House** offers a look at a mining tycoon's ostentatious lifestyle in the silver boom days. It was one of the first homes in the state with central heating and gas lighting, and the deluxe outhouse must surely have been a legend in its day. The two-story, 19-room mansion was originally a modest little residence, but as owner William A. Hamill's mine-camp fortune grew, he not only redecorated the interior (with such touches as a ten-foot-tall handcarved walnut fireplace mantle, camel-hair wallpaper and gold-plated doorknobs) but also added rooms, towers and a solarium to create one of the most impressive mansions in the state. The hand-milled hardwood and marble interiors have been polished to their original rich gleam. Open daily June through September, weekends only October through December; closed January through May. Admission. ~ 305 Argentine Street, Georgetown; 303-569-2840; www.historicgeorgetown.org, e-mail preservation@historicgeorgetown.org.

The Hotel de Paris' restaurant was the first to bring French gourmet cuisine to the mining camps of Colorado, and the kitchen is one of the high points of the hotel tour today.

The history of Silver Plume is recounted with old photos and Victorian memorabilia in the **George Rowe Museum**, housed in the town's old schoolhouse. Closed October through May. Admission. ~ 905 Main Street, Silver Plume; 303-569-2562.

A large population of Rocky Mountain bighorn sheep—about 175 at last count—grazes among the rugged crags above Georgetown, providing highway travelers with their best chance to glimpse Colorado's official state animal. The **Georgetown Watchable Wildlife Viewing Station**, located by Georgetown Lake just north of town and just off the freeway, has telescopes to spot the sheep. Viewing is best in the early morning and late afternoon. ~ Route 6, Georgetown.

One of Colorado's finest scenic routes starts from downtown Georgetown. The **Guanella Pass Road** climbs by switchbacks up the near-vertical mountain slope that looms over the town. Though easier than it looks, the dramatic ascent is not for sightseers who suffer from a fear of heights. After the first two miles of steep grades and sharp turns, the road grows gentle and takes motorists on a wonderful trip through wild mountains that feel as if they couldn't possibly be just a few miles off the interstate. It's a 12-mile drive from Georgetown to the 11,669-foot Guanella Pass summit, the most spectacular viewpoint on the road, above timberline on the west side of Mount Evans. From there, you can either return to Georgetown or drive down the south side of the pass for 15 miles to join Route 285, a main highway linking the Denver area with South Park.

**LODGING**     Located in the very small town of Empire, about five miles north of Georgetown on the other side of Route 70, **The Peck House**

originally opened its doors as a stagecoach stop in 1862 and has been in continuous operation longer than any other hotel in Colorado. The parlor and all 11 guest rooms are so sumptuously decorated in Victorian-era antiques that the Peck House once received the Governor's Award for Historic Restoration. The rates include a continental breakfast. ~ 83 Sunny Avenue, Empire; 303-569-9870, fax 303-569-2743; www.thepeckhouse.com, e-mail info@ thepeckhouse.com. MODERATE.

You'll find affordable lodging at the **Georgetown Mountain Inn**, quietly located well off the interstate. Many of the 32 large rooms have been remodeled with natural aspen and pine log furniture, and some have kitchenettes. All rooms have phones with computer access jacks, and complimentary VCRs and videotapes are available to guests. There's an outdoor hot tub and, in summer, a heated swimming pool. ~ 1100 Rose Street, Georgetown; 303-569-3201, 800-884-3201, fax 303-569-3407; www.george townmountaininn.com, e-mail gtinn@mho.net.

**DINING**

**The Peck House**, Colorado's oldest hotel, is also one of the finest restaurants in the area. The intimate dining room with its rustic antique decor, hardwood furnishings and red-brick fireplace features a traditional beef and seafood menu with a few touches of continental flair. Sunday brunch is extra special here—a gourmet fantasy featuring such exotica as roast quail, assorted pâtés, raspberry duck, venison medallions and beef-and-oyster pie. ~ 83 Sunny Avenue, Empire; 303-569-9870. DELUXE.

In Georgetown, you'll find fine dining at reasonable prices at **The Happy Cooker**. A Victorian-era home freshly decorated with rattan furnishings and a garden motif provides contemporary breakfast and luncheon fare such as European waffles (a house speciality), soups, salads and sandwiches. ~ 412 6th Street, Georgetown; 303-569-3166. BUDGET.

The place locals go for good, affordable food in Georgetown is the **Café Prague**, an unpretentious little café with decor that hints at a central European lineage. The Old World motif carries over into the menu, where you'll find such fare as roast duck with potato pancakes and red cabbage, plus desserts like apple strudel and lingonberry-filled bohemian crêpes. ~ 511 Rose Street, Georgetown; 303-569-2861. BUDGET TO MODERATE.

**SHOPPING**

Georgetown's historic district is home to a growing number of galleries of varying quality. The works of a number of Colorado artists and crafters are shown at the cooperative **Georgetown Gallery**. ~ 614 6th Street, Georgetown; 303-569-2218.

**PARKS**

**ARAPAHO NATIONAL FOREST** 🏃 🐴 ⛵ The part of this large national forest that lies south of Georgetown includes the scenic

Guanella Pass area along the western boundary of the Mount Evans Wilderness and a series of picturesque lakes around Square Top Mountain. Fishing is good for rainbow trout in Murray, Silver Dollar and Flat Top lakes. Facilities include picnic areas, restrooms, hiking trails, pack trails and jeep trails. ~ The main national forest access from Georgetown is Guanella Pass Road (Forest Road 381); 303-567-3000.

▲ Guanella Pass Campground has 18 RV/tent sites (no hookups); closed mid-September to late May; $11 per night. Reservations: 877-444-6777; www.reserveusa.com.

## ▼▼▼▼▼▼▼▼▼▼▼▼▼
## Breckenridge Area

Summit County, a long, narrow mountain region set apart from the outside world by the Continental Divide on the east and Vail Pass on the west, contains more ski slopes and winter resorts than any other Colorado county. The charmingly European-flavored ski town of Breckenridge is the county seat and was also the main population center until recently, but while steep mountain slopes and historic preservation concerns have limited Breckenridge's growth, development has been explosive in the communities of Dillon, Frisco and Silverthorne just off Route 70.

**SIGHTS**    Heading west on Route 70, about 60 miles from Denver, you cross the Great Divide and enter Summit County through the **Eisenhower Memorial Tunnel,** a 9000-foot tunnel carved through a formerly impassable ridgeline on the Continental Divide. When it was opened in 1973, the tunnel streamlined travel on Route 70, which had previously been routed over 11,992-foot **Loveland Pass** to the south. You can still take paved Route 6 over the old pass, now a relatively traffic-free scenic route. Along the old route, three ski areas—**Loveland Basin–Loveland Valley** (303-571-5580), on the east side of the Continental Divide; **Arapahoe Basin** (970-468-0718), on the west side; and **Ski Keystone** (970-496-2316), midway between the pass and Dillon Reservoir—rank as the busiest slopes in Colorado.

The highest-altitude inhabited town in the United States, the isolated former silver camp of **Montezuma** (elevation 10,268 feet) can be reached by turning off Route 6 just east of Keystone onto Montezuma Road, which backtracks east for about seven miles to the mostly ghostly old town. Though the town may not look like much, the setting, in the shadow of Santa Fe Peak's 13,180-foot summit, is spectacular. The history of Montezuma and other mining camps along this part of the Continental Divide is the subject of exhibits at the **Montezuma Schoolhouse Museum,** operated by the Summit County Historical Society. Open for group tours only. ~ Montezuma; 970-453-9022.

Route 70 and the Loveland Pass Road merge again at the foot of the pass beside **Dillon Reservoir.** The west shore of the reservoir has grown into a rather bland, conformist sprawl of townhouses and shopping centers making up the communities of **Dillon, Silverthorne** and **Frisco.** These towns are older than they look, and the curious can still find vestiges of the days when they were logging and mining camps.

Many outgrown old schoolhouses in Colorado mountain towns have been resurrected as local history museums. Dillon's is unusual in that it actually focuses on schooling. The Summit County Historical Society's **Dillon Schoolhouse Museum,** furnished with all the trappings of a typical one-room schoolhouse in the late 1800s, is an eye-opener for modern schoolkids. ~ 403 La Bonte Street, Dillon; 970-453-9022.

Near the southwest shore of Dillon Reservoir, seven rustic buildings dating back to the 1880s make up **Frisco Historic Park.** The structures, including a schoolhouse, a small church and a jail, contain photos and memorabilia from the town's early days. ~ Main and 2nd streets, Frisco; 970-668-3428.

From Frisco, take Route 9 south for ten miles to reach the town and ski area of **Breckenridge.** If ever a mountain town was at risk of becoming "another Aspen," in both the best and worst senses of the term, it is Breckenridge. It is the closest major ski resort to the fast-growing Colorado Springs area, less than two hours' drive away. It is even closer to Denver—not quite as close as Winter Park, Arapahoe Basin, Loveland Basin, Copper Mountain or Keystone—but the town's personality makes the longer drive worth it for many Denverites. As a result, it sometimes gets very crowded. From Thanksgiving through the end of March, skiers descend on Breckenridge in astonishing numbers every weekend, packing the miles of parking lots that lie between the streets of town and the ski slopes, creating long lift lines and bumper-to-bumper traffic up and down Main Street.

If possible, plan your ski trip to Breckenridge during the week, when overcrowding is not a problem, in order to really enjoy your stay. This former gold- and silver-mining town of stately old Victorian homes painted in wild color combinations, often refurbished with Tyrolean-style decorative trim, seems to be the community of choice for ski instructors, restaurateurs, innkeepers and others who choose to relocate from the Alps to the Rockies. At any time of year German and the Scandinavian languages are commonly heard on the streets and in the coffee shops.

HIDDEN ►

Breckenridge has a kind of theme-park quality in the summer months, when the ski mountains are transformed into thrill rides under the collective name **Peak 8 Fun Park**. The SuperChair chairlift runs to the top of the Peak 8 ski slope May through August, providing easy access to trails through 11,000-foot-high alpine meadows for hiking and mountain biking. When you're ready to head back down the mountain, consider the Super Slide (admission). Adults and kids alike plunge down the mountainside on wheeled sleds via a fiberglass chute, at speeds of up to 40 miles per hour—it's like riding a roller coaster that's entirely downhill. And if that's not enough family fun for one day, at the foot of Peak 8 is Amaze'n Breckenridge, Colorado's largest human maze, covering 10,000 square feet and containing more than a mile of passageways; an observation deck above gives you the chance to giggle at family members as they get themselves hopelessly lost. The park also has a climbing wall and a miniature golf course. An all-day activities pass covers everything but bike rentals. ~ Peak 8, Breckenridge; 970-453-5000.

**sights**

**AUTHOR FAVORITE**

When it comes to theme parks, no place in Colorado can match Breckenridge's **Peak 8 Fun Park**, which demonstrates how many things you can do on a ski slope when there's no snow. For example, you can swing up the mountainside on a chairlift, take in the breathtaking view from flower-filled meadows at the top and then ride a wheeled sled down the alpine slide at breakneck speed. When you're done with that, thanks to the one-price-for-everything admission policy, you can do it all over again. Denver's famous theme parks don't take you nearly this high. See above for more information.

As you continue south from Breckenridge on Route 9, you face a series of sudden, tight switchback curves that makes its way up a steep mountain slope to the summit of 11,541-foot Hoosier Pass on the Continental Divide.

A scenic unpaved alternative to the highway over Hoosier Pass is the **Boreas Pass Road**, a wide and well-maintained gravel road that follows an old narrow-gauge railroad route as it gradually climbs above timberline to cross the Continental Divide at an elevation of 11,482 feet. Remains of old ranches and railroad buildings dot the roadside on this spectacular drive, which brings you out at the ghost town of **Como**, northeast of Fairplay on Route 285.

**LODGING**

The lowest-cost accommodations in the area are at **Alpen Hütte**, an unaffiliated hostel with 66 beds in nine spartan dormitory rooms with shared baths, as well as private and family rooms. The lounge area has a fireplace, and there is a reading room and a game room as well as mountain bike rentals. Though the town of Silverthorne lacks character, a free shuttle bus runs to Breckenridge and several ski areas. ~ 471 Rainbow Drive, Silverthorne; 970-468-6336; www.alpenhutte.com, e-mail ahutte@alpenhutte. com. BUDGET.

Among the upscale ski lodges in Breckenridge, it's hard to beat **The Lodge & Spa at Breckenridge**, located high on a mountainside. The lodge's guest-room balconies and picture windows offer some of the most majestic mountain views you're ever likely to experience from the comfort of a luxury suite. The 45 guest rooms, each with a kitchen and sitting room, are individually decorated in contemporary Western, Southwestern and European themes. The lodge has landscaped gardens and a spa complete with jacuzzis, hot tubs, saunas, an indoor swimming pool and an exercise room. Massages and beauty wraps are available. Reservations are required at least three days in advance. ~ 112 Overlook Drive, Breckenridge; 970-453-9300, 800-736-1607, fax 970-453-0625; www.thelodgeatbreck.com, e-mail reservations@thelodgeatbreck. com. ULTRA-DELUXE.

A wide range of modern accommodations can be found in **The Village at Breckenridge**, a huge, 11-building complex with heated walkways that sprawls around the Peak 9 chairlift. A single reservation desk offers rooms in what is virtually a hotel shopping mall consisting of the Village Hotel (standard rooms), the Liftside Inn (studio suites), the Hotel Breckenridge (full suites), the Plaza Condominiums (standard condos) and the Châteaux (deluxe condos). Besides lodging, The Village at Breckenridge complex contains ten restaurants, a full range of shops and two health clubs with swimming pools, hot tubs, saunas and exercise rooms. ~ 535 South Park Street, Breckenridge; 970-547-5725, 877-

428-7829; www.breckresort.com, e-mail breckenridgelodging@
vailresorts.com. DELUXE TO ULTRA-DELUXE.

A perennial favorite among Breckenridge's many bed and
breakfasts is the **Fireside Inn**, a historic 1879 home where lodgings
include four deluxe-priced private rooms decorated with antiques,
including a lavish Victorian-style suite, as well as five budget-
priced youth-hostel dorm rooms. You meet a fascinating assortment of people around the fireplace and the hot tub. Continental
breakfast in summer. ~ 114 North French Street, Breckenridge;
970-453-6456, fax 970-453-9577; www.firesideinn.com, e-mail
fireside@colorado.net. BUDGET TO DELUXE.

The **Evans House** offers six guest rooms and a newly added
suite, individually decorated in Victorian, Old West and Southwestern styles, in a restored 1886 home complete with hot tub,
two blocks from the restaurants and shops of Main Street. A full
breakfast is included in the room rate. ~ 102 South French Street,
Breckenridge; 970-453-5509; www.coloradoevanshouse.com, e-
mail evans15@mindspring.com. MODERATE TO DELUXE.

**DINING**

Breckenridge has more than 50 restaurants, each one apparently
trying to be as different as possible from the others. Northern
Italian cuisine is featured at the **St. Bernard Inn**, housed in a
warmly restored Victorian-era building with its original tin roof.
The restaurant serves its own pasta daily as well as fresh seafood
in creamy sauces. Dinner only. ~ 103 South Main Street, Breckenridge; 970-453-2572. MODERATE.

**Downstairs at Eric's**—where the motto is "Because everywhere
else just sucks"—has a 150-item menu that runs the gamut of basic
restaurant fare from burgers, barbecued ribs and pizza to salads
and rotisserie chicken, including some tantalizingly original variations. They also offer 120 different brands of beer—22 of them
on tap—and a sports-bar ambience. ~ 111 South Main Street,
Breckenridge; 970-453-1401. BUDGET.

**Pierre's Riverwalk Café**, a bistro on the river plaza, specializes
in gourmet American and French cuisine including rack of lamb,
filet mignon, rabbit and crème brûlée, accompanied by your
choice of 150 wines. The café is open for dinner year-round and
for lunch on the terrace in summer. ~ 137 South Main Street,
Breckenridge; 970-453-0989. DELUXE.

History also helps create the romantic mood at the **Briar
Rose**. The finest restaurant in Summit County when it was built
in the early 1960s, soon after the ski slopes were opened, the
Briar Rose provided a new home for many antiques from old-
time Breckenridge. The taxidermy that lines the walls may un-
nerve sensitive diners, but the Victorian-era saloon bar—originally a fixture in the Breckenridge Opera House—is an
atmospheric gem that dominates the restaurant's decor. Specials

featuring buffalo and wild game often supplement a fairly predictable beef and seafood menu. Dinner only. ~ 109 East Lincoln Street, Breckenridge; 970-453-9948. DELUXE.

Down the street, **Poirrier's Cajun Café** serves Cajun and Creole cuisine in an atmosphere of southern hospitality. The menu includes blackened catfish, grilled shrimp, crawfish in gravy and the chef's award-winning bread pudding. ~ 224 South Main Street, Breckenridge; 970-453-1877. MODERATE.

**The Blue Moose,** specializing in salads and vegetarian dishes, also offers burgers, fish and steaks. Dine inside or on the open deck with a great view of the Ten Mile Range. Breakfast and lunch only. ~ 540 South Main Street, Breckenridge; 970-453-4859. BUDGET.

**SHOPPING**  While sporting goods shops dominate the historic main street and adjacent modern shopping centers of Breckenridge, there is also a small but stylish collection of art galleries. Established for more than 30 years, **Breckenridge Gallery** features original artwork from the Rocky Mountain region with an emphasis on landscapes and Western-theme paintings and sculptures. ~ 124 South Main Street, Breckenridge; 970-453-2592; www.breckenridge-gallery.com. Even longer-established, predating the ski slopes themselves, the **Fox Ridge Gallery** specializes in sculpture, blown glass and jewelry. ~ 222 South Main Street, Breckenridge; 970-547-8192. **Colorado Scenics** offers beautiful mounted Colorado landscape photographs and coffee table books. ~ 124 South Main Street, Breckenridge; 970-453-4922.

**NIGHTLIFE**  The **Breckenridge Brewery & Pub,** a lively, youth-oriented après-ski brewpub, is one of the most happening places in Breckenridge

---

**AUTHOR FAVORITE**

For a unique Breckenridge dining experience in winter, take a dinner sleigh ride. **Nordic Sleigh Rides** uses 12-passenger horse-drawn sleighs to deliver you to a re-created 1860s miner's camp. Cooked on an antique wood stove, their steak, chicken or salmon dinner accompanies one of several homegrown stage plays—*The Mountain Man*, *The Dance Hall Girls* or *The Unsinkable Mollie Brown*—that have been running for over a decade. ~ 970-453-2005; www.nordicsleighrides.com. ULTRA-DELUXE. **Two Below Zero** has mule-drawn wooden sleighs and serves top sirloin or chicken breast in heated dining tents in the woods, accompanied by live cowboy music, poetry and comedy. ~ 970-453-1520 or 970-453-1520; www.dinnersleighrides.com. ULTRA-DELUXE.

these days. ~ 600 South Main Street, Breckenridge; 970-453-1550. **Tiffany's** is a disco dance club at the base of Peak 9. ~ Beaver Run Resort, Breckenridge; 970-453-6000.

The **Backstage Theatre** presents plays several nights a week during the summer and ski seasons. ~ Bell Tower Mall, 605 South Park Street, Breckenridge; 970-453-0199; www.backstage theatre.org.

Many of the hottest nightspots in Summit County are not in Breckenridge but in Keystone. The rowdy **Snake River Saloon** has live rock-and-roll on weekends. ~ 23074 Route 6, Keystone; 970-468-2788. For something a little more mellow, enjoy a game of bridge, chess or backgammon in front of the 15-foot fireplace in the **Tenderfoot Lounge**. ~ Keystone Lodge, Keystone; 970-468-2316.

**PARKS**

**DILLON RESERVOIR** Proximity to Route 70 and explosive real estate development in the Silverthorne and Frisco areas have made this large, scenic reservoir surrounded by wooded mountain slopes one of the most popular recreational lakes in the state. Most of the north shore is developed, while the south shore is a series of wooded peninsulas offering secluded campgrounds. Fishing is good for rainbow trout, brown trout, cutthroat and kokanee. Facilities include restrooms and boat launches with marinas at Frisco and Dillon. ~ Located just off Route 70 at exits 203 (Frisco) and 205 (Silverthorne/Dillon). Paved roads encircle the lake, providing access to campgrounds and boat ramps; 970-468-5400.

▲ Five campgrounds operated by the U.S. Forest Service on Dillon Reservoir offer 344 RV/tent sites; $11 to $17 per night. Closed late September to late May. The only RV hookups are at Lowry Campground. Reservations: 877-444-6777.

*HIDDEN* ▶

**ARAPAHO NATIONAL FOREST** Breckenridge is at the southernmost tip of this large national forest. Here the forest encompasses seven mountain peaks over 13,000 feet high, rising steeply on all sides of the town. Unpaved roads left by past mining operations are suitable for mountain biking and cross-country skiing. The forest also lines the south and east shores of Dillon Reservoir. Facilities include picnic areas and restrooms. Giberson Bay has a day-use picnic area. ~ The best forest access from Breckenridge is on unpaved Boreas Pass Road (Forest Road 404). Dillon Reservoir is just off Route 70; Routes 6 and 9 run along the lakeshore; 970-468-5400.

▲ There are five campgrounds located on the shores of Dillon Reservoir (see above). Green Mountain Reservoir has undeveloped campgrounds (no water or RV hookups); $5 to $9 per night.

Vail, site of America's largest ski resort, is still a young town. Taking its name from the pass to the east (which had unglamorously been named for a Depression-era state highway engineer), the resort was built in secrecy within a single year and unveiled to the public in 1962. Lacking the historic patina of towns like Aspen, Crested Butte and Breckenridge, Vail gained a reputation as a snow-swept, artificially Swiss, theme-park sort of place that mocked the "real" Colorado. But Vail's image has mellowed with age as the saplings planted in 1962 have grown into a forest of shade trees enfolding each street and pathway. The windowboxes of Vail Village still contain plastic flowers in ski season, but real ones are substituted in summer.

**Vail Area**

**SIGHTS**

Beyond the busy pseudosuburban zone of Silverthorne and Frisco on the shore of Dillon Reservoir, Route 70 West passes Copper Mountain Ski Area and climbs in a few miles to **Vail Pass** (10,666 feet). The summit is not a lofty ridge but rather an expanse of mountain meadows that's not much to look at. If you're seeking alpine majesty, take **Shrine Pass Road**, just west of the Vail Pass summit. Open in summer only and normally suitable for passenger cars, the unpaved road crests the 11,089-foot pass to the west in about four miles, then descends through a scenic canyon to the tiny mining town of Redcliff on Route 24 between Leadville and Vail. From Vail Pass, the interstate descends into the **Vail Valley**.

In the late 19th century, mail carriers on skis risked life and limb to deliver the winter mail in Colorado's rugged mountain communities.

**Vail Village** is a shimmering neverland of chic galleries, boutiques, offices and luxury hotels, condominiums and private townhouses flowing along the banks of Gore Creek. Motor vehicles are not allowed in the main part of the village. Unless you have hotel reservations, park at the huge lot near the visitors center just off Route 70. Walk from there and luxuriate in the traffic-free environment.

During summer, gondolas and chairlifts carry picnickers, hikers and mountain bikers to the tops of the ski mountains from several points. The **Vista Bahn Express Lift** (970-476-5601; admission) runs from Vail Village up to Mid-Vail, below the summit of Vail Mountain, while about a mile to the west, the **Eagle Bahn Gondola** (970-476-5601; admission) runs up to Eagle's Nest Ridge. Several miles west in Beaver Creek, the **Centennial Express Chairlift** (970-949-5750) runs to Spruce Saddle, high on Beaver Creek Mountain.

The most kid-friendly place in Vail is **Adventure Ridge**, a mountaintop activity center at the top of the Eagle Bahn Gondola. Summer activities include a disk golf course, a BMX bicycle course, courts for horseshoes, croquet and volleyball, mountain biking classes and tours, and Dino Dig, a simulated fossil quarry. There's also an indoor laser tag facility and a large trampoline. In winter, the complex offers tubing, ski biking and ice skating. Activities are individually priced in winter; comprehensive activity passes are available in summer for about $40. ~ Eagle's Nest Ridge; 970-476-9090.

Adjacent to Adventure Ridge is the **Vail Discovery Center**, a nature center jointly operated by Vail Resorts, the National Forest Service and the Gore Range Natural Science School. It offers exhibits and guided nature walks in summer. ~ Eagle's Nest Ridge; 970-479-4675.

The **Colorado Ski Museum and Ski Hall of Fame** traces the history of Colorado skiing with videos and exhibits, including one that demonstrates the evolution of ski equipment from the improbably long, heavy wooden skis of a century ago to the latest in fast, nimble fiberglass skis and high-tech boots. A new exhibit traces the evolution of snowboarding, featuring a snowboard used in a James Bond movie. ~ Route 70, Exit 176, Vail; 970-476-1876; www.skimuseum.net.

The **Betty Ford Alpine Gardens**, adjacent to the Gerald R. Ford Amphitheater just east of town, sparkle in summer with tiny bright blossoms unique to the fragile alpine environment. There is also a children's playground and a broad lawn for picnicking. Open from snowmelt to snowfall; tours on Monday and Thursday in summer. ~ South Frontage Road, Vail; 970-476-0103; www.bettyfordalpinegardens.org, e-mail alpgrdn@vail.net.

The Betty Ford Alpine Gardens are the world's highest public gardens.

Nearby, the **Vail Nature Center** preserves an unspoiled seven-acre sample of the Vail Valley's natural environment and has a visitors center in a restored farmhouse, one of the oldest remaining buildings in the Vail Valley. The nature trails are groomed in winter for cross-country skiing, and in summer the river that runs through it is great for fly fishing and kayaking. Admission. ~ 75 South Frontage Road, Vail; 970-479-2291.

Development has kept expanding westward down the valley to include **Avon** and the newest resort, the family-oriented **Beaver Creek**, below the gleaming slopes of a ski megaresort covering 15 square miles with 25 chairlifts and gondolas and 182 named trails. Although winter visitors may marvel at the astonishing lattice of trails that spans Vail Mountain, the real appeal of this ski area lies hidden behind the mountain's top ridge. The Back Bowls of Vail are every deep-powder skier's fantasy—the most remote and expansive mountain skiing that can be reached by ski lift anywhere in the world.

As you begin to appreciate the scope of this place, you might pause for a moment to imagine how many housekeepers, wait-persons, bartenders, security guards and other service personnel it takes to keep Vail running. If you're curious about where they live, head south from town on Route 24. Just two miles down this highway lies the old, low-rent railroad town of **Minturn**. Nine miles farther along, you come to even smaller, nearly abandoned **Redcliff**, the county seat until 1921. From here a road winds through scenic Turkey Creek Canyon and climbs to the summit of Shrine Pass.

Virtually all accommodations in Vail Village are very expensive, so you might as well go for the best, right? The reigning lodge is **Sonnenalp**, established in the late 1960s by a family of hoteliers who owned another resort of the same name in Bavaria. The original Vail Sonnenalp has been demolished and replaced with Vail's first all-suite lodge. The 88 guest units feature furnishings imported from Germany, gas-log fireplaces and walk-in closets. The resort has its own 18-hole golf course, indoor-outdoor swimming pool and complete spa facilities. Winter rates range from about $500 a night to more than $2000; the cost is less than half off-season. ~ 20 Vail Road, Vail; 970-476-5656, 866-284-4411, fax 970-476-1639; www.sonnenalp.com. ULTRA-DELUXE.

**LODGING**

**Gasthof Gramshammer** is another European-style lodge that radiates that *Sound of Music* charm distinctive to Vail. This 40-room inn, one of the first lodges in Vail, set the style for much of the architecture and decor in Vail Village. Rooms range from standard hotel quarters to two-bedroom suites with full kitchens; all have fireplaces. There's a one-week minimum stay in the winter. ~ 231 East Gore Creek Drive, Vail; 970-476-5626, 800-610-7374; fax 970-476-8816; www.pepis.com, e-mail info@pepis.com. ULTRA-DELUXE.

**The Lodge at Vail** is the longest-established American-style luxury resort hotel in Vail Village. Guest rooms, each with a private balcony, are richly appointed in gleaming mahogany and marble. Facilities include a heated swimming pool, jacuzzis, a sauna, a workout room and tennis courts. Rates include breakfast. ~ 174 East Gore Creek Drive, Vail; 970-476-5011, 800-331-5634; www.lodgeatvail.com. ULTRA-DELUXE.

Low-cost lodging—in Vail? Actually, **The Roost Lodge** is in West Vail, on the other side of the interstate and a mile and a half from Vail Village and the ski slopes; shuttle buses run hourly. This 72-unit, family-run A-frame lodge offers newly remodeled rooms plus a swimming pool, a jacuzzi, a sauna and a continental breakfast. ~ 1783 North Frontage Road, West Vail; 970-476-5451, 800-873-3065, fax 970-476-9158; www.roostlodge.com, e-mail roostldg@vail.net. DELUXE.

Other relatively affordable accommodations are farther west in the Avon–Beaver Creek area. The four-story **Comfort Inn** offers 147 big, comfortable, though otherwise unexceptional guest rooms with two queen-size beds each. There's a giant fireplace in the Santa Fe–style lobby. Other facilities include a heated outdoor pool and a jacuzzi. ~ P.O. Box 5510, Avon, CO 81620; 970-949-5511, 800-423-4374, fax 970-949-7762. DELUXE.

The finest hotel in the Vail Valley may be **The Lodge & Spa at Cordillera**, a European-style mountain lodge secluded in 3200 acres of private forest about three miles from Beaver Creek Resort. Designed by Belgian architects, the lodge is as eclectic as it is elegant, featuring Chinese slate roofs, Spanish wrought-iron filigree, handmade French furnishings and natural wood and stonework from the Colorado Rockies. The 56 rooms feature balconies and queen- or king-size beds with down quilts, and many have fireplaces. The European-style spa has hydrotherapy tubs, a full range of exercise machines, two swimming pools, jacuzzis, a sauna and a steam room. On the grounds are golf courses, tennis courts and miles of mountain-bike trails. ~ Squaw Creek Road, Edwards; 970-926-2200, 800-877-3529, fax 970-926-2486; www.cordillera-vail.com. ULTRA-DELUXE.

**DINING**

Most lodges in Vail serve breakfast, complimentary or otherwise, which may explain why hardly any of the town's numerous restaurants serve breakfast. The exception is **DJ McAdams Diner**, a longtime local hangout that serves gourmet coffee and lots of eggs-and-meat breakfasts, including house variations on eggs benedict. As the name promises, this is an improbably down-home little counter-service restaurant where your waitperson is likely to also be the cook and dishwasher. For lunch, the menu includes pasta, burritos and dessert crêpes, as well as wine and beer. Portions are big, prices are small. ~ 616 West Lionshead Circle; 970-476-2336. BUDGET.

Candlelight dining and French cuisine make **The Left Bank** an excellent choice for fine dining in Vail. Established in 1970 by a top French chef, the restaurant is decorated with family heirlooms and paintings enhanced by a pretty view of Gore Creek. Bouillabaisse is a house specialty, along with rack of lamb, homemade pâté de foie gras, and duck à l'orange, and the wine list offers more than 400 selections. Dinner only. Closed Wednesday. ~ 183 Gore Creek Drive, Vail Village; 970-476-3696. DELUXE.

**Sweet Basil**, a cozy bistro with a pretty, shady creekside view, offers a creative, wonderfully eclectic menu with such items as apple and jicama salad; a portobello mushroom goat-cheese tart with two vinaigrettes; a five-onion appetizer pizza with a port and balsamic vinegar glaze; and seared rare tuna served with leek and parsnip purée and red and yellow peppers. For dessert try the crème brûlée. ~ 193 East Gore Creek Drive, Vail; 970-476-0125. MODERATE TO DELUXE.

Don't be fooled by the funky name: **Beano's Cabin** is the most exclusive restaurant in the Vail Valley. Guests arrive by Sno-Cat–drawn sleigh in winter (horseback or horse-drawn wagon in summer) at this elegantly rustic hunting lodge decorated with pioneer paraphernalia, secluded in the Larkspur Bowl on Beaver Creek Mountain. The prix-fixe menu, which changes daily, features a six-course dinner with a choice of eight entrées, including lamb, beef, poultry and seafood dishes as well as special gourmet pizzas. Dinner only; reservations essential. Closed October to mid-December. ~ Larkspur Bowl, Beaver Creek; 970-949-9090. ULTRA-DELUXE.

Another great possibility for a wilderness splurge, **Game Creek Restaurant** is set in a mountain glade 2000 feet above town. Patrons ride the Eagle Bahn Gondola (free after the ski slopes close and the restaurant opens) up to Eagle's Nest Ridge, where they are met by a shuttle (in summer) or Sno-Cat (in winter) that takes them to the restaurant. The menu offers gourmet prix-fixe four-course dinners, including the "Game Creek trilogy"—a bison medallion, moulard duck breast and lamb cheeks served on a bed of polenta. Favorite dessert: lavender honey crème brûlée. The wine list is said to be the best in Vail. ~ Eagle's Nest Ridge; 970-479-4275. ULTRA-DELUXE.

Also in the Beaver Creek area, the family-oriented **Cassidy's Hole in the Wall** started as a barbecue place. It still offers a full rack of barbecued baby back ribs but has expanded its menu to include more than 80 items, including appetizers, salads, sandwiches and pizza. The decor is Old West–saloon style (later in the evening it turns into a cowboy dance club). ~ 82 East Beaver Creek Boulevard, Avon; 970-949-9449. BUDGET TO DELUXE.

Many of Colorado's most exclusive art galleries are located in Vail. **SHOPPING** The place to start browsing is **Knox Galleries** (100 East Meadow Drive, Vail; 970-476-5171), located in the Village Inn Plaza, which is remarkable for its life-size bronze sculptures of people, ranging from kids at play to Indian warriors and historical figures like Benjamin Franklin, placed around the plaza in front of the gallery.

### SKI-BOOT CAMP

Only a neat grid of abandoned streets and the concrete foundations of a few buildings mark the site of **Camp Hale** (Route 24), a World War II U.S. Army training camp where soldiers of the 10th Mountain Division trained on skis for combat missions in the Alps of wartime Europe. Many graduates of Camp Hale returned after the war to play various roles in the early development of Colorado's ski resorts.

Also in Village Inn Plaza is **Claggett/Rey Gallery** (970-476-9350), featuring traditional and Western paintings and bronze sculptures.

**Vail Fine Art Gallery** exhibits an array of regional and international paintings and prints including works by Renoir, Picasso, Warhol, Dali and Chagall. ~ 141 East Meadow Drive; 970-476-2900. **Bader-Melnick Gallery** shows paintings and sculpture by emerging and established American artists. ~ 141 East Meadow Drive; 970-476-0600. **Aboriginal Art, Inc.** has indigenous art from North and South America, Australia, the South Pacific and Africa. Open by appointment. ~ 970-476-7715.

In summer and ski seasons, the Vail Valley Gallery Association offers Saturday art walks on which you can tour local fine art galleries. Call 970-949-1626 for current information.

Fine jewelry is another Vail specialty. For fun pieces in sterling and semiprecious stones stop by **Karats by the Fountain.** ~ 201 East Gore Creek Drive; 970-476-4760. **Currents** offers imaginative variations on traditional designs in gold and diamonds. ~ 285 Bridge Street; 970-476-3322. Unusual, eye-catching inlaid stone jewelry are featured at **Gotthelf's.** ~ 196 Gore Creek Drive; 970-476-1777. Authentic Western collectibles are highlighted at the **Battle Mountain Trading Post.** ~ Vail Gateway; 970-479-0288.

**NIGHTLIFE** The Vail Valley supports a nightclub scene that runs the gamut from sedate to rowdy. The largest and most popular live-music dance club, **8150** is geared to the 21-to-30 crowd; its most unusual feature is a huge, bouncing dancefloor—yes, it actually moves up and down with the crowd's dance rhythms, sort of like a trampoline for the intoxicated. ~ 143 East Meadow Drive; 970-479-0607. **The Club** features rock music live and loud Tuesday through Saturday. ~ 304 Bridge Street, Vail; 970-479-0556. The **Sanctuary and Tap Room** offers a lively après-ski environment in two bright, narrow bars with a patio and a separate two-story dance-club scene. ~ 333 Bridge Street; 970-479-0500. Pool tables and country music—sometimes live, more often recorded—are found at the **Half Moon Saloon** (2161 North Frontage Road, West Vail; 970-476-4314). You'll find hot deejay music at **Pepi's.** ~ Gasthof Gramshammer, 231 East Gore Creek Drive, Vail; 970-476-5626.

**Mickey's** features a mellow atmosphere and live stylings nightly from the Piano Man, a local fixture for more than 25 years. ~ The Lodge at Vail, 174 East Gore Creek Road, Vail; 970-476-5011. The **Red Lion** has a big selection of specialty draft beers, plus entertainment by co-owner Phil Long, who plays piano renditions of pop favorites. ~ 304 Bridge Street; 970-476-7676.

**PARKS**     **WHITE RIVER NATIONAL FOREST** 🯅 🛶 Two large wilderness areas, part of White River National Forest, surround the Vail area. The Eagle's Nest Wilderness, a spectacular area of serrated mountain ridges and glacial valleys, lies just north of Vail Pass.

Lakes, waterfalls and wetlands characterize the lofty Holy Cross Wilderness south of Vail. Fishing is good for native and stocked trout in many lakes and streams, particularly in the Holy Cross Wilderness. The Colorado Wildlife Commission has designated Gore Creek east of Vail as a Gold Medal Stream, offering exceptional opportunities to catch large trout; special restrictions apply. Facilities are limited to hiking trails. ~ Access to the Eagle's Nest Wilderness is from a trailhead east of the summit of Vail Pass as well as several dead-end hikes lower in the Vail Valley. The main trailheads for the Holy Cross Wilderness are on Forest Roads 707 and 703, which turn off Route 24 between Minturn and Redcliff. Gore Creek Campground is located just off Route 70, four miles east of Vail; 970-827-5715.

▲ Gore Creek Campground has 25 RV/tent sites (no hookups); closed mid-September through May; 14-night maximum stay; $13 per night.

## Leadville Area

Located on top of one of the world's largest concentrations of precious ores—not only the gold and silver that gave rise to so many strike-it-rich stories in the late 19th century but also even rarer metals like molybdenum, manganese and zinc—Leadville was Colorado's second-largest city during the mining boom days. Today, with the mines closed and lacking the ski slopes or casinos that have revived the economies of other historic mining towns, Leadville's population has slid to one-eighth of what it was a century ago. The town's main claim to fame now is a well-preserved historic district that's a must-see for anyone intrigued by Colorado's gold and silver boom years.

## SIGHTS

There was a time when all roads in the Colorado Rockies led to Leadville, and although bypassed by the present-day interstate, the town is still easily accessible from every direction. Route 24 puts the town on the direct approach to most major ski areas from the Colorado Springs region and southern Colorado. It is also a reasonably short drive from the Vail Valley; in fact, many Leadville residents today work in Vail hotels and restaurants, commuting 45 minutes each way on special shuttle buses. For motorists coming from Denver on Route 70, the most direct route to Leadville is Route 91, exiting the interstate at **Copper Mountain Ski Area**. ~ Route 70, Copper Mountain; 970-968-2882, 800-458-8386; www.ski-copper.com. The most curious spot on this 25-mile shortcut is the **Climax Molybdenum Mine**, a massive operation that produced most of the world's supply of molybdenum, a metal used in stainless-steel alloys. The mine shut down in 1980 because of the decline in American steel production and the development of synthetic substitutes. Climax, the company town for the mine workers, has joined the new generation of ghost towns.

Whichever route you take to **Leadville,** the trip is bound to be easier than it was for the people who started a mining camp on this site in 1860 during the Pikes Peak gold rush. Early prospectors followed a narrow track around Pikes Peak and across wind-blasted South Park to reach this inhospitable place at an elevation of more than 10,000 feet, surrounded by the Gore, Mosquito and Sawatch mountain ranges. Many came on foot, transporting their worldly possessions in wheelbarrows. Within 20 years, Leadville grew to be the second-ranking city in Colorado, with a population nine times as large as it is today.

The greatest mining-camp legends of Colorado history came out of these silver fields. There was Leadville Johnny Brown, who found a rich gold vein and built a Denver mansion for his "un-sinkable" wife, Molly. There was David May, who turned his Leadville general store into the largest department-store chain in the Rockies, May D & F. Others who started from the streets of Leadville on their way to wealth and power include Marshall Field and Meyer Guggenheim.

Above all, there were Horace Tabor and Baby Doe, whose story epitomizes the euphoria and tragedy of Colorado's mining past. A shopkeeper by trade, Tabor set up a small general store in Leadville and grubstaked a pair of down-and-out miners for one-third of their claim. A month later, the pair struck a rich silver vein. A confidence man bilked Tabor out of his share of the profits by selling him a "worthless" mine that had been salted with a few ounces of gold buckshot. Tabor dug just a few feet and struck the richest silver lode in Colorado history. Tabor re-named his mine The Matchless. After he was elected to the U.S. Senate, Tabor divorced the wife who had come to Colorado with him in favor of his young Washington mistress, Elizabeth "Baby Doe" McCourt. Together they proceeded to spend Tabor's money lavishly but found it virtually impossible to squander it as fast as it poured in. But then . . .

Despite Tabor's vigorous representation of the silver interests in Washington, in 1893 Congress repealed the law requiring the government to buy silver for minting $1 coins, and the price of silver collapsed—along with Horace and Baby Doe Tabor's for-tunes. Tabor was working for the post office when he died six years later. Penniless, Baby Doe clung to the Matchless Mine for 36 years, hoping the price of silver would recover, living in an adjacent one-room cabin where she was discovered one winter morning during the worst days of the Great Depression, wrapped in newspapers for warmth, frozen. You can visit Baby Doe's cabin and the **Matchless Mine** located one mile east of town on a well-marked road. Admission. ~ East 7th Street, Leadville; www.matchlessmine.com.

With its red velvet seats and ornately hand-painted stage backdrops, the **Tabor Opera House** was the most elegant theater between St. Louis and San Francisco when Horace Tabor built it in 1879. Miners paid large sums to see world-class operas, theatrical presentations and vaudeville shows on this stage. Today, visitors can wander through the opera house on a self-guided tour. Open Saturday and Sunday from Memorial Day weekend through Labor Day weekend. Admission. ~ 308 Harrison Street, Leadville; 719-486-3900.

For more on Leadville's history, visit the **Healy House and Dexter Cabin**. Run by the Colorado Historical Society, the two very different homes—one an early prospector's cabin, the other an ornate Victorian mansion—house a museum of gold-rush and boom-town memorabilia. The most surprising part is the cabin, which an early-day mining millionaire converted into a private poker club. It still looks rustic on the outside but was luxuriously appointed inside with richly polished woodwork. Admission. ~ 912 Harrison Avenue, Leadville; 719-486-0487.

**Leadville–Aspen Area**

# Historic Leadville

Leadville's eight-block-long historic district is ideal for exploring on foot. Devoid of the galleries, boutiques, sporting goods stores and sidewalk cafés that have proliferated in other old mining towns, Leadville's main street still imparts a real sense of its gold-and-silver glory days.

**ICE PALACE PARK**     Start at the north end of Harrison Avenue. The hilltop park at Harrison and 10th Street was the site of the largest ice palace ever built, which was intended to bolster the town's sagging after-the-gold-rush economy by attracting tourism. Made from 5000 tons of ice blocks and 307,000 board feet of lumber—much of which was later used in local houses—it opened on January 3, 1896. Covering five acres and standing 90 feet tall, the ice palace contained an ice rink, a dance-floor, a restaurant, a gaming room, a carousel, ice sculptures and toboggan runs and had an electric lighting system. It melted in an early thaw after eight weeks.

**LEADVILLE'S MUSEUMS**     Across Harrison Avenue from the southeast corner of the park are the **Healy House and Dexter Cabin** (page 153), now a public museum operated by the Colorado Historical Society. A block down on the same side of Harrison at 9th Street, the **Heritage Museum** (see below) was originally the town's public library. Across Harrison is the **National Mining Hall of Fame & Museum** (see below).

**DOWNTOWN LEADVILLE**     With its open Gothic-style bell tower, the **Old Church** has been a Leadville landmark since its completion on December 22, 1889. ~ Harrison Avenue and 8th Street. Across Harri-

Housed in Leadville's historic 1904 Carnegie Library building, the **Heritage Museum** re-creates the town's early days in a series of dioramas and exhibits that include everything from Victorian-era furnishings to memorabilia of the 10th Mountain Division and contemporary paintings by local artists. Closed November to mid-May. Admission. ~ 9th Street at Harrison Avenue, Leadville; 719-486-1878.

The most unusual of Leadville's several historical museums is the **National Mining Hall of Fame & Museum**. The museum is chartered by the federal government, and much of what is on display is on permanent loan from the Smithsonian Institution. There is an amazingly realistic full-size reconstruction of a hard-rock son, the **Leadville City Hall** (c. 1905) served as the U.S. Post Office until 1973. In the next block, the **Delaware Hotel** (page 156) was named for the home state of the three brothers who built it. The three-story brick hotel was renovated in 1992, creating the elegant lobby and restaurant on the first floor, which had once been a department store. Detour a block east on 7th Street to see the stately **Annunciation Church** (c. 1879).

**TABOR HOTEL, HOME AND OPERA HOUSE**    Across Harrison Avenue from the Delaware Hotel, the **Tabor Grand Hotel** was one of the finest, most modern hostelries in the Rockies when it was built in 1885. It operated under various names for 104 years. Condemned in 1989, it was restored and reopened in 1992 as storefronts and apartments. Walk two blocks south on Harrison and turn east for half a block on 5th Street to see the home that shopkeeper Horace Tabor built for his first wife Augusta before he struck it rich, became a senator and divorced her. It is now a city museum. ~ 116 East 5th Street. Return to Harrison Avenue and continue south for two more blocks past 19th-century bank and mercantile buildings (Western Hardware on the southwest corner of Harrison and 5th Street has been in continuous operation since 1881), to the **Tabor Opera House** (page 153) at the corner of Harrison and 3rd Street.

**SINNERS AND SAINTS**    The building next door to the opera house was once a saloon where gunfighter Doc Holliday shot (but didn't kill) his last man. The **Silver Dollar Saloon** (page 158) across the street was one of the first commercial businesses in town. If you detour just one block west on 4th Street you'll find two of Leadville's leading houses of worship—**Temple Israel** at 201 West 4th Street, a Reform Jewish temple built in 1884, and across the street, **St. George's Episcopal Church**, built in 1880 as a miniature replica of the church of the same name in New York City.

mine, as well as a collection of gold nuggets and an exhibit that details the role mining has played in shaping America's history and economy. Admission. ~ 120 West 9th Street, Leadville; 719-486-1229; www.leadville.com/miningmuseum, e-mail national miningmuseum@bemail.com.

The **Leadville, Colorado & Southern Railroad** offers two-and-a-half-hour roundtrips between Leadville and Climax twice daily in summer and once a day from early September through the first weekend in October. Though the trains are of '30s to '50s vintage, the guide's narration focuses on the early boom days of the Leadville area, pointing out abandoned gold and silver mines. ~ 326 East 7th Street, Leadville; 719-486-3936; www.leadville-train.com.

Fifteen miles south of Leadville on Route 24, the Twin Lakes turnoff (Route 82) offers a shortcut from the Front Range cities to Aspen—over 12,095-foot **Independence Pass**, the highest Rocky Mountain pass that can be reached on a paved road.

**LODGING**

En route to Leadville, **Copper Mountain Resort** offers a range of hotel- and condominium-style accommodations in several buildings clustered around the foot of the ski slopes. While lodgings vary in size and amenities (higher-priced units have kitchens, fireplaces and balconies), the mildly Southwestern decor is fairly uniform throughout. Guests have complimentary privileges at the Copper Mountain Athletic Club, where facilities include an indoor swimming pool, hot tubs, saunas, exercise rooms and tennis and racquetball courts. Ski package rates are available. ~ P.O. Box 3117, Copper Mountain, CO 80443; 970-968-2318, 888-219-2441, fax 970-968-6227; www.coppercolorado.com. ULTRA-DELUXE.

The **Leadville Country Inn**, a Queen Anne–style Victorian mansion built in 1893, has eight guest rooms, some in the main house and others out back in the carriage house, with restored polished wood trim, brass beds and claw-foot tubs. A full gourmet breakfast is included in the room rate, and there's a hot tub in the garden for guests' enjoyment. ~ 127 East 8th Street, Leadville; 719-486-2354, 800-748-2354, fax 719-486-0300; www.leadvillebednbreakfast.com, e-mail info@leadvillebednbreakfast.com. MODERATE TO ULTRA-DELUXE.

**Club Lead** is an unaffiliated youth hostel with five six-bunk dorm rooms as well as five private rooms with queen-size beds. There is a hot tub. ~ 500 East 7th Street, Leadville; 719-486-2202, 800-349-2202. BUDGET.

**AUTHOR FAVORITE**

In contrast to the big, pricey, ultramodern hotels that are the norm in the nearby ski areas, I find the authenticity of Leadville's **Delaware Hotel** refreshing. This restored 1886 hotel transports me back to the gold-rush days when legends like Baby Doe Tabor and Leadville Johnny Brown strolled the streets of what was then Colorado's second-largest town. The hotel's 36 rooms feature brass beds with cozy down quilts and lace curtains. Crystal chandeliers and Victorian antique furniture grace the lobby. Rates include breakfast. ~ 700 Harrison Avenue, Leadville; 719-486-1418, 800-748-2004, fax 719-486-2214; www.delawarehotel.com, e-mail info@delawarehotel.com. MODERATE.

In contrast to the highly competitive haute cuisine scene in nearby ski resorts, Leadville eateries seem to have trouble keeping their doors open for more than a single season. Yet there's no shortage of entrepreneurs trying to be exceptions to the rule, especially in the 600 and 700 blocks of Harrison Avenue, where cafés virtually line the street. A good bet for bakery goods and hot beverages is the **Cloud City Coffee House.** ~ 711 Harrison Avenue; 719-486-1317. BUDGET.

Or try the **Columbine Café,** an old standby featuring cooking just like Mom's. ~ 612 Harrison Avenue; 719-486-3599. BUDGET.

Leadville has had a large Hispanic population throughout its history as a mining town, but until recently most Spanish-speaking residents lived in a separate municipality called Stringtown, adjacent to Leadville's southern city limit. Annexed to Leadville in the late '70s, Stringtown still retains its own ethnic identity—and some of the tastiest and most atmospheric no-frills Mexican restaurants in the Rockies.

A long-time favorite is **La Cantina.** Seating is in big wooden booths scarred by time. Mexican jukebox music plays in the background. Enchiladas, tamales and Mexican beer are among the specialties of the house. ~ Leadville; 719-486-0484. BUDGET TO MODERATE.

Another of Leadville's best Mexican restaurants, the **Grill Bar & Cafe** has been run by the Martínez family since 1965 and enjoys a statewide reputation for its Mexican and Southwestern food, featuring excellent New Mexico–style green chili as well as *chiles rellenos* and stuffed *sopapillas.* ~ 715 Elm Street; 719-486-9021. BUDGET.

One of the few places in the area these days where the food is *not* budget-priced is **The Windspirit at Twin Lakes Nordic Inn,** set on the shore of Twin Lakes, 13 miles south of Leadville, in a historic building that has been a stagecoach stop and a brothel at various times in the past. The café specializes in home-style cooking, with a selection of German and American entrées as well as deli fare. The atmosphere is casual and bright, with large windows looking out over the lakes. ~ 6435 Route 82; 719-486-8138. MODERATE.

Leadville has a handful of unpretentious galleries featuring the work of local artists, such as the **Little Cottage Gallery.** ~ 108 West 8th Street, Leadville; 719-486-2411. A number of antique shops specialize in mining-era memorabilia, notably **Sweet Betsy's from Pike.** ~ 122 East 7th Street, Leadville; 719-486-2116. The most unusual gift items to be found around Leadville are mineral specimens and mining artifacts, found at a number of shops including the **Museum Gift Shop and Mother Lode Art Gallery** in the

National Mining Hall of Fame & Museum. ~ 120 West 9th Street, Leadville; 719-486-1229.

**NIGHTLIFE** Leadville's historic old saloons tend to be a tad less sophisticated than the chic nightspots of Breckenridge, Aspen and Vail, but at least a beer costs a lot less. Saturday night on the town means bars with pool tables, country-and-western on the jukebox, and sometimes barroom brawls straight out of the cowboy movies. If this sounds like your idea of a good time, head for the **Silver Dollar Saloon**, a historic gin joint that dates back to the height of the 1879 silver boom and never bothered to close down for Prohibition. The current owners have reinvented it as an Irish pub. ~ 315 Harrison Street, Leadville; 719-486-9914.

**PARKS**  **SAN ISABEL NATIONAL FOREST** 🏃 ⛴ 🚤 This portion of the narrow national forest that extends all the way from Leadville to the New Mexico state line includes one of the most beautifully situated recreational lakes in Colorado, Turquoise Lake, just west of town. A hilly, paved 19-mile loop road encircles the lake at a distance, while more than a dozen access roads lead to secluded campgrounds, picnic areas and fishing spots along the shore. A foot trail meanders among the pines all the way around the lake, hugging the shoreline out of sight of the main road. A popular segment of the Colorado Trail runs from Turquoise Lake to Twin Lakes through the Mount Massive Wilderness. This area of the national forest also encompasses Mount Elbert (elevation 14,433 feet), the highest mountain in Colorado. Fishing is good for cutthroat, rainbow and lake trout and kokanee salmon. Facilities include picnic areas, restrooms and hiking trails. ~ Turquoise Lake is located five miles west of Leadville via Turquoise Lake Road (6th Street). There is also access to alpine tundra in the national forest from the Independence Pass Road (Route 82); 719-486-0749.

▲ Nine lakeside campgrounds have a total of 269 RV/tent sites (no hookups). Among them are Baby Doe Campground, with 50 sites, and Molly Brown Campground, with 49 sites. Closed Labor Day to late May; minimum two-night stay on weekends; $12 to $14 per night.

**TWIN LAKES RECREATION AREA** 🏃 ⛴ 🚤 Two small natural lakes alongside the road up Independence Pass have been augmented by dams to create a pair of reservoirs that merge into a single large lake when the water is high. Although the lakeshore is barren, rocky and unappealing, the spectacular views of Mount Elbert and La Plata Peak more than make up for it. The Colorado Trail skirts the lakeshore. Fishing is good for trout. Facilities include a picnic area, restrooms and a hiking trail. ~ Located

# Colorado's Painted Ladies

In older residential neighborhoods in Denver and Colorado Springs, in historic towns like Aspen and Leadville, even on the open prairie where houses stand solitary, Colorado boasts an abundance of "painted ladies"—Victorian houses that have been given fresh, multihued color schemes to emphasize their ornate architectural elements. Many of these mini-mansions have become bed-and-breakfast inns; others serve as small local museums; many others are private residences.

Colorado's favorite historical style got its start in England during the reign of Queen Victoria (1837–1901). Faced with the challenge of designing new kinds of buildings for the increasingly urbanized society of the newborn Industrial Age, innovative British architects borrowed ornamental elements from a wide range of traditions, including Greek, Roman, Gothic, Elizabethan, Italianate, Queen Anne and French Empire buildings, and combined them in fresh new ways. A house might feature Greek columns, a medieval turret and windows etched with designs from the court of Marie Antoinette. At the time, critics dismissed the Victorian look as superficial and inauthentic, but it caught the public's fancy as no other school of architecture ever had, for the first time offering to the middle class stylistic touches copied from the great palaces of Europe.

This "every man a king" architecture captured America's imagination about the same time the settlement of Colorado began. Its principal building materials—wood and red brick—were readily available in Colorado. As businessmen grew wealthy in the mining districts of the Rockies, rough-and-ready gold and silver boom towns began to sprout the kind of houses originally designed for London's nicer neighborhoods. These homes, often built by tradesmen with little or no formal architectural training, tended to exaggerate eccentric ornamentation known as "gingerbread," giving rise to "frontier Victorian" style buildings.

Victorian homes went out of fashion in the early 20th century. In the cities, they were broken up into apartments as older neighborhoods became slums. As populations declined in the mining towns, big old abandoned houses were torn down for firewood. By the 1970s, these high-ceilinged, energy-inefficient white elephants could be bought very cheaply. When a 1976 change in the law gave special tax breaks for fixing up historic buildings, old Victorian homes suddenly came back into vogue, transforming old-fashioned fixer-uppers into sought-after property. Happily, the trend has lasted, and today Colorado's unique "painted ladies" are the kind of status symbol a ski resort condominium just can't match.

15 miles south of Leadville via Route 24, then six miles west on Route 82; 719-486-0749.

▲ Permitted in a large lakeside parking area with a few tent sites nearby (no hookups); $11 to $12 per night.

▼▼▼▼▼▼▼▼▼▼▼
## Aspen Area

From Twin Lakes south of Leadville, Route 82 follows the North Fork of Lake Creek around the south slope of 14,433-foot Mount Elbert, the highest mountain in Colorado, and then climbs by switchbacks up the granite spine of the Sawatch Range to cross the Continental Divide over 12,095-foot Independence Pass. At the pass summit, where tiny flowers spangle the permafrost tundra in midsummer, you get an incomparable panoramic view of the vast, high mountain wilderness that forms the heart of the central Rockies. A Y-shaped chain of mountains extends 30 miles northward to Vail, 30 miles southward to Salida and 50 miles westward to Redstone, dominated by 20 peaks over 14,000 feet high. Aspen nestles in the notch of the Y, sheltered by a natural fortress of alpine pinnacles that protect it from everyday reality.

Snow banks up to 16 feet deep close Independence Pass in the winter, so the only way to drive to Aspen then is via the fast four-lane segment of Route 82 that links the town with Glenwood Springs and Route 70. This approach creates a much different impression of Aspen, taking you past the suburban rows of custom and tract homes that have all but swallowed the town of Carbondale, where many Aspen locals actually live, and from which they daily commute 30 miles to work through a landscape thick with recently constructed homes and condominiums. By the time you pass the sprawling industrial and warehouse district and big, busy airport and reach the town of Aspen itself, you may feel as if you've reached the downtown area of a fair-sized city.

### SIGHTS

Aspen! In every small town in the Rockies preservationists worry that their corner of the world will become another one, while developers fantasize about being the next one. **Aspen** has served as the prototype for redevelopment of old mountain villages for a half-century, yet there's still only one Aspen—the ultimate ski resort and one of the most expensive places on earth.

Aspen sprang up in 1879 as a silver boom town. It grew slowly and steadily to a population of 12,000 in 1892, when its mines produced $12 million in silver, inspiring one journalist to proclaim it "the greatest silver mining camp in the world today." That same year, the federal government stopped buying silver to mint $1 coins, causing the price of silver to collapse. The mines shut down, the railroad stopped running and, by the following summer, three-quarters of the townspeople had moved away.

Aspen's population had dwindled to a few hundred by 1936, when locals opened the tiny Highlands Bavarian ski resort near Ashcroft. It was the first downhill ski area in Colorado and one of the first in the United States. Austrian-born ski instructor Friedl Pfeifer, who moved to Aspen after World War II, persuaded Chicago cardboard-box tycoon Walter Paepke to invest the kind of money it took to develop a European-style resort, creating the Aspen Skiing Company and the beginning of the present ski slopes on Aspen Mountain.

> Aspen's first ski run had a 16-bed dormitory lodge and a boat tow–style ski lift that cost a dime a ride.

The new ski slopes drew worldwide attention in 1950, when Aspen hosted the World Alpine Ski Championships. Walter Paepke, the Chicago cardboard-box tycoon who was the original investor in Aspen's ski slopes, recognized early that it takes more than snow to make a world-class resort. In fact, he envisioned Aspen primarily as a conference center and secondarily as a ski resort. Paepke restored and reopened the Hotel Jerome and Wheeler Opera House, gave local residents free paint to spruce up their homes, then sponsored Aspen's first major cultural event—a celebration of the bicentennial of Goethe's birth—and brought in an all-star cast of great minds and talents including Albert Schweitzer, Thornton Wilder, Arthur Rubinstein and the Minneapolis Symphony Orchestra. The event became the forerunner of the Aspen Music Festival and School as well as the Aspen Institute of Humanistic Studies.

The town's reputation picked up momentum during the Kennedy administration, when the president and his family and all their friends began coming here for ski weekends. Soon celebrities were everywhere, including a few whose very names evoked fantasies of the Aspen lifestyle, notably John Denver, Hunter Thompson and Claudine Longet. The police grew long hair and drove Japanese compact cars, people smoked marijuana openly on the streets, and Aspen became known as a place where anything went—if you could afford the rent. (But don't even think about lighting up a doobie on Main Street today. Times change.)

Other rundown old mining towns throughout Colorado have blossomed into winter megaresorts, but none has ever matched Aspen's image for glamour. A vacation home in Aspen has become an ultimate status symbol. The Aspen Skiing Company has been bought by Twentieth Century Fox. Aspen now has more movie stars than Yellowstone has bears, and the police have come to take their job—keeping the riffraff out—very seriously. The wild Aspen lifestyle probably still exists, but it's in the hot tubs of huge houses up private lanes protected by armed guards. The closest most visitors are likely to get to it is a glimpse of a celebrity in a restaurant or supermarket.

As for the town's Victorian past, most historic buildings of downtown Aspen have been preserved, though they have been engulfed by more contemporary structures and renovated beyond recognition. The most impressive older building is the **Wheeler Opera House**, one of Colorado's finest opera houses when it opened in 1888. (It is still the tallest building in Aspen.) The opera house was in use for barely five years before the silver market's collapse shut down the nightly performances. Abandoned, it was gutted by fire a few years later. It was restored in 1947 and again in 1989, and today it serves as Aspen's principal indoor stage, hosting concerts, theater performances, opera, ballet, big bands and classical artists almost every night of the year. Guided tours are available by request during the day. Aspen's **visitors information center** is located in the opera house, which was named for Jerome B. Wheeler, who made his fortune as a partner in Macy's department store in New York City and moved to the dismal little mining camp of Aspen in 1883, bringing with him so much investment capital that he is generally remembered as the town's founding father. ~ 320 East Hyman Avenue, Aspen; 970-920-5770; www.wheeleroperahouse.com.

Jerome B. Wheeler lived in the beautiful 1888 Queen Anne–style mansion that now houses the **Wheeler-Stallard House Museum**. Open afternoons only, the museum traces Aspen's history from silver boom to bust and back to its current status as one of the world's premier resorts. Also in the Wheeler-Stallard House are the **Aspen County Historical Archives**, a treasure trove of historical photos, century-old newspapers and historical documents, and a gallery exhibiting photography and fine art shows. Admission. ~ 620 West Bleeker Street, Aspen; 970-925-3721; www.aspenhistory.org.

Oddly enough, the **Aspen Art Museum** has no permanent collection. Instead, this large brick Victorian-era building, originally the town's power plant, provides public visual arts space for rotating painting, sculpture, architecture and design exhibitions. The museum hosts lectures, lunchtime art-history programs, monthly benefit dinners and Thursday-evening cocktail receptions. Admission. ~ 590 North Mill Street, Aspen; 970-925-8050; www.aspenartmuseum.org, e-mail info@aspenartmuseum.org.

The essence of downtown Aspen is its array of expensive galleries, sportswear shops and restaurants; yet less than a mile away from downtown lies roadless wilderness. One way to reach the high mountains is to take an 18-minute ride on the **Silver Queen Gondola** to the 11,212-foot summit of Aspen Mountain. It operates in both winter and summer. In summer, the gondola provides easy access to high-country trails, as well as to the mountaintop Sundeck Restaurant, where Aspen Music School students perform regularly. ~ 970-925-1220.

A very popular spot nearby is **Maroon Lake,** a beautiful mountain lake set at the foot of North and South Maroon Peaks and Pyramid Peak, all over 14,000 feet in elevation. Defoliated by too many visitors, the lake is closed to motor-vehicle traffic during the summer (mid-June through Labor Day) except for overnight campers with hard-to-get U.S. Forest Service permits. Maroon Lake is the trailhead for a vast network of foot and horse trails in the **Maroon Bells–Snowmass Wilderness.** There are also easy, scenic trails around the lake and along the creek.

> Most natural hot springs are free but usually don't feature any amenities. Be sure to bring your own water, towels and bathing suits (!) if you plan to relax in comfort.

Shuttle buses operated by **Roaring Fork Transit Agency** run frequently from the T-Lazy-7 Ranch, partway up Maroon Creek Road. The last bus leaves the lake in late afternoon. Fee. ~ 51 Service Center Drive, Aspen; 970-920-1905.

Today only nine abandoned and tumbled buildings remain of the town of **Ashcroft,** which in the 1880s boasted a population larger than Aspen's. To reach the picturesque old townsite, drive 12 miles south of town on Castle Creek Road. Midway between Aspen and Ashcroft is the turnoff for the Conundrum Creek trailhead. From there it is a long but gentle nine-mile walk from the trailhead to **Conundrum Hot Springs,** a pair of idyllic hot-spring pools, three feet and four feet deep, with water temperatures that fluctuate from 99° to 103°F. Camping is permitted in designated backcountry campsites.

The original class act in town is the **Hotel Jerome.** Originally built by local silver tycoon Jerome B. Wheeler in 1889 with the intention of surpassing even the finest New York hotels, the Jerome was restored in 1950 as the centerpiece of the newly opened ski resort. Since then, the management has added to the decor year by year with museum-like care. Fine Victorian antiques grace not only the common areas but also the 93 guest rooms and suites, each of which is uniquely furnished and decorated. The spacious bathrooms are done in white marble and feature jacuzzi tubs large enough for two. Modern improvements include a heated outdoor swimming pool and a well-equipped workout room. ~ 330 East Main Street, Aspen; 970-920-1000, 800-331-7213, fax 970-925-2784; www.hjerome.com. ULTRA-DELUXE.

**LODGING**

While the Jerome vied with the best New York hotels of the late 19th century, the **St. Regis,** with its contemporary Colorado mountain style, is designed to rival the great hotels of today. Opened in 1991, the Luxury Collection Hotel is presently the darling of top-tier jet setters, so if you plan to stay here, make reservations far in advance. Despite its size, the red-brick exterior of this 257-room hotel merges gently into downtown's remaining Victorian-era architecture. The lobby, a wonderland of fine art and classic luxury, makes an ideal place to loiter and watch for movie stars. The guest rooms feel larger than life, with rich carpeting, flowery upholstery and giant marble-clad bathrooms as well as all the little niceties like fresh flowers, terrycloth robes, three phones (one in the bathroom) and Godiva chocolates on the pillows. ~ 315 East Dean Street, Aspen; 970-920-3300, 888-454-9005, fax 970-925-8998; www.stregisaspen.com. ULTRA-DELUXE.

For well-heeled travelers who shudder at the term "resort hotel," there's the wonderful **Hotel Lenado**, a small, elegant European-style luxury hotel situated in the heart of downtown Aspen. The 19 guest rooms are done entirely in various kinds of wood (*lenado* means "wooded" in Spanish), from the polished wood floors, ceilings and wall paneling to the bentwood beds and sofas. Wood-burning stoves and down comforters add to your comfort on chilly winter evenings. The lobby area features a vaulted ceiling, a two-story-high fireplace and a profusion of windows that lets you view the town streets from the stairway. The common areas include a library, a bar and a hot tub. A gourmet breakfast is included in the room rate. ~ 200 South Aspen Street, Aspen; 970-925-6246, 800-321-3457, fax 970-925-3840; www.hotellenado. com. ULTRA-DELUXE.

> If you have to ask about room rates, overnighting in Aspen is probably a bad idea. Just about every private room in the area is priced in the ultra-deluxe range during ski season, though a few plummet into the deluxe range off-season.

Among Aspen's many bed and breakfasts, **Sardy House** boasts the most historic building. Originally built as a private residence in 1892, this red-brick mansion was one of the first Victorian-style homes in Aspen. Now a 20-unit inn, the Sardy House was expanded with renovation of its carriage house and the addition of a new wing that was carefully designed to mirror the mansion's interior architecture. Exceptional care is evident in the decor and furnishings, which seamlessly blend period antiques with modern items to create a distinctive feel of opulence that transcends time. The lofty, century-old blue spruces in the front yard conceal the additions, creating the illusion that the inn is smaller than it actually is. Guest rooms in both the old and new sections have jacuzzis; a hot tub, a sauna and a swimming pool are behind the main house. Rates include a full breakfast menu. ~ 128 East Main Street, Aspen; 970-920-2525, 800-321-3457, fax 970-920-4478; e-mail hotlsardo@rof.net. ULTRA-DELUXE.

The closest thing in Aspen to low-cost lodging is the **St. Moritz Lodge**—part unaffiliated youth hostel and part hotel, with 12 small dorm rooms sharing communal bathroom facilities, and 13 deluxe-priced lodge rooms and two-bedroom apartments with private baths and kitchens. There's a fireplace in the lobby and a jacuzzi, a sauna and an outdoor swimming pool. Dormitory beds are in the budget range all year. ~ 334 West Hyman Avenue, Aspen; 970-925-3220, 800-817-2069, fax 970-920-4032; www.stmoritz lodge.com, e-mail info@stmoritzlodge.com. BUDGET TO DELUXE.

The stylish, contemporary **Mountain House Lodge** offers in-town bed and breakfast accommodations at relatively reasonable rates. The 24 guest rooms, decorated in Southwestern style, range from economy rooms with one double bed to large suites with a king-size, a queen-size and a Murphy bed, and all have private baths, phones, refrigerators and TVs. Guest facilities include an indoor jacuzzi. ~ 905 East Hopkins Avenue, Aspen; 970-920-2550, 866-920-2550, fax 970-544-0090; www.mountainhouse lodge.com, e-mail mhaspen@aol.com. BUDGET TO DELUXE.

Room rates in nearby Snowmass run slightly lower than in Aspen. Representative of these somewhat affordable lodgings is the 44-room **Snowmass Inn**, a modern four-story ski lodge with crazily compact rooms: each has a wall bed that is stored during the day and pulled out at night, and there's a sofa bed, too, so four people can share a room, albeit in cramped quarters. The lodge has a lobby fireplace, a heated swimming pool, a jacuzzi and a sauna. ~ 61 Daly Lane, Snowmass Village; 970-923-4202, 800-635-3758, fax 970-923-3650; www.snowmassinn.com, e-mail lodging@snowmassinn.com. MODERATE TO DELUXE.

"Aspen Nouveau" may best describe the cuisine at **Piñons**, which is widely considered the best restaurant in town. It is certainly one of the most innovative restaurants anywhere. The constantly evolving menu features such specialties as an appetizer of lobster with morel and chanterelle mushrooms and an entrée of sautéed ahi crusted with sesame seeds. The decor is a light, airy takeoff on western ranch-house style, with log pillars, leather-wrapped banisters and window shutters fashioned from willow twigs. ~ 105 South Mill Street, Aspen; 970-920-2021. ULTRA-DELUXE.

**DINING**

**The Restaurant at the Little Nell,** located in a stylish luxury ski lodge near the foot of the Aspen Mountain gondola, charac-terizes its food as "American alpine cuisine," which apparently means originality and innovation: highly improbable combina-tions of many fresh ingredients that result in surprisingly delicious dishes. For example, there's elk with caramelized onions, apples, sweet-potato crisps and sun-dried cherries. If that doesn't suit, try the roast rack of lamb served with peanut-vegetable rice, tor-tilla salad and a sauce of roasted tomatoes and ancho peppers. Desserts include warm apple-blackberry tarts with cinnamon Calvados ice cream. ~ 675 East Durant Avenue, Aspen; 970-920-4600. ULTRA-DELUXE.

For down-home fare, try **Boogie's Bakers**, where the menu is filled with cutely named selections like the Monster Mash meat-loaf dinner and the Ahi & Harriet sandwich. You'll find an array of heart-healthy and vegetarian options, as well as seductive desserts. ~ Cooper Avenue at Hunter Street, Aspen; 970-925-6610. MODERATE.

**Cache Cache** brings Aspen-style culinary innovation to French-country cooking in a casual bistro setting that glows with pastel hues and art deco touches. Try the osso buco on risotto cake or the free-range chicken Provençal. ~ 205 South Mill Street, Aspen; 970-925-3835. MODERATE TO DELUXE.

**Bentley's at the Wheeler**, an old-fashioned English pub located in the Wheeler Opera House and decorated with Victorian antiques (including a handcrafted hardwood bar that was originally a British bank counter), features traditional fish-and-chips as well as other fresh fish dishes, pasta and homemade cheesecake. ~ 328 East Hyman Avenue, Aspen; 970-920-2240. MODERATE.

Out of town, a fine dining favorite is the **Pine Creek Cookhouse**, an elegantly rustic log cabin decorated in old-fashioned ski-lodge style 12 miles from Aspen near Ashcroft. You can drive there in summer, but in winter the trip itself is a wonderful part of this exceptional dining experience: starting at the Nordic ski center on Castle Creek Road, you can either follow a guide on a 20-minute cross-country ski trek in the moonlight or ride to the restaurant in a horse-drawn sleigh. The menu is limited to three entrées, which are different every night. The Pine Creek Cookhouse also serves a lavish Sunday brunch. ~ 11399 Castle Creek Road, Ashcroft; 970-925-1044; www.pinecreekcookhouse.com, e-mail ast@rof.net. ULTRA-DELUXE.

No survey of Aspen dining would dare omit the legendary **Woody Creek Tavern**, located on Woody Creek Road, six miles down-valley from Aspen. Made famous in the '70s by *Rolling Stone* journalist Hunter Thompson, still a regular here, it attracts resident celebrities like musician Don Henley of the Eagles and "Miami Vice" veteran Don Johnson. Its pool tables, burgers 'n' beer and self-consciously funky ambience offer a welcome change of pace when Aspen chic starts to cloy. The fare includes locally grown ground-beef burgers, tamales, enchiladas, barbecued ribs and chicken, a different homemade soup each day and an array of

**AUTHOR FAVORITE**

A one-of-a-kind dining experience that I've found truly unforgettable is Sunday brunch at the **Pine Creek Cookhouse**, located deep in the mountains near a tumble-down ghost town outside Aspen. Getting there is half the fun, especially in winter when you can ski there cross-country through a sparkling crystal landscape and arrive with the heartiest appetite imaginable. See above for more information.

bar appetizers such as Buffalo hot wings, nachos and bison sausage. ~ 2 Woody Creek Plaza, Woody Creek; 970-923-4585. MODERATE.

**SHOPPING**

Shopping, of course, is a big part of what Aspen is all about. The array of beautiful clothing, jewelry, art and gift items is staggering, and the price tags are mind numbing. You'll find everything from hand-painted silks and black pearls to oriental rugs and trendy faux fur hats. If you like to window-shop, you could easily spend your whole vacation right here. If you like to shop for keeps, you could spend your life savings. Because of sky-high rents on retail spaces, shops and galleries tend to come and go faster than it's possible to keep track of them.

The **Aspen Grove Fine Arts** is one of the area's few galleries that show work by Pitkin County's local artists. ~ 525 East Cooper Avenue, Aspen; 970-925-3717. The **Huntsman Gallery of Fine Art,** showing a full range of nationally known traditional painters, is Aspen's largest gallery. ~ 521 East Hyman Avenue, Aspen; 970-920-1910.

Humor meets art at the **Art Tee Gallery**, where original "wearable art" T-shirts are displayed on the walls like paintings. ~ 401 East Hyman Avenue, Aspen; 970-920-2648.

Last, perhaps, but far from least, you'll find end-of-the-season leftovers from many of Aspen's finest boutiques, along with celebrity cast-off clothing, at the oldest secondhand store in town, **Gracy's**. ~ 517 East Hopkins, Aspen; 970-925-5131.

**NIGHTLIFE**

Summer brings a full schedule of cultural events to Aspen. Drawing some of the country's most talented musicians and enthusiastic audiences, the two-month-long **Aspen Music Festival** offers daily performances in its tent theater on Gillespie Street at the northwest edge of town. Held every summer since the early 1950s, the festival attracts the world's top students and leading virtuosos in a broad range of musical styles, from classical to jazz and avant-garde. ~ 2 Music School Road; 970-925-9042; www. aspenmusicfestival.com. More very lively arts: **Theatre in the Park** (Art Park, Aspen; 970-925-9313), a two-month series of contemporary plays; and the five-day-long **Aspen Filmfest** (110 East Hallam Street, Suite 102, Aspen; 970-925-6882). The **Wheeler Opera House** presents live concerts, plays and dance programs almost every night year-round. ~ 320 East Hyman Avenue, Aspen; 970-920-5770; www.wheeleroperahouse.com.

Aspen's nightclub scene is built to accommodate elbow-to-elbow après-ski crowds during the winter season. In summer, most clubs continue to present live music at least on Friday and Saturday evenings. The **Howling Wolf Brew Pub** has contemporary rock music and a young crowd. ~ 424 East Cooper Avenue, Aspen; 970-920-7771. **Shooters Saloon**, Aspen's only country-

and-western dance club, features nationally known live bands on weekends. ~ 220 South Galena Street, Aspen; 970-925-4567. Shooters is a major sponsor of Gay Ski Week. Although Aspen has a sizeable gay and lesbian community, there are specific places and times where people meet before heading for gatherings in private homes. The biggest are the **Friday Afternoon Club** at the Greenhouse at the Little Nell (675 East Durant Avenue; 970-920-4600) and **Saturday Night** at Harry's Velvet Lounge (316 East Hopkins Avenue; 970-544-4664).

For a more sophisticated scene, there is **Mezzaluna**, which has a reputation as the best club in town for celebrity-gawking. ~ 600 East Cooper Avenue, Aspen; 970-925-5882. The **St. Regis Lobby Lounge** offers live jazz. ~ 315 East Dean Street, Aspen; 970-920-3300. Live jazz can also be heard at the **Greenhouse at the Little Nell**. ~ 675 East Durant Avenue, Aspen; 970-920-4600.

**PARKS**

**WHITE RIVER NATIONAL FOREST** 🏃 🐎 ⤸ This 2.25-million-acre forest is Colorado's largest. Of its eight designated wilderness areas, two—the Maroon Bells–Snowmass Wilderness and the Hunter-Fryingpan Wilderness—flank the town of Aspen. The main trailheads that provide access into the wilderness areas are at Maroon Lake, Ashcroft and near the summit of Independence Pass. The Maroon Bells–Snowmass Wilderness is one of the most heavily used wilderness areas in Colorado, and human impact on the delicate alpine ecosystem has become a serious problem. By contrast, the Hunter-Fryingpan Wilderness offers plenty of pristine solitude. Fishing is good for trout, particularly in mountain lakes in the Hunter-Fryingpan Wilderness. Facilities include jeep, hiking and horse trails. ~ Forest access from Aspen is via Independence Pass Road (Route 82 East), Castle Creek Road (Forest Road 102) and Maroon Creek Road (Forest Road 125). Maroon Lake Campground is at the end of Maroon Creek Road; Difficult Campground is just off Independence Pass Road.

▲ Permitted in designated areas. Eight campgrounds totaling 97 RV/tent sites (no hookups). maximum-stay requirements in summer. Camping fees range from $10 to $15 a night, and maximum stay requirements are as short as five days. Reservations are necessary for the campgrounds closest to Aspen—Difficult, Silver Bar, Silver Bell and Silver Queen; call 970-927-0532.

▼▼▼▼▼▼▼▼▼▼▼▼▼▼▼▼
## Steamboat Springs Area

As you follow the long, sweeping curve of Route 40's steep descent from the summit of 9426-foot Rabbit Ears Pass, the first thing you see when you approach Steamboat Springs is a hillside completely covered with condominiums that fill up on winter weekends. Thriving on the recreation industry, Steamboat Springs has a hip, sporty subculture. It often seems as if everyone in town rides a mountain bike—at the same time. Yet unlike other famous-name ski resorts like Aspen, Breckenridge or Telluride, Steamboat was not a boom-and-bust mining town, and it was never abandoned. Instead, this former rough-and-ready ranching center still retains a bit of its original character.

The downtown area is preserved as the **Steamboat Springs Historic District**. Its storefronts have a look of western small-town Americana with a fresh coat of paint. Unlike almost all other ski towns mentioned in this chapter, Steamboat Springs is low enough (6000 feet) in elevation so that its streets are usually free of snow and ice. The commercial area known as Steamboat Village, around the base of the ski area, is 900 feet higher and stays snowpacked most of the winter.

**SIGHTS**

The **Tread of Pioneers Museum** is home to the local history exhibit. Along with typical assortments of Indian artifacts and ranch relics, the museum contains a fascinating collection of ski memorabilia that shows how far skiing has come since the beginning of the 20th century. Admission. ~ 800 Oak Street, Steamboat Springs; 970-879-2214.

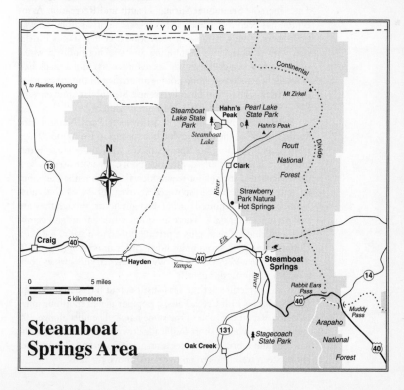

Steamboat
Springs Area

North of town, the lower slope of **Steamboat Ski Area** rises from the jumble of condominiums and ski lodges. Viewing it from below, you can't see a hint of the ski area's true extent. Above the midpoint, a long ridgeline leads back to a maze of slopes and trails spanning the faces of four mountains. The Thunderhead Chairlift and more expensive Silver Bullet Gondola run all summer, carrying mountain bikers to the ski area's mountain-bike trail network, which joins longer trails in adjoining Routt National Forest. ~ 2305 Mt. Werner Circle, Steamboat Springs; 970-879-6111; www.steamboat.com, e-mail info@steamboat.com.

**Steamboat Spring**, for which the town was named, is located alongside two other small springs on the bank of the Yampa River at the 13th Street Bridge. The spring used to spew water and steam 15 feet into the air with a steamboatlike chugging noise that could be heard for miles, but it slowed to a trickle in 1909, the same year the railroad reached the town; local historians speculate that railroad construction "broke" the spring. On the other side of the river, the paved **Yampa River Trail** provides a two-mile scenic route through town.

Many of the 150 other hot springs in the area still work fine. The venerable **Steamboat Springs Health and Recreation Association** has been a spa since 1887, when the first bathhouse was built there. Today, a modern recreational center stands on the site, with several 100°F swimming and soaking pools, a water slide and new sun decks, as well as tennis courts and a snack bar. A small, heart-shaped stone pool is an artifact of the spa's earlier days. Admission. ~ 136 Lincoln Avenue, Steamboat Springs; 970-879-1828; www.sshra.org, e-mail info@sshra.org.

Seven miles north of town, **Strawberry Park Natural Hot Springs** is one of the most idyllic hot springs in Colorado. Water from several scalding hot springs mixes with chilly creek water into three large, hot tub–depth rock pools. This site used to be a closely guarded secret spot where locals went to bathe nude, but so many people have discovered it over the years that now bathing suits are required during daylight hours, though they are still optional after dark. There are a few rustic cabins and campsites available for rent, plus a private pool. Admission. ~ 44200 Country Road 36, seven miles north of Steamboat Springs; 970-879-0342, fax 970-879-6834; www.strawberryhotsprings.com, e-mail hot@springsips.com.

Another picture-perfect spot just beyond the edge of Steamboat Springs is **Fish Creek Falls**, a popular picnic spot four miles east of town on the road of the same name. The falls plunge 200 feet into a canyon. A short trail leads down to a picnic area in the canyon, and a bridge provides a great view of the falls. Another short, steep trail leads to an overlook above the falls.

The **Rabbit Ears Motel** has 65 standard motel rooms in bright colors and an array of thoughtful little appliances such as coffee makers and clock radios. The prices are among the lowest in town, and if that's not enough, guests receive a discount at the Steamboat Springs Health and Recreation hot-springs spa across the street. Rates include continental breakfast. ~ 201 Lincoln Avenue, Steamboat Springs; 970-879-1150, 800-828-7702, fax 970-870-0483; www.rabbitearsmotel.com. MODERATE.

Even more than in most other Colorado ski-resort towns, the lodging scene in Steamboat Springs is dominated by condominiums, from spartan "efficiency condos" (which look suspiciously like motel rooms with kitchenettes) to luxury townhouses with up to five bedrooms. Typical prices are moderate in summer and deluxe to ultra-deluxe during ski season. To learn more, contact **Mountain Resorts** (888-686-8075; mtn-resorts.com, e-mail info@mtn-resorts.com) or **Steamboat Resorts Management** (2350 Ski Trail Lane; 970-879-8000, 800-276-6719; www.steam boatresorts.com, e-mail info@steamboatresorts.com).

Homey and historic, the little **Harbor Hotel** has been in operation since 1939. Of the 113 guest rooms, 66 are in the old hotel and feature Victorian-period furnishings and decor. Two recent annexes contain everything from standard motel rooms to two-bedroom condominiums with full kitchens. Facilities include jacuzzis and a sauna. ~ 703 Lincoln Avenue, Steamboat Springs; 970-879-1522, 800-543-8888, fax 970-879-1737. MODERATE TO ULTRA-DELUXE.

> The Steamboat Bed & Breakfast was originally built in 1891 as the town's first church.

Located downtown, a short shuttle bus trip from the ski slopes, the **Steamboat Bed & Breakfast**, once partly gutted by fire, is now completely renovated into a comfortable little inn. The six guest rooms are furnished with antiques and period reproductions. Facilities include fireplaces, a large hot tub and an outdoor deck overlooking meticulously landscaped gardens. Rates include a full breakfast. ~ 442 Pine Street, Steamboat Springs; 970-879-5724, 877-335-4321, fax 970-870-8787; www.steamboatb-b.com, e-mail info@steamboatb-b.com. DELUXE TO ULTRA-DELUXE.

Set on a hillside between downtown and the ski area, the **Ramada Vacation Suites at the Hilltop** was Steamboat's premier luxury ski lodge until new owners recently converted it to timeshare condos. Units are available for rent when not in use by the co-owners. Besides the 68 uniformly pleasant suites, the complex offers a full complement of facilities including a heated indoor pool, saunas, jacuzzis, tennis courts and a miniature golf course. ~ 1000 High Point Drive, Steamboat Springs; 970-879-2900, 800-438-6494. DELUXE TO ULTRA-DELUXE.

Among the many guest ranches in the Steamboat Springs area, **The Home Ranch**, located 19 miles up the road to Steamboat Lake, stands out as the most luxurious. Some of the six guest units are in the main ranch house, while others are in modern, beautifully appointed cabins a short walk away. Each cabin has its own jacuzzi. Riding and flyfishing lessons are offered, as are treks into the Mount Zirkel Wilderness, and there is a swimming pool and a sauna. The ranch is open from June through September and December through March and offers 25 miles of groomed cross-country ski trails in winter. ~ 54880 County Road 129, Clark; 970-879-1780; www.homeranch.com, e-mail info@home-ranch.com. ULTRA-DELUXE.

A number of resorts dot the area around Steamboat Lake and Hahn's Peak. The one with the most atmosphere is **The Country Inn at Steamboat Lake**. Built in classic style, this eight-room bed-and-breakfast inn has a huge porch and wraparound balcony complete with hot tub overlooking the lake. Rooms are wood-paneled and spacious with contemporary furnishings. ~ 61276 County Road 129, Clark; 970-879-3906. MODERATE TO DELUXE.

**DINING**

For the ultimate in Steamboat Springs dining, take a gondola ride to the top of Thunderbird Peak and **Hazie's**, where china, sterling silver and crystal catch the soft glow of candlelight in a spectacular setting overlooking the town. Fixed-price four-course dinners offer a choice of seafood, chicken, beef and veal entrées plus appetizers, soup, salad and a dessert cart. The gondola ride and live music are included in the dinner price. Closed in fall and spring. ~ Thunderhead Terminal, Silver Bullet Gondola, Steamboat Springs; 970-871-5150. ULTRA-DELUXE.

**La Montaña**, an exceptional Southwestern restaurant located in a shopping center at the foot of the ski slopes near the gondola, serves intriguing variations on traditional New Mexico and Tex-Mex cuisine. Elk meat, a specialty here, turns up in a variety of forms—elk loin with pecans, elk fajitas and braided elk sausage—but you'll also find mesquite-grilled lamb and chorizo sausages as well as *chiles rellenos* and other favorites. The thoroughly modern decor features art photographs, murals, stained glass windows and abundant greenery in a sunny atrium. ~ 2500 Village Drive, Steamboat Springs; 970-879-5800. MODERATE TO DELUXE.

A very popular Mexican restaurant at the slopes, **Dos Amigos** is known for such house specialties as *chiles rellenos* stuffed with Monterey jack cheese and a wide range of enchilada choices, including spinach and mushroom enchiladas, *vegetarino del cocinero* (fresh vegetable enchiladas) and enchiladas *pescador* (seafood enchiladas) with blue-corn tortillas. Adobe-style stucco walls, old-time photos and lots of plants enhance the casual ambience. ~ Ski Time Square, Steamboat Springs; 970-879-4270. MODERATE.

**Antare's,** located in a 1906 building, cultivates an air of casual elegance with polished hardwood floors, parquet tables and an antique bar in the lounge. Its New American cuisine highlights eclectic blends of regional and ethnic recipes adapted to contemporary tastes. Appetizers include prawns sautéed in Thai chili and served on jasmine rice, and ahi encrusted with sesame seeds and herbs. Among the entrées are Maine lobster in mushroom sauce on a bed of chili-pepper linguine; lamb chops with a chutney of melon, mint and chili; and tender veal with a chardonnay and watercress sauce. Closed Sunday and Monday. ~ 57-H 8th Street, Steamboat Springs; 970-879-9939. MODERATE TO DELUXE.

**SHOPPING**

In Steamboat Springs you'll find fine art of the American West at **Two Rivers Gallery,** 56 9th Street; 970-879-0044. **Indian Art of Steamboat** features Indian jewelry. ~ 635 Lincoln Avenue, Steamboat Springs; 970-870-8481. The **Artisans Market of Steamboat** exhibits a wide range of Colorado arts, crafts and antiques. ~ 626 Lincoln Avenue, Steamboat Springs; 970-879-7152. **Mountain Traditions** features wood carvings, prints, sculptures and home furnishings in wildlife motifs. ~ 833 Lincoln Avenue, Steamboat Springs; 970-870-7976. An intriguing place to browse is the **Fair Exchange Company,** a long-established general store that carries everything from Western memorabilia to antiques from around the world. ~ 54 9th Street, Steamboat Springs; 970-879-3511.

**NIGHTLIFE**

In ski season, live rock and reggae are featured at **Heavenly Daze,** a vast, 4000-square-foot brewpub at the foot of the ski mountain. ~ 1360 Ski Time Square, Steamboat Springs; 970-879-8080. In the same shopping center, **The Tugboat** has been serving up televised sports in a country-and-western atmosphere on weekdays and live rock and blues on weekends since 1973. ~ 970-879-7070. **Levelz,** the biggest danceclub in town, features live music every night of the week. ~ 1860 Ski Time Square; 970-870-9090.

### A LOCAL INSTITUTION

A local downtown favorite for breakfast or lunch, **Winona's** serves traditional American food for breakfast, lunch and dinner as well as specialty coffees. This casual café doubles as a bakery, so house specialties include homemade muffins, cinnamon rolls and scones. Other breakfast choices include Belgian waffles, eggs Benedict and huevos rancheros. Lunch features design-your-own hoagie sandwiches, homemade soups and salads. ~ 617 South Lincoln Avenue, Steamboat Springs; 970-879-2483. BUDGET.

**PARKS**

**STAGECOACH STATE PARK**

Stagecoach Reservoir on the Yampa River is the closest recreational lake to Steamboat Springs and provides the most convenient public camping for visitors to the area. The lake is surrounded by hilly native grasslands with distant views of the mountains around Steamboat Springs. Waterskiing and fishing are the main activities, and a hiking trail traces the entire undeveloped south shoreline. Fishing is good for rainbow and Snake River cutthroat trout. Facilities include picnic areas, restrooms, a marina with boat rentals, phones and groceries. Day-use fee, $5. ~ Located 16 miles south of Steamboat Springs via Route 131 and County Road 14; 970-736-2436; www.parks.state.co.us/stagecoach.

Permitted in 92 RV/tent sites (62 sites have electrical hookups); $6 to $14 per night.

**STEAMBOAT LAKE AND PEARL LAKE STATE PARKS**

Located on the pine-clad slopes of Hahn's Peak near the Continental Divide, Steamboat Lake State Park is a popular recreational area for fishing, boating, windsurfing and waterskiing. Smaller, older Pearl Lake State Park, five miles away, is also administered by the Steamboat Lake State Park office. Pearl Lake is set aside for wakeless boating and fly-fishing and lure fishing. Fishing is good for rainbow trout in Steamboat Lake and cutthroat in Pearl Lake. Facilities include picnic areas, restrooms, a marina with rentals and a nature trail. Day-use fee, $5. ~ Both parks are located 24 miles north of Steamboat Springs on paved County Road 129; 970-879-3922; www.parks.state.co.us/steamboat, www.parks.state.co.us/pearl.

Don't get confused if a ranger uses the term "browse." In the wilderness context, it means the shrubs eaten by elk and deer, and has nothing to do with shopping.

There are 198 RV/tent sites (44 with electric hookups) and five camping cabins at Steamboat Lake and 39 RV/tent sites (no hookups) at Pearl Lake; $12 to $16 per night. Yurts and camping cabins are available at $60 a night. Reservations: 800-678-2267.

**ROUTT NATIONAL FOREST** This 1,127,000-acre expanse of forest and high grasslands virtually surrounds Steamboat Springs. It includes the Mount Zirkel Wilderness, one of the first wilderness areas created in Colorado, with its steep, rugged bare granite pinnacles and lush valleys along the Elk and Encampment rivers. Also within the Routt National Forest boundaries are parts of the Flattop Wilderness and the Never Summer Wilderness. Fishing is good for several trout species in streams and alpine lakes. Facilities include picnic areas, restrooms and hiking trails. ~ Main forest access is from the Rabbit Ears Pass area on Route

40 southeast of Steamboat Springs, and from Forest Road 400, which follows the Elk River east from the main road to Steamboat Lake, ending in the main trailhead for the Mount Zirkel Wilderness. Walton Creek Campground is near Rabbit Ears Pass, 18 miles from Steamboat Springs on Route 40. Summit Lake Campground is four miles north of town on County Road 36 and then 13 miles northeast on Forest Road 60; 970-879-1870.

▲ Seven national forest campgrounds in the area include Walton Creek Campground, with 16 RV/tent sites, closed October through June, $10 per night; and Summit Lake Campground, with 8 RV/tent sites and 8 tent-only sites, no drinking water, closed November through June, $10 per night.

▼▼▼▼▼▼▼▼▼▼▼▼

## Outdoor Adventures

### RIVER RUNNING

**BRECKENRIDGE**    The unique **Whitewater Kayak Park**, a free municipal practice area on the Blue River adjacent to the Breckenridge Recreation Center at the north end of town, features splash rocks and other water challenges for all skill levels. ~ 970-453-1734.

**VAIL AREA**    In the Vail area, there is whitewater rafting during the spring runoff (May to mid-July) on the **Eagle River**, which runs among forests of cottonwoods and through the farmlands of the Vail Valley. Half-day and all-day trips are offered by **Timberline Tours** (P.O. Box 131, Vail, CO 81658; 970-476-1414, 800-831-1414; www.timberlinetours.com, e-mail info@timberline tours.com) and **Lakota River Guides** (Lionshead Circle, Vail; 970-845-7238, 800-274-0626; www.lakotariver.com). Both companies also run wetter, wilder raft trips on the rapids of the Colorado River above Glenwood Springs.

**ASPEN AREA**    In Aspen, whitewater enthusiasts run the Roaring Fork River, an exhilarating half-day or all-day trip from sheer-walled red rock canyons to lush evergreen forests. Raft and inflatable kayak trips on the Roaring Fork River are operated by **Colorado Riff Raft**. ~ 555 East Durant Avenue; 970-925-5405, 800-759-3939. **Blazing Adventures** offers a similar selection of rafting trips, but no kayaks. ~ P.O. Box 5068, Snowmass Village, CO 81615; 970-923-4544, 800-282-7238; www.blazingadven tures.com. The **Aspen Kayak School** offers classes for all skill levels on the Roaring Fork River, from one-day and weekend classes to full week-long courses. ~ P.O. Box 1520, Aspen, CO 81612; 970-925-4433; www.aspenkayak.com.

**STEAMBOAT SPRINGS AREA**    Raft trips on the Yampa around Steamboat Springs can be mild or wild depending on the season. Make arrangements through **Moving Mountains Inc.** ~ 2774 Burgess Creek Road, Steamboat Springs; 970-923-4544, 800-282-7238; www.movingmountains.com. **Canyon Canoeing Adventures**

offers guided canoe trips for all skill levels on the upper Colorado, Blue and Yampa rivers. ~ P.O. Box 775363, Steamboat Springs, CO 80477; 888-992-2663.

**BALLOON RIDES & GLIDING**

**ASPEN AREA** Adventures Aloft II (970-925-9497) and Unicorn Balloon Company (970-925-5752) offer hot-air balloon flights over the Aspen area and alpine elk range. Aspen is also the only place in Colorado where you can experience paragliding, a hybrid between skydiving and hang gliding that involves leaping off a mountaintop with a steerable rectangular parachute. Call the **Aspen Paragliding School.** ~ 426 South Spring Street, Aspen; 970-925-7625.

**STEAMBOAT SPRINGS AREA** In Steamboat Springs, balloon trips offered by **Balloons over Steamboat** (P.O. Box 880377, Steamboat Springs, CO 80477; 970-879-3298) and **Pegasus Balloon Tours** (970-879-9191) afford panoramic views of the area from the Flattop Wilderness to Wyoming's Snowy Range.

**DOWNHILL SKIING**

**WINTER PARK–GRAND LAKE AREA** Winter Park Resort is a large ski area covering five mountains. Even though Winter Park has 22 chairlifts with a total capacity of 35,030 skiers an hour, it is often crowded, especially on weekends, because of its nearness to Denver. There are no snowboarding restrictions, and a half-pipe run is for snowboarders only. ~ 239 Winter Park Drive, Winter Park; 970-726-5514, 800-979-0332; www.skiwinterpark.com.

An alternative is the smaller **Silver Creek Golf & Ski Ranch** near Granby. With a vertical drop of 1000 feet and five lifts, Silver Creek offers 33 trails from beginner to advanced, and welcomes snowboarders, snow bikers and tubers. ~ Route 40, Silver Creek; 970-887-3384, 800-757-7669; www.silvercreekski.com. Both ski areas are open Thanksgiving through March.

Near the small ranching center of Fraser, you can rent a giant inner tube and bounce down steep, powdery slopes at the **Fraser Valley Tubing Hill.** ~ Route 40, Fraser; 970-726-5954.

**BRECKENRIDGE AREA** Several major downhill ski areas are located along the Loveland Pass Road (Route 6), which diverges from Route 70 just east of the Eisenhower Memorial Tunnel and rejoins the interstate at Silverthorne.

**Loveland Basin** and **Loveland Valley,** just off Route 70 and 12 miles from Georgetown, receive the second-highest snowfall in the Colorado Rockies—400 inches in an average year. With 11 chairlifts and a vertical drop of 2410 feet, this moderate-size ski area offers 17 percent beginner, 42 percent intermediate and 41 percent advanced slopes. The terrain park keeps boarders happy with natural half pipes and large carving bowls. The slopes are open from mid-November to early April. ~ Route 6; 303-571-5580, 800-736-3754; www.skiloveland.com.

On the other side of 11,992-foot Loveland Pass, **Arapahoe Basin** is America's highest ski area and one of Colorado's first, built in 1946. The highest lift reaches an elevation of 12,450 feet above sea level. With five chairlifts and a vertical drop of 2250 feet, "A-Basin" (as Coloradoans have nicknamed it) may not be among the region's largest ski areas, but it is certainly one of the most dramatic. The slope is so steep it looks almost like a sheer, snowpacked cliff, and 85 percent of the terrain is rated intermediate to advanced. Snowboarding is allowed. The mogul fields at Arapahoe Basin are legendary. A-Basin is open from mid-November to early April. ~ Route 6; 970-468-0718, 888-272-7246; www.arapahoebasin.com.

Its proximity to Denver, plus an absence of lodging at the slopes, means Loveland Basin and Valley is used mainly by Denverites; it is very crowded on weekends but nearly empty on weekdays.

**Keystone Resort** doesn't look like much from the road; steep, tree-covered slopes conceal most of the ski trails higher up the mountain and on its back side, accessible on two gondolas and four chairlifts. The vertical drop is 2580 feet. Only 8 percent of the ski area is suitable for beginners, while 55 percent is rated intermediate and 37 percent expert. There is a snowboarding park, and a large ski school offers downhill and cross-country lessons for kids and adults of all skill levels. Operated by the same management as Arapahoe Basin, Keystone is open from mid-November to late April. ~ Route 6; 970-496-2316, 877-625-1556; www.keystone.snow.com.

The most impressive ski slopes in these parts are at **Breckenridge Ski Area**. Breckenridge covers three mountains with an interconnected trail network served by 23 lifts. About 15 percent of the trails are rated for beginners, 28 percent intermediate and 57 percent advanced and expert. The back bowl of Peak 8 offers the highest-altitude in-bounds skiing in the world (3398-foot vertical drop). The season runs from Thanksgiving to mid-March. ~ Breckenridge; 970-453-5000; www.breckenridge.com.

**VAIL AREA**    The Vail Valley reigns as the world's largest ski development, with a total lift capacity of more than 61,000 skiers per hour. The season runs from Thanksgiving through March.

**Vail Ski Area** alone spans seven miles of mountainside, served by one gondola and 18 chairlifts. The vertical drop is 3360 feet. The front side of the mountain is well balanced for all skill levels, while the much larger bowl area on the back side of the mountain is nearly 90 percent advanced or expert. Snowboarding is permitted. ~ Vail; 970-476-5601; www.vail.com.

Just west of Vail, the **Beaver Creek Ski Area** surpasses Vail in height, with a vertical drop of 4040 feet. Its trails are challenging, but well-distributed for all ski levels. Fourteen lifts cover 1625 acres of skiable terrain. Snowboards have a choice between two terrain parks. ~ Avon; 970-845-9090, 888-830-7669; www. beavercreek.snow.com.

**LEADVILLE AREA**   Leadville's little-known downhill ski area, located ten miles north of town on Tennessee Pass, is **Ski Cooper**. It has two chairlifts and a vertical drop of 1200 feet. Trails are 30 percent beginner, 40 percent intermediate and 30 percent advanced, and there's a backcountry ski bowl plus a snowboard park. Open Thanksgiving through early April. ~ Route 24; 719-486-2277; www.skicooper.com.

**ASPEN AREA**   Aspen has four ski mountains in a row, all under the same management—Aspen Mountain, Aspen Highlands, Buttermilk and Snowmass. Lift tickets are good for any of the mountains. The most expensive ski areas in the United States, in 1996 Aspen's slopes became the first to break the $50 mark for one-day lift tickets. The season for all Aspen ski areas runs from Thanksgiving to the end of March. ~ 970-925-1220, 800-525-6200; www.aspensnowmass.com.

**Aspen Mountain**, the original Aspen ski area, sprawls in plain view just a few blocks from the center of town. With a vertical drop of 3267 feet, it is served by a gondola and seven chairlifts. The 76 trails are not for the faint-hearted: a third of the runs are expert-only, and there are no beginner slopes. Snowboarding is prohibited on Aspen Mountain, though it is allowed on all other Aspen–Snowmass area ski slopes.

**Aspen Highlands** is about the same size as Aspen Mountain, and taller, with a vertical drop of 3635 feet. Although most of the ski area is not visible from below, four chairlifts carry skiers up to the higher reaches of the ski area and a number of challenging ski trails.

**AUTHOR FAVORITE**

There are plenty of good reasons to get into cross-country skiing. Unlike the downhill variety, it's inexpensive, and instead of long lift lines you can enjoy solitude. But my number-one reason is that there are so many great cross-country trails in the Colorado Rockies that you can ski every winter weekend of your life and never visit the same place twice. For the ultimate cross-country adventure, fill up your backpack and spend several days ski-touring the 300-mile **10th Mountain Division Trail System** between Aspen, Vail and Leadville, overnighting in mountain huts. ~ 1280 Ute Avenue, Aspen; 970-925-5775; www.huts.org. See page 180 for more information.

**Buttermilk Mountain,** the smallest of the Aspen ski mountains, is a good midsize ski area in its own right, with seven chairlifts and a vertical drop of 2030 feet. Touting itself as the "premier learning mountain," Buttermilk's trails are balanced for all skill levels—35 percent beginner, 39 percent intermediate and 26 percent advanced.

**Snowmass** is the largest of the Aspen ski areas, nearly as large in area and lift capacity as all the other three combined. Its vertical drop is 4406 feet. It has 20 chairlifts. Its trails are 7 percent beginner, 55 percent intermediate, 18 percent advanced and 20 percent expert.

**STEAMBOAT SPRINGS AREA**    **Steamboat Ski Area** ranks third among Colorado ski areas, after Vail and Aspen. From its deceptively compact base, the big eight-passenger gondola and 19 chairlifts carry skiers up a long ridgeline to trails that cover four mountainsides. The vertical drop is 3668 feet. The trails are 13 percent beginner, 56 percent intermediate and 31 percent advanced. There is a half-pipe run for snowboarders only. ~ 2305 Mount Werner Circle, Steamboat Springs; 970-879-6111, 877-237-2628; www. steamboat.com.

**Ski Rentals**    Among the many ski-rental shops in Winter Park are **Sport Stalker** (Cooper Creek Square; 970-726-8873) and **Flanagan's Ski Rentals** (Route 40; 970-867-2554); both rent cross-country and downhill skis as well as snowboards. In Grand Lake, **Never Summer Mountain Products** rents cross-country skis. ~ 919 Grand Avenue; 970-627-3642.

The Breckenridge area has an overwhelming number of ski-rental shops. For downhill skis, snowboards and cross-country skis, check out **Wilderness Sports** (171 Route 9, Silverthorne; 970-468-5017), **Virgin Islands Ski Rental** (Summit Place Shopping Center, Silverthorne; 970-468-6655), **Mountain View Sports** (22869 Route 6, Keystone; 970-468-0396) and **Rebel Sports** (520 South Main Street, Breckenridge; 970-453-2565). You'll find Nordic equipment at **Mountain Outfitters**. ~ 112 South Ridge Street, Breckenridge; 970-453-2201.

Downhill skis and snowboards are for rent at **Base Mountain Sports**. ~ Landmark Building, Vail; 970-476-4875. **American Ski Exchange** also rents skis and boards. ~ 225 Wall Street, Vail; 970-476-1477. Several ski and snowboard rental shops cluster around the base of Lionshead Gondola, including **Vail SkiTech**. ~ 555 East Lionshead Circle; 970-477-2812, 800-525-5995.

In Steamboat Springs, downhill skis are for rent at **Sport Stalker**. ~ 1835 Central Park Plaza; 970-879-1250. Both alpine and Nordic equipment are available at **Ski Haus**. ~ Pine Grove Road; 970-879-0385. **One Stop Ski Shop** rents downhill and cross-country skis plus snowshoes and snowboards. ~ 729 Yampa Avenue; 970-879-4916.

**CROSS-COUNTRY SKIING**

**WINTER PARK–GRAND LAKE AREA**　More than 60 miles of groomed cross-country ski trails cut through deep evergreen forest and along ridgelines with spectacular mountain views north of Winter Park at **Devil's Thumb Ranch**. ~ County Road 83, Tabernash; 970-726-5632. The **SilverCreek Nordic Center** has three miles of easy, scenic groomed and tracked ski trails and a telemarking slope. ~ Route 40, SilverCreek; 970-887-3384. At Grand Lake, cross-country skiing trails are found at the **Grand Lake Touring Center**. ~ Grand Lake Golf Course; 970-627-8008. They can also be found throughout Rocky Mountain National Park.

**BRECKENRIDGE AREA**　There are 20 miles of challenging groomed trail designed by Olympic silver medalist Bill Koch at the **Frisco Nordic Center**, which also offers lessons and rentals. ~ Frisco; 303-668-0866. **Keystone Cross-Country Center**'s 18 miles of groomed trails include the expert-rated Mountain Top Trail, reached via the ski slope gondola for an additional charge. The center also offers telemarking lessons. ~ Keystone; 970-496-4275. There are also 20 miles of groomed, tracked trails through the pine forest at **Breckenridge Nordic Ski Center**, Colorado's oldest public cross-country ski area. ~ 1200 Ski Hill Road, Breckenridge; 970-453-6855.

**VAIL AREA**　Groomed cross-country ski trail networks include the nine-mile course at **Vail Nordic Center**, which is perfect for snow skating. ~ 1778 Vail Valley Drive, Vail; 970-476-8366. Or ski naked at **Vail Nature Center**'s eight miles of groomed trails. ~ 601 Vail Valley Drive, Vail; 970-479-2291. With 12 miles of trails, Vail's **Golden Peak Nordic Sports Center** offers a gourmet cross-country ski tour with hot drinks, appetizers, entrées and desserts served along the route. ~ Vail Golf Course, Vail; 970-476-3210. Another option is the **Cordillera Nordic Center**, which has more than a dozen loops for varying ski levels off a main ski trail surrounding an exclusive subdivision and golf course. ~ The Lodge at Cordillera, Edwards; 970-926-2200. The 11-mile **Shrine Pass Road**, which starts at Vail Pass and winds up in Redcliff (arrange to have a vehicle waiting at the end), is among the area's best cross-country ski trails.

**LEADVILLE AREA**　**Piney Creek Nordic Center** has 24 miles of groomed trails and a 300-acre telemarking slope. ~ Route 24, Leadville; 719-486-1750.

The **10th Mountain Huts** provides a network of more than 300 miles of trails linking Vail, Leadville and Aspen. Along the way you can stay in mountain huts (reservations required). Located between 9700 and 11,700 feet, the budget-priced huts sleep up to

16 people and are fairly primitive (you'll have to bring your own sleeping bag; water comes from streams or melted snow). There are wood-burning stoves (kitchen supplies are provided). For maps, organized tour information and hut reservations, contact 10th Mountain Division Trail Association. ~ 1280 Ute Avenue, Aspen; 970-925-5775, fax 970-925-5317; www.huts.org, e-mail huts@huts.org.

**ASPEN AREA**    Groomed cross-country trails are found at the **Aspen Cross-Country Ski and Snowshoe Center.** ~ 39551 West Route 82; 970-544-9246. Another Nordic ski area, **Ashcroft Ski Touring Center** has trails that loop around a historic mining ghost town. ~ Castle Creek Road; 970-925-1044.

**STEAMBOAT SPRINGS AREA**    For cross-country skiers, the favorite area near Steamboat Springs is the maze of roads and trails from the vicinity of **Rabbit Ears Pass** in Routt National Forest. **Hahn's Peak** is another popular cross-country area. There are groomed Nordic trails at **Steamboat Ski Touring Center.** ~ Mount Werner Road, Steamboat Springs; 970-879-8180. Or try the small **Howelsen Hill Ski Area.** ~ Steamboat Springs; 970-879-8499.

For information on renting equipment, see the ski-rental section in "Downhill Skiing" above.

**WINTER PARK–GRAND LAKE AREA**    Near Winter Park, the public 18-hole **Pole Creek Golf Club** is the only golf course in Middle Park. Club rentals are available, and the views of the Continental Divide from every hole are impressive. ~ Route 140; 970-726-8847. Built by local golf enthusiasts in the '60s, the 18-hole championship **Grand Lake Golf Course** features challenging narrow fairways nearly 8500 feet above sea level. ~ 1415 County Road 48, Grand Lake; 970-627-8008.

**GOLF**

It is not uncommon to see elk, moose and bears ambling across the greens at Grand Lake Golf Course.

**BRECKENRIDGE AREA**    The **Keystone Ranch Golf Club,** designed by Robert Trent Jones, Jr., is open to nonguests who reserve tee times at least four days ahead. It features a front nine flanked by evergreen forest and a back nine in open meadows with many water hazards. Carts are required, and included in the greens fee. ~ 1437 County Road 150, Keystone; 970-496-4250. Not to be outdone, the **Breckenridge Golf Club** had its course designed by Jack Nicklaus. The terrain of the mountainous 27-hole course is exceptionally varied, and it may be the only place where golfers have to watch out for beaver-pond water hazards. Cart and club rentals are available. ~ 200 Clubhouse Drive, Breckenridge; 970-453-9104.

**VAIL AREA**    A creek meanders the length of the 18-hole **Vail Golf Club,** one of the longest-established courses in the Vail area.

The public course has cart and club rentals. ~ 1778 Vail Valley Drive, Vail; 970-479-2260. Flanked by White River National Forest and the Eagle River, the 18-hole **Eagle-Vail Golf Course** and adjacent nine-hole par-three **Willow Creek Golf Course** offer the best in mountain golfing. Carts are mandatory; players must provide their own clubs; lessons and clinics are available. ~ 431 Eagle Road, Avon; Vail Golf Course: 970-949-5267; Willow Creek Golf Course: 970-845-7273. Designed by Robert Trent Jones, Jr., the 18-hole, semiprivate **Beaver Creek Golf Course** is particularly challenging—some say brutal—on the first three holes. The course has cart and club rentals and exceptionally high green fees. ~ 103 Offerson Road, Beaver Creek; 970-845-5775.

**LEADVILLE AREA** The semiprivate 18-hole **Copper Creek Golf Club** is very mountainous and shorter than most, with a par of 70, many water hazards and abundant wildlife. Carts are mandatory, and clubs are available for rent. ~ 104 Wheeler Place, Copper Mountain; 970-458-8386. At 10,200 feet, the nine-hole **Mount Massive Golf Course** is North America's highest and has views of the two highest mountains in Colorado, Mount Massive and Mount Elbert. Club and cart rentals are available. ~ 259 County Road 5, Leadville; 719-486-2176.

Local tennis courts aren't lit for after-dark play because the cold night air tends to break the lights, which cool too quickly when they are turned off.

**ASPEN AREA** In Aspen, the 18-hole municipal **Aspen Golf Course** is designed as an environmentally sensitive, wildlife-friendly course. Carts and clubs are available for rent, along with just about everything else including golf shoes. There are also putting and chipping greens and a driving range. ~ 22475 West Route 82; 970-925-2145. The more expensive, privately owned golf course at the **Snowmass Lodge and Club**, designed by Arnold Palmer, is open to the public on a limited basis. ~ 239 Club Circle, Snowmass Village; 970-923-3148.

**STEAMBOAT SPRINGS AREA** Steamboat Springs has a nine-hole course with stands of trees and running water throughout at the **Steamboat Golf Club**. Carts and clubs are for rent. ~ Route 40; 970-879-4295. The very expensive **Sheraton Steamboat Golf Club** offers an 18-hole course designed by Robert Trent Jones, Jr., in a mountain setting with abundant deer and other wildlife. ~ 2000 Clubhouse Drive; 970-879-1391.

**TENNIS** In Grand Lake, there are two free public asphalt-surfaced tennis courts at the **Grand Lake Golf Course**. ~ 1415 County Road 48; 970-627-8328. In Breckenridge, there are seven hard-surfaced outdoor public tennis courts at the **Breckenridge Recreation Center** (880 Airport Road; 970-453-1734; fee) and two more in municipal **Carter Park** on High Street. There are also four clay municipal courts in Dillon's **Town Park.** ~ Reservations: 970-468-2403. Vail has 24 hard-surfaced public tennis courts, located in **Ford Park** on South Frontage Road and in the **Gold Peak, Lionshead** and **Booth Creek** town parks. In the Aspen area, 2 indoor and 11 outdoor asphalt tennis courts are open to the public for a steep fee at **Snowmass Lodge and Tennis Garden.** ~ Snowmass Village; 970-923-5600 ext. 5818. Steamboat Springs has three outdoor asphalt tennis courts, open in summer only, at the **Steamboat Springs Health and Recreation Association.** ~ 136 Lincoln Avenue; 970-879-1828.

**WINTER PARK–GRAND LAKE AREA**    In the Grand Lake area, you can rent horses for guided or solo trail rides in Rocky Mountain National Park at **Sombrero Stables.** ~ 304 West Portal Road, Grand Lake; 970-627-3514.

**RIDING STABLES**

**BRECKENRIDGE AREA**    In Breckenridge, guided trail rides and dinner rides are offered at **Breckenridge Stables** at the Peak 8 Fun Park. ~ 970-453-4438. Organized trail rides, including breakfast and dinner rides, through pine and aspen woods on a working cattle ranch surrounded by Arapaho National Forest are available in nearby Silverthorne at **Bar-T Outfitters.** ~ Ranch Road #0605; 970-468-6916.

**VAIL AREA**    In Vail, most horseback riding is in the form of guided rides and pack trips. **Beaver Creek Stables** outfits trail rides for groups of up to 60, ranging from an hour to all day, following the east ridge above Beaver Creek, and offers sleigh rides in winter. Reservations required. ~ Beaver Creek Resort, Avon; 970-845-7770. At **Spraddle Creek Ranch,** horses are available for trail rides only. Rides range from one to three hours, with destinations like Bald Mountain, Elk Springs and Bear Hollow. ~ Spraddle Creek Road, Vail; 970-476-6941.

**LEADVILLE AREA**    **Leadville Stables** rents horses for independent riding and offers guided trail rides into the high country. Many of the organized rides climb above timberline for magnificent views. ~ 131 North Route 91, Leadville; 719-486-1497.

**ASPEN AREA**    **Capitol Creek Outfitters** offers one- to four-hour guided trail rides around Snowmass Village as well as longer rides into the Maroon Bells and Capitol Peak wilderness areas. ~ Snowmass Village; 970-923-4402. Snowmass Stables offers riding lessons, guided trail rides, wilderness pack trips and backcountry fishing expeditions, as well as hay-wagon dinner rides and weekly rodeos. ~ P.O. Box 6088, Snowmass Village, CO 81615; 970-923-3075. Rocky Mountain Cattle Moo-vers, Inc. takes city slickers on day-long cattle drives in the foothills of Mount Sopris, including a steak lunch; they also rent horses for independent riding. ~ P.O. Box 457, Carbondale, CO 81623; 970-963-9666.

**STEAMBOAT SPRINGS AREA** A number of stables and guest ranches that rent horses to the public are located along the road from Steamboat Springs to Steamboat Lake. **Glen Eden Stables** has horses to rent for independent rides and offers guided one-hour to half-day trips through high country where elk are often seen. ~ 22090 County Road 60, Steamboat Springs; 970-879-0687. There are also guided rides at **Sunset Ranch**. ~ 42850 County Road 129, Steamboat Springs; 970-879-0954. **Steamboat Lake Outfitters** offers a full range of guided horseback tours of the mountains surrounding Steamboat Lake, from an hour to overnight and longer. ~ Steamboat Lake; 970-879-4404.

## BIKING

**WINTER PARK–GRAND LAKE AREA** The **Winter Park Mountain Bike Trail System** includes 500 miles of designated trails, eight major loop trips and access to hundreds of miles of logging roads in Arapaho National Forest north of Winter Park. The Grand Lake area has an extensive network of multiple-use trails that are ideal for mountain biking in surrounding areas of Arapaho National Forest.

**BRECKENRIDGE AREA** The favorite mountain-bike trail in the Breckenridge area is the **Peaks Trail** (9 miles), which runs between Breckenridge and Frisco along the Ten Mile Range. Breckenridge and Keystone chairlifts carry mountain bikers to summer trails high on the ski mountains.

**VAIL AREA** In the Vail area mountain bikes can be rented at Eagle's Nest above the **Lionshead Gondola** for riding on the upper ski trails. For road-bike touring, the **Vail Pass Bikeway** parallels the interstate over Vail Pass. The first half of the 40-mile trip is a grueling climb to the pass summit; from there, it's an unforgettable coast down the mountain in either direction—to Frisco or to Vail.

**LEADVILLE AREA** In recent years a growing number of mountain bikers have been discovering the old mining roads that surround Leadville. A number of four-wheel-drive roads, including the spectacular climb over **Mosquito Pass**, also offer mountain-biking challenges.

**ASPEN AREA** Around Aspen, you'll find the rugged trail where mountain biking got its start in the early 1980s—the **Pearl Pass Road**, which climbs from Ashcroft over the 12,700-foot pass and descends to Crested Butte. Easier trails are also found throughout the area.

**STEAMBOAT SPRINGS AREA** The most popular backcountry mountain-biking area around Steamboat Springs is the extensive national forest trail network accessed from trailheads at **Rabbit Ears Pass** on Route 40 southeast of town. For an easier ride, take the paved five-mile **Yampa River Trail** from Steamboat Village to downtown Steamboat Springs; you can continue on a good dirt road that follows the Yampa River for nine miles south of town.

**Bike Rentals**    In Winter Park, you can rent a mountain bike at **Winter Park Sports Shop**. ~ King's Crossing Shopping Center; 970-726-5554. Or visit **Slopeside Gear & Sport**. ~ Winter Park Base; 970-726-1664.

In Breckenridge, the equipment-rental shop at **Peak 8 Fun Park** rents mountain bikes during the summer months and on September weekends. ~ 970-453-5000.

In Leadville, **Bill's Sport Shop** rents mountain bikes and also organizes half-day and all-day group tours to the Twin Lakes area and Mosquito Pass. ~ 225 Harrison Avenue; 719-486-0739.

In Aspen, you can rent mountain bikes by the hour, day, week or month at **Aspen Velo Bike Shop**. ~ 465 North Mill; 970-925-1495. Aspen's oldest bicycle tour outfitters, **Timberline Bicycle Tours**, rents mountain bikes and organizes guided day trips to Ashcroft, Woody Creek and Hunter Creek, including transportation, equipment and food. They also offer three- and five-day hut-to-hut tours between Aspen and Vail. ~ Silver Queen Gondola; 970-925-3586.

For steep road touring in the Aspen area, try the Maroon Lake Road, closed to private motor vehicles in the summer months but open to cyclists.

Mountain bikes, as well as kids' bikes and inline skates, can be rented in Vail at **Vail Bike Tech**. ~ 555 Lionsahead Circle; 800-525-5995. **Venture Sports** rents blades and bikes, too, and can put customers in touch with area mountain-bike tour guides. ~ Avon; 970-949-1318.

In Steamboat Springs, mountain bikes and kids' bikes are for rent at **Sore Saddle Cyclery**, where the shop's staff delights in helping customers plan individually customized rides. ~ 1136 Yampa Avenue; 970-879-1675. **Ski Haus** can also meet your rental needs for mountain bikes, cross bikes, kids' bikes and tandems, along with maps and information on where to ride. ~ 1450 South Lincoln Avenue; 970-879-0385.

All distances listed for hiking trails are one way unless otherwise noted.

## HIKING

**WINTER PARK–GRAND LAKE AREA**    In the Grand Lake area you'll find trailheads for several spectacular, uncrowded trails on the west side of Rocky Mountain National Park. Among the prettiest is the **Cascade Falls Trail** (3.5 miles), which starts near the park visitors center just north of Grand Lake and makes an easy 300-foot ascent to the waterfalls. Farther north in the park, the **Lulu City Trail** (3 miles) leads to old mines and the ghost town of Lulu City. Nearby, the challenging **Timber Lake Trail** (5 miles) climbs more than 2000 feet from marshy meadows to alpine lakes and tundra.

**GEORGETOWN AREA**   You can climb to the twin summits of **Grays Peak and Torreys Peak** on a five-mile trail starting from a marked trailhead on Stevens Gulch Road west of Georgetown. One of the easiest ways to climb to the summit of a 14,000-foot mountain is to hike the **Mount Bierstadt Trail** (2.5 miles) from Guanella Pass above Georgetown.

**BRECKENRIDGE AREA**   Above Breckenridge, Blue Lakes Road near the summit of Hoosier Pass leads to the 2.5-mile hiking trail that leads to the summit of 14,264-foot **Quandary Peak**.

**VAIL AREA**   Near Vail, the **Booth Lake Trail** climbs from a trailhead parking lot beside Route 70 for two miles to 60-foot-high Booth Creek Falls and then climbs for four more miles to Booth Lake in the Eagle's Nest Wilderness. A six-mile trail from the end of Forest Road 707 near Minturn climbs to the 14,003-foot summit of **Mount of the Holy Cross** in the heart of the Holy Cross Wilderness.

The Keystone Resort operates a chairlift for hikers and sightseers during the summer.

**LEADVILLE AREA**   The challenging six-mile hike from the Elbert Creek campground near Turquoise Lake west of Leadville takes you to the 14,421-foot summit of **Mount Massive**, following the Colorado Trail for the first part of the way.

**ASPEN AREA**   In the Aspen area, the popular **East Maroon Creek Trail** (8.5 miles) from Maroon Lake goes to the top of 11,280-foot East Maroon Pass; you can walk as far as you like and return to the lake by the same route. You may wish to plan an expedition with **Town Taxi** (Aspen; 970-349-5543), on which you take the 13-mile, seven- to ten-hour hike from Maroon Lake over East Maroon Pass to the ghost town of Gothic; then a shuttle picks you up, takes you to Crested Butte for the night and returns you to Aspen the next day. You can arrange for your lodging, or they can help you make arrangements as part of the package. Another classic Aspen-area hike is the **Conundrum Creek Trail** (9 miles) to Conundrum Hot Springs, starting from Castle Creek Road.

**STEAMBOAT SPRINGS AREA**   One of the first wilderness areas in Colorado, the Mount Zirkel Wilderness northeast of Steamboat Springs has an extensive trail network that can be accessed from the Slavonia trailhead at the end of Forest Road 400, which turns off County Road 129 south of Steamboat Lake. A magnificent day hike from this trailhead is the **Gilpin Lake Trail** (4 miles), a moderate hike to a 10,000-foot alpine lake.

## Transportation

### CAR

All major areas described in this chapter lie within an hour's drive of **Route 70**. To reach Winter Park, take **Route 40** north from the Empire exit; turn off on **Route 34** at Granby to reach Grand Lake. For Breckenridge, turn off south on **Route 9** at Frisco. Leadville can be reached either from the Copper Mountain exit via **Route 91** or from Vail via **Route 24**. Aspen can be reached via **Route 82** either from the east over Independence Pass from Leadville (closed in winter) or from Glenwood Springs to the west. Three highways—Route 40 from Winter Park; Route 9 north from Silverthorne; or **Route 131** north from Wolcott, at the west end of the Vail Valley—lead to Steamboat Springs.

**AIR**

United Express and Continental Express both have frequent flights from Denver International Airport to Aspen's **Pitkin County Airport,** and both airlines offer a few flights from other U.S. cities. American Airlines and America West Airlines offer direct flights to the **Vail–Beaver Creek Jet Center**. Located about 25 miles west of Steamboat Springs in the town of Hayden, the **Yampa Valley Regional Airport** has commuter service from Denver on Continental Express.

**TRAIN**

The **Rio Grande Ski Train** runs directly from Denver to Winter Park on winter weekends and on Saturdays from mid-June to mid-August. ~ 303-296-4754; www.skitrain.com. **Amtrak** offers passenger service to Winter Park and Granby on the "California Zephyr" or the "Desert Wind." Following the most scenic route on the Amtrak system, the trains run through the Vail Valley but don't stop until they reach Glenwood Springs. ~ 800-872-7245; www.amtrak.com.

**BUS**

**Greyhound** offers bus service to Winter Park (Vasquez Road; 970-726-4118), Aspen (Rubey Park Transportation Center; 970-925-8484), Vail (Vail Transportation Center; 970-476-5137) and Steamboat Springs (500 South Lincoln; 970-879-0866). ~ 800-229-9424; www.greyhound.com.

**CAR RENTALS**

In Aspen, you'll find **Alamo Rent A Car** (800-462-5266), **Eagle Rent A Car** (800-282-2128), **Thrifty Car Rental** (800-847-4389), **National Car Rental** (800-227-7368) and other car-rental desks at the Pitkin County Airport. Four-wheel-drive vehicles are available at **Rocky Mountain Rent A Car**. ~ Aspen; 800-525-2880.

Car rentals are available from **Hertz Rent A Car** (800-654-3131) at the Vail–Beaver Creek Jet Center in Eagle.

**Avis Rent A Car** (800-331-1212), **Budget Rent A Car** (800-527-0700) and **Hertz Rent A Car** (800-654-3131) are located at the Yampa Valley Regional Airport near Steamboat Springs.

**PUBLIC TRANSIT**

**The Lift** provides free summer and winter shuttle service among the hotels, shopping areas and ski slopes of Winter Park. ~ 970-726-4118.

The **Town Trolley** provides shuttle service around Brecken-ridge. ~ 970-547-3140. The free **Summit Stage** carries passengers throughout the area of Frisco, Dillon, Silverthorne/Keystone, Copper Mountain and Breckenridge. ~ 970-668-0999.

**Vail Transit** offers free shuttle service around Vail. **Avon–Beaver Creek Transit** (970-748-4120) provides public transportation throughout the Avon–Beaver Creek area.

The **Eagle County Regional Transportation Authority** runs morning and evening shuttle service to Vail and Beaver Creek, where many Leadville residents work. ~ Leadville Food Town; 970-328-3520.

**Roaring Fork Transit Authority** offers free shuttle service in Aspen and runs commuter buses to Snowmass, Basalt, Car-bondale and Glenwood Springs. ~ Rubey Park; 970-925-8484.

**Steamboat Springs Transit** operates regularly scheduled free shuttle service between downtown Steamboat Springs and the ski area. ~ 970-879-3717.

**TAXIS**

**Home James Taxi Service** provides taxi service in the Winter Park area. ~ 970-726-5060. In Breckenridge, call **Rainbow Taxi** for taxi and limousine service. ~ 970-453-8294. Local transporta-tion in Aspen is provided by **High Mountain Taxi**. ~ 970-925-8294. **Aspen Limo** offers scheduled shuttle service to Aspen's Pitkin County Airport, the Glenwood Springs Amtrak station and Denver International Airport, all twice daily in the winter and summer seasons and once daily in the off-seasons. ~ 970-948-5466. **Vail Valley Taxi** serves the Vail area. ~ 970-476-8294. **Alpine Taxi** (970-879-2800) serves Steamboat Springs.

# Northwestern Colorado

An unpaved road winds through ancient forests, past jumbles of fractured lava rock, among pristine lakes dancing with rainbow trout. It is a broad, nearly level landscape, high enough to be chilly even in midsummer, and except for a few roads like this one, seemingly untouched by civilization. The road ends at the rim of the mesa, and from there you can look off across the farmlands of the Colorado River Valley a mile below and the sandstone and slickrock desert that stretches from there far into Utah. It's like standing on a rocky headland along the coast of a very large yet uninhabited island overlooking an ocean that, a few million years ago, somehow drained away.

Hot springs, secret waterfalls, dinosaur bones, majestic mesa tops and redrock canyonlands—these are a few of the hidden pleasures that await the adventurous traveler who takes time to explore the northwestern corner of Colorado, one of the state's least-visited regions. Tell the folks back home (even if home is as close as the Denver metro area) that you're planning a trip to Grand Mesa, the Flat Tops Wilderness, Browns Park and the Gates of Lodore, and they'll most likely respond with blank stares. Most of northwestern Colorado is far enough removed from both major population centers and popular tourist areas so that if you visit the region at any time of year except the autumn hunting season (which is considered peak season in these parts), you're likely to find yourself completely alone with nature.

The two main towns in the region are Glenwood Springs, a long-established spa resort that has grown in popularity thanks to its proximity to both the trendy Aspen scene and the spectacular scenery of Glenwood Canyon, and Grand Junction, the nontouristy commercial center for the fruit-growing communities that line the banks of the Colorado River. Located 90 miles apart on Route 70, they are the only towns of any size in an area larger than Connecticut, Massachusetts and New Hampshire combined.

In fact, a look at a road map would lead most people to believe that the northwestern quadrant of Colorado is completely empty and featureless. It is the purpose of this chapter to show that this impression is not exactly accurate. This is a landscape full of natural wonders concealed by canyons and mesas as wild and remote as they are beautiful—all in all, the most hidden part of "Hidden Colorado."

# Glenwood Springs Area

Glenwood Springs has had a roller-coaster career as a resort town since the 1880s, when Aspen silver tycoon Jerome B. Wheeler built a hot-springs spa there. He hoped to attract wealthy easterners and Europeans, but the resort soon became a rough-edged playground for the wealthier denizens of nearby mining towns like Aspen and Leadville. Alongside the grand Colorado Hotel, the elegant bathhouse and the polo field stood some of the finest gambling casinos in the West and no fewer than 22 saloons.

Glenwood Springs' popularity waned by the 1920s, though in the '30s it gained notoriety as a mountain hideaway for Al Capone and other gangsters. Until as recently as the 1970s it remained a low-budget party town where college students flocked on weekends. The recreation boom that transformed other nearby towns pretty much bypassed Glenwood Springs until the past few years, when the wave of big-money tourism that poured out of Aspen to create such upscale bedroom communities as Carbondale finally washed over Glenwood Springs like a fresh coat of paint. Now a popular weekend destination for Denverites as well as an easy day trip from Vail, Glenwood Springs is once again one of Colorado's liveliest mountain towns.

**SIGHTS**

The center of the action is **Glenwood Hot Springs**, with the world's largest hot-spring pool: it's 92° to 94°F, two blocks long, holds 1000 bathers and has a water slide. There is also a smaller, hot tub–temperature (104°) therapeutic pool. Lockers and towels are provided, and a shop beside the locker rooms sells bathing suits. Although the pools are outdoors, they are open until 10 p.m. year-round. Admission. ~ 401 North River Street, Glenwood Springs; 970-945-2846.

A short distance from the hot springs is **Yampah Spa and Vapor Caves**, geothermally heated steam baths in three natural caves—two for men and one, the largest, for women. The Ute Indians are said to have revered the caves for their healing powers. The vapor caves feature soft, spacey music; additional amenities include massages and individual hot tubs. Admission. ~ 709 East 6th Street, Glenwood Springs; 970-945-0667.

Glenwood Springs' newest visitor attraction, **Glenwood Caverns** includes a historic old-time tourist sight formerly known as Fairy Caves that was open to the public from 1895 to 1917. Forty years later, spelunkers found a small hole in the wall of Fairy Caves and squeezed through it to discover what is believed to be the

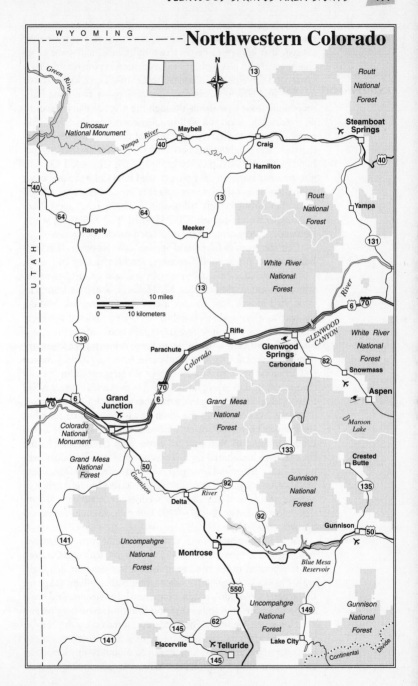

# Northwestern Colorado

second-longest cave in Colorado (the longest, Moaning Cave near the east end of Glenwood Canyon, is not developed for public access). It is known to be over two miles long, and some of its chambers are 50 feet high. It has never been explored to the end. Glenwood Caverns was reopened to sightseers on a limited basis in 1999 and now presents two tour options—a two-hour, half-mile family tour that winds through the original Fairy Caves to an overlook high on the wall of Glenwood Canyon and a wild four-hour tour into rarely seen areas of the cave, on which participants wear lighted helmets and the guides are expert spelunkers. Shuttle vans pick up groups at the Glenwood Caverns gift shop and museum next door to the Hotel Colorado and carry them three miles up the mountainside to the cave entrance. Closed December through April. Admission. ~ 51000 Two Rivers Plaza Road, Glenwood Springs; 970-945-4228, 800-530-1635; www. glenwoodcaverns.com, e-mail info@glenwoodcaverns.com.

One memento of Glenwood Springs' colorful past is **Doc Holliday's grave** in Linwood Cemetery, reached by foot trail from Cemetery Road, two blocks east of the Chamber of Commerce, which is located along Route 82. Holliday, a dentist from Virginia, had moved west to seek a cure for tuberculosis. Making his way as a professional gambler, he gained national notoriety as the subject of a best-selling paperback book, *My Friend, Doc Holliday*, written by lawman Wyatt Earp. Following the legendary gunfight at the OK Corral in Tombstone, Arizona, Holliday moved to Glenwood Springs, where he spent the last year of his life and then succumbed to tuberculosis. Buried in the same cemetery is Kid Curry (a.k.a. Harvey Logan), a member of Butch Cassidy's gang.

More recollections of the town's early days can be found at the **Frontier Historical Society Museum**, where you can see a generous sampling of Victorian-era mine-camp elegance, including the marriage bed shared by silver tycoon and scandal-ridden senator Horace Tabor and his mistress-turned-wife, Baby Doe. There are also American Indian artifacts and a walk-through replica of a coal mine. Closed Tuesday and Wednesday in winter and Sunday year-round. Admission. ~ 1001 Colorado Avenue, Glenwood Springs; 970-945-4448.

In 1993 construction was completed on the formerly narrow winding 12-mile stretch of Route 70 through **Glenwood Canyon**, the last portion of the road to become a four-lane divided highway. Thanks to imaginative engineering, half a billion taxpayer dollars and Colorado's tough, controversial environmental laws, Glenwood Canyon is today the most beautiful scenic area on any U.S. interstate highway. The roadways, terraced up the canyon walls with eastbound and westbound lanes at different levels, stand on concrete pillars up to 80 feet tall to minimize impact on the environment. In the few places where rock cuts or blasting were necessary, the rock was resculpted to make the surface look natural. Contractors were fined for *any* shrubs or trees they destroyed while building the road, the amounts ranging from $35 for a raspberry bush to more than $22,000 for a Douglas fir. A 4000-foot tunnel conceals the freeway from sight of hikers on the Hanging Lake Trail, the most popular recreational spot in the canyon.

At the bottom of the 1800-foot-deep gorge, well below the din of the interstate, the paved **Glenwood Canyon Trail** takes walkers, joggers, cyclists and even rollerbladers along the bank of the Colorado River. Hiking trails start at three rest areas along the way. The most spectacular is the steep 1.2-mile trail that climbs to **Hanging Lake**, where waterfalls feed a gem-blue pool on a narrow terrace 930 feet up the canyon's sheer granite wall. Formerly one of the "hidden" wonders of the Rockies, **Hanging Lake Trail** has become the single most popular hiking trail in Colorado since

## BIKE TOUR
## Glenwood Canyon

**GLENWOOD CANYON RECREATION PATH**   If you're traveling in the
Colorado Rockies during the warm months, you're sure to notice that
mountain bikers are everywhere. Mountain-bike rides can be as challenging as you want, but they don't come any easier—or more scenic—
than the Glenwood Canyon Recreation Path. Running along the canyon
floor, underneath the split-level interstate highway, the wide, paved biking, jogging and skating trail is surprisingly serene. The trail is 19.2 miles
long (one way) but gains only 411 feet in elevation over the whole distance. You can complete the roundtrip, taking time out for hiking and
picnicking, in a day, or turn back earlier for a shorter trip. (For mountain-bike rentals in Glenwood Springs, see page 218.)

**NO NAME CREEK**   The Glenwood Canyon Recreation Path starts on the
east edge of Glenwood Springs at **Yampah Spa and Vapor Caves**
(page 190). The granite walls of the canyon rise quickly as the trail descends along a frontage road for 2.4 miles to **No Name Rest Area**,
where the interstate looms overhead and almost seems to vanish. If
you'd like to test yourself and your bike on a more challenging stretch,
take a side trip up the primitive forest road that follows No Name

completion of the Glenwood Canyon Project. The trail starts
from Sixth Street on the east side of Glenwood Springs, near the
Yampah Vapor Caves. The Hanging Lake trailhead is ten miles
from town. The entire Glenwood Canyon Trail is 20 miles long,
paved all the way.

For a fascinating day trip from Glenwood Springs, take Route
82 south for 12 miles to Carbondale and then fork right on Route
133, which goes around the twin 14,000-foot red-hued mountain
peaks known as the Maroon Bells on the non-Aspen side. Seven-
teen miles down this road lies the tiny village of **Redstone**, originally a turn-of-the-20th-century coal-mining town and now one
of the most secluded luxury resort areas in Colorado. The sight

HIDDEN ►

that makes the trip worthwhile is **Redstone Castle**. Built by the
founder of Colorado Fuel & Iron, which operated the big steel mill
at Pueblo and controlled most of the state's coal mines, the 42-
room castle is one of the most remarkable architectural achieve-
ments of Colorado's early days. The massive red-sandstone mansion was abandoned after only a few years of occupancy when
the owner lost everything in a corporate takeover. It has been restored in lavishly authentic fashion. Now operated as a bed and

Creek north for about seven miles to its source and then continues into the **Flat Tops Wilderness**. Watch for some of the bighorn sheep that have been reintroduced to the No Name Creek area.

**GRIZZLY CREEK TRAILHEAD**    It's another 2.6 miles along the recreation path from No Name to Grizzly Creek, where a hiking trail from the rest area runs along the creek for 3.4 miles. The creek got its name because the largest grizzly bear on record in Colorado was shot here in 1881. There are no more grizzlies, but other wildlife is abundant along the trail.

**HANGING LAKE**    The next four miles of the recreation path take you past the **Shoshone Power Plant**, the uppermost dam on the Colorado River; it has supplied hydroelectric power to Denver since 1909. The rest area at the dam is the trailhead for the steep 1.2-mile Hanging Lake Trail (page 219), Colorado's most popular hiking trails.

**BAIR RANCH REST AREA AND DOTSERO**    The Hanging Lake Trailhead is halfway up the canyon. From there, the recreation path continues for four miles to the Bair Ranch Rest Area, where there are shaded picnic tables, restrooms, drinking water and short trails that follow the river and climb to scenic overlooks. It's five more miles to the end of the recreation path at Dotsero Junction, at the confluence of the Colorado and Eagle rivers. From here, the long downhill coast back to Glenwood Springs is both gentle and breathtaking.

breakfast, the castle welcomes sightseers. Redstone also has a small art center featuring marble sculptures and a tiny historical museum with exhibits on the coal-mining days. The nearby Redstone Inn sponsors afternoon tours of the castle and more expensive lunch tours daily during the summer months. ~ 58 Redstone Boulevard, Redstone; tours: 970-963-2526, fax 970-963-2527; www.redstoneinn.com, e-mail info@redstoneinn.com.

About five miles southeast of Redstone on a well-marked, exceptionally scenic back road is the even smaller village of **Marble**, site of a huge abandoned marble mill, still surrounded by broken slabs and columns of gleaming white marble scattered all about. Continue up the mountain on a dirt road for four miles and you'll find the quarry, which used to produce up to 3000 cubic feet of marble a day. The marble from the quarries and mill here was used to build many federal government buildings and monuments, among them the Lincoln Memorial and the Tomb of the Unknown Soldier.

The AYH-affiliated **Glenwood Springs Hostel** offers 24 dormitory beds and several private rooms, along with kitchen and laundry

**LODGING**

facilities and shared baths. There's also a photographers' dark-room and a book and record library. ~ 1021 Grand Avenue, Glenwood Springs; 970-945-8545, 800-946-7835, fax 970-945-0984; hostelcolorado.com, e-mail info@hostelcolorado.com. BUDGET.

One of the first grand hotels in the Rocky Mountains, the **Hotel Colorado** is over a century old. Modeled after the Villa de Medici and built of native sandstone and Roman brick, the formerly opulent Italianate-style hotel once welcomed President William Taft and was a favorite haunt of Theodore Roosevelt during his presidency. Though it has also served intermittently as a youth hostel, the venerable hotel never closed its doors, and in the 1970s a top-to-bottom renovation transformed it with modern fixtures and period decor. The landscaped courtyard is inviting, the lobby is truly vast, and each of the 126 guest rooms and suites is individually decorated in restful, muted hues. It also has a jacuzzi, a sauna and an exercise room, and the hot springs are just a short walk away. ~ 526 Pine Street, Glenwood Springs; 970-945-6511, 800-544-3998, fax 970-945-7841; www.hotelcolorado.com, e-mail thehotelcolorado@aol.com. DELUXE.

**Hot Springs Lodge** is right across the street from Glenwood Hot Springs; guests get a discount at the hot-spring pool. The decor is contemporary western, the lobby cheerily remodeled, and the 107 guest rooms (most with balconies) are bright and exceptionally spacious, offering a choice of two queen-size beds or one king-size. ~ 415 6th Street, Glenwood Springs; 970-945-6571, 800-537-7946, fax 970-947-2950; www.hotspringspool.com. DELUXE.

The classiest accommodations in town today are at the **Hotel Denver**, across the street from the Amtrak station and a short walk from the hot springs. Built in 1906, the hotel has been completely renovated in art deco–revival style. The rooms are spacious and modern. ~ 402 7th Street, Glenwood Springs; 970-945-6565, 800-826-8820, fax 970-945-2204; www.thehoteldenver.com, e-mail info@thehoteldenver.com. MODERATE TO DELUXE.

**Adducci's Inn Bed & Breakfast** is an antique-decorated B&B in an older downtown residence, this one built in 1900. Adducci's Inn offers five simple, pleasant rooms. Each room has a private WC, but bathtub and showers are down the hall. There's a private hot tub. ~ 1023 Grand Avenue, Glenwood Springs; 970-945-9341. MODERATE TO DELUXE.

You don't have to drive far from Glenwood Springs to get away from it all. Twelve miles out of town, the **Sunlight Mountain Inn** has 20 rustic rooms with private baths in a ranch setting with horses for rent and hiking and fishing close by. ~ 10252 County Road 117; 970-945-5225, 800-733-4757, fax 970-947-1900; www.sunlightinn.com, e-mail innkeeper@sunlightmtn.com. BUDGET TO DELUXE.

In the hideaway community of Redstone, the **Redstone Castle** (also known as the Cleveholm Manor) was the turn-of-the-20th-century home of Colorado's leading coal and steel baron. Today the castle has been restored to the opulence of that era with museum-quality antiques including chandeliers and velvet-upholstered furnishings. It operates as a bed and breakfast with eight rooms and suites as well as eight more modest rooms, once servants' quarters, which share bathrooms. ~ 82 Redstone Boulevard, Redstone; 970-963-2526, 800-748-2524, fax 970-704-9288; www.redstonecastle.com, e-mail redstoneinn@aol.com. MODERATE TO ULTRA-DELUXE.

**DINING**

In contrast to the high cost of eating in Aspen, Glenwood Springs presents an array of good restaurants for every culinary preference at surprisingly low prices.

Centrally located downtown, **Mi Restaurante** is a long-time local favorite. The big, brick-walled restaurant is on the second floor, and the nonsmoking section has picture windows overlooking the main street of town. The menu features home-style American and Mexican food. ~ 720 Grand Avenue, Glenwood Springs; 970-947-9888. BUDGET.

Across the street, the **Italian Underground** is located in the basement of the historic Silver Club Building, originally a turn-of-the-20th-century gambling hall. Northern Italian food, pizzas and ice cream are all homemade. ~ 715 Grand Avenue, Glenwood Springs; 970-945-6422. MODERATE.

The **19th Street Diner** is an authentic '50s-style local hangout decorated entirely in black and white. The large menu features a little of everything, from hamburgers with fries, to chicken-fried steak with mashed potatoes and gravy, to fajitas, *huevos ran-*

**AUTHOR FAVORITE**

Being someone who understands that hot peppers are one of the five basic food groups, I make a point of heading for **The Bayou** whenever I'm in Glenwood Springs. They serve up the spiciest (and just about the only) Cajun food on Colorado's Western slope. Look for the green awning with the bulging frog's eyes on top. The broad outdoor deck has a mountain view, and entrées range from "Wabbit Stuff" like blackened shark salad to "Fowl Stuff" like chicken étouffée and "Udder Stuff" like Cajun rib-eye steak, as well as old standbys such as catfish po'boys, seafood gumbo and sautéed frog's legs. ~ 52103 Route 6/24, Glenwood Springs; 970-945-1047.

*cheros* and fettuccine. ~ 1908 Grand Avenue, Glenwood Springs; 970-945-9133. BUDGET.

The **Rivers Restaurant** perches on the banks above the Roaring Fork River, so that in late spring and early summer diners can sit on the broad outdoor terrace and watch the parade of whitewater rafts. The eclectic bill of fare—beef, fowl, wild game and seafood—comes with some interesting nouveau touches, ranging from light choices such as the Baja duck and orzo salad to entrées such as a lavender-seasoned salmon filet or a red curry and coconut chicken breast. ~ 2525 South Grand Avenue, Glenwood Springs; 970-928-8813. MODERATE TO DELUXE.

> It's a good thing the hot springs stay open until 10 p.m., because Glenwood Springs does not have an abundance of other nightlife.

The elegant Victorian-style **Sopris Restaurant** is widely considered the best in the Glenwood Springs area. Fresh flowers and candlelight set the mood. For starters, there are salads topped with raspberry vinaigrette and appetizers like escargot and snow crab claws. Entrées include veal, rack of lamb and vegetarian dishes. ~ 7215 Route 82, Glenwood Springs; 970-945-7771. MODERATE TO DELUXE.

The **Buffalo Valley Inn**, located in a building that used to be a local historical museum, has a saloonlike atmosphere and a bar inlaid with 1000 silver dollars. Beef dominates the menu in the form of steak, prime rib and barbecued ribs, and there is a large, elaborate salad bar. ~ 3637 Route 82, Glenwood Springs; 970-945-5297. BUDGET TO DELUXE.

**SHOPPING**    A standout among the galleries and gift shops lining Grand Avenue in Glenwood Springs, **The Watersweeper and The Dwarf** has been in business in the same location since 1976. It exhibits a whimsical array of fine one-of-a-kind handicrafts. ~ 717 Grand Avenue, Glenwood Springs; 970-945-2000. Other intriguing little shops have sprung up nearby, including the fanciful **Treasures Under the Stairs**. ~ 812 Grand Avenue, Glenwood Springs; 970-945-2168. The work of local craftspeople is exhibited at **Mountain Valley Weavers**. ~209 8th Street, Glenwood Springs; 970-928-0774.

The Redstone area is well on the way to becoming a full-fledged artists' colony, and several local galleries have opened there, including one at **Redstone Art Center**, showing works by more than 80 local and regional artists and artisans. ~ 173 Redstone Boulevard, Redstone; 970-963-3790; www.redstoneart.com. There's also the nearby **Wild Horse Enterprises**, which displays Western art, jewelry and antiques. ~ 306 Redstone Boulevard, Redstone; 970-963-8100. The **Redstone Country Store** has a broad spectrum of crafts and gifts, including a room filled with garden ornaments and birdhouses and another with Christmas decorations. It shares the premises with **The Teddy Bear Factory**, which has stuffed toys for both cuddlers and collectors. ~ 117 Redstone Boulevard; 970-963-9912.

The **Buffalo Valley Inn** has live music on weekend nights, sometimes rock-and-roll or big-band, other times country-and-western. Its dancefloor is said to be the largest in the state. ~ 3637 Route 82, Glenwood Springs; 970-945-5297. You'll also find live music on weekends in the Hotel Colorado's **Palm Court Lounge**. ~ 526 Pine Street, Glenwood Springs; 970-945-6511.

**NIGHTLIFE**

**WHITE RIVER NATIONAL FOREST** 🏃 🚴 ⚓ Glenwood Springs is surrounded by White River National Forest, one of the oldest and largest national forests in the Rocky Mountains, which also includes the forest around Aspen and Vail (see Chapter Four). The forest is split into two separate units by Glenwood Canyon, a strip of Bureau of Land Management land that follows the Colorado River. With the exception of Glenwood Canyon, most of which lies within a corner of the national forest boundary, direct access to the national forest from the Glenwood Springs area is mainly limited to jeep trails. Many miles of such trails follow creeks among the ridgelines and plateaus north of town. A good road, suitable for passenger cars, leads from the upper end of Glenwood Canyon to the Heart Lake area, a cluster of lakes at the 10,500-foot elevation on the White River Plateau north of Glenwood Springs. Fish for rainbow and brown trout in Heart Lake, Deep Lake and other lakes on the White River Plateau, as well as in the area's many streams. There are parking areas, picnic areas, restrooms, bike trails, hiking trails and jeep trails. ~ To reach the Heart Lake area, take Route 70 Exit 133 17 miles east of Glenwood Springs at the upper end of Glenwood Canyon and follow Forest Road 600 (Coffee Pot Road) for 27 miles; 970-328-6388.

**PARKS**

▲ There are no national forest campgrounds in the Glenwood Springs vicinity. The remote Heart Lake area has Supply Basin Campground, with 8 RV/tent sites and the Deep Lake Campground, with 21 RV/tent sites; $6 per night. There are no hookups or drinking water at either campground. Both are closed from November through June.

▼▼▼▼▼▼▼▼▼▼

Continuing west on Route 70 from Glenwood Springs, motorists leave the mountains behind and enter a rugged land of dry hills and high mesas. Northwestern Colorado is part of the vast expanse of small mountain ranges and rocky desert basins that reaches from here across Utah and Nevada to the foot of California's High Sierra. Little-known and far from major population centers, northwestern Colorado is largely undeveloped as a tourist destination; the busiest time of

## Rifle/Craig Area

year is the fall hunting season. This is one of the least populated and most pristine areas in the lower 48 United States, and its beauty lies hidden in some of the least likely places.

**SIGHTS**

From the interstate, the most direct gateway to northwestern Colorado is the small town of Rifle, 27 fast miles west of Glenwood Springs. To realize that there's more to this area than first impressions would suggest, all you have to do is take a 20-minute detour to **Rifle Falls** (for directions, see "Parks" below). Suddenly you find yourself in a lush creekside forest. A short walk takes you to the falls themselves, three separate cascades that arc outward from a limestone canyon rim. A short but strenuous and precarious trail climbs to the top of the falls and continues along the rim to loop back to the parking area and campground.

HIDDEN ►

Sixteen miles west of Rifle, the odd little town of **Parachute** boomed during the energy crisis of the 1970s, when the Union Oil Company of California opened large-scale oil shale operations in the canyons north of town. The cream-colored shale rock there is so permeated with petroleum that you can actually light it with a match; unlike coal, the rock remains after the fire burns out. The oil company believed that skyrocketing world petroleum prices would make it profitable to mine the shale and extract the oil from it. Unfortunately, prices soon declined, operations were halted at the multimillion-dollar facility, and Parachute was virtually abandoned. You can see several units of the oil shale plant as you drive about 12 miles up Parachute Creek Canyon as it slices its way through the center of the mesa into a labyrinth of smaller canyons, still owned by the oil company and off-limits to the public.

If you take Route 13 north from Rifle, a 39-mile drive will bring you to the little town of **Meeker**, which is remembered in Colorado history as the site of the "Meeker Massacre." In 1879, recently appointed Indian agent Nathan C. Meeker and ten employees were killed by a Ute war party—with justification, according to most accounts. The government responded by banishing the Northern Ute people from Colorado to a reservation south of Vernal, Utah. They were the last Indian tribe to be driven out of Colorado and, ironically, almost all the land that was taken from them remains uninhabited to this day. Meeker's history is recounted in photos, antiques and artifacts—including items belonging to President Theodore Roosevelt, who used to go elk hunting in the Flat Tops—in the free **White River Museum**, located behind the red-flagstone Rio Blanco County Courthouse in a log Army barracks built after the massacre. ~ 565 Park Street, Meeker; 970-878-9982.

HIDDEN ►

The best reason for going to Meeker is that it is the starting point for the **Flat Tops Trail Scenic Byway**. The road heads east for 82 miles to the equally out-of-the-way town of Yampa, on

Route 131 midway between Vail Valley and Steamboat Springs. The middle 40 miles, within the White River National Forest boundary, are unpaved but wide and well graded. The scenic by-way climbs to the broad mesa top and continues through gently rolling hills covered with aspen, fir and spruce. Frequent overlooks provide views of the Flat Tops themselves, sheer stone buttes formed in geological antiquity as gigantic volcano plugs, rising to elevations over 11,000 feet, accessible only on foot or horse-back. A detour from the main route takes you to **Trappers Lake,** the largest of many lakes that dot the mesa. The lake and the road leading in to it are completely surrounded by the untamed Flat Tops Wilderness.

Continuing north from Meeker on Route 3 will bring you to **Craig,** a crossroads community on the Yampa River. The major industries here are three large coal mines and a coal-fired power plant that supplies electricity to several states. The **Museum of Northwest Colorado** displays not only local history and railroad exhibits, rare 19th-century wildlife photographs by A. G. Walli-han, cowboy and Indian artifacts and geological specimens, but also one of the West's largest collections of old-time gunfighter memorabilia. Closed Sunday. ~ 590 Yampa Street, Craig; 970-824-6360; www.museumnwco.org.

"**Marcia,**" a private railroad car built in 1906 for Denver rail-road magnate David H. Moffat, stands alongside Victory Street near Craig's city park. Tours of the ultra-luxurious coach's re-stored interior—a real eye-opener for modern RV travelers—can be arranged by calling the Craig Visitors Center (970-824-5689).

West of Craig lies the emptiest part of Colorado, an arid stretch of shale badlands. The main point of interest in this part of the state is **Dinosaur National Monument,** which straddles the Colorado–Utah state line. The main entrance to Dinosaur National Monu-ment, where some of the first complete dinosaur skel-etons ever assembled for museums were unearthed as early as 1909, is 12 miles east of Vernal, Utah, via Route 149, 20 miles west of the Colorado state line. Admission. ~ Route 149; 970-374-3000; www.nps.gov/dino.

Although Dinosaur National Monument encompasses a vast area of desert canyon wilderness, the Dinosaur Quarry is the only spot where dinosaur bones can be seen.

Sixty-five million years ago, a sandy barrier island at the mouth of a river delta lush with tropical forest became the final resting place for dinosaurs that drowned when the river flooded. Over the eons, thousands of them were entombed in sandy sediments that later hardened into sandstone. The fossil remains of prehis-toric giants such as the vegetarian aptosaurus, diplodocus and stegosaurus as well as the meat-eating allosaurus have been shipped to museums around the world. Today paleontologists continue to expose dinosaur bones at the quarry, but do not remove them. The sandstone face with its still-emerging jigsaw puzzle of fossil skeletons forms one wall of the **Dinosaur Quarry**, the main sightseeing attraction at this national monument.

Just inside the monument boundary is a huge parking lot at the Dinosaur Quarry Visitors Center. During the busy summer months, visitors must park here and take a shuttle bus to the quarry; exhibits and a short slide show at the visitors center are designed to keep people occupied as they wait as long as half an hour for their shuttle. In the off-season, you can drive directly to the quarry. Past the visitors center, the Cub Creek Road leads along the Green River to campgrounds, hiking trails, Indian petroglyphs and an early settler's cabin. The two-hour **Harper's Corner Scenic Drive** rounds out an all-day visit with a spectacular expedition into the center of the park. ~ Located 25 miles east via Route 40 on the Colorado side of the state line.

This side of the park is wild canyon country that includes 44 miles of the Green River, 48 miles of the Yampa and the two rivers' confluence. There are no roads and only a few two-track jeep trails through the northern backcountry of the park; the main access is by river raft. Taking a marked turnoff from Route 318, motorists can reach the launch point for trips down the Green River. From there it's an easy hike to an overlook view of

*HIDDEN* ► the **Gates of Lodore**, dramatic quartzite cliffs that rise suddenly to an elevation of 2300 feet above the river. Plunging through the Canyon of Lodore, the water pounds over Disaster Falls and gushes through Hell's Half Mile before slowing to mirrorlike serenity as it makes its way through python bends that shelter

*HIDDEN* ► sandy beaches nearing the raft pullout point at **Echo Park**, close to the south side of the national monument. A paved scenic road that starts just east of the town of Dinosaur, three miles from the state line, runs twenty-five miles through slickrock country to an overlook that offers an awe-inspiring view of Echo Park. From this paved park road, a 14-mile unpaved side road bounces its way to the riverbank tent campground at Echo Park itself.

Continuing west from the turnoff to the Gates of Lodore,

*HIDDEN* ► Route 318 passes through a remote desert valley known as **Browns Park** (or sometimes "Browns Hole"). In earlier times, mild winters and abundant grass made Browns Park a favorite wintering place for nomadic Indians, mountain men and outlaws. Today the area attracts mostly birdwatchers, who come to visit **Browns Park National Wildlife Refuge**, a major stopover and nesting area for migratory waterfowl on the Green River. ~ Route 318, 55 miles west of Maybell; 970-365-3613. Other points of interest in the Browns Park area include **Vermillion Falls**, a pretty canyon cascade a short distance south of the highway, and **Irish Canyon**, a colorful canyon that offers picnicking and hiking areas, rock climbing and Indian petroglyphs, reached by taking unpaved County Road 10N north from Route 318. A few miles farther on, another unpaved road turns south to the remains of the hand-hewn log buildings of the **Two Bar Ranch**, which was one of the largest cattle ranches in Colorado in the early 1900s. Nearby, a meeting hall and well-preserved old cemetery mark the location of **Lodore**, which formerly served area ranches, but is now a ghost town. Just before you reach the state line on Route 318, unpaved County Road 83 veers off to the south; along the way to scenic Crouse Canyon on the Utah side, the road offers a cheap thrill as it crosses the Green River on a one-lane swinging wooden bridge.

Just off Route 70, Rifle offers a fair selection of low-priced independent motels. The two-story, 89-unit **Rusty Cannon Motel** scores slightly above the competition because it has a heated swimming pool and sauna. The guest rooms themselves are about as conventional as motel rooms can be, simply decorated in brown and blue hues. The owners are Rifle natives who also operate a backcountry guide service and are full of suggestions for touring the area. ~ 701 Taughenbaugh Street, Rifle; 970-625-4004. MODERATE.

**LODGING**

Battlement Mesa, across the highway from the oil shale ghost town of Parachute, got its start in the 1970s as a bedroom community for oil company executives, complete with its own golf course, indoor swimming pool and racquetball courts. Today, Battlement Mesa is primarily a retirement community but also serves as a resort for vacationers who don't mind that the location is not very convenient to any tourist destination. One- and two-bedroom condominium-style suites with kitchenettes rent by the night or week. For rental information and reservations, call **Battlement Mesa Guest Suites**. ~ 73 Sipprelle Drive, Parachute; 970-285-9579, 800-275-5687. MODERATE.

In Meeker, the **Meeker Hotel** is a handsome red-brick historic hotel dating back to 1896. The 24 refurbished guest rooms, some

**AUTHOR FAVORITE**

For a night of total peace and quiet in a tiny, quaint town far off the beaten path, I highly recommend the **Brick House Bed & Breakfast** in Meeker. Built by the same craftspeople as Redstone Castle and Denver's Brown Palace Hotel, the turn-of-the-20th-century house has just three luxurious guest rooms, each with antique decor and a queen-size bed, and shade trees in the yard. The residential neighborhood location is away from the two-lane highway that passes for Meeker's main street, and it's within walking distance of . . . well . . . everything. ~ 687 Garfield Street, Meeker; 970-878-5055. MODERATE.

with shared baths, are modern and modest, and the lobby features a mural of the Meeker Massacre along with more than a dozen big-game trophy heads. Teddy Roosevelt slept here. ~ 560 Main Street, Meeker; 970-878-5255. MODERATE.

Great wilderness lodging is available at **Trappers Lake Lodge**, on the shore of a beautiful lake off the Flat Tops Trail Scenic Byway. Guest accommodations are in 14 simple cabins with cooking stoves; guests share central restrooms. Canoes, fishing skiffs and saddle horses are for rent, and the main lodge has a dining room and store. ~ 7700 Trappers Lake Road, Meeker; 970-878-3336; www.trapperslake.com, e-mail info@trapperslake.com. MODERATE.

Craig has more than a dozen unexceptional, budget-priced motels. For something a bit more special, try the **Williams Fork Bed & Breakfast**, 13 miles south of Craig in the small community of Hamilton. The four-unit contemporary log home sits on the bank of Williams Creek. The rates include a continental breakfast. ~ 17559 South Route 13, Hamilton; 970-824-3322. MODERATE.

**DINING**

In Rifle, an attractive alternative to the array of famous-name fast-food joints is the Asian atmosphere and succulent stir-fry fare at **Shanghai Gardens**. ~ 1538 Railroad Avenue, Rifle; 970-625-4430. BUDGET TO MODERATE.

Fresh homemade breads and pastries enhance breakfast, lunch or dinner from **The Bakery**. ~ 265 6th Street, Meeker; 970-878-5500. BUDGET TO MODERATE.

Craig has dozens of fast-food joints and family restaurants. Among the most attractive of them, the **Golden Cavvy Restaurant & Lounge** serves steaks, seafood, soup, sandwiches and salads in a casual, friendly atmosphere. ~ 538 Yampa Avenue, Craig; 970-824-6038. BUDGET.

The best Mexican food in northwestern Colorado is found at the modest **La Plaza Restaurant**. ~ 994 Yampa Avenue, Craig; 970-824-7345. BUDGET.

**PARKS**

**RIFLE GAP STATE PARK** ⚓ 🛶 ⛷ 🏕 🚣 This reservoir flanked by limestone cliffs on the way to Rifle Falls is popular among western Colorado water-sports enthusiasts because of its easy access from Route 70. Besides boating, waterskiing, windsurfing and fishing, the lake is a popular spot for scuba diving because of its unusually clear water. Fish here for walleye and large- and smallmouth bass, as well as some rainbow trout. There are restrooms, picnic areas, a swimming area and a winter play area. Day-use fee, $5. ~ Located on Route 325, eight miles north of Rifle, which is 27 miles west of Glenwood Springs on Route 70; 970-625-1607; www.coloradoparks.org/rifle_gap.

▲ There are 47 RV/tent sites (no hookups) in four campgrounds; $12 per night.

# Dinosaur Hunting in Colorado

**M**ore dinosaur fossils have been found in Colorado than anywhere else on earth. This is due in large part to the Morrison Formation, a 400-foot-thick layer of red sandstone that extends from Utah and northern Arizona to Colorado's Front Range, which formed as sandy muck in the wetland marshes and shallow shoals of a long-forgotten sea about 140 million years ago. It was the last geological stratum to form during the Jurassic era, the time when dinosaurs grew the largest and were the most numerous.

So why are more dinosaur fossils found in Colorado than in neighboring states that also have the Morrison sandstone layer beneath them? For two reasons: For millions of years, most of the formation was under the surface of the sea, while only its eastern edge (what is now Colorado) was shoreline. Here land-dwelling dinosaurs could wade and graze, the swampy wetlands offering slow herbivores some measure of protection from fast-moving predators. Then, too, the uplifting of the Rocky Mountains some 80 million years later fragmented the Morrison Formation, pushing it up through the earth's surface like splinters along both sides of the mountain range, leaving more of this particular geological layer exposed in Colorado than in other regions.

All it takes is a visit to the Denver Museum of Nature and Science, where some of the best Colorado fossil finds are on permanent exhibit, to visualize these giant creatures roaming the lush, green world of Colorado's Jurassic era. In fact, fragmentary fossilized dinosaur skeletons are displayed in glass cases in the local history museums of more than a dozen towns in all parts of the state. But for the truly spectacular, nothing can compete with the far northwestern part of Colorado and the rugged, colorful tangle of sandstone canyons that extends from the Grand Junction area to Dinosaur National Monument.

You might expect that the best dinosaur sight around would be the national monument, where the world's largest dinosaur quarry is located. You'd be half right, especially if you included the dinosaur museum and Jurassic sculpture garden in Vernal, Utah, west of the monument's main entrance. Grand Junction, however, is quickly emerging as Colorado's dinosaur capital. The Museum of Western Colorado's Dinosaur Journey museum in neighboring Fruita is also a working paleontology lab where visitors can watch fossil experts at work. The active fossil digs at Riggs Hill, Dinosaur Hill and Rabbit Valley also offer a close-up look at the painstaking work involved in searching for hints about the nature of these amazing beings that inhabited Earth long before the Rocky Mountains were born.

**RIFLE FALLS STATE PARK** 🏃 A 45-minute drive from Glenwood Springs, Rifle Falls is hidden in a shale canyon in northwestern Colorado's dry plateau country. Rifle Creek splits into several cascades that spill side by side into the canyon, creating an oasis lush with ferns, mosses and wildflowers. Among the falls and along the canyon wall are marked entrances to several small caves that are easy to explore with a flashlight. Facilities include picnic areas, restrooms and a nature trail. Day-use fee, $5. ~ Located on Route 325, 12 miles north of Rifle; 970-625-1607; www.coloradoparks.org/rifle_falls.

▲ There are 7 tent sites and 12 RV sites with electric hookups; $12 to $16 per night.

**RIFLE MOUNTAIN PARK** 🏃 This municipal park is actually an extension of Rifle Falls State Park, continuing up the canyon to the national forest boundary. Picnic spots and campsites lie along the banks of a tree-lined creek. Several caves, some of them extending for more than a mile, open along the base of the limestone cliffs, including at least two perpetually frozen ice caves. The park also has several rock-climbing practice walls. There are picnic areas, restrooms and hiking trails. Day-use fee, $5 per vehicle. ~ Located on Route 325, 13 miles north of Rifle.

▲ There are 19 RV/tent sites (no hookups); $10 per night.

**WHITE RIVER NATIONAL FOREST** 🏃 🏊 🎣 The northern unit of White River National Forest encompasses the wild mesa area called the Flat Tops, where rolling hills dotted with small natural lakes surround the steep cliffs of truncated mountains—mesas upon the mesa top—that give the area its name. More than half of this section of the forest lies within the Flat Tops Wilderness, and is laced with hiking trails and full of wildlife. This wilderness area is accessible from several trailheads along the Flat Tops Trail Scenic Byway. Swimming is permitted at Trappers Lake. Fishing is good for rainbow trout and Snake River cutthroat in Lake Avery; exceptional for native cutthroat in Trappers Lake. There are parking areas, a grocery store and trailheads. ~ The principle access to the Blanco Unit is the Flat Tops Trail Scenic Byway, an 82-mile road (40 miles unpaved) between Meeker and Yampa. The forest road that continues beyond Rifle Falls State Park and Rifle Mountain Park provides unpaved access to the southwestern part of the forest. Trappers Lake is located 41 miles east of Meeker on the Flat Tops Trail and then 10 miles south on Forest Road 15205; Blanco Ranger District, 970-878-4039.

▲ There are eight national forest campgrounds along the Flat Tops Trail Scenic Byway, including four at Trappers Lake. Among them, Trappers Lake–Shepard's Rim Campground has 20 RV/tent sites (no hookups), closed mid-November to mid-

June; and nearby Trappers Lake–Cutthroat Campground has 14 RV/tent sites (no hookups), closed October to mid-June. Fees are $14 per night at all Trappers Lake area campgrounds.

The Colorado River pours from a mountain canyon into the Grand Valley, where fruit orchards line its banks and fill the air with the

▼▼▼▼▼▼▼▼▼▼▼▼▼▼
## Grand Junction Area

scent of blossoms in the spring. Route 70 follows the river through Grand Junction, named for its location—where the Colorado River (once known as the Grand River) and the Gunnison River meet— and the largest city in Colorado west of the Continental Divide.

Grand Junction is a long, narrow city, bounded by Route 70 on the

**SIGHTS**

north and the Colorado River on the south. Venturing off the main thoroughfares into the downtown area, you will find a graceful neighborhood of older homes harking back to the more prosperous era when Grand Junction was a major railroad center. Follow Main Street as it meanders from 2nd Street to 7th Street through

Grand Junction Area

the **Downtown Shopping Park**. This city center, imaginatively rede-
veloped back in 1963, combines the amenities of a pedestrian mall
with a single traffic lane that curves between too few parking spaces.

School-age kids will find plenty of hands-on learning play at
the **Doo Zoo Children's Museum**, where top attractions include a
cage full of plastic balls and a working model post office. Closed
Sunday. Admission. ~ 421 Colorado Avenue, Grand Junction;
970-241-5225.

The main location of the **Museum of Western Colorado**, the
largest museum between Denver and Salt Lake City, features a time-
line exhibit that traces regional history from 1880 to the present.
The recently expanded museum also displays American Indian artifacts, flora and fauna and historical documents and photographs,
as well as a working weather station, a walk-through full-scale
replica of a uranium mine, a 1921 fire truck, Colorado's largest
collection of historic firearms and an exhibit recounting the story
of Alferd Packer, the "Colorado cannibal." Closed Monday in
winter. Admission. ~ 462 Ute Avenue, Grand Junction; 970-242-
0971; www.wcmuseum.org.

Another unit of the Museum of Western Colorado is **Cross
Orchards Historic Site**. Traditional farm life of the early 1900s
is re-created at this open-air museum, originally the headquarters of one of Colorado's largest apple orchards. A portion of the
orchard, along with the summer house, workers' bunkhouse,
blacksmith shop, barn and packing house, is open to the public.
Other exhibits include a collection of road-building machinery
and railroad memorabilia. Living-history demonstrations are held
daily from mid-April through October; special events include
workshops where students learn traditional farming methods
using teams of draft horses, antique appraisal sessions and classes
on making cornhusk dolls. Closed November through April. Admission. ~ 3073 F (Patterson) Road, Grand Junction; 970-434-
9814.

The Museum of Western Colorado also operates **Little Park
Desert Preserve**, on Grand Junction's southern city limits. The
1200-acre wilderness area has trails for hiking and mountain
biking. The museum also conducts ongoing fossil digs at **Riggs
Hill** and **Dinosaur Hill**, situated near the west and east entrances
of Colorado National Monument, as well as at **Rabbit Valley**, 24
miles west of town. All three digs have self-guided walking trails
that are open to visitors.

Located in a former elementary school building two miles
from downtown, the **Western Colorado Math and Science Center**,
meant primarily to accommodate school field trips from all over
the region, is also open to the public. The center has more than
125 hands-on interactive displays on topics ranging from mag-

netism and ecology to nuclear energy and artificial intelligence, designed to prove to young minds that math and science are cool. Closed to the public Sunday through Tuesday. ~ 2660 Unaweep Avenue, Grand Junction; 970-243-0028.

The nearby town of Fruita is home to **Dinosaur Journey**, a branch of the Museum of Western Colorado that replaces the former Dinosaur Valley in Grand Junction. The new, expanded facility features half-size robotic dinosaurs and dinosaur skeletons (including a casting of a huge legbone from what was the world's largest dinosaur skeleton when it was discovered on nearby Dinosaur Hill in 1900), exhibits about dinosaur digs and a working paleontology laboratory. ~ Jurassic Court (across from the Colorado Welcome Center at Route 70 Exit 19), Fruita; 970-858-7282, 888-488-3466; www.dinosaurjourney.com, e-mail jcron@westcomuseum.org.

The **Grand Valley** is wider than the Grand Canyon and nearly half as deep. Orange sandstone cliffs form a wall 2000 feet high along its south side, and from the top rim of the cliffs above Grand Junction you can see that they form one side of a canyon carved by the Colorado River. On its far side, 14 miles away, stands its other wall—the inaccessible, purple-gray Book Cliffs. **Colorado National Monument** encompasses 32 square miles of the south rim between Grand Junction and the smaller town of Fruita nearby, providing a small sample of the cliffs and side canyons that enclose the Grand Valley. What makes this particular segment of the rim special is that you can reach it in a passenger car. **Rim Rock Drive**, built by the Civilian Conservation Corps during the 1930s, climbs by switchbacks to the upper rim from either the east park entrance on the outskirts of Grand Junction or the west entrance near Fruita. The 23-mile drive offers more than a dozen scenic view points, some overlooking the orchards, towns and farmlands of the valley, others affording glimpses of secluded side canyons. For most travelers, the dramatic one-hour drive through the national monument alone is worth the price of admission. Admission. ~ Fruita; 970-858-3617; www.nps.gov/colm.

> Caution: The clay surface of the road to Rattlesnake Canyon gets so slippery when wet that even four-wheel-drive vehicles can't travel on it.

◄ HIDDEN

**Rattlesnake Canyon** may be one of the best-kept secrets in "Hidden Colorado." Huge natural arches of beige and red sandstone, some with spans of more than 100 feet, line the eastern rim of the canyon. A century ago, visitors arriving in Grand Junction by train rode horseback to Rattlesnake Canyon in such numbers that President Theodore Roosevelt declared it a national monument. A generation later, when the age of motorcars began, tourism dropped off so much that the National Park Service abandoned Rattlesnake Canyon National Monument, turning the canyon over to the Bureau of Land Management. By the time four-wheel-drive vehicles made the canyon accessible again, it was long forgotten. The turnoff for the canyon is just outside the back entrance to Colorado National Monument, off West Glade Park Road. You need a four-wheel-drive vehicle to reach the trailhead in the Black Ridge Wilderness.

There is plenty of spectacular canyon scenery to be found in the uninhabited public lands along the cliffs at the base of the Uncompahgre Plateau for 65 miles south and east of Grand Junction. Little-known canyons can be reached on unpaved ranch roads off Route 50 between Grand Junction and Montrose. For instance, **Dominguez Canyon**, on the Gunnison River, offers 20 miles of hidden canyonlands with a marvelous range of environments—from desert to riverbank beaches, from cottonwood forests to waterfalls that plummet down sheer sandstone cliffs. A campground and wilderness trailhead are accessible by car.

HIDDEN ►

For more information on Rattlesnake Canyon or Dominguez Canyon, as well as other scenic canyons on BLM land, contact the Bureau of Land Management, Grand Junction District Office. ~ 2815 H Road, Grand Junction, CO 81506; 970-244-3000.

First-time visitors to **Grand Mesa**, east of Grand Junction, often expect to find dry, scrubby terrain like that of Mesa Verde and other northwestern Colorado mesas. They are surprised to discover instead a cool mountain landscape of Douglas-fir trees studded with lakes like blue sapphires at elevations of more than 10,000 feet above sea level and a mile above the Grand Valley. Motorists who take the paved, 55-mile **Grand Mesa Scenic Byway** (Route 65) over the mesa top between Routes 50 and 70 feel as if they are climbing the steep, aspen-covered slopes of a mountain the size of Pikes Peak or Mount Evans—except that Grand Mesa's summit looks as if it had been neatly sliced off at timberline to create the world's largest flat-topped mountain. Grand Mesa's unique landscape was formed by an ancient lava flow that protected the softer layers of sandstone and shale beneath as the surrounding terrain eroded away. The mesa top, with its gently rolling, low hills, more than 300 lakes and innumerable streams, is a favorite destination for anglers in summer and cross-country skiers in winter. Despite a handful of rustic resort lodges, most of the mesa seems practically untouched by humankind. Two graded, unpaved roads, Land's End Road and Trickle Park Road, branch off the Grand Mesa Scenic Byway and lead deep into the forest. Land's End Road runs west along the rim of the mesa to offer spectacular views of the Grand Valley and the small crater of the volcano that created the mesa. Trickle Park Road runs east, providing access to the area's largest concentration of lakes as well as a number of four-wheel-drive roads and hiking trailheads. Because of the altitude, deep snowdrifts remain until the Fourth of July.

Grand Junction, the only major town on an otherwise empty **LODGING**
200-mile stretch of Route 70, has about 30 motels with a total
of more than 2000 guest rooms. For exceptional accommodations in town, reserve one of the seven individually decorated
rooms—some with wrought-iron beds and Shaker armoires—at
**Los Altos Bed & Breakfast.** Each window offers spectacular
views of the Colorado National Monument and Grand Mesa,
while French doors open onto a wraparound deck. Bonuses include afternoon tea, a meeting room and a living room with a
fireplace. ~ 375 Hillview Drive, Grand Junction; phone/fax 970-
256-0964, 888-774-0982; e-mail losaltos@wic.net. MODERATE
TO ULTRA-DELUXE.

Most national motor-inn chains are represented in Grand
Junction. Room rates at these places are some of the lowest in the
state. One option is the **Value Lodge.** ~ 104 White Avenue, Grand
Junction; 970-242-0651. BUDGET. There's also the large, reason-
ably priced **Adams Mark Hotel.** ~ 743 Horizon Drive, Grand
Junction; 970-241-8888, 800-444-2326, fax 970-242-7266. MOD-
ERATE TO DELUXE.

For more unique lodging, a good prospect is the **Historic
Melrose House** in downtown Grand Junction. This turn-of-the-
20th-century railroad hotel operates as an IYH hostel and has 12
individual guest rooms with private baths as well as even more
affordable dormitory accommodations. It's modestly furnished
with antiques and bursting with youthful energy. ~ 337 Colorado
Avenue, Grand Junction; 970-242-9636. BUDGET.

A bed-and-breakfast charmer, **Tomorrow Hill Farm** offers
three guest rooms, individually decorated with contemporary furnishings and queen- or king-size beds, in an 1890s-style two-story
farmhouse. The farm's orchards and gardens provide organic fruits
and vegetables used in making guests' full gourmet breakfast. They
also attract an abundance of bird life, and if you amble along the
half-mile nature trail you may spot hummingbirds, quail, wood-
peckers or kestrels. Closed in winter. ~ 945 24 Road, Grand
Junction; 970-255-8080 or 877-258-8080; www.tomorrowhill
farm.com. MODERATE.

◆◆◆◆◆◆◆◆◆◆◆◆◆◆◆◆◆◆◆◆◆◆◆◆◆◆◆◆◆◆◆◆◆◆◆◆◆◆◆◆◆◆◆◆◆◆◆◆◆◆◆◆◆◆◆◆◆

### SCULPTORS TAKE IT TO THE STREETS

Grand Junction's **Art on the Corner** program, initiated in 1989, has transformed the five-block Downtown Shopping Park into an outdoor sculpture
gallery. Under the program, artists from all over Colorado loan their
sculptures to the city for one year. At any given time more than 30
works of art wait along the downtown sidewalks to be seen, touched
and admired. All are for sale.

There are several forest lodges atop Grand Mesa, all of them small and secluded. **Alexander Lake Lodge** has seven rustic cabins, some with kitchens and fireplaces, and a main lodge with a dining room and a huge fireplace built from 200 tons of stone. The lodge fills up with snowmobilers and cross-country skiers in winter. Due to the "range war" between the two groups, the forest service working with the lodges on Grand Mesa has set aside one vast forest area for cross-country skiing and a separate, equally extensive area for snowmobiling. ~ Grand Mesa; 970-856-2539. BUDGET TO DELUXE.

Another popular year-round forest lodge on Grand Mesa is **Spruce Lodge**. There are 11 cabins; some have kitchens with microwaves and refrigerators. The lodge has a restaurant and a bar. ~ Grand Mesa; 970-856-6240, 800-850-7221, fax 970-856-6241. MODERATE.

**Grand Mesa Lodge** has 16 units including both housekeeping cabins and motel-style duplex units on Island Lake, the largest lake on Grand Mesa. There is a grocery store on the premises but no restaurant. Boat rentals are available. ~ Grand Mesa; 970-856-3250, 800-551-6372. BUDGET TO MODERATE.

For a unique alternative to Colorado's conventional dude ranches, book a stay at the **Cedar's Edge Llamas Bed & Breakfast**, near the little town of Cedaredge at the south end of Grand Mesa. There are just four guest rooms—two with private baths in the main ranchhouse and two others that share a separate guesthouse. The owner-operators love to introduce their llamas to guests—especially kids. ~ 2169 Route 65, Cedaredge; 970-856-6836; e-mail rrecord2@juno.com. MODERATE.

**DINING**

Grand Junction's only Japanese restaurant and sushi bar, **Suehiro Japanese Restaurant** serves authentic, traditional dishes includ-

**AUTHOR FAVORITE**

One of the things that make northwestern Colorado so special is its abundance of all-but-unknown scenic drives. Here's one of my personal favorites: Follow either of the two paved roads that lead from the back entrances of Colorado National Monument up into **Glade Park**. The roads pass through cool, dreamlike ranchlands to intersect at the Glade Park General Store, the pastoral setting providing a dramatic contrast to the desertlike landscapes below. About eight miles west of the store on a well-marked, unpaved road is Grand Mesa's top sightseeing highlight, **Miracle Rock**, a balanced rock teetering on the edge of a cliff and said by some to be the largest of its kind on earth.

ing tempura, sukiyaki and beef or chicken teriyaki, accompanied by sake, plum wine or Asian beer. Closed Sunday. ~ 541 Main Street, Grand Junction; 970-245-9548. MODERATE.

There is an abundance of Chinese restaurants along North Avenue, including the long-established **Far East Restaurant**, a spacious tri-level place that specializes in Szechuan and Cantonese cuisine. ~ 1530 North Avenue, Grand Junction; 970-242-8131. MODERATE.

Creative twists on New Mexican food are featured at **W. W. Peppers**. Specialties include chimichangas and crabmeat enchiladas. Steaks and more conventional seafood dishes are also served. The decor strives for the look of contemporary Santa Fe. Dinner only. ~ 753 Horizon Court, Grand Junction; 970-245-9251. MODERATE.

For just plain good food at the lowest prices in town, try **Starvin' Arvin's**. Particularly known as a breakfast spot—the hotcake stacks are formidable and the biscuits and gravy are legendary among Route 70 truckers—the restaurant also serves sandwiches and dinner specials. The decor consists of the owner's snapshots of people rafting, biking and generally enjoying the outdoors in the Grand Junction area. ~ 752 Horizon Drive, Grand Junction; 970-241-0430. BUDGET.

**SHOPPING**

As Grand Junction's more practical stores have abandoned the downtown area for the North Avenue commercial strip just a few blocks away, the smaller storefronts of Main Street Mall have reopened as modest galleries, boutiques and antique shops.

**Original Accents Gallery** has an impressive selection of contemporary American crafts and jewelry. ~ 321 Main Street, Grand Junction; 970-256-7870. The best antique shopping in town is at **Haggle of Vendors Emporium**. ~ 510 Main Street, Grand Junction; 970-245-1404.

For the largest selection of dinosaur-motif gift items you're likely to find anywhere, check out the gift shop at **Dinosaur Journey** in Fruita. ~ Jurassic Court, Fruita; 970-858-7272, 888-488-3466; www.dinosaurjourney.com.

**NIGHTLIFE**

The main music venue in Grand Junction, the **Mesa Theater and Club** presents deejays or live bands nightly and has a vast dancefloor. ~ 538 Main Street, Grand Junction; 970-241-1717. For someplace more intimate, try **Station 234**, a small club with live musicians and a pool table. ~ 234 Main Street, Grand Junction; 970-242-3620.

**PARKS**

**GRAND MESA NATIONAL FOREST** 🏃🏇⛵ This 360,000-acre reserve encompasses the world's largest flat-topped mountain, a vast expanse of lakes, lava fields and Douglas-fir forest ranging between 10,000 and 11,000 feet above sea level. Although this forest has no federally designated wilderness area, roads into the central part are for four-wheel-drive vehicles, and much of the eastern half of the mesa is accessible only by hiking and horse trails. The Land-O-Lakes area, on the western part of the mesa, has more than 300 lakes, many of them connected by a maze of streams and creeks that are legendary among trout fishermen. There's excellent fishing here for rainbow, cutthroat and brook trout. At the western tip of the mesa, Land's End overlooks the Grand Valley a mile below. There are five picnic areas, all with tables, drinking water and restrooms. ~ The main access to Grand Mesa National Forest is via the Grand Mesa Scenic Byway (Route 65). The 55-mile scenic road runs between Cedaredge, a small town 15 miles off Route 50 near Delta, and the Island Acres/Mesa exit from Route 70, about 15 miles east of Grand Junction. (For the adventurous, the Land's End Road starts from Route 50 about 12 miles east of Grand Junction and climbs to the mesa top by a series of 18 tight, unpaved switchbacks.) It is usually passable by passenger cars but not by trailers or motor homes; inquire at the ranger station for current road conditions; 970-874-6600.

If it's solitude you want, the Plateau Unit of the Uncompahgre National Forest is a good place to look for it.

▲ Grand Mesa has 18 national forest campgrounds for tents and RVs (no hookups). Those along or near the paved Grand Mesa Scenic Byway include Jumbo (27 sites), Spruce Grove (16 sites), Island Lake (42 sites), Valley View (8 sites), Little Bear (40 sites), Carp Lake (20 sites) and Ward Lake (26 sites). All are open from late May through Labor Day; $10 to $12 per night. More campgrounds can be reached via the unpaved Trickle Park Road, which starts near Valley View Campground and runs east from the scenic byway for about 14 miles.

**UNCOMPAHGRE NATIONAL FOREST** 🏃 Two separate areas make up Uncompahgre National Forest. The rolling juniper-and-pine-forest terrain of the Uncompahgre Plateau, a vast, uninhabited island in the sky 9000 feet above sea level, extends south of the Grand and Gunnison valleys for 65 miles, from the Grand Junction area to the Montrose area. The Plateau Unit, which has neither high mountains nor significant bodies of water, is not widely used for recreation. Deer are abundant on the plateau; so are mountain lions and bobcats, though these nocturnal predators usually avoid human contact. Uncompahgre National Forest also includes the northern part of the San Juan Mountains around Telluride, Ouray and Lake City, described in Chapters Seven and Eight. ~ There is no paved road access. Divide Road, a wide, graded forest road, climbs to the north end of the plateau from

Route 141 south of Grand Junction, runs its length and descends to Montrose. The Delta-Nucla Road, another graded dirt road, climbs southwest from Delta to join Divide Road; 970-874-6600.

▲ The Uncompahgre Plateau has two small campgrounds for RVs and tents (no hookups). Columbine Campground (6 sites; free) is located southwest of Delta. Iron Spring Campground (7 sites; free) is southwest of Montrose. Neither campground has water; both are open from June through October, weather permitting.

**COLORADO RIVER STATE PARK–ISLAND ACRES** Originally a large island in the Colorado River used as a landmark and encampment site by Ute Indians and mountain men, Island Acres was later planted with peach orchards. In 1967, the State of Colorado converted the island into a recreation area by building a dike to link it with the riverbank, leaving four lakes for swimming, fishing and nonmotorized boating. There are rainbow trout in spring and fall and catfish, bluegill and carp year-round; ice fishing in winter. Facilities include picnic areas with tables, drinking water and restrooms, and a nature trail (.75 mile). Day-use fee, $5. ~ Located 15 miles east of Grand Junction on Route 70 at the exit for the Grand Mesa Scenic Byway; 970-434-3388.

▲ There are 80 RV/tent sites (50 with full hookups); $12 to $20 per night; dump station for RVs.

**VEGA STATE PARK** The largest body of water in the Grand Valley area, two-mile-long Vega Reservoir is a local favorite for waterskiing, windsurfing and jet skiing. Abundant wildflowers and the subalpine beauty of its mountain setting attract nature lovers to the lake's shore. Visitors sometimes spot deer, elk, beaver, blue grouse and wild turkeys here. The park affords access to Grand Mesa trails for hikers, mountain bikers and four-wheel-drive vehicles. The lake has trout in the spring and fall and is a very popular ice-fishing spot in winter. There are picnic areas with tables, drinking water, restrooms and a nature trail. Day-use fee, $5. ~ Exit Route 70 at Colorado River State Park—Island Acres and follow Route 330 east through the town of Collbran to the park, a distance of about 35 miles; 970-487-3407..

▲ There are 109 RV/tent sites (no hookups); $12 per night; dump station for RVs.

**HIGHLINE LAKE STATE PARK** Surrounding two lakes amid Grand Valley farmland near Fruita, this park provides a full range of water recreation. Highline Lake, a 160-acre manmade reservoir, is used for waterskiing, jet skiing and windsurfing; it also offers an overlook where birders watch the many species of migratory birds that use the lake as a rest stop.

Boating on the smaller Mack Mesa Lake is limited to electric and hand-propelled craft, and there is a wheelchair-accessible fishing pier. Highline Lake has good warm-water fishing for catfish and crappie. Mack Mesa Lake offers excellent early-season trout fishing. Facilities include picnic areas with tables, drinking water, restrooms and a phone. Day-use fee, $5. ~ Located seven miles northwest of Loma near Route 139; 970-858-7208.

▲ There are 28 RV/tent sites (no hookups); $12 per night; showers.

## Outdoor Adventures

### RIVER RUNNING

**GLENWOOD SPRINGS AREA** In Glenwood Springs, raft trips both through Glenwood Canyon on the Colorado River and down the Roaring Fork River are offered by **Rock Garden Rafting**. ~ 1308 County Road 129; 970-945-6737. Also contact **Whitewater Rafting** for raft trips on the Colorado River. ~ 51100 Route 6/24; 970-945-8477.

**RIFLE/CRAIG AREA** Raft trips through the wild reaches of the Snake and Yampa rivers in Dinosaur National Monument can be arranged through **Moving Mountains Inc.** ~ 2774 Burgess Creek Road, Steamboat Springs; 970-870-9359, 877-624-2538; www. movingmountains.com. There are also outfitters in Vernal, Utah, that serve this area.

Near Fruita, the favorite stretch of the Colorado River for rafting runs through Ruby and Horse Thief canyons, where you may see ducks, beaver, coyote, mule deer and even eagles.

**GRAND JUNCTION AREA** Rimrock Adventures offers full-day raft trips through the canyons, as well as shorter guided trips and raft, canoe and tube rentals. The trips range from one hour to a half-day. Rimrock also has all-day combination horseback and rafting trips. ~ P.O. Box 608, Fruita, CO 81521; 970-858-9555.

### DOWNHILL SKIING

**GLENWOOD SPRINGS AREA** Downhill skiing in the Glenwood Springs area is at the relatively small **Ski Sunlight**. Although this ski area has only three chairlifts, its trails—20 percent beginner, 55 percent intermediate, 20 percent advanced and 5 percent expert— offer a fairly impressive vertical drop of 2010 feet. The season is from Thanksgiving to mid-April. ~ 10901 Four Mile Road, Glenwood Springs; 970-945-7491; www.sunlightmtn.com.

**GRAND JUNCTION AREA** Powderhorn Ski Area is a small intermediate-level ski area with four lifts and a 1650-foot vertical drop on the north slope of Grand Mesa. Located 40 miles east of Gunnison, the ski area has rentals and a ski school. Open December through March. ~ Route 65, Grand Mesa National Forest; 970-268-5700; www.powderhorn.com, e-mail ski@powderhorn.com.

**Ski Rentals** For downhill and cross-country skis, telemarking equipment, snowshoes and snowboards, visit **Sunlight Ski and**

**Bike Shop**. ~ 309 9th Street, Glenwood Springs; 970-945-9425.
**BSR Sports** rents snowboards. ~ 210 7th Street, Glenwood Springs;
970-945-7317.

**GLENWOOD SPRINGS AREA**   **Ski Sunlight Nordic Center** has
miles of groomed cross-country trails, including several that are
accessed by chairlifts. ~ 10901 Four Mile Road, Glenwood Springs;
970-945-7491, 800-445-7931; www.sunlightmtn.com.

**GRAND JUNCTION AREA**   Cross-country skiing is an incomparable experience among the lakes, Douglas-fir forests and lava
hills atop Grand Mesa. The **Grand Mesa Nordic Council**, a local
nonprofit group of skinny-ski enthusiasts, grooms nearly 70 kilometers of trails each winter. ~ P.O. Box 3077, Grand Junction,
CO 81501; 970-434-9753. The **Powderhorn Nordic Center**
grooms six miles of gently sloping cross-country trails, particularly suited for telemarking, within Powderhorn Ski Area. ~ Route
65, Grand Mesa National Forest; 970-268-5700, 800-241-6997;
www.powderhorn.com, e-mail ski@powderhorn.com.

**GLENWOOD SPRINGS AREA**   Glenwood Springs has two nine-
hole executive courses—the **Glenwood Springs Golf Club** (193
Sunny Acres Road; 970-945-7086) and the **Westbank Ranch
Golf Course** (1007 Westbank Road; 970-945-7032). Local duf-
fers head down the interstate to the Rifle Creek Golf Club—see
below.

**RIFLE/CRAIG AREA**   Public golf courses include the 18-hole **Rifle
Creek Golf Club**, adjacent to Rifle Gap Reservoir. This beautiful
course offers a dramatic contrast between the front and back
nines: Golfers on the front nine holes make their way through
canyons between sandstone cliffs, while the back nine run through
mountain meadows along the banks of Rifle Creek. Cart and club
rentals are available. ~ 3004 Route 325, Rifle; 970-625-1093. At
**Battlement Mesa Golf Course**, the 18-hole course with views of
the Colorado River was designed by Joe Finger and Ken Dye. ~
Battlement Mesa; 970-285-7274. In Meeker, there's the modest
(but hardly ever crowded) nine-hole **Meeker Golf Course**. ~ 903
County Road 13, Meeker; 970-878-5642.

**GRAND JUNCTION AREA**   Grand Junction's main public golf
course, the 18-hole **Tiara Rado Golf Course** is located near the
entrance to Colorado National Monument. ~ 2063 South Broadway; 970-245-8085. In the nearby community of Fruita is the
27-hole **Adobe Creek National Golf Course**. It consists of three
interlocking nine-hole courses—Mesa, Monument and Desert;
golfers sign up to play any two. ~ 876 18 1/2 Road; 970-858-0521.

**RIFLE/CRAIG AREA**   Horseback riding is one of the best ways to
explore the vast Flat Tops Wilderness. Horses can be rented by

**CROSS-
COUNTRY
SKIING**

**GOLF**

**RIDING
STABLES**

the hour or day at **Trappers Lake Lodge.** ~ P.O. Box 1230, Meeker, CO 81641; 970-878-4288.

**GRAND JUNCTION AREA**   **Rimrock Adventures,** near the Route 340 entrance to Colorado National Monument, offers guided horseback trips into the back canyons of the national monument and the nearby Black Ridge Wilderness. ~ P.O. Box 608, Fruita, CO 81521; 970-858-9555.

**BIKING**

**GLENWOOD SPRINGS AREA**   The *sine qua non* bike ride in the Glenwood Springs area is the paved **Glenwood Canyon Trail,** suitable for both mountain bikes and ten-speed touring bikes.

**GRAND JUNCTION AREA**   One of the most ambitious and memorable mountain-biking trips anywhere is **Kokopelli's Trail,** a route established in 1989 by the Colorado Plateau Mountain-Bike Trail Association in cooperation with the Bureau of Land Management. The trail begins at the Loma Boat Launch, off Route 70 near Fruita, and runs 128 miles along back roads and trails generally following the course of the Colorado River, all the way to Moab, Utah. ~ Grand Junction; 970-241-9561. Another ultimate mountain-bike route is the **Tabeguache Trail,** which goes south from Grand Junction for 142 miles along the Uncompahgre Plateau, climbing to 10,000-foot altitudes. For detailed information on both trails, contact the Bureau of Land Management. ~ 2815 H Road, Grand Junction; 970-244-3000. Or you may call the Colorado Plateau Mountain-Bike Trail Association. ~ P.O. Box 4602, Grand Junction, CO 81501; 970-241-9561.

**Bike Rentals**   Bicycles are for rent in Glenwood Springs at **Sunlight Ski and Bike Shop.** ~ 309 9th Street; 970-945-9425. Also try **BSR Sports** for rentals. ~ 210 7th Street, Glenwood Springs; 970-945-7317. **Canyon Bikes** will not only rent you a mountain bike but will shuttle you to the upper end of Glenwood Canyon so you can coast the 16 miles back to town. ~ Located in the Hotel Colorado, 526 Pine Street; 970-945-8904. In Grand Junction, mountain bikes can be rented at **The Bike Peddler.** ~ 710 North 1st Street; 970-243-5602.

**HIKING**

All distances listed for hiking trails are one way unless otherwise noted.

**GLENWOOD SPRINGS AREA**   Besides the **Hanging Lake Trail,** the most popular hiking trail in Colorado, a number of lesser-known trails start from the paved Glenwood Canyon Trail and climb to the upper reaches of the canyon. Among them are **No Name Trail** and **Grizzly Creek Trail,** each about two miles long. From the end of 8th Street in town, the well-marked 1.5-mile trail up Lookout Mountain offers spectacular views of the town and the Roaring Fork Valley.

**RIFLE/CRAIG AREA**  The fairly steep **Battlement Mesa Trail** (3 miles) runs through varied terrain of scrub oak, spruce, fir and aspen forests and offers views of the Colorado River Valley as it makes its way up to Battlement Reservoirs. To reach the trailhead, take County Road 320 from Rifle for three and a half miles, then turn left on Beaver Creek Road and continue for seven miles to the trailhead.

The four-mile shoreline trail around **Trappers Lake**, off the Flat Tops Trail Scenic Byway east of Meeker, serves as a hub for trails that head off in every direction into the Flat Tops Wilderness, providing access to more than 400 miles of maintained trails. Good day hikes include the trails to **Little Trappers Lake** (2 miles) and **Wall Lake** (5 miles), and the **Fraser Creek Trail** to **Parvin Lake** (4 miles).

The **Sandrocks Nature Trail** (1 mile), just north of Craig on Alta Vista Drive, follows the base of a sandstone cliff where visitors can see hundreds of petroglyphs carved by Indians over a period of at least a thousand years.

**GRAND JUNCTION AREA**  Colorado National Monument has about 44 miles of trails. The most remote and challenging hike in the park is **No Thoroughfare Canyon** (8.5 miles), studded with juniper and enclosed by sheer cliffs 400 feet high. Midway up the canyon, the intermittent stream at the bottom plunges over two waterfalls about three-quarters of a mile apart whenever the water is flowing—usually in late spring. Another great hike in Colorado National Monument is the **Liberty Cap Trail** (5.5 miles), a fairly level trail that follows a ridge to an "island in the sky" overlooking the Grand Valley. The park also has a number of shorter trails suited to hikes of a half-hour to four hours.

One of the best hikes in the Grand Junction area is **Rattlesnake Canyon**, where rock formations include a dozen large nat-

**AUTHOR FAVORITE**

Decades ago, before Glenwood Canyon was discovered by tourists, the steep 1.2-mile trail up to **Hanging Lake**, an idyllic pool with a spectacular view, was one of my favorite hikes. It has since become Colorado's most popular hiking trail. Parking can be a problem, and you're lucky if you can see the little lake for the crowds, but it still ranks among my favorites for a different reason: It's the place every Aspen visitor comes to experience "mountain climbing," and on any given day if you sit midway up the trail for a while, there's a good chance that you'll see a movie star gasping for breath.

ural arches. Take Black Ridge Road, which exits from West Glade Park Road just outside the back entrance to Colorado National Monument. The 11-mile drive to Rattlesnake Canyon takes about an hour. Passenger cars can negotiate the first nine miles, but visitors without four-wheel drive must walk the last two miles. From the road's end, a steep foot trail descends through the first arch, and you reach eight others on a two-mile loop hike.

On Grand Mesa, the main hiking trail is the **Crag Crest Trail** (10 miles). The trail keeps to the high ground as it winds among the lakes and through the fir-and-aspen forests, commanding sweeping views of the mesa, the valley below and the San Juan Mountains in the distance.

▼▼▼▼▼▼▼▼▼▼▼▼

## Transportation

**CAR**

Glenwood Springs, Rifle and Grand Junction are on **Route 70**. Meeker, and Craig are on **Route 13** north of Rifle. From Craig, **Routes 40 and 318** head west to the Dinosaur National Monument and Browns Park area.

**AIR**

**Walker Field Public Airport**, located in Grand Junction, has flights to and from Denver on Continental Airlines, Mesa Airlines/United Express and Sky West/Delta Connection.

**BUS**

**Greyhound** (800-229-9424; www.greyhound.com) offers bus service to Glenwood Springs. ~ West 6th and Laurel streets; 970-945-8501. There's also a station in Grand Junction. ~ 230 South 5th Street; 970-242-6012.

**TRAIN**

**Amtrak** offers passenger service to Glenwood Springs and Grand Junction on the "California Zephyr" or the "Desert Wind." Both trains follow the same route through the Rockies between Denver and Salt Lake City. ~ 800-872-7245; www.amtrak.com.

**CAR RENTALS**

Grand Junction has a full complement of name-brand car-rental agencies. Most are located at Walker Field Airport, including **Avis Rent A Car** (800-331-1212), **Budget Rent A Car** (800-527-0700), **Hertz Rent A Car** (800-654-3131) and **National Car Rental** (800-227-7368).

**TAXIS**

Cab service in Grand Junction is provided by **Sunshine Taxi**. ~ 970-245-8294.

# Pikes Peak Region

From the summit of Pikes Peak, theoretically you can see parts of Wyoming, Nebraska, Kansas, Oklahoma, Texas and New Mexico—in addition to more than half of Colorado. Of course, the visible parts of these six states are merely indistinguishable segments of the flat, featureless horizon 200 miles away, blurring toward the north into the murky atmosphere that conceals both Denver and the horizon beyond, but the panoramic view of the immediate surrounding area is worth the drive, train ride or hike to the top of the mountain.

Jutting up out of the prairie like an 8000-foot pyramid, Pikes Peak offers a study in contrasts. Though it reaches to within five miles of downtown Colorado Springs, the mountain's 450 square miles of alpine tundra and evergreen forest is wilderness so slightly touched by humans that black bears, mountain lions, elk and bighorn sheep make it their home. To the north, the gentle, low mountains of the Rampart Range cradle the Garden of the Gods and the U.S. Air Force Academy. Looking west, the casino glitter and forgotten gold mines of Cripple Creek mark the gateway to South Park and the neat row of 14,000-foot peaks in the Collegiate Range. Cheyenne Mountain, which reaches southward toward the Arkansas River, the Royal Gorge and its namesake, Cañon City, appears to be a pristine wilderness of steep slopes and deep canyons, but in fact the mountain conceals a huge, bizarre underground military complex, a remnant of the Cold War era.

It's easy to see why "Pikes Peak or Bust!" was the rallying cry that carried more than 100,000 pioneers west in 1859, pursuing dreams of gold strikes deep in the unexplored wilderness of the Colorado Rockies. As they crossed the Great Plains in wagons or on foot with handcarts, Pikes Peak was the first mountain peak to break the skyline, announcing the end of the two-month journey. The huge mountain marked the gateway to the land where veins of gold and silver lay waiting to be claimed. Colorado City, at the foot of Pikes Peak, marked the start of a road many gold seekers took on their way to South Park and Leadville, and formed the nucleus of modern Colorado Springs.

The Pikes Peak region boasted Colorado's first major tourist resorts as early as the 1870s, when travelers came by train from the East Coast and Europe to hike to the top of Pikes Peak or bask in the soothing waters of world-famous Manitou Springs at the foot of the mountain.

More than 30 years after the "Pikes Peak or Bust!" gold rush put the area on the map and made the mountain a household word, a new and even larger gold find on the west side of Pikes Peak brought a tidal wave of population and prosperity to the region. At the turn of the 20th century, Colorado Springs emerged as the financial center of the gold boom, setting the stage for an era of Roaring '20s elegance that added to the town's tourist appeal.

Gold mines come and gold mines go. Although many locals believe the rich gold veins that still remain in the earth beneath Cripple Creek to be merely an offshoot of a fabulous mother lode in the center of Pikes Peak, the mines were abandoned in the 1930s as changes in federal law made gold mining unprofitable. Summer tourism, however, has sustained the region through bad times and good. Since the 1960s, Colorado Springs' beautiful setting and dry, sunny climate have also helped attract many high-tech industries to the area, swelling the population and making tourism relatively less important to the city's economy; yet the economy of most other towns in the Pikes Peak region—including the Colorado Springs suburbs of Old Colorado City and Manitou Springs—still depends on tourist dollars.

▼ ▼ ▼ ▼ ▼ ▼ ▼ ▼ ▼ ▼ ▼ ▼ ▼ ▼ ▼ ▼
## Colorado Springs Area

In 1872, railroad builder William Jackson Palmer ran 60 miles of track south from Denver, then founded Colorado Springs so people would have someplace to go on his railroad. The city's name is a synthesis of Colorado City and Manitou Springs, already a famous spa. There never were any springs in Colorado Springs.

As it grew into an exclusive resort, Colorado Springs was nicknamed "Little London" for its popularity with British nobility. Later still, it came to be known as "Newport in the Rockies" for its elegant mansions. From the 1890s to the 1960s, Colorado Springs was one of the wealthiest communities per capita in the country, the Aspen of another era.

**SIGHTS**

Today, **Colorado Springs** is by far the largest community in the Pikes Peak area—in fact, the second-largest city in Colorado and the third largest in the Rocky Mountain West. The population of Colorado Springs quadrupled between 1969 and 1972 as military personnel returning from Vietnam were discharged from the Army at Fort Carson south of town. Electronics firms built plants on the north side. Suburbs and shopping malls sprawled farther and farther out across the eastern plains. But the old-time tourist towns in the hills and canyons along the west edge of the city, seemingly oblivious to the metropolis bustling along on the other side of the freeway, have changed little in two generations, though, like many historic districts in tourist areas, they've been spiffed up lately.

Traveling south from Denver on Route 25, motorists leave the farthest reaches of Front Range suburbia upon passing the town of **Castle Rock** and the towering butte for which it is named, then crest a 9000-foot ridge inaccurately called **Monument Pass**. From here, the highway begins a long, slow 100-mile descent toward the Arkansas River.

About ten miles before reaching the outskirts of Colorado Springs, travelers come to the **United States Air Force Academy**, where college-age cadets train to become career officers in a rigorous four-year program. With more than one million visitors a year, the academy is the most-visited tourist attraction in the Pikes Peak region. The buildings of greatest interest to visitors include the Barry Goldwater Visitors Center, the planetarium, the athletic field house, and the cadet chapel with its 17 futuristic spires. On weekdays during the school year, visitors are welcome to watch the noon formation (it's actually at 12:30 p.m.), in which 4400 cadets assemble in rank and file on the central parade ground before marching to lunch. ~ 2346 Academy Drive, Colorado Springs; 719-333-1110; www.usafa.af.mil.

**Pikes Peak Region**

A visit to the **Western Museum of Mining & Industry**, near the Air Force Academy's north gate, can enhance travelers' understanding and appreciation of the gold mines they will see in the Cripple Creek area and other parts of Colorado. Exhibits demonstrate the complete process of gold mining, from prospecting through drilling and blasting to refining the ore. Closed Sunday from October through May. Admission. ~ 1025 Northgate Road, Colorado Springs; 719-488-0880, 800-752-6558; www.wmmi.org.

Between the Air Force Academy and the Garden of the Gods, the **Pro Rodeo Hall of Fame and American Cowboy Museum** presents short films on rodeo riding and the more mundane work of punching cattle. The highlight of the museum, the Pro Rodeo Hall of Fame commemorates legendary bronco and Brahma riders. Admission. ~ 101 Pro Rodeo Drive, Colorado Springs; 719-528-4764.

On the city's northwestern outskirts lies the **Garden of the Gods**. The 1350-acre city park is filled with orange sandstone spires and monoliths and bordered by an escarpment of pink alabaster. Take a hike or just drive through the park on paved roads to see Balanced Rock, Steamboat Rock and the Kissing Camels, some of the most photographed rock formations in the West. Although climbing without a permit is prohibited, on weekends you're sure to see expert rock climbers challenging the 200-foot-high faces of the Gateway Rocks. One route into the park is north from Old Colorado City on 31st Street; others are from Manitou Springs and the Garden of the Gods Road exit from Route 25 north of Colorado Springs. The free **Museum of Natural and Cultural History** has a theater presentation on geology, and offers guided tours and transportation throughout the park. ~ 1805 North 30th Street; 719-634-6666.

Near the north entrance to the Garden of the Gods is **Rock Ledge Ranch Living History Site**. This city-operated living museum re-creates early-day farms of the Pikes Peak area. Buildings include a 1868 homestead, a 1895 ranch house, and a bigger 1907 home. Guides in period costume enact old-time lifestyles, and the fields and pastures of the ranch are worked by means of traditional 19th-century farming methods. Admission. ~ Gateway Road, Colorado Springs; 719-578-6777.

HIDDEN ►     Nearby, **Glen Eyrie Conference Center** was the mansion of Colorado Springs' founder, Denver & Rio Grande Railroad tycoon William Jackson Palmer. When it was built in 1904, the 67-room Tudor-style castle with its 700 acres of grounds was the largest and most expensive home west of the Mississippi. It had its own steam-powered electrical generator and a four-story elevator. A mile-long chimney tunnel that carried smoke from the mansion's 24 fireplaces far up the canyon reveals the dislike of smoke and soot that Palmer developed during his years as a railroad builder. The same aversion prompted him to include the nation's first air-pollution laws in the original Colorado Springs city charter. Glen Eyrie is now the headquarters of a Christian youth group called the Navigators. In summer, daily public tours of the estate are offered at 1:00 p.m., and a formal Victorian high tea is served at 2:30 p.m. in the castle's music room. Admission. ~ 3820 North 30th Street, Colorado Springs; 719-634-0808; home.navigators. org/us/gleneyrie.

If you continue through the Garden of the Gods to one of its several west entrances, you will join Route 24 in Old Colorado City or Manitou Springs, both historic, visitor-oriented suburbs of Colorado Springs; Manitou Springs is outside the city limits, nd Old Colorado City is inside. (Manitou Springs is covered separately in the "Pikes Peak Area" section later in this chapter.)

Colorado City, founded in 1859 during the Pikes Peak gold rush, was the first town in the area. Now part of Colorado Springs'

# Colorado Springs

**POINTS OF INTEREST**

Ⓐ Broadmoor Hotel
Ⓑ Cheyenne Mountain Zoo
Ⓒ Colorado Springs Fine Arts Center
Ⓓ Colorado Springs Pioneer Museum
Ⓔ Garden of the Gods
Ⓕ Ghost Town Museum
Ⓖ Glen Eyrie
Ⓗ McAllister House Museum
Ⓘ Old Colorado City
Ⓙ Pro Rodeo Hall of Fame and American Cowboy Museum
Ⓚ Rock Ledge Ranch Living History Site
Ⓛ Rocky Mountain Motorcycle Museum
Ⓜ Seven Falls
Ⓝ U.S. Olympic Training Center
Ⓞ Van Briggle Art Pottery
Ⓟ Will Rogers Shrine of the Sun

west side, the old wooden storefronts and red-brick Victorian office buildings along the main street of **Old Colorado City** were refurbished in the 1970s and 1980s and reborn as a historic district of cafés and cute shops. Located on West Colorado Avenue between 24th and 31st streets (take Cimarron Street/Route 24 west from Route 24 and turn left on 26th Street), Old Colorado City is a centrally located starting point for touring the major tourist attractions of the Colorado Springs area. You'll find exhibits on the area's early days and redevelopment at the **Old Colorado City Historical Society History Center**. ~ 1 South 24th Street; 719-636-1225.

It is possible to see all the major sights of the Pikes Peak area without going into the downtown or east-side areas of Colorado Springs. Visitors who take the time to explore these parts of town, however, can find a few unique places. The **Colorado Springs Pioneers Museum**, in the old county courthouse across the street from the present courthouse and jail at the south end of downtown, has two floors of exhibits ranging from antique Van Briggle pottery to firearms. The restored courtroom upstairs dates back to 1903. Closed Sunday off-season and Monday year-round. ~ 215 South Tejon Street, Colorado Springs; 719-385-5990; www.cspm.org.

The 1903 courtroom at Colorado Springs Pioneers Museum has been used as a set for motion pictures and the "Perry Mason" television series.

North of downtown, the **McAllister House Museum** preserves the one-and-a-half-story brick home of Major Henry McAllister, one of the city's founding fathers. His enduring contribution was to plant 5000 trees along the now-shady streets north of downtown. Built in 1873, the McAllister House was the first brick residence in Colorado Springs. The exhibits consist entirely of the home's original furnishings, which offer a look at the lifestyle of one of the city's wealthiest residents in the late 19th century. Admission. ~ 423 North Cascade Avenue, Colorado Springs; 719-635-7925.

One mile north of downtown, adjacent to the Colorado College campus, is the **Colorado Springs Fine Arts Center**. The building is said to be the finest example of an odd architectural style called "Pueblo Deco"—a 1930s art deco variation inspired by the Indian architecture of New Mexico. The permanent exhibits also have a Southwestern flavor, with Pueblo and Navajo Indian collections and a replica of a *penitente* chapel. Three of the museum's five exhibition halls are used for traveling exhibits of folk art and contemporary art, many of them on tour from the Smithsonian Institution. The museum also houses one of the largest theaters in town, used by several community organizations for plays, concerts and dance performances. Closed Monday. Admission. ~ 30 West Dale Street, Colorado Springs; 719-634-5581; www.csfineartscenter.org.

Next to the Fine Arts Center is the **Museum of the American Numismatic Association**. Although the museum space appears small, it contains one of the world's largest exhibits of antique and exotic money; in the United States, only the Smithsonian's collection is larger. Displays include early American coins and currency, medals, privately minted coins of the gold-rush era, and a world history of money from 600 B.C. to the present. Admission. ~ 818 North Cascade Avenue, Colorado Springs; 719-632-2646; www.money.org.

East of downtown, the **U.S. Olympic Training Center** occupies a former U.S. Air Force base that was abandoned as the city grew to surround it. Each year, more than 15,000 Olympic hopefuls attend training camps at the 37-acre complex. The visitors center has a muralled rotunda containing a hall of fame, as well as art exhibits and a sculpture garden. Regularly scheduled tours take visitors through the athletic facilities. ~ 1 Olympic Plaza, Colorado Springs; 719-578-4618; www.olympic-usa.org/about_us/visitor_ctr.html.

Perhaps the least-known and most unusual museum in the Pikes Peak region, the **Rocky Mountain Motorcycle Museum** focuses on the pioneers of motorcycling and has more than 50 fully restored vintage and antique motorcycles dating back as far as 1913, along with a large collection of photographs and memorabilia including pins, dealer signs, riding leathers and accessories. ~ 308 East Arvada Street, Colorado Springs; 719-633-6329.

◄ HIDDEN

To tour the sights of the Broadmoor area on the southwest edge of Colorado Springs, start from Old Colorado City or Route 24 west and take 21st Street south. Near the intersection of 21st Street and Route 24 is a cluster of commercial tourist attractions, including **Ghost Town Museum**, which contains Old West antiques and re-creations of frontier buildings. Admission. ~ 400 South 21st Street, Colorado Springs; 719-634-0696.

Across the parking lot from Ghost Town Museum is **Van Briggle Art Pottery**. The legacy of famed ceramic artist Artus Van Briggle, the sculptural and free-form pottery is made in various styles, including some art deco designs from the '30s. The free tour shows how artisans throw clay on potters' wheels, shape it, glaze it and fire it. Visitors can buy the pottery at the showroom. Van Briggle's is in the old railroad roundhouse where ore trains from Cripple Creek turned around. Across the street, a tall smokestack is all that's left of the old mill where gold was refined and cast into bars. Closed Sunday. ~ 600 South 21st Street, Colorado Springs; 719-633-4080, 800-847-6341; www.vanbriggle.com.

Continue south on 21st Street for about two miles, past Cheyenne Boulevard and Cheyenne Road, to reach the extensive resort complex of the **Broadmoor Hotel**. Even if the ultra-deluxe rates discourage you from staying there, stop in to see this magnificent hotel, ranked as the finest resort west of the Mississippi during the 1920s. In 1918, Cripple Creek refinery tycoon Spencer Penrose, who made a fortune establishing gold refineries in the Cripple Creek district, built the original hotel on the site of an earlier gambling casino and dairy farm. In the era between the World Wars, the Broadmoor was the place where the crowned heads of Europe and Asia stayed when they visited the American West. Located on the shore of its own idyllic private lake, the Broadmoor was reopened in 1992 after a $76 million restoration of the original hotel, in the course of which the old Mediterranean-style building was stripped to its concrete structure, more than 6,000 tons of debris were removed and the marble interior was entirely rebuilt. ~ 1 Lake Avenue, Colorado Springs; 719-634-7711; www.broadmoor.com.

The tennis club, spa and other facilities that surround the hotel itself are just the tip of the iceberg. Past the golf course and up the side of Cheyenne Mountain, the Broadmoor has not only its own ski slopes but also its own zoo. The **Cheyenne Mountain Zoo**, perched midway up the mountainside, has the most spectacular location of any zoo we've seen and more than 500 animals, including an impressive herd of giraffes. Admission. ~ 4250 Cheyenne Mountain Zoo Road, Colorado Springs; 719-633-9925, fax 719-633-2254; www.cmzoo.org.

The paved road through the zoo continues in a series of steep switchbacks up the mountain to the **Will Rogers Shrine of the Sun**. The four-story stone tower, which commands perhaps the finest possible view of the Colorado Springs area, was originally conceived as Cripple Creek gold tycoon and Broadmoor founder Spencer Penrose's monumental tomb. Before it was completed, humorist Will Rogers, a friend of Penrose's, died in a plane crash, and the tower was dedicated to him. Penrose and his wife (but not Will Rogers) are buried under the floor of the small room in the base of the shrine, making him perhaps the only man in history to successfully promote his own grave as a tourist attraction. ~ 719-578-5367.

From the Broadmoor area, head west on either Cheyenne Boulevard or Cheyenne Road; they merge and less than a mile later divide again at the mouth of Cheyenne Canyon. **Seven Falls**, in the south fork of the canyon, is one of the region's oldest commercial tourist attractions. South Cheyenne Creek tumbles into this box canyon down a near-vertical granite cliff in a stairstep series of waterfalls—count 'em, seven—for a total drop of about 300 feet. In winter, when the falls are frozen, and in spring, when snowmelt swells the creek into a torrent, the falls are truly spectacular. It is not possible to see all the falls from the bottom of the canyon. A series of stairways goes up the cliff beside the falls, and another goes to a lookout point from which all can be seen.

An incline elevator also goes up to the lookout. Near the foot of the falls are a small pavilion where American Indian dancers perform. At night, colored floodlights illuminate the cliffs for a mile down the canyon, all the way to the tollgate. Admission. ~ 2850 South Cheyenne Canyon Road, Colorado Springs; 719-632-0765; www.sevenfalls.com.

Drivers who turn right instead of left at the Seven Falls turnoff find themselves in **North Cheyenne Canyon**, which is quite different from South Cheyenne Canyon. For one thing, it's free. Like the Garden of the Gods, North Cheyenne Canyon is a Colorado Springs city park. And as in the Garden of the Gods, you're likely to see expert rock climbers challenging the 400-foot-high granite walls in the middle part of the canyon. The paved road twists steeply in places, to **Helen Hunt Falls**, a classic mountain waterfall that looks exactly like the one on Coors Beer labels.

In peak tourist season, when South Cheyenne Creek often slows to a trickle, recirculating pumps supplement Mother Nature to keep the Seven Falls in operation.

Not far past the falls, the North Cheyenne Canyon Road joins the narrow, unpaved **Gold Camp Road**, originally the trackbed for the Cripple Creek Short Line standard-gauge railroad, which carried ore down from the goldfields at the turn of the 20th century. Until a 2002 tunnel collapse closed the road to auto traffic indefinitely, it ran through Pike National Forest around the south side of Pikes Peak for 36 slow miles, returning to the pavement near Victor. You can still drive one of the most spectacular segments of the road by turning right at the top of North Cheyenne Canyon for an eight-mile return trip to Colorado Springs. The road follows the rim of the canyon, goes through two railroad tunnels and traverses the mountainside high above the city. Despite appearances, there *is* room for two vehicles to pass each other.

The Gold Camp Road comes back to town on 26th Street, across Route 24 from the Old Colorado City area. The road descends from the mountainside into Bear Creek Regional Park. The solar-heated **Bear Creek Nature Center**, at the northwest side of the park, has exhibits on the wildlife of the park's foothills and streamside forests, which can be explored on a network of nature trails. ~ 245 Bear Creek Road, Colorado Springs; 719-520-6387.

The most direct route between Colorado Springs and Cañon City is Route 115, which runs along the perimeter of a military reserve used for maneuvers by the mechanized infantry forces at Fort Carson army base. The 42-mile trip takes less than an hour. Nine miles outside of Colorado Springs, an iron sculpture of a beetle larger than a man marks the entrance to the private, eccentric little **May Natural History Museum**. The museum contains more than 7000 mounted insects of the tropics, some of them brightly colored and others incredibly large. There is also a new space exploration wing featuring photos from Voyager and other space probes. Open May through September; winter visits by appointment. Admission. ~ Route 115, Colorado Springs; 719-576-0450.

As you drive along Route 115, the mountain ridge that rises steeply on your west is **Cheyenne Mountain**. From a distance it's easy to visualize why, in Ute Indian legend, the mountain represented the Dragon of Thirst, who ended a great primordial flood by drinking up the water that covered the earth and has lain sleeping ever since. Even stranger and absolutely true is the fact that tunnels inside the mountain house the **North American Air Defense Command Headquarters**, a Cold War–era control center for U.S. and Canadian missiles built on giant shock absorbers that theoretically would withstand the shock of a direct nuclear strike. Public tours of the facility are rare (though not unheard of), but you can glimpse the massive steel-doored entrance to the facility from the highway about three miles south of the Colorado Springs city limit.

**LODGING**  If you dream of spending a night or two in a European castle, **Glen Eyrie** may be the next best thing. General William Jackson Palmer, Colorado Springs' founder, collected large fireplaces from cathedrals in England and Holland and even imported the roof from an Italian castle to build his majestic home in a secluded canyon near Garden of the Gods. Today it offers incomparable bed-and-breakfast accommodations at a wide range of rates. The castle also serves as the headquarters of the Navigators, a Christian youth group, so you may encounter a little polite proselytizing. No smoking or alcohol; not gay-friendly. ~ 3820 North 30th Street, Colorado Springs; 719-634-0808, 800-944-4536; home. navigators.org/us/gleneyrie.

There are a number of older, low-priced motels along West Colorado Avenue between Old Colorado City and Manitou Springs, relics from the pre-freeway era when this street was the main highway to Pikes Peak and points west. For a country feel in the middle of town, rent one of the 24 cabins nestled among tall shade trees at **Timber Lodge**. Rustic in appearance, all have renovated interiors and modern conveniences including TVs and

**AUTHOR FAVORITE**

The **Broadmoor Hotel** has traditionally been considered the finest resort hotel in Colorado and who am I to argue. Guests can relax by the pool, stroll the extensive grounds, or bike into nearby Cheyenne Canyon. If that doesn't appeal to you, don't worry. There are plenty of other things to do—or not. See page 232 for more information.

phones, and some have full kitchens or kitchenettes. A creek flows through the grounds, and there's a swimming pool. Two- or three-night minimum stay requirements apply to some cabins. ~ 3627 West Colorado Avenue, Colorado Springs; 719-636-3941, 800-448-6762.

Another good bet in this area is the **Garden of the Gods Motel**, a two-story motel offering the most ordinary rooms imaginable and an indoor heated swimming pool within easy walking distance of Old Colorado City. ~ 2922 West Colorado Avenue, Colorado Springs; 719-636-5271, 800-637-0703, fax 719-477-1422. BUDGET TO MODERATE.

An 1897 Victorian just down the street from Old Colorado City, **Our Hearts Inn Old Colorado City Bed & Breakfast** has three distinctively decorated guest rooms with private baths in the main house, as well as a private Western-decor cottage with a fireplace, jacuzzi tub and kitchenette. ~ 2215 West Colorado Avenue, Colorado Springs; 719-473-8684, 800-533-7095; www.inn-colorado-springs.com, e-mail hearts@inn-colorado-springs.com. MODERATE TO DELUXE.

The newest lodging in Old Colorado City, the **Old Town Guest House** was built in 1997 in a red-brick architectural style designed to harmonize with its Victorian surroundings. The three-story building contains just eight guest rooms, each spacious and uniquely decorated, with period-style furnishings and modern touches such as VCRs, CD players and computer ports. A full breakfast is included in the room rate. ~ 115 South 26th Street, Colorado Springs; 719-632-9194, 888-375-4210, fax 719-632-9026; www.oldtown-guesthouse.com, e-mail luxury@oldtown-guesthouse.com. MODERATE TO DELUXE.

Located in the residential part of historic Old Colorado City, the **Holden House 1902 Bed and Breakfast Inn** has five suites in a Victorian-era Colonial Revival home and carriage house. Some suites feature fireplaces and Roman marble tubs large enough for two. ~ 1102 West Pikes Peak Avenue, Colorado Springs; 719-471-3980, 888-565-3980, fax 719-471-4740; www.holdenhouse.com, e-mail mail@holdenhouse.com. DELUXE.

Downtown Colorado Springs is dominated by the **Antlers Adams Mark Hotel**, a modern 292-room high-rise that stands on the site of an earlier Antlers Hotel built by the founder of Colorado Springs. The hotel has a gleaming all-marble lobby and spacious guest rooms with king-size beds and exceptional quality furnishings. All rooms have computer dataports, many have views of Pikes Peak, and some have whirlpool baths. ~ 4 South Cascade Avenue, Colorado Springs; 719-473-5600, 800-444-2326, fax 719-444-0417. ULTRA-DELUXE.

The finest bed and breakfast in downtown Colorado Springs is the **Hearthstone Inn**, an 1885 Victorian mansion built by a paper bag tycoon, located near Colorado College, the Colorado Springs Fine Arts Center and Monument Valley Park. The inn-keepers annexed the neighboring building, built in 1885 as a tuber-culosis sanatorium, and extensively remodeled both buildings to create an antique-filled 25-room hostelry that glows with warm elegance. Rates include a full breakfast. ~ 506 North Cascade Avenue, Colorado Springs; 719-473-4413, 800-521-1885, fax 719-473-1322; www.hearthstoneinn.com, e-mail info@hearthstone inn.com. MODERATE TO ULTRA-DELUXE.

The Roaring Twenties are meticulously preserved at the ele-gant **Broadmoor Hotel**. Instead of slipping into decay like so many other grand hotels, for decades the Broadmoor has been pursu-ing an expansion program designed to keep up with the finest new resorts worldwide. Three hotel annexes have brought the total number of rooms to 700. Rooms in both the old and new parts of the hotel are furnished with antiques, and the hotel's common areas are filled with original paintings by Toulouse-Lautrec and Maxfield Parrish as well as priceless Asian artworks. The lobby areas of the original historic hotel have been renovated, expand-ing the space for shops; for picnickers and in-room snackers, the gourmet food shop is a particularly welcome addition. Among the recreational facilities are three golf courses, three swimming pools, 16 tennis courts, a spa, stables, and a hot-air balloon. ~ 1 Lake Avenue, Colorado Springs; 719-577-5775, 800-634-7711, fax 719-577-5779; www.broadmoor.com. ULTRA-DELUXE.

**DINING**

**Jose Muldoon's**, a sort of cross between a Mexican restaurant and a fern bar, serves contemporary south-of-the-border fare—fajitas are a specialty—as well as a varied selection of steak, chicken and seafood options. Start your meal with the best gazpacho soup in town. The atmosphere in this half-bar, half-restaurant is dark and congenial, with a large courtyard patio for summer dining. ~ 222 North Tejon Street, Colorado Springs; 719-636-2311. BUDGET TO MODERATE.

Another long-time favorite is **Michelle's**, a candy shop, soda fountain and café operated by a Greek family since 1950. The front part of the café is a shop displaying candies made on the premises. In the back part, people gorge themselves on big, elab-orate concoctions of homemade ice cream. Though fewer than one out of ten patrons actually comes here to eat a meal, there is a limited but tasty lunch and dinner menu ranging from cheese-burgers to Greek hero sandwiches, and it's one of the few places downtown that serves breakfast. ~ 122 North Tejon Street; 719-633-5089. There's a second location in the city's main shopping mall. ~ 750 Citadel Drive East; 719-597-9932. BUDGET.

A favorite hangout of the Colorado College crowd since 1975 (though not in the same location), **Poor Richard's Restaurant and**

**Bookstore** features a full range of sandwiches and creative vegetarian choices. ~ 324½ North Tejon Street, Colorado Springs; 719-632-7721. BUDGET.

Since 1950, when Mexican food was almost unknown in these parts, **Nemeth's El Tejon** has been serving great, authentic enchiladas and tacos. They also offer less-familiar Mexican dishes such as *camarones* (shrimp) Mazatlan, seafood burritos and *machaca* (spicy shredded beef). The cozy little restaurant is decorated with a hodgepodge of south-of-the-border mementos ranging from wrought-iron chachkas and pottery to a stuffed marlin. ~ 1005 South Tejon Street; 719-471-0240.

The most exclusive restaurant in Colorado Springs is the Broadmoor Hotel's **Charles Court**. Located in the hotel's modern annex on the west side of the lake, Charles Court is decorated in elegant Tudor style and features fare that changes seasonally, including a sumptuous wild game mixed grill. The presentation, by a serving staff that often seems to outnumber the diners, is impeccable, and the wine cellar—over 100,000 bottles representing 650 wineries—will impress even the most jaded connoisseur. Jackets are required for men. ~ 1 Lake Avenue, Colorado Springs; 719-634-7711. ULTRA-DELUXE.

Also in the Broadmoor Hotel, the Victorian-style **Penrose Room** presents traditional gourmet cuisine with a French flair, including appetizers such as Breton lobster and fava beans, and entrées including châteaubriand and breast of Breton Marsh duck. High tea is served from 2 p.m. to 4 p.m., May through September. There is live music in the evening, and a dancefloor. Jackets are required for men. ~ 1 Lake Avenue, Colorado Springs; 719-634-7711. ULTRA-DELUXE.

The **Lake Terrace Dining Room** serves breakfast daily in elegant surroundings befitting the venerable 1920s part of the Broadmoor Hotel. The pièce de résistance comes on Sundays,

### AUTHOR'S FAVORITE

Decades ago, when I was a student in Colorado Springs, Giuseppe's was the hangout where everybody went for pizza and beer in an atmosphere filled with smoke and folk music. Later it turned respectable and moved to the old train station, but **Giuseppe's Depot** still serves the same great pizza and huge submarine sandwiches, alongside more sophisticated fare such as steak, lasagna, a selection of fresh seafood, Key lime pie and kahlua chocolate mousse, as well as a good selection of wine. Windows overlook the railroad yards, where coal trains still rumble by. ~ 10 South Sierra Madre Street, Colorado Springs; 719-635-3111. BUDGET TO MODERATE.

when the dining room serves a buffet brunch complete with ice sculptures, a piano player, and more than 70 items to choose from. ~ 1 Lake Avenue, Colorado Springs; 719-634-7711. DELUXE.

If down-home food—and lots of it—sounds good to you, check out the **Hungry Farmer**, a huge restaurant on the north side of town that was designed to resemble a barn. Waiters wear overalls, waitresses wear granny dresses and the decor is way cuter than any real farmyard ever was. A bottomless bucket of thick, hearty soup, homemade oatmeal muffins and cinnamon rolls come with all meals. Entrées include seafood, steaks and country-style cooking. ~ 575 Garden of the Gods Road, Colorado Springs; 719-598-7622. MODERATE.

**SHOPPING**  Despite high-volume tourism, Colorado Springs and the Pikes Peak area have never developed the high-priced, arts-oriented retail shops that characterize so many Colorado resort areas.

**Old Colorado City**, a formerly rundown three-block area along Colorado Avenue, has blossomed into new life with an array of artisans' shops.

**Simpich Character Dolls** is both factory and gallery for these unique, individually made collectible dolls, which are sold nationwide; factory tours are available. ~ 2413 West Colorado Avenue, Colorado Springs; 719-636-3272.

Artist Michael Garman, famous in the world of cowboy art for his finely detailed sculptural miniatures of Old West street scenes, had his factory-like studio in Old Colorado City long before the neighborhood became trendy; today, his works are on display in the big **Michael Garman Gallery**, now operated by his son Mike, who is following in his father's famous footsteps. Adjoining the Gallery is **Michael Garman's Magic Town**, a miniaturized city neighborhood where 18 old-fashioned buildings form the backdrop for changing scenes of everyday life of yesteryear. Admission. ~ 2418 West Colorado Avenue, Colorado Springs; 719-471-9391.

The **Pine Creek Art Gallery** exhibits paintings and sculpture by local and national artists. ~ 2419 West Colorado Avenue, Colorado Springs; 719-633-6767.

**NIGHTLIFE**  **Loonies Comedy Corner** is Colorado Springs' top comedy club and features adult humor. ~ 1305 North Academy Boulevard, Colorado Springs; 719-591-0707.

A favorite singles danceclub is **Meadow Muffins**, a perennial favorite even though it presents deejayed dance music only. ~ 2432 West Colorado Avenue, Colorado Springs; 719-633-0583. A lively alternative danceclub that does have live bands is **The Underground**. This student-oriented hotspot offers a variety of goings-on, from poetry slams to hip-hop and '80s nights. It's located in the basement of the once-staid, historic building that housed the Colorado Springs Mining Exchange, a major stock market during the gold rush days. ~ 110 North Nevada Avenue, Colorado Springs; 719-633-0590. Also downtown, **Rum Bay** has contemporary dance music in one room and '60s oldies rock in the other, as well as 200 different kinds of rum. ~ 120 North Tejon Street, Colorado Springs; 719-634-3522. The place to go for Caribbean and salsa music is **King's Palace**, which also has darts, pool, shuffleboard, a small basketball court and a cigar bar. ~ 2815 East Platte Avenue, Colorado Springs; 719-472-7410.

For adults, the classic Colorado Springs hangout is the **Golden Bee**. A sing-along ragtime piano player encourages a party atmosphere; the crowd is a mix of the Broadmoor's well-heeled guests and Colorado Springs locals who come here for fun. This is where you can watch sophisticated women dripping in diamonds, as well as lawyers and bankers competing to see who can chug a "yard" of beer (a three-foot-tall carafe) the fastest. ~ Broadmoor Hotel, 1 Lake Avenue, Colorado Springs; 719-634-7711.

Bear Creek Regional Park and Bear Creek Canyon Park are especially beautiful in autumn, when the forest along the creek bursts into a riot of reds, oranges and golds.

A long-established gay-friendly club (in fact, it's often said to be the oldest alternative lifestyles club in the state), the **Hide N' Seek** features deejay dance music. The dark, warehouselike club has one of the town's largest dancefloors. There is also a country bar and a restaurant. ~ 512 West Colorado Avenue, Colorado Springs; 719-634-9303.

**BEAR CREEK REGIONAL PARK AND BEAR CREEK CANYON PARK** 🧍🏇 Birdwatchers, equestrians and joggers meet on this network of trails among the scrub oak foothills on the west side of Colorado Springs. The visitors center contains exhibits on bird and animal life found within the park boundaries. While the west half of the park is rugged and wild, the east half has neat lawns, tennis courts and soccer and football fields. Bear Creek Canyon Park, adjoining the west side of Bear Creek Regional Park and continuing south to Gold Camp Road, follows the creek for about two miles and offers numerous parking areas and picnic sites. Facilities include picnic areas, restrooms, a visitors center, game fields and nature trails. ~ Located south of Route 24 between 21st Street and 26th Street, which becomes Bear Creek Canyon Road and joins the Gold Camp Road; 719-520-6387.

**PARKS**

Besides the huge granite massif that dominates the skyline west of Colorado Springs, the Pikes Peak region includes an assortment of towns and scenic routes that surround the mountain on all sides. Manitou Springs, the quaint old tourist town at the foot of Pikes Peak's east face, is the natural starting point for exploring the town and the region. From

## Pikes Peak Area

there, the main highway skirts the north side of the mountain, following an old railroad route known as Ute Pass (though it is not a true pass because it has no summit). Other former railroad routes—the Gold Camp Road from Colorado Springs and the Phantom Canyon Road from Cañon City—provide access to the rugged forest and canyon country on the south side of the Peak. On the west side, the Cripple Creek District was once the richest goldfield in the Rockies, supporting a city that ranked as one of the region's largest at the turn of the century—long since abandoned but recently revived as a gambling center. Allow at least four days to explore all sides of Pikes Peak, beginning with an ascent to the summit.

**SIGHTS**    About two miles west of Old Colorado City, **Manitou Springs** is the actual site of the 26 mineral springs for which Colorado Springs was named. Beginning in the 1870s, people from the East and even Europe began to flock to Manitou Springs for the dry mountain climate and the healing waters, which were thought to cure everything from tuberculosis to polio. In those days, the circular building in the center of town was a fashionable spa, and a geyser spurted at regular intervals on Manitou Avenue. Most of the springs were later capped or clogged by mineral deposits. Since the late 1980s, the nonprofit **Manitou Springs Foundation** has been working to restore the springs to their original flow during the spa era. The organization conducts guided "Springabout" tours and offers free walking-tour maps.~ 354 Manitou Avenue, Manitou Springs; 719-685-5089.

Today, a number of old-time tourist attractions live on in this quaintly old-fashioned town. Up the hill, easier to reach from the Route 24 bypass than from the town itself, the **Cave of the Winds** has been one of the Pikes Peak area's top commercial sites for more than a century. The cave is long, narrow and twisting, with plenty of stalactites, stalagmites, crystal formations and colored lights. Admission. ~ Cave of the Winds Road, Manitou Springs; 719-685-5444; www.caveofthewinds.com.

Just down the highway from the cave, the **Manitou Cliff Dwellings Museum** is a group of Anasazi cliff dwellings that were found in a canyon near Dolores in southwestern Colorado and moved to a sandstone cliff above Manitou Springs in the 1920s. It probably made sense at the time, when few travelers could reach the area of Dolores and Mesa Verde. Today, the most remarkable fact about these reconstructed cliff dwellings is that they were disassembled into tens of thousands of individual stones, each marked for position, and reassembled 300 miles away. Admission. ~ Route 24, Manitou Springs; 719-685-5242, 800-354-9971; www.cliffdwellingsmuseum.com.

The best Manitou Springs tourist attractions are on Ruxton Avenue, which leads south up a canyon from the center of town.

**Miramont Castle** is a restored 1895 stone mansion built by a ◄ HIDDEN
wealthy French priest who had come to Manitou Springs to seek a cure for his tuberculosis. It was opened to the public as a museum in the late 1970s. A fantasyland of eclectic architecture, the castle incorporates nine different styles—among them Romanesque, Gothic, Tudor and Byzantine. Some rooms have been restored with period furnishings, while others house miscellaneous collections such as dolls. Closed Monday. Admission. ~ 9 Capitol Hill Avenue, Manitou Springs; 719-685-1011.

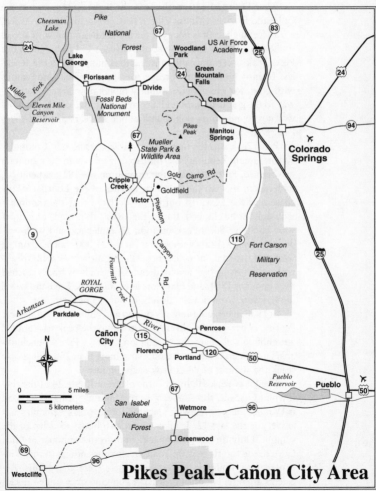

**Pikes Peak–Cañon City Area**

At the end of Ruxton Avenue is the depot for the **Pikes Peak Cog Railway**, certainly the easiest way to climb the peak. The railroad uses Swiss-made two-car diesel trains to climb the otherwise-inaccessible west face of Pikes Peak. The trains run from May through October, twice daily during the spring and fall, as many as eight times a day during peak season. The round trip takes between three and four hours. Reservations are essential. Admission. ~ 515 Ruxton Avenue, Manitou Springs; 719-685-5401, fax 719-685-9033; www.cograil way.com, e-mail info@cograilway.com.

The Pikes Peak Cog Railway, the highest in the United States, climbs grades as steep as 26 percent.

Pikes Peak (14,110 feet) is not the highest mountain in the Colorado Rockies (Mount Elbert, between Leadville and Aspen, is 323 feet higher). It is not even the highest mountain with a road to the top. (Mount Evans, west of Denver, is 154 feet higher.) But Pikes Peak is certainly the most famous mountain in the Rockies. To early pioneers and prospectors its name was synonymous with gold, for the massive, solitary mountain marked the gateway to the goldfields around Fairplay and Leadville—though gold was not found on its slopes until about 35 years after the Pikes Peak gold rush.

Pikes Peak was the first major tourist attraction in Colorado. When Captain Zebulon Pike, the explorer for whom the mountain was named, failed to reach the summit on his 1810 expedition, undertaken to map the southern reaches of the Louisiana Purchase and the Mexican border, he declared that the mountain would never be climbed. But by the 1870s, thousands of visitors were climbing Pikes Peak on foot, on muleback and by horse-drawn carriage. A fancy resort hotel at the 11,000-foot level on the west side, its ruins now lost beneath the surface of a city reservoir, did a thriving business for decades. Cog railway tracks reached the summit in 1891, and two years later, Katherine Lee Bates wrote the lyrics to "America the Beautiful" on top of the peak.

In 1916, when gold-refinery tycoon and philanthropist Spencer Penrose converted the old carriage road up the peak to a graded automobile toll road, the assault on Captain Pike's "unclimbable" mountain began in earnest. Now, more than 250,000 people reach the summit of Pikes Peak each summer.

The **Pikes Peak Highway** turns off from Route 24 at the tiny town of Cascade, three miles west of Manitou Springs. The road is 19 miles long, paved with blacktop for the first seven miles and gravel for the last 12. It takes about two hours to drive to the summit. Only on the switchback climb from the house at Glen Cove to the top ridge is the road precipitous enough to make inexperienced mountain drivers wish there were guard rails. Accidents are rare, but breakdowns are common since some vehicles need fuel-system adjustments to run at such high altitudes. Motorists who are inexperienced at mountain driving would be well advised to take the cog train instead, which ascends the east face of the mountain at a straight, steep angle from Manitou Springs. Admission. ~ 719-385-7325.

Whichever mode of transportation you choose, morning is the best time to climb Pikes Peak. The view is clearer then because there's less smog over Colorado Springs and Denver, and the weather is more reliable in the morning. Even in August, afternoon lightning storms can bring snowdrifts, closing the road temporarily and stranding motorists on top until the snowplows come. Visitors to Pikes Peak soon learn what a climatic difference elevation makes. Temperatures at the summit fall below freezing every night and, even on the sunniest days, typically run 40 degrees lower than in Colorado Springs.

Above timberline, Pikes Peak's long ridgeline is carpeted with delicate arctic tundra—tiny plants and flowers that can grow in the thinnest layers of soil and survive severe cold. Visitors taking either the toll road or the cog railway are likely to see some of the Rocky Mountain bighorn sheep that graze on the tundra, as well as alpine rodents—big, rotund golden marmots and smaller animals called picas that look something like prairie dogs. The very top of the mountain is so high that not even tundra can grow; the only life native to the boulder-strewn summit is lichen.

The Pikes Peak summit has a large curio shop, snack bar and observation deck. From the top, on a clear day, you can see most of Colorado, from the Continental Divide to the boundaries of Kansas, Oklahoma and New Mexico. The eastern horizon is about 175 miles away. While on the summit, keep in mind that there is not much oxygen at 14,000 feet. Excessive exercise can cause altitude sickness—dizziness, nausea, fainting. Alcoholic beverages, which have a much more powerful effect at high altitudes, should be avoided. Another high-altitude effect many people experience is sleepiness on the way down the mountain.

In addition to the interpretive exhibits at the visitors center on Pikes Peak's summit, two small museums tell more about the mountain and its history. The **Pikes Peak Auto Hill Climb Race Car Museum** traces the traditional Fourth of July road race to the summit, presents video views of what driving in the race is like, and displays some of the cars that have raced up the peak in past years. Admission. ~ 135 Manitou Avenue, Manitou Springs; 719-685-4400. The **Ute Pass Cultural Center**, housed in what was the first high school in the bedroom community of Woodland Park back in the 1930s, has a small art exhibit and a visitor information center. ~ Located 18 miles from Manitou Springs up Route 24 on the way to Cripple Creek, 210 East Midland Avenue, Woodland Park; 719-687-5284.

## DRIVING TOUR
# Gold Belt Loop

The backroad Gold Belt Loop connects Cañon City and the Cripple Creek district. The trip takes you along the south slope of Pikes Peak, up and down 122 miles of 19th-century narrow-gauge railroad and stagecoach routes that were graded into auto roads but never paved. If you drive an SUV, this kind of road is why you got it, but you can also make the trip in a regular automobile. (Do *not* try it in a motorhome or if you're terrified of narrow roads with sharp dropoffs.) If you're starting from Cripple Creek, you'll join the middle of the tour as described here.

**PHANTOM CANYON ROAD**     From Cañon City, drive east on Route 50 for seven miles to the intersection with Route 67, which continues south to Florence. Turn left and drive north on County Road 67. The pavement soon ends as the road crosses grazing lands before passing through a notch in a hogback ridge at **Indian Springs Trace Fossil Site**, where paleontologists study fossilized rodent holes. Then it follows Eightmile Creek into Pike National Forest between the steep cliffs of **Phantom Canyon** (page 251). Spectacular with some narrow, edgy parts, the road is the former trackbed of what was the first rail route to Cripple Creek (until the train derailed on the steel bridge you drive across today). The route continues for 35 miles, climbing about 5000 feet in elevation to the high aspen forest. Uphill traffic has the right of way, but you can't assume that drivers coming downhill know that. East of the road lies the vast, roadless **Beaver Creek Wilderness Study Area**, home to abundant elk, beaver, bears, bighorn sheep and the largest concentration of mountain lions in the state.

**GOLDEN LOOP HISTORIC PARKWAY**     As you approach the town of **Victor** (page 244), the Phantom Canyon Road rejoins the pavement.

The stretch of Route 24 between Manitou Springs and Woodland Park, commonly called **Ute Pass** although it is a canyon and not a true pass, follows the route of the Colorado Midland, a standard-gauge train that carried gold ore from Cripple Creek to Colorado Springs for processing. Tall smokestacks south of Route 24 between 8th and 21st streets mark the site of the former refinery. On the way up the "pass," the village of **Green Mountain Falls** is one of the region's prettiest mountain communities. The waterfall for which it is named is well hidden on a secluded dirt road without signs, but the lake in the center of town makes a good picnic spot.

The **Victor/Battle Mountain Interpretive Site** affords a view of the mining district and information on some of the major mines and processing mills. Turn right (east) to take the backroad into Cripple Creek. It takes you past the old mining town of **Goldfield**, just past which is a marked trailhead on the left for the **Vindicator Valley Trail**, a two-mile walk among mines of the gold boom era. Continuing on the same road will take you past active gold mines on the way into **Cripple Creek** (page 241).

SHELF ROAD    After visiting Cripple Creek, follow Route 67 south. Signs will say you're going toward Victor. Halfway there, a tight hairpin curve marks the ghost town of **Anaconda**. The unpaved road that turns off to the left is the Shelf Road (County Road 88), a stagecoach route from the 1890s that will take you back to Cañon City. It follows the creek for which Cripple Creek was named into a steep, rocky canyon, then under a massive granite arch called **Window Rock** (watch for bighorn sheep) to the **Shelf Road Rock Climbing Area**, before reaching the narrow, cliffhanger stretch of road that traverses a "shelf" across a near-vertical slope. The road descends out of the mountains to **Red Canyon Park** and the **Garden Park Fossil Area**, where the first stegosaurus skeleton was discovered. You'll rejoin Route 50 on the east side of Cañon City.

ALTERNATE ROUTE    If you found the Phantom Canyon Road scary, you'll find the Shelf Road even scarier. You'll be traveling downhill, and since uphill traffic has the right of way, you may have to back up on especially narrow stretches. You can avoid this (and miss some of the most dramatic "hidden" views in the region) by taking **High Park Road** from Cripple Creek back to Cañon City instead. Follow Florissant Road (the extension of Cripple Creek's main street) west to 11 Road near Wrights Reservoir and turn left. This road becomes High Park Road and makes it's way across open rangeland called the **Bare Hills** before reaching Route 50 near **Royal Gorge** (page 251), west of Cañon City.

No tour of the Pikes Peak region is complete without a visit to the **Cripple Creek–Victor Historic District**, located at 9600 feet above sea level on the west slope of Pikes Peak, about an hour's drive from Colorado Springs. To get there, take Route 24 west for 25 miles to the crossroads town of Divide, then Route 67 south for 18 miles. In the summer tourist season and on weekends year-round, expect long lines of traffic at the one-lane, stoplight-controlled tunnel on Route 67.

The town of **Cripple Creek** was founded in 1891 after a local rancher spotted gold nuggets in the mountain stream of the same name. The discovery touched off the last great gold rush in the lower 48 United States, and by 1900, the Cripple Creek metropolitan area had become the largest city in Colorado, with a population of more than 60,000 including nearby Victor and several smaller settlements. The district boasted 150 saloons, 91 lawyers, and 15 newspapers. The mines of the Cripple Creek district produced some 625 tons of gold, worth more than eight billion dollars at today's gold prices.

Twenty years after the town was founded, most of the mines in the Cripple Creek district had closed down. Little by little, the 100 or so blocks of residential neighborhoods vanished as the few remaining residents tore down abandoned buildings for firewood until only bare, grassy hillsides remained. A stark reminder of the transitory nature of mortals' works and wealth set against a background of Pikes Peak's massive, timeless crags, Cripple Creek gradually developed a low-key tourism economy, and by the late 1960s a number of shops had opened along the main street to sell arts and crafts, antiques and curios.

In 1991, the Colorado legislature legalized casino gambling in Cripple Creek. The idea was to generate money to preserve the historic buildings, many of which were crumbling away with neglect. When the casinos opened in 1993, the interior of every building on Bennett Avenue had been spruced up with pseudo-Victorian glitz. Slot machines and blackjack tables had displaced almost every other business in town, and huge tracts of vacant land had become parking lots. How gambling will ultimately reshape Cripple Creek's character is anybody's guess. Meanwhile, wild donkeys, great-grandchildren of beasts that pulled ore carts in the old days, still wander the streets, and several tourist attractions from the pre-casino days continue to operate.

The two-story **Cripple Creek District Museum**, at the east end of town, offers a look at the mining district's heyday, including its seamy or otherwise unpleasant aspects: fast money, deadly epidemics, labor violence, gambling and prostitution. One of the most interesting exhibits is a model showing the vast underground network, many miles of tunnels reaching thousands of feet into the earth, in just one of the district's 500 gold mines. Open weekends only in winter. Admission. ~ Bennett Avenue, Cripple Creek; 719-689-2634.

HIDDEN ▶

Don't miss the unique **Old Homestead House Museum**, originally a brothel in the middle of Cripple Creek's red-light district. Despite its raunchy past, tours of the old parlor house and nearby cribs are family-friendly. They offer plenty of history about Cripple Creek and the gold rush. Open June through September. Admission. ~ 353 Myers Avenue, Cripple Creek; 719-689-3090.

Near the museum, the **Cripple Creek and Victor Narrow Gauge Railroad** takes passengers on a 45-minute narrated trip through the goldfields in open railcars pulled by an old-time steam loco-

# Gold Camp Luck

Greed, more than any other factor, attracted settlers to Colorado. From 1858 through the 1890s, newspapers regularly carried stories of prospectors who ventured into the mountains, spotted a flash in a streambed or rock cliff, and came back rich beyond their wildest imaginings. Never mind that of the hundreds of thousands of people who risked everything to seek their fortunes in the goldfields, only a few hundred found the wealth they hoped for, or that most of those few did it through retail commerce, real estate deals or speculative stock issues, rather than by actually finding silver or gold. Still, every once in a while, against all odds, people actually did "strike it rich."

Every junior-high student in Colorado learns how Horace Tabor was fleeced into trading his store for a worthless Leadville gold mine, only to discover that it contained the richest silver vein in the Rockies. (Then, as the richest man in Colorado, he became a U.S. senator only to lose his fortune when the price of silver crashed.) The same mining boom also made a rich man of prospector Leadville Johnny Brown. (Rebuffed by Denver high society, Brown used his wealth to build the city's most elegant hotel, the Brown Palace, and divorced his wife, who later survived the sinking of the *Titanic*, earning national notoriety.)

The Cripple Creek District, too, spawned its share of get-rich-quick tales. Between 1893, when Cripple Creek became a town, and 1899, four local storekeepers, two druggists, two real estate agents, two schoolteachers, a lawyer, a butcher, a sawmill owner, a coal delivery man, a race horse trainer and a former sheriff from Iowa all became overnight millionaires by discovering veins of gold.

Most famous of all Cripple Creek prospectors was Winfield Scott Stratton, a Colorado Springs carpenter who used to spend his summers exploring various gold districts around Colorado. After years of fruitless searching, Stratton promised his wife that he would give up his daydreams and stay home and attend to his family and trade. He settled down and specialized in making hand-carved fireplace mantles that are valued as antiques today, but within a few years Stratton succumbed to temptation and went to take a second look at a claim he had once staked in Cripple Creek. On his second day there, he discovered the vein that would become the Independence Mine, the largest in Cripple Creek history. Stratton later sold the mine to British investors for $11 million. Though he built a hospital and bought bicycles for all the city's working women, Stratton's fortune earned interest faster than he could give the money away, and he is remembered as the most generous philanthropist in Colorado Springs history.

motive. The old mines and other abandoned buildings along the way are off-limits to sightseers these days. A mining company is recovering gold from the low-grade ore found in mine tailings through a highly toxic cyanide leaching process. The train operates May through mid-October. Admission. ~ 520 East Carr Street, Cripple Creek; 719-689-2640.

About a mile out of town, the **Molly Kathleen Gold Mine** offers tours into a gold mine. An elevator drops visitors down a shaft to a tunnel 1000 feet underground to see where miners blasted and drilled along a gold vein. Everyone who takes the tour receives a sample of gold ore. Closed intermittently between November and April. Admission. ~ Route 67, Cripple Creek; 719-689-2465.

Seven miles south of Cripple Creek, at the other end of the mining district, lies **Victor.** By some legislative whim, gambling was legalized in Cripple Creek but not in Victor, so visitors to the small near–ghost town can get a good idea of what Cripple Creek was like before casinos. Among the town's points of historic interest are the city hall building, where soon-to-be world heavyweight boxing champion Jack Dempsey trained while making his living as a prizefighter in the bars of the Cripple Creek district, and a saloon with a mine entrance inside.

Victor's main attraction is the **Victor–Lowell Thomas Museum,** which contains newspaper articles, photos and memorabilia on the life and worldwide travels of the journalist-adventurer who grew up here and began his distinguished career as a cub reporter on the *Victor Record.* The museum also has an exhibit on miners and promoters who struck it rich in the Cripple Creek District. Lowell Thomas buffs can also see the outside of his modest boyhood home at 225 South 6th Street and visit the Victor Record Building, a weekly newspaper office with a thick patina of history, at 118 South 4th Street. The museum is open during summer only, from Wednesday through Sunday. ~ 3rd Street at Victor Avenue, Victor; 719-689-5509.

From the west end of Bennett Avenue in Cripple Creek, unpaved County Road 1 passes the perfect little volcanic cone of **Mount Pisgah** and runs through ranchland for about 20 miles and intersects Route 24 at Florissant, eight miles west of the main Cripple Creek turnoff at Divide. The road past Mount Pisgah

HIDDEN ► takes motorists to **Fossil Beds National Monument,** a 6000-acre expanse where volcanic ash covered a sequoia forest 35 million years ago, preserving 1100 species of butterflies, dragonflies, beetles, bees and other prehistoric bugs, as well as plants, fish, birds and mammals, and providing the most detailed information anywhere on the natural history of the Eocene era. The monument's most striking feature is a forest of giant petrified tree stumps. Equally interesting is the visitors center's display of remarkably detailed small fossils found in the monument. Admission. ~ Florissant; 719-748-3253; www.nps.gov/flfo.

Manitou Springs is full of small ma-and-pa motels, cottages and guest houses dating back to the early 20th century, when this little town in the shadow of Pikes Peak was one of the most popular tourist resorts in the region. Some are rundown and only marginally acceptable by modern standards; most are remarkably affordable. One of the nicer old cabin compounds is **Town-n-Country Cottages**, which has ten recently renovated Spanish-style one- to three-room cabins with full baths and furnished kitchens. The four-acre grounds have an outdoor swimming pool, a hot tub, barbecue grills, a laundromat, a game room and a children's playground. A stream runs through the property, and there is easy access to hiking trails. ~ 123 Crystal Park Road, Manitou Springs; 719-685-5427, 800-366-3509; www.townncountryc.com, e-mail inquiries@townncountryc.com. MODERATE.

**LODGING**

Santa Fe–style architecture sets the **El Colorado Lodge** apart from other long-established Manitou Springs motels. Most of the 26 guest cabins have rough-hewn beam ceilings and fireplaces, and all have light, cheerful color schemes with earthtone accents. Eight have kitchenettes complete with dishes and utensils. The heated outdoor swimming pool is the largest one in town. ~ 23 Manitou Avenue, Manitou Springs; 719-685-5485, 800-782-2246. MODERATE.

Situated in the middle of the Manitou Springs Historic District, the **Two Sisters Inn** offers four guest rooms in a charming Victorian bungalow that was originally a boardinghouse for the town's schoolteachers, plus a separate "honeymoon cottage." The atmosphere here is light and airy, and fresh flowers are everywhere. Works by local artists are on exhibit in the lobby, and the

---

### RETIRE TO ROOSEVELT'S ROOM

Built in 1871, the **Red Crags B&B** was a favorite vacation spot of President Theodore Roosevelt. The eight guest rooms, including five suites, which were renovated in 1991, feature Victorian-era antique decor. All have private baths and king-size European-style beds with down mattresses, and five have fireplaces. The private patio has a Pikes Peak view and a jacuzzi. The landscaping of the two-acre grounds includes a duck pond and herb gardens. Rates include a full breakfast. ~ 302 El Paso Boulevard, Manitou Springs; 719-685-1920, 800-721-2248, fax 719-685-1073; www.red crags.com, e-mail info@redcrags.com. MODERATE TO ULTRA-DELUXE.

parlor has a large fireplace and antique piano. Rates include a gourmet three-course breakfast, formally served with crystal and silver. ~ 10 Otoe Place, Manitou Springs; 719-685-9684, 800-274-7466; www.twosisinn.com, e-mail info@twosisinn.com. MODERATE TO DELUXE.

Setting the standard for luxury accommodations in Manitou Springs, the recently restored **Cliff House** dates back to the late 1850s, when it was a stagecoach station and boarding house for gold-seekers on their way to Leadville. In 1886 it was converted to a luxury resort, complete with a tunnel to the old Manitou Spa across the street. In its heyday, as the finest hotel in the region before the Broadmoor was built, its guests included Theodore Roosevelt, Thomas Edison, Henry Ford, P. T. Barnum, Clark Gable and J. Paul Getty. But the Cliff House deteriorated and became a low-rent apartment building before catching fire and closing in 1981. It stood vacant for 16 years. A California developer sank $9 million to restore the hotel to its original Victorian-era architecture and decor while adding modern technology and amenities. Today, the Cliff House has 55 elegant guest units. The standard studio rooms as well as the suites are individually decorated with handmade furnishings, and some suites have special features such as gas fireplaces, two-person jacuzzis and towel warmers. The location couldn't be more central. ~ 306 Cañon Avenue, Manitou Springs; 719-685-3000, 888-212-7000; www.thecliff house.com, e-mail info@thecliffhouse.com. ULTRA-DELUXE.

Another historic luxury hotel, the **Rockledge Country Inn** is set in a historic 20-room Tudor-style mansion built in 1912 as the summer home of an oil tycoon. It's situated on 3.5 terraced, landscaped, gated acres. The four spacious guest suites have feather beds and spectacular mountain views, and some have fireplaces. The main living room has an 1875 Steinway grand piano, and there is more room for lounging in the solarium and on the large, secluded patio. Typical of the full gourmet breakfasts served is a Rocky Mountain trout quiche served with fruit juice, new potatoes and fruit cobbler. Colorado wines and hors d'oeuvres are served each evening. ~ 328 El Paso Boulevard, Manitou Springs; 719-685-4515, 888-685-4515, fax 719-685-1031; www.rockledge inn.com, e-mail info@rockledgeinn.com. ULTRA-DELUXE.

For low-priced lodging with a touch of antique atmosphere, check out the **Buffalo Lodge**, on the boundary between Colorado Springs and Manitou Springs. The venerable old creekside lodge has 46 units ranging from small, threadbare motel rooms with dark and dreary wood paneling to contemporary accommodations, plus a large, beautifully rustic lobby right out of a century past. ~ 2 El Paso Boulevard, Colorado Springs; 719-634-2851, 800-235-7416; www.buffalolodge.com, e-mail information@buffalo lodge.com. BUDGET TO MODERATE.

The **Pikes Peak Paradise B&B**, a five-bedroom inn on a dirt backroad in the ponderosa pine forest 25 minutes west of the city resembles a Southern mansion and offers a romantic atmosphere with plenty of privacy. Amenities include a sundeck, fireplaces and hot tubs in all rooms. A full breakfast is included. ~ 236 Pinecrest Road, Woodland Park; 719-687-6656, 800-728-8282, fax 719-687-9008. ULTRA-DELUXE.

The **Cripple Creek Hotel** offers modern hotel rooms in a stately 1899 building that served as the Cripple Creek High School until 1975. You can tell by the slate blackboards in many rooms—perfect for guests who have the urge to doodle on the walls or tally their gambling gains (or losses). ~ 350 East Carr Avenue, Cripple Creek; 719-689-3709. MODERATE.

The **Imperial Hotel** was Cripple Creek's most elegant hotel when it was built in 1896 at the peak of the gold boom. When the city was largely abandoned, the hotel kept its doors open by presenting authentic Victorian melodramas that have been imitated throughout the West. The big draw these days is gambling. The Imperial's casino occupies drawing rooms on three floors of the hotel. Most of the 29 guest rooms and suites have been remodeled with original period oil paintings and antique or period furnishings; 11 have private baths. ~ 123 North 3rd Street, Cripple Creek; 719-689-7777, 800-235-2922, fax 719-689-1008. MODERATE.

Zeke's opens at 3:30 a.m. to serve breakfast to gold miners on their way to work, and serves breakfast, lunch and dinner all day; miners also come here to drink after work, keeping the doors open until 2 a.m.

The **Victorian Lady of Cripple Creek** is a small showcase bed and breakfast dating back to 1898. The exterior features ornate Victorian gingerbread trim. Inside are turn-of-the-20th-century frescoes, an original carved wood fireplace, stained glass windows, a gold chandelier and antique furniture that includes an 1890s piano. The four guest rooms feature vintage brass-and-wood beds and clawfoot tubs. The only anachronism is a modern hot tub. ~ 127 West Carr Avenue, Cripple Creek; 719-689-2814; cripple-creek.co.us/victorianlady.com. MODERATE TO DELUXE.

**DINING**

A long-standing favorite for fine dining in Manitou Springs is the **Craftwood Inn**, with its romantic ambience in a lovely 1912 Tudor-style home that was once a woodcrafter's studio and shop. The à la carte menu specializes in wild game—caribou, elk, pheasant, venison, quail, duck, rabbit, antelope and Colorado mountain bass—but also has some excellent vegetarian dishes, plus unique desserts such as jalapeño white-chocolate mousse and white chocolate ravioli. The owner is a connoisseur of wines, so the wine list contains some of the most expensive selections anywhere. ~ 404 El Paso Boulevard, Manitou Springs; 719-685-9000. DELUXE.

Fine dining is also offered at the **Briarhurst Manor**, serving contemporary international cuisine in a turn-of-the-20th-century mansion that is one of Manitou Springs' historic showpieces. The ambience is lavish with polished hardwood, ceramic fireplaces and wall tapestries. House specialties include braised rabbit dijonnaise and blackberry salmon. Dinner only. ~ 404 Manitou Avenue, Manitou Springs; 719-685-1864; www.briarhurst.com. DELUXE.

Casual dining beside a shady creek is offered at the **Stagecoach Steak & Ale House,** housed in the building that was originally the stage stop for Manitou Springs in the 1870s. Rustic Victorian-era decor sets the stage for such fare as buffalo, prime rib, rotisseried chicken, and an assortment of pastas and vegetarian entrées. Dinner only. ~ 702 Manitou Avenue, Manitou Springs; 719-685-9400. MODERATE.

International and vegetarian cuisine is the focus of the **Adams Mountain Café**. The restaurant–coffee shop maintains a friendly, casual atmosphere amid Victorian antique furnishings. Typical of the international no-meat offerings is orzo Mediterranean (orzo with broccoli, sun-dried tomatoes, onions, cucumbers, dill and garlic). White poultry and shrimp are also served. Desserts such as chocolate-hazelnut torte and a list of fine wines, beers and gourmet coffees round out the menu. Closed for dinner Sunday and Monday. ~ 110 Cañon Avenue, Manitou Springs; 719-685-1430. MODERATE.

**Zeke's** is the oldest continuously operating business in the area; the owners' ancestors started their first restaurant in Victor in 1888, even before the start of the gold boom, and moved to the present location in 1899. The walls are of old red bricks and the tables, each different, are wooden and old. The menu ranges from hamburgers and hot dogs to full meals such as pork steak with mashed potatoes and mixed vegetables. The chili is said to be world famous—that is, Lowell Thomas once praised it in a newspaper column. ~ 108 South 3rd Street, Victor; 719-689-2109. BUDGET.

All Cripple Creek casinos have restaurants, or at least fast-food bars; and conversely, just about all restaurants have slot machines. A standout is the Imperial Hotel, where the quiet, elegantly appointed **Stratton's Grill** serves such specialties as crab legs and prime rib. Also in the hotel, the **3rd Street Deli** offers sandwiches, burgers and wraps. ~ 123 North 3rd Street, Cripple Creek; 719-689-7777.

**SHOPPING**   The region supports a fair number of artists and craftspeople, found in highest concentration in Manitou Springs, adjoining the western city limit of Colorado Springs along Manitou Avenue (Business Route 24). You can see a representative sampling of local arts and crafts at the **Commonwheel Artists Co-op,** one of the region's longest-established co-op galleries. ~ 102 Cañon Avenue, Manitou Springs; 719-685-1008; www.commonwheel.com. The newer **Business of Art Center** houses galleries, shops and studios featuring local artists' works in all media. Closed Monday. ~ 513 Manitou Avenue, Manitou Springs; 719-685-1861.

In summer, the top nighttime tourist attraction in the Colorado Springs area is **Laser Canyon.** You may have seen laser light shows before; you may even have seen better ones—this program seems a bit "dumbed down" for mass appeal with an uncomfortable mix of educational lecture, flag-waving old-time pop songs and a too-brief taste of hard rock—but this is probably the only place where you'll see computer-animated laser imaging projected onto an 800-foot-high limestone canyon wall. Spectacular. Admission. ~ Cave of the Winds, Manitou Springs; 719-685-5444, fax 719-634-2887.

**NIGHTLIFE**

A tradition in Manitou Springs for more than four decades, the **Iron Springs Melodrama Dinner Theater** serves up old-time stage productions played strictly for laughs, followed by a singalong and vaudeville olio. The all-you-can-eat fried chicken and barbecued beef dinner is served from 6 to 7 p.m., with the play beginning at 8:00, nightly except Monday in the summer and on weekend evenings the rest of the year. ~ 444 Ruxton Avenue, Manitou Springs; 719-685-5104.

On the other side of Pikes Peak, Cripple Creek is one of the three historic mining towns where casino gambling ($5-per-bet limit) is legal. All of its 18 gambling casinos (fewer than there used to be, but more than in all the rest of the state, including Indian reservations) are located along three blocks of Bennett Avenue. The reigning queen is the relatively classy **Midnight Rose,** with six blackjack tables, four poker tables and 325 video poker and slot machines. ~ 256 East Bennett Avenue, Cripple Creek; 719-689-0303. **Bronco Billy's Sports Bar & Casino** features not only blackjack tables and slot machines but also a sports

## BAR-HOPPING

It is traditional to have a drink in each of the Imperial Hotel's five turn-of-the-20th-century-style bars. One might suspect that this tradition originated with the hotel's management in the early days of tourism, since the 9500-foot altitude doubles the potency of alcoholic beverages and makes driving back to Colorado Springs both hazardous and illegal. So if you're spending the night here, enjoy.

bar with 45 TV sets and a 70-inch big-screen showing sporting events nonstop. ~ 233 East Bennett Avenue, Cripple Creek; 719-689-2142. **Womack's/Legends Saloon & Gaming Parlor** is the only casino in town that features off-track betting. ~ 200 East Bennett Avenue, Cripple Creek; 719-689-0333.

For gaming in an authentic Victorian setting, you can't beat the casino in the **Imperial Hotel** where blackjack tables and banks of slot machines are scattered through a number of intimate parlor rooms. ~ 123 North 3rd Street, Cripple Creek; 719-689-7777.

**PARKS**

**PIKE NATIONAL FOREST** 🏃 🚲 ⛵ 🏕️ 🚣 This forest, which includes all of Pikes Peak as well as the Rampart Range between Colorado Springs and Denver, encompasses more than a million acres of pine, aspen and fir forests and alpine tundra. More visitors use it for recreation than any other national forest in Colorado. In the winter, the U.S. Forest Service operates a small downhill ski area beside the Pikes Peak Highway; cross-country skiing is also popular on trails near Colorado Springs. You may fish for rainbow trout in Rampart Reservoir. Facilities include picnic areas, restrooms, jeep and bike trails and a ski area. ~ Primary access to Pike National Forest is via the Pikes Peak Highway, the Gold Camp Road between Colorado Springs and Cripple Creek, and the Rampart Range Road between Colorado Springs and Sedalia. The Crags Campground is two and a half miles in on Forest Road 383, four miles south of Divide off of Route 67; 719-636-1602.

▲ Camping opportunities are limited on Pikes Peak itself. On the west side of the peak along the route to Cripple Creek, the Crags Campground has 17 RV/tent sites (no hookups); closed November to mid-May; $10 per night. Other national forest campgrounds are located along the Rampart Range Road north of Woodland Park. Official campgrounds along the Gold Camp Road have been closed, but there are several spots suitable for informal RV camping and hike-in tent camping along this route.

**MUELLER STATE PARK AND WILDLIFE AREA** 🏃 🚣 This 12,000-acre mountain park provides camping in the vicinity of Cripple Creek. It also has an 80-mile network of hiking trails through a variety of habitats ranging from aspen and conifer forests to spectacular rock formations and open meadows ablaze with wildflowers. Abundant wildlife includes deer, elk, wild turkeys, bears and bighorn sheep. Fishing is good for rainbow trout in Fourmile Creek. There are picnic areas, restrooms and showers. Day-use fee, $5. ~ Located three and a half miles west of Divide off Route 67; 719-687-2366; www.coloradoparks.org/mueller.

▲ There are 22 walk-in tent sites, $12 per night; and 110 RV/tent sites with electrical hookups, $16 per night.

Cañon City, a quiet ranching town on the Arkansas
River, is named for the geological wonder that has
become its claim to fame and fortune. The Royal
Gorge is owned by the municipal government, and visitor admission fees have provided the town's main source of revenue since 1929. Despite hundreds of thousands of visitors each year, Cañon City has retained so much of its old-fashioned, small-town character that as you wander along the downtown sidewalks you may feel as if you'd stumbled into a Norman Rockwell painting.

## Cañon City Area

It is possible to make a loop tour and see the Cripple Creek district and the Royal Gorge in the same day by taking the steep, narrow, unpaved and spectacularly scenic road that starts near Victor and winds between the reddish granite walls of **Phantom Canyon** to reach Route 50 at Florence, a few miles east of Cañon City. The 35-mile drive takes about two and a half hours. The Phantom Canyon Road was originally a narrow-gauge railroad route. In their haste to build the first railroad to the Cripple Creek district in 1893, the engineers cut a few corners, and on the first Florence-to-Cripple Creek run the train tumbled off a trestle into the canyon. By the time the tracks were reopened, the Midland Railroad route from Colorado Springs had won the race to the goldfields.

**SIGHTS**

◀ HIDDEN

The **Royal Gorge** is one of the deepest canyons in Colorado, 1053 feet from the rim to the Arkansas River at the bottom. Visitors can descend to river level on an incline railway or glide across the gorge on an aerial tramway. The canyon's main attraction, however, is the world's highest suspension bridge, built in 1929.

**AUTHOR'S FAVORITE**

**sights**

From the bridge more than 1000 feet above, I used to watch the freight trains glide alongside the Arkansas River at the bottom of Royal Gorge and think how great it must have been in the olden days when people could ride a passenger train on those tracks. Now, once again, we can. The **Royal Gorge Route** runs sightseeing trains through the gorge three times daily in the summer and once a day on weekends the rest of the year. The highlight of the two-hour, 24-mile roundtrip is crossing a hanging bridge that clings to a sheer cliff. While diesel-powered trains have been used on the route up to now, plans were under way in late 2004 to relocate the 19th-century steam trains that had previously been used on the Georgetown Loop railroad to the Royal Gorge. ~ 401 Water Street, Cañon City; 303-569-2403, 888-724-5748; www.royal gorgeroute.com.

Clatter across it by car or simply walk out to the middle for a swaying, dizzying view of the gorge. The scrub oak–covered parkland surrounding the canyon rim is home to many tourist-friendly mule deer. The management recently started a petting zoo to discourage visitors from feeding or otherwise molesting the wild deer. (Frequent people food makes them unable to digest their natural diet of vegetation and tree bark, leading to starvation in winter.) Other attractions to keep families occupied while waiting their turn on the incline or tram include burro rides, a scale-model train, a carousel and a storytelling theater. Admission. ~ 719-275-7507; www.royalgorgebridge.com, e-mail rgb@ris.net.

Just outside the Royal Gorge entrance gate is **Buckskin Joe**, a movie-set town of pioneer buildings collected from around the state and placed below the stunning backdrop of the Sangre de Cristo Range. Some of the buildings came from a real town called Buckskin Joe, 80 miles to the northwest near present-day Alma. When not in use as a film location, Buckskin Joe does a roaring business as a stagecoaches-and-shootouts tourist theme park. Admission. ~ County Road 3A; 719-275-5149, fax 719-275-8035; www.buckskinjoes.com, e-mail info@buckskinjoe.com.

Motorists who enjoy mountain driving should not miss **Skyline Drive**, a three-mile scenic detour on the way back from Royal Gorge to Cañon City. Built in 1915 by an automobile club to prove the feasibility of asphalt highways, it was the first paved road west of the Mississippi. The narrow one-way road runs above the town along the top of a hogback ridge with 800-foot dropoffs on both sides.

The **Museum of Colorado Prisons** was in use as a state maximum-security facility until the late 1970s, when the Colorado Supreme Court ruled that to confine prisoners there was "cruel and unusual punishment." Since then, the old stone prison has been opened to the public, providing a close-up look at the section where women prisoners were held and an antique electric chair that was used for more than 100 executions. Open daily in summer, Friday through Sunday off-season. Admission. ~ 201 North 1st Street, Cañon City; 719-269-3015.

> The first stegosaurus skeleton dug up in the Garden Park Fossil Area was in 1886; it now resides in the National Museum of Natural History in Washington, DC.

In town, the **Cañon City Municipal Museum** has a log cabin and a settler's stone house from the 1880s, as well as a mixed bag of Indian artifacts, fossils, guns, antiques and big-game hunters' trophies. Closed Sunday and Monday in winter. Admission. ~ 612 Royal Gorge Boulevard, Cañon City; 719-276-5279.

As you drive through Cañon City on Route 50, it's hard to miss the life-size allosaurus that stands in front of the old train station, which has been transformed into **Dinosaur Depot**, a museum devoted to dinosaurs that inhabited the area during the Jurassic period. Besides fossil exhibits, visitors can see the paleontology laboratory, where trained volunteers prepare rock-encased fossils for display. Dinosaur Depot is owned and operated by the Garden Park Paleontology Society, and staffers also offer guided tours of the Garden Park Fossil Area just north of Cañon City. Admission. Closed Monday and Tuesday from Labor Day to Memorial Day. ~ 330 Royal Gorge Boulevard, Cañon City; 719-269-7150, 800-987-6379, fax 719-269-7227; www.dino saurdepot.com, e-mail office@dinosaurdepot.com.

To reach Route 25 from Cañon City, take Route 50 east for 39 miles to Pueblo.

Cañon City's historic **St. Cloud Hotel** dates back to 1883, when it was built in the mining boom town of Silvercliffe. When the silver mines played out, the entire four-story building was moved to Cañon City, where it got a new lease on life providing overnight lodging for railroad passengers. Today, guests can ride the antique Otis elevator or climb the white-spindled staircase to their rooms, each refurbished in neo-Victorian style and individually decorated with antique pieces. All 35 rooms have ceiling fans and private baths, and some have old-fashioned clawfoot tubs and stained glass transoms. One- and two-bedroom suites with kitchens or kitchenettes are available. ~ 631 Main Street, Cañon City; 719-276-2000; www.stcloudhotel.com, e-mail st cloud@stcloudhotel.com. MODERATE TO DELUXE. **LODGING**

Close to town, the modern **Cañon Inn** has 152 oversized rooms with all standard amenities. Facilities include six indoor hot tubs and an outdoor heated swimming pool. ~ 3075 East Route 50 (at Dozier Street), Cañon City; 719-275-8676, 800-525-7727, fax 719-275-8675; www.canoninn.com, e-mail info@ canoninn.com. MODERATE.

Located near Royal Gorge, the **Cactus Rose** is a venerable mom-and-pop motel with 18 rooms decorated in the style of the Old West. All rooms are nonsmoking. For groups and families, the Cactus Rose also has a two-bedroom home for rent with a full kitchen, dining room and breakfast bar. ~ 44058 West Route 50, Cañon City; phone/fax 719-269-7673; www.cactusrosemotel. com, e-mail cactus@aculink.net. BUDGET TO MODERATE.

A daydream on Elm Street, the **Deweese Lodge**, dates back to 1896 and features four guest rooms with shared baths in the main house, as well as a suitelike guest house. The lodge has a large veranda furnished with rocking chairs, ideal for watching the world go by on lazy afternoons. Rates include breakfast. ~ 1226 Elm Street, Cañon City; 719-269-1881. MODERATE.

In Cañon City, fine dining is found at **Merlino's Belvedere**, operated by an Italian family of long-time residents. The emphasis is on Italian food—veal parmesan, fettuccine—but the menu also **DINING** includes salmon, shrimp, trout, prime rib, filet mignon and great desserts (try the "chocolate suicide cake"). ~ 1330 Elm Avenue, Cañon City; 719-275-5558. MODERATE TO DELUXE.

**Ortega's** is a longtime favorite out of the many family-owned Mexican restaurants in the Cañon City area. The atmosphere is Southwestern and modest, and the specialty of the house is *chiles rellenos*. They also serve standard Mexican combination plates and New Mexican–style dishes, as well as imported beer and margaritas. Closed Monday and Tuesday. ~ 2301 East Main Street, Cañon City; 719-275-9437. BUDGET.

North of Penrose, the **Juniper Valley Ranch Dining Room** has been serving the same menu since it opened in 1951, and it continues to be so popular that you'll want to phone ahead for reservations. Dinner specialties include skillet fried chicken and baked ham, served family-style in a rustic ranch-house setting. The dinner prices include beverages and homemade desserts. Closed Monday and Tuesday and December through April. ~ Route 115, 15 miles north of Penrose; 719-576-0741. MODERATE.

**SHOPPING**    As was true in most of Colorado's older tourist areas, Cañon City used to have more than its share of rock shops where you could buy crystals, geodes, arrowheads, turquoise, gold ore and other geological curiosities. Check out the **Rock Stop**, one of the last survivors of this vanishing breed. ~ 1318 Main Street, Cañon City; 719-275-8497.

You'll find stained glass, blown glass and art glass at the **Persnickety Shoppe**, along with a year-round Christmas room offering a wide array of imported European ornaments. ~ 312 South 9th Street, Cañon City; 719-276-1902.

If you've always wanted a bearskin rug, the place to buy one is **Traders of the Bighorn**, which also has buckskin clothing, old-fashioned firearms, vintage American Indian items and books about the frontier. ~ 402 Royal Gorge Boulevard, Cañon City; 719-275-3205.

The little town of Florence, a few miles southeast of Cañon City, appears to survive solely on the sale of antiques. At the **Oil City Merchants Antique Shoppes** you'll find 25 dealers under one roof. Among the wares featured are hardwood furniture, 1920s lighting, glassware and art glass, pottery, cowboy tools and Victoriana. ~ 126 West Main Street, Florence; 719-784-6582. Across the street, **Mezzanine Arts and Antiques** has 30 more dealers. ~ 127 West Main Street, Florence; 719-784-4598. And **Golden Era Antique Mall** has 15 more. ~ 131 B West Main Street, Florence; 719-784-1228. Among the individual shops located in the same block are **Cottage Collectibles** (119 West Main Street; 719-784-1125) and **Fox Den of Antiquity** (123 West Main Street; 719-784-2303).

**SAN ISABEL NATIONAL FOREST** 🚶 🚴 This long, narrow strip
of national forest contains the eastern slope of the Sangre de
Cristo Range southwest of Cañon City as well as the Wet Mountains to the south. The Sangre de Cristo Wilderness, reaching from
the north end of the range near the town of Salida
as far south as the Great Sand Dunes, encompasses 226,000 acres. It was the largest of the wilderness areas created by the 1993 Wilderness Act.
There are hiking trails and a ski area. ~ The easiest
access to the Sangre de Cristo portion of San Isabel
National Forest is via several unpaved roads that run
west from the town of Westcliffe into the mountains. To
get to Westcliffe, take Route 50 west to Route 69 south.
To reach Alvarado Campground from Westcliffe, continue
south on Route 69 for three miles, then head west on County
Road 140 for five miles. Wet Mountain access is via Route 165;
719-269-8500.

> Much of San Isabel
> National Forest is hard
> to reach because the
> Sangre de Cristos are
> so steep that not
> even jeep trails
> climb them.

▲ Among the few forest service campgrounds in the area is
Alvarado Campground, with 30 RV-only sites and 17 RV/tent sites
(no hookups); open late May to mid-September; $11 per night.

South Park is a sparsely populated basin of high
ranchlands between Pikes Peak and the Collegiate **South Park Area**
Peaks. Despite its windswept emptiness, South Park
is where three key highways converge, an important crossroads
for motorists touring Colorado. From Buena Vista, Route 24
heads east toward Cripple Creek and Colorado Springs and north
toward Leadville and Breckenridge, while Route 285 goes north
to Fairplay and, eventually, Denver, or south to Salida. From Salida, Route 50 follows the Arkansas River east down a long
canyon to Cañon City and Pueblo, and west over Monarch Pass
to Gunnison, while Route 285 continues south across the San
Luis Valley.

**Salida**, at the south end of South Park, is an older town that has **SIGHTS**
recently broken the tourism barrier to become the most popular
travelers' destination in the area. The main industry in this unpretentious little Victorian-era town is whitewater rafting on the
Arkansas River, with dozens of local outfitters running river trips
through Browns Canyon and downriver toward the Royal Gorge
and Cañon City. Skiing at nearby Monarch Ski Area also con-
tributes to the town's rising popularity. The four-block-long historic district, consisting of red-brick two-story buildings with
Victorian-era stone ornamentation, takes visitors back to an earlier time. The small **Salida Museum**, located next to the visitor
information center at the main highway turnoff, contains displays on the town's early history, including mining equipment

and ranching gear. Closed in winter. ~ 406 West Rainbow Boulevard, Salida; 719-539-2311.

The **Salida Hot Springs Pool** uses geothermal water piped from springs five miles away in the high mountains to heat a municipal swimming pool that is claimed to be the largest spring-fed pool in the state. There are also six individual European-style hot baths and a 100-degree therapeutic soaking pool. The main pool is also used for kayak instruction. Admission. ~ 410 West Rainbow Boulevard, Salida; 719-539-6738.

To the north of Salida is **Buena Vista**, ranch center for South Park and home of the Colorado State Reformatory. The town may not look like much, but its setting, where the high plains of South Park meet the solid wall of the **Collegiate Peaks**, defies comparison. Colorado's greatest concentration of 14,000-foot peaks stands in a row just west of Buena Vista: Mount Oxford (14,153 feet), Mount Harvard (14,420 feet), Mount Columbia (14,075 feet), Mount Yale (14,196 feet) and Mount Princeton (14,197 feet). In the southernmost part of the Collegiate range is **Mount Princeton Hot Springs**, where geothermal swimming pools are open to the public. Admission. ~ 15870 County Road 162, Nathrop; 719-395-2447, 888-395-7799.

Continuing north on Route 285, Fairplay is the site of **South Park City**, an open-air museum that gives visitors glimpses into the details of everyday life during the gold-rush era. More than 30 buildings have been moved here from abandoned mining towns in the area and filled with antiques and artifacts of the time to create the quintessential Colorado ghost town. Among the historic structures are miners' cabins, a bank, a general store, a stagecoach station and a brewery. This is not one of those movie-set/tourist-trap assemblages of old western buildings; it's well worth visiting for the powerful sense of the past it evokes. Closed mid-October to mid-May. Admission. ~ Fairplay; 719-836-2387; www.southparkcity.org.

**HIDDEN ▶**

North of Fairplay at the tiny town of Alma, take unpaved County Road 8 and then Forest Road 415 for a total distance of about six miles to the **Bristlecone Pine Scenic Area**, one of several alpine areas in Colorado where these stunted, slow-growing trees are twisted by the wind into fantastic and grotesque shapes. The trees are some of the oldest living organisms on earth. Some have been determined to be almost 5000 years old—twice as old as California's giant redwoods.

**HIDDEN ▶**

A favorite jeep route in the South Park region, **Mosquito Pass Road** lumbers from Alma over a 13,188-foot pass, then descends into Leadville (see Chapter Four). The first seven miles of the road, past the remains of old mines and the ghost town of Park City, are usually fine for passenger cars; the last three miles to the pass summit are steep and rocky and can be negotiated only by high-clearance, four-wheel-drive vehicles.

Salida's historic district has recently sprouted an impressive number of bed and breakfasts. Noteworthy among them is the **Gazebo Country Inn**, a 1901 Victorian home built for a prominent Salida merchant during the railroad era. Set in a quiet residential neighborhood of shade trees and white picket fences, the two-story inn has flower gardens and a redwood deck with views of the surrounding 14,000-foot mountains. The four guest rooms are accented with floral prints and down comforters. Rates include a full breakfast. ~ 507 East 3rd Street, Salida; 719-539-7806, 800-565-7806; www.gazebocountryinn.com, e-mail info@gazebo countryinn.com. MODERATE.

The **River Run Inn**, situated on the bank of the Arkansas River, once served as the county poor farm, where, for more than 50 years, indigents were sent to work for room and board. Today, it has been refurbished in light, contemporary style as a combi-

**LODGING**

**South Park Area**

nation hostel–bed-and-breakfast inn, with a 13-bed dormitory on the top floor and seven individual guest rooms—some with shared baths, others private. The countryside location offers trout fishing and great mountain views. ~ 8495 County Road 160, Salida; 719-539-3818, 800-385-6925; www.riverruninn.com, e-mail river run@amigo.net. BUDGET TO MODERATE.

HIDDEN ▶

Nestled among the evergreens at the foot of the dramatic Chalk Cliffs, **Mount Princeton Hot Springs Resort** has been the site of one hotel after another since 1870. In the 1920s a magnificent four-story hotel that then stood at the springs was one of the most elegant hot-spring spas in the West. Today, a modern lodge and adjacent motel offer pleasant, spacious accommodations, a dining room and a spacious sun deck. Four of the largest among many hot springs in the vicinity feed the resort's three outdoor swimming pools and two private hot tubs. Undeveloped hot springs that line the creek and hillsides nearby include Hortense Spring, the hottest hot spring in Colorado—a scalding 183°F. To find this secluded resort, drive eight miles south from Buena Vista on Route 285 to Nathrop and turn west on the well-marked county road; the resort is five miles up the road. ~ 15870 County Road 162, Nathrop; 719-395-2447, 888-395-7799, fax 719-395-6249; www.mtprinceton.com. MODERATE.

Open only during the summer months, the **Trout City Inn** is located on 9346-foot Trout Creek Pass eight miles east of Buena Vista. A century-old narrow-gauge train station and two old-time railroad cars have been refurbished to create four guest accommodations so authentically decorated in elegant Victorian fashion and in such a remote location that they're the next-best thing to a time machine. A full breakfast is included in the rates. ~ Route 24/285, Buena Vista; 719-395-8433. MODERATE.

**DINING**

In Salida, try **Country Bounty** for huge portions of home cookin'. This family-style restaurant features a long menu that ranges from fresh-caught Arkansas River trout, homemade soups and Mexican combination plates to specialties such as almond chicken Shanghai in a sesame-ginger sauce, as well as elkburgers and numerous vegetarian options. The ambience is more like a gift shop than a restaurant, with country crafts, Indian jewelry and curios—all with price tags—wherever you look. ~ 413 West Rainbow Boulevard, Salida; 719-539-3546. BUDGET TO MODERATE.

The **Laughing Ladies Restaurant** offers intriguing international specialties, as well as vegetarian entrées, thick steaks with butter-garlic sauce, fresh bakery goods, and brew-pub beers. The atmosphere is Victorian and friendly. ~ 128 West 1st Street, Salida; 719-539-6209. BUDGET TO MODERATE.

Near the main highway, away from the historic district, the family-style **Windmill Restaurant** offers a selection ranging from fajitas and Tex-Mex taco salads to steak and seafood. The main attraction here is the decor, featuring an extensive collection of old-time advertising memorabilia. ~ 720 East Rainbow Boulevard, Salida; 719-539-3594. BUDGET.

The restaurant choice elsewhere in South Park is more limited but far from hopeless. The hands-down favorite in Buena Vista is **Casa Del Sol**, an outstanding Mexican restaurant that features dishes made from regional recipes collected throughout Mexico, from seafood quesadillas to *enchiladas suizas* and *pollo en mole*. Mexican guitar music, kachina and chile ristra decor and summer outdoor dining add spice to the homey atmosphere. ~ 303 Route 24, Buena Vista; 719-395-8810. MODERATE.

## ARKANSAS HEADWATERS RECREATION AREA 🏃 ⛵ 🚣 🚤 — PARKS

Established through a unique partnership between the federal Bureau of Land Management and the Colorado state parks, this recreation area spans the first 148 miles of the Arkansas River, from its origin just below Leadville's Turquoise Lake to Pueblo Reservoir. Highways trace the entire length of the river, just above the bank in some places and miles away in others, making this one of the most popular rivers in the West for recreational use. More commercial rafting outfitters use it than any other stretch of river in the United States, and on weekends in June and July, when the flow is highest, hundreds of private canoes and kayaks also shoot its challenging rapids. The most remote part of the river, Browns Canyon, is home to many wildlife species, including mule deer, mountain lions, bobcats and peregrine falcons. The section of the river below Salida, from Wellsville to Parkdale, is bighorn sheep habitat. There are picnic areas and restrooms. Day-use fee, $5. ~ Route 25 follows the river from Leadville to Buena Vista, Route 285 from Buena Vista to Salida, and Route 50 from Salida to Pueblo. Access to the remote Browns Canyon area is via the three-mile unpaved Hecla Junction Road, which leaves Route 285 midway between Buena Vista and Salida; 719-539-7289.

The Collegiate Peaks are named for the Ivy League schools for good reason: their mountaineering teams were the first to reach the summits in the early years of the 20th century.

▲ There are a total of 100 RV/tent sites (no hookups) in four campgrounds—Ruby Mountain and Hecla Junction upriver from Salida, Rincon downriver from Salida and Five Points above Cañon City and Railroad Bridge; $10 per night.

## PIKE NATIONAL FOREST 🏃 ⛵

Much of the east half of South Park is part of Pike National Forest. The 15,000-acre wilderness area includes scenic Elevenmile Canyon and the roadless Lost Creek Wilderness, an area of rugged terrain with spectacular sandstone and granite formations and abundant wildlife. Fishing is available for northern pike in Tarryall Reservoir. There are jeep trails here. Day-use fee, $3. ~ Trailheads for the Lost Creek Wilderness can be reached on County Road 77, which runs between Route 24 north of Buena Vista and Route 285 at Jefferson, passing small Tarryall Reservoir on the way. Elevenmile Canyon Road runs from Route 24 at Lake George to Elevenmile Reservoir—a distance of 11 miles; 719-836-2031.

▲ There are seven forest service campgrounds along Elevenmile Canyon Road. Among them are Spruce Grove Campground, with 20 RV/tent sites (no hookups) and 8 tent-only sites; and Blue Mountain Campground, with 20 RV/tent sites (no hookups) and one tent-only site. Both are open April through October; $10 per night.

**SAN ISABEL NATIONAL FOREST** 𝕩 ♞ ⌣ The vast Collegiate Peaks Wilderness, which covers 159,000 acres west of Buena Vista, is divided equally between Pike and San Isabel national forests. This forest also includes large expanses of pine woods east of Buena Vista and Salida. You may fish for rainbow trout in Chalk Creek, Cottonwood Creek, Browns Creek and other area streams. There are picnic areas, restrooms and jeep trails. ~ The main access to this part of the national forest is on Chalk Creek Road (Forest Road 211), which leaves Route 285 at Nathrop and passes Mount Princeton Hot Springs. All public campgrounds in the area are along this road; 719-539-3591.

▲ There are four national forest campgrounds along Chalk Creek at the base of Mount Princeton, including Cascade Campground, with 23 RV/tent sites; and Mount Princeton Campground, with 17 RV/tent sites. Both are open mid-May to mid-September and cost $12 per night.

▼▼▼▼▼▼▼▼▼▼▼▼▼▼

## Outdoor Adventures

### FISHING

The upper **Arkansas River** is a favorite fishing area. It's particularly known for brown trout (fishermen rate flyfishing on the Arkansas as the world's best for brown trout), and rainbow, cutthroat and brook trout are abundant in many of the river's tributary streams. **Cottonwood Lake**, off Cottonwood Pass Road west of Buena Vista, is legendary for big rainbow trout. Tarryall Reservoir is stocked with northern pike. Fishing tackle is sold in Salida at **Salida Sporting Goods**, which is also a good source of information on fishing spots and guides. ~ 509 East Rainbow Boulevard, Salida; 719-539-6221. In Buena Vista, head for **Hi Rocky**. ~ 111 Cottonwood, Buena Vista; 719-539-2258.

### RIVER RUNNING

The Salida area, on the southern edge of South Park near the headwaters of the Arkansas River, is one of the top whitewater rafting areas in Colorado. Nearly 100 tour operators operate there, including **Wilderness Aware Rafting**. ~ P.O. Box 1550, Buena Vista 81211; 719-395-2112, 800-824-3795. Another Buena

Vista–based company is **Noah's Ark Whitewater Rafting.** ~ P.O. Box 850, Buena Vista 81211; 719-395-2158. Also contact **Dvorak Kayaking & Rafting Expeditions** for rafting information. ~ 17921 Route 285, Nathrop; 719-539-6851, 800-462-7238. Trips are also available though **Canyon Marine.** ~ 129 West Rainbow Boulevard, Salida; 719-539-7476, 800-643-6707. You may also try **American Adventure Expeditions.** ~ 228 North F Street, Salida; 800-288-0675. Between Salida and Cañon City, you'll find **Arkansas River Tours.** ~ Cotapaxi; 800-321-4352. **RaftMasters** offers free wetsuits and river boots for those who want to shoot the rapids without getting soaked. ~ 2315 East Main Street, Cañon City; 800-568-7238.

**PIKES PEAK AREA** The Forest Service operates a small ski hill with a T-bar lift, open only when natural snowfall permits, about eight miles up the Pikes Peak Highway. For real downhill skiing, the closest ski areas are at Breckenridge, 150 miles away (see Chapter Four), and Monarch, 120 miles away (see Chapter Seven).

**SKIING**

The best cross-country skiing is found at **The Crags** and **Mueller State Park,** both off Route 68 on the west side of Pikes Peak en route to Cripple Creek.

**Ski Rentals** In Colorado Springs, cross-country skis, telemarking skis and snowshoes are available at **Mountain Chalet.** ~ 226 North Tejon Street; 719-633-0732.

**COLORADO SPRINGS AREA** Public courses in Colorado Springs include the 27-hole **Patty Jewett Golf Course,** a municipal course with cart and club rentals and a close-in location. ~ 900 East Española Street; 719-578-6825. The 18-hole **Pine Creek Golf Club** boasts generous fairway landing areas, subtly breaking greens, dramatic elevation changes, bunkers, trees, creeks and lakes. ~ 9850 Divot Trail; 719-594-9999. There's also

**GOLF**

### ICE SKATING

Colorado Springs has traditionally been one of the major ice-skating capitals in the United States, thanks to the Broadmoor Skating Club, which sponsored and trained Olympic figure-skating champions such as Peggy Fleming. The Broadmoor's ice rink is gone now. Olympian training, along with hockey games and sometimes national and world skating championships, have moved to the new **World Arena Ice Hall.** Visitors can watch practices during the daytime, and the rink is open for public skating in the evenings. ~ 3185 Venetucci Boulevard; 719-477-2100; www.world arena.com.

the 18-hole **Valley Hi Municipal Golf Course.** ~ 610 South Chelton Road; 719-578-6351.

**CAÑON CITY AREA**   In Cañon City, the 18-hole **Shadow Hills Country Club Golf Course** is open to the public on weekdays, but is members-only until 3 p.m. on weekends. ~ 1232 County Road 143; 719-275-0603.

**SOUTH PARK AREA**   **Collegiate Peaks Golf Course** has a nine-hole course with cart and club rentals. ~ 28775 Fairway Drive, Buena Vista; 719-395-8189. There's also the nine-hole public **Salida Golf Course.** ~ 404 Grant Street, Salida; 719-539-6373.

**TENNIS**

Colorado Springs has four public tennis courts at **Monument Valley Park.** ~ Monument Creek; 719-578-6636. There are also four courts at **Bear Creek Regional Park.** ~ 21st and Argus streets. Four more public courts are located at **Memorial Park.** ~ East Pikes Peak Avenue at Hancock Street; 719-578-6676. All are first-come, first-served, and are lighted for night play.

**RIDING STABLES**

**COLORADO SPRINGS AREA**   Horses for riding in the Garden of the Gods may be rented at **Academy Riding Stables**, which also offers easy one- and two-hour guided trips, often with 50 or more riders. ~ 4 El Paso Boulevard, Colorado Springs; 719-633-5667. Unique (but pricier) rides can be arranged at the **Broadmoor Hotel Stables**, where guides lead groups along alpine trails on Cheyenne Mountain. The hotel's private reserve is stocked with wildlife, and you can expect to see elk, bison and llamas grazing there. Reservations required. ~ 719-577-5775, 800-634-7711; www. broadmoor.com.

**AUTHOR'S FAVORITE**

While I was in college, I had a summer job was as a tour guide on the Pikes Peak Highway. Once each summer I'd take a busman's holiday and hike up Pikes Peak on the **Barr Trail** from Manitou Springs. Though the 17-mile trail makes for one of the longest ascents of the 14,000-foot mountain, it has the advantage of starting at the same place as the Pikes Peak Cog Railway, so upon reaching the summit you can ride the train back down. Another option is to ride the train up and hike back down. Sounds easier, but in fact—unlike trekking uphill—the downhill hike will paralyze you for a week with sore leg muscles. Besides, climbing the peak provides a thrill of accomplishment, whereas riding up and walking back down some-how seems like cheating. For more information, see page 264.

**CAÑON CITY AREA** Near Cañon City, guided one-hour to full-day rides through 3500 acres of foothill and arroyo country with views of the Royal Gorge area are offered by **Fort Royal Stables**. ~ 44899 Route 50 West, Cañon City; 719-275-2962, 866-678-8880.

**SOUTH PARK AREA** Horse rentals and guided hour-long to all-day trail rides on forested mountain slopes are available at **Mount Princeton Riding Stables**, located three miles west of Nathrop. ~ Nathrop; 719-395-6498; www.coloradotrailrides.com. Overnight llama treks are offered by **Spruce Ridge Llama Adventure Treks**. ~ 4141 County Road 210, Salida; 719-539-4182, 888-686-8735.

**PIKES PEAK AREA** The unpaved **Gold Camp Road**, the track-bed for a standard-gauge railroad that brought gold ore from Cripple Creek to refineries in Colorado Springs, was a popular backcountry auto road until a 2002 tunnel cave-in closed it to motor vehicles indefinitely—much to the delight of mountain bikers, who now have this spectacular 26-mile route around the south side of Pikes Peak all to themselves. Another great area for dirt-road bike touring is the **Rampart Range Road** between the Garden of the Gods and the mountain town of Woodland Park. West of Cañon City, the three-mile **Tunnel Drive**, which leads to an overlook near Royal Gorge, has been closed to motor vehicles and is now a popular bike route.

**BIKING**

**SOUTH PARK AREA** In the Fairplay area, mountain bikers use the 35 miles of marked trails in the **Fairplay State Snowmobile Trail System**, two and a half miles north of town on Forest Road 659. Around Salida, popular rides include **Bighorn Sheep Canyon**, which starts in downtown Salida and follows the Arkansas River for 12 miles to Coaldale.

**Bike Rentals** In Colorado Springs, mountain bikes are for rent at **Criterium Bike Shop**. ~ 6150 Corporate Drive; 719-599-0149; www.criterium-bicycles.com. **Team Telecycle** also has mountain bikes. ~ 615 South Baldwin Street, Woodland Park; 719-687-6165. **Absolute Bikes** rents front-suspension, full-suspension and tandem mountain bikes in Salida. ~ 330 West Sackett Street; 719-539-9295.

All distances listed for hiking trails are one way unless otherwise noted.

**HIKING**

**COLORADO SPRINGS AREA** On the southwest edge of Colorado Springs, North Cheyenne Canyon has several outstanding, easy-to-reach hiking trails. The **Mount Cutler Trail** (1.75 miles) climbs 500 feet from the middle part of the canyon up to the ridge between North and South Cheyenne canyons for a view of Seven Falls. The **Columbine Trail** (5 miles) runs the length of the North Cheyenne Canyon from its lower end all the way to Helen Hunt Falls.

**PIKES PEAK AREA**    The ultimate Colorado Springs–area hike is the **Barr Trail** (17 miles) from Manitou Springs to the summit of Pikes Peak. The first three miles of the trail, from the Pikes Peak Cog Railway parking lot on Ruxton Avenue to the top of Mount Manitou, is the steepest portion. From there it's an easy ridgeline walk to Barr Camp at timberline on the east face of Pikes Peak. The last few miles of switchbacks, up rocky alpine slopes, are difficult not so much because the trail is steep but because the air is thin. There is also a short trail up Pikes Peak from The Crags, a National Forest campground on a marked dirt road off Route 67 on the west face of the peak near Cripple Creek.

Near Cripple Creek, Mueller State Park has an 85-mile network of hiking trails, ranging from the easy, spectacular **Outlook Ridge Trail** (2 miles) to the long, strenuous **Four Mile Overlook Trail** (9 miles), which commands dramatic views of remote Four Mile Canyon.

**SOUTH PARK AREA**    In the Collegiate Peaks, a longer and more challenging ascent that requires no special equipment is the 8.5-mile trail that goes to the summit of **Mount Harvard** (14,420 feet). The upper portion of the climb follows the Colorado Trail, which runs 420 miles from Denver to Durango.

Another popular hiking route, the **Browns Pass Trail** starts from the Denny Creek Trailhead 12 miles west of Buena Vista and climbs four miles to a pass on the Continental Divide, then descends for half a mile to a century-old prospector's cabin.

▼ ▼ ▼ ▼ ▼ ▼ ▼ ▼ ▼ ▼ ▼
**Transportation**

**CAR**

Colorado Springs is 70 miles south of Denver on Route 25. From Colorado Springs, **Route 24** heads west toward South Park, with turnoffs to Pikes Peak and Cripple Creek. **Route 115** goes south from Colorado Springs to the Cañon City area.

**AIR**

**Colorado Springs Airport** is served by America West, American Airlines, Continental Airlines, Delta Air Lines and Mesa Airlines. Built about the same time, the Colorado Springs Airport has been competing aggressively with the problem-ridden Denver International Airport for airline hub routes; as a result, airfares are often significantly lower if you fly into Colorado Springs instead of Denver. ~ www.flycos.com.

**RideFinders Transportation Center** provides low-cost bus service to and from the airport. ~ 719-385-7433.

**TNM&O Coaches**, a Greyhound affiliate, provides service to Colorado Springs. ~ 120 South Weber Street; 719-635-1505.    **BUS**

Among the many car-rental agencies at or near the Colorado Springs airport are **Alamo Rent A Car** (800-327-9633), **Avis Rent A Car** (800-331-1212), **Dollar Rent A Car** (800-800-4000), **Hertz Rent A Car** (800-654-3131) and **Budget Car Rental** (800-527-0700).    **CAR RENTALS**

Colorado Springs municipal buses are operated by **Colorado Springs Transit**. ~ 1015 Transit Drive; 719-385-7433.    **PUBLIC TRANSIT**

**Yellow Cab** is the local taxi company in Colorado Springs. ~ 719-634-5000.    **TAXIS**

# SEVEN

# South Central Colorado

Colorado changes character south of the Arkansas River. The slender green valleys of the north give way to turquoise-gray sagebrush desert. Spring sandstorms whip across the arid flats and wash against the steep slopes of the Sangre de Cristo Range like typhoon waves on a rocky shore, piling dunes to heights unknown elsewhere in America. Forbidding and fascinating, this strange landscape speaks of the awesome scope and power of nature wherever you look. At the heart of the region, the San Luis Valley is the oldest, poorest, driest, coldest part of the state—a perfect place to search for "Hidden Colorado."

The towns are different, too. Other than Pueblo, there is no community in south central Colorado that could be characterized as a city. Alamosa, the largest town after Pueblo, has a population of less than 8000. The names of most towns, as well as rivers, mountains and other landmarks, are Spanish, the language still spoken by about half the people who live in the region. Their forefathers arrived in neighboring New Mexico by wagon train from Mexico City more than two centuries before Zebulon Pike led the first United States expedition into what is now Colorado. Gradually, generation by generation, the descendants of these Spanish immigrants moved northward along the Río Grande from Santa Fe and Taos. Their spirit endures in the arts and crafts, religion and language of the region, and in an austere rural way of life not far removed from the pioneer tradition.

The land south of the Arkansas River and east of the San Juan Mountains belonged to Mexico until 1848, when it became United States territory in the treaty that ended the Mexican War. No battles were ever fought here, though; the fighting took place more than a thousand miles to the south, where American troops invaded Mexico and seized Mexico City. At the time, there were not yet any Mexicans in the region that is now southern Colorado. Apache and Comanche Indian refugees who had been driven out of Texas by non-Indian settlers had laid claim to the mountains, prairies and desert of southern Colorado as their new homeland and sought to keep it by waging a campaign of terror against anyone who tried to start a farm or ranch farther north than Taos. The soldiers sent to secure United States owner-ship of New Mexico also provided protection from Indian raids, making it safe for settlers from New Mexico to homestead in southern Colorado.

Even today, south central Colorado is sparsely inhabited. The rapid growth that has swollen northern Colorado's population into the millions has bypassed south central Colorado completely. No significant gold strike was ever discovered in the Sangre de Cristos—only coal, which held out the dismal promise of life as a mine laborer without the corresponding possibility of striking it rich. The lack of water limited agriculture to family farms operating at subsistence level, and cattle quickly overgrazed the fragile grasslands, transforming them into desert with hardly a trace of fertile soil. Today, the economy of the region still depends mainly on small veg-etable farms and, more and more, on specialty agriculture including herb farms and llama and bison ranches.

Tourism in south central Colorado bears little resemblance to the major in-dustry that has brought such prosperity to resort towns in the northern part of the state. Although there are expanses of mountain wilderness with abundant wildlife, they are so remote and inaccessible that few hikers or hunters ever venture into them. Restaurants and motels tend to be simple, unpretentious little places with prices to match. Yet travelers who take the time to explore the Sangre de Cristos, the San Luis Valley, and the Gunnison River area discover scenery and recreational opportunities as exciting in their way as any to be found in the better-known and more crowded Colorado tourist areas.

South central Colorado has something to offer just about every traveler. The recently expanded and upgraded Great Sand Dunes National Park merits a ranking alongside the Grand Canyon and Carlsbad Caverns as one of the premier natural wonders of the American Southwest. History echoes in the whistle of the steam locomotive that pulls the Cumbres and Toltec narrow-gauge passenger train, as well as in the artsy little revival mining town of Creede and the ghost-town remains of other such communities that did not survive. Although most of the region covered in this chapter has no ski slopes, the two exceptions—Monarch and Crested Butte—afford more relaxed alternatives to northern Colorado resort scenes such as Aspen and Vail. The annual crane migration draws birders to wildlife refuges along the Rio Grande, and fishing and boating lure water sports enthusiasts to Blue Mesa Reservoir, Colorado's largest lake. Mountain biking was born on the jeep trails around Crested Butte, where fat-tire bicycles now seem to outnumber cars.

## Pueblo Area

With 104,000 residents, Pueblo is Colorado's fourth-largest city; it was the second largest before Colorado Spring's and Aurora's prodigious growth spurts and may soon be sur-passed by Boulder as well. Pueblo thrived because in 1875 the Colorado Fuel and Iron Company (later CF&I Steel), which domi-nated coal mining in Colorado for generations, chose this location as the site of its huge steel mill, which shut down in 1982. Today, Pueblo is the only Front Range city that is not experiencing a population explosion. The shutdown of the mill improved air quality, but the economy has not yet fully recovered, though the mill was recently acquired by Oregon Steel, which reopened it on a smaller scale and retooled it to manufacture rails for train tracks.

**SIGHTS**    Certainly Pueblo's top sightseeing highlight is **Rosemount Museum**. This three-story, 37-room stone mansion, one of the grandest in Colorado, was built for a banker in 1893. On display in the servants' quarters, the McClelland Collection of curiosities from around the world strikes a fun-loving counterpoint to the opulence of Rosemount's polished wood-and-marble interiors. Look for the rose motif, which appears somewhere in each room of the home. Closed Monday. Admission. ~ 419 West 14th Street, Pueblo; 719-545-5290; www.rosemount.org, e-mail vol@rose mount.org.

Tourism has not figured much in Pueblo's development over the years. It has a plain but comfy hometown feel, and the main points of interest are meant primarily for residents to enjoy. The story of the town's early years awaits at the free **Pueblo County Historical Museum** in the Union Avenue Historic District. The museum's collection of Pueblo paraphernalia features an impressive collection of locally made saddles. Open Tuesday through Saturday afternoons. ~ 217 South Grand Avenue, Pueblo; 719-543-6772; www.pueblohistory.org, e-mail info@pueblohistory.org.

At the northeast end of Pueblo's historic district, the modern **Sangre de Cristo Arts and Conference Center** has three galleries that show changing exhibits, works by regional artists and shows on national tour, as well as a permanent collection of Western art. There are also a children's museum and a theater that presents local theater and dance productions. Closed Sunday. Admission. ~ 210 North Santa Fe Avenue, Pueblo; 719-295-7200.

On Pueblo's southwest side near the state fairgrounds is **El Pueblo Museum**. Operated by the Colorado Historical Society, the museum is a re-creation of the adobe Fort Pueblo trading post, built on the site in 1842. Plains Indian artifacts, buffalo robes and long, black-powder rifles are on display. Admission. ~ 324 West 1st Street, Pueblo; 719-583-0453.

To the northwest, on the way out to Lake Pueblo, is Pueblo's **City Park**, with green lawn and picnic tables surrounding a duck pond, as well as a children's playground, a baseball diamond, tennis courts and a 1911 carousel—one of only 170 all-wood hand-carved carousels in existence. The park is also the home of the **Pueblo Zoo**. The small zoo features an "ecocenter" containing artificial environments that range from tropical rainforest to penguin habitat. There are also a children's petting zoo and a sizable collection of snakes and other reptiles. City Park also has a restored antique carousel that children can ride for a small charge. Admission. ~ 3455 Nuckells Avenue, Pueblo; 719-561-1452; www. pueblozoo.org, e-mail director@pueblozoo.org.

*Text continued on page 272.*

South Central Colorado

## San Luis Valley

Visiting Great Sand Dunes National Park presents a planning challenge because the dunes can become so hot in the middle of the day that your feet can get burned right through the soles of your sneakers. Whether you're camping in the park or spending the night in Alamosa, you'll want to visit early and late in the day, when it's pleasantly cool and the sun is low enough to cast the long shadows that make the dunes most photogenic. With the remainder of your weekend getaway, you can explore more of the San Luis Valley, a land sheltered by mountain ranges, where the Spanish heritage of centuries past lives on.

**Day 1**
- For a weekend visit, get an early start and plan to arrive at **Great Sand Dunes National Park** (page 282) by noon. From anywhere in the Denver–Boulder–Colorado Springs area, it takes three to four hours to reach the park. The driving time is similar from other major tourist destinations in the region such as Vail, Durango, Taos or Santa Fe. If you're planning to camp in the park, go there first to stake out your site in the first-come, first-served campground. If you plan to spend the night in Alamosa and already have reservations, you may want to spend some time relaxing at the park's popular "beach" area, where the cold mountain spring water of Medano Creek splays out across the sand flats at the base of the dunes. An hour or so should be plenty in the sun's midday glare.

- Leaving the park, head south on Route 150 for five miles to the **Zapata Falls Natural Area** for a great view of the San Luis Valley below. Take the short, steep hike to the waterfalls, which plunge into a narrow gorge. Bring a lunch to enjoy in the picnic area below the falls.

- In the afternoon, take a trip around the southern part of the San Luis Valley on the **Los Caminos Antiguos Scenic and Historic Byway** loop route. Continue south on Route 150 for nine more miles to Route 160. Turn left and go east for ten miles to Fort Garland and the **Fort Garland Museum** (page 284), Kit Carson's command post. Then proceed south for 16 miles to **San Luis** (page 284), the oldest town in Colorado.

- Head west from San Luis on Route 142. Visit the village of **San Acacio**, where you can see the rustic old adobe and wood church and learn about the miracle that caused it to be built. After crossing the Rio Grande, you'll come to **Manassa** (page 284), where the main attraction is the **Jack Dempsey Museum** (page 284). Near the village of **Romeo** is a restoration of the stockade where explorer Zebulon Pike and his men spent the winter of 1807, not realizing that they were invading Mexico. The distance from San Luis to Romeo is 34 miles.

• Head south on Route 285 for seven miles to Antonito, northern terminus of the **Cumbres & Toltec Scenic Railroad** (page 284). Take a short side road to the neighboring town of Conejos to see **Our Lady of Guadalupe Church**, a Spanish-colonial mission church that is home to the oldest parish in Colorado. Take Route 17 for seven miles west of Antonito to see **Las Mesitas Church**, another picturesque old Catholic church. If it's a hot afternoon, there's no better way to beat the heat than to follow Route 17 for another 20 miles into the cool forests around **Cumbres Pass** (page 285).

• Returning to Romeo, take Route 285 for 28 straight miles north to Alamosa, then continue for 14 more miles to Mosca, where a right turn will put you on the road back to the Great Sand Dunes National Park entrance. By now the time should be right for a late afternoon walk in the dunes. You might start at the campground and hike through the "lost forest," where ancient ponderosa pines have been engulfed by the dunes.

**Day 2**   • Rise early the next morning for a more ambitious dunes hike. Starting from the Medano Creek "beach," it will take about an hour to reach the top of the highest sand dune you can see. When you finally get there, you'll see more dunes just as high, extending in an unbroken expanse of sand for many miles. How can you top that experience? Maybe it's time to head back to the beach for a picnic lunch, and start home.

**Hose Company No. 3**, Pueblo's firefighters museum, shows kids of all ages the workings of a traditional fire station, and features an old-time, hand-drawn fire hose cart, a 1917 fire truck, and memorabilia including tributes to acts of bravery by local firemen. Closed Saturday and Sunday. ~ 116 Broadway, Pueblo; 719-544-4548.

The look of downtown Pueblo has recently been transformed by the **Arkansas Riverwalk**. Diverted away from downtown with levees after a catastrophic 1921 flood, the river has been restored to its original course and impounded to widen it. Pedestrian paths now follow the parklike shoreline past plazas and pavilions, sculptures and fountains. Excursion boats run every day and evening during the summer and offer one-hour cruises complete with cocktails and hot hors d'oeuvres on Friday and Saturday nights. There's also a trailhead for the Pueblo Greenway bike trail, which runs out to Lake Pueblo. ~ 200 West 1st Street, Pueblo; 719-595-0242, 719-595-1589 (cruise reservations); www.pueblo harp.com, e-mail info@puebloharp.com.

The free **Weisbrod Aircraft Museum** and **International B-24 Museum**, located on opposite sides of the road at the airport, contain major collections of World War II–era aircraft. The Weisbrod Museum has 26 airplanes, including a B-29 bomber and an RB-37, with interpretive plaques. The B-24 Museum traces the development of the B-24 Liberator, one of the most successful bombers of World War II, and its crewmen who trained in Pueblo. ~ Pueblo Airport, Pueblo; 719-948-9219.

From Pueblo, the mountains barely break the western skyline. Motorists with plenty of time can leave Route 25 on a scenic detour that takes three times longer than the drive from Pueblo to Walsenburg on the interstate and takes you as close to the mountains as it's possible to go by car. Take Route 96 west from Pueblo for 52 miles, across the low Wet Mountains, to the small ranching town of **Westcliffe**, the all-but-undiscovered base camp for recreation along the steep eastern slope of the Sangre de Cristos. The range is a jagged, impassable wall of granite that runs unbroken for 75 miles without a single road over it. Route 69 heads southeast along the base of the mountain range, returning to Route 25 at Walsenburg, 57 miles away.

Twenty-nine miles southeast of Westcliffe near the junction of Routes 165 and 78 is the unique **Bishop Castle**, a project that owner Jim Bishop has been working on since 1969. Built with more than 1000 tons of stone gathered by hand from the surrounding mountains, the three-story castle features medieval walls, flying buttresses, a 130-foot-tall tower, gold minarets and a wrought-iron bridge. Future plans call for a moat and a drawbridge. Bishop, who has dedicated the project to the spirit of working men around the world, asserts that the castle is the largest

structure ever built in the United States by a single in
Route 165, Beulah; 719-485-3040.

With only a couple of notable exceptions, lodging option
Pueblo consist of name-brand motor inns and a scattering of li
ma-and-pa motels, mostly clustered around Route 25 Exit 10
(the junction with Route 50 westbound) at the north end of town.
That's where you'll find the city's largest hotel, the **Holiday Inn
of Pueblo,** which bills itself as the city's only full-service hotel,
with amenities that include a laundromat and room service, not

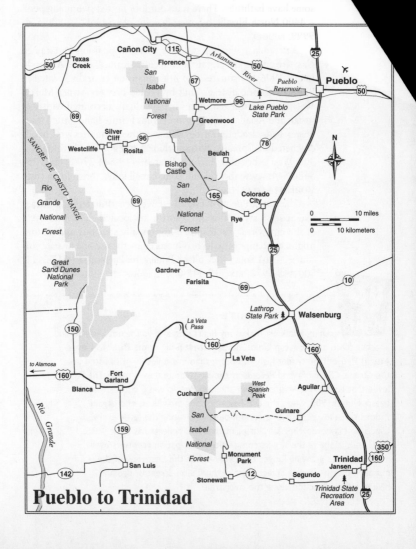

**Pueblo to Trinidad**

munications links and a fitness center.
nporary, with cheerful color schemes,
y-per-view movies on TV. There are
d a cocktail lounge. ~ 4001 North
43-8050, fax 719-545-2271; www.

und side-by-side with the major
paralleling Route 25 between
lotel has 29 clean units with
ur units have two double beds, and
ere is an outdoor heated swimming pool.
izabeth Street, Pueblo; 719-543-4173, 800-524-
GET.

A veranda, a winding staircase, inlaid wood floors and stained glass are among the elegant architectural features of the **Abriendo Inn**, a 1906 foursquare-style brick mansion centrally located in Pueblo's historic district. Built by Pueblo brewery owner Martin Walter, each of the ten rooms is individually decorated with Victorian and Asian antiques. Some rooms feature handcrafted four-poster beds, leaded and beveled windows, armoires and hand-crocheted bedspreads. Rates include a full gourmet breakfast. ~ 300 West Abriendo Avenue, Pueblo; 719-544-2703, fax 719-542-6544; www.abriendoinn.com, e-mail info@abriendoinn.com. MODERATE TO DELUXE.

The **Inn at Pueblo West**, a Best Western affiliate, is an attractive Spanish-style 80-room resort hotel located eight miles west of the city. Guest rooms are exceptionally spacious and feature bright, contemporary decor. Guests enjoy the use of a nearby golf course. ~ 201 South McCulloch Boulevard, Pueblo; 719-547-2111, 800-448-1972, fax 719-547-0385. BUDGET TO MODERATE.

**AUTHOR FAVORITE**

Unique folk art makes my heart sing, and you're not likely to find another piece of folk art in Colorado as just-plain-big as the **Pueblo Levee Mural Project**. Sixty feet high and more than five miles long, it's listed in the *Guinness Book of World Records* as the largest mural ever made. The levee that guides the Arkansas River through Pueblo was a graffiti-riddled eyesore until 1980, when the city began inviting individuals and organizations to paint sections of a continuous mural along the levee every Cinco de Mayo, recycling surplus paint that was collected as toxic waste. The result is one of the largest community-participation artworks ever made—and it's growing longer each year. ~ For the best view of the murals, park on Corona Street west of the Union Street bridge and hike in either direction along the river trail.

You'll find Continental cuisine at affordable prices at **La Renais-** **DINING**
**sance**, which has been operating in a converted 1886 church since
the early 1970s. High ceilings and stained glass add a touch of
class to the casual ambience. Specialties include baby back ribs
and prime rib. Lunch "sometimes"—call first. Closed Sunday. ~
217 East Routt Avenue, Pueblo; 719-543-6367. MODERATE.

**Ianne's Whisky Ridge** is a good Italian restaurant with white
linen tablecloths and a seductive menu featuring such selections as
pasta primavera, chicken piccata, veal Marsala, linguini, scampi,
calamari and escargot. Dinner only. ~ 4333 Thatcher Avenue,
Pueblo; 719-564-8551. MODERATE.

The **Gold Dust Saloon** serves what are reputed to be the best
cheeseburgers and fries in town, as well as homemade soups, salads, sandwiches and big pitchers of beer, in a neighborhood-style
bar and grill with Old West decor. You also get free peanuts so
that you can contribute to the crunchy drifts of shells that cover
the floor, sometimes ankle-deep. Closed Sunday. ~ 217 South
Union Avenue, Pueblo; 719-545-0741. BUDGET.

The ambience is all-natural at the **Café del Rio**, which offers
outdoor dining alongside the Arkansas River near the Pueblo
Greenway and Nature Center. In spite of the Spanish name, the
eclectic menu leans toward French fare such as chicken Provençal,
pork tenderloin *moutarde* and beef *tournedo au poivre*. ~ 2200
Nature Center Road, Pueblo; 719-549-2009. MODERATE.

There are plenty of good Mexican restaurants in Pueblo, most
of them hidden away in neighborhoods where tourists are rarely
seen. A family-run favorite that has been in business since 1975 at
the same location is **Don Carlos Mexican Foods**. The ancestors of
the family that runs it lived in northern New Mexico for centuries,
and this is one of the best places in Colorado to get authentic green
chile stew. Other specialties include a giant pork and avocado
burrito, and there's an all-you-can-eat salad bar. ~ 1234 South
Prairie Avenue, Pueblo; 719-566-1447. BUDGET TO MODERATE.

Artists and crafters have discovered that Pueblo offers low rents    **SHOPPING**
and a central location between the Denver and Santa Fe art markets, and new studios, arts and crafts galleries and gourmet shops
have been revitalizing the neighborhood around Union Avenue,
Pueblo's original main street, and the Pueblo Union Depot. Despite
their enthusiasm, business was slow in the Union Avenue Historic
District until the Arkansas Riverwalk opened in 2000; now it's
the region's liveliest arts scene. Southwestern Indian jewelry can be
found at **Avanyu**. ~ 313 South Union Avenue; 719-543-8112.
You can hunt for antiques at **Granny's Attic**. ~ 331 South Union
Avenue; 719-545-5245. **Tivoli's** also has a selection of antiques.
~ 325 South Union Avenue; 719-545-1448. Crafts studios include
**Heart's Song**. ~ 311½ South Union Avenue; 719-545-2297. Other

shops deal in old and rare books, flower arrangements and antique radios.

**NIGHTLIFE**   **Peppers Niteclub** bills itself as the hottest nightclub between Denver and Albuquerque, although not everyone would agree. The club features mainly recorded music with occasional live bands. The sound is '60s, '70s and early '80s pop except on Thursday, College Night, when techno-alternative music is the main attraction. Nationally known comedy acts are featured on Saturday night. Cover. ~ 4109 Club Manor Drive, Pueblo; 719-542-8629.

Located next to the old CF&I steel mill, **Gus's Place** was the after-work hangout for generations of steelworkers. According to "Ripley's Believe It or Not!," it used to serve more beer per barstool than any other tavern in the world. Today the bar is spruced up and decorated with so much CF&I memorabilia that it's virtually a steel mill museum. ~ 1201 Elm Street; 719-542-0756. Another long-time Pueblo favorite, the **Irish Brew Pub and Grille**, a bar attached to a restaurant that serves steaks, salads and pasta in addition to Irish dishes, draws a largely professional afterwork crowd that slops over into the late evening in a mellow, conversational atmosphere. Closed Sunday. ~ 108 West 3rd Street, Pueblo; 719-542-9974.

As for the performing arts, Pueblo supports several local groups including the **Broadway Theater League**. ~ 719-545-4721. There's also the **Impossible Playhouse**. ~ 719-542-1121. The **Pueblo Choral Society** holds performances. ~ 719-544-4455. You may see the **Pueblo Symphony** and the **Sangre de Christo Ballet Theatre** at the **Sangre de Cristo Arts and Conference Center**. ~ 210 North Santa Fe Avenue, Pueblo; 719-543-0130.

**PARKS**   **LAKE PUEBLO STATE PARK** 🏃 ⛵ 🐟 🚣 🚤 🎣 Surrounded by arid prairie and limestone cliffs, with mountain views to the west, windswept Pueblo Reservoir is a favorite sailing and windsurfing lake. Swimming is prohibited in the lake but permitted in

---

### MEET AN EAGLE FACE-TO-FACE

Part of the Pueblo Greenway and Nature Center, the **Raptor Center of Pueblo** rescues injured eagles, hawks, falcons and owls that are reported or brought in to the center. Most are victims of gunshot wounds. One of the few raptor rehabilitation facilities in the United States, the center succeeds in returning about half the birds it treats to the wild. Handlers introduce some of the nonreleasable birds to visitors in the center's "Birds of Prey" educational program. Call 719-549-2327 for program times.

the Rock Canyon area below Pueblo Dam. Fishing is good for bass, carp, catfish and other lake species. The recreation area also takes in a wide strip of wild land around the lake, providing habitat for coyotes, deer, wild turkeys and many other denizens of the high plains. This backcountry is accessible via a number of hiking and horse trails. There are picnic area, restrooms, marinas, cruise boats and a visitors center. Day-use fee, $5. ~ Located four miles west of Pueblo, with access from Route 50 at the town of Pueblo West via Nichols Road or McCulloch Boulevard; also accessible from Route 96; 640 Pueblo Reservoir Road, 719-561-9320; North Marina, 719-547-3880; South Marina, 719-564-1043.

▲ There are five campgrounds around the lake with a total of 401 tent/RV sites; $12 to $14 per night with no hookups, $16 to $18 per night with electricity. The campgrounds are usually full on weekends. Reservations: 800-678-2267.

**PUEBLO GREENWAY AND NATURE CENTER** 🚶 🚲 The Pueblo Greenway, which follows the banks of the Arkansas River west from Pueblo Boulevard to Lake Pueblo, is a popular cycling and jogging path. Midway along the greenway, the nature center has exhibits about flora and fauna of this prairie and riparian habitat designed with kids in mind. There are nature trails and restrooms. ~ Located a mile west of Pueblo Boulevard at 5200 Nature Center Road; 719-549-2414.

Motorists heading south from Pueblo on Route 25 will find a landscape so vast and empty that it strikes a startling contrast to the busy, heavily populated Front Range corridor of northern Colorado. Walsenburg and Trinidad are the only two towns on the 100-mile route from Pueblo to the New Mexico state line, and neither is generally regarded as a tourist destination. Those who prefer to avoid the interstate and stick to secondary highways will discover leisurely, scenic backroads along the base of the Sangre de Cristo Range.

## Walsenburg–Trinidad Area

Aside from the lake and trails of Lathrop State Park, **Walsenburg** has little but fuel and fast food to entice travelers off the interstate. But the massive stonework of its old courthouse, high school and other buildings, quarried locally in the early 20th century, when Walsenburg was an important railroad junction, gives this unpretentious little town far from anyplace else a rare feeling of permanence. The Huerfano County Historical Society's **Walsenburg Mining Museum**, located in the town's old jail, focuses on the region's coal mining heritage. Open summer weekdays only. Admission. ~ Walsenburg; 719-758-1992.

**SIGHTS**

West of Walsenburg, on the way up La Veta Pass where Route 160 crosses the mountains to Alamosa, the main sight in the small town of La Veta is the **Fort Francisco Museum**, built in 1862 as one of several army outposts designed to protect settlers in south central Colorado from Comanche attacks. The plaza-like fort is now an open-air museum with a collection of period buildings including a blacksmith shop, a schoolhouse and a saloon. Admission. ~ Route 160, La Veta; 719-742-5501.

Southwest from Walsenburg, the **Highway of Legends Scenic Byway** (Route 12) loops around the back side of the Spanish Peaks and returns to the interstate at Trinidad. The **Spanish Peaks** (12,683 feet and 13,626 feet) are the easternmost mountains in the Rockies except for Pikes Peak. Formed by volcanic activity independent of the upheavals that created the Sangre de Cristo Range, the twin peaks are almost disconnected from the main mountain range. The 82-mile paved highway reaches only 9941 feet in elevation as it passes between the Spanish Peaks and the Sangre de Cristos. Along the route lie lakes like mirrors, crumbled adobe ruins, abandoned mines and mills, modern vacation cabins, some of Colorado's most colorful fields of wildflowers and the strange natural formations called the **Great Dikes**, hundreds of narrow rock walls up to 100 feet high and 14 miles long. At Stonewall Gap, the road goes through a natural gateway in the dikes.

A few miles farther up the road, eight miles outside of Trinidad, the **Cokedale National Historic District** preserves the largest of more than 50 coal-mining camps that once brought prosperity to the Spanish Peaks area. Cokedale had a population of 1500 before the company town's owner and sole employer, the American Smelting and Refining Company, shut down its coke ovens here in 1947. Well-preserved homes, small and now mostly abandoned, are scattered through the ghost town. They are overshadowed by the remains of huge ovens that were used to heat coal, refining it into a fuel that burned longer and hotter for use in making steel. Beside the ovens, giant heaps of black slag, a byproduct of the coking process, give visitors some idea of the quantities of coal that were refined here.

Located in the foothills and canyons below Raton Pass, the low, often stormy summit that marks Colorado's boundary with New Mexico, **Trinidad** got its start in the 1830s as a way station on the Santa Fe Trail and became a busy railhead for shipping coal from area mines. The center of town, now preserved as the **Corazon de Trinidad National Historic District**, presents a distinctive blend of New Mexican adobe construction with Colorado's architecture. It's the birthplace of "Santa Fe–style" pueblo-revival architecture. Local architect Isaac Rapp was also the leading building designer in Santa Fe in the early 20th century, when New Mexico was not yet a state and had no architect-licensing board.

The heart of the historic district is the **Trinidad Historical Museum**, which includes the Baca House, Bloom House and Santa

Fe Trail Museum as well as historic gardens. The main attractions are two mansions—the **Baca House**, an 1870 Territorial-style adobe hacienda that belonged to a Mexican cattle baron, and the **Bloom House**, a three-story Victorian mansion built in 1882 for the town banker. The contrast between the two exemplifies the cultural clash that shaped Trinidad's unique personality. The houses are furnished with antiques of the period. Behind the Baca House, the small **Santa Fe Trail Museum**, in the former servants' quarters, contains local memorabilia including substantial collections of weapons and historical photographs. Other exhibits tell the history of the Santa Fe Trail, which connected Kansas City with the capital of New Mexico, and honor Colorado's Hispanic heritage. Closed October through April. Admission. ~ 312 East Main Street, Trinidad; 719-846-7217.

In a restored 1906 department-store building, the **A. R. Mitchell Memorial Museum and Gallery** displays a large collection of works by celebrated local artist Arthur Roy Mitchell depicting life in the Old West, along with paintings by other cowboy artists of the early and mid-20th century. Within the Mitchell Museum, the **Aultman Collection** displays a large exhibit of historic pictures by a longtime local photographer along with his old-time cameras and darkroom equipment. ~ 150 East Main Street, Trinidad; 719-846-4224.

The **Trinidad Children's Museum** is housed in Firehouse #1, the town's original fire station. In addition to firefighting memorabilia, the museum contains a model train, original jail cells and a reconstruction of a 1900 school classroom. ~ 314 North Commercial Street, Trinidad; 719-846-8220.

The first towns in the region were established in the early 1850s, several years before the "Pikes Peak or Bust!" gold rush brought the first wave of settlers to northern Colorado.

Located on the Trinidad State Junior College campus, the **Louden-Henritz Museum of Archaeology** contains exhibits about prehistoric human life in the area. Of special interest is a diorama re-creating Trinchera Cave, which was occupied by nomadic Indians for an estimated 3000 years. The museum also has large collections of arrowheads, fossils and geological samples. ~ Freudenthal Memorial Library, Trinidad State Junior College, Trinidad; 719-846-5508.

**LODGING**

The frontage strip between downtown Walsenburg and the north interstate exit has several nondescript motels, of which perhaps the nicest is the **Best Western Rambler Motel**. This motor inn has 32 rooms decorated in cool earthtone color schemes, and there's a heated pool. ~ Route 25 Exit 52, Walsenburg; 719-738-1121, fax 719-738-1093; www.bestwestern.com. MODERATE.

In Trinidad, the **Stone Mansion** is a B&B in a 1904 three-story home. Built by well-known local architects Isaac and William

Rapp, the unusual house represents an experimental fusion of Victorian shingle-style and arts-and-crafts stonemasonry. The interiors feature original golden oak woodwork and are decorated with museum-quality oil paintings and family heirlooms. One of the three rooms has a private bath, and the others share a bath. ~ 212 East 2nd Street, Trinidad; 719-845-1625, 877-264-4279.

Travelers won't be disappointed with the spacious, contemporary rooms at the 55-unit **Best Western Trinidad Inn**. This motor inn with its hillside location commands a view of Trinidad and the interstate. Many of the bright, spacious rooms overlook the municipal golf course. It has an outdoor swimming pool, a jacuzzi and an exercise room. ~ 900 West Adams Street, Trinidad; phone/fax 719-846-2215, 800-359-4827, fax 719-846-2480; www.bestwestern.com. MODERATE.

The **Days Inn** has 70 clean motel rooms in cheerful color schemes. The two-level complex has an outdoor heated pool, spa, exercise room and restaurant. The rooms are standard fare, but lower in price than most of the comparable motels clustered around the town's interstate exits. ~ 702 West Main Street, Trinidad; phone/fax 719-846-2271. MODERATE.

**DINING**

In Walsenburg, you'll find fresh donuts, a breakfast buffet and a full lunch menu, plus 5,000 books to browse through, at **La Plaza Café & Bookstore**, located on the ground floor of La Plaza Inn. ~ 118 West 6th Street, Walsenburg; 719-738-5700. BUDGET TO MODERATE.

Another good dining bet in Walsenburg is the **Iron Horse**, a family restaurant located in the city's old armory and decorated with small-town memorabilia. Specialties include barbecued ribs and pasta. ~ 503 West 7th Street, Walsenburg; 719-738-9966. BUDGET TO MODERATE.

**Estivins Mexican Family Restaurant** offers Mexican food as authentic as you're likely to find in this largely Hispanic town, featuring an outstanding combination plate. The prices are hard to beat. ~ 525 San Juan Street, Trinidad; 719-846-7491. BUDGET.

**ONCE AND AGAIN**

Originally built as a hotel in 1907, Walsenburg's historic **La Plaza Inn** has recently been restored and reopened as a bed and breakfast. The 16 guest rooms, all with private baths, are uniquely decorated in various themes ranging from Victorian to Southwestern. One features antlers and wildlife art on the walls, and another is furnished with antiques from the owner's ancestral family farm. ~ 118 West 6th Street, Walsenburg; 719-738-5700, fax 719-738-6220. MODERATE.

Nana & Nono Monteleone's Deli & Pasta House serves fettuccini, spaghetti and other pasta entrées with a full range of tantalizing sauces. An unpretentious blend of Italian and Mexican decorations sets the stage for low-priced romantic dinners in this cheerful, student-oriented restaurant, which is also the best place in town to pick up the makings for a picnic lunch. ~ 418 East Main Street, Trinidad; 719-846-2696. BUDGET.

**PARKS**

**SAN ISABEL NATIONAL FOREST** 🚶🛶 A 19,000-acre detached unit of San Isabel National Forest surrounds the Spanish Peaks. The Peaks themselves became the Spanish Peaks Wilderness with the passage of the 1993 Wilderness Act. There are hiking trails around and between the two peaks, and a trail leads to the summit of West Spanish Peak. You may fish for rainbow and brown trout in Cucharas Creek and other area streams. ~ Access to the Spanish Peaks is by the Highway of Legends Scenic Byway (Route 12), which circles both mountains; 719-269-8500.

▲ Along Cucharas Creek, west of Route 12 on Forest Road 413, are Blue Lake and Bear Lake Campgrounds, totalling 30 tent and RV sites (no hookups). Both campgrounds are open late May to mid-September; sites cost $11 per night.

**LATHROP STATE PARK** 🚶🚴 ⚓🛶🎣🚤🛥🛶 The park's twin lakes, Martin Lake and Horseshoe Lake, are quite small, but that doesn't stop Walsenburg area residents from flocking here for waterskiing, sailboarding and fishing. A hiking trail wanders among rock formations on its way up to a hogback ridge, and the campground offers a view across Martin Lake to the Spanish Peaks. Its convenience to Route 25 makes Lathrop State Park a welcome oasis on a long, desolate highway drive. Fishing is good for rainbow trout, bass, catfish, walleye and tiger muskie. There are picnic areas, restrooms, showers, a visitors center and a golf course. Day-use fee, $5. ~ Located off Route 160, three miles west of Walsenburg; 719-738-2376.

▲ Yucca Campground has 21 RV/tent sites (no hookups); $12 per night. Pinon Campground has 79 RV/tent sites (about half with electrical hookups); $12 to $16 per night. Reservations: 800-678-2267.

**TRINIDAD STATE RECREATION AREA** 🚶🎣🛶🛥🛶 Trinidad Lake, which hides old coal mines in its depths, offers fishing, boating and windsurfing in the pretty Purgatoire River Valley above the town of Trinidad. Nine miles of backcountry hiking trails within the park take you among hills studded with piñon and juniper. They connect with a vast network of jeep roads and trails into the surrounding San Isabel National Forest. The lake is populated with rainbow trout, walleye, largemouth bass, channel catfish and bullheads. There are picnic areas and restrooms. Day-use fee, $5. ~ Located four miles west of Trinidad on Route 12; 719-846-6951.

▲ There are 62 RV/tent sites (most with hookups); $12 to $16 per night. Reservations: 800-678-2267.

## Alamosa Area

▼▼▼▼▼▼▼▼▼▼▼

The San Luis Valley is probably the least-visited area in the Colorado Rockies. An oval of flat land 120 miles long and 60 miles wide surrounded by soaring mountain peaks, it was settled in the 1800s by Spanish colonists from nearby Taos. Most people of the valley, descendants of Spanish New Mexican pioneers, live on truck farms along the Rio Grande or in small, poor villages near the foot of the mountains. The valley's inhospitable climate discourages newcomers. Alamosa's winter low temperatures often register as the coldest in Colorado, and the wind blows all year long.

### SIGHTS

Visitors to **Alamosa**, the valley's largest town, may find little more than a long stretch of roadside strip development, though a detour through the old, tree-lined residential neighborhood north of Route 160 reveals a number of Victorian-vintage homes. Founded as the northern terminus of the Denver & Rio Grande Railway's "Chili Line," which followed the Rio Grande Valley south to Espanola, New Mexico, much of Alamosa was erected almost overnight with plain, portable buildings brought here on flatbed rail cars. Since then, the railroad has declined, the weather has continued to be as notoriously bad as ever year-round, and Alamosa has remained a plain, utilitarian town whose most notable feature is the low rents that have attracted a growing community of artists and crafters in recent years.

One of the most extraordinary natural phenomena in the state lies 36 miles northeast of Alamosa. **Great Sand Dunes National Park** is a 50-square-mile expanse of shifting sand, carried by windstorms and deposited over millions of years in this notch at the foot of the Sangre de Cristo Range. Rising 900 feet high, they are the largest sand dunes in the United States. In the summer months, visitors by the thousands flock here to climb the dunes or just play on the half-mile-wide "beach" along the broad, shallow, constantly shifting streams of chilly mountain water where Medano Creek makes its way across the sand. A four-wheel-drive road provides access to primitive campgrounds in remote areas of the dunes. Formerly a national monument, Great Sand Dunes was granted national park status in November 2000. The upgrade was conditioned on the Nature Conservancy completing a series of transactions to acquire and turn over the Medano-Zapata Ranch, formerly a bison ranch bordering the park (the bison herd still grazes along the approach to the park), so signs and brochures did not reflect the new status until 2005. Parts of Rio

Grande National Forest were also added, for a total park expansion of 110,000 acres including grasslands, wetlands, cottonwood and aspen forests and six peaks over 13,000 feet with alpine lakes and tundra. Admission. ~ 11999 Route 150, Mosca; 719-378-2312.

One of the more unlikely attractions in the area is **Colorado 'Gators**, also known as the Two Mile Creek Wildlife Habitat. Located 17 miles north of Alamosa, this colony of more than 80 'gators is the northernmost and highest-altitude outdoor alligator colony in the world. The alligators were brought in to provide a means for disposal of the tons of waste created by a fish processing plant at the facility, which produces tilapia fillets that are shipped fresh to cities throughout the United States and Canada. Admission. ~ 9162 County Road 9 North, Mosca; 719-378-2612; www.gatorfarm.com.

◄ HIDDEN

**Alamosa National Wildlife Refuge,** located three miles east of town on a meandering stretch of the Rio Grande, protects wetlands that provide migratory habitat for ducks, egrets and herons, and, in late winter, bald and golden eagles. There is a nature trail along the river and a 12-mile-long auto tour loop. ~ Route 160, Alamosa; 719-589-4021.

Off Route 160 east of the turnoff to Great Sand Dunes, **Fort Garland Museum** preserves the old U.S. Army fort established in 1858, shortly after the United States won the territory at the end of the Mexican War. Active for 25 years, the fort was the final command in the military career of Colonel Kit Carson, the Southwest's most notorious Indian fighter. The only real test of the fort's effectiveness came in 1863, when a family known as "the bloody Espinozas" mounted a reign of terror in the valley after the Virgin Mary appeared in a vision and told them to drive the Anglos out of the San Luis Valley. The buildings house exhibits of 19th-century military uniforms, weapons and everyday items. Closed Tuesday and Wednesday. Admission. ~ 29477 Route 159, Fort Garland; 719-379-3512.

South of Fort Garland, little **San Luis** is the oldest town in Colorado. The **San Luis Museum and Cultural Center** presents the folk art and history of the valley's people. Exhibits include an outstanding collection of carved wooden saints, known as *bultos*, a display of *colchas*—pictorial quilts unique to the San Luis Valley—and a reconstruction of a traditional *penitente* chapel. ~ 401 Church Place, San Luis; 719-672-3611.

HIDDEN ▶

Beginning at a trailhead near the junction of Routes 159 and 142 in San Luis, a 1.25-mile walking trail leads up past a series of life-size bronze statues by local sculptor Humberto Maestas depicting the **Stations of the Cross**. The 14 life-sized sculptures depict scenes from the Passion—Christ's trial and suffering leading to His crucifixion. On Good Friday and Easter weekend, hundreds of pilgrims walk from other San Luis Valley communities to perform devotions at the stations along this path. At the path's terminus, the top of the mesa, a Crucifixion scene looms over the valley.

HIDDEN ▶

A few miles away, the even smaller town of **Manassa** is locally famous as the birthplace of boxer Jack Dempsey, who as a teenager fought for prize money in mining-camp saloons from Durango to the Cripple Creek district and went on to win the world's heavyweight title in 1919. The **Jack Dempsey Museum** exhibits a collection of Dempsey mementos contributed by residents. Manassa was established in the mid-1870s as the first Mormon colony in the region, and its population (988 people) is still entirely Mormon. The San Luis Valley as a whole has a Mormon population of about 3500—who make up most of the area's non-Hispanic residents. Closed October through May. ~ 412 Main Street, Manassa; 719-843-5207.

At the southwestern edge of the valley, Antonito is the northern terminus of the **Cumbres & Toltec Scenic Railroad**. Two separate narrow-gauge steam trains run each morning from Antonito, Colorado, and Chama, New Mexico, climbing by sweeping loops through forests of aspen up to Osier, a mountain ghost town that is inaccessible by car. In the afternoon, passengers can return along the same route or, for a higher fare, continue all the way to Chama and take a van back in the evening. The 64-mile Antonito-to-Chama trip is America's longest and highest narrow-gauge steam train route operating today. The train runs from Memorial Day to mid-October. Antonito is in the process of converting the town's only mansion into the Conejos Museum, which will focus on the history of the railroad. ~ 719-376-5483, 888-286-2737; www.cumbrestoltec.com.

Both fish and reptiles at Colorado 'Gators are able to survive the sub-zero San Luis Valley winters because the water in which they live is warmed by hot springs.

Motorists can take a scenic drive different from, but comparable to, the train route by taking paved Route 17 over La Manga Pass (10,230 feet) to the summit of **Cumbres Pass** (10,022 feet), where the narrow-gauge tracks parallel the road for several miles. The ghost town of Cumbres, near the summit of the pass, was home to railroad workers who kept the trains running year-round back in the 1880s.

Motorists going west toward Wolf Creek Pass and Durango on Route 160 pass through the towns of Monte Vista and Del Norte. Monte Vista is best known for the **Monte Vista National Wildlife Refuge**, well known among birders as a stopover for as many as 20,000 sandhill and whooping cranes migrating south to New Mexico each October and November. Bald eagles and thousands of ducks spend the winter months in these wetlands. ~ Route 15, Monte Vista; 719-589-4021.

Del Norte's **Rio Grande County Museum** focuses on the multicultural history of American Indians, Spanish settlers and Anglo trappers and traders along the upper Rio Grande. Exhibits range from ancient petroglyphs to relics from the failed 1848 expedition of mountain man John C. Fremont, who lost 11 of his 33 men to hypothermia in a fruitless wintertime search for a year-round route over the Continental Divide. The museum also hosts history and nature lectures and local art programs. Admission. ~ 580 Oak Street, Del Norte; 719-657-2847.

Toward the north end of the San Luis Valley, the tiny, remote village of **Crestone** has become a New Age phenomenon. The old mining town's population had shrunk to 61 by 1978, when developers bought a nearby ranch and subdivided it into homesite lots. Inspired by a vision of international spiritual harmony (not to mention the tax advantages), the promoters donated lots to be used as spiritual retreats by Carmelite nuns, Tibetan Buddhists and other groups including the Sri Aurobindo Learning Center, the Crestone Mountain Zen Center, the Haidakhandi Universal Ashram, the Naropa Institute and Lindesfarne Temple, as well as several environmental projects. In 1996, renowned Tibetan shaman Kardum Sonam came to Crestone to consecrate the 41-foot-tall Stupa of Many Auspicious Doors, one of the largest Buddhist stupas in the Western Hemisphere. Today, Crestone has a year-round population of 500 and hosts spiritual conferences that draw thousands of participants from throughout the world.

**LODGING**    Alamosa's hotel and restaurant selection is on the slim side. A welcome find is the **Cottonwood Inn & Gallery**, a big pink-and-gray Victorian several blocks from the main highway in a quiet, shady neighborhood. It has nine antique-furnished guest rooms, most with private baths, including four suites. The common areas feature changing exhibits by local artists. ~ 123 San Juan Avenue, Alamosa; 719-589-3882, 800-955-2623, fax 719-589-6437; www.cottonwoodinn.com, e-mail relax@cottonwoodinn.com. MODERATE TO DELUXE.

The **Alamosa Lamplighter Motel** is actually two motels under the same management but several blocks apart, with a total of 70 guest rooms. The rooms, which are about as conventional as motel rooms get, are a bargain when you consider that the rent includes the use of the indoor swimming pool and sauna at the main motel and the jacuzzi in the annex. There is also a restaurant on the premises. ~ 425 Main Street, Alamosa; 719-589-6636, 800-359-2138. BUDGET.

Other lodging options in Alamosa consist of a scattering of motels and motor inns along Route 160. For example, modern, spacious, air-conditioned lodgings and an indoor swimming pool, hot tub and sauna, can be found at the 121-unit **Best Western Alamosa Inn**. The rooms, available with two double beds or one king-size, are clean and contemporary. Most face the interior pool area instead of the highway and are quieter than an average motel room. ~ 1919 Main Street, Alamosa; 719-589-2567, 800-528-1234, fax 719-589-0767. BUDGET TO MODERATE.

**AUTHOR FAVORITE**

Who can resist spending a night or two at a hot springs spa? One of the most unusual and affordable spa experiences around is to be found at **Joyful Journey Hot Springs Spa**, located at the north end of the San Luis Valley. The spa has a large, neck-deep outdoor hot pool and two smaller, waist-deep soaking pools, all fed by the hottest, clearest natural hot springs in Colorado and maintained at 98° to 108°F. The mountain views from the pools and surrounding deck are spectacular, especially at sunset. There's a sauna and complete spa services such as therapeutic massage, shiatsu and herbal wraps. And to top it all off, you can spend the night in a Mongolian-style yurt (shared bath). There's no restaurant—only snacks and beverages—but you can bring your own food and dine in the picnic area. ~ Route 17, Mineral Hot Springs (50 miles north of Alamosa); 719-256-4328; www.joyfuljourneyhotsprings.com. BUDGET.

The closest accommodations to the national park, **Great Sand Dunes Lodge** has motel-plain rooms in a calming blue-and-rose color scheme, each with two queen-size beds. There's a heated indoor pool. ~ 7900 Route 150 North, Mosca; 719-378-2900, fax 719-378-2901; www.gsdlodge.com, e-mail information@gsd lodge.com. MODERATE.

Travelers can spend the night in a nunnery at **El Convento Bed & Breakfast**. Set in the center of a small village that dates back to the Spanish Colonial era, this historic building served as a Catholic school and convent before the church decided to remodel it and open it to the public as a bed and breakfast. The four rooms are decorated in authentic Southwestern style, with handcrafted furniture and *horno* fireplaces. ~ 512 Church Place, San Luis; 719-672-4223. MODERATE.

At the other end of the valley, **Kelloff's Movie Manor Motel** harks back to the 1950s and the height of America's infatuation with automobiles. In all 60 units of this otherwise-ordinary motel, big picture windows look out onto the big screen of the Star Drive-In Theater next door. The movie soundtrack plays through speakers installed in each room. Although the drive-in operates during the summer months only, the motel is open year-round. ~ 2830 West Route 160, Monte Vista; 719-852-5921, 800-771-9468, fax 719-852-0122; e-mail kellgeju@fonenet.com. MODERATE.

Crestone has a handful of small bed and breakfasts geared to the town's New Age tourist trade. Representative of the genre is **Dome Sweet Dome B & B, Retreat & Spa**, a two-story geodesic dome home with three private guest rooms (shared bath), a sauna, meditative walking paths and a nearby Tibetan stupa. Massage, reflexology, aromatherapy and body wrap treatments are available. ~ 4179 Rarity Way, Crestone; 719-256-4374, fax 719-256-4370; www.creativehealthcenter.com. BUDGET.

**DINING**

In Alamosa, you can get breakfast all day—until the 2 p.m. closing hour—at **Bauer's Campus Pancake House and Restaurant**, which caters to the students at Adams State College. Giant cinnamon rolls are the most popular item on the menu. The restaurant also serves weekday lunch specials. Closed Tuesday. ~ 435 Poncha Avenue, Alamosa; 719-589-4202. BUDGET.

A good carry-out option is **Lara's First Street To-Go Café**, featuring homemade Italian entrées along with steaks, shrimp and lobster and Mexican combination plates. ~ 2040 1st Street, Alamosa; 719-589-6769. BUDGET.

A local favorite, **Taqueria Calvillo** serves authentic Mexican food such as *chiles rellenos*, tacos and enchiladas, using homemade tortillas and fresh sauces. Closed Monday. ~ 119 Broadway, Alamosa; 719-587-5500. BUDGET.

Enchiladas and hot chili stew are everyday fare for many local people in the San Luis Valley. Mexican restaurants in the area serve good, spicy food at low prices in a simple atmosphere. One such restaurant, **El Charro Café**, has been run by the same family for more than 50 years. No alcohol. Closed Monday. ~ 421 6th Street, Alamosa; 719-589-2262. BUDGET.

Diners who prefer their Mexican food with margaritas or imported beer might try **Mrs. Rivera's**, where a house specialty is *chiles rellenos*—green chili peppers stuffed with cheese. The decor features touches of Old Mexico. ~ 1019 6th Street, Alamosa; 719-589-0277. BUDGET.

The main restaurant in Crestone is **Desert Sage**, a big, bright, modern place with seating for up to 150 people. The specialty is pizza, though the menu contains a range of other offerings including vegetarian fare. ~ Crestone; 719-256-4402. MODERATE.

Other Crestone restaurants tend to be on the tiny side, like **Iktomi's Kitchen**, which serves organic foods and smoothies. Open weekdays. ~ Crestone; 719-256-5157. BUDGET.

**SHOPPING**  A fair number of contemporary artists and craftspeople make their homes in the San Luis Valley, where the cost of living is low. While most sell their work in other localities, some also show at galleries in Alamosa. **Firedworks Gallery** exhibits paintings, pottery and weavings by the studio-gallery's owners and other area artists. ~ 608 Main Street, Alamosa; 719-589-6064. A block down the street, **Gallery West** features paintings, sculptures, graphics, ceramics and fiber art by San Luis Valley artists. ~ 718 Main Street, Alamosa; 719-589-2275.

Traditional arts and crafts from Spanish colonial times, including tinwork and religious wood carving, are still practiced. The most noteworthy folk-art specialty of the San Luis Valley is pictorial quilting. Examples are found in museums around the West, and examples can usually be purchased in the area. A good place to shop for local arts and crafts is **Centro Artesano**. This little gallery run by the Catholic church shares the building with El Convento Bed & Breakfast, providing exhibit space for the valley's traditional artisans. ~ 512 Church Place, San Luis.

Another church-sponsored gallery, the **San Juan Art Center**, is located in the Chapel of San Juan Bautista in the small village of La Garita, eight miles off Route 285 at the foot of the mountains on the northwest side of the San Luis Valley. Open in summer only.

**NIGHTLIFE**  Alamosa's nightlife is pretty much limited to the lounges of the two biggest motor inns such as **Clancy's** at the Holiday Inn. ~ 333 Santa Fe Avenue, Alamosa; 719-589-5833. The other lounge is **Alamosa Inn Restaurant and Lounge,** which features Monday

# Colorado's Hispano Heritage

Colorado's largest ethnic subculture, accounting for more than 15 percent of the population, is Hispanic. The Latino heritage in Colorado dates back more than two centuries. All of present-day Colorado became Spanish territory in 1762, when France ceded the Louisiana Territory (which reached from the Mississippi River to the Pacific) to the King of Spain. Acquisition of the vast new territory inspired the government of Spanish colonial Nuevo Mexico to send the first European explorers into Colorado.

In 1765, Don Juan Maria de Rivera led an expedition through the San Juan Mountains to the Gunnison River in search of gold and silver—which they did not find. In 1786, Don Juan Bautista de Anza, governor of the Spanish colony of Nuevo Mexico, led an army of almost 600 Spanish soldiers from Santa Fe north through the San Luis Valley and down the Arkansas River, where he picked the site for the town of San Carlos (present-day Pueblo). Unfortunately, this first settlement failed within a year.

No permanent Spanish settlement was ever established in Colorado by Spain, or later by Mexico. But within a few years after it became a U.S. territory in 1848 as part of the treaty of Guadalupe Hidalgo ending the Mexican War, Spanish-speaking settlers began moving into southern Colorado, and through most of the 1850s more Coloradoans spoke Spanish than English. It was during this era that most towns, rivers and mountains in southern Colorado received the Spanish names by which they are known today.

A second wave of Spanish-speaking inhabitants came to Colorado in the 1920s, as the growth of the sugar-beet industry created a big demand for seasonal farm labor. With no immigration restrictions between Mexico and the United States, contractors brought thousands of Mexican workers north to Colorado each summer, and many stayed. But as the Great Depression brought unemployment, a racist backlash against Mexicans swept through Colorado. The Ku Klux Klan vowed to drive Catholics (meaning Hispanics) out of the state, and Mexicans were increasingly segregated into barrios in the Front Range cities and into separate satellite towns, often lacking public utilities, on the outskirts of mountain towns.

Only since the 1960s have Chicano activists made progress toward ending the discrimination. Today, the Mexican holiday Cinco de Mayo is one of the biggest holiday celebrations in Denver and other Colorado communities. Spanish is taught in Colorado public schools from the second grade on. And Hispanic candidates have won the offices of mayor of Denver and governor of Colorado.

night football and the rest of the week . . . TV. ~ 1901 Main Avenue, Alamosa; 719-589-4943.

**PARKS**

**RIO GRANDE NATIONAL FOREST** 🏃 🚣 This horseshoe-shaped, two-million-acre national forest surrounds the San Luis Valley. The eastern part, which runs along the western slope of the Sangre de Cristo Range, is virtually roadless. Much of it has been designated the Southern Sangre de Cristo Wilderness. Most trails are only a few miles long, following gulches up the slope of the high, jagged, unbroken wall of 13,000-foot peaks. There are also jeep trails. You may fish for trout in area streams. ~ The easiest trail access is from the Mosca Pass trailhead, off Route 150 in Great Sand Dunes National Park; 719-852-5941.

**SAN LUIS LAKES STATE PARK** 🏃 🎣 🚣 🛥 🚤 🚣 Shallow, natural San Luis Lake, just west of the Great Sand Dunes, is a locally popular spot for waterskiing, fishing, sailing and windsurfing. The north portion of the lake, as well as the wetlands and smaller Head Lake, are off-limits to boats but laced with wide, level trails for nature lovers to observe wildlife such as migrating whooping cranes and bald eagles, as well as native waterfowl, songbirds, coyotes and pronghorns. Fishing is excellent year-round for trout. The park adjoins the second-largest bison ranch in the United States. Facilities include picnic areas with tables and restrooms. Day-use fee, $3. ~ Located ten miles east of Mosca on Six Mile Lane; 719-378-2020.

▲ There are 51 RV/tent sites with electric hookups, tables and fireplaces, drinking water, showers and laundry facilities; $16 per night. Reservations: 800-678-2267.

▼▼▼▼▼▼▼▼▼▼▼▼▼▼▼▼
## Creede–Lake City Area

The San Juans of southwestern Colorado are the largest, wildest and least populated mountains in the state. Compared to the western side of this vast range, where adventurous Durango and Telluride visitors often mob old mining roads with hundreds of mountain bikes and four-wheel-drive vehicles, the eastern side adjoining the San Luis Valley has a refreshingly undiscovered feel. The area's main towns—unexpectedly artsy little Creede and the even tinier Texan stronghold of Lake City—are short on development and long on personality. The Silver Thread Scenic Byway, which connects the two towns, takes motorists through some of the most spectacular mountain scenery anywhere.

**SIGHTS**

Following the Rio Grande toward its source high in the mountains by way of paved Route 149 brings travelers to **Creede**, one of several spectacularly situated, spruced-up old mining towns turned mountain hideaways in the San Juans. (Others include Telluride, Ouray and Silverton, which are covered in Chapter Eight.) Creede is the only one east of the Continental Divide. Founded in 1889 upon the discovery of the richest silver lode in Colorado, Creede is also remembered in history as one of the wildest Western boom towns. Such legendary characters as the James Gang, "Calamity Jane" Canary, "Poker Annie" Tubbs, con artist "Soapy" Smith and lawman Bat Masterson passed through Creede during its heyday. The boom lasted for only four years, but unlike other similar mine camps, Creede was never completely abandoned. A self-guided auto tour takes visitors to the steep, narrow canyon above town and several of the mines on which Creede's fortunes rose and fell a century ago. Creede is also home to the finest summer repertory theater in south central Colorado.

A magnificent scenic drive, the 48-mile **Silver Thread Scenic Byway** (Route 149) climbs from Creede to meander gently through

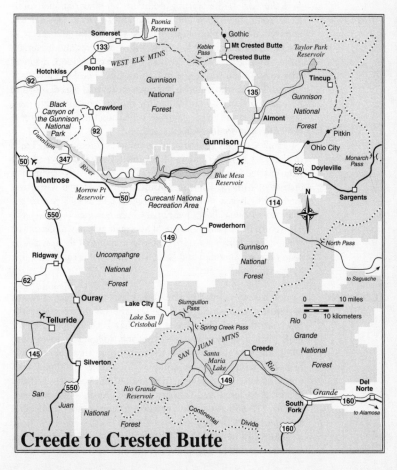

**Creede to Crested Butte**

lush green mountain meadows where streams flow together to form the headwaters of the Rio Grande. The only difficult part of the drive on the byway is the steep descent from 11,361-foot Slumgullion Pass. Stop at the overlook near the top of the pass for a look at **Slumgullion Slide**, where a huge mudslide eight centuries ago slipped down the slopes below Slumgullion Pass to block the valley and dam the river, forming **Lake San Cristobal**, the second-largest natural body of water in Colorado. Its namesake, the tiny village of **Lake City**, is the Hinsdale County seat—and, in fact, the only town in the county, which otherwise consists of national forest land. Lake City had its beginnings in 1875 as a gold camp, and many wooden storefronts and churches date back to that period. By 1960 it had declined to only six residents, but burgeoning tourism has boosted Lake City's present-day population to 223.

HIDDEN ►    Lake City is the starting point for another national forest scenic route, the **Alpine Loop Backcountry Byway**. This narrow, unpaved 63-mile mountain road is very rocky and steep in places, suitable only for four-wheel-drive vehicles and mountain bikes. Passenger cars can take the first stage of the loop, Engineer Pass Road, as far as the site of **Capitol City**. Local ore processor George T. Lee, who founded the town, believed it was destined to become the state capital, but today the site contains only scattered traces of the lavish governor's mansion that Lee built there soon after Colorado attained statehood.

From Capitol City the road deteriorates quickly as it climbs to the 12,800-foot summit of Engineer Pass and descends the wind-blasted south face of Engineer Peak to the early-day mining district of **Mineral Point** and **Animas Forks**, strewn with rusty mementos of past prosperity. To return to Lake City, take the road from Animas Forks west over Cinnamon Pass (12,620 feet). The return route passes the site of **Sherman**, which was destroyed when a dirt dam burst upriver. Little remains of the town. The road between Sherman and Lake San Cristobal is easily passable by passenger car.

**LODGING**    Creede has a few small bed and breakfasts in the upstairs rooms of refurbished historic buildings on the main street near the repertory theater. **The Creede Hotel** has been in operation for more than a century and was the only lodging in town until 1992. The four guest rooms in the main house are rather sparsely furnished with mining-era antiques. Two other buildings, with four additional units, have been renovated and opened as bed and breakfasts. Closed mid-October through April. ~ Main Street, Creede; 719-658-2608; www.creedehotel.com, e-mail creedehotel @amigo.net. MODERATE.

**The Old Firehouse No. 1 B&B**, decorated with firefighting memorabilia and historic photos of old-time Creede, has four guest rooms and a sitting room with a library and games. On the ground floor is an old-fashioned soda fountain. Open in summer only. ~ Main Street, Creede; 719-658-0212; e-mail oldfirehouse@creede. com. MODERATE. Across the street, **Blessings Inn** offers four antique-filled rooms with private baths. Open in summer only. ~ Main Street, Creede; 719-658-0215, 877-506-9252; www.blessingsinn. com, e-mail info@blessingsinn.com. MODERATE.

The tiny hideaway town of Lake City offers a fine selection of vacation accommodations. Foremost among them is **Crystal Mountain Lodge**, secluded in fir-and-aspen forest on the Lake Fork of the Gunnison River near Lake San Cristobal. The lodge offers 18 simple guest rooms, including five with full kitchens and four housekeeping cabins. The dining room serves the best gourmet meals in town. Amenities include hiking trails, a hot tub and a sundeck with a spectacular view of nearby Crystal Peak. Closed November and April. ~ 2175 Route 149 South, Lake City; 970-944-2201, 877-465-6343, fax 970-944-2503; www. crystallodge.net, e-mail crystallodge@lakecity.net. MODERATE TO DELUXE.

A long-established riverbank cabin complex, **Texan Resort**, nestled at the base of a maroon-colored canyon wall on the Lake Fork of the Gunnison River, has 16 housekeeping cabins with full kitchen facilities as well as outdoor barbecue grills. It's an easy walk to a 65-foot waterfall nearby. ~ Route 149 South, Lake City; 970-944-2246. BUDGET TO DELUXE.

For travelers who prefer to stay in town, the **Cinnamon Inn Bed & Breakfast** has four guest rooms and suites in an 1878 two-story Victorian residence that belonged to the town jeweler in Lake City's heyday. Each room is individually decorated with period furnishings. A full country breakfast is included in the room rates. ~ 426 Gunnison Avenue, Lake City; 970-944-2641, 800-337-2335. DELUXE.

◆◆◆◆◆◆◆◆◆◆◆◆◆◆◆◆◆◆◆◆◆◆◆◆◆◆◆◆◆◆◆◆◆◆◆◆◆◆◆◆◆◆◆◆◆◆◆◆◆◆◆◆

**THE "OTHER" RED MEAT . . .**

Lake City is best known as the home of Colorado's most macabre historical figure, Alferd Packer, who was convicted of murdering—and eating—five prospectors who had hired him as a guide in 1874. Cannibal jokes have had a place in Colorado culture ever since: The official name of the main student dining hall at the University of Colorado in Boulder (thanks to a student vote a generation ago) is the Alferd E. Packer Memorial Cafeteria, and prominent Coloradoans often receive invitations to join a venerable social club called The Friends of Alferd E. Packer. The club's motto: "Serving our fellow man since 1874."

**DINING**    In Creede, the place to eat is the **Creede Hotel Dining Room**. This little restaurant on the ground floor of a frontier Victorian-style bed and breakfast near the repertory theater serves a full menu of homemade entrées each evening, including tamari-honey chicken, prime rib, baked salmon and fettuccine Alfredo. Can you resist the pecan brandy apple pie? Make reservations well in advance for theater nights. Lunch and dinner daily from mid-May through September; dinner only on the weekends the rest of the year. ~ Main Street, Creede; 719-658-2608. MODERATE.

Eighteen miles southwest of Creede, a rustic-elegant restaurant stands secluded in the heart of Rio Grande National Forest. The **Bristol Inn** serves lobster, roast beef and quail with a Continental flair. It is busiest around noon on Sundays, when an early dinner provides a tantalizing excuse for people all over south central Colorado to go for a drive in the mountains. The inn has an art gallery that exhibits works in various media by 11 local artists. Reservations required. Dinner only. Closed Monday and Tuesday. Open in summer only. ~ 39542 Route 149, Creede; 719-658-2455, 888-238-4281; www.thebristolinn.com. MODERATE TO DELUXE.

**SHOPPING**    Creede has a mini-arts district on its main street near the repertory theater. **Rare Things**, a studio-gallery, spotlights a horse-hair jewelry collection. ~ Main Street, Creede; 719-658-2376. There's also **Abbey Lane Gallery**. ~ Main Street, Creede; 719-658-2736. And right down the street is **Quiller Gallery**, which features water-color landscapes. ~ Main Street; 719-658-2741. The **Basky Gallery** shows serigraphs, monoprints and paintings by local artists. ~ 150 Main Street; 719-658-0407.

**AUTHOR FAVORITE**

Culture in the Rockies pops up in some of the most unlikely places. In 1966, a local pastor in Creede recruited drama students from the University of Kansas. With a $32 budget, they began to stage plays in hopes of attracting tourists to the run-down old mining town. Who'd have thought that the **Creede Repertory Theatre** would win a reputation as the top summer-stock company in the southern Colorado Rockies and become the nucleus of an arts renaissance that would transform the town? Today, actors from coast to coast vie for roles in a summer and fall schedule of plays that includes Broadway comedies and musicals on the main stage and more serious plays on the smaller upstairs stage. Order tickets well in advance (CRT Box Office, P.O. Box 269, Creede, CO 81130). ~ 124 North Main Street, Creede; 719-658-2540, 866-658-2540; www.creederep.org.

**RIO GRANDE NATIONAL FOREST** 🧍🛶🛥️⛵ The west side **PARKS**
of this national forest covers the eastern slope of the San Juans,
offering boundless hiking possibilities in the vast Weminuche
Wilderness and the smaller La Garita Wilderness, both in the
vicinity of Creede. Forest roads off the paved Silver Thread
Scenic Byway (Route 149) provide access to campgrounds and
natural and artificial lakes in the high country. Fishing is good
for trout in Rio Grande Reservoir, Tucker Ponds, Poso Creek
and many other lakes and creeks; the upper Conejos River is famous for rainbow trout and kokanee salmon. There are picnic
areas, restrooms and an archery range. ~ Main access roads to
the national forest are Route 160 below Wolf Creek Pass, and
the Silver Thread Scenic Byway (Route 149) beyond Creede.
Silver Thread Campground is 25 miles southwest of Creede on
Route 149; 719-852-5941.

▲ There are seven campgrounds in the Creede area, including
Silver Thread Campground, with 11 RV/tent sites (no hookups);
closed mid-September through May; $11 per night. Most camp-
grounds in the Lake City area are small, little-known spots along
the Cebolla Creek Road (Forest Road 788), which turns off Route
149 to the north at Slumgullion Campground on Slumgullion Pass.
Slumgullion, Hidden Valley, Spruce and Cebolla Campgrounds
have a total of 19 tent/RV sites (no hookups). Closed October to
mid-June; no charge.

From Lake City, Route 149 fol-
lows the Lake Fork of the Gun-    ▼▼▼▼▼▼▼▼▼▼▼▼▼▼▼▼▼▼▼▼▼▼
nison River northeast through a    **Gunnison–Crested Butte Area**
red-cliff gorge and then descends arid foothills to Curecanti National Recreation Area, joining Route 50 in the Gunnison area. In
the summer, many visitors to the Gunnison area come for the fishing, as well as other water sports, on Blue Mesa Reservoir, Colorado's largest reservoir. In nearby Crested Butte, mountain biking
is the most popular summer sport. Gunnison National Forest surrounds Gunnison and Crested Butte with jeep roads to old mining camps and a network of foot trails that could keep a hiker
busy all summer. In the winter, Crested Butte enjoys a wealthier
lifestyle as a famous ski resort. Motorists can also reach the Gunnison area on Route 50 from Cañon City and Salida up a series
of switchbacks to the summit of Monarch Pass (11,846 feet)—a
hard pull for those who are headed for Curecanti National Recreation Area with boats in tow.

The town of **Gunnison** is situated among dry hills beside a raging    **SIGHTS**
whitewater stretch of the Gunnison River. Gunnison has been the
site of **Western State College** since 1911. The campus is located

at the east edge of town. ~ 600 North Adams Street, Gunnison; 970-943-0120.

Nearby, the **Pioneer Museum** occupies eight historic buildings, including Gunnison's original one-room schoolhouse. On exhibit are a restored narrow-gauge steam train, early-day automobiles and assorted collections of arrowheads, rocks, farming tools and other memorabilia dating as far back as 1874, when Gunnison was founded as a transportation and supply center for mining camps in the surrounding mountains. Admission. ~ South Adams Street at Route 50, Gunnison; 970-641-4530.

A few miles west of Gunnison, **Curecanti National Recreation Area** encompasses the three basins of 20-mile-long Blue Mesa Reservoir, the largest manmade lake in Colorado, as well as the smaller and more secluded Morrow Point Reservoir and long, narrow Crystal Lake, which winds through the upper part of the Gunnison River Gorge. In the summer, the National Park Service operates daily boat cruises with naturalist guides on Morrow Point Reservoir (reservations required; 970-641-2337 ext. 242). ~ Route 50; 970-641-2337; www.nps.gov/cure.

Downriver from Curecanti National Recreation Area, beyond the dam that impounds Crystal Lake, lies **Black Canyon of the Gunnison National Park**, which contains the most spectacular 12 miles of the Gunnison River Gorge. This is the last national park created in the 20th century, upgraded from a national monument by act of Congress in October 1999. Although 10,000 additional acres were added to the monument's 21,000 acres, it remains the third-smallest national park in America. Whatever it may lack in land area, however, is more than made up for by spectacular, rugged beauty. The canyon's dark gray cliffs of schist and gneiss, almost 3000 feet deep, rise so steeply that in some places the canyon is deeper than its width from rim to rim. The south rim, easily accessed from Route 50 via a paved park road, has a large campground, a visitors center and numerous overlooks and short hiking trails. The more remote north rim is reached only by a long unpaved road from the little town of Crawford on Route 92. The bottom of the canyon can be reached by river raft or by any of four steep one- to three-mile trails that descend the cliffs from rim trailheads which are themselves hard to reach. ~ Montrose; 970-641-2337; www.nps.gov/blca.

North of Gunnison on Route 135 is the historic district of **Crested Butte**, which began in 1879 as a way station on the road between Gunnison and Aspen. It became a mining town when Colorado Fuel & Iron, the Rockefeller family's steel company, discovered large deposits of coal there. Coal mining continued in Crested Butte until the 1950s, saving the beautiful frontier Victorian town from the decay and abandonment that erased so many other Colorado mining towns from the map. Ski-resort development came within a few years after the mines closed. The historic district retains a lot of authenticity and old-time charm beneath new coats of paint. Across the valley, not quite adjoining the old town, is **Mount Crested Butte**, a development of custom homes and luxury condominiums that stands in dramatic contrast to the old town. Among the modern town's part-time residents is former president Gerald Ford, who put Crested Butte in the news during his brief administration in the mid-1970s.

Mountain bikes seem to outnumber cars for most of the summer around Crested Butte. To find out why, one needs only look at a Gunnison National Forest map (buy one—$4 plus tax—from the ranger station at 216 North Colorado Street, Gunnison; 970-641-0471 or any of several Crested Butte cycle shops) and marvel at the array of dirt roads and jeep trails that lead into the surrounding mountains.

There's even a **Mountain Bike Hall of Fame and Museum**—well, almost. Legendary mountain bikers have been inducted into the hall of fame annually since 1988 and now number 82 individuals and three groups. The museum founders have amassed the world's largest collection of historic mountain-biking photographs. The photos go all the way back to 1896 when Buffalo Soldiers were sent to test the military feasibility of using customized bicycles in mountainous terrain by riding 800 miles from Yellowstone to Missoula, Montana, and back. Still, the museum currently only exists in cyberspace and private homes. The historic building at 331 Elk Avenue, which will eventually house the exhibits, is undergoing restoration and will open its doors to the public in 2003. ~ P.O. Box 845, Crested Butte, CO 81224; 800-454-4505; www. mtnbikehalloffame.com.

One of the most spectacular routes that is accessible by passenger car is the unpaved **Kebler Pass Road**, which starts at the west end of White Rock Avenue in Crested Butte and goes 31 miles over Kebler Pass (10,000 feet) to Paonia Reservoir. Following an

## THE BIRTHPLACE OF MOUNTAIN BIKES

In the 1970s, according to local legend, a bunch of Crested Butte locals made a friendly wager: they would race to Aspen on jeep roads over a 12,700-foot pass on the crest of the Sawatch Range—but instead of jeeps they would ride old-fashioned newspaper bicycles. The race evolved into Fat Tire Bike Week, the world's largest mountain-bike gathering, held each July, and the legend gave rise to Crested Butte's reputation as a mountain-biking mecca.

abandoned railroad bed, the road offers panoramic views of the high peaks of the West Elk Wilderness and provides access to aspen forests, alpine meadows and fishing lakes such as **Lost Lake** and **Lake Irwin**. Near Lake Irwin, a graveyard is just about all that remains of **Irwin**, a silver-mining town that was founded in 1879, flourished briefly with a peak population of almost 5000 and was abandoned by 1884. The saloons, stores and banks have long since been stripped for firewood and their rubble sunk in the soggy marsh that was once the main street.

Some of Colorado's most picturesque old mining towns can be found in the Sawatch Range east of Gunnison and Crested Butte. Eight miles north of Crested Butte on unpaved Forest Road 317 is the site of **Gothic**, a gold-prospecting town that boomed between 1879 and 1881 to 4000 people and 400 buildings—mostly boardinghouses, saloons and bordellos. Unfortunately, none of the eager prospectors who swarmed over the mountainsides around Gothic ever found gold in sufficient quantities to mine, and the town was abandoned in a few years. For the past 60 years, the townsite has been owned by the **Rocky Mountain Biological Laboratory**, which conducts environmental studies there. A number of the old buildings remain standing along the main road, and there are campgrounds nearby. Guides from the laboratory lead flora and fauna tours around Gothic several days a week during the summer. ~ 970-349-7231; www.rmbl.org.

Other old mining towns in varying states of disrepair lie secluded in the mountains east of Gunnison and Crested Butte. **Pitkin**, a notoriously lawless silver-mining town of 1500 people, lasted less than 20 years—from 1879 to 1898—before the mines played out and a rash of fires destroyed the business district. Yet the town was never entirely abandoned; as of the 1990 census, it had a full-time population of 58. Along the paved road to Pitkin, which turns off Route 50 about 12 miles east of Gunnison, lie the ruins of **Ohio City**, a more enduring gold and silver town where mining continued until World War II. A few scattered structures there have been kept up as summer homes.

In its day—from 1881 to 1910—the Alpine Tunnel was recognized as an engineering masterpiece, especially since the monumental amount of heavy labor was done in the rarefied air 11,500 feet above sea level.

A mile or so past Pitkin, a rocky dirt road branches off and climbs an old railroad grade for ten miles to the west portal of the **Alpine Tunnel**. It took 18 months for a work crew of 400 men to dig this 1771-foot tunnel through the sheer wall of granite that is the crest of the Sawatch Range. Today, the scope of the accomplishment remains evident even though both portals of the tunnel have collapsed. Nearby are the ruins of Woodstock, where railroad workers lived until 1884, when it was wiped out by an avalanche.

Visitors traveling in high-clearance vehicles can continue on the unpaved road from Pitkin over 12,000-foot Cumberland Pass to Tincup, one of the most remote mountain communities in the state. Like Pitkin, Tincup earned a reputation in the early mining days as a wide-open, violent town. With a population of 3000, it had 20 saloons and four graveyards. Abandoned in 1918, Tincup was all but forgotten until the 1950s, when radio host Pete Smythe started broadcasting his popular talk show from "East Tincup" (meaning Denver) and rekindled interest in the old ghost town. Now Tincup has a country store, a church and a cluster of summer homes. The original town is preserved as a historic district.

Beyond Tincup, the road descends to **Taylor Park Reservoir,** a large lake with fishing and boating facilities and campgrounds in a high mountain valley. A paved road follows Taylor Canyon down to join Route 135 between Crested Butte and Gunnison.

◄ HIDDEN

For affordable elegance in Gunnison, the best bet is the **Mary Lawrence Inn.** This seven-unit bed and breakfast, located in a two-story former rooming house built in 1885 and situated on a tree-shaded side street, has lovingly decorated theme rooms and suites—Victorian, Southwestern Indian, flowery and downright lovely. A gourmet breakfast is included in the room rate. ~ 601 North Taylor Street, Gunnison; 970-641-3343, fax 970-641-6719; e-mail marylinn@gunnison.com. MODERATE TO DELUXE.

**LODGING**

◄ HIDDEN

Most of your other lodging choices in Gunnison are the standard-issue motels and motor inns lying along Tomichi Avenue (Route 50). There are independent places such as the plain-and-simple 24-unit **ABC Motel.** ~ 212 East Tomichi Avenue, Gunnison; 970-641-2400, 800-341-8000, fax 970-641-6342. BUDGET TO MODERATE. There is also the reasonably priced luxury of the Southwestern-style, 49-unit **Best Western Tomichi Village.** Rates include continental breakfast. ~ Route 50 East, Gunnison; 970-641-1131, 800-641-1131, fax 970-641-9554; e-mail bestwest@gunnison.com. BUDGET TO DELUXE.

One of the nicer guest ranches in the Gunnison–Crested Butte area is **Waunita Hot Springs Ranch.** Set among the pines at 9000 feet in the mountains 27 miles northeast of Gunnison, the ranch has a picture-perfect hot-spring pool. No nude bathing here—the staff is cheerfully Christian and holds nondenominational church services on summer Sundays. The rooms are simple, with wood paneling; designed for families and groups, many have bunk beds. The lodge is heated geothermally with water from the springs. The family-oriented ranch has a petting farm and group activities that include fishing, hiking, horseback riding, river trips, hayrides and four-wheel-drive excursions. Rates include all meals and all activities in summer, with a six-night minimum stay. Open in winter for cross-country-ski and snowmobile groups (no individual bookings), with a two-night minimum. ~ 8007 County Road 887, Gunnison; 970-641-1266; www.waunita.com. DELUXE.

Luxurious lodging is not why people come to **Irwin Lodge**; isolation is. Situated in the Elk Mountains at 10,700 feet and overlooking Lake Irwin, the lodge is reached via ten miles of unpaved forest roads (transportation is provided from Crested Butte). The barnlike lodge has 24 very simple, spacious rooms with queen-size beds and foldout couches. The rooms open off the long, narrow common room with its 30-foot ceiling. Although snow closes the road to the lodge for about five months of the year, the lodge stays open as a very exclusive ski resort. Sno-Cats carry skiers from the lodge to 2500 acres of remote ski bowls. Après-ski amenities include a giant fireplace and two 20-person jacuzzis. Summer rates for bed and breakfast are in the moderate price range, while winter rates including all meals, skiing and transportation are ultra-deluxe (three-night minimum stay). ~ 311 5th Street, Crested Butte; 970-349-9800.

Several modern ski lodges and condominium complexes lie at the foot of the Mount Crested Butte ski area. The largest of the lodges, the **Club Med Crested Butte**, offers 262 bright, contemporary guest rooms and suites with whirlpool baths as well as balconies, refrigerators, king-size beds and queen-size fold-out sofas. The lodge has an indoor swimming pool, outdoor hot tubs, a sauna and a spa. ~ 900 Gothic Road, Mount Crested Butte; 970-349-9700, 800-358-2633. ULTRA-DELUXE.

Nearby, the **Nordic Inn** offers cozy, ski-from-your-doorstep lodging, with 27 guest units plus two chalets in a distinctive Scandinavian-style lodge. After a day on the slopes, guests relax around the large fireplace that dominates the lobby or soak in the hot tub. Rates include a generous continental breakfast. ~ 14 Treasury Road, Mount Crested Butte; 970-349-5542, 800-542-7669, fax 970-349-6487; e-mail acox@csn.net. ULTRA-DELUXE.

One good choice in Crested Butte is the **Crested Butte Club**, a seven-room bed and breakfast in a frontier-style building with a false facade on the town's main street. Originally a social club for Croatian immigrants who worked in the coal mines a century ago, the 1886 building is listed on the National Register of Historic Places. The rooms are large and lavishly decorated in Victorian style, with flowery furniture, old-fashioned fireplaces and copper bathtubs, as well as such modern amenities as four-poster waterbeds. This bed and breakfast is also a health club, so guests have access to a lap pool, steam rooms, weights and exercise machines, as well as aerobic and fitness classes. ~ 512 2nd Street, Crested Butte; 970-349-6655, 800-815-2582, fax 970-349-7580; www.crestedbutteclub.com, e-mail info@crestedbutte club.com. ULTRA-DELUXE.

The **Claim Jumper,** is whimsical, fun and the most eccentric bed and breakfast in town. The decor—satirical taxidermy and creative clutter that includes a jukebox, a man-eating fish and an in-room putting green—exudes a slightly warped sense of humor, making this six-unit inn a place travelers either love or hate. Each room has its own theme—cowboys, gold miners, sailing ships or sports. ~ 704 White Rock Avenue, Crested Butte; 970-349-6471. DELUXE.

Accommodations in Crested Butte can be hard to find during the winter months. Travelers can save a lot of calls in search of a vacancy by telephoning the **Crested Butte–Mount Crested Butte Chamber of Commerce.** ~ 970-349-6438, 800-545-4505; www. crestedbuttechamber.com.

**DINING**

The established favorite for fine dining in Gunnison is the **Cattlemen Inn.** The decor is ranch-style, and the menu offers a full assortment of hand-cut steaks, from sirloin and rib eye to T-bone and filet mignon, as well as chicken and seafood entrées. ~ 301 West Tomichi Avenue, Gunnison; 970-641-1061. MODERATE TO DELUXE.

**The Trough,** west of Gunnison on the way to Curecanti National Recreation Area, serves steak, wild game and seafood favorites in a relaxed, casual environment of natural wood and dim lighting. Swordfish, salmon and catch-of-the-day specials make this the best place in the area to satisfy a craving for fish. ~ 37550 West Route 50, Gunnison; 970-641-3724. MODERATE TO DELUXE.

Inexpensive meals, from chicken-fried steak to chimichangas, can be found at the **Sundae Shoppe Restaurant**. As the name suggests, the restaurant also offers a tantalizing array of banana splits, hot-fudge sundaes, chocolate malts and pies. Closed Sunday. ~ 901 West Tomichi Avenue, Gunnison; 970-641-5051. BUDGET TO MODERATE.

The cuisine scene is considerably more interesting in Crested Butte. For starters, the little resort town boasts more French cuisine than the rest of south central Colorado put together. Top of the line is **Le Bosquet,** a small French restaurant decorated in pink hues, lace and photos of French provincial life. The menu features such entrées as elk medallions in cabernet sauce and roasted half

**UP-CLOSE AND PERSONAL**

Lodgings are generally smaller and more homelike in the old town of Crested Butte, about three miles from the slopes. In the winter, shuttle buses run constantly from town to the ski area. In fact, staying in town offers a wider selection of restaurants and nightlife within walking distance.

duck with cherry sauce. ~ Majestic Plaza, 6th Street and Belleview Avenue, Crested Butte; 970-349-5808. DELUXE.

Another French restaurant, **Soupçon**—pronounced "soup's on"—has a more rustic ambience—it's in a historic log cabin in the alley behind Kochevar's Bar. The frontier feel of the restaurant sets off the sheer elegance of the cuisine. The gourmet menu, which changes daily, typically features fresh fish and lamb entrées. Classic appetizers include escargot, caviar and duckling mousse. ~ 127 Elk Avenue, Crested Butte; 970-349-5448. DELUXE.

**Karolina's Kitchen**, adjoining Kochevar's Bar, serves assorted soups, salads, sandwiches and steaks in a historic building that once served as Crested Butte's blacksmith shop. Vintage photographs and fragments of old-time machinery and equipment, including a moonshine still, decorate the wall. ~ 127 Elk Avenue, Crested Butte; 970-349-6756. MODERATE.

The two-story **Timberline** features a variety of creative Continental dishes, from venison medallions to herb-seasoned pasta in butter sauce and smoked trout. The decor is that of an old miner's cabin, though the restaurant is large enough to seat 60 diners. ~ 21 Elk Avenue, Crested Butte; 970-349-9831. DELUXE.

Located in a picturesque Old West false-front building, the **Slogar Bar & Restaurant** serves delicious home-style fried chicken with all the fixings—cole slaw, fresh vegetables, mashed potatoes and flaky biscuits. Dinner only. ~ 517 2nd Street, Crested Butte; 970-349-5765. MODERATE.

An affordable and often lively place for breakfast or lunch is the **Paradise Cafe**. The small restaurant, which occupies part of the large, tourist-oriented general store known as the Company Store, has eclectic decor reminiscent of the South Seas and offers a menu of health-conscious breakfasts and overstuffed deli sandwiches. Dinner is also served during ski season. ~ 303 Elk Avenue, Crested Butte; 970-349-2274. BUDGET.

**AUTHOR FAVORITE**

The **Wooden Nickel** is the oldest restaurant in the Crested Butte historic district. The original restaurant on the site had been in business for 56 years when it burned to the ground in 1985, so the same owners built this modern restaurant on the same spot. The decor is a clutter of antiques and oddities, including an intricate wooden ship over the fireplace and a number of deer heads. The menu offers just about anything people are likely to crave after a day on the ski slopes, from jalapeño cheese potato skins to steak and lobster. Dinner only. ~ 222 Elk Avenue, Crested Butte; 970-349-6350. MODERATE TO DELUXE.

For Mexican food in Crested Butte, it's **Donita's Cantina**. This cozy restaurant and lounge, built around a big rock fireplace, features not only predictable taco-and-burrito fare but also such unconventional options as spinach enchiladas. Portions are large and prices are reasonable. ~ 330 Elk Avenue, Crested Butte; 970-349-6674. MODERATE.

Shopping possibilities in Gunnison are limited for the most part to hunting and fishing supplies. **The Great Wall**, the town's oldest art gallery, specializes in limited-edition Southwestern lithographs. ~ 125 North Main Street, Gunnison; 970-641-4680. There's also the **Johnson Building Gallery**. ~ 124 North Main Street, Gunnison; 970-641-4790. The **Porter Gallery** offers work by local artists and handcrafters. ~ 320 North Main Street, Gunnison; 970-642-1253. The **Gunnison Rockery** carries Indian-style jewelry, decorative rocks and other souvenir items. ~ 107 North Main Street, Gunnison; 970-641-1503.

**SHOPPING**

Crested Butte offers a larger range of shops and galleries. **Paragon Art Gallery** in the old town hall shows works by craftspeople and local artists. ~ 132 Elk Avenue, Crested Butte; 970-349-6484. Another good bet for gifts is the **Rocky Mountain Chocolate Factory**, which creates attractive gift baskets of handmade chocolates and cookies. ~ 314 Elk Avenue, Crested Butte; 970-349-0933. Equally unusual is **The Natural Butte**, a shop that sells all-natural, locally made bath and body care products and creates individualized scents for its customers. ~ 326 Elk Avenue, Crested Butte; 970-349-7775.

Surprisingly, for a college town Gunnison is practically devoid of nightlife. **The Trough** has comedy shows on Thursday and live rock bands Friday and Saturday nights. ~ 37550 West Route 50, Gunnison; 970-641-3724.

**NIGHTLIFE**

Up the hill in Crested Butte, rowdy après-ski clubs line the main street and rock on all year long. **Kochevar's Bar** retains the feel of an Old West saloon; memorabilia on the walls recall the days when the place was a casino and house of ill repute. Today, pool tables and occasional bands keep the bar lively well past midnight. ~ 127 Elk Avenue, Crested Butte; 970-349-6350.

A block down the street, the **Idle Spur** microbrewery has a spacious bar and restaurant with a large stone fireplace in the middle. Rock bands play in the back room on Thursday, Friday and Saturday nights. ~ 226 Elk Avenue, Crested Butte; 970-349-5026.

A bit more upscale, the **Wooden Nickel** gradually metamorphoses from restaurant to rock-and-roll bar as the evening wears on. ~ 222 Elk Avenue, Crested Butte; 970-349-9945.

Well-heeled après-ski revelers gather for happy hour at **The Rafters** and party on into the night once the live rock bands get warmed up. ~ Ski Area Central, Mount Crested Butte; 970-349-2298.

**PARKS**

**GUNNISON NATIONAL FOREST** 🏃 🚲 ⛵ 🛥 ⛷ This 1.7-million-acre forest contains 27 mountain peaks over 12,000 feet high. The forest surrounds the towns of Gunnison and Crested Butte, reaching south to include Slumgullion Pass and the mountains above Lake City. On the north, it borders three other national forests—Grand Mesa, White River and San Isabel—in the highest and most remote part of the Colorado Rockies. The West Elk Wilderness, an expanse of granite peaks and alpine ridges southwest of Crested Butte, is a popular backpacking area. East of Gunnison and Crested Butte, the Sawatch Range was a major mining district in the late 19th century. Today, unpaved forest roads and jeep trails lead back to ghost towns and hidden fishing lakes throughout the district. A bowl in the mountains east of Crested Butte forms the spectacular setting for Taylor Park Reservoir, a popular boating and fishing lake.

Katherine Bates was apparently inspired to write "America the Beautiful" after a trip to Colorado in 1893.

Fishing is good for trout in Taylor Park Reservoir, Spring Creek Reservoir, Lake Irwin, Lost Lake and many smaller lakes and streams. Facilities include boat ramps at Taylor Park and Spring Creek reservoirs, and picnic areas with tables in Taylor Canyon. ~ Paved routes that provide access to the national forest include Taylor Canyon (Forest Road 742), from Route 135 north of Gunnison to Taylor Park Reservoir; and Quartz Creek (76 Road) from Route 50 east of Gunnison to the ghost town of Pitkin. The unpaved Kebler Pass Road winds through alpine lake country to connect Route 135 at Crested Butte with Route 133 near Paonia to form the West Elk Scenic Loop. Lake Irwin Campground is seven miles west of Crested Butte on County Road 2, then three miles north on Forest Road 826. Lost Lake Campground is 15 miles west on Route 135, then three miles south on Forest Road 706; 970-874-6600.

▲ There are several campgrounds in the Crested Butte area, including the Lake Irwin Campground, with 32 RV/tent sites (no hookups; no drinking water); closed October through May; $12 per night; and Lost Lake Campground, with 10 RV/tent sites (no hookups; no drinking water); closed mid-November to late June; $10 per night.

**CURECANTI NATIONAL RECREATION AREA** 🏃 ⛷ 🚣 ⛵ ⛴ ⛵ Colorado's largest lake, Blue Mesa Reservoir, is the centerpiece of this boating and fishing area, which also encompasses two smaller reservoirs, Morrow Point Reservoir and Crystal Lake. Blue Mesa Reservoir is used for waterskiing and speedboating; boating on both of the smaller lakes, which have no boat ramps, is limited to hand-carried craft. Fishing is good for rainbow, brook, brown and mackinaw trout and kokanee salmon. An area of Blue Mesa Reservoir called the Bay of Chickens is a favorite wind-surfing area. The recreation area also includes many miles of back-country in the foothills around the lake, although the water is very cold for swimming. There are restrooms, picnic areas and groceries. ~ Located along Route 50 from about 5 to 25 miles west of Gunnison; there are numerous turnoffs to areas of the lakeshore; 970-641-2337; www.nps.gov/cure.

▲ Permitted in eight campgrounds totaling 352 RV/tent sites (no hookups); $5 to $15 per night.

Hundreds of lakes, rivers and mountain streams throughout south central Colorado offer great fishing for several species of trout; most areas are stocked annually by the Colorado Division of Wildlife.

## Outdoor Adventures

### FISHING

Rainbow and brown trout are the most common, and some areas have kokanee (freshwater salmon). There is bass fishing on some of the larger reservoirs.

Most fishing east of the mountains is in warm-water reservoirs such as Pueblo Reservoir near Pueblo and Trinidad Lake near Trinidad. The catch in these lakes can include largemouth bass, channel catfish, pike, bluegill, carp, bullhead, perch and crappie.

**ALAMOSA AREA**   West of Antonito, at the southern end of the San Luis Valley, the **Conejos River** is highly regarded by fly-fishers.

**GUNNISON–CRESTED BUTTE AREA**   Between Gunnison and Crested Butte, the **Roaring Judy State Wildlife Area** permits fly-fishing in the East River, both upstream and downstream from the state fish hatchery there. It is a catch-and-release area, so all fish under 12 inches long must be returned to the water. **Willowfly Anglers** offers trout-fishing float trips on the upper Gunnison River. ~ 130 County Road 742, Almont, CO 81229; 970-761-3474. The Curecanti National Recreation Area includes Blue Mesa Reservoir and two other reservoirs on the Gunnison River that are stocked with fish. Eight tributary creeks offer good rainbow, brown, brook and cutthroat trout fishing. Fishing guides, as well as tackle and in-formation, are available in Gunnison at **High Mountain Drifters**. ~ 115 South Wisconsin Street, Gunnison; 970-641-4243.

**ALAMOSA AREA**   Near Alamosa, the shallow, natural San Luis Lake (the largest of several lakes in San Luis Lakes State Park) is a locally popular spot for waterskiing, fishing, sailing and wind-surfing. There are no boat rentals, though.

### BOATING

**GUNNISON–CRESTED BUTTE AREA**   A few miles west of Gun-nison, Curecanti National Recreation Area offers water sports on 20-mile-long Blue Mesa Reservoir. The recreation area has two rental concessions with identical rates. You can rent a fishing boat, pontoon boat or cruiser at **Elk Creek Marina** on Route 50 or **Lake**

Fork Marina on Route 92; call the recreation area headquarters for information. ~ Route 50; 970-641-2337.

A more secluded recreational lake is Taylor Park Reservoir, in the mountains east of Crested Butte. Boat rentals there are available through **Taylor Park Marina**. ~ Taylor Park; 970-641-2922.

**RIVER RUNNING**

Scenic River Tours runs the Gunnison and Upper Taylor rivers, with trips ranging from the gentle and sublime to fast-action whitewater thrills, including expeditions through the Black Canyon of the Gunnison. ~ 703 West Tomichi Avenue, Gunnison; 970-641-3131.

**DOWNHILL SKIING**

Located 28 miles north of Gunnison, **Crested Butte Ski Area**, a midsize winter resort, offers excellent downhill runs for skiers of all abilities. The total vertical drop is 2775 feet, and there are 14 chairlifts. Many consider the north face, where telemarking was invented, to be Colorado's ultimate "extreme skiing" run. The ski area is open Thanksgiving to mid-April. ~ 12 Snowmass Road, Crested Butte; 970-349-2222, fax 970-349-2397; www.crestedbutte.org.

**Monarch Ski Area**, 45 miles east of Gunnison, is only about one-third the size of Crested Butte but has 670 skiable acres. Since the ski lifts start beside the summit of Monarch Pass (11,950 feet), you ski above timberline on the highest part of the mountain. The resort is used mainly by weekenders from Colorado Springs and Denver, but the four chairlifts run almost empty on winter weekdays. Though some of the trails are suitable for beginners, the majority are for intermediate and expert skiers. Ski and snowboard rentals are available. Open Thanksgiving to mid-April. ~ Route 50, Monarch Pass; 719-530-5000, 888-996-7669; www.skimonarch.com.

**Ski Rentals** Flatiron Sports rents downhill and cross-country skis. ~ 10 Crested Butte Way, Mount Crested Butte; 970-349-6656.

**CROSS-COUNTRY SKIING**

More than 20 kilometers of groomed cross-country ski trails, maintained by the Crested Butte Nordic Council, start from the outskirts of Crested Butte. For equipment rentals, maps and information on other cross-country ski routes in the area, go to **Alternative Ski & Sport**. ~ 309 6th Street, Crested Butte; 970-349-1320.

**GOLF**

**PUEBLO AREA** Pueblo's best public course is the 18-hole **Walking Stick Golf Course**. Designed by Arthur Hill, the course rambles over rolling hills on the city's west side. It has cart and club rentals, a restaurant and a bar. ~ 4301 Walking Stick Boulevard; 719-584-3400. You can also rent a cart and clubs for the day at the 27-hole **City Park Golf Course**. ~ 3900 Thatcher Avenue; 719-

561-4946. The public is also welcome at the privately owned 18-hole **Desert Hawk at Pueblo West** golf course. ~ 2515 McCullock Boulevard; 719-547-2280.

**WALSENBURG–TRINIDAD AREA** The nine-hole course at **Walsenburg Golf Club** has a beautiful location adjoining Lathrop State Park. ~ Route 160 West; 719-738-2730. Trinidad also has a nine-hole course, the **Trinidad Municipal Golf Course**. ~ 1415 Nolan Drive; 719-846-4015.

**ALAMOSA AREA** The only option in the Alamosa region is the 18-hole **Cattails Golf Club**. ~ 6615 North River Road, Alamosa; 719-589-9515.

**GUNNISON–CRESTED BUTTE AREA** On the outskirts of Gunnison, the 18-hole **Dos Rios Golf Club** is open to the public in the summer months; cart and club rentals are available. ~ 501 Camino del Rio, Gunnison; 970-641-1482. Near the foot of the ski slopes at Crested Butte, the 18-hole golf course at the **Club at Crested Butte** is ranked as one of the best in America. Cart usage is included in the greens fee; club rentals are available. ~ 385 Country Club Drive, Mount Crested Butte; 970-349-6131.

**TENNIS**

Pueblo has a 17-court tennis complex in **City Park**. ~ 800 Goodnight Avenue; 719-566-1745. Crested Butte has three municipal tennis courts in **Town Park**, open to the public at no charge on a first-come, first-served basis.

**RIDING STABLES**

Near Gunnison, guided daytrips and pack trips are available at **7-11 Ranch,** an old-style working cattle and horse ranch. ~ Gunnison; 970-641-0006. Horse rentals and guided daytrips are also offered by **Coal Creek Outfitting**. ~ P.O. Box 903, Gunnison, CO 81230; 970-641-1227. One-hour to all-day guided trail rides on Crested Butte Mountain are offered by **Lazy F Bar Outfitters**, located two miles past the Crested Butte Airport. ~ 2991 County Road 738, Gunnison; 970-641-0193.

**BIKING**

**PUEBLO AREA** The **Pueblo Greenway** offers 30 miles of multi-use trails suitable for biking along the Arkansas River, from Lake Pueblo east through Pueblo.

◆◆◆◆◆◆◆◆◆◆◆◆◆◆◆◆◆◆◆◆◆◆◆◆◆◆◆◆◆◆◆◆◆◆◆◆◆◆◆◆◆◆◆◆◆◆◆◆◆◆◆◆◆◆◆◆◆◆◆◆

### BIG HORN, TAKE ME AWAY!

**Big Horn Balloon Company** takes passengers on hour-long early-morning flights among the mountain crags that surround the ski resort of Crested Butte. It bills itself as the world's highest-altitude balloon operation. ~ 14522 Mustang Lane, Montrose; 970-596-1008; www.balloon-adventures.com, e-mail hotair@balloon-adventures.com.

**ALAMOSA AREA**   The flat, straight roads of the **San Luis Valley** make the area ideal for bicycle touring. Besides the main highways, a grid of farm roads crisscrosses the valley with very little traffic.

**CREEDE–LAKE CITY AREA**   There are national forest jeep roads suitable for mountain biking in the **Cumbres Pass** area west of Antonito. For information, contact the Rio Grande National Forest Headquarters. ~ 1803 West Route 160, Monte Vista; 719-852-5941. In the Creede area, contact Rio Grande National Forest, Creede Ranger District for information. ~ P.O. Box 270, Creede, CO 81130; 719-658-2556.

**GUNNISON–CRESTED BUTTE AREA**   Since the sport was invented in Crested Butte in the late 1970s, mountain biking has become Colorado's most popular summer sport. World-class, organized events include Crested Butte's Fat Tire Bike Week in July. Some popular mountain-biking routes in the area are **Kebler Pass Road** and the roads from **Pitkin** to the west portal of the **Alpine Tunnel** and over Cumberland Pass to **Tincup** and **Taylor Park Reservoir**. For details on these and many other forest roads that make good bike routes, get a Gunnison National Forest map from the ranger station. ~ 216 North Colorado Street, Gunnison; 970-641-0471.

The spectacular mountain setting is one of the reasons former president Gerald Ford says the Club at Crested Butte is his favorite golf course.

**Bike Rentals**   In Alamosa, **Kristi Mountain Sports** provides mountain-bike rentals. ~ Villa Mall, 7565 West Route 160; 719-589-9759. In Creede, **San Juan Sports** rents mountain bikes. ~ 102 Main Street; 719-658-2359. In Gunnison, mountain-bike rentals are at **Tomichi Cycles**. ~ 134 West Tomichi Avenue; 970-641-9069. Bicycling is a big industry in Crested Butte, where rentals are available at half a dozen shops including **Flatiron Sports**. ~ 10 Crested Butte Way; 970-349-6656. Or you may contact **Crested Butte Sports Ski & Bike Shop**. ~ 35 Emmons Road; 970-349-7516.

**HIKING**   All distances listed for hiking trails are one way unless otherwise noted.

**WALSENBURG–TRINIDAD AREA**   In San Isabel National Forest, the short, steep **West Spanish Peak Trail** (3 miles) to the 13,626-foot summit west of Trinidad is one of several outstanding trails among the Spanish Peaks. A longer but easier trail, the **Wahatoya Trail** (10 miles), climbs over the saddle between the two peaks; the distance from the trailhead on Huahatolla Valley Road to the upper ridge is four miles, and from there it is possible to leave the established trail and scramble across rocky alpine terrain to the summit of **East Spanish Peak**.

**ALAMOSA AREA**   Although no permanent trails mar the sands of **Great Sand Dunes National Park**, it is virtually impossible to get lost. Yet the dunes are so vast that hikers with plenty of water can explore the dune field for days (backcountry hiking permit required). Also in the national monument, the **Mosca Pass Trail** (3.5 miles) climbs to the crest of the Sangre de Cristo Range for spectacular views of the San Luis and Wet Mountain valleys.

**CREEDE–LAKE CITY AREA** Various trailheads in the vicinity of Creede provide access to the Weminuche Wilderness. They range from the fairly easy climb to Ruby Lake on the **Fern Creek Trail** (3.5 miles) to the 80-mile stretch of the **Continental Divide Trail** that crosses the wilderness from Stony Pass to Wolf Creek Pass.

**GUNNISON–CRESTED BUTTE AREA** Curecanti National Recreation Area has hiking trails through a wide range of habitats: the lush streamside greenery of the five-mile **Neversink Trail**; the dry, rugged **Curecanti Needle Trail** (2.5 miles) to the base of the spirelike rock formation for which it is named; and the steep **Curecanti Creek Trail** (2 miles) down to Morrow Point Reservoir in the Black Canyon of the Gunnison. Within **Black Canyon of the Gunnison National Monument**, four trails, ranging in distance from one to three miles, descend from the rim to the river; a high-clearance vehicle is necessary to reach the trailheads.

Hikers can explore the West Elk Wilderness west of Gunnison and Crested Butte on the **Mill Creek Trail** (15 miles), which climbs to heights of over 12,000 feet. There is an extensive network of interconnecting trails from **Cement Creek**, seven miles south of Crested Butte. Perhaps the ultimate hike in the Crested Butte area is the **Conundrum Trail** (14 miles), which starts above the ghost town of Gothic and crosses the Continental Divide to Conundrum Hot Springs and, from there, descends toward Aspen.

▼ ▼ ▼ ▼ ▼ ▼ ▼ ▼ ▼ ▼

## Transportation

### CAR

South central Colorado has two main east–west highways, each of which crosses the Continental Divide over a high switchback pass. **Route 50** exits from Route 25 at Pueblo, winding its way over Monarch Pass (11,312 feet) and then descending into the Gunnison–Crested Butte area. **Route 160** exits from Route 25 at Walsenburg and, after an easy climb over La Veta Pass (9413 feet), descends into the San Luis Valley and the Alamosa area, then continues over Wolf Creek Pass (10,850 feet).

Several north–south highways connect Route 50 with Route 160. The straightest and fastest roads are **Route 285** and **Route 17**, both of which run the length of the San Luis Valley, meeting Route 50 at Poncha Springs and Route 160 at Salida. **Route 149**, also known as the Scenic Thread Scenic Byway, meets Route 50 at Gunnison, goes through Lake City and Creede and intersects Route 160 at Del Norte.

**AIR**

The **Pueblo Memorial Airport** has America West, Continental Express and Trans World Airlines flights; both **City Cab** (719-543-2525) and **City Bus** provide airport ground transportation.

Mesa Airlines/United Express has flights between Denver and **Alamosa–San Luis Valley Regional Airport**. Visitors arriving by air may wish to arrange shuttle service through their lodging; no public transportation is available in Alamosa.

United and United Express (in ski season only) fly into **Gunnison County Airport**. The airport, which serves both Gunnison and Crested Butte, also handles ski-trip flights from other parts of the United States during the winter months. Airport shuttle service is offered by **Alpine Express**. Reservations required. ~ 970-641-5074, 800-822-4844. Shuttle service is also available from **Gunnison Valley Shuttle**. Reservations required. ~ 1 Meridian Lake Road; 970-349-0278, 800-349-1778.

**TRAIN**

**Amtrak**'s "Southwest Limited" crosses southern Colorado with a stop in Trinidad on its route between Chicago and Los Angeles. Call for schedule information and reservations. ~ 800-872-7245.

**BUS**

**TNM&O Coaches**, a Greyhound affiliate, provides service to Pueblo. ~ 116 North Main Street; 719-543-2775. TNM&O also services Trinidad. ~ 639 West Main Street; 719-846-7271.

**Greyhound Bus Lines** has bus service to Alamosa and Gunnison. ~ 800-231-2222.

**CAR RENTALS**

**Avis Rent A Car** (800-331-1212) and **Hertz Rent A Car** (800-654-3131) are at the Pueblo Memorial Airport.

Rental cars are scarce in the Alamosa area. Try **L & M Auto Rentals** (719-589-4651) or **Budget Rent A Car** (800-527-0700), both at the Alamosa San Luis Valley Regional Airport.

Agencies at the Gunnison County Airport include **Avis Rent A Car** (800-331-1212), **Budget Rent A Car** (800-527-0700) and **Hertz Rent A Car** (800-654-3131). **Flatiron Sports** also rents four-wheel-drives. ~ 10 Crested Butte Way; 800-821-4331. In Lake City, **Rocky Mountain Jeep Rental** provides jeeps. ~ 549 South Gunnison Avenue, Wade's Addition; 970-944-2262. Also try **Lake City Auto & Sports Center**. ~ 809 Route 149; 970-944-2311.

**PUBLIC TRANSIT**

Pueblo public transportation is provided by **City Bus**. ~ 719-542-4306.

**TAXIS**

Taxi service is provided in Pueblo by **City Cab**. ~ 719-543-2525. In Crested Butte taxi service is available through **Town Taxi**. ~ 970-349-5543.

# EIGHT

# Southwestern Colorado

Stone towers stand silent watch over hidden canyons littered with painted pot shards and marked with shamanic petroglyphs, remnants of an ancient civilization that arose among the juniper-covered mesas a thousand years ago and then vanished; today, only wild horses live in the canyons. Unknowable and often baffling even to archaeologists, the mysteries of these ruins tug at a visitor's imagination. Meanwhile, an hour's drive up the highway, tourists line up to board the old-time steam train that will carry them on an all-day excursion through Colorado's most dramatic mountain scenery, inching across sheer cliffs and dizzying trestles to a born-again Victorian-era mining town high in the San Juan Mountains.

The San Juans are so vast that they can accommodate every kind of recreation. As motorists take in the thrill-a-minute scenery along the 200-mile highway loop coined the San Juan Skyway, mountain bikers and off-roaders explore the web of hundreds of miles of dirt wagon roads and railroad beds leading to forgotten ghost towns that once yielded fortunes in gold and silver. Elsewhere in the same mountains, Colorado's largest wilderness areas offer backcountry trails where hikers can go for a week or more without crossing a single road, paved or otherwise. Mountain climbers liken the challenges presented by the jagged, spirelike peaks to those found in the Swiss Alps. And in an even more remote part of the mountains, many people believe, the last grizzly bears in Colorado make their home far from the reach of human eyes.

Southwestern Colorado emerged as a tourist area much later than the state's other major destinations. At the time the Pikes Peak region, Estes Park and Aspen began striking it rich in the tourist business, about the most exciting thing happening in this distant corner of the state was the pinto bean crop. Surrounded on three sides by Indian reservations and on the fourth by high mountains, the Durango area was almost three hundred miles from any larger town. To reach it, motorists had to maneuver their way over steep Wolf Creek Pass, one of the last highways in Colorado to be paved. The region was so hard to reach that during the 1920s an archaeologist actually disassembled an ancient cliff dwelling in McElmo Canyon stone by stone and reassembled it on a cliff face above Manitou Springs west of Colorado Springs—so that visitors could see for themselves a cliff dwelling of the Ancestral Pueblo culture whose empire spanned the Four Corners region, without making the long, arduous journey all the way to the southwestern mesas. The Ancestral Puebloans were known to archaeologists as Anasazi (Navajo for "ancient enemies") until 1997, when their Hopi descendants persuaded the U.S. government to declare the term Anasazi politically incorrect and change it at all national parks and monuments.

As roads improved, attendance figures grew gradually at Mesa Verde National Park, site of the most elaborate cliff dwellings. But it was not until the late 1970s, with the opening of the Durango & Silverton Narrow-Gauge Railroad and the emergence of Telluride as Colorado's most out-of-the-way ski resort in winter and leading music and art festival venue in summer, that visitors began coming to Durango in numbers comparable to other Colorado tourist destinations.

Tourists may be more common these days, but much of the region has retained its traditional character. In fact, southwestern Colorado is the only part of the state where Indians live on tribal land today. The Ute people who live south of the Durango area—and formerly claimed the entire region as their homeland—add an additional dimension to the local cultural heritage. Although their reservation appears small on the map, it and the adjoining Navajo and Hopi reservations form a bloc of Indian lands larger than the states of Massachusetts, Connecticut and Vermont combined. Nor are Indians the only distinctive subcultures that help shape southwestern Colorado's unique character. Buckskin-clad mountain men still live in the wild San Juans, and the hills east of Durango are home to a traditional rural community of Basque sheepherders.

▼▼▼▼▼▼▼▼▼▼▼▼▼▼

## Pagosa Springs Area

One of the largest and hottest geothermal springs in the United States, the Great Pagosa Hot Spring has been held sacred in American Indian tradition since ancient times for the curative power of its sulphurous mineral water. It was used for healing by Ute, Navajo and Apache people, and probably in earlier times by the Ancestral Pueblo people living at nearby Chimney Rock. The town of Pagosa Springs sprang up in connection with developers' attempts to convert the spring into a European-style spa (the water's mineral content is similar to that of the famous Karlsbad Spa in the Czech Republic), but none of the spas flourished until recent times, when basking in geothermals pools became the preferred après-ski pastime for skiers at nearby Wolf Creek Ski Area. Though the area has seen steady, modest development in recent years, its vast mountains and cozy town center seem "undiscovered" compared to most areas of southwestern Colorado.

**SIGHTS**   Motorists coming from the eastern slope on Route 160 reach the Durango area by way of **Wolf Creek Pass** (10,850 feet), one of the highest and steepest passes on any U.S. highway. At the foot of the winding descent down the west side of the pass lies **Pagosa Springs,** a likable little town named for the steamy, slightly sulfurous **Great Pagosa Hot Spring** located behind the visitors information center in the middle of town. The depth of the spring is unknown; it has been plumbed to 850 feet without reaching the bottom. The bathing area, operated as a spa by the Spring Inn, is arranged in a series of cooling pools that dilute the scalding 154°F spring, said to be the hottest natural mineral spring in the world.

The springs were traditionally used as a gathering place and wintering ground by nomadic Indians of the region, who built a 50-foot-long pool to mix the scalding geothermal water with chilly river water for bathing. In 1878 the U.S. Army built a fort here, and 13 years later the town was established by developers who hoped to popularize it as a hot springs spa. But Wolf Creek Pass presented a formidable barrier that inspired travelers to visit other, easier-to-reach spas instead. The Pagosa Springs economy has traditionally depended on timber cutting in the surrounding national forest, and as logging operations in the area have been

**Southwestern Colorado**

phased out in favor of recreational uses, the town has evolved
into a low-key resort area. The history of the hot springs and the
area's Ute Indian inhabitants and early settlers is recalled in displays of photos and artifacts at the **San Juan
Historical Society Pioneer Museum.** Other exhibits
include a one-horse open sleigh and a fully equipped
blacksmith shop. ~ 1st and Pagosa streets, Pagosa
Springs; 970-264-4424.

*"Pagosa" is the Ute word
for "healing water."*

Two miles west of town is the **Fred Harman Art Museum,** exhibiting collected works by the late Pagosa
Springs artist whose cowboy comic strip, "Red Ryder,"
was syndicated worldwide in the 1950s. ~ Route 160,
Pagosa Springs; 970-731-5785.

Between Pagosa Springs and Durango, three miles off Route
160 on the road to Navajo Lake, the **Chimney Rock Archaeological Area** is open to visitors from mid-May to mid-September by
guided tour only; the rest of the year, only group reservations are
offered. Nine hundred years ago, this ancient Ancestral Pueblo site
was the most distant "outlier," or colony, of the huge settlement at
Chaco Canyon in New Mexico. Archaeologists believe that mostly
single men lived at the Chimney Rock pueblo, which served as both
a ceremonial center and a lumber camp from which logs were
floated down the Piedra River for use as roof beams in Chaco Canyon. Admission. ~ Route 151; 970-883-5359 (mid-May through
September), 970-264-2287 (October to mid-May); www.chimney
rockco.org.

**LODGING**

In Pagosa Springs, the classiest place to stay is three and a half miles
west of town at the newly refurbished 100-room **Pagosa Lodge.**
The lodge is on a private lake in a resort community of custom-
built vacation homes and condominiums with a golf course, tennis courts and a swimming pool, all under a spectacular mountain
skyline. Touches of Southwestern decor and furnishings as tasteful
as they are durable brighten the rather condominium-like guest
rooms. ~ 3505 West Route 160, Pagosa Springs; 970-731-4141,
800-523-7704, fax 970-731-4343; www.pagosalodge.com, e-mail
pagosalodge@pagosasprings.net. MODERATE TO DELUXE.

Right in the center of town, the **Pagosa Springs Resort** has 37
rooms done in Southwestern-style, pastel decor with double or
king- size bed, phone, shower and cable TV; suites are also available. They also offer one big difference: guests have unlimited use
of the inn's 17 outdoor geothermal pools set in a landscaped fantasy oasis on the bank of the San Juan River. It's one of the best
hot-springs facilities in southern Colorado. ~ 165 Hot Springs
Boulevard, Pagosa Springs; 970-264-4168, 800-225-0934; www.
pagosaspringsresort.com. MODERATE TO DELUXE.

Guests can also soak in hot-spring pools at the **Best Western Oak Ridge Lodge**, a conventional mid-range establishment where the rooms have air conditioning and offer a choice of two double beds or one queen-size. ~ 158 Hot Springs Boulevard, Pagosa Springs; 970-264-4173, fax 970-264-4472; e-mail oakridge@outer bound.net. MODERATE.

There are individual geothermal tubs at the nearby, no-frills **Spa at Pagosa Springs**, where the rooms are tidy, well lit and close to the pool. ~ 317 Hot Springs Boulevard, Pagosa Springs; 970-264-5910, 800-832-5523, fax 970-261-2624; e-mail thespa @frontier.com. BUDGET TO MODERATE.

The 10,000-square-foot **Echo Manor Inn**, known among locals as "the castle," was a typical Queen Anne–style residence until a previous owner—inspired by a visit to Disneyland, so the story goes—started building on towers, gables and sprawling additions, creating an architectural curiosity of such mammoth proportions that cars often stop on the highway to take snapshots. The lodge has a game room, a sun deck, a hot tub and a fantastic view of the San Juans. There are nine rooms, each individually decorated in country style with antiques and a handmade quilt, and there is a three-bedroom suite with a kitchen and fireplace. ~ 3366 Route 84, Pagosa Springs; 970-264-5646, fax 970-264-4617. MODERATE.

**DINING**

Most Pagosa Springs restaurants are several miles out of town. The **Ole Miner's Steakhouse**, east of Pagosa Springs, specializes in surf and turf. There is a wider selection of seafood here than in most other southern Colorado restaurants—including lobster, Alaskan King crab, rainbow trout, catfish, flounder and shrimp. The restaurant is designed for privacy, with cozy dining nooks containing one or two tables each, separated by rough-hewn wood dividers. The decor is like a mining museum, with shovels, rusty machinery, old photographs and an antique bathtub that serves as a salad bar. Dinner only. ~ 3825 East Route 160, three miles east of Pagosa Springs; 970-264-5981. DELUXE.

At the **Branding Iron Bar-B-Q**, next door to Ole Miners, the menu is simple: your choice of Texas-style barbecued beef, pork ribs, sausage or chicken, served with potatoes, pinto beans and corn-on-the-cob, plus pecan pie for dessert. The simple dining room has rustic pine-paneled walls decorated with branding irons and Indian rugs, and there is more seating on the small outdoor patio. Closed November through April; closed Sunday. ~ 4101 East Route 160, three miles east of Pagosa Springs; 970-264-4268. BUDGET.

The **Greenhouse**, a contemporary two-story restaurant with picture windows that provide great views of Pagosa Peak and the nearby airport, offers something for everybody; choose from filet mignon, grilled salmon, roast turkey or pizza, as well as home-made soups. ~ Piedra Road, three miles west of Pagosa Springs; 970-731-2021. MODERATE TO DELUXE.

**PARKS**

**SAN JUAN NATIONAL FOREST** 🏃 🚣 🐟 This two-million-acre forest includes a 130-mile expanse of mountains north of Pagosa Springs and Durango, from the Continental Divide on the east to the Dolores River on the west. The part of the forest around Pagosa Springs includes Williams Reservoir and portions of two major wilderness areas—the 459,000-acre Weminuche Wilderness to the north and the 128,000-acre South San Juan Wilderness to the east. Fishing is good for rainbow trout, brook trout and koka-nee salmon in Williams Creek Reservoir. There are picnic areas, restrooms and pack trails. ~ There is trail access to the national forest from Route 160. Major trailheads for the South San Juan Wilderness are near East Fork Campground, ten miles northeast of Pagosa Springs off Route 160, and Forest Roads 662/665 east of Pagosa Springs. Access to Weminuche Wilderness trailheads and Williams Creek Reservoir is via Forest Road 631, which leaves the main highway two miles west of town. The distance to the reservoir is 22 miles; 970-247-4874.

▲ Of the eight forest service campgrounds in the Pagosa Springs area, the closest to town is East Fork Campground, with 26 RV/tent sites (no hookups); open mid-May to mid-November; $8 per night. At Williams Creek Reservoir, Williams Creek Camp-ground has 69 RV/tent sites (no hookups); open mid-May to mid-November; $9 per night.

**NAVAJO LAKE STATE PARK** 🛶 🚤 🚢 🐟 Thirty-five-mile-long Navajo Lake wanders among pine-forested hills and reaches into a hundred hidden side canyons. The reservoir was created in 1962 when the San Juan River was dammed to provide irriga-tion for the Navajo Indian Reservation. Most of the lake lies in New Mexico, where there is another state park of the same name. At the opposite end of the lake from the dam, Colorado's Navajo Lake State Park combines a wild, remote feel with a few modern conveniences such as an airstrip for fly-in campers and the largest boat ramp in the state (80 feet wide and a quarter-mile long). Fishing and waterskiing are the main water sports. The lake is populated by bluegill, catfish, crappie, largemouth bass, kokanee salmon and rainbow, brown and brook trout. The visitors center displays Ancestral Pueblo and Ute artifacts found in the canyons that were flooded by the lake. Wildlife in the park includes bald eagles, wild turkeys, beaver, mink, foxes, deer and elk. Mountain lions inhabit the backcountry but are rarely seen. Facilities in-clude picnic area with tables and restrooms, boat ramp, airstrip, marina with boat, ski and fishing tackle rentals and groceries. Food and lodging are two miles away in Arboles. Day-use fee, $5. ~ Located two miles south of Arboles and Route 151. Navajo Lake State Park is 35 miles south of Pagosa Springs and 45 miles southeast of Durango; 970-883-2208.

▲ The 71-site campground is situated on a peninsula so that most sites have water frontage; $12 to $16 per night ($7 per night in the primitive tent area). There are showers, flush toilets and a dump station; four sites have electric hookups. Reservations: 800-678-2267.

## Durango Area

Durango is the largest town in southwestern Colorado and the natural hub for exploring the Four Corners area. The San Juans, the most spectacular mountains in the central Rockies, dominate the region's skyline wherever you go. The Durango area is a full day's drive from any major population center, giving it an off-the-beaten-path feel.

Despite its rather isolated location, Durango boasts one of Colorado's most popular tourist attractions—the narrow-gauge railroad to Silverton. The town also serves as a base camp for the many thousands of outdoor enthusiasts who each year venture into the San Juan Mountains by car, jeep or mountain bike or on horseback or foot to gaze with awe upon a panorama of unvanquished mountain crags that has often been likened to the Swiss Alps.

## SIGHTS

About 25 miles northeast of Durango is **Vallecito Reservoir**, a popular boating and fishing area. The shore is lined with campgrounds, marinas, motels, lodges, bed and breakfasts, restaurants and cocktail lounges. Not far away is the less-developed Lemon Reservoir. Both reservoirs are manmade.

Routes 501 and 240 make for a pretty back-road trip between Bayfield and Durango through sheep-ranching country. Many of the sheepherders in this area are Basques who retain their unique language and many traditions brought from the Pyrenees between Spain and France.

**Durango** got its start in 1880 as a smelter town where gold and silver ore from the mining camps in the San Juan Mountains was refined. Within two years the boom town rivaled Denver as the richest city in Colorado. Although the gold-mining era ended, the town slid into poverty and many structures in Durango were abandoned, the solidly built, elaborately ornamented red-brick buildings downtown endured through the decades. Good times began returning to Durango in the mid-1950s, when Fort Lewis College was established there and the popularity of nearby Mesa Verde

> Though steam locomotives pull sightseeing trains through many parts of the West these days, the Durango & Silverton trip, with its trestles hundreds of feet above the Animas River and its thrilling climb along a narrow shelf cut into the sheer Animas River Canyon wall, remains unsurpassed.

National Park began to grow and boosted the local economy. When the Durango & Silverton Narrow-Gauge Railroad was revived in 1981, the town saw a surge of tourism that lifted it to a new level of prosperity. Today, Durango throbs with youthful exuberance thanks to the college students who make up a sizable part of its population. The town also has far more than its share of latter-day mountain men, old and young, who live in the wilderness of the San Juans, at least during the warm months, and who come into town for supplies and celebrations.

Each morning from May through October, the **Durango & Silverton Narrow-Gauge Railroad** fills Durango's downtown historic district with steam and tumult as it loads passengers for the 45-mile trip to Silverton in the heart of the San Juan Mountains. The trip to Silverton takes three hours. Passengers have a three-hour stay, plenty of time for lunch and shopping. The two-hour return trip arrives in Durango at dinnertime. Passengers can choose to spend one or more nights in Silverton before returning to Durango. One-way tickets allow backpackers to get off the train at the Needleton or Elk Park trailhead and trek into the Weminuche Wilderness. The Durango & Silverton Narrow-Gauge Railroad is one of the most popular tourist attractions in Colorado, carrying more than 200,000 passengers a year; reservations are essential and should be made at least a month in advance. Admission. ~ 479 Main Avenue, Durango; 970-247-2733, 888-872-4607, fax 970-259-3570; www.durangotrain.com, e-mail info@durangotrain.com.

North of Durango up the Animas River Canyon, Route 550 passes **Durango Mountain Resort** (formerly Purgatory Ski Area). In the summer months, the ski lift carries thrill seekers up the slopes to careen down an **alpine slide** on vehicles that look like a cross between a sled and a skateboard. Admission. ~ Route 550, Durango; 970-247-9000.

The perfect ending to a Durango day is a relaxing dip in **Trimble Hot Springs**. The original resort on the site was built in 1883. Recently rebuilt and reopened, the present hot springs have an Olympic-size swimming pool and a smaller, hotter pool; the water comes from underground at $119°F$ and is diluted to $104°F$ before being piped into the pool. The hot springs are open late into the evening year-round and are especially popular in the winter months, when people stop there on the way back to Durango from the Purgatory ski slopes. Admission. ~ 6475 County Road 203, Durango; 970-247-0111; www.trimblehotsprings.com.

**LODGING**   The shores of Vallecito Reservoir, northeast of Durango, are lined with cabins, most of them in small rental-cabin compounds referred to as lodges. Try **Circle S Lodge**, situated at the north end of the lake near the edge of the Weminuche Wilderness. The 14 cabins are spacious enough to accommodate up to nine people and have carpeting, kitchenettes and fireplaces. ~ 18044 County Road 501, Bayfield; 970-884-2473, fax 970-884-2470. DELUXE.

Farther along the east shore of the lake, two miles past the end of the pavement, **Elk Point Lodge** offers ten cabins, most with fireplaces, and also rents horses and boats. The cabins vary in size and range in price. ~ 21730 County Road 501, Bayfield; 970-884-2482; e-mail elkpoint@frontier.net. BUDGET TO DELUXE.

At the top of the list of Durango's restored historic lodgings is the **Strater Hotel**, which has been in continuous operation since

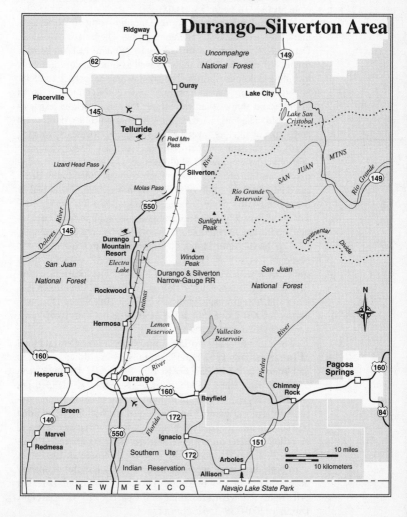

**Durango–Silverton Area**

Ridgway

Uncompahgre National Forest

Placerville

Ouray

Lake City

Lake San Cristobal

Telluride

Red Mtn Pass

Lizard Head Pass

Silverton

SAN JUAN MTNS

Rio Grande

Molas Pass

Rio Grande Reservoir

Continental Divide

Dolores River

Durango Mountain Resort

Sunlight Peak

Electra Lake

Windom Peak

San Juan National Forest

Rockwood

Durango & Silverton Narrow-Gauge RR

Animas

Hermosa

Lemon Reservoir

Vallecito Reservoir

Piedra River

San Juan National Forest

Pagosa Springs

Hesperus

River

Durango

Chimney Rock

Breen

Bayfield

Marvel

Florida

Redmesa

Ignacio

Southern Ute

Arboles

Indian Reservation

Allison

Navajo Lake State Park

NEW MEXICO

0    10 miles

0    10 kilometers

N

1887, when it was one of the most luxurious hotels in the West. Beautifully maintained, the interior of the five-story hotel now glows with a soft patina of authentic frontier elegance. Twelve-foot-high mirrors and gold-papered walls brighten the lobby, where a big writing desk looks out upon Main Avenue. Since the second coming of the railroad brought prosperity back to Durango, the guest rooms have been upgraded to grand-hotel quality with flowery carpets and ornate 100-year-old walnut furnishings. Rates include breakfast. ~ 699 Main Avenue, Durango; 970-247-4431, 800-247-4431, fax 970-259-2208; www.strater. com. MODERATE TO ULTRA-DELUXE.

A block down the street stands Durango's other historic landmark hostelry, the **General Palmer Hotel**. The hotel's namesake, Denver & Rio Grande Railroad owner William Jackson Palmer, founded the town of Durango, as well as other Colorado towns including Colorado Springs. The hotel, which dates back to 1898, is restored with period antiques and reproductions. It looks brighter and shinier than the Strater though somehow less genuinely old. The long, narrow lobby has brass fittings, dark wood trim, pink wallpaper, overstuffed armchairs, loveseats, rocking chairs and carpeting in Victorian floral patterns. There is a library with a picture window on Main Avenue, as well as a window display room full of teddy bears. Each room is individually decorated and features a full- or queen-size poster bed, pewter bed or brass bed. ~ 567 Main Avenue, Durango; 970-247-4747, 800-523-3358, fax 970-247-1332; www.generalpalmerhotel.com, e-mail gphdurango@yahoo.com. MODERATE TO ULTRA-DELUXE.

The **Jarvis Suite Hotel**, in a former theater listed on the National Register of Historic Places, offers 22 sunny, modern suites, each with a fully equipped kitchen. The location, within easy walking distance of the railroad station and downtown galleries and restaurants, is ideal. ~ 125 West 10th Street, Durango; phone/fax 970-259-6190, 800-824-1024; e-mail jarvis@frontier. net. DELUXE TO ULTRA-DELUXE.

For a low-priced Victorian atmosphere, try the **Central Hotel of Durango**. This 1892 hotel is upstairs from a downtown pool hall known as the El Rancho Tavern, where Jack Dempsey won $50 in a prizefight in 1915, four years before he claimed the world's heavyweight championship title; the event is commemorated in a mural painted on the side of the building. The hotel had sunken into musty decrepitude before new management and an influx of adventure-oriented budget travelers arrived to rejuvenate it. Today it's one of the best youth hostels in Colorado, with both dormitory accommodations and a handful of sparely decorated private rooms. Youthful exuberance abounds here, but prize fights in the bar are a thing of the past. ~ 975 Main Avenue, Durango; 970-259-3562. BUDGET.

The largest hotel in Durango, with 154 guest rooms, the **Doubletree Hotel Durango** feels more like a big-city business travelers' hotel than a vacation retreat. Rooms are colorful, contemporary and unusually spacious. The motor inn has an indoor swimming pool, a spa and an exercise room. ~ 501 Camino del Rio, Durango; 970-259-6580, 800-222-8733, fax 970-259-4398; www.doubletree.com. DELUXE.

For those who prefer more conventional roadside lodging, the three-mile-long commercial strip along Route 550 on the northern outskirts of Durango is lined with standard highwayside motels. There are enough choices that travelers should be able to spot a few "vacancy" signs even during peak season. While in-season rates for private rooms aren't cheap anywhere in Durango, more reasonable rates can be found at well-maintained independent motels such as the **Caboose Motel**. ~ 3363 Main Avenue, Durango; 970-247-1191, fax 970-259-4887. BUDGET TO MODERATE. The **Alpine Motel** is another choice. ~ 3515 North Main Avenue, Durango; 970-247-4042. MODERATE.

Rates at Durango motels drop by 50 percent or more in the winter—a great bargain for skiers at nearby Purgatory.

Farther from downtown—but more convenient to the ski slopes at Durango Mountain Resort—the **Iron Horse Inn** is Durango's other large, upscale motor inn. Each of the 140 guest accommodations is a suite with a loft bedroom and a fireplace. An indoor swimming pool, a sauna and a whirlpool are on the premises. Rooms facing the railroad tracks are more desirable; the steam train comes by only twice a day, while the highway keeps on rolling all night long with big trucks roaring slowly up the canyon. ~ 5800 North Main Avenue, Durango; 970-259-1010, 800-385-4791, fax 970-748-2990; www.ironhorseinndurango.com, e-mail information@ironhorseinndurango.com. MODERATE TO DELUXE.

Durango also has more than 20 bed-and-breakfast inns. In the historic residential neighborhood adjoining downtown, just five blocks from the narrow-gauge railroad station, the **Gable House** has antique-furnished guest rooms, each with its own private entrance, in a large, three-story Queen Anne Victorian home with a beautifully landscaped yard. The inn is open during the summer months only. ~ 805 East 5th Avenue, Durango; 970-247-4982. MODERATE.

The **Rochester Hotel**, one of Durango's oldest hotels, has been in operation since 1892, when—under the name Peeple's Hotel—it rivaled the Strater and the General Palmer in prestige. It continued to thrive until the 1950s, then became a boardinghouse, a residential hotel and finally a flophouse with the cheapest rates in town—but no heat. New owners rescued the hotel in 1993, converting its 33 old rooms to 15 spacious ones individually renovated in the spirit of various movies filmed in the Durango area, including *How the West Was Won, Butch Cassidy and the Sundance Kid* and *City Slickers*. The hotel lobby is like a cowboy movie museum, its walls festooned with vintage posters and publicity stills. Rates include a full breakfast. ~ 726 East 2nd Avenue, Durango; 970-385-1920, 800-664-1920, fax 970-385-1967; www. rochesterhotel.com, e-mail stay@rochesterhotel.com. DELUXE TO ULTRA-DELUXE.

The **Leland House Bed & Breakfast Suites**, a circa-1927 apartment building across the street from the New Rochester Hotel and under the same management, has one ultra-deluxe-priced, one-bedroom suite with full kitchen and living room and a plainer deluxe-priced single room with kitchenette and private bath, both decorated with pre-Depression antiques from around Colorado. ~ 721 East 2nd Avenue, Durango; 970-385-1920, 800-664-1920, fax 970-385-1967; www.leland-house.com, e-mail stay@leland-house.com. DELUXE TO ULTRA-DELUXE.

Away from downtown, Durango-area bed and breakfasts tend to be modern, luxurious and located in spectacular settings. Consider, for example, the **River House Bed & Breakfast**, whose eight guest rooms and one cottage overlook the Animas River from a county road just north of town. As late sleepers soon discover, the narrow-gauge train steams right past the house a little before nine each morning. Gourmet breakfasts are served in a sunny 928-square-foot atrium with a waterfall. Other features include a living room with fireplace and wet bar, a snooker table, a sauna and an exercise room. Some of the individually decorated guest rooms have skylights or clawfoot tubs, and one is entirely lined with shelves of books. ~ 495 Animas View Drive, Durango; 970-247-4775, 800-254-4775, fax 970-259-1465. MODERATE.

Also north of town, the **Apple Orchard Inn** was transformed by new owners into one of the area's most spectacular B&Bs, with six lavishly decorated cottages on landscaped grounds with river-

**AUTHOR FAVORITE**

Three miles west of town, the award-winning **Lightner Creek Inn** is regularly cited as one of the finest bed and breakfasts in the state. The imposing white inn stands amid acres and acres of carefully manicured lawn complete with a duck pond and gazebo, looking like a Connecticut country estate magically transported to the Rockies. The seven guest rooms and three carriage-house suites feature brass beds, cute stuffed toys and a plethora of antique decor. The breakfast here is exceptional. ~ 999 County Road 207, Durango; 970-259-1226, 800-268-9804, fax 970-259-9526; www. lightnercreekinn.com, e-mail info@lightnercreekinn.com. MODERATE TO ULTRA-DELUXE.

fed streams and a small private lake. The farmhouse-style main lodge has four more rooms, a sitting room with a river-rock fireplace and original artwork. All rooms and cottages have elegant country furnishings including featherbeds, down comforters and armoires; some cottages have fireplaces and jacuzzis. Memorable breakfasts are prepared by the European-trained chef/co-owner. ~ 7758 County Road 203, Durango; 970-247-0751, 800-426-0751; www.appleorchardinn.com, e-mail info@appleorchardinn. com. MODERATE TO ULTRA-DELUXE.

Several of the finest guest ranches in the state are located in the vicinity of Durango. **Colorado Trails Ranch**, near Vallecito Reservoir, boasts one of the finest Western and English-style riding instruction programs offered anywhere. It also has a Western village complete with opera house and trading post. The family-oriented ranch offers activity programs organized by age group and supervised by full-time counselors. Other amenities include a heated swimming pool, tennis courts, a fishing pond and archery, rifle target and trap ranges. Guest accommodations are in individual cabins with modern furnishings, carpeting and private baths. Rates include all meals. Week-long stays only. Closed October through May. ~ P.O. Box 848, Durango, CO 81302; 970-247-5055, 877-7711-7843, fax 970-385-7372; www.colotrails.com, e-mail info@coloradotrails.com. DELUXE.

Perhaps the ultimate resort ranch experience in southwestern Colorado is to be found at **Tall Timbers Resort**. With just ten modern, split-level suites in duplexes secluded in a shimmering forest of aspens, the resort is so exclusive that it can't be reached by road—only by the narrow-gauge train or helicopter. The suites have high vaulted ceilings, loft bedrooms and marble baths. Among the resort's amenities are three hot tubs, a riding stable, a nine-hole golf course, tennis courts, a solar-heated swimming pool, an exercise room and a basketball court. Programs include fly-fishing coaching, massage therapy and high peaks trekking in the San Juan National Forest surrounding the lodge. Rates, as you might expect, are high—as much as $1600 per person for a three-night minimum stay. Meals are included in the rate. Closed November to mid-May. ~ 1 Silver Star Road, Durango; 970-259-4813; www. talltimberresort.com. ULTRA-DELUXE.

North of Durango, just three miles from the slopes of the Durango Mountain Resort, is the 325-unit **Lodge at Tamarron**. Built for $50 million in the early 1970s, Tamarron has become known as one of the state's top resorts, with a golf course that ranks among the best in the Rocky Mountain region. The resort also offers tennis courts, nature trails, riding stables, an indoor-outdoor pool and exercise rooms, as well as easy access to the ski slopes and miles of groomed ski trails. Guest rooms, decorated in pastel hues and Southwestern patterns, are on the small side but still include king-size beds and kitchenettes. Three-bed-room condominiums are also available. ~ 40292 Route 550 North, Durango; 970-259-2000, 800-678-1000, fax 970-382-7822; www.durangomountainresort.com, e-mail reservations@lodgeattamarron.com. MODERATE TO ULTRA-DELUXE.

**DINING**
Besides the array of family-style restaurants and familiar fast-food places along the three-mile-long Route 550 commercial strip on the northern outskirts of Durango, you'll find a good selection of places to eat in the downtown historic district. In a turn-of-the-20th-century red-brick building next to the narrow-gauge train station, the **Palace Restaurant** offers mesquite-grilled chicken and other dishes such as honey duck and brandy pepper steak in an elegant Victorian-style ambience. Dinner only. ~ 505 Main Avenue, Durango; 970-247-2018. DELUXE TO ULTRA-DELUXE.

Family dining meets 19th-century elegance in the stately old Strater Hotel at **Henry's Chop House & Italian Bistro**, with its Tiffany lightshades, ornate moldings and trim and red-leatherette padded chairs and booths. The menu features such house spe-cialties as veal osso buco, grilled buffalo steak, walnut chicken fettuccini and pistachio halibut. ~ 699 Main Avenue, Durango; 970-247-4431. MODERATE TO DELUXE.

**Francisco's Restaurante y Cantina**, established in 1968 by a family from northern New Mexico, is one of the best Mexican restaurants in Colorado and certainly the most popular restaurant in Durango, with seating for 250 people amid a labyrinth of adobe walls and Santa Fe–style decor. Try the enchiladas Durango, beef wrapped in blue-corn tortillas and smothered in green chili. Be-sides Mexican food, entrées include steak, chicken, trout and lob-ster. ~ 619 Main Avenue, Durango; 970-247-4098. MODERATE.

**AUTHOR FAVORITE**

I don't know about you, but after I've been traveling for a few days—especially in the Colorado outback, where "local cuisine" often con-sists of beef (ground or otherwise) and stuff that goes with beef (like French fries)—I tend to get a powerful craving for vegetables. That's why I like **Nature's Oasis**, Durango's largest natural foods market. The store has a complete deli with organic salads, soups, sandwiches, gourmet cof-fee, fruit smoothies and a vegetable juice bar, plus a few pleasantly healthy surprises. Try the kung pao tofu or the brown-rice *nori* rolls filled with avocado and carrots. You can eat on the premises, then stock up for the road in the produce section. ~ 1123 Camino del Rio, Durango; 970-247-1988. BUDGET.

Downtown Durango has more than its share of breakfast places, all designed to entice visitors before they board the narrow-gauge train. The unpretentious-looking **Carver Brewing Company** serves healthy breakfast specials such as granola pancakes. For dinner try the fajitas—beef or chicken fried in tequila salsa with green chili and onions, served with black beans, black olives and sour cream. Vegetarian entrées are also featured, and four varieties of home-brewed beer are available. No dinner on Sunday. ~ 1022 Main Avenue, Durango; 970-259-2545. BUDGET.

**SHOPPING**

At first glance, Main Avenue in Durango's nine-block downtown historic district seems to consist entirely of sporting goods stores. Look closer and you'll find that there are also a lot of factory outlet stores.

The tourism boom that has turned once-sleepy little Durango into prime retail space has also spawned a growing number of art galleries. They exhibit traditional American Indian art as well as works by area artists and craftspeople reflecting the full range of visual and spiritual imagery to be found in the Four Corners area. The largest gallery in town, **Toh-Atin**, offers high-quality Indian arts and crafts from around the Southwest, including fine selections of both replica Ancestral Pueblo pottery and authentic modern Pueblo pottery. ~ 145 West 9th Street, Durango; 970-247-8277; www.toh-atin.com. The **New West Gallery** displays sculptures and paintings of Southwestern subjects as well as an overwhelming selection of turquoise-and-silver jewelry. ~ 747 Main Avenue, Durango; 970-259-5777. One of the most distinctive traditional folk art galleries in town is the **Martin-Roll Gallery**, featuring Navajo weavings, Spanish colonial antiques, Huichol bead art among its many delights. ~ 635 East 2nd Avenue, Durango; 970-247-2211.

**Termar Gallery** offers an array of Indian, Spanish and Anglo fine arts, jewelry and pottery, as well as works by many of the best-known Southwestern artists. ~ 780 Main Avenue, Durango; 970-247-3728.

Railroad memorabilia and rare books can be found at **Southwest Book Trader**. ~ 175 East 5th Street, Durango; 970-247-8479.

If your head is aching for a custom-fitted cowboy hat, try **O'Farrell Hat Company**. They make fur felt hats by hand, the old-fashioned way, and have produced customized models for Robin Williams, Bruce Willis, Ronald Reagan and George H.W. Bush. ~ 563 Main Avenue, Durango; 970-259-2517; www.ofarrell hats.com.

**NIGHTLIFE**

In the Strater Hotel, the **Diamond Circle Theatre** presents a campy rendition of Victorian melodrama nightly during the summer season. ~ 970-247-3400, 877-325-3400; www.diamondcirclemelo drama.com. Also here is the **Diamond Belle Saloon,** which has a ragtime piano player and hosts live bluegrass on Sunday. ~ 699 Main Avenue, Durango; 970-247-4431.

**Farquahrts,** a student hangout, serves pizza as well as drinks and features live music at night during the summer months. ~ 725 Main Avenue, Durango; 970-247-9861. The dark-wood elegant **Mahogany Grille** serves up live jazz nightly along with cordials and two dozen varieties of cutely named martinis, including a banana splitini and the basic "Bill Clinton martini"—a very dirty vodka martini with olives. ~ 7th & Main Avenue; 970-247-4433.

**PARKS**

**SAN JUAN NATIONAL FOREST** 🏃 🚵 🐎 🏊 🏠 ⚓ ⛷ ⛵ This vast national forest encompasses all the mountains north of Durango (see "San Juan Skyway Area Parks" later in this chapter), as well as the popular recreation area of Vallecito Reservoir. Fishing is good for rainbow and brown trout and kokanee salmon in the Animas River, Vallecito Reservoir and Lemon Reservoir. There are picnic tables, restrooms, pack trails and jeep trails. ~ The main roads for forest access from the Durango area include the San Juan Skyway (Route 550), Vallecito Road (County Road 501) to Vallecito Reservoir from Bayfield, and Junction Creek Road (Forest Road 171) from the north side of Durango; 970-247-4874.

▲ Most forest service campgrounds in the area are at Vallecito Reservoir, including Graham Creek Campground, with 25 RV/tent sites (no hookups); closed mid-November through April; $12 per night. Reservations: 970-385-7224.

▼▼▼▼▼▼▼▼▼▼▼▼
# Mesa Verde Area

With the explosive growth of tourism in southwestern Colorado in recent years, Mesa Verde has emerged as one of the most-visited places in the U.S. national park system. Park Service officials say more European visitors visit Mesa Verde than the Grand Canyon, Yellowstone or Yosemite. The spectacle of these unique ancient ruins is well worth braving the crowds for. Once you've been there and done that, why not head for one of the smaller, more remote archaeological sites in the area, such as Hovenweep or Lowry Ruins, where you're likely to find yourself alone with ancient spirits?

**SIGHTS**

West of Durango off Route 160, **Mesa Verde National Park** protects one of the greatest wonders of pre–Columbian America—a community of castlelike stone pueblos built in niches high up the sheer cliffs of the mesa. Mesa Verde is the northernmost site of the ancient Ancestral Pueblo people, whose civilization dominated the Southwest for centuries and who evolved into the modern-day Pueblo Indians. Visitors drive up a long, steep road on the north side of the mesa to the nearly level top, then drive all the way to the south end of the mesa where the cliff dwellings are located, a half-hour's drive from the entrance. The miniature forest of juniper and piñon on the mesa top, plus some spectacular views of the distant mountains and the surrounding desert 3000 feet below set the stage for a visit to what may be the biggest mystery in Colorado's past. Admission. ~ 970-529-4465.

Although there are thousands of Ancestral Pueblo ruins in southwestern Colorado and neighboring New Mexico, Arizona and Utah, no other cliff dwellings rival those at Mesa Verde in size or architectural elegance. The people who built them had started a permanent community on top of Mesa Verde around A.D. 500, when they learned to cultivate corn and abandoned their previous nomadic way of life. Around A.D. 950, faced with the pressures of a growing population, they built an extensive system of irrigation ditches and reservoirs that allowed them to cultivate more land. After living in individual pit houses for six centuries, around A.D. 1100 they began building large pueblos on the mesa top. Examples of both the pit houses and the pueblos have been excavated and restored to provide visitors with a look at both stages of development.

Around A.D. 1200, for reasons archaeologists cannot agree on, the Mesa Verde people moved off the mesa top and into new

Mesa Verde Area

**DRIVING TOUR**

## On the Road to Ruins

Thousand-year-old structures built and later mysteriously abandoned by the ancestors of the Pueblo people are a source of fascination for many visitors to the Four Corners region. Visitors often have the mistaken impression that these ancient ruins are only found at Mesa Verde and a handful of other national park units in New Mexico and Arizona. The fact is, the entire region had a larger population in A.D. 1000 than it does today. You can spot cliff dwellings on the south-facing sides of most canyons, and you're never far from the remains of ancient village walls. This driving tour will take you to the best Ancestral Pueblo ruins that are open to the public.

**MESA VERDE**     Start your exploration of Southwestern Colorado's ancient heritage at **Mesa Verde National Park** (page 326), the most-visited pre-Columbian archaeological site in the United States (the rest of this tour will take you to other, far less crowded Ancestral Pueblo ruins). More extensively restored than any other Indian ruins in southwestern Colorado, the cliff dwellings on the sides of **Chapin Mesa** will help you imagine what other sites must have looked like in their prime, as will the dioramas in the museum. Plan to spend the morning on the main tour loop, then return to **Farview Visitors Center** for lunch and a bus tour to **Wetherill Mesa** to see the ongoing excavation and restoration of a mesatop pueblo.

**ANASAZI HERITAGE CENTER**     The main gate at Mesa Verde marks the beginning of a 106-mile, all-day driving tour of other ancient ruins. Leaving the national park, turn left on the main highway and drive west on Route 160 for nine miles to the intersection with Route 145. Turn right and go north for ten miles to Route 184. Turn left again and go west for a short distance to the Anasazi Heritage Center (page 330), where you can see the partially excavated ruins of Escalante and Dominguez pueblos. The visitors center here serves as the headquar-

dwellings built into the overhanging cliffs in canyons that sliced into the sides of the mesa. Experts who date Indian ruins by analyzing the tree rings of roof beams to see when they were cut have determined that almost all the great Mesa Verde cliff dwellings were built at the same time. Construction took just a few years, and they were not added on to later. Nobody knows for sure why they suddenly decided to build these unique dwellings. For many years, the theory was that warfare drove the people off the mesa top because the cliff dwellings were easier to defend.

ters for several sites in the area, including Lowry Ruins and Canyons of the Ancients. Allow one hour.

**LOWRY RUINS**    Continue west on Route 184 for eight miles to the junction with Route 666. Turn right and drive north for nine miles to the little town of Pleasant View. In the middle of town, watch for the "Lowry Ruins" sign at CC Road. Turn left on this partly paved road and drive straight for nine miles, ignoring side roads. After a slight curve to the left you'll see a turnoff to the parking area for Lowry Ruins (page 331). Allow one-half to one hour to see this strange pueblo ruin built on top of a great kiva.

**HOVENWEEP NATIONAL MONUMENT**    Leaving Lowry Ruins, go back the way you came for about three miles to 10 Road and turn right. Driving south for 19 miles, you'll cross into Utah and soon come to the visitors center for Hovenweep National Monument (page 331), which straddles the state line. You can see the visitors center and the unique **Square Tower** site in an hour or less. If you decide to explore the rough backroads that lead to other ruins groups, you're likely to find yourself spending the rest of the day here.

**McELMO CANYON**    Continuing south from the Hovenweep visitors center, after four miles you'll come to a "T" intersection. Turn left and drive two more miles to reach **McElmo Canyon Road** (page 332), also called Road G. Turn left again and you'll almost immediately cross the state line back into Colorado. Although some pasturage along the sides of the road is private, everything beyond it is part of the vast **Canyons of the Ancients National Monument** (page 332). Though several rugged four-wheel-drive roads lead back into canyons along the way, only **Sand Canyon Trail** (page 357) is officially open to national monument visitors. The trailhead is on your left 19 miles east of the state line. Hike all or part of the six-mile trail up the canyon to view a series of unnamed and almost unknown cliff dwellings and pueblos. From Sand Canyon, continue on McElmo Canyon Road for 12 more miles to return to Cortez and the junction of Routes 160 and 666.

But no extraordinary numbers of burials have been found that would indicate battles, and no burials reveal evidence of wounds from warfare. A more recent theory is that after inhabiting the mesa for 700 years, they may have been running out of firewood. The cliff dwellings, experts point out, might be easier to heat than the older pueblos.

Then comes the biggest mystery of all. About 100 years after the Ancestral Pueblo moved into the cliff dwellings, they abandoned them and left Mesa Verde for good. Most experts believe the Mesa Verde people migrated southward around A.D. 1300, briefly inhabiting the abandoned pueblos at Aztec and Chaco Canyon—which had been abandoned 50 years before by another Ancestral Pueblo group—and then establishing Acoma Pueblo on a high mesa near Grants, New Mexico. The reason they left Mesa Verde has been a subject of ceaseless speculation among archaeologists. War? Disease? Again, no large number of burials or corpses has been found that would indicate such a catastrophe. Drought or famine? Abandoned storerooms containing corn and beans make the food shortage theory doubtful. Again, the most appealing theory is that their civilization ended in an energy crisis when they burned the last wood on the mesa. This theory, however, does not explain why the people walked away leaving weapons, jewelry and kitchen utensils around as if they would be back by nightfall.

The main ruins area at Mesa Verde is below the rim of Chapin Mesa, 21 miles from the park entrance. There is an **archaeology museum** at the starting point of the two six-mile loop drives that take motorists and cyclists along canyon rims to sites such as **Cliff Palace** and **Balcony House**. Exploring the largest ruins involves some climbing on ladders and narrow trails. An unpaved road from Far View Visitors Center leads to the more remote pueblo sites of **Step House** and **Long House** on Wetherill Mesa. Public access to most parts of Mesa Verde is restricted to protect unexcavated archaeological sites. The strict visitor controls makes the park seem very crowded much of the time, but the expanse of land untouched by humans harbors an abundance of wild animals, which often show themselves by the roadside. Keep your eyes peeled for mule deer and wild horses. Mountain lions, bears and bighorn sheep are also spotted sometimes, and the mesa provides habitat for more than 160 species of birds.

The town of **Dolores**, located 17 miles northwest of Mesa Verde's entrance gate via Route 160 West and Route 145, seems so low-key that you may wonder whether anybody lives there. In truth, things have livened up a lot since the completion of **McPhee Reservoir**, just west of town, boosted the bait-and-tackle business. Near the lake is the Bureau of Land Management's **Anasazi Heritage Center** (the name was not changed when the National Park Service expunged the word "Anasazi" elsewhere as politically incorrect), which displays Pueblo Indian artifacts from the classic period (11th to 13th centuries) that were found in canyons now flooded by the reservoir. Nearby are two partially excavated Ancestral Pueblo sites. ~ Route 184, Dolores; 970-882-4811, fax 970-882-7035; www.co.blm.gov.

If you'd like to get a taste of an archaeological dig yourself, contact **Crow Canyon Archaeological Center**, which offers hands-on day programs for adults at surprisingly reasonable prices. ~ 2339D Road K, Dolores; 970-565-8975, 800-422-8975; www. crowcanyon.org.

In Dolores you can see **Galloping Goose #5**, a gas-powered hybrid—part Buick passenger bus and part boxcar—that carried passengers on the narrow-gauge trail routes of the San Juans from 1931 to 1951. The local historical society has been working since 1987 to restore the strange vehicle so that it can run again on a track up Lost Canyon.

In addition to corn, the Ancestral Pueblo grew beans, squash and to-bacco and raised turkeys for meat.

For most travelers, Dolores is a stop on the San Juan Skyway, from which Route 145 will take them to Telluride (see "San Juan Skyway Area" later in this chapter). But if you want to explore more ancient Ancestral Pueblo ruins—or just want to go around the mountains instead of over them—Route 666 takes you northwest to **Dove Creek**, from which a long and not particularly interesting Route 141 will lead you to either Grand Junction or Montrose. A dirt-road detour on 10.00 Road just south of town will bring you to a remote campground on the rim of the **Dolores River Canyon** for a panoramic view of the red canyon walls and the wild river far below.

The main point of interest worth searching the maze of parallel farm roads in the Dove Creek area for is **Lowry Ruins**, a small ◄ HIDDEN Ancestral Pueblo located about eight miles west of the hamlet of Pleasant View on a straight dirt road marked by small but plentiful signs. The three-story pueblo, built in stages over a period of 30 years in the late 11th century, contained 40 rooms and eight round kivas believed to have been used for religious rituals. Entering one of the rooms at the front of the pueblo, you descend into a lower room behind it and another behind and below that one, to find yourself on the rim of a large kiva built beneath the center of the pueblo. Traces of stucco murals that decorated the kiva walls are still visible. Down the hill from the main pueblo, a very large great pueblo stands alone. The size of the great kiva and the number of smaller ones is out of proportion to the size of the pueblo, which could only have housed about 100 people. Archaeologists believe it must have served as a ceremonial and government center. Some speculate that it may not have been lived in by families at all but by an elite group of priests. The site was abandoned around A.D. 1150 after only 80 years of use. It has no visitors center or other facilities. ~ Pleasant View; 970-247-4082.

From Lowry Ruins or from Route 666 near Pleasant View, several dirt roads are marked with small signs that keep you aimed in the right direction for **Hovenweep National Monument**, which ◄ HIDDEN straddles the Colorado–Utah state line. One of the least-visited

National Park Service units in Colorado, Hovenweep is far enough off the beaten path so that you're likely to have the place completely to yourself—a welcome change from the crowds of Mesa Verde for anyone who wants to contemplate the mysteries of the Ancestral Pueblo in solitude and silence. Admission. ~ 40 miles west of Cortez off Route 666; 970-562-4282; e-mail hoveninfo@nps.gov.

The main ruins, the **Square Tower group**, has a ranger station and campground (but no food, water, firewood or gasoline; stock up on what you may need before venturing out here). An interpretive trail leads around the canyon rim to several small pueblos and the most distinctive feature of the Hovenweep ruins: several tall, square towers both at the bottom of the canyon and along the rim. They are unique to the Hovenweep sites, and their function is unknown. There are also five other ruins groups in Hovenweep—the Holly, Hackberry Canyon, Cutthroat Castle, Goodman Point and Horseshoe sites. All are in remote locations along rough back roads that are not well marked and may require high-clearance or four-wheel-drive vehicles at some times of the year. Ask for a map and check on current road conditions at the Square Tower Ruins ranger station.

HIDDEN ▶ The partially unpaved **McElmo Canyon Road** (also called Road G) from Hovenweep National Monument takes you 40 miles east through a lonely red-rock canyon to join Route 160 near Cortez. Almost all the land north of the road, and some of the land to the south, is part of the new **Canyons of the Ancients National Monument**. The 164,000-acre park was set aside by presidential proclamation in June 2000 to protect the more than 20,000 archaeological sites hidden away in its remote canyons. No facilities have been built yet in the monument, most of which is inaccessible to visitors. There is one hiking trail. ~ Anasazi Heritage Center, Route 184, Dolores; 970-882-5200, fax 970-882-7035; www.co.blm.gov/canm.

South of Mesa Verde are the adjoining **Southern Ute and Ute Mountain Indian reservations**, the only Indian lands in Colorado. In addition to **Navajo Lake** and the **Ute Mountain Casino** in Towaoc, visitor attractions on the Ute reservations include the **Southern Ute Indian Cultural Center**, the only tribally owned and operated museum in Colorado, with exhibits of Ute beadwork, leatherwork and other arts and crafts as well as ancient Ancestral Pueblo artifacts found on the reservation. Admission. ~ Ignacio; 970-563-4531.

There's also the **Ute Mountain Tribal Park**, a remote group of Ancestral Pueblo cliff-dwelling ruins that can be visited only with an Indian guide on a fairly strenuous hike or mountain-bike tour. The most interesting feature of these cliff dwellings is a kiva containing one of the few surviving examples of Ancestral Pueblo ceremonial murals. ~ Towaoc; 970-565-3751 ext. 330, 800-847-

5485, fax 970-564-5317; www.utemountainute.com/tribalpark. htm, e-mail utepark@fone.net.

In the southwestern corner of the Ute Mountain Indian Reservation is the spot where the Colorado–Utah and Colorado–New Mexico state lines intersect, the only place in the United States where four states touch one another (Arizona is the fourth state). At the **Four Corners Monument Navajo Tribal Park**, a large plaque inlaid in granite and brass just off Route 160 in the middle of nowhere says so. Navajos sell jewelry from the tailgates of pickup trucks in the monument parking lot. There is nothing else around.

The only lodging in Mesa Verde National Park is at **Far View Lodge** on the summit of Navajo Hill, commanding a spectacular panoramic view out over the valleys that lie to the south, clear to the huge rock formation known as Shiprock in New Mexico and the Lukachukai Mountains in the Navajo lands of Arizona. The lodge's 150 nonsmoking rooms are in duplex and four-plex units scattered across juniper-covered hillsides. The spacious rooms are decorated in Ancestral Pueblo motifs and have private sun porches. Closed late October to mid-April. ~ 970-529-4421, 800-449-2288, fax 970-529-4411; www.mesaverde.com. MODERATE.

**LODGING**

If your taste runs to something a little more secluded, there's **Jersey Jim**, an isolated fire lookout tower that has been converted into a guest cabin. After driving 14 miles from Mancos along an unpaved national forest road, you have to climb several flights of stairs to reach your room at the top. Amenities include a stove,

◄ HIDDEN

**AUTHOR FAVORITE**

It's a little disconcerting to find T-1 high-speed internet access and videoconferencing facilities in a remote "ghost town" that looks as if it shouldn't even have electricity. Could this be the future of tourism? Nestled in a green valley adjoining San Juan National Forest, **Dunton Hot Springs** has 12 new luxury guest cabins with modern amenities, reconstructed using materials from 19th-century mine-camp buildings. Each is individually decorated with antiques, handcrafted furniture and folk art, and has a fireplace or vintage wood-burning stove. The resort has a bathhouse with a large geothermal pool, another hot spring in a tepee, and several open-air hot springs around the grounds. Activities include horseback riding, massage therapy, trout fishing and, in winter, heliskiing. Private group retreats are the focus here, so call ahead to check availability. ~ Route 145, Dolores; 970-882-4800; www.duntonhotsprings.com. ULTRA-DELUXE.

a refrigerator and lanterns; bring your own sleeping bag. Water can be brought from a campground four miles away via a pulley system. No TV or phone. Accessible late May to mid-October. Reservations required; you can make them up to a year in advance. ~ Call the Jersey Jim Foundation at 970-533-7060. BUDGET.

In Dolores, the **Rio Grande Southern** has eight small rooms filled with antiques—quite possibly the original furnishings; the hotel has been in operation since 1894. A full breakfast is included in the room rate. Closed January. ~ 101 5th Street, Dolores; 970-882-7527, 800-258-0434. MODERATE.

**HIDDEN ►** Off McElmo Road between Cortez and Hovenweep National Monument, at the doorstep of the new Canyons of the Ancients National Monument, you'll find **Kelly Place**. The three adobe casitas and the main lodge with its seven guest rooms are surrounded by fruit orchards at the mouth of a sandstone canyon. You can explore Ancestral Pueblo ruins on the 100-acre grounds. Breakfast is included in the room rate. ~ 14663 Road G, Cortez; 970-565-3125, 800-745-4885, fax 970-565-3540; www.kelly place.com, e-mail kellypl@fone.net. MODERATE.

The casino resorts operated by the Ute Indian tribes offer spacious new guest rooms at amazingly reasonable rates. The **Sky Ute Casino and Lodge**, located southeast of Durango near Navajo Lake in Ignacio, the capital of the Southern Ute Reservation, has 32 standard motor inn units opening onto a courtyard with a heated swimming pool. ~ 14826 Route 172 North, Ignacio; 970-563-3000, 800-876-7017; www.skyutecasino.com. BUDGET TO MODERATE. Its rival, the four-story **Ute Mountain Casino, Hotel & Resort**, located south of Cortez on the way to Four Corners Monument, has 106 guest rooms and suites and a swimming pool. ~ 3 Weeminuche Drive, Towaoc; 970-565-8837, 800-258-8007; www.utemountaincasino.com, e-mail rjones@fone.net. BUDGET TO MODERATE.

**DINING**  In Mesa Verde National Park, the **Metate Room** at Far View Lodge serves an unexotic assortment of Southwestern dishes, and

---

## A MEAL IN MANCOS

The best dining in the Mesa Verde area is at **Millwood Junction**, seven miles east of the park boundary in Mancos. The dining room may look rough-hewn, but the fare is first-rate, featuring such entrées as steak and lobster, châteaubriand and blackened catfish. The salad bar is a vegetarian's dream. Lunch and dinner mid-May to mid-October; dinner only, Thursday through Sunday, the rest of the year. ~ 101 Railroad Avenue, Mancos; 970-533-7338. MODERATE TO ULTRA-DELUXE.

also has steak, shrimp and a great view. ~ 970-529-4423. MODERATE TO DELUXE. The nearby **Far View Terrace Café** (actually a cafeteria), serves an uninspired selection of burgers, sandwiches and salads, along with Navajo tacos (fry bread topped with chili *con carne*, lettuce and cheese). ~ 970-529-4481. BUDGET TO MODERATE. Similar fare is available in the ruins area at **Spruce Tree Terrace**. ~ 970-529-4521. BUDGET TO MODERATE.

The sleepy little town of Dolores boasts one of the finest restaurants along the San Juan Skyway, the **Old Germany Restaurant & Lounge**. In a renovated turn-of-the-20th-century home, the restaurant is decorated with memorabilia imported from Bavaria, including 800-year-old antiques. The food is also authentically Bavarian. Savor a delicacy such as *paprikaschnitzel* sausage or sauerbraten with German potato salad. ~ 200 South 8th Street, Dolores; 970-882-7549. BUDGET TO MODERATE.

The Sky Ute Lodge has two restaurants, both set just off the casino floor. The sunny, soft-pink **Pino Nuche Restaurant** specializes in Southwestern food with New Mexico–style dishes and a few native options such as Indian tacos (standard taco toppings served flat over fry bread.) The **Rolling Thunder Cafe** serves simple fare such as burgers, pizza and deli-style sandwiches and is open late. ~ 14826 Route 172 North, Ignacio; 970-563-3000 or 800-876-7017; www.skyutecasino.com. BUDGET.

Although it is the larger of the two Indian gaming resorts, the Ute Mountain Casino, Hotel & Resort, has only one restaurant—**Kuchu's**, which serves a wide range of food, from Mexican and Indian dishes to steaks and Alaskan king crab legs. It also has Vegas-style all-you-can-eat buffets for lunch and dinner, with a seafood buffet on Fridays and a brunch buffet on weekends. The restaurant prides itself on its desserts. ~ 3 Weeminuche Drive, Towaoc; 970-565-8837, 800-258-8007; www.utemountainca sino.com. BUDGET TO MODERATE.

**SHOPPING**

In Mesa Verde National Park, curio concessions at Morefield Campground, Far View Visitors Center and Chapin Mesa sell a full range of T-shirts and trinkets as well as a good selection of books on the region's natural history and Indian cultures. Among the more interesting gift items are Navajo and Zuni jewelry and reproductions of Mesa Verde–style pottery manufactured by non-Indians. Here and elsewhere in southwestern Colorado you will also find Ute Mountain pottery, manufactured near Towaoc by the Ute people. This factory-made pottery is not a traditional Ute craft; like most nomadic Indians, ancestral Utes made their vessels of less fragile materials like leather and gourds. But it is pretty. You can see the pottery made and buy it from the source, at the **Ute Mountain Pottery Plant**. ~ 156 Route 160, Towaoc; 970-565-8548.

**NIGHTLIFE** The Ute Indian tribes operate two casinos on their reservations south of Durango and Cortez. Although both are in the middle of nowhere, they operate free shuttles to and from major towns in the area and rank among the most popular gambling houses in the state. However, unlike other Colorado casinos, the ones on tribal land do not allow alcoholic beverages. The **Sky Ute Casino** on the Southern Ute Reservation has blackjack and three-card poker tables as well as bingo, video poker and, of course, slot machines. Special events, from poker championships and boxing matches to musical concerts, are scheduled on most weekends. Open round the clock. ~ 14826 Route 172 North, Ignacio; 970-563-3000 or 800-876-7017; www.skyutecasino.com. Roughly twice as large, the **Ute Mountain Casino** in Towaoc, the capital of the Ute Mountain Indian Reservation south of Cortez, has table games, keno, high-stakes bingo and 500 slot machines. Open until 4:00 a.m.~ 3 Weeminuche Drive, Towaoc; 970-565-8837, 800-258-8007.

**PARKS** **MANCOS STATE PARK** 🏃 🛶 ⛴ ⛵ ⛴ A three-mile road winds into the mountains above Mancos to Jackson Lake, the reservoir that provides the small town with drinking and irrigation water. The lake is open to nonmotorized boating and fishing (rainbow and brown trout). A four-mile trail runs from the lake along slopes and ridgelines bright with wildflowers to join a larger trail network in the adjoining San Juan National Forest. The park is open in the winter for cross-country skiing. There are restrooms and a picnic area with tables. Day-use fee, $3. ~ From Mancos, go north on Route 184 for one-half mile, then right on County Road 42 for four miles and left on County Road N; 970-533-7065.

▲ There are 33 RV/tent sites (no hookups) scattered along the lakeshore; $12 per night. Drinking water is available.

▼▼▼▼▼▼▼▼▼▼▼▼▼▼▼▼

# San Juan Skyway Area

To experience the San Juans by car, drive the 231-mile San Juan Skyway, which follows paved Routes 160, 184, 145, 62 and 550 to form a loop beginning and ending in Durango. The route is clearly marked with "Scenic Byway" signs. In fact, the San Juan Skyway was one of the first routes selected under a 1988 federal law directing the National Forest Service to designate the most scenic driving routes in national forests as scenic byways. But you don't really need special road signs to tell you that you're on one of America's most spectacular drives.

I recommend traveling the San Juan Skyway clockwise, mainly because drivers unaccustomed to edgy mountain roads will find that the road that climbs south from Ouray is much easier to drive uphill than downhill. (If I had to choose either the Dolores–Telluride leg of the trip or the Ouray–Silverton leg as a one-way route between Durango and the Gunnison or Grand Junction area, it would be a hard decision indeed; the whole loop route is filled with variety and scenic beauty on a grand scale. However, the segment between Ouray and Silverton has what is probably the most breathtaking scenery.)

First, drive west from Durango on Route 160 to Mancos, the small town near the turnoff to Mesa Verde National Park; from there, go northwest on Route 184 to Dolores (see the "Mesa Verde Area" in this chapter). Follow Route 145 north from Dolores. At

**SIGHTS**

San Juan
Skyway Area

the tiny community of Stoner a side road turns off to follow the **West Fork of the Dolores River**, a popular fishing area. Unpaved forest roads provide access to the aspen-covered plateau above the rim of Dolores Canyon. Route 145, the main highway up the East Fork of the river, is equally scenic. Past Stoner, the highway begins its long climb into the high mountains and ultimately to the summit of **Lizard Head Pass** (10,222 feet), where there is a trailhead for a hiking trail to the top ridgeline of Lizard Head Peak, the mountain with the 400-foot spire of granite on top. Rock climbers rate the monolith as one of the most difficult technical ascents on earth.

Past Lizard Head Pass, a side trip along the San Juan Skyway brings you to **Telluride**. No other ski town in Colorado is as far from a major city. This fact alone has made the town irresistible to skiers who want to *really* escape the outside world. In fact, only Aspen, in its glitzier way, can rival Telluride for away-from-it-all-ness. But when it comes to mountain scenery, Telluride, set in a basin surrounded by peaks over 13,000 feet high, actually has Aspen beat. Out past the end of 1st Street, Ingram Falls plunges hundreds of feet down craggy cliffs that stand like castle walls. All around, snow-capped mountain turrets protect the town and its residents from the outside world.

For the best view imaginable, ride the **gondola**. It sweeps sightseers, hikers, bikers and cross-country skiers 2000 feet up to the top of Coonskin Ridge, providing easy access to the surrounding peaks, and then swoops down the other side of the ridge to Mountain Village, an exclusive Euro-style condo development, spa and shopping area that makes for a striking contrast to Victorian-style Telluride. Built as a unique municipal public transportation project, the gondola is free to all. It runs nonstop year-round except for the off-season months of April and mid-October to mid-November, when it shuts down for inspection and servicing.

Telluride was founded in 1875 as a gold-mining camp. The town's rebirth started in 1971, when plans to build a ski area there were unveiled. Even before the first ski lift was running, a motley assortment of ski bums, trust-fund babies, realtors, lawyers and Aspen dropouts had moved into the near-deserted old mining town to buy up abandoned buildings for back taxes. Many of the newcomers had seen resort money swallow the souls of other historic Colorado gold-rush towns, so the new city fathers promptly adopted rigid preservation laws. Today, the historic district is free of new buildings, and turn-of-the-20th-century structures have been refurbished instead of replaced. Historic landmark buildings include the **Sheridan Opera House**, where Sarah Bernhardt once performed and William Jennings Bryan made a speech, and the **Bank of Telluride**, the first bank Butch Cassidy ever robbed. The bygone glory of the gold era is recalled at the **Telluride His-**

torical **Museum**, located in the town's restored Old Miners' Hospital. Stop in to find out about the days when Telluride supported 26 saloons and 12 houses of ill repute and the miners returned home on winter days by sledding on shovels from the mines down the mountainside to town. Closed in spring and fall. ~ 201 West Gregory Avenue, Telluride; 970-728-3344.

Visitors can drive up to the old **Idarado Mine and Mill**, the town's biggest employer for more than 50 years in the late 19th and early 20th centuries. Nearby, **Bridal Veil Falls** has the longest vertical drop of any waterfall in Colorado—365 feet.

North of Telluride, Route 145 descends from the mountains. To continue on the San Juan Skyway loop route, turn east on Route 62 at Placerville and then south on Route 550 at Ridgway. Route 550 goes all the way back to Durango.

**Last Dollar Road** (Forest Road 638), an unpaved route that turns off the main road three miles west of Telluride and runs north over high mesa country to rejoin the San Juan Skyway near Ridgway, is a favorite with four-wheel-drivers—especially in the fall—because of the picturesque old ranch buildings and dazzling stands of aspen along the way. The first few miles from the Telluride end are the roughest, and motorists in low-clearance two-wheel-drive cars should inquire locally before trying it. An abbreviated version of the trip can be made from the Ridgway end, taking a left fork that returns you to the highway before reaching the rugged, rocky stretch of Last Dollar Road.

◄ HIDDEN

Most motorists on the San Juan Skyway barely notice the little town of **Ridgway** as they drive through it. Situated in the center of a broad bowl-shaped ranching valley walled in by distant mountain ridgelines, its charms present themselves less dramatically than other towns along the route. Yet a milder climate, longer hours of direct sunlight and a central location within half an hour's drive of Telluride, Ouray and Montrose give Ridgway a quiet appeal.

**sights**

**AUTHOR FAVORITE**

Two natural features that add to Ouray's unique character are the dramatic cliffs that enfold the town and the many waterfalls that plunge over them. The best place to get up close to both is the spectacular **Box Canyon Falls and Park**. The 285-foot-high falls have sliced a canyon so narrow that when you walk into its misty depths along the narrow boardwalks and century-old steel bridge, you'll feel as if you're in a cave filled to overflowing with the noise and spray of down-rushing water. It's the only waterfall in the area where you have to pay an admission charge, and it's worth every penny. ~ Route 550 South, Ouray; 970-325-4464.

More celebrities have homes here than in any other town on the San Juan Skyway; General Norman Schwartzkopf owns a vacation home in the area, actor Dennis Weaver lives here and operates a restaurant and an environmental foundation, and designer Ralph Lauren owns a vast cattle ranch just west of town.

In the farming community of **Montrose**, is the **Ute Indian Museum**. Landscaped with columbines of many colors, the museum occupies land that was once the farm of Chief Ouray, the great statesman of the Ute people. He is remembered for negotiating an 1873 treaty with the U.S. government that established a Ute homeland in the San Juan Mountains. Soon after Ouray's death in 1880, the treaty was broken and his people were forced into the badlands of Utah to make way for gold prospectors. Visitors to the museum can see beaded costumes and artifacts, photographs of Ouray and other Ute leaders and a bigger-than-life copy of the broken treaty. Admission. ~ 17253 Chipeta Road, Montrose; 970-249-3098.

**Chipeta Park**, a grassy expanse adjoining the museum, is named for Chief Ouray's wife. The highway re-enters the mountains through the Uncompahgre River Canyon, whose maroon walls rise so steeply that mountain streams plunge over the rim and fall hundreds of feet before splashing against the cliffs. The deepest part of the canyon is the dramatic setting for the village of Ouray.

With neither a ski area nor a railroad, **Ouray** has been spared the kind of industrial tourism that has swallowed other Colorado mining towns whole. The town's slightly old-fashioned charm is as authentic as can be. Most buildings in town date back to the turn of the 20th century and before. Some have been refurbished and painted in rainbow color schemes; others, such as the shell of the grand old Ouray Hotel, built in 1887 and closed in 1964, stand vacant. Main Street has endured good and bad times, and local businesses keep on keeping the spirit of small-town Colorado alive.

Ouray's special claim to fame is its hot springs. At the northern edge of town, the municipal **Ouray Hot Springs Pool** has an Olympic-size swimming pool and a smaller, hotter (104°F) pool. Admission. ~ Route 550, Ouray; 970-325-4638. Other options include the private outdoor hot tub, available to the public by the hour with reservations, at the European-style **Wiesbaden Hot Springs Spa**. Admission. ~ 625 5th Street, Ouray; 970-325-4347; www.wiesbadenhotsprings.com.

At **Orvis Hot Springs** between Ridgway and Ouray, you'll find a sand-bottomed natural pool with a hot waterfall and a smaller, very hot pool (both bathing suits–optional) as well as an indoor pool (suits required). Admission. ~ 1585 County Road 3, Ridgway; 970-626-5324; www.orvishotsprings.com.

Waterfalls are another Ouray specialty. A dozen or more of them plummet down the cliffs surrounding the town. The most accessible is **Lower Cascade Falls**, reached by a half-mile trail that starts a few blocks uphill from Main Street. Farther up the cliffs, the same stream takes an earlier and even longer fall at **Upper Cascade Falls**, reached by a steep trail two and a half miles long that begins at the natural amphitheater south of town.

Ouray is also an excellent base for exploring old mining roads by mountain bike or four-wheel-drive vehicle. **Engineer Pass Road** ◀ HIDDEN leads to the early-day mining district around Mineral Point and Animas Forks, one of Colorado's best ghost towns, to join the **Alpine Loop Backcountry Byway** (see "Creede–Lake City Area" ◀ HIDDEN in Chapter Seven). From there other jeep roads go to Lake City and Silverton. Another great four-wheel-drive trip is on rugged **Camp Bird Road**, which leads past the abandoned mines and ghost towns ◀ HIDDEN of what was once the busiest gold and silver district of the San Juans to Yankee Boy Basin, a broad expanse of alpine meadows that bursts with red, yellow and purple wildflowers in summer.

An easier way to explore the Ouray district's mining heritage is to tour the **Bachelor-Syracuse Mine**. Mine carts take visitors two-thirds of a mile into the mountain to see where hard-rock miners followed veins of gold and silver ore for a hundred years before the mine ceased operations in 1984. Admission. ~ 122 County Road 14, Ouray; 970-325-0220.

Mining is also the focus of the small **Ouray County Museum**. Exhibits include an ore train and a re-creation of an assay office, as well as several rooms of Victorian-era antiques and an old-time law office. The building that houses the museum was originally a hospital, and several upstairs rooms have been restored to offer a glimpse of 19th-century health care. Admission. ~ 420 6th Avenue, Ouray; 970-325-4576.

South of Ouray, Route 550 climbs steep cliffs in a sweeping series of switchbacks and finally reaches the summit of **Red Moun-**

### THE MOST CELEBRATIONS PER CAPITA IN THE WEST

Telluride's 300-inch annual snowfall makes the town a skiers' mecca. During the summer, Telluride is the festival capital of Colorado. In the mid-1970s, residents hatched a plan to boost the local economy during the no-snow season by hosting the Telluride Bluegrass Festival. It drew huge crowds, and spinoffs in the form of a jazz festival and a film festival came quickly. Today, all three have attained international stature, and other festivals completely fill the town's calendar from mid-May through September except for one weekend in July, when the annual Telluride Nothing Festival packs 'em in.

tain Pass (11,008 feet), the highest point on the San Juan Skyway. Well above timberline, this part of the route offers the most spectacular views of the remote Needle Mountains in the Weminuche Wilderness to the east. Long before the Forest Service dubbed it part of the San Juan Skyway, the stretch of Route 550 between Ouray and Silverton was known as the **Million Dollar Highway**. Some say the name came from the high cost of building the road back in the days when a million dollars was a lot of money for road construction, while others say the road's foundation, built with mine tailings, contains $1 million worth of gold ore. It may well be the most scenic 23 miles of highway in America.

**Silverton** was founded in 1874 as the center of what would prove to be one of the wealthiest mining districts in southwestern Colorado. Large deposits of gold, silver, copper and lead were located here, but the town could be reached only by crossing high mountain passes, so only limited amounts of ore could be shipped out until the **Denver & Rio Grande Railroad** (now the Durango & Silverton Narrow-Gauge Railroad) reached the town in 1882. As Silverton boomed to a population of 4000 in the next few years, it saw the construction of elegant false-front Victorian buildings along Main Street. The boom faded slowly, until finally the last of the mines closed during World War II. Nearly abandoned, the town became nothing more than a roadside curiosity on Route 550. Motion-picture companies occasionally slapped fresh coats of paint on the old buildings and used Main Street as an Old West location. The revival of the Durango & Silverton Narrow-Gauge Railroad as a scenic train for tourists brought a new wave of prosperity to Silverton, whose sidewalks and curio shops bustle with train passengers every day from about 11 a.m. to 2 p.m. The rest of the time, the town is very quiet.

> Silverton's mines have never shut down but continue producing silver, lead, zinc and other minerals, giving rise to the local motto, "The town that never quit."

The **San Juan County Museum** is housed in the former county jail adjacent to the county courthouse. The memorabilia and photographs on display there recount the mining era in Silverton and several other mining towns that have since faded into oblivion. There are displays about mining, including an exhibit of minerals from local mines, and railroads, including one of the last railcars remaining from the days when the Denver and Rio Grande ran narrow-gauge trains between Durango and Silverton, but perhaps the most interesting aspect of the museum is the old jail itself, with its colorful anecdotes of mine camp law and order. Admission. ~ 1559 Greene Street, Silverton; 970-387-5838.

On the hillside west of Silverton stands **Christ of the Mines**, a larger-than-life statue of Jesus with outstretched arms, carved from a 12-ton block of marble. The sculpture is dedicated to the protection of miners, although it was only erected in 1959, long after the mining era had ended in most Colorado towns. Tenth Street leads out of town and climbs the hillside to the statue.

Besides allowing you to stroll the streets and browse through the town during off-hours, driving to Silverton lets you explore back roads in the surrounding national forest. A short distance north of town, Main Street becomes Forest Road 586. The pavement soon ends, but the road continues past the scattered remains of the old mining towns of Howardsville and Eureka. It is passable without four-wheel-drive as far as **Animas Forks**, one of the most picturesque ghost towns in the San Juans thanks to its dramatic timberline setting. Beyond that, rough roads suited only for four-wheel-drive vehicles and mountain bikes climb to join the Alpine Loop Backcountry Byway in the heart of the San Juans.

◄ HIDDEN

**LODGING**

Telluride's grand old hotel, the three-story red-brick **New Sheridan Hotel**, operated for 30 years—from 1895 to 1925—and then stood abandoned for more than a half-century. Thanks to a meticulous restoration completed in 1977, the hotel's lobby and guest rooms have recaptured the glory of bygone days with rich, warm period decor. The guest accommodations vary in size from rather small rooms with shared baths to larger rooms with private baths and a single opulent suite with impressive views of the town and the mountains. Room rates vary wildly, from the ultra-deluxe range with a five-night minimum stay during peak ski season to the budget range with no minimum stay on summer weeknights. ~ 231 West Colorado Avenue, Telluride; 970-728-4351, 800-200-1891, fax 970-728-5024; www.newsheridan.com, e-mail info@ newsheridan.com. MODERATE TO ULTRA-DELUXE.

A great Telluride bed and breakfast is **San Sophia**. Although situated in the historic district, San Sophia is of recent vintage, designed and built as an inn, with gabled dormers and a central tower. The 16 guest rooms, each named after a gold mine, have soothing pastel interiors appointed with brass beds, etched mirrors, stained glass windows and extra-large bathtubs. A full gourmet breakfast and afternoon wine and hors d'oeuvres are included in the rates. Closed mid-October to mid-November and mid-April to mid-May. ~ 330 West Pacific Avenue, Telluride; 970-728-3001, 800-537-4781, fax 970-728-6226; www.sansophia.com, e-mail info@sansophia.com. DELUXE TO ULTRA-DELUXE.

The **Bear Creek Bed & Breakfast** is located on the upper floors of a historic brick building at the east end of Telluride's main street, making it the closest accommodation to the stage area for the various summer music festivals. The nine rooms are contemporary in style, and the rooftop hot tub is one of the best spots in town from which to watch the sunset. ~ 221 East Colorado Avenue,

Telluride; 970-728-6681, 800-338-7064, fax 970-728-3636; www.
bearcreektelluride.com, e-mail info@bearcreektelluride.com.
MODERATE TO ULTRA-DELUXE.

Another Telluride bed and breakfast, **Pennington's Mountain
Village**, ranks as one of the most luxurious and expensive B&Bs
in Colorado. It is located by the 12th fairway of the golf course
in Telluride Mountain Village, the newly built area on the mesa
five miles from the historic district. The inn's ridgeline site affords
spectacular panoramic views from every window and balcony. A
magnificent circular staircase leads up to 12 guest rooms, each
with its own whirlpool bath and private deck. The rooms are
decorated in French country style. Common areas include a sunken
library and sitting room with a big fireplace and a game room with
a pool table. ~ 100 Pennington Court, Telluride; 970-728-5337,
800-543-1437, fax 970-728-5338. ULTRA-DELUXE.

Although Telluride lodging tends to be very expensive in peak
season, there is one affordable hostelry in town—the **Oak Street
Inn**. This hostel, situated in a building that was originally a Meth-
odist church and affiliated with American Youth Hostels (AYH),
provides very plain private rooms and also has six-bed dormitory
rooms at youth hostel prices. All rooms have shared baths. The
best features are the coed sauna and the upstairs TV lounge
where a young, enthusiastic crowd often hangs out. Closed mid-
April to mid-May. ~ 134 North Oak Street, Telluride; 970-728-
3383. BUDGET.

Santa Fe–style charm sets the **Chipeta Sun Lodge** in Ridgway
apart from other bed-and-breakfast accommodations along the
San Juan Skyway. The 12-unit inn, built in 1994, is warmed by
passive solar heat from the two-story picture windows that fill
the south wall of the spacious lobby. Guest rooms have queen-
or king-size beds with down comforters, rustic Southwestern furniture and Mexican-tile private baths, including one with a private spa tub. Centrally located between Telluride, Montrose and
Ouray, this is a great base camp for touring the area—and it's
surprisingly affordable compared to other San Juan Skyway B&Bs.
~ 304 South Lena, Ridgway; 970-626-3737, 800-633-5868, fax
970-626-3715. MODERATE TO DELUXE.

Ouray offers affordable luxury in lodging along the San Juan
Skyway. Even during the peak summer season, rates here are less
than they would be for comparable accommodations in Telluride.
In winter, skiers can actually save hundreds of dollars on lodging
by staying in Ouray and driving an hour to Telluride Ski Resort.
Many Ouray inns participate in a continuing co-promotion campaign that gives visitors who stay there during the winter discounts
on Telluride lift tickets and free admission to Ouray's municipal
hot springs.

Ouray's original landmark hostelry, the Beaumont Hotel (circa 1887), kept its doors open until 1964, then closed them for good. The shell of the elegant old building still dominates Main Street, and maybe someday investors will come along to restore it. In the meantime, two smaller historic hotels operate in town. Back in the 1880s, the **St. Elmo Hotel** was a low-rent boardinghouse for mine laborers' families, but times have changed. Today, this intimate nine-room hotel is full of antiques and period reproductions, stained glass, polished wood and brass trim. Guest rooms, each one individually decorated, have brass beds, lace curtains and ornate mining-era wallpaper. ~ 426 Main Street, Ouray; 970-325-4951, 866-243-1502, fax 970-325-0348; www.stelmo hotel.com, e-mail innkeeper@stelmohotel.com. DELUXE.

The **Historic Western Hotel** opened as a hotel in 1891 and operated as a boardinghouse for mine workers until World War II. Closed but never quite abandoned—it served for a while as office space and a local museum—the three-story wood-frame hotel with its grandiose whitewashed facade is mostly original, refurbished but not rebuilt. The period antiques that grace the 14 small guest rooms and the common areas are genuine but not fancy; they speak with eloquence of daily life in the Old West. Most rooms have shared baths. A bar and restaurant are on the premises. ~ 210 7th Avenue, Ouray; 970-325-4645, 888-624-8403, fax 970-325-0773; www.historicwesternhotel.com. BUDGET TO MODERATE.

The most elegant of Ouray's bed-and-breakfast inns, the **China Clipper** is a three-story, 7800-square-foot mansion on a quiet residential street. The sitting room and elegant formal dining room are accented with antiques and mementos from the owners' Asian travels. Eleven individually decorated guest rooms have queen-size beds and private baths, and some are outfitted with fireplaces and two-person jacuzzis. The house has a hot tub for guests' use in a

**EX-SPA-RIENCE**

A different kind of hot-spring experience awaits at the **Wiesbaden Hot Springs Spa and Lodgings**. Originally started as Mother Buchanan's Bathhouse in 1879 and later used as a hospital, the place was converted into a European-style spa in the late 1970s. The lodgings are small, conventional motel rooms, apartments and cottages, most of them redecorated with Old World antiques. Guests have full use of the spa facilities, which include a natural vapor cave, a sauna and soaking pool, an outdoor swimming pool and a fully equipped exercise room. ~ 625 5th Street, Ouray; 970-325-4347, fax 970-325-4845; www.wiesbadenhotsprings. com. DELUXE.

pretty enclosed garden. ~ 525 2nd Street, Ouray; 970-325-4190, 800-315-0565, fax 970-325-0565; www.chinaclipperinn.com, e-mail china5@mindspring.com. MODERATE TO ULTRA-DELUXE.

A more modest Ouray B&B, **The Manor** is a tastefully restored 1890 Georgian Revival home with seven guest rooms. All are on the second and third floors, with mountain views. Decor is simple and evocative of the Old West, though now they have queen-size European featherbeds and down comforters. ~ 317 2nd Street, Ouray; 970-325-4754, 800-628-6946. MODERATE.

**Box Canyon Lodge & Hot Springs** is essentially a standard midrange motel with a spectacularly scenic location and one other distinction: It has outdoor hot tubs fed by natural mineral springs located on the property. The clean, modern guest rooms hint at European sensibilities in their decor and furnishings. There are also two luxury suites with fireplaces and fully equipped kitchens. ~ 45 3rd Avenue, Ouray; 970-325-4981, 800-327-5080; www.boxcanyonouray.com, e-mail bcm@boxcanyonouray.com. BUDGET TO MODERATE.

In Silverton, the historic landmark hotel is the 40-room **Grand Imperial Hotel**. Its understated elegance shows in the lobby with its leather-upholstered sofas and in the rooms with their brass beds, crystal chandeliers and oak bathroom fittings. The Old West–style saloon on the main floor is open only during daytime hours when the train is in town. The hotel itself is open only from mid-March through September. ~ 1219 Greene Street, Silverton; phone/fax 970-387-5527, 800-341-3340; www.grandimperialhotel.com, e-mail info@grandimperialhotel.com. MODERATE TO DELUXE.

The **Wyman Hotel and Inn** is a restored 1902 building of local red sandstone with high ceilings and arched windows. The 17 guest rooms are comfortably furnished with king- or queen-size beds, period pieces and antiques, and all have private baths and TVs with VCRs and 600 movies available free to guests. Rates include a full gourmet breakfast and afternoon tea with home-made cookies. ~ 1371 Greene Street, Silverton; 970-387-5372, 800-609-7845, fax 970-387-5745; www.thewyman.com, e-mail thewyman@frontier.net. MODERATE TO DELUXE.

There are also a number of smaller, bed-and-breakfast-style lodgings around Silverton. **Smedley's** has just three suites above an ice-cream parlor. The guest suites have period furniture and full kitchens. ~ 1314 Greene Street, Silverton; phone/fax 970-387-5713. MODERATE.

The same innkeepers operate the **Teller House Hotel,** a former miners' boardinghouse. You'll find five shared-bath guest rooms and four private-bath accommodations, all decorated in early Victorian. ~ 1250 Greene Street, Silverton; phone/fax 970-387-5423, 800-342-4338. BUDGET.

Nearby is the **Wingate House,** an ornate mansard-roofed Victorian home filled with floral patterns and lace. The five antique-furnished guest rooms share two baths. ~ 1045 Snowden Street, Silverton; phone/fax 970-387-5520, call before faxing. MODERATE TO DELUXE.

**DINING**

Telluride has about two dozen restaurants, many of which are designed for an upscale resort clientele. Poshest of them all is **La Marmotte**, where Continental cuisine and fine wines are served in an intimate environment that looks much like an old wine cellar but in fact was once the town icehouse. Closed October and May. ~ 150 West San Juan Avenue, Telluride; 970-728-6232. DELUXE.

The **Cosmopolitan Restaurant,** in the restored, very Victorian Columbia Hotel, serves a broad range of meals for all tastes and budgets, from pizzas to chicken cordon bleu and wild-mushroom calzones. Eat in the elegant dining room or outside on the deck with a view of the ski slopes. Closed October through November and April through May. ~ 300 West San Juan Avenue, Telluride; 970-728-1292. MODERATE TO DELUXE.

One of the liveliest restaurants in Telluride is the **Floradora Saloon,** specializing in beef and offering a large salad bar as well. The Old West saloon atmosphere makes the Floradora a perfect après-ski spot. Lunch only. Closed October and November. ~ 103 West Colorado Avenue, Telluride; 970-728-3888. BUDGET.

Two blocks down the main street, **South Park Café** serves gourmet pizzas, pasta and overstuffed sandwiches on an outdoor deck with one of the best views in town. ~ 300 West Colorado Avenue, Telluride; 970-728-5335. BUDGET TO MODERATE.

Top of the line in Ouray is the **Bon Ton Restaurant,** serving northern Italian fare in an atmosphere that emphasizes the historic Victorian building with its bare brick walls and cut-glass accents. Although the menu may have changed over the years, the restaurant has been in continuous operation since the 1880s. The Sunday brunch is the best in town. ~ 426 Main Street, Ouray; 970-325-4951. DELUXE.

Another good place to eat is **Pricco's Restaurant.** Victorian woodwork complements the exposed brick interior of the restaurant. Family-owned since 1906, Pricco's features Philly steaks, cobb

**HASTY HARVEST**

Silverton's extremely short growing season—less than two weeks—means local gardeners can successfully grow only one crop: rhubarb. The community celebrates an annual Rhubarb Festival in August, and rhubarb pie is a specialty in many restaurants.

salads, steak hoagies and chicken Santa Fe, as well as vegetarian options. ~ 736 Main Street, Ouray; 970-325-4040. MODERATE.

The **Piñon Restaurant** is a modern little café with a tavern upstairs. Try the vegetarian burrito, stuffed with black beans, zucchini, carrots, onions and celery, or the trout with piñon nuts. ~ 737 Main Street, Ouray; 970-325-4334. MODERATE.

In Silverton, train passengers flock to **Handlebars Restaurant**, which is defined as much by the clutter of antiques that passes for decor as for its conventional menu of salads, burgers, homemade soups and barbecued ribs. Some patrons may find it disconcerting to eat under the gaze of all the big-game trophies (mounted animal heads). ~ 117 13th Street, Silverton; 970-387-5395. BUDGET TO MODERATE.

Another good place for breakfast, lunch or dinner is the **Pickle Barrel**, which was operating as a restaurant long before the railroad started running again. In a building that dates back to 1880 and was originally a general store, the restaurant serves sandwiches, steak and trout. Closed in winter. ~ 1304 Greene Street, Silverton; 970-387-5713. BUDGET TO MODERATE.

**SHOPPING**  Telluride has plenty of T-shirt shops and pricey sporting goods stores. It also has a handful of quite upmarket art galleries. As in Durango, the galleries in Telluride feature predominantly American Indian arts and Southwest-style paintings and sculptures, including some pieces that cost as much as a car. A good places to gaze longingly at such artworks is the **Telluride Gallery of Fine Art**. ~ 130 East Colorado Avenue, Telluride; 970-728-3300. The **McNair Gallery** features American Indian artwork and has a fascinating collection of historical photographs. ~ 209 East Colorado Avenue, Telluride; 970-728-3617. The **Brody Art Gallery** also displays American Indian artwork. ~ 575 West Colorado Avenue, Telluride; 970-728-3734.

Souvenir shopping in Ouray offers an intriguing ambience. Some of the stores along Main Street look as if they haven't changed in 50 years. Check out, for example, **Ouray V & S Variety**, a traditional small-town general store. ~ 700 Main Street, Ouray; 970-325-4469. In recent years, many artists and craftspeople have settled in Ouray because living is cheaper there than in most southwestern Colorado towns. Their work is exhibited in a half-dozen Main Street galleries, including the **Ago Fine Art Gallery**, where the works of over 50 Colorado artists and crafters are exhibited. ~ 735 Main Street, Ouray; 970-325-0270. There's also the **Ouray Gallery**. ~ 518 Main Street, Ouray; 970-325-4110.

Silverton's main industry is curio shops, which cluster along Greene Street between 11th and 14th streets. None stands out. You can also find San Juan Mountains guidebooks and maps as well as hiking and camping gear. **Clear Mountain Pottery** has original stoneware handmade in Silverton from local clay. ~ 1025 Blair Street, Silverton; 970-381-0115.

Telluride's most venerable drinking establishment is the **Sheridan Bar,** a dignified old hotel bar that harks back to the Victorian era but can become rowdy during ski season. ~ 225 West Colorado Avenue, Telluride; 970-728-3911. For really loud fun, though, the place to go is the **Fly Me to the Moon Saloon.** It presents live rock, R&B or reggae bands nightly during the ski and festival seasons and has an underground dancefloor. Cover. ~ 132 East Colorado Avenue, Telluride; 970-728-6666.

**MCPHEE NATIONAL RECREATION AREA** 🚶 🚴 ⚓ 🛶 🚤 🛥️ ⚓ Completed in 1987, McPhee Reservoir flooded the lower portion of the Dolores River Canyon and a network of tributary canyons to create a long, narrow lake that provides almost boundless opportunities for backcountry boating and fishing. Before it was flooded, the canyon was the site of a number of Ancestral Pueblo ruins and home to a wide assortment of wildlife. A "mitigation area" surrounding the lake protects habitat for birds and animals, including bobcats, coyotes, mountain lions, ospreys, beavers and mule deer, that previously lived in the canyons where the lake is today. Fishing is good for rainbow, brown and cutthroat trout as well as largemouth bass. There are picnic areas with tables, drinking water, restrooms, boat ramps and hiking trails. ~ Located 12 miles west of Dolores off Route 184; 970-882-7296.

> Archaeological surveys performed during the McPhee Reservoir's construction yielded numerous artifacts, many of which are on exhibit at the Anasazi Heritage Center nearby.

▲ McPhee Recreation Complex, on the lake's western shore, and House Creek Campground, on the eastern shore, have 106 RV/tent sites (33 with electric hookups) with drinking water and dumping stations; $12 per night. Reservations: 877-444-6777.

**RIDGWAY STATE PARK** 🚶 🏊 🚤 🛥️ ⚓ Recreational facilities are located in two separate areas along the shoreline of 80,000-acre Ridgway Reservoir. The main recreational site, on a promontory at the lake's south shore, has a boat ramp, a public swimming beach, two campgrounds and four miles of hiking trails. The mile-long, paved main trail leads to the Dallas Creek Recreation Site, at the east end of the reservoir where both Dallas Creek and the Uncompahgre River flow in. The Dallas Creek site has picnic areas, as well as walkways and bridges that provide pedestrian access to the lake's north shore. There are rainbow and brown trout and ice fishing is available in the winter. Facilities include picnic areas with tables and restrooms, and a marina (970-626-5094) with boat rentals, which is open Friday through Sunday only. Day-use fee, $5. ~ Located five miles north of Ridgway on Route 550, about midway between Telluride and Ouray; 970-626-5822.

▲ The Dakota Terraces, Pa-co-chu-puk and Elk Ridge campgrounds offer a total of 264 RV/tent sites and 25 walk-in tent sites; $12 to $18 per night. Most have electric hookups. There are showers, flush toilets, laundry facilities and a dump station.

### SAN JUAN NATIONAL FOREST 🏃🚴🐎🏊🏄🏠⬆️🚣🚤

San Juan National Forest surrounds the San Juan Skyway and includes the jagged, lofty Needle Mountains, which rise to the east of the Skyway, and the narrow-gauge railroad in the vast Weminuche Wilderness. Parts of the Lizard Head and South San Juan wilderness areas also lie within San Juan National Forest. The San Juan Mountains were a rich gold-mining district in the 1870s to 1920s, containing numerous mines, camps and wagon roads and narrow-gauge tracks; today, more than 2000 miles of unpaved forest roads, many of which require four-wheel-drive vehicles or are suitable for mountain biking, provide access to many areas of the forest. For serious backpackers, San Juan National Forest is one of the most popular playgrounds in the Rocky Mountains. Fishing is good for rainbow and other trout in more than 90 natural lakes and 280 streams throughout the forest. Facilities include picnic areas, restrooms, pack trails and jeep trails. ~ Access is via the San Juan Skyway Scenic Byway—Route 145 between Dolores and Lizard Head Pass and Route 550 between Durango and Silverton. Purgatory Campground, South Mineral Campground and most other campgrounds and trailheads are found along these highways; 970-247-4874.

Uncompahgre National Forest's waters are best in July and August for rainbow, brown and brook trout, especially in Owl Creek and Beaver Lake east of Ridgway.

▲ Among the numerous campgrounds along the San Juan Skyway is Purgatory Campground, located near Durango Mountain Resort midway between Durango and Silverton, with eight RV/tent sites (no hookups) and five tent-only sites; closed mid-September to mid-May; $10 per night. South Mineral Campground near Silverton has 21 RV/tent sites (no hookups); closed mid-October to late May; $12 per night.

### UNCOMPAHGRE NATIONAL FOREST (SOUTHERN UNIT) 🏃🚣

This part of Uncompahgre National Forest (see also "Grand Junction Area Parks" in Chapter Five) encompasses the mountains around Telluride and Ouray. Big Blue Wilderness contains Uncompahgre Peak (14,309 feet) and Wetterhorn Peak (14,015 feet) near Ouray. Other areas (without roads) include the Mount Sneffels and the Lizard Head wilderness areas, both near Telluride. All are destinations for serious mountain-climbing expeditions. There are picnic areas, restrooms, hiking trails, pack trails and jeep trails. ~ Access is via the San Juan Scenic Skyway—Route 145 between Lizard Head Pass and Telluride and Route 550 between Ouray and Silverton. Most trailheads and campgrounds, including Matterhorn, Sunshine and Amphitheater campgrounds, are along these highways; 970-327-4261.

**▲** Matterhorn and Sunshine Campgrounds near Telluride offer 43 RV/tent sites (no hookups; open Memorial Day through September; $12 per night. Amphitheater Campground near Ouray has 30 RV/tent sites (no hookups); closed late September to late May; $14 per night.

## Outdoor Adventures

### FISHING

**PAGOSA SPRINGS AREA** The east and west forks of the **San Juan River** above Pagosa Springs are known for especially good trout fishing, with rainbow and brown trout at lower elevations and cutthroat trout higher upstream. A broad spectrum of fishing options, from largemouth bass in the shallows to kokanee salmon in the deeps, can be found at **Navajo Lake State Park**.

**DURANGO AREA** Directly east of Durango, **Vallecito Reservoir**, a large fishing lake, offers bass fishing.

**SAN JUAN SKYWAY AREA** The **Dolores River** is reputed to be one of the finest dry flyfishing areas in the West. In particular, the stretch of river below **McPhee Reservoir** teems with large rainbow and brown trout and Snake River cutthroats. Guides for wading or horseback flyfishing expeditions on the Dolores River and its tributaries can be arranged through **West Fork Guide Service**. ~ P.O. Box 300, Dolores, CO 81323; 970-882-7959, 888-882-8001.

They say 12- to 18-inch rainbow and brown trout are the norm in the San Miguel River near Telluride. **Telluride Flyfishers** offers combination flyfishing schools. ~ 150 West Colorado Avenue, Telluride; 970-728-4477, 800-828-7547. For flyfishing guide services, call **Telluride Angler**. ~ P.O. Box 685, Telluride, CO 81435; 970-728-3895, 800-831-6230; www.tellurideoutside.com.

### BOATING

**PAGOSA SPRINGS AREA** On Navajo Lake, **San Juan Marina** has a full spectrum of rentals, from little fishing skiffs to 24-foot pontoon boats and 50-foot houseboats. ~ 1526 County Road 982; 970-883-2343.

**DURANGO AREA** Vallecitos Reservoir, east of Durango, is the most popular lake in the Durango region for water sports. **Mountain Marina** provides boat rentals. ~ 14810 County Road 501, Bayfield; 970-884-9450.

**SAN JUAN SKYWAY AREA** You can rent fishing boats, pontoon boats on McPhee Reservoir at **McPhee Marina**. ~ 25021 Route 184, Lewis; 970-882-2257, 800-882-2038.

**RIVER RUNNING**

**PAGOSA SPRINGS AREA** Pagosa Rafting Outfitters offers raft trips on the San Juan River as well as special two- and three-day expeditions. ~ P.O. Box 222, Pagosa Springs, CO 81147; 970-731-8060.

**DURANGO AREA** Durango rafting companies run the lower Animas River south from town past old mining ruins, down a series of wet-and-wild rapids and through the Southern Ute Reservation. **Mountain Waters Rafting** runs Class I through V rapids on the Animas and Piedra. ~ 643 Camino del Rio, Durango; 970-259-4191, 800-585-8243; www.durangorafting.com. **Flexible Flyers Rafting** provides rafting and scenic float trips. ~ 2344 County Road 255, Durango; 970-247-4628. A smaller, more personalized company is **Watermelon Adventure Rafting**. ~ Durango; 970-946-7238.

**SAN JUAN SKYWAY AREA** When the water's high, **Telluride Outside** offers half- and full-day trips on the San Miguel and Dolores rivers. ~ P.O. Box 685, Telluride, CO 81435; 970-728-3895, 800-831-6230; www.tellurideoutside.com.

**BALLOON RIDES & GLIDING**

For a unique perspective on the spectacular San Juan Mountains, try drifting silently on the updrafts above the mountain slopes in a glider or hot-air balloon. Both are among the pricier thrills to be found in the region; the cost of a glider ride—including glider rental, pilot and tow plane, is about the same as hot-air ballooning. Either way, you'll come away with an experience that's sure to remain a vivid memory.

**PAGOSA SPRINGS AREA** **Rocky Mountain Balloon Adventures** offers hot-air balloon flights from Pagosa Springs or Durango above lush meadows in the San Juan Mountains and champagne afterward. Reservations required. ~ P.O. Box 4095, Pagosa Springs, CO 81147; 970-731-8060.

**DURANGO AREA** Scenic glider rides over Durango and the Animas Valley can be arranged through the **Durango Soaring Club**. ~ Val-Air Gliderport, Route 550, Durango; 970-247-9037.

**SAN JUAN SKYWAY AREA** Glider rides among the spectacular mountains that surround Telluride are offered by **Telluride Soaring**. ~ Telluride airport, Telluride; 970-209-3497. **San Juan Balloon Adventures** offers one-hour balloon flights over the Ridgway Valley every morning year-round (weather permitting) from Ridgway. There's a good chance of spotting wildlife, and passengers enjoy a champagne breakfast when they land. ~ P.O. Box 66, Ridgway, CO 81421; 970-626-5495. Another popular sky sport in Telluride is paragliding; with **Telluride Paragliding** you can launch from the ski slope summit and float more than 3500 feet down into town. ~ 970-369-4696.

**PAGOSA SPRINGS AREA** Wolf Creek Ski Area receives more snowfall than any other ski area in the state—over 400 inches a year. The ski area near the Wolf Creek Pass summit is 65 miles west of Alamosa and 75 miles east of Durango. It has a vertical drop of 1425 feet and five chairlifts as well as a magic carpet and a Snow Cat shuttle to transport people back from the ungroomed trails of the "outback" area. The runs are almost evenly divided between beginner, intermediate, advanced and expert, with a slight emphasis on intermediate. Snowboarding is permitted. Open Thanksgiving through April. There is a rental shop at the base. ~ Route 160, Wolf Creek Pass; 970-264-5639, fax 970-264-5732; www.wolfcreekski.com, e-mail wolfcreekski@wolfcreekski.com.

**DOWNHILL SKIING**

**DURANGO AREA** What you see from the highway near **Durango Mountain Resort** is just a hint of the complex 75-mile groomed trail network that works its way around the broad side of the mountain, making this relatively small ski area, with its 2029-foot vertical drop, wider than it is high. There are 11 chairlifts. Located 25 miles north of Durango, the ski area has rentals, child care and a ski school. Half the runs are intermediate, with the rest divided between beginner and advanced/expert. Snowboarding is allowed on most runs. Open Thanksgiving to late April. ~ Route 550; 970-247-9000, 800-982-6103; www.durangomountainresort.com.

> Telluride Ski Resort's Plunge and Spiral Stairs, running down the front face, are the longest, steepest mogul runs in Colorado.

**SAN JUAN SKYWAY AREA** Telluride Ski Resort has a reputation as an "experts only" ski mountain. Developers in the early 1970s ran into financial problems after completing only the incredibly steep runs on the front side of the mountain. Today, more than 60 percent of the runs are for beginning and intermediate skiers, but these runs are hidden on the back side of the mountain. The vertical drop is an awesome 3552 feet. There are 12 chairlifts and a gondola, as well as a snowboarding park. There are also ski rentals and a ski school. This ski resort offers the most spectacular mountain scenery in the state. Open from Thanksgiving through April. ~ Route 145, Telluride; 970-728-6900; www.telski.com, e-mail skitelluride@telski.com.

**Ski Rentals** In Telluride, rent downhill and cross-country equipment at **Telluride Sports**. ~ 150 West Colorado Avenue; 970-728-4477. **Paragon Sports** also rents equipment. ~ 213 West Colorado Avenue; 970-728-4525.

**DURANGO AREA** Durango Mountain Nordic Center offers rentals, cross-country ski lessons and more than 15 kilometers of groomed trails. ~ Route 550, Purgatory; 970-247-9000 ext. 3196, 800-982-6103; www.durangomountainresort.com.

**CROSS-COUNTRY SKIING**

**SAN JUAN SKYWAY AREA**   Telluride Nordic Center maintains 30 kilometers of groomed trails and offers rentals. ~ Town Park; 970-728-1144. In Ouray, cross-country ski rentals and information about groomed trails in the national forest can be obtained at **Ouray Mountain Sports.** ~ 722 Main Street, Ouray; 970-325-4284.

For more information on renting equipment, see the ski-rental section in "Downhill Skiing" above.

**GOLF**    **PAGOSA SPRINGS AREA**   The **Pagosa Springs Golf Club,** located at the Fairfield Resort west of Pagosa Springs, features three nine-hole mountain courses designed by Johnny Bulla. Each course is different, and there is a reduced fee for playing any two in tandem. Club and cart rentals are available. ~ 1 Pines Club Place, Pagosa Springs; 970-731-4755.

**DURANGO AREA**   In Durango, the 18-hole **Hillcrest Golf Club** has spectacular mountain views from a mesa top overlooking Durango. There are cart and club rentals and a driving range. ~ 2300 Rim Drive; 970-247-1499. Also near Durango is the semi-private 18-hole **Dalton Ranch Golf Course**, designed by Ken Dye, dramatically set among the red cliffs of the Animas Valley. ~ 435 County Road 252; 970-247-7921. A scenic mountain course designed by Arthur Hills, the **Cliffs Golf Course** at the prestigious Sheraton Tamarron Resort is open to nonguests on a standby basis—only guests can reserve tee times in advance. Greens fees for nonguests are among the highest in the state. Dress code. ~ 40292 Route 550 North, Durango; 970-382-6700.

**SAN JUAN SKYWAY AREA**   The **Fairway Pines Golf Club,** an 18-hole championship course, is open to the public. It is set at 8000-feet elevation on a broad mesa, surrounded by mountain skylines. Cart and club rentals are available, and there is a driving range. ~ 117 Ponderosa Drive, Ridgway; 970-626-5284.

**TENNIS**    In summer, hard-surface tennis courts and racquets are rented to the public at **Fairfield Pagosa Resort;** reservations required. ~ Route 160, Pagosa Springs; 970-731-8000. In Durango, **Fort**

---

### CLAMP ON YOUR CRAMPONS

From November through May, ice-climbing enthusiasts from all over the world come to the Uncompahgre Gorge in Ouray to pit their strength and skill against the 140-foot-tall frozen manmade waterfalls in **Ouray Ice Park**. ~ 970-325-4288. For equipment rentals and event information, visit **Ouray Mountain Sports**. ~ 722 Main Street, Ouray; 970-325-4284; www.ouraysports.com.

Lewis College has 12 asphalt tennis courts, which are open to the public when they're not in use for school activities. ~ College Heights; 970-247-7010. Telluride, Ouray and Silverton each have two municipal tennis courts in their respective town parks.

**PAGOSA SPRINGS AREA**  Wolf Creek Outfitters leads guided horseback rides, ranging in length from an hour to all day, into the high country around Wolf Creek Pass. ~ West Fork Road, Pagosa Springs; 970-264-5332.

**RIDING STABLES**

**DURANGO AREA**  Vallecito Reservoir has several riding stables. **Outlaw West Livery at Five Branches Camper Park** offers guided rides. ~ 4677 County Road 501A, Bayfield; 970-884-9631, 970-884-2070 (winter), 800-447-3395.

West of Durango, **Mayday Livery** rents horses by the hour and offers guided rides in La Plata Canyon. ~ 4432 County Road 124, Hesperus; 970-385-6772.

**MESA VERDE AREA**  Near the entrance of Mesa Verde National Park, the **Mesa Verde Riding Stable** guides small-group tours of up to ten people, ranging from hour-long to all-day, and rents horses by the day for personal use in the park's hilly piñon and juniper woodlands. ~ Route 160 West, Mancos; 970-533-7269. In Dolores, you can ride at **Circle K Ranch**. ~ 27758 Route 145; 970-562-3826, 800-477-6381.

**SAN JUAN SKYWAY AREA**  Horses and tours are available in Telluride at **Many Ponies Outfit**. ~ 122 South Townsend Avenue; 970-728-6278. **Telluride Horseback** organizes guided one and two-hour trail rides for up to 30 people on Turkey Creek Mesa near Wilson Peak as well as all-day and overnight trips by advance arrangement. ~ 9025 Route 145; 970-728-9611. **Deep Creek Sleighs & Wagon Rides** offers horse-drawn sleigh and wagon rides with dinner nightly. ~ Telluride; 970-728-3565.

**Ouray Livery Barn** rents horses for guided rides. ~ 834 Main Street, Ouray; 970-325-4606.

A pack trip into the southern Colorado Rockies can turn a vacation into an adventure. For those who want to hike long distances into the high country but don't want to be burdened with backpacks, llama trekking may be just the ticket. Besides being an extraordinary hiking companion, the llama carries your lunch, camera gear and fishing tackle—up to about a 40-pound load.

**PACK TRIPS & LLAMA TREKS**

**DURANGO AREA**  In Bayfield, **Outlaw West Livery** has guided rides of varying lengths, including seven-day full-service pack trips in the Weminuche Wilderness. ~ 4677 County Road 501A, Bayfield; 970-884-9631, 800-447-3395. **Engine Creek Outfitters & Cascade Stables** also offers trips. ~ 50827 Route 150, Durango; 970-259-2556. Near Durango, the **Buckhorn Llama Company**

takes visitors on trips into the high San Juans. ~ 1834 County Road 207, Durango; 970-318-9454.

**SAN JUAN SKYWAY AREA** In Silverton, **Silverado Outfitters** lead ten-day horse pack trips on the Colorado and Continental Divide trails. ~ Mineral Street; 970-387-5747.

**BIKING**

**PAGOSA SPRINGS AREA** An easy ride near Pagosa Springs, the **Turkey Springs Trail** (six miles) offers views of Pagosa Peak. A more challenging route, the **Willow Draw Trail** (16 miles), starts at Pagosa Springs City Park and climbs high into the hills before the thrilling downhill run back into town.

**DURANGO AREA** The chairlift at **Durango Mountain Resort** is equipped in the summer to take riders and their bikes to the summit, where they can ride the four-mile **Harris Park Loop** across the alpine **Hermosa Creek Valley** on the back side of the mountain. Admission. ~ Route 550, Durango; 970-247-9000. A longer and more challenging ride, the **Hermosa Creek Trail** (23 miles) takes cyclists through high meadows and along the rim of the Hermosa Cliffs. Just up the highway from Purgatory, the graded **Lime Creek Road** (11 miles) makes for a gentle ride through aspen forests with sweeping panoramic views of the surrounding mountains.

**SAN JUAN SKYWAY AREA** Telluride's gondola is equipped to let you transport a mountain bike to the high ridge above town for access to more than 100 miles of alpine trails. Unpaved **Ilium Road** is a favorite among mountain bikers in the Telluride area. The eight-mile road takes you to historic mining sites and waterfalls in a deep canyon. For an ultimate all-terrain biking experience, the trail to **Bear Creek Falls** climbs 1100 feet in elevation on its way to one of the most beautiful canyons in the area. **Ingram Falls Road** is a steep three-mile ascent to Bridal Veil Falls, at the upper end of the canyon overlooking town. For a week-long mountain-bike trek, the **San Juan Hut System**, a series of six shelters along a 215-mile bike route between Telluride and Moab, Utah, crosses varied terrain from alpine tundra to slickrock desert.

Unpaved, rugged four-wheel-drive roads leading to abandoned mines in the San Juan Mountains make for challenging mountain-bike trips. Around Ouray, great mountain-bike routes include the jeep trail from near Amphitheater campground up to the Portland and Chief Ouray mines. Another starts above Lake Lenore on the way to the Bachelor Mine and runs past the Wedge Mine to the Bridge of Heaven.

**Bike Rentals** In Pagosa Springs, you'll find bicycles at **Juan's Mountain Sports**. ~ 155 Hot Springs Boulevard; 970-264-4730. In Durango, try **Hassle Free Sports** (mid-April through October). ~ 2615 Main Avenue; 970-259-3874. There's also **Mountain**

Bike Specialists (May through October). ~ 949 Main Avenue; 970-247-4066. Places to rent bicycles in Telluride include **Telluride Sports.** ~ 150 West Colorado Avenue; 970-728-4477. Or you can contact **Paragon Ski and Sport.** ~ 217 West Colorado Avenue; 970-728-4525. **Ouray Mountain Sports** rents mountain bikes in the summer. ~ 722 Main Street; 970-325-4284.

All distances listed for trails are one way unless otherwise noted.

**HIKING**

**DURANGO AREA** Durango has an overwhelming number of hiking options. The ultimate trail in the area is the **Colorado Trail** (469 miles), which goes all the way from Durango to Denver, following the Continental Divide most of the way. The first segment of the trail goes from Durango to Silverton, a distance of about 70 miles through the rugged La Plata Mountains.

Another magnificently ambitious hike is the **Needle Creek Trail,** which starts at the ghost town of Needleton, a stop on the Durango & Silverton Narrow-Gauge Railroad route. The trail climbs into the jagged peaks of the Weminuche Wilderness to join a network of other trails, including the spectacular **Chicago Basin** route, which follows alpine valleys all the way to Creede—a 75-mile trip that takes about a week. Backpackers without train tickets use a longer route to reach the high wilderness, starting at Vallecito Reservoir and taking the **Vallecito Trail** or the **Pine River Trail.** Still other trails into the Weminuche Wilderness start from Route 550.

Among the many day-hike options in the Durango area are **Red Creek Trail** (six miles), on Missionary Ridge above town, and **Twin Buttes Trail** (four miles), overlooking town.

**AUTHOR FAVORITE**

When you visit Mesa Verde National Park in midsummer, you find yourself engulfed by crowds of theme-park proportions. For me, it was a relief to find that there are lesser-known ruined pueblos and cliff dwellings all over this corner of Colorado—most of them unexcavated, unvisited and tantalizing in their mystery. For a real archaeological adventure free from national park crowd control, explore the **Sand Canyon Trail,** the only official trail in the vast new Canyon of the Ancients National Monument, which goes six miles up a secluded canyon, passing several cliff dwellings and pueblos along the way. Take lots of water! ~ From the M&M Truck Stop on Route 666 south of Cortez, go west on Road G for 12 miles to the unmarked but obvious trailhead on the north side of the road; 970-882-4811.

**SAN JUAN SKYWAY AREA** Telluride is hiker's heaven in the summertime. Short, challenging trails like the steep one-mile climb to **Bridal Veil Falls** start from the outskirts of town. For an all-day or overnight hike, the **Bear Creek Trail** passes another waterfall and climbs high in the mountains to join the **Wasatch Trail** for a descent to Bridal Veil Falls, making a strenuous ten-mile loop. For mountaintop vistas without the pain, hikers can ride the chairlift (which operates all year) up the Telluride ski slopes and hike along at 10,500-foot elevation alpine ridges.

In Ouray, short hikes include the **Lower Cascade Falls Trail** (.5 mile), which starts just a few blocks from the center of town, and the steep **Upper Cascade Falls Trail** (2.5 miles), which starts from the natural amphitheater south of town. For an all-day hike, try **Bear Creek Trail** (7.25 miles), which passes several old mining operations on its way to the summit of Engineer Pass.

Near Silverton, the **Highland Mary Lakes Trail** (2.5 miles) takes you through a landscape thoroughly probed by miners a century ago and leads up to a pair of alpine lakes. This trail joins the Canada-to-Mexico **Continental Divide Trail** as it passes through the Weminuche Wilderness. The **Molas Pass Trail** (3 miles) starts at Molas Lake on Route 550 and descends steeply to the Animas River and the Durango & Silverton train tracks a thousand feet below, offering breathtaking views and a hard climb back up to your car.

## Transportation

**Route 160** goes over Wolf Creek Pass (10,850 feet) between Pagosa Springs and the Durango area.

**Route 550** and **Route 145** together are known as the San Juan Skyway Scenic Byway. Route 550 leaves Route 160 at Durango and goes through Silverton and Ouray. Route 145 leaves Route 160 at Mancos, a short drive west of Durango, and goes through Dolores and Telluride.

**CAR**

**AIR**

Daily commuter flights from Denver to **Durango–La Plata Airport** are provided by AmericaWest Express, American Airlines, Continental Express and Mesa Airlines/United Express. Airport shuttles are operated by **Durango Transportation Inc.** ~ 970-259-4818.

AmericaWest Express, Continental Express, Mesa Airlines/United Express and Skywest/Delta Connection serve the **Telluride Regional Airport**; the Continental and Mesa flights also land at **Montrose Regional Airport**. Ground transportation at both airports is available during ski season from **Telluride Transit Company Airport Shuttle Service**. ~ 970-728-6000.

**BUS**

**Greyhound Bus Lines** has bus service to Durango. ~ 275 East 8th Avenue; 970-259-2755, 800-231-2222.

Car-rental agencies at Durango–La Plata Airport include **Avis Rent A Car** (800-331-1212), **Budget Rent A Car** (800-527-0700), **Dollar Car Rental** (800-800-4000), **Hertz Rent A Car** (800-654-3131) and **National Car Rental** (800-227-7368). You can rent either a late-model used car or a four-wheel-drive vehicle at **Rent A Wreck**. ~ 21760 Route 160 West; 970-259-5858, 800-682-5858.

Along the San Juan Skyway, four-wheel-drive vehicles are for rent at **Switzerland of America Jeep Rentals**. ~ 226 7th Avenue, Ouray; 970-325-4059. **Colorado West Jeep Rentals** provides rentals. ~ 701 Main Street, Ouray; 970-325-4014, 800-648-5337. **Triangle Rent A Jeep** also rents four-wheel-drive vehicles. ~ 864 Greene Street, Silverton; 970-387-9990, 800-522-2354.

**CAR RENTALS**

The **Durango Lift** provides in-town, fixed-route bus service during the summer months and shuttle service from Durango to the slopes at Purgatory during ski season. ~ 949 East 2nd Avenue, Durango; 970-259-5438.

**PUBLIC TRANSIT**

In Durango, the taxi company is **Durango Transportation**. ~ 970-259-4818. In Telluride, it's **Skip's Taxi**. ~ 970-728-6667.

**TAXIS**

## NINE

# The Eastern Plains

Sunflowers, a common cash crop along the plains that make up Colorado's eastern state line, face Kansas in the morning. The flowers rotate in unison to follow the sun, pointing the way to the Rocky Mountains in the afternoon. This seemingly arcane bit of information can be important to know if you leave the main route without a compass to venture into the gridwork of forgotten two-lane blacktop highways and gravel farm-to-market roads that segment the prairie out past the horizon where the mountains cannot be seen and all directions look pretty much the same.

Forty percent of Colorado's land area lies east of the Rocky Mountains and the major Front Range population centers. If Colorado's arbitrary boundaries were redrawn according to geography, economy or cultural heritage, the eastern plains would belong to Kansas or perhaps Nebraska, certainly not to Colorado. The region is arid, nearly flat land used for cattle ranching and dryland farming, the main crops being corn and wheat. Tourism is not a significant factor in eastern Colorado's economy.

It's not that the plains of eastern Colorado are devoid of things to see or do. It's just that the distances are vast and the sights so modest that they can't begin to rival those found in any other part of the state. The information presented in this chapter is for motorists and bus passengers bound for Colorado's cities and resort areas from points east. Then, too, my search for points of interest in this nearly empty land has sometimes led me to special spots on the most remote reaches of the prairie where few people have set foot since the days of the pioneers. I include these spots for the benefit of the rare traveler driven by curiosity to seek out the most thoroughly "hidden" places in the entire state.

Three main highway routes cross the eastern plains. Route 76 follows the South Platte River from Nebraska, where it branches off Route 80, entering the northeast corner of Colorado and angling down toward Denver, where it merges with Route 70. Colorado's early Anglo settlers turned off the Oregon Trail, the main covered-wagon route west, following the Overland Trail southwest from Nebraska along this fork of the river to establish new communities at the foot of the Rocky Mountains.

Route 70 follows no river or historical trail. A path first used by stagecoaches in the 1850s, it is simply the most direct line across the Great Plains from Kansas City west to Denver. Burlington and Limon, the two main agricultural towns along the 200-mile stretch of divided highway between the Colorado–Kansas state line and Denver, seem to be affected little by the high-speed traffic flow along their outskirts. Only occasionally do highway travelers stop for longer than it takes to fill up with gas and fast food.

Route 50 traces the Arkansas River and the Santa Fe Trail, one of the most important historical routes of the 19th century. The first explorers from the United States to set foot in Colorado came this way, and the first goods traded between the United States and Mexico were carried in wagons along this route. Today, this is the least-used of the three routes because it is somewhat slower than the interstate highways and it does not go to Denver. Travelers bound for the southern part of Colorado from points east may find that this is the easiest—and most interesting—route.

The weather on the eastern plains tends to be more extreme than along the Front Range Corridor, which is sheltered by the rain shadow of the Rocky Mountains. The prairie slopes slightly downward from the foothills east to the state line. The elevations of Julesburg and Burlington, for instance, are more than 1000 feet lower than that of Denver, and Lamar, the lowest point in Colorado at 3500 feet above sea level, is nearly half a mile lower than Colorado Springs. The difference in elevation translates into hotter summer temperatures. Thermometers commonly read 100 degrees on summer afternoons; large thunderstorms, tornadoes and golfball-size hail are fairly common, alternating with the sometimes devastating dry spells that earned the region the name "Great American Desert" in the days before irrigation or wells. Winter weather, though variable, can also be severe. Snowstorms are typically accompanied by high winds that create blinding blizzard conditions and road-blocking snowdrifts.

Despite the apparent drawbacks of prairie life, as you cross Colorado's eastern plains you will see that people do live way out here. They may live so spread out that no ranch or farm house is within sight of any other, and they may routinely drive forty miles to the nearest town, which may consist of a grain silo and a convenience store that also sells diesel fuel, but the people of the prairie fight hard to survive the economic problems that threaten small farmers and ranchers throughout in the Great Plains and hold on to their ties with the land. In eastern Colorado it can truly be said that America's pioneer spirit lives on.

## South Platte River Area

History (along with grain silos and cattle feed lots) reigns supreme in northeastern Colorado. Most historical points of interest in the area are left over from the period between 1860 and 1868, when the Overland Trail was the busiest route in the American West. The trail branched off the Oregon Trail in central Nebraska to follow the South Platte River southwest to Denver and other newly founded towns along the Rocky Mountain foothills.

**SIGHTS**

In 1860, a year after Congress created Jefferson Territory (which would later be renamed Colorado), the Pony Express established the first courier service to the new territory by building a station at **Julesburg**—less than two miles from the Nebraska border. Mail arriving at the station might not be delivered promptly, though, because Pony Express did not extend its route farther into the territory until 1862. The station was closed in 1868, when the arrival of the railroad made the Pony Express obsolete. The ruins of the **Pony Express station**, located just west of town on Route 138, the old, empty highway across the river from Route 76, are one of the few points of interest in present-day Julesburg. The little farm town's past is the focus of the **Fort Sedgwick Depot Museum**, with its modest displays of American Indian and pioneer artifacts. ~ 202 West 1st Street, Julesburg; 970-474-2264. Other Overland Trail historic sites along Route 138 include the remains of the **Lillian Springs and Spring Hill stage coach stops** at the tiny town of **Crook**.

One early Oregon Trail pioneer described the **South Platte River** as "a mile wide and an inch deep." The South Platte looks much different than any of the other major rivers—such as the Arkansas, the Rio Grande and, of course, the Colorado—that originate in the Colorado Rockies. From the main highway, all that can be seen of the river is a skyline of tall trees in the middle distance. Fortunately, you can get a better look from any of the numerous bridges that span the river to reach towns on the other side, revealing the South Platte as a braid of many small channels that wind their ways among long, slender islands overgrown with bushes. Because the South Platte occasionally lets loose with a flood like a tidal wave, farms and buildings are set well away from its banks, leaving the river area wild and, in many places, so thickly tangled with vegetation as to be almost impenetrable.

You can get close to the river at any of several state wildlife areas designed for duck hunting in the fall and rarely visited at other times of year except by local fishermen. The biggest and best is **Tamarack Ranch State Wildlife Area**, which takes in both banks of the river for almost 20 miles. The 10,600-acre wild area also includes a large tract of natural prairie, as well as plots of farmland where part of the crop is left for the birds. Notable among the many bird species seen at Tamarack Ranch year-round are wild turkeys and greater prairie chickens, an endangered species. White-tailed and mule deer are also abundant. ~ Route 138, Crook; 970-474-2711.

**Sterling**, an agriculture and railroad shipping center with a population of about 10,000, is the largest town on Colorado's eastern plains. The tallest building in town is a grain silo. Sterling was founded in 1873 by a group of settlers from Tennessee and Mississippi who abandoned the war-ravaged South to build new lives on the frontier. Sterling's most unusual sights are its so-called

**HIDDEN ▶**

**Eastern Plains**

**Living Trees**, actually colossal wood sculptures, most of them more than ten feet tall, carved from the trunks of dead trees by local artist Brad Rhea. Sixteen (so far) of the fanciful sculptures—among them a golfer, a plainsman, giraffes and a mermaid—are scattered all over town in parks and public buildings. You can see one outside the **Visitors Information Center** at the Route 6 exit from Route 76 and pick up a map there that shows the way to each of the others and provides an excuse to spend a couple of hours exploring Sterling.

Across the highway from the visitors center stands an even larger sculpture—the **Overland Trail Monument**, a 20-foot-tall, 40-foot-long concrete rendition of a covered wagon pulled by a team of oxen. Nearby, the **Overland Trail Museum** offers a look at the migration route that brought thousands of settlers and gold hunters to Colorado from 1862 to 1868, when the coming of the railroad made wagon trains obsolete. The main museum building, a replica of an old fort, houses a collection of buckskin clothes, dolls, arrowheads and other artifacts from the pioneer era, as well as one of the world's largest branding-iron collections. Grounds landscaped with native wildflowers and prairie grasses and strewn with covered wagons and old-time farm machinery surround a cluster of historic buildings including a one-room schoolhouse, a blacksmith shop and a Lutheran church. Admission. ~ Route 6, Sterling; 970-522-3895.

*HIDDEN* ▶

History buffs can also get directions at the Sterling Visitors Information Center to the small monument marking the **Summit Springs Battlefield** southwest of Sterling near Atwood. The 1869 battle, which ended in the killings of 50 Cheyenne and Arapaho men and the rescue of two kidnapped pioneer women from Kansas, was the last armed conflict between U.S. Army troops and American Indians in eastern Colorado.

*HIDDEN* ▶

Although most visitors arrive in Sterling with the impression that there's nothing but flat grasslands for a hundred miles in any direction, surprisingly dramatic scenery can be found at **Chimney Canyons**, 20 miles north on County Road 37 (7th Avenue) and then 8 miles west of town on County Road 70, where the plains give way to 250-foot chalk cliffs.

**Fort Morgan**, the next large town on the Platte River west of Sterling, was originally the site of a military fort that protected pioneers on the Overland Trail from 1864 to 1868. The cavalry outpost is the subject of a permanent exhibit at the **Fort Morgan Museum**, which also contains plains Indian artifacts, a fully equipped soda fountain from the 1920s, and a gallery commemorating 1930s and '40s big-band superstar Glenn Miller, whose boyhood home was in Fort Morgan. ~ 414 Main Street, Fort Morgan; 970-867-6331. Located at Route 76 and Main is **Riverside Park**, a 180-acre natural area by the South Platte with trails along the riverbank and through verdant woodlands. Adjacent to the park, the **James Marsh Arch Bridge** (Route 53) is the only rainbow arch–design bridge in the state, a source of pride for Fort Morgan and presumably a thrill for bridge architecture buffs.

Much of the arid prairie land that lies north of the South Platte River is within the boundaries of **Pawnee National Grassland**, the Great Plains equivalent of a national forest. The grasslands were formerly in private ownership, first as part of the vast domain of late-19th-century cattle baron John Wesley Iliff, later transformed into small, marginally productive dryland farms by homesteaders between 1910 and 1918. Brutal winters, a deadly influenza epidemic and finally the Dust Bowl drought of the 1930s forced the abandonment of virtually all farm and ranch land in the area. In the late '30s, the federal government began an ambitious reclamation plan to dig wells, construct small reservoirs called catch basins, replant the ruined meadow land with hardy crested wheatgrass from the Russian steppes, and plant stands of trees for windbreaks and wildlife habitat. Restoration of the prairie has been more pragmatic than environmentally aesthetic, and today the national grasslands are managed by the National Forest Service according to a "multiple use" philosophy under which the land is shared by birdwatchers, grazing cattle, oil rigs and Air Force missile silos.

For hiking and wildlife viewing, the best place in Pawnee National Grassland is **Pawnee Buttes**, twin white sandstone formations rising 350 feet above the surrounding plain. Many fossil skeletons of prehistoric mammals have been found at the buttes. A hiking trail leads to the base of the buttes. Rock climbing is discouraged and, during the March-to-June raptor nesting season, prohibited. ~ To get there, follow Route 14 west from Sterling

◄ *HIDDEN*

for 42 miles to County Road 103 (known as the Keota Turnoff) and carefully follow the signs to Pawnee Buttes, a circuitous 16-mile route from the main highway on paved county roads; 970-346-5200; www.fs.fed.us/arnf.

**LODGING**

Accommodations in the towns along Route 76 are limited to conventional motels and motor inns, most of them offering very reasonable rates compared to those in other parts of the state.

The **Platte Valley Inn**, a two-story, 59-unit motel, has clean, nicely furnished rooms with phones and cable TV. The swimming pool is a welcome sight after a long, hot drive across Nebraska. ~ Route 76 Exit 180, Julesburg; phone/fax 970-474-3336, 800-562-5166. BUDGET.

For a touch of cowtown class, stay at Sterling's **Ramada Inn**, a two-story complex with 100 spacious, contemporary guest rooms that serves as the area's main conference center. Facilities include an indoor swimming pool, sauna, hot tub and exercise room. ~ Route 76 at Route 6, Sterling; 970-522-2625, 888-298-2054, fax 970-522-1321. MODERATE.

> Keep an eye out for birds of prey when visiting Pawnee Buttes: the buttes are a major nesting area for golden eagles, Swainson's hawks and other species of hawks, falcons and kestrels.

A decent, inexpensive place to spend the night in Sterling is the 14-unit **Colonial Motel**, located across the street from a city park that contains several of the town's "Living Tree" sculptures. The rather plain guest rooms have cable TV and coffeemakers; some have bathtubs. There's no swimming pool, but the motel has a children's playground and basketball court. ~ 915 South Division Street, Sterling; 970-522-3382; e-mail colonialmotel@sosinc.net. BUDGET.

In Fort Morgan, the **Affordable Inn** has an outdoor swimming pool and 42 comfortable guest rooms with cable TV. Overnight valet laundry service is available. ~ 1409 Barlow Road, Fort Morgan; 970-867-9481, fax 970-867-3145. BUDGET.

**DINING**

Look for home-style cooking in Julesburg at the **D & J Café**, a classic roadside diner serving sandwiches and full dinners ranging from spaghetti to chicken-fried steak, as well as daily specials. ~ 114 Cedar Street, Julesburg; 970-474-3556. BUDGET.

The restaurant scene in Sterling offers more variety than you'll find in other towns in the area. Spicy, authentic Mexican food can be found at the small, friendly **Cocina Alvarado**. ~ 715 West Main Street, Sterling; 970-522-8884. BUDGET.

Another very popular Mexican restaurant, **Delgado's Dugout** serves selections such as guacamole tostadas and beef-stuffed sopapillas in the low-ceilinged, romantically rustic basement of a building that was formerly Sterling's original Baptist church. ~ 116 Beech Street, Sterling; 970-522-0175. BUDGET.

Dim lighting and exotic decor set the stage for Mandarin and Szechuan cuisine at the **Wonderful House.** ~ 100 Broadway Street, Sterling; 970-522-0101. BUDGET TO MODERATE.

In Fort Morgan, a good dining bet is **Maverick's Country Grill** in the Affordable Inn, where you'll find a family atmosphere and a varied menu with daily specials and an emphasis on heart-healthy selections. ~ 1409 Barlow Road, Fort Morgan; 970-867-9482. MODERATE.

**SHOPPING**

Far more than mountain towns, the eastern plains of Colorado are prime antiquing territory. Family treasures dating back to the pioneer era are often discovered in remote farmhouses and tiny prairie towns, and a number of dealers specialize in offering them to collectors.

**Antiques & Artisans** has a little bit of everything: furniture, ceramics, farm collectibles, country dolls, jewelry and vintage clothing. ~ 101 Cedar Street, Julesburg; 970-474-2363. Hand-crafted gifts and antiques are found at **Heart of the Plains Antiques**. ~ 103 Main Street, Sterling; 970-521-9519. Antique hunters will also want to stop in at **M & M Collectibles**. ~ 331 Ensign Street, Fort Morgan; 970-867-4780.

**PARKS**

**NORTH STERLING RESERVOIR STATE PARK** 🏃 ⛵ ⛴ 🚤 🛥 Impounded since the turn of the 20th century, this 3000-acre manmade lake was the first large-scale irrigation project in eastern Colorado. It is one of Colorado's newest state parks, though, opened for recreational use in 1992. Sailing, waterskiing and fishing are the main recreational activities except during the November waterfowl hunting season, when the lake is closed to boaters. The state park also includes more than 1000 acres of wild prairie lands that offer opportunities for hiking and wildlife watching. The area provides habitat for deer, eagles, pelicans, coyotes and many species of water birds. Fishing is good for warm-water fish including walleye, crappie, perch, bass, bluegill, catfish and wiper. There are restrooms and a marina with boat rentals (970-522-1511). Day-use fee, $5. ~ Located 11 miles north of Sterling on County Road 33. Take 7th Avenue north from town and follow the signs; 970-522-3657.

▲ Elks Campground has 50 RV/tent sites (electric hookups); $16 to $18 per night. Chimney View has 54 RV/tent sites (no hookups) and Inlet Grove has 47 RV/tent sites (no hookups); $12 to $14 per night.

**JACKSON LAKE STATE PARK** ⛵ ⛴ 🚤 🛥 🛥 This prairie reservoir northwest of Fort Morgan has sandy beaches and shore-front campsites. Although recreational boating, fishing, water-skiing and windsurfing are the main sports, the lake also has a reputation as a good birding spot during migration season, when bald eagles, long-eared owls, sandhill cranes and pelicans by the hundreds, as well as flocks of up to 20,000 ducks, stop over at the lake. (In the fall, duck hunters also congregate here.) The lake is populated by wiper, rainbow trout, walleye, perch, crappie, catfish, northern pike, bluegill, carp and bullhead. There are restrooms, a marina with boat rentals and picnic areas. Day-use fee, $4. ~ Located ten miles north of Wiggins. Take Route 39 north from Route 76 and follow the signs to the state park entrance; 970-645-2551.

▲ There are 262 RV/tent sites; $12 to $18 per night.

▼▼▼▼▼▼▼▼▼▼
**Route 70**

Route 70 is the fastest and, for the most part, least interesting route from the Great Plains to the Colorado Rockies.

It can take you 177 miles from the state line to downtown Denver in less than three hours, and you'll only have to turn the steering wheel twice. The highway does not follow a river. Instead, it traces the old Lawrence & Pikes Peak stagecoach route, which dates back to 1859. It slices straight through the least-populated area in the state, a land so empty that it is has come to be known as "the outback." Still, travelers who want to take their time and look around can find a handful of interesting sights.

**SIGHTS**

Motorists arriving in Colorado from the east on Route 70 reach **Burlington** 14 miles after leaving Kansas. A small town serving the ranches of sparsely populated Kit Carson County, Burlington boasts one of the most unusual little tourist attractions in the state.

*HIDDEN* ►

The **Kit Carson County Carousel** was built in 1905 and bought by the county commissioners in 1928 to serve as a centerpiece for the county fair. Accused of squandering public funds on the merry-go-round, the commissioners were forced from office, and within a few years the county fair was discontinued and the carousel was shut down. Thanks to a 20-year, $250,000 restoration effort, the carousel now operates from Memorial Day to Labor Day, carrying kids of all ages for just a quarter. Now a National Historic Landmark, it is the only antique carousel in the United States that still has its original paint. ~ County Fairgrounds, Burlington.

Burlington's **Old Town Museum** contains 23 historic structures gathered from plains towns of eastern Colorado and western Kansas, among them a jail, a saloon, a railroad depot, a newspaper office, a two-story farmhouse and an immense barn, all restored with antique furnishings. The museum also has a 25,000-square-foot indoor exhibit area where antique vehicles and farm implements are displayed. Admission. ~ 420 South 14th Street, Burlington; 719-346-7382.

The **World's Wonder View Tower,** located in the tiny town of    ◀ *HIDDEN*
Genoa 11 miles east of Limon, was built in 1934 as a sightseeing
attraction for early-day motorists. When it was completed, the
U.S. Geological Survey determined that the tower was the highest
point between Denver and New York City. Promoters claimed that
people who climbed to the top of the 75-foot stone tower could
see six states—Colorado, Wyoming, Nebraska, Kansas, Oklahoma
and Texas. It's hard to judge, since all the land on the distant
horizon looks pretty much the same. There is an old-time museum of curiosities containing two-headed calves and other livestock mutations as well as collections of branding irons, old guns
and ranch memorabilia, more than 20,000 Indian artifacts and
a 75,000-year-old imperial mammoth skeleton found nearby.
Admission. ~ 30121 Frontage Road, Genoa; 719-763-2309.

**Limon** got its start in 1888, when it became the dividing point
for Rock Island Railroad routes to Denver and Colorado Springs.
Today it continues to serve as eastern Colorado's central shipping
hub, where Route 70 to Denver and Route 24 to Colorado
Springs meet Routes 40, 71 and 287. Although the surrounding
terrain may look flat, this town of 1800 people is situated on one
of the highest points in the eastern plains—officially 86 feet

**Route 70**

higher than Denver. For motorists driving west on Route 70, the first glimpse of the Rockies comes when Pikes Peak springs into view on the western horizon at Limon.

Limon's original railroad depot has been restored to house the **Limon Heritage Museum and Railroad Park**. Staffed by volunteers, the homegrown museum complex includes collections and cultural efforts started by private citizens around the Limon area. Among them are the Don Bailey Saddle Collection, Doug Morrison's scale model of the Limon railyards circa 1940, the Gladys Liggett Memorial Little Theater, the Limon Education Association's Pioneer Schoolhouse Museum and Dan Houtz's American Indian Collection and Medicine Tipi. ~ 899 1st Street, Limon; 719-775-2373.

Between Limon and Denver, in Strasburg, the free, volunteer-operated **Comanche Crossing Museum** is a collection of antique-furnished historic buildings surrounding the town's old railroad depot, which now houses exhibits of everything from bibles to barbed wire. With advance registration, second- through sixth-grade kids can attend one of the teacher-supervised classroom sessions held in August in the museum's 1904 one-room school-house. Open June through August. ~ Strasburg; 303-622-4690.

**LODGING**

Burlington and Limon have more than a dozen motels each, and all of them offer budget room rates. You can almost always find a decent room in either town without advance reservations.

In Burlington, the 39-unit, single-story **Chapparal Budget Host** has air-conditioned, blandly furnished rooms, a heated swimming pool and a hot tub. ~ 405 South Lincoln Street, Burlington; 719-346-5361. BUDGET.

Burlington also has a small bed and breakfast, the **Twelfth Street Station**. This Victorian house on a quiet back street has two guest rooms and one shared bath. ~ 350 12th Street, Burlington; 719-346-7180. BUDGET.

In Limon, a good family bet is the two-story, 28-room **Safari Motel**. It offers a quiet location away from the highway with a heated pool, kids' playground and laundry room. Guest rooms are air-conditioned and have king- or queen-size beds, direct-dial phones and cable TV; two-bedroom family units are available. ~ 637 Main Street, Limon; 719-775-2363. BUDGET.

For something a little more atmospheric, spend the night at the **Midwest Country Inn**. This three-story, 32-room establishment combines all the amenities of a quality motor inn—cable television, air conditioning, direct-dial phones, and king- or queen-size beds—with touches of elegance in the antique-filled lobby and individually decorated guest rooms featuring handcrafted accents and designer fabrics. In trendier parts of the state, accommodations

like this come at deluxe rates, but not out here on the prairie. ~
795 Main Street, Limon; 719-775-2373, 888-610-6683. BUDGET.

In both Burlington and Limon, you'll find most of the familiar **DINING**
fast-food franchises that grace interstate highway exits from coast
to coast. Aside from these, dining options are few.

If you're desperate for a romantic candlelight dinner on the
prairie, your best bet is the **Burlington Country Club**. You don't
have to be a member to eat here. The atmosphere is on the casual side, and the bill of fare is almost all
beef—not surprisingly, since most patrons      Arts and crafts traditions from
here are cattle ranchers. ~ 48680 Snead        pioneer times, including wheat
Drive, Burlington; 719-346-7266. MODERATE      weaving, tatting, quilting and
TO DELUXE.                                     wood carving, are alive and
                                               well and on display in gift
For simpler fare, try **The Diner**, a family-style   shops or artists' coopera-
place serving an assortment of breakfasts all day,   tives in several eastern
burgers and other sandwiches, and a limited selec-   Colorado towns.
tion of full dinners. ~ 100 Rose Avenue, Burlington;
719-346-8322.

One of Limon's more satisfying eateries is the
**Country Fare Restaurant**, located in Rip Griffin's Truck-Travel
Center and open 24 hours a day. The varied menu, daily buffet,
homemade pastries and salad bar confirm that the best highway
food really is found where the most truck drivers stop. ~ Routes
70 and 24, Limon; 719-775-2811. BUDGET.

When passing through Burlington, antique hunters will want to **SHOPPING**
check out the **Old Town Emporium**, a shop located within the
Old Town Museum. ~ 420 South 14th Street, Burlington; 719-
346-8484.

There's also a selection of antiques and gifts for sale at the
**World's Wonder View Tower**. ~ 30121 Frontage Road, Genoa;
719-763-2309.

In Limon, **Treasures Unlimited** sells antiques, art and gift items
on consignment for more than 60 local craftspeople and collectors. ~ 973 Main Street, Limon; 719-775-2057.

**BONNY LAKE STATE PARK** 🐟 ⛵ 🚤 🛥️ This large flood-   **PARKS**
control reservoir on the Republican River north of Burlington
makes for a relaxing detour from Route 70. On weekends it is busy
with fishermen, boaters and waterskiers from the surrounding area.
On weekdays the lake is practically deserted, letting visitors experience this oasis and its abundant bird and animal life, including
osprey and golden and bald eagles as well as deer, badgers, coyotes, bobcats and beavers. Some 250 bird species rest here during
spring and fall migrations, and 30,000 to 50,000 birds including

snow geese, Canada geese and pelicans winter here. In addition to the lake, the park encompasses more than 5000 acres of natural bluestem loess prairie land. A short nature trail near the North Cove campground has markers identifying many of the various plant species of the plains. There is swimming at two beaches; fishing is exceptional for northern pike, freshwater drum, walleye, white bass, largemouth and smallmouth bass, crappie, bluegill, bullhead, channel catfish and wipers. Facilities include a picnic area, restrooms, showers, laundry, a telephone and a marina with boat rentals. Day-use fee, $5. ~ Located 25 miles north of Burlington on Route 385; 970-354-7306; www.coloradoparks.org/bonny.

▲ There are four campgrounds totaling 200 RV/tent sites (26 with electric hookups); $12 to $18 per night. Reservations are advised on weekends; call 800-678-2267.

## Arkansas River Area

Unlike the other highway routes described in this chapter, Route 50 across eastern Colorado is not an interstate highway, nor does it form a direct link between major cities. To the east is Dodge City, Kansas; to the west is Pueblo, Colorado; and like these cities, the route that follows the Arkansas River across Colorado's eastern plains has far more historical significance than meets the eye today.

In 1806, U.S. Army Lieutenant Zebulon Pike and his party of 22 soldiers followed this route to become the first American explorers ever to set foot in what is now Colorado. Pike and his men ignored warnings from the local Pawnee that the region had long been claimed by Spain as part of colonial Nuevo Mexico, and they soon found themselves arrested by the Spanish army, to be held prisoner in Santa Fe and Chihuahua on espionage charges for six months and finally deported back to the United States. Subsequent explorations of Colorado followed the South Platte instead.

The Arkansas River route suddenly became important 15 years later, when Mexico gained independence from Spain and opened its borders for the first time to trade with the United States. As word of the new policy got out, merchants rushed to organize wagon expeditions along the Santa Fe Trail, earning enormous profits by trading hardware, textiles and other factory-made goods for Mexican gold, silver and furs. The wagon road that became Route 50 was known as the Mountain Branch of the Santa Fe Trail, longer but less hazardous than the hot, bone-dry Cimarron Cutoff route over the *llano* of eastern New Mexico. The Arkansas River route was the busiest road in what is now Colorado for the next forty years, reaching its height in the late 1850s with the "Pikes Peak or Bust" Gold Rush. Soon afterwards, the Atchinson, Topeka and Santa Fe Railroad began laying tracks, still used by Amtrak passenger trains today, along the old Santa Fe Trail route.

Today, plenty of Santa Fe Trail history awaits the curious all along Route 50. The easternmost major town, 32 miles west of the Kansas state line, is **Lamar**. The largest town for more than 100 miles in any direction, Lamar boasts a population of 8300. Founded by the Santa Fe Railroad in 1886 as a cattle-shipping terminal, Lamar still retains a lot of old-time cowboy character. It's classic small-town America with broad-brimmed hats and gun racks in the rear windows of pickup trucks. The local economy still depends completely on ranching and the railroad.

The **Big Timbers Museum** displays collections of household antiques, ranch memorabilia, Indian artifacts, old guns and historical

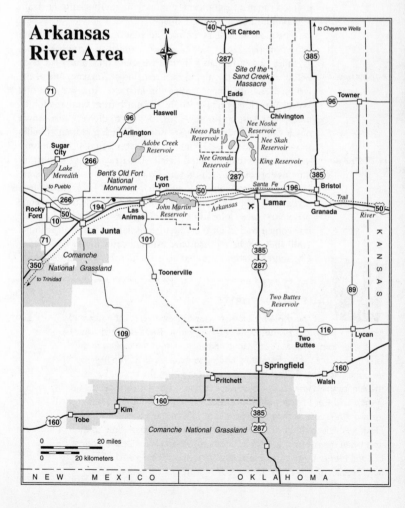

photos from the Lamar area. The museum is named after the three-quarter-mile-wide Big Timbers cottonwood forest, which lines the Arkansas River for 45 miles up and downstream from Lamar and served as a landmark and oasis for travelers on the Santa Fe Trail. ~ Route 50 North at Route 196, Lamar; 719-336-2472.

The **Madonna of the Trail Monument**, a statue of a pioneer woman and her children, is one of 12 madonna monuments, each in a different state, placed by the Daughters of the American Revolution in 1928 to mark the 12 officially designated National Old Trails in the United States. Lamar was selected as the site for the Santa Fe Trail madonna monument because the Big Timbers was deemed the most significant landmark along the Santa Fe Trail. ~ Main and Beech streets, Lamar.

The area also offers the morbidly curious traveler a glimpse or two of the darker side of American history. From Granada, 17 miles east of Lamar, a short drive south on County Road 25 HIDDEN ► will bring you to the abandoned remains of **Amache**, one of the largest U.S. internment camps for Japanese Americans during World War II. If you take Route 385 north from Granada for 23 miles, turn west on Route 96 for 13 miles to the very small town of Chivington, and take County Road 54 north for about 10 miles to where it ends at a "T" intersection, you'll find a small monu-HIDDEN ► ment on the **Site of the Sand Creek Massacre**, one of the most infamous episodes in 19th-century Colorado history. In 1864, state National Guard Colonel John Chivington led his regiment in a predawn "disciplinary action" intended to persuade the Cheyenne people to leave Colorado by attacking a camp occupied mainly by women and children. Chivington claimed his troops killed 1000 Indians there (historians' estimates run somewhat lower); Chivington's troops suffered no casualties. He was subsequently

**AUTHOR FAVORITE**

Of the three major east–west highways across the Colorado prairie, my favorite is Route 50 along the Arkansas River. Although, like the others, its scenery doesn't offer much distraction from the tedium of the long drive, there's some fascinating history to make up for it. The highway follows the Old Santa Fe Trail, the first trade route from the United States to the American Southwest. The best place to appreciate this early heritage is **Bent's Old Fort National Monument**, the oldest permanent settlement on the route between Independence, Missouri, and Santa Fe, Nuevo Mexico. A visit to the restored fort sweeps you back through time to the days when the river marked the Mexican border and Plains Indians and U.S. and Mexican traders crossed paths here, decades before "civilization" reached the territory. See page 375 for more information.

awarded a medal of honor by Colorado's territorial governor and court-martialed by the U.S. Army.

History buffs may also wish to visit the stone foundations of Old Fort Lyon and **Bent's New Fort (Fort Wise)**, located adjacent ◀ **HIDDEN** to one another, one mile south of Route 50 on a marked gravel road that turns off 12 miles west of Lamar. A trading post and Indian agency were established on the site in 1852 by William Bent, the younger of the two brothers who had previously operated Bent's Old Fort (see below) 35 miles to the west. Although the new enterprise never equalled the Bent brothers' original trading post, it served Santa Fe Trail travelers and troops at the army fort for more than a decade. With hostilities mounting between Indians and settlers, the Bent family saga culminated tragically in 1864 as George Bent, the son of William and his Cheyenne wife, Owl Woman, was forced into service as a scout for Colonel Chivington and eyewitnessed the slaughter of his Indian relatives at Sand Creek. The Bents turned over their fort to the army and left in disgust.

On the outskirts of Las Animas is the site of **Boggsville**, a sheep- and cattle-ranching community founded in 1862 that was the original county seat for 9000-square-mile Bent County. Two restored adobe ranch houses and dozens of historical markers line the trail system winding through the historic restoration district. Adobe bricks are made at the site to aid in the reconstruction of other buildings of the pioneer community, including a general store, stage stop, one-room schoolhouse and Kit Carson's last home. ~ Route 101, Las Animas; 719-384-8113.

The most interesting of all the historic sites along the Arkansas River is **Bent's Old Fort National Monument**, located between Las Animas and La Junta on the other side of the river from Route 50. This adobe fortress is a reconstruction of the original trading post established by brothers Charles and William Bent in 1833 as the first permanent Anglo settlement on the Santa Fe Trail and the headquarters for a vast commercial empire that served not only pioneers from the U.S. but also Mexican, Navajo, Southern Cheyenne, Arapaho, Ute, Northern Apache, Kiowa and Comanche people of the region. Bent's Old Fort operated until the late 1840s, when the Mexican War, increasing hostilities between Anglo settlers and Indians, the violent death of Charles Bent and finally a cholera epidemic drove William Bent and his family to abandon it. Today, the impressive complex has been fully restored, and antique furnishings and volunteers in period costume re-create the frontier way of life. Admission. ~ 35110 Route 194; 719-383-5010.

In La Junta, the **Koshare Indian Museum** provides an ironic ◀ **HIDDEN** coda to the tragic history of Colorado's plains Indians. The Koshare Indian Dancers, a local troop of non-Indian Boy Scouts, have been performing since 1933. The proceeds from their performances are used to add to the collections in this museum of American Indian art objects and paintings depicting Indians. Admission. ~ 115 West 18th Street, La Junta; 719-384-7411.

The **Otero Museum,** located in the century-old Sciumato Grocery Store, has exhibits on the history of Otero County, focusing on the arrival of the railroads and growth of the sugar-beet industry, as well as a display about the World War Two Army Air Corps bomber base—one of the nation's largest—that was located near La Junta. Closed November through May. ~ 2nd and Anderson streets, La Junta; 719-384-4411.

South of the Arkansas River corridor lies a truly vast expanse of arid and almost completely uninhabited prairie, much of it contained within the 420,000 acres of **Comanche National Grassland** (719-384-2181). The most accessible area of the national grassland for recreational purposes is **Picket Wire Canyonlands,** a hiking and mountain-biking area south of La Junta. Visitors can see a large dinosaur-track site with more than 1300 tracks preserved in sandstone. Indian rock art in the area is believed to date back as much as 4500 years. In the canyonlands are the abandoned remnants of a Mexican mission and cemetery and an 1870s cattle ranch. ~ To get there, follow Route 109 south from La Junta for 13 miles; turn west on County Road 802 (David Canyon Road) and go eight miles; then turn south on County Road 25 (Rourke Road) and go six more miles to the canyonlands entrance. From there, four-wheel-drive vehicles can make it two miles in on rough Forest Road 500 before reaching a locked gate. Only hiking, horseback riding and mountain biking are allowed beyond the gate.

Deeper into Comanche National Grassland, in Colorado's southeast corner near the Oklahoma state line, **Picture Canyon** is perhaps the most remote recreation area in Colorado. The canyon has natural arches and caves, abundant bird and animal life, and many Indian petroglyphs and pictographs. Unique rock art designs found here closely resemble *ogham,* a form of writing developed in ancient Ireland, leading some scholars to contend that Celtic explorers may have come here around 200 B.C. ~ To get there, follow Route 287 south from Springfield (which is 48 miles due south of Lamar) for 20 miles to the tiny crossroads of Campo; turn west on County Road J and go 10 miles to the marked turnoff for Picture Canyon.

**LODGING**    Lamar's best accommodations are at the big **Cow Palace Inn.** The only convention facility in this part of the state, this 100-room motor inn has modern, spacious rooms decorated in earth tones with king- or queen-size beds, direct-dial phones and cable TV. There are an indoor swimming pool, a hot tub and an indoor tropical garden. ~ 1301 North Main Street, Lamar; 719-336-7753, 800-528-1234, fax 719-336-9598. MODERATE.

Lamar also has a good selection of low-priced motels such as the **El Mar Budget Host Motel**, a 40-unit motel with clean, comfortable guest rooms, some with kitchenettes, and a heated pool. ~ 1210 South Main Street, Lamar; 719-336-4331, fax 719-336-3731. BUDGET.

Lodging options in La Junta are even more limited than in Lamar. A good choice among the handful of family-run motels in town, the **Mid-Town Motel** has a central location that would be wonderfully convenient if the town had much of anything to be convenient to. The 25 guest units are routine and clean. ~ 215 East 3rd Street, La Junta; 719-384-7741. BUDGET.

The closest thing to fine dining in Lamar is the **Oasis Restaurant** at the Cow Palace Inn, with both indoor and courtyard seating. As you might expect, the menu is mostly steak and potatoes; for vegetarian travelers, however, the impressively long salad bar is probably the best bet in the area. ~ 1301 North Main Street, Lamar; 719-336-7753. MODERATE TO DELUXE.

**DINING**

Lamar also has an exceptionally good Chinese restaurant, the **Green Garden**. All-red Oriental decor sets the stage for Mandarin and Szechuan specialties such as chicken, black mushroom and abalone soup, and velvet chicken and scallops. ~ 601 East Olive Street, Lamar; 719-336-3264. BUDGET.

In La Junta, try the **El Camino Inn**, a homey little Mexican restaurant that has been operated by the same family for more than 30 years. House specialties include spicy red enchiladas and *chiles rellenos*, green chile peppers stuffed with cheese, breaded and fried. ~ 816 West 3rd Street, La Junta; 719-384-2871. BUDGET.

In Las Animas, take a look at the exquisite local stained glass work exhibited at **Glass Designs by Jackie**. ~ 475 Bent Avenue, Las Animas; 719-456-0200.

**SHOPPING**

**AUTHOR FAVORITE**
**Rocky Ford**, a small town 12 miles west of La Junta, grows cantaloupes that are reputed to be the best in the country. This claim to fame supports an abundance of roadside produce stands along Route 50, as people come from as far away as Denver during the fall harvest season to buy the melons. The stands also sell watermelons, sweet corn and honey.

**NIGHTLIFE** The Koshare Indian Dancers, Boy Scouts in American Indian garb, perform traditional dances on Friday and Saturday nights during the summer months at the kiva of the **Koshare Indian Museum** on the Otero Junior College campus in La Junta. ~ 115 West 18th Street, La Junta; 719-384-4411.

**PARKS**  **JOHN MARTIN RESERVOIR STATE PARK** 🚤 🛶 🎣 🏕️ 🚣 🏊 ⛵ This large flood-control reservoir managed by the U.S. Army Corps of Engineers is used for boating and waterskiing. A 75-acre excavation originally dug to obtain earthfill for the dam was filled with water to create Lake Hasty, now used for swimming, canoeing, windsurfing and fishing. The lake is populated by rainbow trout, walleye, channel catfish, largemouth bass and bluegill. A fenced area north of the lake preserves a half-mile stretch of the original wagon ruts of the Santa Fe Trail. There is a visitors center, restrooms, a picnic area and playground. ~ From Route 50, 21 miles west of Lamar and 14 miles east of Las Animas, take Route 260 south for two miles to the park entrance. Day-use fee, $5. ~ 719-336-1690.

▲ There are 65 RV/tent sites, including 12 with electric hookups; $10 to $14 per night.

# Outdoor Adventures

**FISHING**

**SOUTH PLATTE RIVER AREA** Once it leaves the mountains, the South Platte River runs so wide and shallow that it is an uninviting place for fish and fishermen alike. Fishing here focuses on several reservoirs: **Julesburg Reservoir** (commonly called Jumbo Lake) near Julesburg, **North Sterling Reservoir** near Sterling and **Jackson Lake** near Fort Morgan. All three lakes have good-sized catfish and walleye. **Shoreline Marina** at Jackson Lake rents fishing boats and has bait and tackle. ~ 970-768-6011. North Sterling Reservoir's **Bayside Marina** also has boat rentals. ~ 970-522-1511.

**ROUTE 70** The only body of water in this part of the state, **Bonny Lake State Park** offers an assortment of warm-water fish including walleye, northern pike, freshwater drum, white bass, largemouth and smallmouth bass, crappie, bluegill, bullhead, channel catfish and wipers.

**ARKANSAS RIVER AREA** Lake Hasty, the manmade recreational lake adjoining John Martin Reservoir, is stocked with rainbow trout, walleye, channel catfish, largemouth bass and bluegill. Other area reservoirs that offer good warmwater fishing include **Adobe Creek Reservoir** (also called Blue Lake) north of Las Animas and a cluster of neighboring lakes—**Nee Skah, Nee Noshe and Nee Gronda reservoirs**—all north of Lamar.

**BOATING**  **SOUTH PLATTE RIVER AREA** North Sterling Reservoir (970-522-3657) near Sterling and **Jackson Lake** (970-645-2551) near

Fort Morgan are popular areas for recreational boating, waterskiing and windsurfing. A favorite of sailboat enthusiasts, **Bayside Marina** at North Sterling Reservoir has boat rentals ranging from paddleboats to waterski and pontoon boats, daily in summer and weekends only the rest of the year. ~ 970-522-1511.

**ROUTE 70  Bonny Lake State Park** attracts recreational boaters and waterskiers from all around this arid part of the Colorado and Kansas plains. There is a marina with fishing boats, pontoon boats and jet skis for rent. ~ 970-354-7339.

**ARKANSAS RIVER AREA  John Martin Reservoir** offers a full range of water sports. The main reservoir is used for recreational boating and waterskiing. Adjoining the reservoir is Lake Hasty, a smaller manmade lake that is off-limits to motorized boats and is used for canoeing and windsurfing. ~ 719-336-1690.

**SOUTH PLATTE RIVER AREA**  Platte River golf courses include the **Riverview Golf Course**, an 18-hole public course and driving range with cart and club rentals. Designed by Val Heim, the course takes advantage of the rolling prairie terrain, incorporating no fewer than 48 sand traps. ~ 3064 North Riverview Road, Sterling; 970-522-3035. There's also the 18-hole **Fort Morgan Golf Course**, where the front nine holes have been in use since 1929. Lined by mature shade trees, the traditional course has cart and club rentals. ~ Riverside Park, Fort Morgan; 970-867-5990.

**GOLF**

Its shoreline choked with tamarisk and scrub brush, the Arkansas River does not attract anglers in large numbers, though it is said to have some large native catfish.

**ROUTE 70**  In Burlington, there's the very hilly nine-hole **Prairie Pines Golf Club**. Cart and club rentals are available. ~ 48680 Snead Drive; 719-346-8207. You'll find nine more holes half an hour to the west at the **Mossland Memorial Golf Course**. ~ 100 3rd Street, Flagler; 719-765-4659. Designed by Henry Hughes, the nine-hole **Tamarack Golf Course** is laid out around two lakes and has challenging sand traps. Cart and club rentals are available. ~ Route 71 South, Limon; 719-775-9998.

**ARKANSAS RIVER AREA**  Lamar has the **Spreading Antlers Golf Course**, a nine-hole course along Willow Creek with small greens and luxuriant bluegrass fairways, as well as a pro shop, carts and club rentals. ~ South Route 287; 719-336-5274. Other links along the Arkansas River include the **Las Animas Golf Course**, a level nine-hole course designed by Ray Hardy with five water hazards; cart and club rentals are available. ~ 220 Country Club Drive; 719-456-2511. You may also tee off at the nine-hole public **La Junta Golf Club**; cart and club rentals are available. ~ 27696 Harris Road; 719-384-7133. The challenging, hilly nine-hole course at the **Rocky Ford Country Club** is also open to the public and has cart and club rentals. ~ 91 Play Park Hill; 719-254-7528.

**TENNIS**    You'll find two free asphalt-surfaced outdoor public tennis courts, lighted for night play, in Sterling at **Pioneer Park**. ~ West Main Street, Sterling.

**BIKING**    The prairie of eastern Colorado is crisscrossed by a gridwork of literally thousands of miles of straight, featureless, relatively level, infrequently used farm and ranch roads. A bike trip along any of them gives you a chance to fully appreciate the sights, sounds and scents of the high plains.

**ARKANSAS RIVER AREA**    The most exciting mountain biking on the eastern plains is in **Picket Wire Canyonlands** south of La Junta. Eleven miles of multiple-use trails and primitive roads take you along the Purgatoire River to an old Mexican cemetery, dinosaur tracks, Indian rock art and the remains of a 19th-century cattle ranch.

**HIKING**    All distances listed for hiking are one way unless otherwise noted.

**SOUTH PLATTE RIVER AREA**    You'll find a network of short trails among the fascinating rock formations of Chimney Canyon north of Sterling. Farther north, a two-mile hiking trail leads to the foot of **Pawnee Buttes** in Pawnee National Grassland (see "South Platte River Area" earlier in this chapter).

**ROUTE 70**    There is little hiking here. Your best bet is a walk through the cottonwoods and natural prairie along the lakeshore in **Bonny Lake State Park**.

**ARKANSAS RIVER AREA**    The **Picket Wire Canyonlands** trail described above under "Biking" also makes for a good all-day hike. On the route from La Junta to the canyonlands described elsewhere in this chapter, there is a scenic 2.25-mile loop trail in **Vogel Canyon**—watch for the marked entrance road off County Road 802 one mile west of the turnoff from Route 109. Along the Vogel Canyon trail you'll find Indian rock art and the ruins of an old homestead and a stage station. Farther southeast in Comanche National Grassland, a four-mile loop trail runs through **Picture Canyon**, offering a look at some of the best examples of Indian rock art in the state and an area of fantastic rock formations known as Hells Half Acre.

**Transportation**

**CAR**

Route 76 follows the Platte River and the old Overland Trail through the towns of Julesburg, Sterling and Fort Morgan. **Route 70** runs through Burlington and Limon. The two interstate routes meet in Denver. **Route 50** follows the Arkansas River and the old Santa Fe Trail to Pueblo through Lamar, Las Animas and La Junta.

There is no commercial air service to the towns covered by this **AIR**
chapter. The nearest major airports are Denver and Colorado
Springs.

**Amtrak**'s "Southwest Chief," which provides service between **TRAIN**
Chicago and Los Angeles, traces the entire length of the old Santa
Fe Trail, making stops in Lamar and La Junta. ~ 800-872-7245.

**Greyhound Bus Lines** (800-231-2222) buses go through Jules- **BUS**
burg, Sterling and Fort Morgan on Route 76 and Burlington and
Limon on Route 70. The driver can let you off at any of these
towns on request; to make arrangements to board a bus on its
way through any of these towns, you must call the bus terminal
in Denver. ~ 303-293-6555.

   **TNM&O Coaches** (800-231-2222) has a bus route along
Route 50 through Lamar and La Junta. To make arrangements
to board a bus, call the terminal in Pueblo. ~ 719-543-2775.

# Index

# Lodging Index

# Dining Index

## HIDDEN GUIDES

Adventure travel or a relaxing vacation?—"Hidden" guidebooks are the only travel books in the business to provide detailed information on both. Aimed at environmentally aware travelers, our motto is "Where Vacations Meet Adventures." These books combine details on unique hotels, restaurants and sightseeing with information on camping, sports and hiking for the outdoor enthusiast.

## PARADISE FAMILY GUIDES

Ideal for families traveling with kids of any age—toddlers to teenagers— Paradise Family Guides offer a blend of travel information unlike any other guides to the Hawaiian islands. With vacation ideas and tropical adventures that are sure to satisfy both action-hungry youngsters and re-laxation-seeking parents, these guides meet the specific needs of each and every family member.

Ulysses Press books are available at bookstores everywhere. If any of the following titles are unavailable at your local bookstore, ask the bookseller to order them.

You can also order books directly from Ulysses Press
P.O. Box 3440, Berkeley, CA 94703
800-377-2542 or 510-601-8301
fax: 510-601-8307
www.ulyssespress.com
e-mail: ulysses@ulyssespress.com

## HIDDEN GUIDEBOOKS

____ Hidden Arizona, $16.95
____ Hidden Bahamas, $14.95
____ Hidden Baja, $14.95
____ Hidden Belize, $15.95
____ Hidden Big Island of Hawaii, $13.95
____ Hidden Boston & Cape Cod, $14.95
____ Hidden British Columbia, $18.95
____ Hidden Cancún & the Yucatán, $16.95
____ Hidden Carolinas, $17.95
____ Hidden Coast of California, $18.95
____ Hidden Colorado, $15.95
____ Hidden Disneyland, $13.95
____ Hidden Florida, $18.95
____ Hidden Florida Keys & Everglades, $13.95
____ Hidden Georgia, $16.95
____ Hidden Guatemala, $16.95
____ Hidden Hawaii, $18.95
____ Hidden Idaho, $14.95
____ Hidden Kauai, $13.95
____ Hidden Los Angeles, $14.95
____ Hidden Maui, $13.95

____ Hidden Miami, $14.95
____ Hidden Montana, $15.95
____ Hidden New England, $18.95
____ Hidden New Mexico, $15.95
____ Hidden New Orleans, $14.95
____ Hidden Oahu, $13.95
____ Hidden Oregon, $15.95
____ Hidden Pacific Northwest, $18.95
____ Hidden San Diego, $14.95
____ Hidden Salt Lake City, $14.95
____ Hidden San Francisco & Northern California, $18.95
____ Hidden Seattle, $13.95
____ Hidden Southern California, $18.95
____ Hidden Southwest, $19.95
____ Hidden Tahiti, $17.95
____ Hidden Tennessee, $16.95
____ Hidden Utah, $16.95
____ Hidden Walt Disney World, $13.95
____ Hidden Washington, $15.95
____ Hidden Wine Country, $13.95
____ Hidden Wyoming, $15.95

## PARADISE FAMILY GUIDES

____ Paradise Family Guides: Kaua'i, $16.95
____ Paradise Family Guides: Maui, $16.95
____ Paradise Family Guides: Big Island of Hawai'i, $16.95

Mark the book(s) you're ordering and enter the total cost here ⇨ [_____]

California residents add 8.25% sales tax here ⇨ [_____]

Shipping, check box for your preferred method and enter cost here ⇨ [_____]

❏ BOOK RATE                    **FREE! FREE! FREE!**

❏ PRIORITY MAIL/UPS GROUND     cost of postage

❏ UPS OVERNIGHT OR 2-DAY AIR   cost of postage

[_____]

Billing, enter total amount due here and check method of payment ⇨

❏ CHECK          ❏ MONEY ORDER

❏ VISA/MASTERCARD _____ EXP. DATE _____

NAME _____ PHONE _____

ADDRESS _____

CITY _____ STATE _____ ZIP _____

MONEY-BACK GUARANTEE ON DIRECT ORDERS PLACED THROUGH ULYSSES PRESS.

## ABOUT THE AUTHOR

**RICHARD HARRIS** has written or co-written 35 other guidebooks including Ulysses' *Hidden Miami*, *Hidden Baja*, *Hidden Belize*, *Hidden Cancún and the Yucatán*, *Hidden Highways Arizona*, *Weekend Adventure Getaways: Yosemite Tahoe* and the best-selling *Hidden Southwest*. He has also served as contributing editor on guides to Mexico, New Mexico, and other ports of call for John Muir Publications, Insight Guides, Fodor's, Birnbaum and Access guides. He is a past president of PEN New Mexico and currently president of the New Mexico Book Association. When not traveling, Richard writes and lives in Santa Fe, New Mexico.


## ABOUT THE ILLUSTRATOR

**DOUG McCARTHY**, a native New Yorker, lives in the San Francisco Bay area with his family. His illustrations appear in a number of Ulysses Press guides, including *Hidden British Columbia*, *Hidden Tennessee*, *Hidden Georgia*, *Hidden Bahamas* and *The New Key to Ecuador and the Galápagos*.